Width

Microsoft® Word 2010

COMPLETE

by Pasewark and Pasewark*, Morrison, Pinard

COURSE TECHNOLOGY
CENGAGE Learning™

Australia • Brazil • Japan • Korea • Mexico • Singapore • Spain • United Kingdom • United States

Microsoft® Word 2010

COMPLETE

by Pasewark and Pasewark*, Morrison, Pinard

William R. Pasewark, Sr., Ph.D.
Professor Emeritus, Business Education,
Texas Tech University

Scott G. Pasewark, B.S.
Occupational Education, Computer Technologist

William R. Pasewark, Jr., Ph.D., CPA
Professor, Accounting, Texas Tech University

Carolyn Denny Pasewark, M.Ed.
National Computer Consultant, Reading and Math
Certified Elementary Teacher, K-12 Certified Counselor

Jan Pasewark Stogner, MBA
Financial Planner

Beth Pasewark Wadsworth, B.A.
Graphic Designer

Connie Morrison, M.A.
Consultant, Encore Training, Inc

Katherine T. Pinard
Contributing Author

*Pasewark and Pasewark is a trademark of the Pasewark LTD.

COURSE TECHNOLOGY
CENGAGE Learning™

Australia • Brazil • Japan • Korea • Mexico • Singapore • Spain • United Kingdom • United States

COURSE TECHNOLOGY
CENGAGE Learning™

Microsoft Word 2010 Complete
Pasewark and Pasewark, Morrison, Pinard

Author: Connie Morrison

Contributing Author: Katherine T. Pinard

Executive Editor: Donna Gridley

Product Manager: Allison O'Meara McDonald

Development Editors: Rachel Biheller Bunin,
  Robin M. Romer, Karen Porter

Associate Product Manager: Amanda Lyons

Editorial Assistant: Kim Klasner

Senior Content Project Manager: Catherine DiMassa

Associate Marketing Manager: Julie Schuster

Director of Manufacturing: Denise Powers

Text Designer: Shawn Girsberger

Photo Researcher: Abigail Reip

Manuscript Quality Assurance Lead: Jeff Schwartz

Manuscript Quality Assurance Reviewers:
  Green Pen QA, Marianne Snow

Copy Editor: Michael Beckett

Proofreader: Green Pen Quality Assurance

Indexer: Sharon Hilgenberg

Art Director: Faith Brosnan

Cover Designer: Hannah Wellman

Cover Image: © Neil Brennan / Canopy Illustration / Veer

Compositor: GEX Publishing Services

For product information and technology assistance, contact us at
Cengage Learning Customer & Sales Support, 1-800-354-9706
For permission to use material from this text or product, submit all requests online at **www.cengage.com/permissions**
Further permissions questions can be emailed to
permissionrequest@cengage.com

Library of Congress Control Number: 2010936380

Hardcover:
ISBN-13: 978-1-111-52951-2
ISBN-10: 1-111-52951-5

Course Technology
20 Channel Center Street
Boston, Massachusetts 02210
USA

Cengage Learning is a leading provider of customized learning solutions with office locations around the globe, including Singapore, the United Kingdom, Australia, Mexico, Brazil, and Japan. Locate your local office at:
international.cengage.com/region

Cengage Learning products are represented in Canada by Nelson Education, Ltd.

To learn more about Course Technology, visit **www.cengage.com/coursetechnology**

Visit our company website at **www.cengage.com**

Any fictional data related to persons or companies or URLs used throughout this book is intended for instructional purposes only. At the time this book was printed, any such data was fictional and not belonging to any real persons or companies.

To access additional course materials [including CourseMate], please visit www.cengagebrain.com. At the CengageBrain.com home page, search for the ISBN of your title (from the back cover of your book) using the search box at the top of the page. This will take you to the product page where these resources can be found.

Printed in the United States of America
1 2 3 4 5 6 7 14 13 12 11 10

ABOUT THIS BOOK

Microsoft Word 2010 Complete is designed for beginning users of Microsoft Word 2010. Students will learn to use the application through a variety of activities, simulations, and case projects. *Microsoft Word 2010 Complete* demonstrates the tools and features for this program in an easy-to-follow, hands-on approach.

This self-paced step-by-step book with corresponding screen shots makes learning easy and enjoyable. End-of-lesson exercises reinforce the content covered in each lesson and provide students with the opportunity to apply the skills that they have learned. It is important to work through each lesson within a unit in the order presented, as each lesson builds on what was learned in previous lessons.

Illustrations provide visual reinforcement of features and concepts, and sidebars provide notes, tips, and concepts related to the lesson topics. Step-by-Step exercises provide guidance for using the features. End-of-lesson projects concentrate on the main concepts covered in the lesson and provide valuable opportunities to apply or extend the skills learned in the lesson. Instructors can assign as many or as few of the projects at the end of the lesson as they like.

In the **Introductory Word** unit, students start by learning the basics of document creating and editing, and then move on using Word commands to apply formatting, styles, and themes, and create elements such as numbered and bulleted lists and tables. Then students learn how to create specialized documents with multiple columns and graphics, and how to work with longer documents by adding headers, footers, and page numbers and working with document properties. Finally, students learn how to use the Mail Merge feature, how to review documents using tracked changes and comments, and how to combine different versions of a document.

The lessons in the **Advanced Word** unit introduce students to details and special features that will help them achieve a higher level of expertise in word processing skills. Students learn how to customize styles, themes, tables, and charts. To improve productivity, there is full coverage of creating merge documents for letters, envelopes, labels, emails, and directories. Students learn how to protect documents and restrict access when sharing documents. To work more efficiently, students learn to create citations and bibliographies for research papers, and also how to create indexes, tables of contents, tables of figures, and tables of authorities for long documents. Students also learn to create macros for repetitive tasks and to customize the Word application settings.

Please note that some concepts introduced in the Introductory unit will be expanded upon in the Advanced unit.

To complete all lessons and end-of-lesson material, this book will require approximately 33 hours.

Start-Up Checklist

Hardware

- Computer and processor: 500-megahertz (MHz) processor or higher
- Memory: 256 megabytes (MB) of RAM or higher
- Hard disk: 3.5 gigabyte (GB) available disk space
- Display 1024 × 768 or higher-resolution monitor

Software:

- Operating system: Windows XP with Service Pack 3, Windows Vista with SP1, or Windows 7

INSIDE THIS BOOK

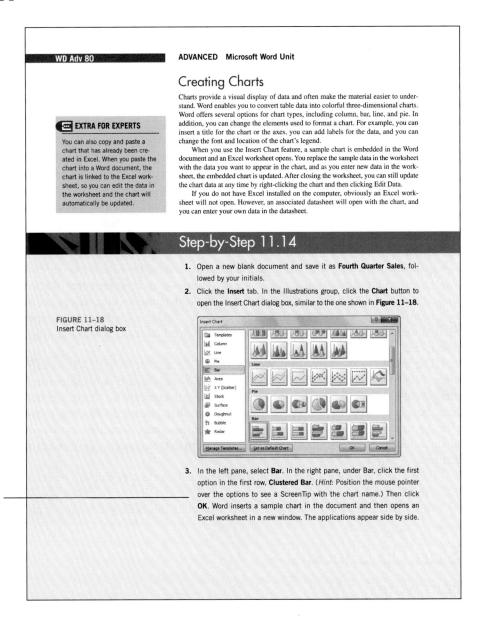

ADVANCED Microsoft Word Unit

Creating Charts

Charts provide a visual display of data and often make the material easier to understand. Word enables you to convert table data into colorful three-dimensional charts. Word offers several options for chart types, including column, bar, line, and pie. In addition, you can change the elements used to format a chart. For example, you can insert a title for the chart or the axes, you can add labels for the data, and you can change the font and location of the chart's legend.

When you use the Insert Chart feature, a sample chart is embedded in the Word document and an Excel worksheet opens. You replace the sample data in the worksheet with the data you want to appear in the chart, and as you enter new data in the worksheet, the embedded chart is updated. After closing the worksheet, you can still update the chart data at any time by right-clicking the chart and then clicking Edit Data.

If you do not have Excel installed on the computer, obviously an Excel worksheet will not open. However, an associated datasheet will open with the chart, and you can enter your own data in the datasheet.

⊞ EXTRA FOR EXPERTS

You can also copy and paste a chart that has already been created in Excel. When you paste the chart into a Word document, the chart is linked to the Excel worksheet, so you can edit the data in the worksheet and the chart will automatically be updated.

Step-by-Step 11.14

1. Open a new blank document and save it as **Fourth Quarter Sales**, followed by your initials.

2. Click the **Insert** tab. In the Illustrations group, click the **Chart** button to open the Insert Chart dialog box, similar to the one shown in **Figure 11–18**.

FIGURE 11–18
Insert Chart dialog box

3. In the left pane, select **Bar**. In the right pane, under Bar, click the first option in the first row, **Clustered Bar**. (*Hint*: Position the mouse pointer over the options to see a ScreenTip with the chart name.) Then click **OK**. Word inserts a sample chart in the document and then opens an Excel worksheet in a new window. The applications appear side by side.

Step-by-Step Exercises offer "hands-on practice" of the material just learned. Each exercise uses a data file or requires you to create a file from scratch.

Lesson opener elements include the **Objectives**, **Suggested Completion Time**, and **Vocabulary Terms**.

End of Lesson elements include the **Summary**, **Vocabulary Review**, **Review Questions**, **Lesson Projects**, and **Critical Thinking Activities**.

Instructor Resources Disk

ISBN-13: 978-0-538-47523-5
ISBN-10: 0-538-47523-4

The Instructor Resources CD or DVD contains the following teaching resources:

The Data and Solution files for this course.

ExamView® tests for each lesson.

Instructor's Manual that includes lecture notes for each lesson and references to the end-of-lesson activities and Unit Review projects.

Answer Keys that include solutions to the end-of-lesson and unit review questions.

Critical thinking solution files that provide possible solutions for critical thinking activities.

Copies of the figures that appear in the student text.

Suggested Syllabus with block, two quarter, and 18-week schedule

Annotated Solutions and Grading Rubrics

PowerPoint presentations for each lesson.

Spanish glossary and Spanish test bank.

Appendices that include models for formatted documents, an e-mail writing guide, and a letter writing guide.

Proofreader's Marks

ExamView®

This textbook is accompanied by ExamView, a powerful testing software package that allows instructors to create and administer printed, computer (LAN-based), and Internet exams. ExamView includes hundreds of questions that correspond to the topics covered in this text, enabling students to generate detailed study guides that include page references for further review. The computer-based and Internet testing components allow students to take exams at their computers, and save the instructor time by grading each exam automatically.

Online Companion

This book uses an Online Companion Web site that contains valuable resources to help enhance your learning.

- Student data files to complete text projects and activities
- Key terms and definitions for each lesson
- PowerPoint presentations for each lesson
- Additional Internet boxes with links to important Web sites
- Link to CourseCasts

CourseCasts

CourseCasts—Learning on the Go. Always Available…Always Relevant.

Want to keep up with the latest technology trends relevant to you? Visit our site to find a library of podcasts, CourseCasts, featuring a "CourseCast of the Week," and download them to your mp3 player at http://coursecasts.course.com.

Our fast-paced world is driven by technology. You know because you're an active participant—always on the go, always keeping up with technological trends, and always learning new ways to embrace technology to power your life.

Ken Baldauf, a faculty member of the Florida State University Computer Science Department, is responsible for teaching technology classes to thousands of FSU students each year. He knows what you want to know; he knows what you want to learn. He's also an expert in the latest technology and will sort through and aggregate the most pertinent news and information so you can spend your time enjoying technology, rather than trying to figure it out.

Visit us at http://coursecasts.course.com to learn on the go!

SAM 2010 *SAM*

SAM 2010 Assessment, Projects, and Training version 1.0 offers a real-world approach to applying Microsoft Office 2010 skills. The Assessment portion of this powerful and easy to use software simulates Office 2010 applications, allowing users to demonstrate their computer knowledge in a hands-on environment. The Projects portion allows students to work live-in-the-application on project-based assignments. The Training portion helps students learn in the way that works best for them by reading, watching, or receiving guided help.

- SAM 2010 captures the key features of the actual Office 2010 software, allowing students to work in high-fidelity, multi-pathway simulation exercises for a real-world experience.
- SAM 2010 includes realistic and explorable simulations of Office 2010, Windows 7 coverage, and a new user interface.
- Easy, web-based deployment means SAM is more accessible than ever to both you and your students.
- Direct correlation to the skills covered on a chapter-by-chapter basis in your Course Technology textbooks allows you to create a detailed lesson plan.
- SAM Projects offers live-in-the-application project-based assignments. Student work is automatically graded, providing instant feedback. A unique cheating detection feature identifies students who may have shared files.
- Because SAM Training is tied to textbook exams and study guides, instructors can spend more time teaching and let SAM Training help those who need additional time to grasp concepts

Note: This textbook may or may not be available in SAM Projects at this time. Please check with your sales representative for the most recent information on when this title will be live in SAM Projects.

MESSAGE FROM THE AUTHORS

About the Pasewark Author Team

Pasewark LTD is a family-owned business with more than 90 years of combined experience authoring award-winning textbooks. They have written over 100 books about computers, accounting, and office technology. During that time, they developed their mission statement: To help our students live better lives.

Pasewark LTD authors are members of several professional associations that help authors write better books. The authors have been recognized with numerous awards for classroom teaching and believe that effective classroom teaching is a major ingredient for writing effective textbooks.

Connie Morrison, M.A. Consultant, Encore Training, Inc.

Connie Morrison has more than 35 years of combined experience in education and educational publishing. She began her career teaching business education at the high school and college levels, and then became an education consultant in the publishing industry. Connie currently works as a consultant for Encore Training, Inc., providing staff training and professional development.

This book represents a true team effort, and it was a pleasure working with everyone. My appreciation goes to all the members of the team who made this book possible. I owe special thanks to the following individuals: Donna Gridley, Allison O'Meara, and Cathie DiMassa for their direction and support in the development of this book; Karen Porter, for her meticulous editing and valuable input; and my family, Gene, Al, Amy, and Chris, for their continued support. — **Connie Morrison**

From the Contributing Author

Thank you especially to Donna Gridley for again giving me the opportunity to contribute to this book. Thank you to my co-conspirators, Robin, Jess, and Rachel for putting up with me. As always, the talented team at Course Technology worked together to create a fantastic book under impossible deadlines. Thanks to Cathie DiMassa, our production editor, and Allison O'Meara McDonald and Amanda Lyons, our product managers, for their tireless efforts. And as always, thank you to my family for picking up the slack while I was chained to my desk. — **Katherine T. Pinard**

ADDITIONAL MICROSOFT OFFICE 2010 TITLES

Microsoft® Office 2010 Advanced
Casebound
ISBN-13: 978-0-538-48129-8
ISBN-10: 0-538-48129-3
Hard Spiral
ISBN-13: 978-0-538-48142-7
ISBN-10: 0-538-48142-0
Soft Perfect
ISBN-13: 978-0-538-48143-4
ISBN-10: 0-538-48143-9

Microsoft® Access® 2010 Complete
Hardcover
ISBN-13: 978-1-111-52990-1
ISBN-10: 1-111-52990-6

Microsoft® Excel® 2010 Complete
Hardcover
ISBN-13: 978-1-1115-2952-9
ISBN-10: 1-111-52952-3

Microsoft® PowerPoint® 2010 Complete
Hardcover
ISBN-13: 978-1-1115-2953-6
ISBN-10: 1-111-52953-1

CONTENTS

INTRODUCTORY UNIT

INTRODUCTORY MICROSOFT WORD 2010

ADVANCED MICROSOFT WORD 2010

WORD 2010 COMPLETE
DATA FILES GRID

APPLICATION	LESSON	DATA FILE	SOLUTION FILE
INTRODUCTION	1	Class Descriptions.docx	Blackfoot Resort.pptx
		Clients.accdb	Final Spectrum Follow-up.docx
		Historic Preservation.pptx	First Qtr Sales.xlsx
		January Sales.xlsx	Historic Housing.pptx
		JC's Data.mdb	JC's Updated Data.accdb
		Sales Report.xlsx	Revised Sales Report.xlsx
		Spectrum Follow-up.docx	Updated Class Descriptions.docx
			Updated Clients.accdb
INTRODUCTORY WORD	1	Interview.docx	Cosmic Connections Flyer.docx
		Lecture.docx	Holiday Sale Flyer.docx
		Sale.docx	Interview Tips.docx
			\My Letters\Thank You Letter.docx
			\My Tasks\My To Do List.docx
INTRODUCTORY WORD	2	Interview.docx	Customer Letter.docx
		Letter.docx	Interview Preparation.docx
		Tournament.docx	Spelling List.docx
		Web Site.docx	Tournament Notice.docx
		Workshop.docx	Web Site Tips.docx
			Workshop Checklist.docx

APPLICATION	LESSON	DATA FILE	SOLUTION FILE
INTRODUCTORY WORD	3	Application.docx	Application Letter.docx
		Lancaster Memo.docx	Club Minutes.docx
		Memo.docx	Fall Classes Memo.docx
		Minutes.docx	Lancaster Voting Memo.docx
		Museum.docx	Museum Visit.docx
INTRODUCTORY WORD	4	Certificate.docx	Break Room Poster.docx
		Checking Account.docx	Checking Account Info.docx
		Flyer.docx	Employee Certificate.docx
		Golf Tournament 2.docx	Employee Handbook.docx
		Handbook.docx	Formatted Golf Tournament Notice.docx
		Poster.docx	Race Track Flyer.docx
INTRODUCTORY WORD	5	Diet Guidelines.docx	Agenda.docx
		Diet.docx	American Diet.docx
		Interview 2.docx	American Diet Guidelines.docx
		Invitation.docx	American Diet Title Page.docx
		NADA Memo.docx	Break Room Poster 2.docx
		Poster 2.docx	Exercise Plan.docx
		Shipping.docx	Government.docx
			Health Plan.docx
			Interview Preparation Tips.docx
			NADA Office Supplies Memo.docx
			Overnight Shipping.docx
			Resume for Jeffrey.docx
			Wedding Invitation.docx

APPLICATION	LESSON	DATA FILE	SOLUTION FILE
INTRODUCTORY WORD	6	Invitation2.docx	Garage Sale.docx
		Memo2.docx	HH Newsletter.docx
		Newsletter.docx	Holiday Invitation.docx
		Shelter.docx	Org Chart Memo.docx
			Park Map.docx
			Shelter News.docx
INTRODUCTORY WORD	7	Diet2.docx	Correspondence Guidelines.docx
		Guidelines.docx	Diet Final.docx
		References.docx	References Formatted.docx
		Sales.docx	References Unformatted.docx
			Sales Leaders.docx
INTRODUCTORY WORD	8	Bank Customers.docx	Bank Fax.docx
		Checking.docx	Bank Letter.docx
		Subscription.docx	Bank New Customer Letters.docx
		Telephone 2.docx	Bank Template.dotx
		Telephone.docx	Combined Bank Letter.docx
			Envelope.docx
			Final Bank Letter.docx
			Hodges Envelope.docx
			Hodges Labels.docx
			Journal Addresses.docx
			Journal Subscription.dotx
			Labels.docx
			Letter with Changes Accepted.docx
			Letter with Comments.docx
			Merged Journal Letters.docx
			My Resume.docx
			Telephone Combined Solution.docx
			Telephone Etiquette 2.docx
			Telephone Etiquette.docx

APPLICATION	LESSON	DATA FILE	SOLUTION FILE
INTRODUCTORY WORD	Unit Review	Bagels.docx	Bagel Mania.docx
		Internet.docx	Ergonomics.docx
		Menu.docx	Greeting Card Sample.docx
		Properties.docx	Internet Terms.docx
		Recycling.docx	Island West Properties.docx
		Tenses.docx	Java Menu.docx
			Recycling Flyer.docx
			Star Contacts.docx
			Star Envelope.docx
			Star Letter.docx
			Star Merge.docx
			Star Template.dotx
			Verb Tenses.docx
ADVANCED WORD	9	Get Fit.docx	Enhanced Get Fit 1.docx
		Invitation.docx	Enhanced Get Fit 2.docx
		Lead Out.docx	Enhanced Get Fit 3.docx
		Plastic.docx	Enhanced Get Fit 4.docx
		Recycling symbol.jpg	Enhanced Invitation.docx
		Trees.docx	Enhanced Lead Out 1.docx
			Enhanced Lead Out 2.docx
			Enhanced Plastic 1.docx
			Enhanced Plastic 2.docx
			Enhanced Plastic 3.docx
			Enhanced Plastic 4.docx
			Enhanced Trees.docx
ADVANCED WORD	10	Agenda.docx	Agenda Template.dotx
		Certificate.docx	Certificate Template.dotx
		Credit Letter.docx	Final Events.docx
		Events.docx	Final Flyer.docx
		Flyer.docx	Final Waste.docx

APPLICATION	LESSON	DATA FILE	SOLUTION FILE
ADVANCED WORD	10	LCCU Building Blocks.docx	November Agenda.docx
		Pharmacy.docx	Pharmacy 1.docx
		Quick Parts.docx	Pharmacy 2.docx
		Waste.docx	Pharmacy 3.docx
			Pharmacy 4.docx
			Updated Credit Letter.docx
			Weber Certificate.docx
			Your Name Template.dotx
ADVANCED WORD	11	Accounts Receivable.docx	Balances Due 1.docx
		Employee.docx	Balances Due 2.docx
		Expenses.xlsx	Countries.xlsx
		Green Bucket.docx	Country Requests.docx
		Rates.docx	Employee Data 1.docx
		Rates.xlsx	Employee Data 2.docx
		Sales.xlsx	Employee Data 3.docx
			First Quarter Expenses.xlsx
			First Quarter Report.docx
			Fourth Quarter Sales.docx
			Green Bucket Letter.docx
			Monthly Sales 1.docx
			Monthly Sales 2.docx
			New Members.docx
			New Rates.docx
			Past Due Accounts 1.docx
			Past Due Accounts 2.docx
			Past Due Accounts 3.docx
			Payroll.docx
			Products 1.docx
			Products 2.docx
			Purchase Order.docx
			Quarterly Sales.xlsx

APPLICATION	LESSON	DATA FILE	SOLUTION FILE
ADVANCED WORD	11		Recycling Rate.docx
			Regional Sales.xlsx
			Sales Report 1.docx
			Sales Report 2.docx
			Sales Report 3.docx
ADVANCED WORD	12	Account Holders.docx	Account Holders Data Source.docx
		Catalog.docx	Catalog Main Document.docx
		Clients.docx	Client Envelopes Main Document.docx
		Course Catalog.docx	Clients Data Source.docx
		Courses.docx	Courses Catalog Main Document.docx
		Customers.docx	Courses Data Source.docx
		Donation Letter.docx	Customer Labels Main Document.docx
		Order Confirmation.docx	Customers Data Source.docx
		Orders Shipped.docx	Donation Letter Main Document.docx
		Orders.docx	Membership Contacts Data Source.mdb
		Overdraft Letter.docx	Merged Client Envelopes.docx
		Products.docx	Merged Customer Labels.docx
		Prospects.docx	Merged Donation Letters.docx
		Shipped Message.docx	Merged Order Confirmations.docx
		Sponsors Letter.docx	Merged Overdraft Labels.docx
		Staff.docx	Merged Overdraft Letters.docx
			Merged Product Catalog.docx
			Merged Prospects Envelopes.docx
			Merged Shipped Messages.docx
			Merged Sponsors Letters.docx
			Merged Spring Courses Catalog.docx
			Merged Staff Messages.docx
			Order Confirmation Main Document.docx
			Orders Data Source.docx
			Orders Shipped Data Source.docx
			Overdraft Labels Main Document.docx
			Overdraft Letter Main Document.docx

DATA FILES

APPLICATION	LESSON	DATA FILE	SOLUTION FILE
ADVANCED WORD	12		Products Data Source.docx
			Prospects Data Source.docx
			Prospects Envelopes Main Document.docx
			Selian Letter.docx
			Shipped Message Main Document.docx
			Sponsors Data Source.mdb
			Sponsors Letter Main Document.docx
			Staff Data Source.docx
			Staff E-mail Main Document.docx
ADVANCED WORD	13	Bill of Sale.docx	Certified Employee Evaluation.docx
		Board Minutes RD.docx	Certified Employee Evaluation.xps
		Board Minutes RE.docx	Completed Challenge.docx
		Board Minutes.docx	Confidential Employee Evaluation.docx
		Challenge.docx	Final Bill of Sale.docx
		Completed Employee Evaluation.docx	Final Board Minutes.docx
		Consultation Call.docx	Final Emergency Contacts.docx
		Emergency Contacts 1.docx	Final Employee Evaluation.docx
		Emergency Contacts 2.docx	Final Job Description.docx
		Employee Evaluation.docx	Protected Consultation.docx
		Job Description RA.docx	Restricted Consultation Call.docx
		Job Description RB.docx	Restricted Employee Evaluation 1.docx
		Jones.jpg	Restricted Employee Evaluation 2.docx
		Sales Goal.docx	Restricted Employee Evaluation 3.docx
		Will Draft 1.docx	Revised Board Minutes 1.docx
		Will Draft 2.docx	Revised Board Minutes 2.docx
			Revised Board Minutes 3.docx
			Revised Board Minutes 4.docx
			Revised Board Minutes 5.docx
			Revised Sales Goal.docx
			Signed Bill of Sale.docx
			Updated Will.docx

DATA FILES

APPLICATION	LESSON	DATA FILE	SOLUTION FILE
ADVANCED WORD	14	Apollo 11.docx	Apollo 11 Revised.docx
		Apollo 12.docx	Family Disaster Plan.docx
		Apollo 13.docx	Final Lease.docx
		Apollo Resources.docx	Final Soil.docx
		Extreme Heat.docx	Journeys to the Moon 1.docx
		Family Disaster Plan.docx	Journeys to the Moon 2.docx
		Floods.docx	Journeys to the Moon 3.docx
		Landslides.docx	Journeys to the Moon 4.docx
		Lease.docx	Journeys to the Moon 5.docx
		Mission Highlights.docx	Journeys to the Moon 6.docx
		Moon Missions.docx	Journeys to the Moon 7.docx
		Natural Disasters Sources.docx	Journeys to the Moon 8.docx
		Returning Home.docx	Journeys to the Moon 9.docx
		Soil.docx	Journeys to the Moon 10.docx
		Tornadoes.docx	Journeys to the Moon 11.docx
			Journeys to the Moon 12.docx
			Journeys to the Moon Readability.docx
			Preparing for Natural Disasters 1.docx
			Preparing for Natural Disasters 2.docx
ADVANCED WORD	15	Apollo Missions 11-17.docx	Apollo Missions 1.docx
		Calories.docx	Apollo Missions 2.docx
		Disaster Index Entries.docx	Apollo Missions 3.docx
		Financial Review.docx	Apollo Missions 4.docx
		Fohey Case.docx	Apollo Missions 5.docx
		Foreign Trade.docx	Apollo Missions 6.docx
		Freedman Case.docx	Apollo Missions 7.docx
		Index Entries.docx	AutoMark Index Entries.docx
		Natural Disasters.docx	Fohey Case Summary.docx
		Nutrition Facts.docx	Freedman Case Summary.docx
			Revised Financial Revew.docx
			Revised Foreign Trade.docx

APPLICATION	LESSON	DATA FILE	SOLUTION FILE
ADVANCED WORD	15		Revised Natural Disasters 1.docx
			Revised Natural Disasters 2.docx
			Revised Nutrition Facts.docx
			Updated Disaster Index Entries.docx
ADVANCED WORD	16	Investment Club.docx	Final Resume.docm
		Profile.docx	Final Resume.xps
		Registrations.docx	Investment Club Agreement 1.docx
		Resume.docx	Investment Club Agreement 2.docx
		Revised Profile 1.docx	Personal Template 2.dotm
			Personal Template 3.dotm
			Quick Access Toolbar Screenshot.docx
			Revised Profile 1.docx
			Revised Profile 2.docx
			Updated Registrations 1.docm
			Updated Registrations 2.docm
			Updated Registrations 3.docm
			Updated Registrations 4.docm
ADVANCED WORD	17	LLDPE Blends and Coextrusions.docx	Custom Ribbon Screenshot.docx
		Member Directory.docx	Custom Ribbon Settings.exportedUI
			Members.dic
			Personal Template 4.dotx
			Revised LLDPE Blends and Coextrusions.docx
			Revised Member Directory.docx
			Toolbar Screenshot.docx
			Ultratech.dic
			Word Customizations.exportedUI

APPLICATION	LESSON	DATA FILE	SOLUTION FILE
ADVANCED WORD	Unit Review	Home Remedies Entries.docx	Envelopes Main Document.docx
		Home Remedies.docx	Final Home Remedies.docx
		Kick City.docx	Final Kick City.docx
		Managers.docx	Final Kick City.xps
		Pet Travel 1.docx	Final Pet Travel.docx
		Pet Travel 2.docx	Final Sales Letter.docx
		Pyramid.jpg	Marketing.dic
		Sales Letter.docx	Merged Sales Letter 1.docx
		Ski Club.docx	Merged Sales Letter 2.docx
			Merged Sales Letter Envelopes 1.docx
			Merged Sales Letter Envelopes 2.docx
			Personal Template 5.dotm
			Quarterly Sales Chart.docx
			Revised Sales Letter.docx
			Sales Letter Main Document.docx
			Ski Club Flyer.docx
			Ski Club Flyer.xps
			Updated Managers 1.docx
			Updated Managers 2.docx

ADVANCED

INTRODUCTION

LESSON 1   2 HRS.

Microsoft Office 2010 and the Internet

LESSON 1

Microsoft Office 2010 and the Internet

■ OBJECTIVES

Upon completion of this lesson, you should be able to:

- Apply basic Microsoft Word, Excel, Access, PowerPoint, and Outlook features.
- Search for information on the World Wide Web.
- Evaluate Web sites.
- Bookmark favorite Web sites.
- Manage the history of the Web sites visited.

■ VOCABULARY

bookmark

browser

hits

keywords

search engine

wildcard

Microsoft Office 2010 is a complete set of computer applications that equips you with the tools you need to produce a variety of documents and files, and to help streamline your everyday computing activities. This course focuses on the more complex and advanced capabilities of the Word, Excel, Access, PowerPoint, and Outlook applications.

This lesson provides a review of basic application features and will help you refresh your application skills. In this lesson, you will also learn more about how to access resources on the World Wide Web.

Applying Word Features

As you know, Microsoft Word is a powerful, full-featured word processor with comprehensive writing tools. You've already learned many of the basic features that enable you to complete common word-processing documents. The Word lessons in this course will introduce you to features that will enable you to further enhance the appearance of your documents and save time preparing and editing documents. Developing a document often involves multiple team members, and Word offers several tools to help you share documents and effectively collaborate on projects.

However, before you begin to explore these and other advanced features in Word, complete the following Step-by-Step, which provides a review of many basic Word skills.

Step-by-Step 1.1

1. Launch Word and then open the **Class Descriptions.docx** file from the drive and folder where your Data Files are stored. Save the document as **Updated Class Descriptions**, followed by your initials.

2. Edit the document as shown in **Figure 1–1**.

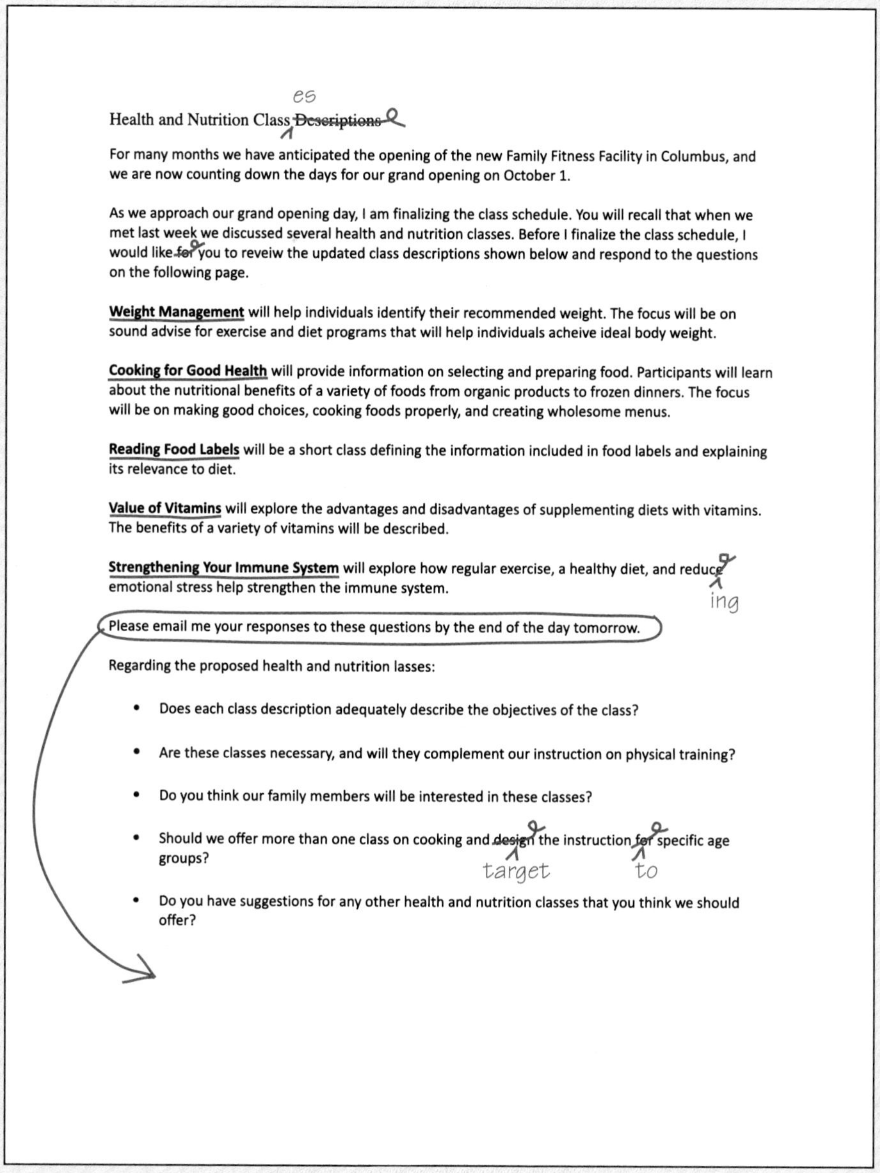

FIGURE 1–1
Edits for document in
Step-by-Step 1.1

Health and Nutrition Class ~~Descriptions~~ *es*

For many months we have anticipated the opening of the new Family Fitness Facility in Columbus, and we are now counting down the days for our grand opening on October 1.

As we approach our grand opening day, I am finalizing the class schedule. You will recall that when we met last week we discussed several health and nutrition classes. Before I finalize the class schedule, I would like ~~for~~ you to reveiw the updated class descriptions shown below and respond to the questions on the following page.

Weight Management will help individuals identify their recommended weight. The focus will be on sound advise for exercise and diet programs that will help individuals acheive ideal body weight.

Cooking for Good Health will provide information on selecting and preparing food. Participants will learn about the nutritional benefits of a variety of foods from organic products to frozen dinners. The focus will be on making good choices, cooking foods properly, and creating wholesome menus.

Reading Food Labels will be a short class defining the information included in food labels and explaining its relevance to diet.

Value of Vitamins will explore the advantages and disadvantages of supplementing diets with vitamins. The benefits of a variety of vitamins will be described.

Strengthening Your Immune System will explore how regular exercise, a healthy diet, and reduc*ing* emotional stress help strengthen the immune system.

Please email me your responses to these questions by the end of the day tomorrow.

Regarding the proposed health and nutrition lasses:

- Does each class description adequately describe the objectives of the class?

- Are these classes necessary, and will they complement our instruction on physical training?

- Do you think our family members will be interested in these classes?

- Should we offer more than one class on cooking and *target* ~~design~~ the instruction *to* ~~for~~ specific age groups?

- Do you have suggestions for any other health and nutrition classes that you think we should offer?

3. Center and bold the title, and then change the font to Arial 18 point. Change the title text to all uppercase.

4. Select the paragraphs that describe the five classes and format all the paragraphs with a left indent of 0.5" and a right indent of 5.5" (0.5" from the right margin).

5. Select the list of bulleted questions at the end of the document and apply the number format (1., 2., 3.) to create an enumerated list.

6. Position the insertion point anywhere in the first numbered paragraph and add space after the paragraph. Then use the Format Painter feature to copy the new paragraph format to the other paragraphs in the numbered list.

7. Search for the word *email* and replace it with **e-mail**.

8. Change the document margins to **Office 2003 Default** setting (1" top and bottom and 1.25" left and right).

9. Position the insertion point in front of the paragraph that begins *Regarding the proposed...* and insert a page break.

10. Create a header for only the second page of the document. Use the Blank (Three Columns) format for the header, and then type the title **Health and Nutrition Classes** in the center of the header.

11. Check the document for spelling and grammar and make any necessary corrections. The spelling checker doesn't catch mistypes if they are the same as correctly spelled words.

12. Save the changes. Close the document, and then exit Word.

Applying Excel Features

Excel is the spreadsheet application in the Office suite. As you've discovered, spreadsheets are used for entering, calculating, and analyzing data. You should now be familiar with the basic features for creating, editing, and formatting worksheet information. Excel's advanced features enable you to perform complex calculations and in-depth analysis that you'd normally leave up to an economist or mathematician! With Excel's data analysis tools, you can generate reports, charts, and tables that are every bit as professional looking and accurate as those created by the experts. In this course, you'll also learn how to share workbooks with colleagues.

Before you venture into the advanced features of Excel, complete the following Step-by-Step, which provides a review of the Excel basic skills.

Step-by-Step 1.2

1. Launch Excel and then open the **Sales Report.xlsx** file from the drive and folder where your Data Files are stored. Save the workbook as **Revised Sales Report**, followed by your initials.

2. Go to cell M5 and type the column heading **TOTAL**.

3. Go to cell M6 and enter a formula to calculate the sum of the numbers in cells B6:L6. Fill the formula down through cell M12.

4. Go to cell A14 and type the row heading **TOTAL**.

5. Go to cell B14 and enter a formula to calculate the sum of the numbers in cells B6:B13. Fill the formula across through cell M14.

6. Insert a new column to the left of the *TOTAL* column. In the new column, type the heading **Dec**, and then enter the following data in the new column:

   61258

   50211

   61858

   50212

   61855

   50215

   61852

7. Copy the formula in cell L14 and paste it in cell M14.

8. Merge and center the title *Division Sales Report* over cells A1:N1. Format the title text bold and italic, and change the font size to 14 point.

9. Delete rows 2 and 3.

10. Format the column and row headings bold, and then center the column headings.

11. Apply a currency format to all the numeric data, with no decimal points. If necessary, automatically adjust the column widths.

12. Create a 3-D pie chart on a new sheet, using only the data in the cell ranges A4:A10 and N4:N10. Add the title **Total Sales by Division** to the chart and apply a chart style of your choice.

13. Format the worksheet to fit on one page in landscape orientation.

14. Save the changes. Close the file, and then exit Excel.

Applying Access Features

Access is the database application in the Office suite that is used for storing and organizing information. Databases are made up of objects, including tables, queries, forms, and reports. You now should be familiar with the basic techniques for creating these objects. In the advanced lessons, you will learn about features that give you even more control over how database records are viewed, edited, and professionally analyzed. You'll learn how to streamline data entry and editing and to present the data in an attractive, reader-friendly manner.

Before you begin exploring advanced features in Access, walk through the following Step-by-Step to review the application's basic features.

Step-by-Step 1.3

1. Launch Access and open the **JC's Data.accdb** file from the drive and folder where your Data Files are stored. Save the database as **JC's Updated Data**, followed by your initials.

2. Open the EMPLOYEE table in Design View. Between the *Employee ID* and *Last Name* fields, insert a new field titled **Department**. Define the field data type as **Text**.

3. Save the changes to the table and then switch to Datasheet View.

4. Sort the table alphabetically by last name and then update the records to include the department name in which each employee works:

Dominquez:	**Marketing**
Gonzalez:	**Administrative**
Keplinger:	**Sales**
Mann:	**Accounting**
Pullis:	**Accounting**
Thomsen:	**Sales**
Ti:	**Marketing**
Wong:	**Sales**

5. Sort the table by Employee ID, and then add a new record to the table and enter the following information:

Employee ID:	**9**
Department:	**Sales**
Last Name:	**Barkin**
First Name:	**Dave**
Salary:	**$145,000**
Home Phone:	**608-555-5121**
Date Hired:	**3/24/13**

6. Adjust the column widths to show all the data, and then show the table in Print Preview.

7. Change the page layout to **Landscape** and close Print Preview. Save the changes and close the table.

8. Open the PRODUCTS table and filter the data to show only those products with a price greater than $10. The filter should produce eleven records. Remove the filter and close the table. When prompted, save the changes.

9. Use the Form Wizard to create a form based on the EMPLOYEE table.

   a. Include all the fields in the form.

   b. Select the **Columnar** layout.

   c. Name the form **EMPLOYEE FORM**.

10. Use the Report Wizard to create a report based on the EMPLOYEE table.

    a. Include all the fields except *Salary* and *Date Hired*.

    b. Group the records by **Department**.

    c. Sort the records in ascending order by **Last Name**.

    d. Apply the **Stepped** layout and **Portrait** orientation.

    e. Name the report **EMPLOYEE TELEPHONE REPORT**.

11. Close the report and the form, and then exit Access.

Applying PowerPoint Features

PowerPoint is a presentation graphics program that enables you to create presentation materials for a variety of audiences, including slide shows using a projector and online presentations that everyone on a network can view. In the PowerPoint unit, you will explore some of its more advanced features. To make your presentations more interesting and effective, PowerPoint provides tools to add multimedia effects to your slides. The many customizing features PowerPoint offers enable you to create your own color schemes, backgrounds, and design templates. When preparing for your final presentation, PowerPoint has many options for distributing your slide show, including sharing via e-mail or presenting it remotely over a Web page or network.

Before you explore these advanced PowerPoint features, complete the following Step-by-Step to review your PowerPoint skills.

Step-by-Step 1.4

1. Launch PowerPoint, and then open the **Historic Preservation.pptx** file from the drive and folder where your Data Files are stored. Save the presentation as **Historic Housing**, followed by your initials.

2. On the title slide, replace *Your Name* with your own first and last names.

3. Add a new slide after the title slide, using the **Two Content** layout for the new slide.

4. In the title placeholder, type **Stabilization**. In the text placeholder on the left, type the following two lines of text. The text should automatically be formatted with bullets.

   Reestablish structural stability.

   Maintain essential form.

5. Move slide #5 (with the title *Resources)* so it is the last slide in the presentation.

6. Add graphics to slides 2–9. If possible, search Office.com for the graphics. *Hint*: Try search terms such as *house, fix, historic, tools,* and *blueprints.*

7. Apply a built-in design, and, if desired, change the color theme and/or fonts.

8. Apply a transition to all slides in the presentation. Adjust the timing of the transitions as needed.

9. Apply custom animations to the text and graphics on slides 2–10 to control when and how the objects appear.

10. Run the slide show and observe your transitions and animations, and make any necessary changes.

11. Save your changes. Close the presentation, and then exit PowerPoint.

Applying Outlook Features

Outlook is a desktop information management application. As you already know, using Outlook helps you keep track of e-mail messages, appointments, meetings, contact information, and tasks you need to complete. In this course, you will explore some of Outlook's more advanced features. You will learn about features that make it even easier to manage contact information, manage e-mails, and communicate with others. You will also learn about many features and tools that make it easier for you to schedule events and track progress on tasks.

Before you explore Outlook's advanced features, complete the following Step-by-Step to review the basic skills and features for Outlook.

Step-by-Step 1.5

1. Launch Outlook. Open a new journal entry and enter the information below. Then start the timer and leave the journal entry open.

   Subject: **Step-by-Step 1.5**

   Entry type: **Task**

2. Open the Contacts folder. Create a new contact group and name the group **Fitness Trainers**.

3. Add the following contacts to the new group and save the group.

   Name: **Sharon McKee**

   E-mail: **smckee@familyfit.xyz**

   Name: **Ronald DeVilliers**

   E-mail: **rdevillers@familyfit.xyz**

   Name: **Alisa Mandez**

   E-mail: **amandez@familyfit.xyz**

4. Create a new e-mail message. Send the message to the Fitness Trainers group, and type **Health and Nutrition Classes** in the Subject box. Then type the following in the message area:

   Please review the attached document and give me your feedback by the end of the day tomorrow.

5. Attach your solution file **Updated Class Descriptions.docx** to the e-mail message, and save the e-mail message as a draft. Do not attempt to send the e-mail.

6. Create the following two notes:

   Upload the health and nutrition class descriptions to the Web site.

   Confirm yoga class schedule with Bonnie.

7. Open the Calendar and show the calendar for a week from the current date. Create an appointment with your dentist for 10 a.m. and set a reminder. The appointment should last 45 minutes.

8. Open the Tasks folder and create the following new task. Give the task high priority and specify that it be completed within a week.

   Gather information for dental bills to submit for insurance.

9. Delete the dentist appointment.

10. Delete the contact group and contacts you created, and then delete the e-mail draft.

11. Delete the insurance task.

12. Delete the two notes.

13. Return to the journal entry and pause the timer. Make note of how much time you spent on this activity, and then delete the journal entry.

14. Exit Outlook.

Accessing Internet Resources

Microsoft Office 2010 is designed to give you quick and easy access to the World Wide Web, regardless of which Office application you are currently using. A *browser* is a program that connects you to remote computers and gives you the capability to access, view, and download data from the Web. Microsoft's browser program is Microsoft Internet Explorer.

▶ **VOCABULARY**
browser

Searching for Information and Evaluating Web Sites

Each day, millions of people use the World Wide Web to find information. To get the information they're looking for, they must navigate through an enormous amount of data. As a result, even with high-speed connections and powerful search engines, searching for specific information can be very time consuming.

▶ **VOCABULARY**
search engine
keywords
hits
wildcard

A *search engine*, such as Microsoft's Bing, is a tool designed to find information on the Web. When you enter *keywords*, words that describe the information you are seeking, the search engine generates a list of Web sites that potentially match the search criteria. These search results (the best matching Web sites) are often referred to as *hits*. Searches often produce a long list of hits; if you wish to narrow the search results, you need to be more specific in the keywords that you provide. **Table 1–1** describes several options for refining a search so you can find information quickly and effectively.

TABLE 1–1   Options for refining searches

SEARCH OPTIONS	DESCRIPTION
Capitalization	If you want the results to include occurrences of both upper and lowercase letters, enter the keywords using all lowercase letters. However, if you want to narrow your results to words that begin with capital letters (such as Central Intelligence Agency) or all capital letters (such as CIA), enter the keywords with the same capitalization.
Plurals	Most search engines consider singular keywords as both singular and plural. For example, results for the keyword *agent* will include hits with the word *agents*. If you want the results to include only hits with a plural word, be sure the keyword is plural.
Phrases	Search for a group of words by including quotation marks before and after the sequence of words. With the quotation marks, only hits with all of the words in the exact same sequence will appear in the results. Without the quotation marks, the results will include hits that contain all or most of the words anywhere within a Web site.
Operators	Narrow or broaden the search using operators including *+*, *&*, *and*, *-*, *not*, and *or*. For example, if you are searching for information about international exchange students, use the following keywords in the search engine to exclude hits for currency exchange rates: **+international +exchange +students -currency** or **international and exchange and students not currency**
Related pages	Many search engines provide options to include hits for Web pages with similar information. Look for links such as *Similar pages*, *Also try*, or *Related searches*.
Truncation	Some search engines support the use of a symbol, sometimes referred to as a **wildcard**, that allows for variations in the spelling of words. When an asterisk (*) symbol is used in a word, the search results include hits with alternate spellings for the word at the point that the asterisk appears. For example, *extra** generates hits for Web pages with *extra*, *extras*, *extract*, and *extraordinary*.
Domains	You can limit search results to a specific domain, such as an educational institution or a government Web site. For example, to find information about environmental research at an educational institution, in the search engine, enter the following keywords: **+domain:edu +environmental +research** or **domain:edu and environmental and research**

When the search results appear, read the information carefully before clicking any of the links. You can determine the validity of some of the hits by looking at the URLs. For example, if you're looking for information about deadlines for filing forms for personal income taxes, you want to click a link that includes IRS in the URL. Also, domain name extensions help to identify the type of entity. **Table 1–2** shows common domain extensions and the type of entity related to them.

EXTRA FOR EXPERTS

Most search engines include links that provide information about advanced search features. Be sure to access these links to learn how to make your searches more effective.

TABLE 1–2   Common domain extensions

DOMAIN EXTENSIONS	DESCRIPTIONS
.com	Commercial business
.edu	Educational institution
.gov	Governmental institution
.org	Nonprofit organization
.mil	Military site
.net	Network site
.us	Abbreviation that indicates a country; for example: .us (United States), .ja (Japan), .uk (United Kingdom), .ca (Canada), and .hk (Hong Kong)

TIP

Clicking a link on a Web site can distract you and take you off task. Before you click a link, try to determine if the link will take you where you want to go. If you click a link and see that the target is not what you expected, click the Back button to return to the previous Web page and stay on task.

Just about anyone can publish information on the Web—often for free, and usually unmonitored. So how do you know if you can trust the information that you find? When you depend on the Web for sources of information, it is your responsibility to determine the integrity and validity of the information and its source. **Table 1–3** provides questions that will guide you through an evaluation process.

TABLE 1–3   A guide for evaluating information on the Web

QUESTIONS TO ASK	WHAT TO CONSIDER
Is the information relevant to my query?	The information should help you to accomplish your goals and objectives. Make sure you analyze the information and determine if it meets your needs.
Is the information current?	Check for a date on the Web page that indicates when the information was last updated.
Is the Web site published by a company or an entity, or is it a personal Web site?	The URL often includes a company name. If you are familiar with the company or entity, consider whether you trust information from this source. If you are not familiar with the company, or the individual, look for links such as *About Us*, *Background*, or *Biography*.
What is the purpose of the Web site?	Use the domain name to identify the type of Web site. For example: a domain name ending with .com is a business, and the intent of the Web site is to sell or promote a product or service.
Who is the author?	Look for information that explains who the author is and how the author is connected to the subject. Verify that the author is qualified to address the subject. Individuals sometimes falsify their credentials, so research the author's background and confirm that the author is credible. For example, if information at the Web site indicates that the author is a professor at a university, go to the university Web site and check the faculty roster.
Is the author biased in his/her opinion?	When looking for facts, be sure the author provides objective viewpoints and cites information with credible sources.
Is the Web site presented professionally?	Information should be well organized and presented accurately, free from spelling and grammar errors.
Are the links legitimate and credible?	Confirm that links are up to date. Links to a credible Web site, such as a business or an organization, do not mean that the business or organization approves of or supports the content on the linked Web page.

Step-by-Step 1.6

1. If necessary, log onto the Internet and open your browser.

2. In the address bar, type **www.bing.com** and then press **Enter** to open the Bing search engine.

3. In the Bing search box, type **lake tahoe ski** and then click the **Search** button, or press **Enter**.

4. Note that the number of hits is indicated at the top of the search results. Scroll down and review the first set of results. Each link provides a brief preview of the Web page content, and the keywords are highlighted in the preview. Occurrences of the word *skiing* may also appear highlighted in the previews.

5. Edit the text in the search box to read **+lake +tahoe +ski -water**. Click the **Search** button, or press **Enter**. Scroll down through the first set of results. Note that the number of hits is greatly reduced, and the word *water* is not found in any of the previews.

6. Edit the text in the search box to read **"lake tahoe water ski"** and then click the **Search** button, or press **Enter**. Note that the number of hits is considerably less because adding more keywords often narrows the search.

7. Delete the text in the search box and then type **domain:org and tahoe and ski**. Click the **Search** button, or press **Enter**. Scroll down through the first set of results. Notice every URL has a .org extension.

8. Type **www.nasa.gov** in the address bar and then press **Enter**. The NASA home page opens.

9. Navigate the Web site and find the following information:
   a. the date when the site was last updated
   b. NASA locations
   c. blogs
   d. the names of the authors of the site's articles and blogs
   e. any available information about the authors' backgrounds
   f. information for contacting NASA

10. Return to the home page for the NASA Web site.

11. Leave the NASA Web site open for the next Step-by-Step.

Revisiting Web Sites

As you rely more and more on the Web as a primary source of information on any topic, you'll find that there are sites you visit frequently or that you know you'll want to access again. You can create a bookmark for quick and easy access to a Web page. A *bookmark* is a link that navigates you to the Web page, and it is saved in a Favorites folder. You can create additional folders inside the Favorites folder to keep the list of sites organized.

▶ **VOCABULARY**
bookmark

Your browser keeps track of the sites you have visited, so you can also quickly revisit a site by selecting the Web site from the History list. The History list can be organized by date, site, most visited, and the order the sites were visited on the current day. You can easily delete the History list, as well as temporary Internet files, cookies, form data, and passwords.

Step-by-Step 1.7

The following steps describe bookmarking Web pages using Internet Explorer features. If you are not using Internet Explorer as your browser, you can still explore the features for creating the bookmarks, but these steps will not exactly describe your browser features.

1. If necessary, log onto the Internet, open your Internet Explorer browser, and open **www.nasa.gov**. Or navigate to the NASA home page, if necessary.

2. Click the **Favorites** button on the Command bar in the upper-left corner of the screen, as shown in **Figure 1–2**.

FIGURE 1–2
Favorites button on
the Internet Explorer browser

Favorites button

3. If necessary, click the **Favorites** tab to show a list of your favorite sites. Your favorites list will be different than the one shown in **Figure 1–3**.

FIGURE 1–3
Folders on the Favorites tab

History tab

Favorites list

4. Click the **Add to Favorites** button to open the Add a Favorite dialog box shown in **Figure 1–4**.

FIGURE 1–4
Add a Favorite dialog box

TIP

You can also quickly add Web sites to the Favorites folder using the shortcut keys Ctrl+D.

5. In the Name text box, *NASA - Home* appears. Leave the name as is and click **New Folder** on the dialog box. The Create a Folder dialog box similar to the one shown in **Figure 1–5** opens. In the Folder Name text box, type **Research** and then click **Create**. The Add a Favorite dialog box is still open. Click **Add**.

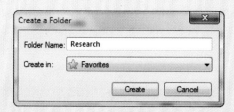

FIGURE 1–5
Create a Folder dialog box

6. Click the **Favorites** button to show your list of favorites. Click the new folder **Research** and you will see the *NASA - Home* site. You can move favorites into folders by dragging the site name to the desired folder.

7. Click the **History** tab on the Favorites pane. Click the **View By...** button at the top of the History list, and then click **View By Order Visited Today**. Notice that the NASA Web page is included in the list of documents and Web sites accessed today. Click the **View By...** button at the top of the History list again, then click **View By Most Visited**. The list is rearranged.

8. Right-click one of the Web sites in this list, click **Delete** in the shortcut menu, and then click **Yes** to confirm the deletion.

9. Click the **Favorites** button, and on the History tab, click any one of the site names on the History list. The Web page opens.

10. Click the **list arrow** at the right side of the address bar in the browser, as shown in **Figure 1–6**. A history of accessed Web sites is displayed, as well as a list of favorite sites. Click anywhere outside the History list to close it.

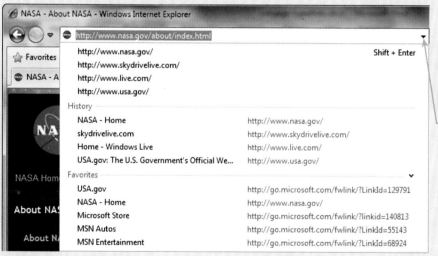

FIGURE 1–6
History and Favorites lists on the address bar

Click to display history of accessed Web sites and favorite sites

11. Click the **Safety** button on the browser toolbar, as shown in **Figure 1–7**.

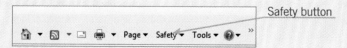

Safety button

FIGURE 1–7
Safety button on browser toolbar

12. Click **Delete Browsing History** to open the dialog box in **Figure 1–8**. If necessary, change the settings so they match those shown in the figure, and then click **Delete**.

FIGURE 1–8
Delete Browsing History
dialog box

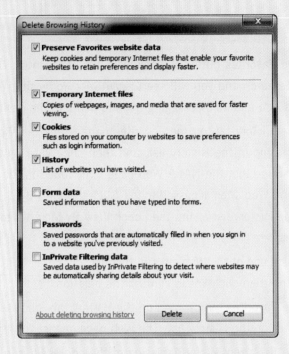

13. Click the **Favorites** button. Click the **Favorites** tab, and in the Favorites list, right-click the **Research** folder, and then click **Delete** in the shortcut menu. Click **Yes** to confirm the deletion.
14. Close Internet Explorer.

SUMMARY

In this lesson, you learned:

■ Microsoft Word is a powerful, full-featured word processor. Its advanced features enable users to further enhance the appearance of documents and save time preparing and editing documents. Developing a document often involves multiple team members, and Word offers several tools to help you share documents and effectively collaborate on projects.

■ Excel is the spreadsheet application in the Microsoft Office suite. Spreadsheets are used primarily for calculating and analyzing data, and Excel's advanced features enable you to perform complex calculations and in-depth analysis. Excel includes many features that enable you to generate accurate and professional-looking reports, charts, and tables.

■ Access is the database application in the Office suite. Databases are used for storing and organizing information. The advanced features in Access give you more control over how database records are viewed, edited, and professionally analyzed. Effectively designed forms and reports help to streamline data entry and editing.

■ Microsoft PowerPoint is a presentation graphics program that enables you to create materials for presentations of many kinds. Its advanced features include several tools for customizing slide designs and using multimedia effects to enhance your content. Remote publishing features in PowerPoint enable you to share presentations over the Internet or a network.

- Microsoft Outlook is a desktop information management program that provides several tools for scheduling appointments and meetings, managing and delegating tasks, and communicating with others. Advanced features help you customize the tools to fit your needs.

- An enormous amount of information is available on the World Wide Web. Effective search strategies not only save you time, but they also lead you to more relevant sources.

- When you depend on the Web for sources of information, it is your responsibility to determine the integrity and validity of the information and its source.

- You can bookmark Web sites that you visit frequently and save the links to the Favorites folder. You can create additional folders to organize your Favorites list.

- You can also quickly revisit a site by selecting the Web site from the History list, which can be organized by date, site, most visited, and the order the sites were visited on the current day.

VOCABULARY REVIEW

Define the following terms:

bookmark	hits	search engine
browser	keywords	wildcard

REVIEW QUESTIONS

MATCHING

Match the most appropriate application in Column 2 to the application described in Column 1.

Column 1

_____ 1. A graphics application with multimedia capabilities that can be used to create materials to present and share information with others

_____ 2. An application designed for entering, calculating, and analyzing data

_____ 3. An application used for storing and organizing information

_____ 4. A desktop information management application

_____ 5. An application that provides comprehensive writing tools for sharing information with others

Column 2

A. Microsoft Outlook

B. Microsoft PowerPoint

C. Internet Explorer

D. Microsoft Word

E. Microsoft Excel

F. Microsoft Access

MULTIPLE CHOICE

Select the best response for the following statements.

1. A _____ is a program that gives you the capability to access, view, and download data from the Web.

   A. search engine   C. browser

   B. Web page   D. tracking device

2. _____ are used to broaden or narrow an online search.

   A. Keywords   C. Operators

   B. Phrases   D. all of the above

3. Non-profit organizations commonly use the _____ extension in the domain name.

   A. .net   C. country abbreviation

   B. .org   D. .com

4. _____ are the results generated by a search engine.

   A. Hits   C. Wildcards

   B. Domains   D. Quick links

5. You can organize your Internet Explorer History list based on _____.

   A. the date sites were accessed   C. the order in which sites were visited today

   B. the names of the sites   D. all of the above

WRITTEN QUESTIONS

1. Explain how the search results are affected when you include quotation marks before and after a group of words when entering keywords in a search engine.

2. Explain how the domain name can help you identify the purpose of a Web site.

3. Give an example of when you would include operators with the keywords in a search engine.

4. How can you validate that a Web site author has credibility?

5. Name some examples of related pages options provided by some search engines.

■ PROJECTS

If you have a SAM 2010 user profile, your instructor may have assigned an autogradable version of the indicated project. If so, log into the SAM 2010 Web site at *www.cengage.com/sam2010* to download the instruction and start files.

PROJECT 1–1

1. Launch Word, then open the **Spectrum Follow-up.docx** data file from the drive and folder where your Data Files are stored. Save the document as **Final Spectrum Follow-up**, followed by your initials.

2. Make the edits indicated in **Figure 1–9**.

3. Change the left and right margins to 1.25 inches.

4. Justify the alignment of the paragraphs in the body of the letter.

5. Indent the bulleted list .5 inches from the left margin.

6. Adjust the paragraph spacing as needed to fit the entire document on one page.

7. Proofread and check for spelling and grammar errors, and make any necessary corrections.

8. Save the changes and leave the document open for the next project.

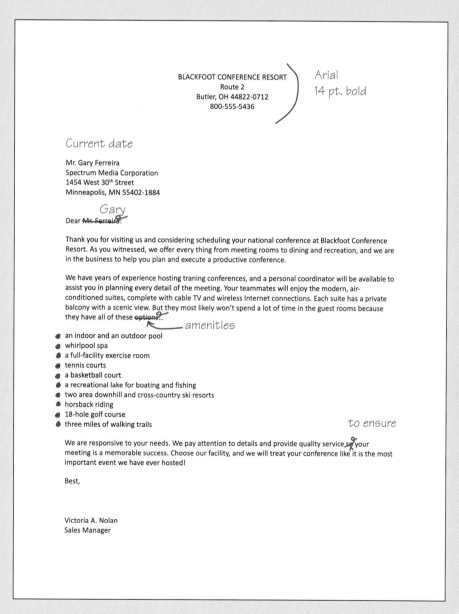

FIGURE 1–9   Edits for the Word document in Project 1–1

◣ SAM PROJECT 1–2

1. Launch PowerPoint and open a new presentation. Save the presentation as **Blackfoot Resort**, followed by your initials.

2. Create a slide show highlighting the guest amenities described in the Blackfoot Conference Resort letter in Project 1-1. This presentation will be distributed on the Internet to promote the resort.

3. Add pictures and graphics to help viewers visualize the amenities.

4. Add a creative title slide at the beginning of the presentation, and add a slide for closure at the end of the presentation.

5. Apply an appropriate design or background colors to the slides.

6. Add transitions to the slides, animations to the text, and objects on the slides to produce special effects and keep the viewer's attention.

7. Save the changes and exit PowerPoint.

PROJECT 1–3

1. If necessary, log onto the Internet and open your browser.

2. In the address bar, type **www.bing.com** and press Enter.

3. Enter the keywords **Conference Resorts Ohio** to search for Ohio-based conference resort sites that offer options for guests that are similar to the options described in the Blackfoot Conference Resort document you edited in Project 1-1.

4. When you find at least two Web sites promoting a conference center similar to the Blackfoot Conference Resort, save the sites to your Favorites list in a Conference Resort folder. *Hint*: Several hits may be sites that showcase multiple resorts, and you will need to navigate to the individual resort pages to get the required information.

5. Evaluate the Web sites and answer the following questions about each Web site.
   a. Were you able to find relevant information to compare resorts?
   b. Is the information at the site current?
   c. When was the site last updated?
   d. Is the site organized well, and is the information presented accurately and professionally?
   e. Does the site provide background information about the resort?
   f. Can you easily access information to contact the resort?
   g. Would you recommend this resort? Explain the reasons for your answer.

6. Close the browser.

PROJECT 1–4

1. Launch Excel and open the **January Sales.xlsx** file from the drive and folder where your Data Files are stored. Save the workbook as **First Qtr Sales**, followed by your initials.

2. In cell C1, type the column heading **February**. In cell D1, type the column heading **March**. In cell E1, type the column heading **Total**. In cell A7, type the row heading **Total**.

3. Enter the following data in the new columns.

	February	March
Byron Store	23112	42109
Fenton Store	38432	41002
Holly Store	31902	48111
Howell Store	27656	39202
Linden Store	29211	43007

4. Proofread the data entries to make sure you entered the numbers correctly.

5. Apply the Accounting number format to all the cells with numbers and remove the decimal places.

6. Enter a formula to calculate the sum of the cell range B2:D2 in cell E2, then fill the formula down through cell E6.

7. Enter a formula to calculate the sum of the cell range B2:B6 in cell B7, then fill the formula across through cell E7.

8. Create a 3-D column chart on the same sheet showing total sales by store. Apply a design of your choice.

9. Add a centered overlay title and type **First Qtr. Sales**. Turn off the legend options.

10. Reposition the chart on the sheet so you can see the sales data in the worksheet.

11. Save the changes and close the document.

PROJECT 1–5

1. Launch Access and open the **Clients.accdb** file from the drive and folder where your Data Files are stored. Save the database as **Updated Clients**, followed by your initials.

2. Open the CLIENTS table in Datasheet View.

3. Delete the record for Daniel Warner.

4. Update the address for Helen Sanderson. Her street address is now **709 Vienna Woods Drive, Cincinnati, OH 45211**.

5. In Design View, add a new field named **Mobile Phone**. Save the changes to the table and then switch back to Datasheet View.

6. Delete the home phone number for Paula Trobaugh and add her mobile phone number, **513-555-4465**.

7. Add two new clients:

   Penelope Rausch

   5074 Signal Hill

   Cincinnati, OH 45244

   Home Phone 513-555-0133

   Mobile Phone 513-555-0899

   Roger Williamson

   722 Red Bud Avenue

   Cincinnati, OH 45229

   Mobile Phone 513-555-1055

8. Save and close the database, then exit Access.

 # CRITICAL THINKING

ACTIVITY 1–1

Excel and Access have some similarities because both applications are used to organize data. If possible, look at two computer screens, side by side. On one computer, open an Excel worksheet. On the other computer, open an Access database table in Datasheet View. Compare the two screens, and create a list of similarities and differences between the worksheet and the database table. You should point out at least four similarities and four differences.

ACTIVITY 1–2

Open your browser and go to *www.bing.com*. Search for the keywords *Top Ten Search Engines*. Find the most current information available, and confirm that the sources are credible. Then, from the two sources, choose two search engines that you have never used and explore the features in each. Write a brief description of the features you like and why you would use them.

INTRODUCTORY UNIT

MICROSOFT WORD 2010

LESSON 1

Microsoft Word Basics

■ OBJECTIVES

Upon completion of this lesson, you should be able to:

- Start Word and understand the ways to view your document.
- Enter text in a document and navigate a document.
- Use Backspace and Delete to correct errors.
- Save a document.
- Open an existing document.
- Use Full Screen Reading view.
- Change the page orientation of a document. Preview and print a document.
- Exit Word.

■ VOCABULARY

Draft view

Full Screen Reading view

insertion point

landscape orientation

Outline view

portrait orientation

Print Layout view

Quick Access Toolbar

Ribbon

status bar

toolbar

view buttons

Web Layout view

word processing

word wrap

Zoom

Introduction to Word Processing

Word processing is the use of computer software to enter and edit text. When using word-processing software such as Word, you can easily create and edit documents such as letters and reports. You can even create more complex documents such as newsletters with pictures and other graphics. These documents can be used in your school, career, personal, and business activities.

The lessons in this unit contain step-by-step exercises for you to complete using a computer and Word. You'll learn how to start Word, enter and edit text, save and open a document, and switch among the various ways to view a document. You'll also learn how to change the orientation of a page, preview and print a document, and exit Word.

Starting Word

To start Word, click the Start button on the taskbar. Click All Programs on the Start menu, and then click Microsoft Office on the submenu. Click Microsoft Word 2010. A screen displaying copyright information appears briefly, followed by a window containing a blank page in which you can create and edit documents. See **Figure 1–1**.

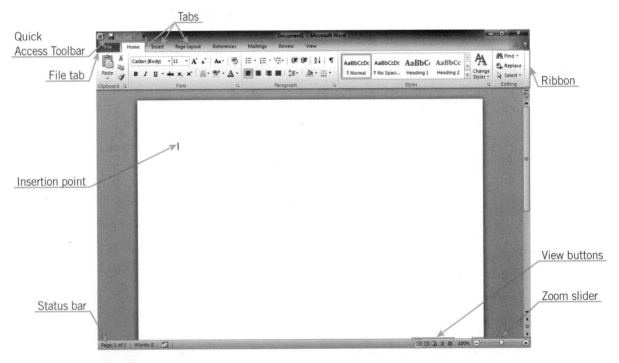

FIGURE 1–1   Opening screen in Word

Step-by-Step 1.1

1. Click the **Start** button 🌑 on the taskbar.

2. Click **All Programs**. The Start menu changes to show all the programs installed on the computer.

3. On the Start menu, click the **Microsoft Office** folder. The list of programs in the folder appears. Click **Microsoft Word 2010** on the submenu. Word starts and a blank document appears in the program window, as shown in Figure 1–1.

4. Leave the blank Word document open for the next Step-by-Step.

Identifying Parts of the Word Program Window

Look carefully at the parts of the Word program window labeled in Figure 1–1, and find them on your screen. Many of these elements appear in other Office applications. **Table 1–1** describes some of the commonly used elements of the program window.

heading ⇒ título

TABLE 1–1   Understanding the Word program window

ELEMENT	FUNCTION
Ribbon	Contains commands for working with the document, organized by tabs.
Quick Access Toolbar	Contains buttons (icons) for common commands.
Insertion point	Shows where text will appear when you begin typing.
Status bar	Displays information about the current document and process.
View buttons	Allows you to change views quickly.
Zoom slider	Allows you to increase or decrease the size of the document on-screen.

When the pointer is in the document window, it looks like an uppercase letter *I* and is called the I-beam pointer. When you move the pointer out of the document window toward the Ribbon or the status bar, it turns into an arrow to allow you to point to and click the buttons. The pointer changes into other shapes for performing certain tasks.

Understanding Document Views

As you work with a document, you might want to change the way it looks on the screen. Word provides five ways to view a document on the screen: Print Layout, Full Screen Reading, Web Layout, Outline, and Draft. **Table 1–2** describes each view.

TABLE 1–2 Document views

VIEW	DESCRIPTION
Print Layout	Shows how a document will look when it is printed
Full Screen Reading	Shows text on the screen in a format that is easy to read and hides the Ribbon
Web Layout	Simulates the way a document will look when it is viewed as a Web page; text and graphics appear the way they would in a Web browser
Outline	Displays headings and text in outline form so you can see the structure of your document and reorganize easily
Draft	Displays only the text of a document without showing the arrangement of the text; if your document includes any pictures, they would not appear

To switch between views, on the Ribbon, click the View tab, and then in the Document Views group, click the button that corresponds to the view you want. You can also click one of the *view buttons* at the bottom-right of the document window, to the left of the Zoom slider. Switching views changes only the way the document looks on the screen. It does not change the way it looks when you print it. You will work in Print Layout view most of the time.

▶ **VOCABULARY**

view buttons

insertion point

word wrap

Inserting Text and Understanding Word Wrap

To enter text in a new document, you begin typing. The text appears in the document window at the *insertion point*. As you type, the insertion point moves to the right and the word count indicator in the status bar changes to show the number of words in the document. If the text you are typing extends beyond the right margin, it automatically moves to the next line. This feature is called *word wrap* because words are "wrapped around" to the next line when they do not fit on the current line.

When you press Enter, a blank line is inserted automatically and you start a new paragraph. Most documents in the business world are typed with a blank line between paragraphs, rather than indenting the first line of each paragraph. The settings in Word help you do this easily.

Step-by-Step 1.2

1. Type the following text. As you type, watch how the words at the end of lines wrap to the next line. If you type a word incorrectly, just continue typing. You learn how to correct errors later in this lesson.

   You should take the time to plan and organize your work. To help you meet your goals, it can be helpful to list the tasks you need to accomplish, and then you can rank them by importance.

2. Press **Enter**. The insertion point skips a line and appears blinking at the left margin, as shown in **Figure 1–2**.

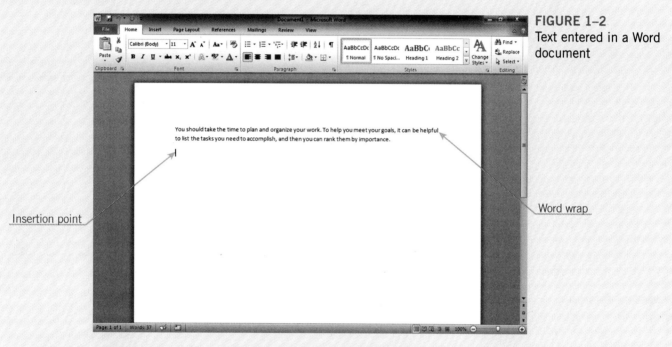

FIGURE 1–2
Text entered in a Word document

Insertion point

Word wrap

3. Type the following text. Press **Enter** at the end of each paragraph.

   Start by listing everything you need to accomplish today. Include both tasks that you must complete, as well as tasks you would like to complete.

   Next, examine the tasks you listed, and then number them in order of importance. Once you have the items in order, you have a plan!

4. Leave the document open for the next Step-by-Step.

Navigating a Document

To correct errors, insert new text, or change existing text, you must know how to reposition the insertion point in a document. You can move the insertion point in a document by using the mouse or the keyboard. To reposition the insertion point using the mouse, move the mouse so that the pointer moves to the position where you want the insertion point to appear, and then click the left mouse button. The blinking insertion point appears at the point you clicked.

When working with a long document, it is faster to use the keyboard to move the insertion point. **Table 1–3** lists the keys you can press to move the insertion point.

TABLE 1–3   Keyboard shortcuts for moving the insertion point

PRESS	TO MOVE THE INSERTION POINT
Right arrow	Right one character
Left arrow	Left one character
Down arrow	To the next line
Up arrow	To the previous line
End	To the end of the line
Home	To the beginning of the line
Page Down	To the next page
Page Up	To the previous page
Ctrl+right arrow	To the beginning of the next word
Ctrl+left arrow	To the beginning of the previous word
Ctrl+End	To the end of the document
Ctrl+Home	To the beginning of the document

In Table 1–3, two keys are listed for some of the movements. When you see an instruction to press two keys at once, press and hold the first key, press the second key, and then let go of both keys.

Step-by-Step 1.3

1. Press **Ctrl+Home**. The insertion point jumps to the beginning of the document.
2. Press **Ctrl+right arrow** four times to move to the fourth word (*time*) in the first line.
3. Press **End**. The insertion point moves to the end of the first line.
4. Press **down arrow** to move to the end of the next line.
5. Press **Ctrl+End**. The insertion point jumps to the end of the document.
6. Press **Ctrl+Home** to move back to the beginning of the document.
7. Leave the document open for the next Step-by-Step.

Using Backspace and Delete

[handwritten: retroceso]

If you make a mistake typing, or you just want to change text, you might need to delete characters or words. There are two ways to delete characters: Use Backspace or Delete. Pressing Backspace deletes the character to the left of the insertion point. Pressing Delete deletes the character to the right of the insertion point.

[handwritten notes in margin:
clipboard ⇒ portapapeles
desktop ⇒ escritorio
recycle bin ⇒ papelera de reciclaje
System tray ⇒ bandeja de sistema
bold ⇒ audaz, atrevido, enérgico]

Step-by-Step 1.4

1. Position the insertion point after the word *should* in the first sentence of the document.

2. Press **Backspace** until the words *You should* are deleted.

3. Press **Delete** twice to delete the space and the lowercase letter *t* in the word *take*, and then type **T**.

4. In the second sentence of the first paragraph, position the insertion point before the third word instance of the word *you* (after the word *then*).

5. Press **Delete** until the words *you can* and the space after *can* are deleted.

6. Look over the document. Position the insertion point as needed, and then use Backspace or Delete to correct any typing errors you made.
   [handwritten: hacer una revisión]

7. Leave the document open for the next Step-by-Step.

[handwritten: underlining ⇒ subrayado]

Saving a Document

When you save a document for the first time, you can click the Save button on the *Quick Access Toolbar*. You can also click the File tab, and then on the navigation bar, click the Save or Save As command. In all three cases, the Save As dialog box

▶ **VOCABULARY**
Quick Access Toolbar

appears, as shown in **Figure 1–3**. This is where you name your file and choose a location to save it in.

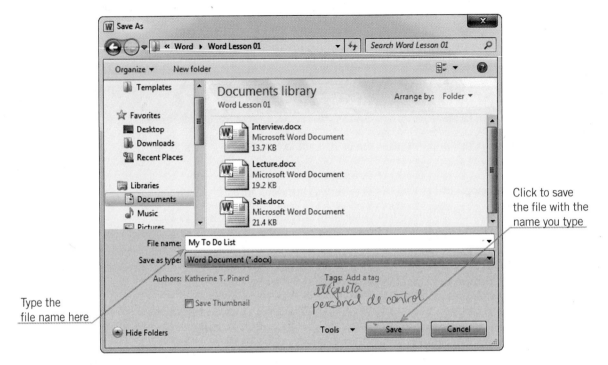

FIGURE 1–3   Save As dialog box

Once you have saved a document for the first time, you can click the Save button on the Quick Access Toolbar, or you can click the File tab, and then on the navigation bar, click the Save command, and Word saves the changes you made in the document by copying over the previous version. If you don't want to copy over the original version of your document, you can use the Save As command to open the Save As dialog box and save it using a different name or to a new location.

Creating Folders

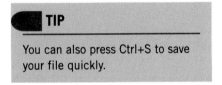
Folders can help you organize files. You can create a new folder in the Save As dialog box. To create a new folder within your current folder, click the New folder button on the toolbar in the Save As dialog box. A new folder appears in the list with the temporary name "New folder" highlighted in blue, as shown in **Figure 1–4**. Because the name is highlighted, you can just type the new folder name, and the text you type will replace the old name. When you are finished, press Enter. The folder name is changed and the folder opens to become the current folder.

New folder button

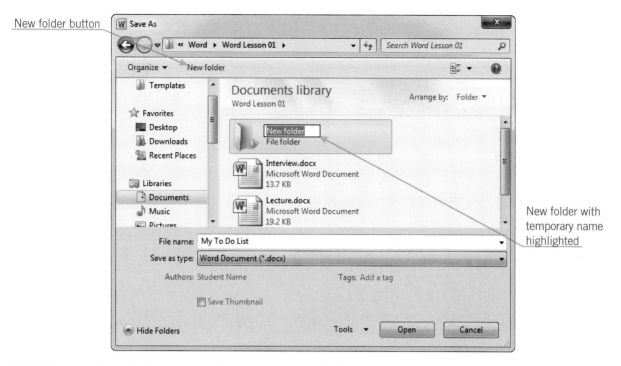

New folder with temporary name highlighted

FIGURE 1–4   Save As dialog box after creating a new folder

Step-by-Step 1.5

1. On the Ribbon, click the **File** tab, and then on the navigation bar, click the **Save As** command. The Save As dialog box appears. Refer back to Figure 1–3.

2. Navigate to the drive and folder where your Data Files are stored.

3. Double-click the **Word** folder, and then double-click the **Word Lesson 01** folder.

4. On the toolbar, click the **New folder** button. A new folder appears in the list in the dialog box with the name highlighted. Refer back to Figure 1–4.

5. Type **My Tasks**, and then press **Enter**. Click **Open**. The Address bar at the top of the Save As dialog box changes to indicate that My Tasks is the current folder.

6. In the File name box, select the entire name of the file, if necessary. Type **My To Do List** followed by your initials.

7. Click **Save**. Word saves the file in the folder you created, and the dialog box closes. The new file name appears at the top of the document window.

8. Click the **File** tab, and then on the navigation bar, click the **Close** command to close the document without exiting Word.

9. Keep Word open for the next Step-by-Step.

Locating and Opening an Existing Document

You can open an existing document by clicking the File tab, and then on the navigation bar, clicking the Open command. This displays the Open dialog box, as shown in **Figure 1–5**, where you can open a file from any available disk and folder. If you worked on the document recently, you can click the File tab, on the navigation bar, click Recent, and then in the middle pane, click the name of the document in the list of recently opened and saved documents.

Click the file name in the list

Click to open the file you select

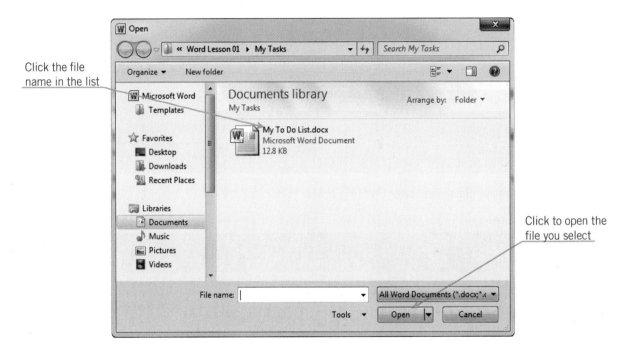

FIGURE 1–5   Open dialog box

Opening a New, Blank Document

You can open a new, blank document by clicking the File tab, and then on the navigation bar, clicking New. This opens the New tab in Backstage view, as shown in **Figure 1–6**. In the Available Templates list in the center, the Blank document button is selected. Click the Create button in the pane on the right to close Backstage view and open a new, blank document.

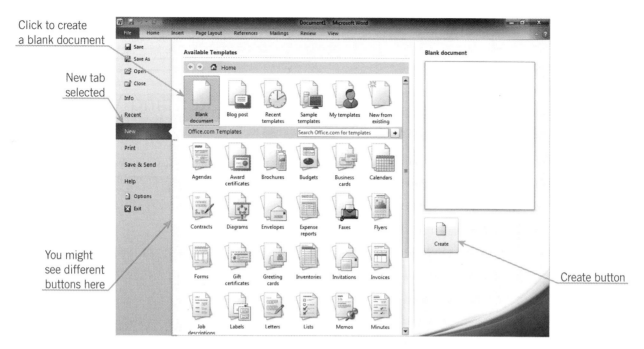

Click to create
a blank document

New tab
selected

You might
see different
buttons here

Create button

FIGURE 1–6   New tab in Backstage view

Step-by-Step 1.6

1. With Word still running, click the **File** tab, and then on the navigation bar, click the **Open** command. The Open dialog box appears.

2. If necessary, navigate to the drive and folder where your Data Files are stored.

3. If necessary, double-click the **Word** folder. Double-click the **Word Lesson 01** folder. Finally, double-click the **My Tasks** folder. The saved file My To Do List.docx appears in the dialog box.

4. Click **My To Do List.docx** in the list. Click **Open**. The My To Do List document appears on the screen.

5. Leave the document open for the next Step-by-Step.

TIP

You can also open a file by double-clicking it in the Open dialog box.

WARNING

If the yellow Protected View bar appears at the top of the document window when you open the document, click the Enable Editing button, and then continue with Step 5.

Zooming a Document

You can use the *Zoom* feature to magnify and reduce your document on the screen. Zoom is measured in percentage. A zoom percentage of 100% shows the document at its normal size. The higher the percentage, the larger the document appears; the lower the percentage, the smaller the document appears. The easiest way to change the percentage is to drag the Zoom slider at the bottom-right of the screen, or to click the Zoom In or Zoom Out buttons on either end of the Zoom slider. You can also click the Zoom level

▶ **VOCABULARY**
Zoom

percentage to the left of the Zoom slider to open the Zoom dialog box. Finally, you can click the View tab on the Ribbon, and then click one of the buttons in the Zoom group to zoom to a preset percentage, or click the Zoom button to open the Zoom dialog box.

Switching to Full Screen Reading View

▶ **VOCABULARY**
Full Screen Reading view
toolbar

Full Screen Reading view removes the Ribbon and the status bar from the screen. It leaves only the document and, in place of the Ribbon, a small bar called a *toolbar* that contains buttons for performing commands. See **Figure 1–7**. Full Screen Reading view is useful for reading the document on the screen. It does not show how the document will look when printed on paper.

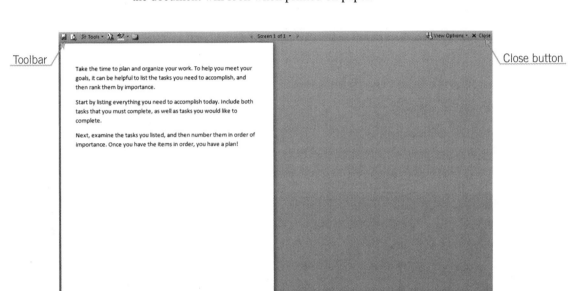

Toolbar

Close button

Take the time to plan and organize your work. To help you meet your goals, it can be helpful to list the tasks you need to accomplish, and then rank them by importance.

Start by listing everything you need to accomplish today. Include both tasks that you must complete, as well as tasks you would like to complete.

Next, examine the tasks you listed, and then number them in order of importance. Once you have the items in order, you have a plan!

FIGURE 1–7   Document in Full Screen Reading view

To use Full Screen Reading view, click the View tab on the Ribbon, and then in the Document Views group, click the Full Screen Reading button. You can also click the Full Screen Reading button on the status bar to the left of the Zoom slider. To return to Print Layout view, click the Close button on the toolbar at the top of the screen.

Step-by-Step 1.7

1. At the lower-right of the document window, drag the **Zoom slider** ⎁ all the way to the left. The zoom percentage is changed to 10% and the document appears as a small piece of paper in the upper-left of the document window.

2. At the right end of the Zoom slider, click the **Zoom In** button ⊕ five times. The zoom percentage increases by 10 each time you click the Zoom In button. The zoom percentage is now 60%.

3. On the Ribbon, click the **View** tab. The Ribbon changes to show the View commands. In the Zoom group, click the **Page Width** button. The document just about fills the screen. See **Figure 1–8**.

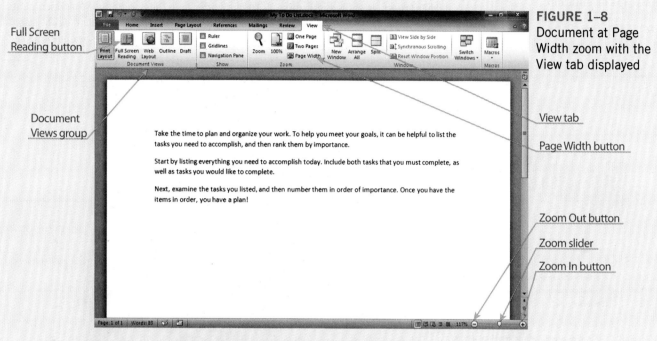

Full Screen
Reading button

Document
Views group

FIGURE 1–8
Document at Page
Width zoom with the
View tab displayed

View tab

Page Width button

Zoom Out button

Zoom slider

Zoom In button

4. On the View tab, in the Zoom group, click the **One Page** button. The zoom changes to show the whole page on the screen.

5. On the View tab, locate the Document Views group. Click the **Full Screen Reading** button. The view changes to Full Screen Reading view.

6. At the right end of the toolbar, click the **Close** button. You return to Print Layout view.

7. Leave the document open for the next Step-by-Step.

Selecting a Page Orientation

▶ **VOCABULARY**
portrait orientation
landscape orientation

Word has two ways to print text on a page. Documents printed in ***portrait orientation***, as shown in **Figure 1–9**, are longer than they are wide. By default, Word is set to print pages in portrait orientation. In contrast, documents printed in ***landscape orientation***, as shown in **Figure 1–10**, are wider than they are long. Most documents are printed in portrait orientation. Some documents, such as documents with graphics or numerical information, look better when printed in landscape orientation.

HOW CAN I BUILD A GOOD RELATIONSHIP WITH MY SUPERVISOR?

❖ Do not let personal problems affect your work
❖ Show you are willing to assume responsibilities
❖ Be loyal to your company
❖ Be reliable

HOW CAN I BUILD GOOD RELATIONSHIPS WITH MY CO-WORKERS?

❖ Avoid unnecessary conversations at work
❖ Treat co-workers' property with respect
❖ Use good manners, not bad language
❖ Treat others with respect

Join us for the

Time Management Techniques Seminar

Easy to use time saving techniques for those who want to learn to set priorities and defeat procrastination. Registration deadline is February 1st.

February 3, 8:00 a.m. to Noon
Conroe Building – Room 110
Business Council of Rapid City

FIGURE 1–9   Portrait orientation
retrato

FIGURE 1–10   Landscape orientation
paisaje

You can change the orientation of the document you want to print. To do this, click the Page Layout tab on the Ribbon, and then, in the Page Setup group, click the Orientation button, as shown in **Figure 1–11**. On the menu, click the option you want.

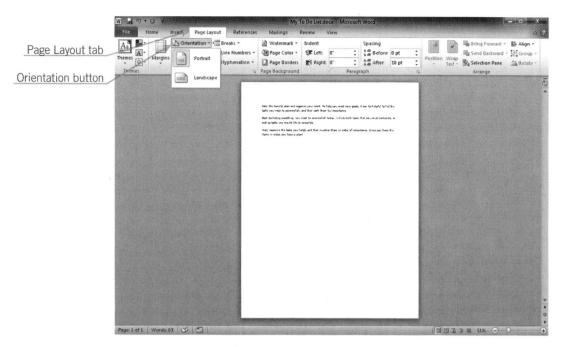

FIGURE 1–11   Changing page orientation on the Page Layout tab

You can also change the orientation on the Print tab in Backstage view. After displaying the Print tab, click the Portrait Orientation button or the Landscape Orientation button in the Settings section, and then click the orientation you want to use on the menu.

go over ⇒ revisar.
set up ⇒ crear, establecer.

Step-by-Step 1.8

1. On the Ribbon, click the **Page Layout** tab. The Page Layout commands appear on the Ribbon.

2. In the Page Setup group, click the **Orientation** button. Notice that Portrait is selected. Because the document is in One Page zoom, you can clearly see this.

3. Click **Landscape** on the menu. The page orientation of the document changes to landscape.

4. On the Ribbon, click the **File** tab, and then on the navigation bar, click **Print**. Notice in the preview that the page orientation of the document is landscape.

5. In the Settings section in the center pane, click the **Landscape Orientation** button. A menu opens.

6. On the menu, click **Portrait Orientation**. The orientation of the document changes back to portrait.

7. On the Ribbon, click the **File** tab. Backstage view closes and the Page Layout tab is selected again. You can see the entire page in portrait orientation.

8. On the Quick Access Toolbar, click the **Save** button ▣.

9. Leave the document open for the next Step-by-Step.

Previewing and Printing a Document

The Print tab in Backstage view enables you to look at a document as it will appear when printed before you actually print it. To open the Print tab, click the File tab on the Ribbon, and then on the navigation bar, click Print. The Print tab appears as shown in **Figure 1–12**. A preview of how the document will print using the current settings appears on the right. You should always look at the preview to make sure the document will print as you expect.

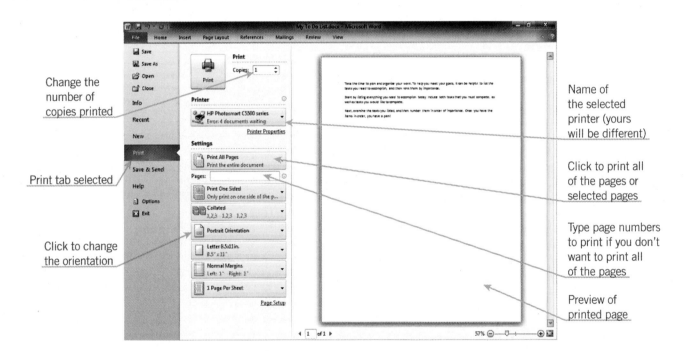

FIGURE 1–12   Print tab in Backstage view

The Print tab contains settings for printing your document. You can change the orientation, paper size, margins, and whether to print more than one page per sheet of paper or automatically shrink text to fit it on a page. You can zoom in on the document using the Zoom slider in the lower-right corner of Backstage view.

After you select the settings you want, to print a document, click the Print button in the center pane on the Print tab in Backstage view.

Step-by-Step 1.9

1. Use the **Zoom slider** ▽ to return to 100% view.

2. Press **Ctrl+End** to jump to the end of the document, press **Enter**, and then type your name.

3. On the Ribbon, click the **File** tab, and then on the navigation bar, click **Print**. The Print tab appears in Backstage view.

4. At the top of the center pane, click the **Print** button to print the document using the default settings.

5. Leave the document open for the next Step-by-Step.

Exiting Word

When you are finished working, you can close your document and exit Word. To close the document without exiting Word, click the File tab, and then on the navigation bar, click the Close command. To exit Word, click the Close button in the upper-right corner of the document window. You can also click the File tab on the Ribbon, and then on the navigation bar, click the Exit command.

Step-by-Step 1.10

1. On the Ribbon, click the **File** tab.

2. On the navigation bar, click the **Close** command. A dialog box opens asking if you want to save any changes.

3. Click **Save**. The document closes, but Word is still running.

4. In the upper-right corner of the window, click the **Close** button ⬛✕⬛. Word exits and the Word program window closes.

SUMMARY

In this lesson, you learned:

■ You can view the document screen in Print Layout view, Full Screen Reading view, Web Layout view, Outline view, and Draft view. The key elements of the screen in Print Layout view are the Ribbon, Quick Access Toolbar, insertion point, status bar, view buttons, and Zoom slider.

■ When text is entered, the word wrap feature automatically wraps words to the next line if they will not fit on the current line.

■ When corrections or additions need to be made, you can place the insertion point anywhere within a document using the mouse or keyboard, and then delete text using Backspace and Delete.

- When you save a document for the first time, the Save As dialog box opens. This is where you name your file and choose a location in which to save it. After you have saved a document the first time, you use the Save command to save your changes in the document or use the Save As command to save it with a different file name or to a new location.

- You can create new folders for storing documents in the Save As dialog box.

- You can locate and open an existing document using the Open dialog box.

- You can use the Zoom slider to magnify or reduce the size of your document on the screen.

- Full Screen Reading view makes it easier to view the entire document on the screen by removing the Ribbon and status bar and displaying only the text, not the layout, of the document.

- You can use the Orientation command to change the page orientation to portrait orientation or landscape orientation.

- You can preview and print a document by using the Print tab in Backstage view.

■ VOCABULARY REVIEW

Define the following terms:

Draft view	Print Layout view	Web Layout view
Full Screen Reading view	Quick Access Toolbar	word processing
insertion point	Ribbon	word wrap
landscape orientation	status bar	Zoom
Outline view	toolbar	
portrait orientation	view buttons	

■ REVIEW QUESTIONS

MULTIPLE CHOICE

Select the best response for the following statements.

1. In Full Screen Reading view, which of the following is visible?

   A. Ribbon

   B. Zoom slider

   C. toolbar

   D. status bar

2. Which dialog box do you use to save a file for the first time?

   A. Save

   B. Save As

   C. Save File

   D. Locate File

3. Dragging the Zoom slider to the left

   A. magnifies the document on-screen.

   B. reduces the size of the document on-screen.

   C. switches the document to Full Screen Reading view.

   D. changes the way the document will look when it is printed.

4. The feature that causes text you type to automatically move to the next line when it does not fit on the current line is called

   A. paragraphing.

   B. word processing.

   C. jumping.

   D. word wrap.

5. Commands for working with the document are organized into tabs on the

   A. Ribbon.

   B. status bar.

   C. Zoom slider.

   D. Quick Access Toolbar.

FILL IN THE BLANK

Complete the following sentences by writing the correct word or words in the blanks provided.

1. _____ view shows how a document will look when it is printed.

2. The _____ shows where text will appear when you begin typing.

3. Pressing Enter starts a new _____ in a document.

4. _____ can help you organize files on your disks.

5. Documents printed in _____ orientation are wider than they are tall.

TRUE / FALSE

Circle T if the statement is true or F if the statement is false.

T   F   **1.**   When the pointer is positioned in the document window, it takes the shape of the I-beam pointer.

T   F   **2.**   Word provides seven different views, including Web Layout view.

T   F   **3.**   Pressing Delete deletes the character immediately to the left of the insertion point.

T   F   **4.**   Pressing Ctrl+Home moves the insertion point to the beginning of the document.

T   F   **5.**   You can preview a document on the Preview tab in Backstage view.

◼ PROJECTS

If you have a SAM 2010 user profile, your instructor may have assigned an autogradable version of the indicated project. If so, log into the SAM 2010 Web site at *www.cengage.com/sam2010* to download the instruction and start files.

PROJECT 1–1

Match the key or keys in the first column to the description in the second column.

Column 1

_G_ 1. Right arrow
_B_ 2. Left arrow
_D_ 3. Down arrow
_J_ 4. Up arrow
_F_ 5. End
_E_ 6. Home
_K_ 7. Page Down
_C_ 8. Page Up
_L_ 9. Ctrl+right arrow
_I_ 10. Ctrl+left arrow
_A_ 11. Ctrl+End
_H_ 12. Ctrl+Home

Column 2

A. Moves to the end of the document
B. Moves left one character
C. Moves to the previous page
D. Moves to the next line
E. Moves to the beginning of a line
F. Moves to the end of the line
G. Moves right one character
H. Moves to the beginning of the document
I. Moves to the previous word
J. Moves to the previous line
K. Moves to the next page
L. Moves to the next word

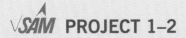 **PROJECT 1-2**

1. Start Word. Open the **Lecture.docx** document from the drive and folder where your Data Files are stored. This is a flyer announcing an upcoming program at the planetarium.

2. Save the document as **Cosmic Connections Flyer** followed by your initials.

3. Scroll down so you can see the lines of text below the drawing. Place the insertion point at the end of the first sentence (after *galaxy.*), press the spacebar, and then type: **Dr. Scott Wycoski will be the guest lecturer.**

4. Place the insertion point after the word *Park* in the next line, and then use Backspace to delete that word and the extra space.

5. Create a new paragraph after *Green Hills Planetarium*. Type the following: **Thursday, May 9, 7 p.m. to 8 p.m.**

6. Change the view to Full Screen Reading.

7. Close Full Screen Reading view.

8. Change the zoom to One Page.

9. Change the orientation of the document to landscape.

10. Change the zoom back to 100%, press Ctrl+End, press Enter, and then type your name.

11. Save, print, and close the document. Exit Word.

√**PROJECT 1-3**

1. Start Word. You will write a letter thanking Dr. Wycoski for his presentation.

2. Type today's date, using the format *May 10, 2013*.

3. Press Enter twice, and then type the following text:

Dear Dr. Wycoski,

Thank you for participating in our lecture series. Your presentation was very interesting! Thanks to your clear explanations, we now understand much more about the origins of the galaxy. Thank you again for helping to make our lecture series a great success.

Sincerely,

4. Press Enter twice to insert enough blank space after *Sincerely* for you to sign your name, and then type your name.

5. Change the document to Full Screen Reading view.

6. Close Full Screen Reading view.

7. Change the zoom to One Page.

8. Open the Save As dialog box. Navigate to the drive and folder where you want to save the file. Create a new folder in this location. Name the folder **My Letters**.

9. Make sure the My Letters folder is the current folder. Save the document as **Thank You Letter** followed by your initials.

10. Print and close the document. Exit Word.

PROJECT 1–4

1. Start Word, and then open the **Sale.docx** document from the drive and folder where your Data Files are stored. You will modify this advertisement for a department store sale.

2. Save the document as **Holiday Sale Flyer** followed by your initials.

3. Change the Zoom percentage to 110%.

4. Scroll down, and then position the insertion point in front of the sentence starting with *These great bargains*. Type: **Hurry now to Carville's for sale prices on all holiday products.** Press the spacebar.

5. Position the insertion point before the word *now* in the sentence you just typed, and then use Delete to delete that word and the space after it. Position the insertion point to the right of the word *products* in the second line in the document. Use Backspace to delete that word, and then type **items**.

6. Press Ctrl+End to move the insertion point to the end of the last sentence.

7. Press Enter, and then type your name.

8. Change the orientation of the document to **portrait**.

9. Save the document.

10. Preview and print the document. Close the document, and exit Word.

PROJECT 1–5

1. Start Word. Open the **Interview.docx** document from the drive and folder where your Data Files are stored. Save the document as **Interview Tips** followed by your initials. You will revise a page in this informational pamphlet provided as a resource for people seeking employment.

2. Change the zoom to Page Width.

3. Change to Full Screen Reading view.

4. Read the document to become familiar with it.

5. Close Full Screen Reading view.

6. Press Ctrl+Home to position the insertion point at the beginning of the document, if necessary.

7. Press Ctrl+right arrow five times to move the insertion point after the word *job* and before the word *ahead*. Type **interview**, and then press the spacebar.

8. Press Ctrl+End to position the insertion point at the end of the document. Press the spacebar, and then type: **The third thing you should do is to prepare a list of questions about the position for which you are interviewing. Make sure you do not ask about the salary at this point.**

9. Start a new paragraph and type: **After the interview, write a thank you note as soon as possible to the person who conducted the interview. A handwritten note will make a better impression than an e-mail. In addition to being good manners, it reminds the interviewer who you are, and it sets you apart from the other candidates.**

10. Proofread the document. Use Backspace or Delete to correct any errors.

11. Jump to the end of the document, insert a new paragraph, and then type your name.

12. Save, preview, print, and close the document. Exit Word.

■ CRITICAL THINKING

ACTIVITY 1–1

Thank you notes are easier to write when done promptly, preferably the day you receive a gift or attend an event. Using what you have learned in this lesson, start Word and write a thank you note to someone who has done something special for you recently. Save the document with a file name of your choice, print it, and then close the document and exit Word.

ACTIVITY 1–2

With Windows, a file name may contain up to 255 characters and include spaces. You should use a descriptive file name that will remind you of what the file contains, making it easy to find.

Read each item below. From the information given, create a file name for each document. Create a new Word document and type the file name next to the appropriate number in a list. Each file must have a different name. Strive to develop descriptive file names. Choose a file name for the document you created, and then save the document. Print and close your document, and then exit Word.

1. A letter to Binda's Boutique requesting a catalog.

2. A report entitled "Possible Problems Due to Global Warming" written by the environmental foundation, Earth!. The report will be used to develop a grant proposal.

3. A letter that will be enclosed with an order form used to place an order with Binda's Boutique.

4. A letter of complaint to Binda's Boutique for sending the wrong merchandise.

5. An announcement for a reception to be given in honor of a retiring executive, Serena Marsh.

6. A memo to all employees explaining new vacation time policies at Sheehan Global Enterprises.

7. Minutes of the November board of directors' meeting of Eastern Seaboard Insurance Company.

8. A press release written by Earth! to the media about a one-day event called *Live in Harmony with Nature*.

9. A mailing list for sending newsletters to all employees of Sheehan Global Enterprises.

10. An agenda for the December board of directors' meeting of Eastern Seaboard Insurance Company.

ACTIVITY 1–3

When you open the New tab in Backstage view, you see a variety of options for creating a new document. In addition to creating a blank document, you can create a document based on a template, which is a special type of document that contains sample text and formatting. When you open a template, it opens as a new document that you need to save with a file name.

Use the Help system in Word to find out more about creating a document from a template, and then use this information to create a new document based on one of the templates located in the Sample Templates folder (at the top of the New tab in Backstage view). Save the new document you create with the file name **Document Based on Template** followed by your initials. Close this document when you are finished.

Next, create a new, blank Word document, and then type the answer to the following questions based on the information presented in this Activity and in Help. Save the document you create using an appropriate file name, and then preview and print it. Close the document and exit Word.

■   What is a template and why would you use one?

■   Can a template contain text?

■   How do you create a new document based on a template?

LESSON 2

Basic Editing

■ OBJECTIVES

Upon completion of this lesson, you should be able to:

- Show and hide formatting marks.
- Select text.
- Create paragraphs without blank space between them.
- Undo, redo, and repeat recent actions.
- Move and copy text using drag-and-drop and the Clipboard.
- Use the Office Clipboard.
- Find and replace text, and use the Go To command.
- Identify the number of words in a document or a selection.

■ VOCABULARY

Clipboard

copy

cut

drag

drag-and-drop

format

Office Clipboard

paste

select

toggle

Editing Text

Word's features and tools make it easy to edit documents. In this lesson, you will learn how to show and hide formatting marks, select text, and remove extra space after paragraphs. You will also undo and redo actions, move and copy text, and locate and replace text. Finally, you will learn how to jump to a specific location in the document, and count the number of words in a document or a selection of text.

Showing Formatting Marks

Many times it is easier to select and edit sentences and paragraphs if you can view the paragraph marks and other formatting symbols. The Show/Hide ¶ command allows you to see these hidden formatting marks, as shown in **Figure 2–1**. To view the formatting marks, click the Show/Hide ¶ button in the Paragraph group on the Home tab. The formatting marks do not appear when you print your document.

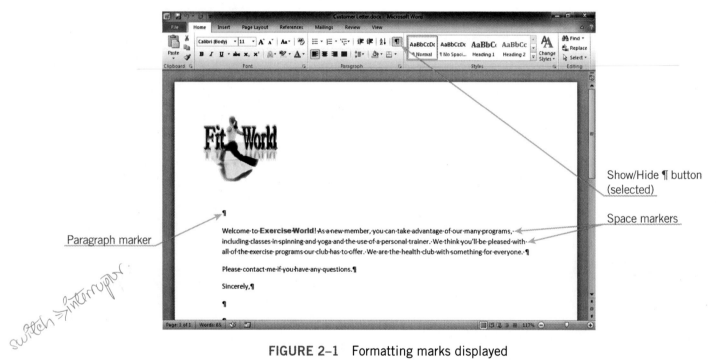

FIGURE 2–1   Formatting marks displayed

Understanding Toggle Commands

Clicking the Show/Hide ¶ button once displays paragraph and formatting marks; clicking the button again hides them. Switching between two options in this manner is known as *toggling*, so a command that you use by turning a feature on or off is sometimes known as a toggle command. Word contains several toggle commands that turn a feature on or off. When a toggle command on the Ribbon is selected, it is orange. Toggle commands can also appear on a menu. When a toggle command on a menu is selected, a check mark appears next to it.

Selecting Text

[handwritten annotation: puntos culminantes destacar, sbracqer]

To *select* text means to highlight a block of text. Blocks can be as small as one character or as large as an entire document. After selecting a block of text, you can work with the entire block of text as a whole. You can select text using the mouse, using the keyboard, or using the keyboard in combination with the mouse.

To select text with the mouse, position the I-beam pointer to the left of the first character of the text you want to select. Hold down the left button on the mouse, drag the pointer to the end of the text you want to select, and release the button. This is called *dragging*. To remove the highlight, click the mouse button.

To select text with the keyboard, press and hold down Shift, and then press an arrow key in the direction of the text you want to select. Pressing Shift extends the selection in the direction of the arrow key you press. To select a word at a time, press and hold Shift+Ctrl, and then press the left or right arrow key. To select a paragraph at a time, press and hold Shift+Ctrl, and then press the up or down arrow key. **Table 2–1** summarizes additional ways to select text.

> **VOCABULARY**
>
> **select**
>
> **drag** *[handwritten: arrastrar, rastrear]*

> **TIP**
>
> To quickly select everything in a document, press and hold Ctrl+A or on the Home tab, in the Editing group, click the Select button, and then click Select All.

> **EXTRA FOR EXPERTS**
>
> To select blocks of text that are not next to each other, select the first block of text, press and hold down Ctrl, and then use the mouse to select additional blocks of text.

TABLE 2–1   Selecting blocks of text

TO SELECT THIS	DO THIS
Characters	Click to the left of the first character you want to select, press and hold Shift, and then click to the right of the last character you want to select.
Word	Double-click the word.
Line	Position the pointer in the left margin next to the line so that it changes to ⟍, and then click.
Multiple lines	Position the pointer in the left margin next to the first line so that it changes to ⟍, press and hold the left mouse button, and then drag down or up in the margin to select as many lines as you want.
Sentence	Press and hold down Ctrl, and then click anywhere in the sentence.
Paragraph	Triple-click anywhere in the paragraph. Or Position the pointer in the left margin next to the paragraph so that it changes to ⟍, and then double-click.
Entire document	Triple-click in the left margin. Or Position the pointer in the left margin next to any line so that it changes to ⟍, press and hold down Ctrl, and then click in the left margin

Step-by-Step 2.1

1. Open the **Letter.docx** document from the drive and folder where your Data Files are stored. Save the document as **Customer Letter** followed by your initials.

2. On the Home tab, in the Paragraph group, click the **Show/Hide ¶** button [¶]. The paragraph marks and other hidden formatting marks appear on your screen, and the Show/Hide ¶ button on the Ribbon changes to orange to show that it is selected, as shown in Figure 2–1.

3. Position the pointer in the left margin to the left of the word *Welcome* so that it changes to ⌐. Click once. The first line in the document is selected, as shown in **Figure 2–2**.

FIGURE 2–2
A selected line of text

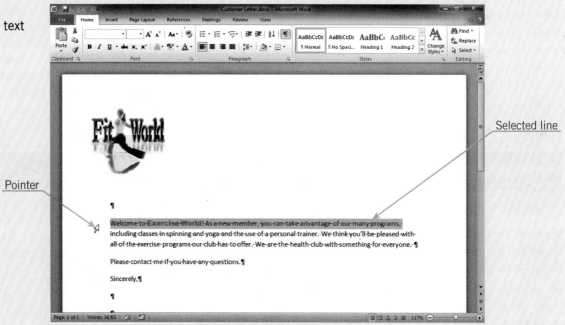

Pointer

Selected line

4. Click anywhere in the document. The text is deselected.

5. Double-click the word **Welcome** at the beginning of the first paragraph. The word is selected.

6. Click anywhere in the document to deselect the text.

7. Triple-click anywhere in the first paragraph. The entire paragraph is selected. Deselect the text.

8. In the first paragraph at the beginning of the second sentence, position the I-beam pointer before the letter *A* in the word *As*. Press and hold the left mouse button, and then drag to the right and down to just before the last sentence in the first paragraph (just before *We are the health club...*). Release the mouse button. The text you dragged the pointer over is selected.

TIP

You can also press an arrow key to deselect text.

9. On the Home tab, in the Editing group, click the **Select** button, and then click **Select All**. The entire document is selected. Deselect the text.

10. Press **Ctrl+A**. The entire document is selected again. Deselect the text.

11. Click the **Show/Hide ¶** button ¶. The formatting characters are hidden again.

12. Leave the document open for the next Step-by-Step.

Creating Paragraphs Without Blank Space Between Them

When you press Enter, you create a new paragraph. When you create a new paragraph, the default style is for extra space to be added after the original paragraph. The extra space is helpful when you are typing because you don't need to press Enter twice to insert space between paragraphs. But there may be times when you don't want that extra space to appear. For example, when you type a letter, extra space should not appear between the lines in the inside address.

You can format a paragraph so that it does not have extra space after it. To *format* text or paragraphs means to change its appearance. To do this, you can use the Line and Paragraph Spacing button, which is located in the Paragraph group on the Home tab. When you click this button, a gallery opens, as shown in **Figure 2–3**. To remove the space after the selected paragraphs, click Remove Space After Paragraph at the bottom of the menu. Notice that the command above this lets you add space before the paragraph. These commands change depending on the settings applied to the selected paragraphs. For example, if the selected paragraphs did not have space after them, the bottom command would be Add Space After Paragraph.

▶ **VOCABULARY**
format

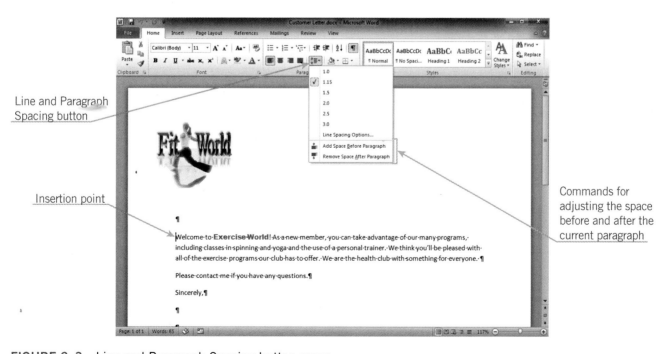

Line and Paragraph Spacing button

Insertion point

Commands for adjusting the space before and after the current paragraph

FIGURE 2–3 Line and Paragraph Spacing button menu

Step-by-Step 2.2

1. Click the **Show/Hide ¶** button ¶. The formatting marks are displayed.

2. In the vertical scroll bar, drag the scroll box to the top. Position the insertion point in the blank paragraph below the logo and above the first paragraph. Type **May 13, 2013**. Press **Enter**. A blank line is inserted and the insertion point is blinking at the beginning of a new paragraph.

3. Type **Karen DeSimone**.

4. On the Home tab, in the Paragraph group, click the **Line and Paragraph Spacing** button. A gallery opens as shown in Figure 2–3.

5. At the bottom of the menu, click **Remove Space After Paragraph**. The space after the current paragraph is removed. See **Figure 2–4**.

FIGURE 2–4
Paragraph with spacing after removed

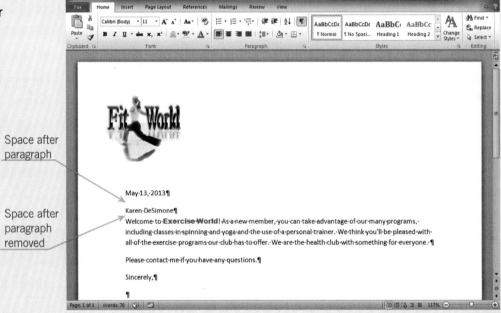

Space after paragraph

Space after paragraph removed

6. Press **Enter**. A new paragraph is created, but no space appears between the two paragraphs. Type **47 Bradford St.**, press **Enter**, and then type **Salem, RI 02922**. The inside address is complete.

7. In the Paragraph group, click the **Line and Paragraph Spacing** button, and then click **Add Space After Paragraph**. Space is inserted below the current paragraph.

8. Press **Enter**. A new paragraph is created. Because you changed the paragraph formatting before you pressed Enter, space was added after the previous paragraph.

9. Type **Dear Ms.**

10. On the Quick Access Toolbar, click the **Save** button to save your changes to the document. Leave the document open for the next Step-by-Step.

Using the Undo, Redo, and Repeat Commands

When working on a document, you might delete text accidentally or change your mind about editing or formatting changes that you made. The Undo command is useful in these situations because it reverses recent actions. To use the Undo command, click the Undo button on the Quick Access Toolbar.

You can keep clicking the Undo button to continue reversing recent actions, or you can click the arrow next to the Undo button to see a list of your recent actions. The most recent action appears at the top of the list, as shown in **Figure 2–5**. Click an action in the list, and Word will undo that action and all the actions listed above it.

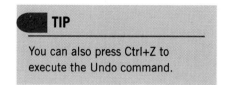

TIP

You can also press Ctrl+Z to execute the Undo command.

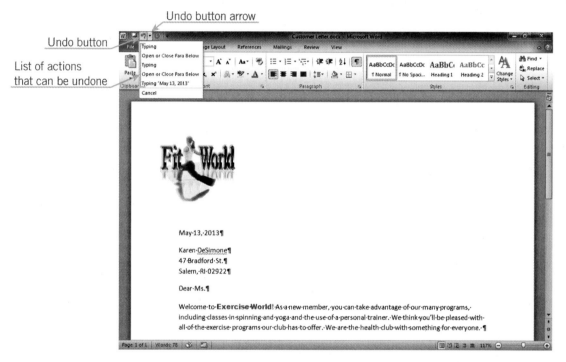

FIGURE 2–5   List of actions on the Undo button

The Redo command is similar to the Undo command. The Redo command reverses an Undo action. To use the Redo command, click the Redo button on the Quick Access Toolbar. Unlike the Undo command, you cannot open a list of actions to redo.

The Redo button does not appear on the Quick Access Toolbar until you have undone something. Until then, the Repeat button appears next to the Undo button. The Repeat command repeats the most recent action. For example, if you type something, and then click the Repeat button, the same text will appear on the screen. If you select text, delete it, and then select more text, clicking the Repeat button deletes the selected text. To use the Repeat command, click the Repeat button on the Quick Access Toolbar. The Repeat button is sometimes visible but light gray, which means that it is unavailable; that is, you can't repeat the most recent action.

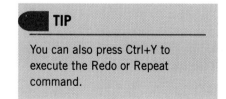

TIP

You can also press Ctrl+Y to execute the Redo or Repeat command.

Step-by-Step 2.3

1. On the Quick Access Toolbar, click the **arrow** next to the Undo button ⟲. The list of actions that can be undone appears, similar to Figure 2–5. You might see additional actions on your list.

2. Point to the third item in the list. The action you point to as well as all of the actions above it are selected. The command at the bottom of the list changes from Cancel to Undo 3 Actions.

3. Click the third item on the Undo list. The last three actions are undone, and some of the text you typed disappears from the letter. Also note that the Redo button now appears next to the Undo button on the Quick Access Toolbar.

4. On the Quick Access Toolbar, click the **Redo** button ⟳ three times. The actions you undid are redone and all the text is restored to the document. The Redo button on the Quick Access Toolbar changes to the Repeat button, which is now light gray, so clicking it will have no effect.

5. Double-click the word **Ms** in the salutation to select it. Press **Delete**. The selected word is deleted. On the Quick Access Toolbar, the Repeat button is now available.

6. Double-click the word **Dear** in the salutation to select it. On the Quick Access Toolbar, click the **Repeat** button ⟳. The last action is repeated and the selected word is deleted.

7. On the Quick Access Toolbar, click the **arrow** next to the Undo button ⟲. Click the second **Clear** in the list. The salutation is restored.

8. Deselect the text, and then save your changes to the document. Leave the document open for the next Step-by-Step.

Using Drag-and-Drop to Move and Copy Text

At some point when you are editing a document, you will probably want to move or copy text to a different location. The easiest way to move text is to select it, position the pointer on top of the selected text, and then drag the selected text to the new location. This is called *drag-and-drop*. As you drag the selected text, a vertical line follows the pointer indicating where the text will be positioned when you release the mouse button, as shown in **Figure 2–6**. If you want to copy the text instead of move it, you must press and hold Ctrl while you drag it.

▶ **VOCABULARY**
drag-and-drop

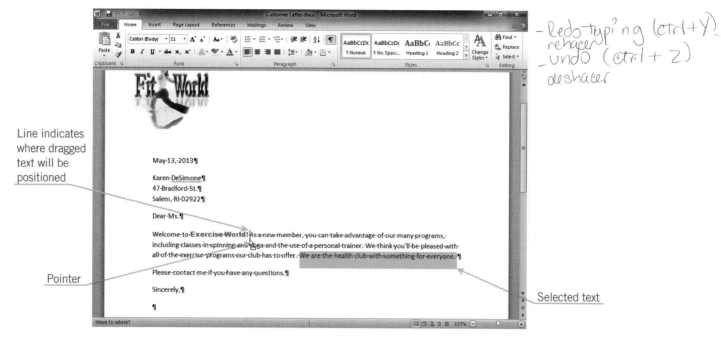

Line indicates where dragged text will be positioned

Pointer

Selected text

- redo Typing (ctrl+Y).
rehacer
- undo (ctrl + z)
deshacer

FIGURE 2-6   Using drag-and-drop to move selected text

Step-by-Step 2.4

1. Press and hold **Ctrl**, click the last sentence of the first paragraph to select it, and then release Ctrl.

2. Position the insertion point on top of the selected text. The pointer changes to ▷.

3. Press and hold the left mouse button, and then drag the pointer up to the first line in the first paragraph until the vertical line following the pointer is positioned just before the word *As*, as shown in Figure 2–6. Release the mouse button. The selected sentence moves from the end of the first paragraph to become the second sentence in the first paragraph.

4. In the inside address, double-click **DeSimone**. The last name is selected.

5. Press and hold down **Ctrl**, and then drag the selected text to the salutation line so that the vertical indicator line is positioned between the period after Ms. and the paragraph mark. Release the mouse button and Ctrl. A copy of the selected text is positioned in the salutation line, and the original text is still in the inside address.

6. Press the **right arrow** key to deselect the text and move the insertion point after *DeSimone*, and then type **:** (a colon).

7. Save your changes to the document. Leave it open for the next Step-by-Step.

Using the Clipboard to Move and Copy Text

Another way to move or copy text is to use the Clipboard. The ***Clipboard*** is a temporary storage place in the computer's memory. To use the Clipboard, you cut or copy text. When you ***cut*** selected text, it is removed from the document and placed on the Clipboard. When you ***copy*** selected text, it remains in its original location and a copy of it is placed on the Clipboard. Once you have placed text on the Clipboard, you can then ***paste*** whatever is stored on the Clipboard into the document.

The Clipboard can hold only one selection at a time, so each time you cut or copy text, the newly cut or copied text replaces the text currently stored on the Clipboard. The Clipboard is available to all the programs on your computer, and it is sometimes called the system Clipboard.

Cutting and Pasting to Move Text

To move text from one location to another using the Clipboard, you need to use the Cut command and then the Paste command. First, select the text you want to move. Then, on the Home tab, in the Clipboard group, click the Cut button.

To paste the text stored on the Clipboard to a new place in the document, position the insertion point at the location where you want the text to appear. On the Home tab, in the Clipboard group, click the Paste button. The text currently stored on the Clipboard is pasted into the document. Moving text in this manner is referred to as *cutting and pasting*.

Copying and Pasting Text

To copy text in one location to another location, you need to use the Copy command. Select the text you want to copy. On the Home tab in the Clipboard group, click the Copy button.

To paste the copied text, you use the Paste command in the same manner as when you move text. This procedure is sometimes referred to as *copying and pasting*.

Using the Paste Options Button

When you use the Paste command, the Paste Options button appears below and to the right of the pasted text. Click this button to open a gallery of options. You can also click the arrow below the Paste button in the Clipboard group on the Home tab to see the Paste Options buttons. You can point to the buttons to see the effect using each one would have on the pasted text. See **Figure 2–7**. The Paste Options buttons change depending on what you pasted in the document. Usually when text is on the Clipboard, you can choose to paste the text so its appearance matches the original appearance (source formatting), so its appearance matches or merges with the text in the location where it is being pasted (destination formatting), or so it is pasted as text only, with no custom formatting. This means that it will match the formatting of the location where it is being pasted.

> **TIP**
>
> When you press Delete or Backspace, the text you delete is not placed on the Clipboard; it is simply removed from the document.

> **TIP**
>
> Press Ctrl+X to cut selected text; press Ctrl+C to copy selected text; and press Ctrl+V to paste text from the Clipboard into the document at the insertion point.

Arrow below the
Paste button

Paste Options
buttons

ScreenTip
identifying button
being pointed to

Live Preview of
text to be pasted

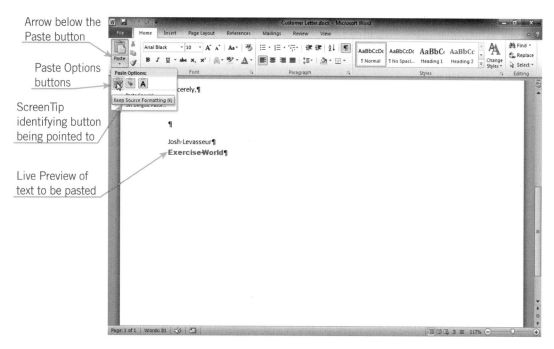

FIGURE 2-7   Paste Options buttons

Step-by-Step 2.5

1. Select the last sentence in the first paragraph (*We think you'll be pleased...*). On the Home tab, in the Clipboard group, click the **Cut** button. The selected sentence disappears from the screen and is placed on the Clipboard.

2. Position the insertion point at the beginning of the second sentence in the first paragraph (immediately to the left of *We are the health club...*).

3. On the Home tab, in the Clipboard group, click the **Paste** button. The sentence you cut is pasted at the location of the insertion point. The Paste Options button appears just below the pasted text.

4. In the first sentence in the first paragraph, select the blue text **Exercise World**. On the Home tab, in the Clipboard group, click the **Copy** button. The text stays in the document and is also placed on the Clipboard, replacing the sentence that you had previously cut and placed on the Clipboard.

5. Press **Ctrl+End**. The insertion point moves to the end of the document, in the blank paragraph below the closing.

6. On the Home tab, in the Clipboard group, click the **arrow** below the Paste button. The Paste Options buttons appear.

7. Position the pointer on top of the **Keep Source Formatting** button. The text you copied appears in the document with the same formatting as the original. See Figure 2-7.

EXTRA FOR EXPERTS

You can also access the Cut, Copy, and Paste commands by right-clicking the selected text, and then choosing the commands from the shortcut menu.

8. Position the pointer on top of the **Merge Formatting** button 🖱. The formatting of the text to be pasted changes to match the formatting of the text in the current paragraph.

9. Position the pointer on top of the **Keep Text Only** button 🅰. The formatting of the text to be pasted is plain, unformatted text. This formatting looks exactly the same as the formatting that appears when you pointed to the Merge Formatting button. This is what happens most of the time with these two options.

10. Click the **Merge Formatting** button 🖱.

11. Save your changes to the document. Leave it open for the next Step-by-Step.

Using the Office Clipboard

If you want to collect more than one selection at a time, you can use the Office Clipboard. The **_Office Clipboard_** is a special clipboard on which you can collect up to 24 selections. It is available only to Microsoft Office programs.

Unlike the system Clipboard, which is available all the time, you must activate the Office Clipboard to use it. On the Home tab, in the Clipboard group, click the Clipboard Dialog Box Launcher. (Remember, the Dialog Box Launcher for a group is the small square with an arrow in the lower-right corner of the group.) This opens the Clipboard task pane on the left side of the window. Once the Clipboard task pane is open, each selection that you cut or copy is placed on it. See **Figure 2–8**. The task pane displays up to 24 items. When you cut or copy a twenty-fifth item, it replaces the first item.

EXTRA FOR EXPERTS

You can use the Office Clipboard in other Office programs, such as Excel. For example, you can copy a chart you created in Excel to a report you are writing in Word.

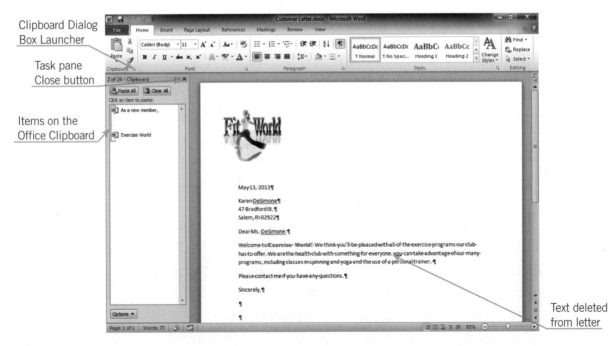

FIGURE 2–8   Clipboard task pane with two items collected on it

Step-by-Step 2.6

1. Press **Ctrl+Home** to jump to the beginning of the document.

2. On the Home tab, in the Clipboard group, click the **Clipboard Dialog Box Launcher**. The Clipboard task pane opens on the left side of the window. The item currently on the system Clipboard, the text *Exercise World*, is the first item in the task pane.

3. In the first paragraph of the letter, at the beginning of the fourth sentence, select the text **As a new member,** (including the comma).

4. On the Home tab, in the Clipboard group, click the **Cut** button ✂. The text is deleted from the paragraph and appears in the Clipboard task pane, as shown in Figure 2–8.

5. Position the insertion point in the first paragraph at the beginning of the second sentence (it begins with *We think you'll be pleased...*).

6. In the Clipboard task pane, click **As a new member,**. The text is pasted at the location of the insertion point.

7. Press **Delete**, and then type **w**. If there is no space between the comma after the word *member* and the word *we*, press the **left arrow** key, and then press the **spacebar**.

8. Position the insertion point in the first paragraph at the beginning of the fourth sentence (it begins with *you can take advantage*). Type **At**, and then press the **spacebar**.

9. In the Clipboard task pane, click **Exercise World**. If there is no space between *World* and *you*, press the **spacebar**.

10. In the title bar at the top of the Clipboard task pane, click the **Close** button ✖. The task pane closes.

11. Save your changes to the document. Leave it open for the next Step-by-Step.

> **TIP**
>
> You can clear the Office Clipboard by clicking Clear All at the top of the Clipboard task pane, and you can paste all of the items on the Office Clipboard at once by clicking Paste All.

> **WARNING**
>
> Clicking the Paste button or pressing Ctrl+V pastes the contents of the system Clipboard into the document, not the contents of the Office Clipboard.

Using the Find and Replace Commands

Find and Replace are useful editing commands that let you locate specific words in a document quickly and, if you wish, change them instantly to new words. Both commands are located in the Editing group on the Home tab.

Finding Text with the Navigation Pane

When you click the Find button, the Navigation pane appears on the left side of the program window, as shown in **Figure 2–9**. The tab whose ScreenTip is "Browse the results from your current search" is selected. To find every occurrence of a specific word or phrase in a document, click in the Search Document box in the Navigation Pane, and then type the word or phrase. All of the occurrences of the text for which you are searching appear in a list in the Navigation pane, and they are highlighted in yellow in the document. If you continue typing in the Search Document box, the list and highlighting change to match what you type.

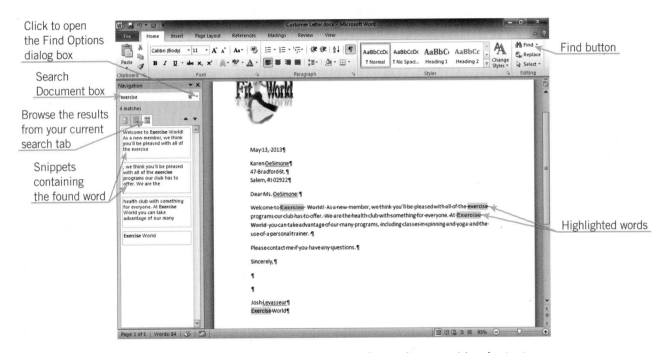

FIGURE 2–9   Navigation Pane after searching for text

The highlighting and the list of items in the Navigation Pane matches the exact text you type in the Search Document box, even if it's in the middle of another word. For example, you can find the word *all* or any word with *all* in it, such as *fall*, *horizontally*, or *alloy*. Find also ignores capitalization when finding words. For example, if you search for *run*, the list of results will include *Run* as well as *run*.

You can make your search more specific. Click the small arrow on the right end of the Search Document box in the Navigation Pane. (The ScreenTip identifies this as the "Find Options and additional search commands" button.) Click that button, and then click Options on the menu that appears to open the Find Options dialog box. The options in this dialog box are described in **Table 2–2**.

TABLE 2–2   Find options

OPTION	DESCRIPTION
Match case	Searches for words with the same capitalization as the text that you type.
Find whole words only	Finds only the exact word or phrase you entered in the Find what box. (For example, choose this option if you want to find the word *all*, but not words with all in them, such as *fall*, *horizontally*, or *alloy*.)
Use wildcards	Makes it possible to search for words using **wildcards**, which are special characters that represent other characters. The most common wildcards are ? (the question mark), which represents any one character, and * (the asterisk), which represents any number of characters. For example, *a??* finds all three-letter words that begin with the letter *a*, including *all* and *ask*, and *a** finds all words of any length that begin with the letter *a*, including *all*, *apple*, or *arithmetic*.
Sounds like (English)	Locates homonyms—words that sound alike but are spelled differently. For example, if you type the word *so*, Word would also find the word *sew*.
Find all word forms (English)	Finds different forms of the entered word. For example, if you search for the word *run*, Word would also find *ran*, *runs*, and running.
Highlight all	Highlights all the found words in the document. This is selected by default.
Incremental find	Finds the text as you type. This is selected by default. If you deselect this, you need to click the Search button in the Search Document box in the Navigation Pane to find the text.
Match prefix	Finds words that begin with the text you type in the Search Document box.
Match suffix	Finds words that end with the text you type in the Search Document box.
Ignore punctuation characters	Finds words that match the text in the Search Document characters box, but ignores any punctuation in the words in the document. For example, if you type *its* in the Search Document box, it will find *it's* as well as *its*.
Ignore white-space characters	Finds text that matches the text in the Search Document box even if there is a space between some of the characters in the document. For example, if you type *Maryellen* in the Find what text box, it will also find *Mary Ellen*.

Step-by-Step 2.7

1. On the Home tab, in the Editing group, click the **Find** button. The Navigation Pane appears. The insertion point is blinking in the Search Document box at the top of the Navigation Pane.

2. Type **exercise**. All four instances of the word *exercise* are highlighted in the document, and the four snippets of text containing the word appear in the Navigation Pane.

3. If necessary, drag the scroll box in the vertical scroll bar up until you can see all four instances of highlighted text in the window, similar to Figure 2–9.

4. In the Navigation Pane, click the **top snippet**. The first highlighted word in the document is selected.

5. In the Navigation Pane, click in the **Search Document** box. The text in the box is selected.

6. Press the **right arrow** key, press the **spacebar**, and then type **w**. One of the snippets in the list in the Navigation Pane is removed, the yellow highlighting disappears from the instance of the word *exercise* in the document that is not followed by a space and the letter *w*, and the highlighting on the other three instances is extended to the *W* in the word *World*.

7. Click anywhere in the document, and then press **Ctrl+Home** to move the insertion point to the beginning of the document.

8. In the Navigation Pane, click the **Close** button ✖. The Navigation Pane closes.

9. Save the document, and leave it open for the next Step-by-Step.

Replacing Text

> **TIP**
>
> You can use the Find tab in the Find and Replace dialog box to find occurrences of a word or phrase.

If you want to replace text you find with other text, you can use the Replace command. To do this, click the Replace button in the Editing group on the Home tab to open the Find and Replace dialog box with the Replace tab selected, as shown in **Figure 2–10**. To replace a word or phrase, type it in the Find what box, and then type the replacement word or phrase in the Replace with box. The Find what box has the same purpose as the Search Document box in the Navigation Pane. The replacements can be made one at a time by clicking Replace, or all at once by clicking Replace All. To make the search more specific, click More to see the same options that appear in the Find Options dialog box.

Replace tab

Type text to find here

Type replacement text here

Click to replace the selected instance of the text in the Find what box and then jump to the next instance

Click to replace all instances of the text in the Find what box

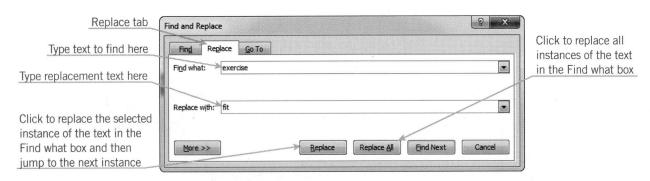

FIGURE 2–10   Replace tab in the Find and Replace dialog box

Step-by-Step 2.8

1. On the Home tab, in the Editing group, click the **Replace** button. The Find and Replace dialog box opens with the Replace tab selected. The text you typed in the Search Document box in the Navigation Pane, *exercise w*, appears in the Find what box in the dialog box.

2. Click in the **Find what** box to the right of the *w*, and then press **Backspace** twice to delete the *w* and the space after *exercise*.

3. Click in the **Replace with** box, and then type **fit**. See Figure 2–10.

4. Click **Find Next**. The first instance of the word *exercise* is selected in the document.

5. Click **Replace**. The selected word is replaced with *fit*, and the next instance of the word *exercise* is selected. Notice that the first letter of the word *fit* was automatically changed to an uppercase letter to match the case of the word it replaced. Also note that because this instance of the word *exercise* was formatted in blue and italics, the replacement word is formatted in the same way. The instance of the word *exercise* that is now selected should not be replaced with *fit*.

6. Click **Find Next**. The next instance of *exercise* is selected.

7. Click **Replace**. The selected text is replaced with the word *fit* and the next instance of *exercise* is selected. Click **Replace** to replace this instance of the word. A dialog box opens telling you that Word has completed its search of the document.

8. Click **OK** to close this dialog box. The Find and Replace dialog box is still open.

9. Click **Close**. The Find and Replace dialog box closes.

10. Save your changes to the document, and leave it open for the next Step-by-Step.

> **TIP**
>
> To replace all instances of the Find what text with the Replace with text, click Replace All. But watch out for replacements of words that contain the text you are replacing rather than whole words.

Using the Go To Command

One of the quickest ways to move through a long document is to use the Go To command. Go To allows you to jump to a specific part of a document. On the Home tab, in the Editing group, click the arrow next to the Find button, and then click Go To on the menu. The Find and Replace dialog box opens with the Go To tab on top. See

Figure 2–11. In the Go to what list, select the type of location you want to move to, and then enter the corresponding number or other information in the box on the right. After you click Next, Word moves the insertion point to the location you specified.

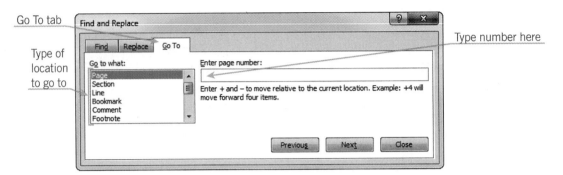

FIGURE 2–11   Go To tab in the Find and Replace dialog box

Step-by-Step 2.9

1. On the Home tab, in the Editing group, click the **arrow** next to the Find button. Click **Go To**. The Find and Replace dialog box appears with the Go To tab on top, as shown in Figure 2–11.

2. In the Go to what box, click **Line**. The box to the right of the Go to what box changes to the Enter line number box.

3. Click in the **Enter line number** box, and then type **10**.

4. Click **Go To**. The insertion point jumps to the tenth line in the document (the paragraph above the closing, which begins *Please contact me...*).

5. Click **Close**. The Find and Replace dialog box closes.

6. Save your changes to the document, and leave it open for the next Step-by-Step.

Identifying the Number of Words in a Document or Selection

As you type and edit a document, you may want to know how many words it contains. The number of words in a document appears in the status bar and is updated as you type. If you select text, the status bar displays the number of words in the selection. You can also find out the number of characters, paragraphs, and lines in a document by opening the Word Count dialog box. To do this, you can click the number of words in the status bar, or you can click the Review tab on the Ribbon, and then, in the Proofing group, click the Word Count button. See **Figure 2–12**.

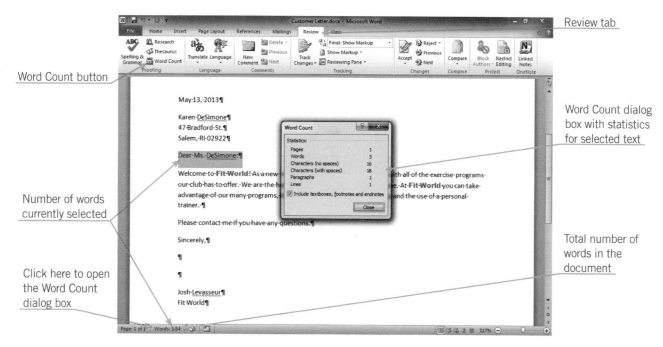

FIGURE 2–12   Word count on the status bar and in the Word Count dialog box

Step-by-Step 2.10

1. Scroll up so that you can see all the text in the document. Look at the word count in the status bar. The document contains 84 words.

2. Select the entire salutation (**Dear Ms. DeSimone:**). The word count indicator in the status bar shows that three out of a total of 84 words are selected in the document.

3. In the status bar, click the word count indicator. The Word Count dialog box opens, as shown in Figure 2–12. Because text is currently selected, this dialog box displays information about the selected text. The selected text consists of 16 characters if you don't count spaces, and 18 if you do.

4. In the dialog box, click **Close**. The Word Count dialog box closes.

5. Deselect the text in the document.

6. On the Ribbon, click the **Review** tab. In the Proofing group, click the **Word Count** button. The Word Count dialog box opens again. Because no text is selected, it tells you that the document contains 383 characters not including spaces, 458 characters if you do count the spaces, 10 paragraphs, and 15 lines. (Remember that a new paragraph is created every time you press Enter.) Because you might have inserted or removed a space when you cut or copied text, the character count with spaces in the dialog box on your screen might be slightly higher or lower than 458.

7. Click **Close**. The Word Count dialog box closes.

8. On the Ribbon, click the **Home** tab. In the Paragraph group, click the **Show/Hide ¶** button ¶. The button is deselected, and the formatting marks disappear from the screen.

9. At the bottom of the document, select the name **Josh Levasseur**, and then type your name.

10. Save, print, and close the document.

SUMMARY

In this lesson, you learned:

■ You can select blocks of text to perform operations on the entire block of text at once, such as cutting, copying, and pasting.

■ The Show/Hide ¶ command allows you to view hidden formatting marks. The Show/Hide ¶ button is a toggle command, which means you can turn the feature on or off.

■ You can change the space before and after a paragraph by using the Line and Paragraph Spacing button in the Paragraph group on the Home tab.

■ You can undo recent actions by using the Undo command. When you click the arrow next to the Undo button, a list of your recent actions appears. You can redo an action using the Redo button and repeat an action using the Repeat button.

■ You can drag selected text to a new location in the document. You can press and hold the Ctrl key to copy the selected text rather than move it when you drag.

■ You can send text to the Clipboard by using either the Cut or Copy command. You can paste text stored on the Clipboard by

using the Paste command. If you want to collect more than one item at a time to paste, you can use the Office Clipboard.

■ The Find command opens the Navigation Pane with the "Browse the results from your current search" tab selected. You type a word or phrase in the Search Document box to highlight every instance of the word in the document and display a list of snippets containing the word in the Navigation Pane.

■ The Replace command opens the Replace tab in the Find and Replace dialog box, finds the next occurrence of the word or phrase for which you are searching and replaces it with the word or phrase you type in the Replace with box.

■ The Go To command moves the insertion point to a part of the document that you specify.

■ You can see the number of words in a document or a selection by checking the status bar. You can see the number of characters, paragraphs, and lines in a document or selection by opening the Word Count dialog box.

■ VOCABULARY REVIEW

Define the following terms:

Clipboard	drag-and-drop	select
copy	format	toggle
cut	Office Clipboard	
drag	paste	

H verses   I-beam

■ REVIEW QUESTIONS

TRUE / FALSE

Circle T if the statement is true or F if the statement is false.

(T) F   **1.**   You can hide formatting marks.

(T) F   **2.**   You can undo more than one action at a time.

(T) F   **3.**   You can remove the extra space that normally appears after a paragraph.

T (F)   **4.**   The Office Clipboard can store up to 48 items.   *44 items max.*

T (F)   **5.**   The only way to find out how many words are in a document or selection is to open the Word Count dialog box.

WRITTEN QUESTIONS

Write a brief answer to each of the following questions.

1. How do you use the keyboard to select text?

Ctrl + A.
shift and left or right mouse

2. How do the Cut and Copy commands differ?

Ctrl + X cut
ctrl + c copy

3. Describe how to move and copy text using drag-and-drop.

4. Describe the Paste Options button and how to use it, including how to preview the effects.

5. Which dialog box contains the Go To tab?

FILL IN THE BLANK

Complete the following sentences by writing the correct word or words in the blanks provided.

1. The _____ is a special clipboard on which you can collect up to 24 selections.

2. The _____ opens when you click the Find button in the Editing group on the Home tab.

3. To jump to a specific part of a document, use the _____ command.

4. Commands that turn a feature on or off are known as _____ commands.

5. To automatically replace a word or phrase with another one, use the _____ command.

■ PROJECTS

If you have a SAM 2010 user profile, your instructor may have assigned an autogradable version of the indicated project. If so, log into the SAM 2010 Web site at *www.cengage.com/sam2010* to download the instruction and start files.

PROJECT 2–1

1. Open a new Word document. Show hidden formatting marks. Remove the space after the current paragraph.

2. Type the list of commonly misspelled words shown below.

   Committee

   Occurrence

   Occasional

   Collectible

   Received

   Jewelry

   Correspondence

   Judgment

   Absence

   Accommodate

3. Type **Until** below *Occurrence*.

4. Undo the last action. The word *Until* disappears.

5. Redo the undone action. The word *Until* reappears.

6. Use the Go To command to move the insertion point to line 5.

7. Use the drag-and-drop technique to alphabetize the word list.

8. Hide formatting marks.

9. Press Ctrl+End, press Enter twice, and then type your name.

10. Save the document as **Spelling List** followed by your initials. Print and close the document.

SAM PROJECT 2–2

1. Open the **Workshop.docx** Data File. Save the document as **Workshop Checklist** followed by your initials.

2. Show hidden formatting marks.

3. Use the Go To command to move the insertion point to line 2.

4. Type the following sentence at the beginning of line 2:

   We are pleased that you have applied to be part of the Summer Language Workshop at Granville University.

5. Use the drag-and-drop technique to move the line *Nonrefundable $15 application fee* to the end of the checklist.

6. Select the entire document. Copy the selection to the Clipboard.

7. Press Ctrl+End to move to the end of the document. Paste the contents of the Clipboard. Press Backspace to remove the second blank paragraph at the end of the document.

8. Use the Find command to find all instances of the word *items*. Then change the word you are looking for to *necessary*. Close the Navigation Pane.

9. Use the Replace command to replace all instances of the word *necessary* with *needed*.

10. Jump to the end of the document, and then type your name in the blank paragraph at the end of the document. Hide formatting marks.

11. Print, save, and close the document.

PROJECT 2–3

1. Open the **Web Site.docx** Data File. Save the file as **Web Site Tips** followed by your initials.

2. Highlight all instances of the word *sight* in the document. Replace them with the word **site**. There should be 10 replacements.

3. Make the insertions and deletions indicated by the proofreader's marks in **Figure 2–13**.

4. Display formatting marks. Move to the blank paragraph below tip number 6, type **Document word count:**, press the spacebar, and type the number of words currently in the document.

5. Remove the space after the current paragraph, and then press Enter. Type **Introductory paragraph word count:**, and then press the spacebar.

6. Create another paragraph. Type **Introductory paragraph character count with no spaces:**, and then press the spacebar.

7. Select all of the text in the introductory paragraph, and determine the number of words in the selection. Move to the end of the document, and then type this number after the phrase you typed in Step 5.

8. Determine the number of characters without counting spaces, in the introductory paragraph, and then type this number after the phrase you typed in Step 6.

9. Add space after the last paragraph, press Enter twice, and then type your name. Hide formatting marks.

10. Save, print, and close the document.

Publicizing Your Web Site

If your company has a Web site, it needs to be publicized so that people will visit it. Here are _six_ tips for publicizing your site.

1. Submit the URL to as many search engines as possible.

2. Submit the URL to _as many_ Internet directories, _as possible_

3. Trade links with _other, related_ Web sites. For example, you could ask the owners of the Business Electronics Online site to add a link to your page, and you can add a link on your Web site to theirs.

4. Advertise your site online by sponsoring a Web page or purchasing advertising space on a relevant Web site.

5. Send out press releases to newspapers, television stations, radio stations, and magazines announcing your site and any unique information or services it provides consumers.

6. Print the URL of your site on all _of_ your business correspondence including business cards, letterhead, and brochures. Also include the URL in any printed or broadcast advertising.

FIGURE 2–13

PROJECT 2–4

1. Open the **Tournament.docx** Data File. Save the document as **Tournament Notice** followed by your initials.

2. Display formatting marks. Position the insertion point in the blank paragraph between the document heading and the first paragraph. Type the following:.
   Where: Forest Hills Golf Club
   When: August 10–11
   Time: Tee times begin at 8:00 a.m.
   Cost: $50 entry fee per person

3. Select the first three lines you typed (from the line staring with *Where* through the line starting with *Time*). Remove the space after these paragraphs.

4. Select the word *Where*. Type **Location**.

5. Undo the change you made in Step 4.

6. Open the Office Clipboard. Cut the four lines you typed at the beginning of the document. Cut the last sentence in the first paragraph.

7. Copy all the text in the heading, but do not copy the paragraph marker in the paragraph.

8. Paste the four lines you typed below the paragraph in the document. Paste the *For more information* sentence in a paragraph below the four lines you typed.

9. Paste the heading at the end of the first sentence in the document, after **Sixth Annual**. Use the Paste Options button to match the format of the first paragraph. Close the Clipboard task pane.

10. Use the Find command to find the text *Robert Shade*, and then replace it with your name. Close the Navigation Pane.

11. Hide formatting marks. Save, print, and then close the document.

PROJECT 2–5

1. Open the **Interview.docx** Data File. Save the document as **Interview Preparation** followed by your initials.

2. Replace all instances of the word *notes* with the word **information**. You should have two replacements.

3. Use the Find command to find the word *these*. Select the word *these*, and then type **this**. Close the Navigation Pane.

4. In the second paragraph, in the first line, cut the text *be sure to*.

5. Use the Repeat command to cut the second paragraph.

6. Paste the paragraph you just cut below the last paragraph in the document.

7. At the end of the document, type your name in the empty paragraph.

8. Save, print, and close the document.

■ CRITICAL THINKING

ACTIVITY 2–1

Work with a classmate to create a new Word document listing qualities employers look for in a job applicant. Some examples are a person who is responsible, detail-oriented, and cooperative. Then, each of you create another document, and list a personal inventory of your strengths and weaknesses as a potential applicant for a job of your choice.

ACTIVITY 2–2

A coworker asks you the following questions about using the Office Clipboard to copy and paste items. Use Help to answer the questions.

1. Can I use the Office Clipboard without displaying the Clipboard task pane?

2. Is there another way to display the Office Clipboard?

3. How do I delete an item from the Office Clipboard? How do I delete all the items from the Office Clipboard?

LESSON 3

Helpful Word Features

■ OBJECTIVES

Upon completion of this lesson, you should be able to:

- Use AutoCorrect.
- Use AutoFormat As You Type.
- Create, insert, and delete Quick Parts.
- Use AutoComplete.
- Insert the current date and time.
- Check the spelling and grammar in a document.
- Use the Thesaurus.
- Insert symbols.

■ VOCABULARY

AutoComplete

AutoCorrect

AutoFormat As You Type

automatic grammar checking

automatic spell checking

building block

contextual spell checking

format

Quick Part

Thesaurus

Using Automatic Features

Word provides many helpful features and commands. For example, as you type, some types of errors correct automatically, and some text is formatted automatically. You can also take advantage of a feature that completes the month names and the days of the week after you type a few letters, or you can simply insert the current date using a button on the Ribbon. If there's text you use all the time, you can save the text as a special item that you can insert with a few clicks. Word provides a feature that checks the spelling and grammar in a document, and you can use a built-in feature to find a synonym for a word. You can also insert symbols that aren't on the keyboard. In this lesson, you will learn how to take advantage of all of these features.

Understanding Automatic Features

Word provides many types of automated features that can help you create documents. The AutoCorrect feature corrects errors as you type, and AutoFormat As You Type, as the name implies, applies built-in formats as you type. You can create and use Quick Parts to insert frequently used text. The AutoComplete feature "guesses" days of the week and month names as you type, and then suggests the complete word.

Using AutoCorrect

▶ **VOCABULARY**
AutoCorrect

AutoCorrect corrects common capitalization, spelling, grammar, and typing errors as you type. You can also customize AutoCorrect by adding or removing words or by changing the types of corrections made.

Using AutoCorrect in a Document

When you type something that is in the AutoCorrect list, the automatic correction occurs after you press the spacebar or Enter. For example, you can specify that when you type the letters *nyc,* they will always be replaced with *New York City.* Or if you start typing a new sentence after some ending punctuation, and you forget to capitalize the first letter of the first word in the new sentence, it will be capitalized automatically when you press the spacebar.

Step-by-Step 3.1

1. Start Word. Open the **Memo.docx** Data File from the drive and folder where your Data Files are stored. Save the document as **Fall Classes Memo** followed by your initials. Ignore the words in the document that are misspelled for now.

2. Position the insertion point at the end of the second paragraph in the memo (immediately following the period after *time*).

3. Press the **spacebar**, type **if**, and then press the **spacebar** again. Notice that as soon as you pressed the spacebar, the word *if* was capitalized because the AutoCorrect feature recognized it as the first word in a new sentence.

hyperlink ⇒ blue mail.

4. Type the following (with the lowercase *i* and the misspelled word *accomodate*): **possible, i will accomodate**, and then press the **spacebar**. AutoCorrect recognized that you meant to type *I* and automatically changed it, and automatically corrected the misspelled instance of *accommodate*.

5. Type **you.** (Be sure to type the period.)

6. Save the document and leave it open for the next Step-by-Step.

Customizing AutoCorrect

You can add or remove words from the AutoCorrect list and change the AutoCorrect options. To do this, you need to open the AutoCorrect dialog box. Click the File tab, and then in the navigation bar, click Options. This opens the Word Options dialog box. You can customize many Word features using this dialog box. Clicking a category on the left side of the Word Options dialog box changes the commands displayed on the right side of the dialog box. To open the AutoCorrect dialog box, click Proofing in the list on the left side of the dialog box. The right side of the dialog box changes to display commands for customizing tools you use to help proofread your document in Word. See **Figure 3–1**. *personalizar.*   *corregir.*

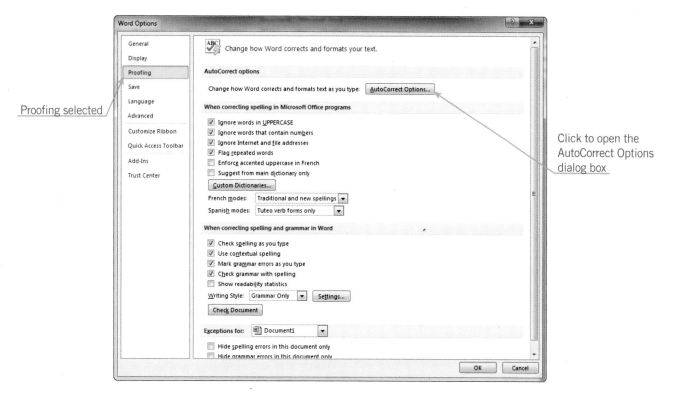

FIGURE 3–1   Proofing options in the Word Options dialog box

On the right side of the dialog box, click AutoCorrect Options. The AutoCorrect dialog box opens with the AutoCorrect tab on top, as shown in **Figure 3–2**. The check boxes at the top of the tab control the AutoCorrect options. Commonly misspelled or mistyped words are listed in the box at the bottom of the tab. The correct spellings that AutoCorrect inserts in the document when you press Enter appear on the right side of the list. Notice in the figure that the first few items listed in the box are not misspellings but are characters that represent a symbol. If you type the sequence of characters, AutoCorrect automatically inserts the symbol in place of the characters.

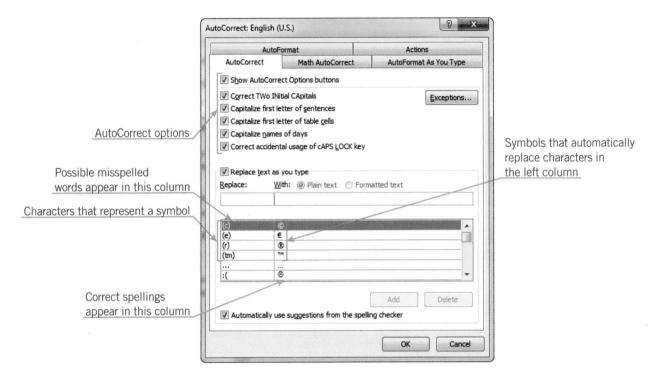

FIGURE 3–2   AutoCorrect tab in the AutoCorrect dialog box

You can also open the AutoCorrect dialog box using the AutoCorrect Options button. When you position the pointer over text that has been automatically corrected, a small blue box appears just below the first character in the word or below the symbol. When you point to the box, it changes to the AutoCorrect Options button. You can click the AutoCorrect Options button to open a menu of commands for changing the AutoCorrect action. Click Control AutoCorrect Options to open the AutoCorrect dialog box.

Step-by-Step 3.2

1. Click the **File** tab, and then in the navigation bar, click **Options**. The Word Options dialog box opens.

2. In the list on the left, click **Proofing**. The commands for customizing proofing tools in Word appear in the right side of the dialog box, as shown in Figure 3–1.

3. On the right side of the dialog box, click **AutoCorrect Options**. The AutoCorrect dialog box opens, as shown in Figure 3–2.

4. In the Replace box, type your initials. If the list under the Replace box scrolls and displays an entry that is the same as your initials, add another letter to your initials.

5. Press **Tab** to move to the With box. In the With box, type your name. Near the bottom of the dialog box, click **Add**. AutoCorrect is now customized with your name.

6. Click **OK** to close the AutoCorrect dialog box, and then click **OK** to close the Word Options dialog box.

7. In the memo, next to the word *From:*, select **David Chofsky**. Type your initials, and then press the **spacebar**. AutoCorrect replaces the initials with your name.

8. Move the pointer on top of your name. A small blue box appears below the first part of your name. Point to the **blue box**. The box changes to the AutoCorrect Options button.

9. Click the **AutoCorrect Options** button [image]. A menu opens, as shown in **Figure 3–3**. The top two commands on the menu allow you to undo the correction or stop making that particular type of correction. The last command opens the AutoCorrect dialog box.

FIGURE 3–3
AutoCorrect Options button in a document

You might not see the Developer tab on your screen

Your name and initials appear here

AutoCorrect Options button

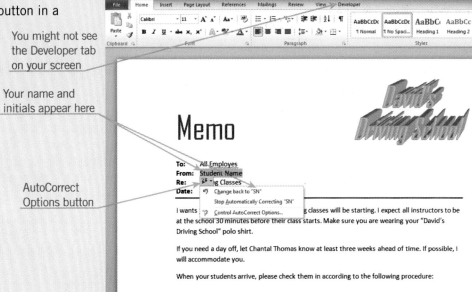

10. On the menu, click **Control AutoCorrect Options**. The AutoCorrect dialog box opens with the AutoCorrect tab on top.

11. In the list at the bottom, scroll down until you see your initials. (Note that the list is organized so that the Replace column is in alphabetical order.)

12. In the list, click your initials. The whole line is selected. Below the list, click **Delete**. Your initials and your name are removed from the list.

13. Click **OK** to close the AutoCorrect dialog box. Save the document and leave it open for the next Step-by-Step.

TIP

To quickly jump to an item in the list, start typing it in the Replace with box.

Understanding Formatting

▶ **VOCABULARY**
format

Formatting means to change the look of text. You can format specific words or entire paragraphs. Examples of text formatting are adding bold, italics, or underlining to words to emphasize them. Examples of paragraph formatting are indenting the first line of a paragraph or double-spacing the lines of text in a paragraph. A paragraph format can also include text formatting. For example, a paragraph format for headings (like the preceding "Understanding Formatting" heading) can include extra space above and below it (paragraph formatting), as well as formatting the text as blue and in a larger font size.

Using AutoFormat As You Type

The *AutoFormat As You Type* feature automatically applies built-in formats to text as you type. In a new paragraph, for example, if you type the number *1* followed by a period, and then press Tab, Word assumes that you are trying to create a numbered list. The AutoFormat As You Type feature changes the text you just typed and the new paragraph you just created to the List Paragraph Quick Style and formats it as a numbered list. If you type something in the list, and then press Enter, the number *2* followed by a period and a tab space is automatically inserted on the next line. Another example of text automatically formatted by the AutoFormat As You Type feature is certain fractions. For example, when you type *1/2*, it changes it to ½.

You can choose which automatic formatting options you want to use on the AutoFormat As You Type tab in the AutoCorrect dialog box, shown in **Figure 3–4**.

▶ **VOCABULARY**
AutoFormat As You Type

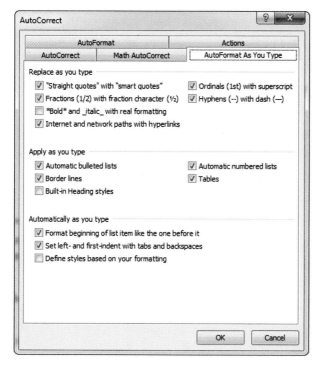

FIGURE 3–4   AutoFormat As You Type tab in the AutoCorrect dialog box

Step-by-Step 3.3

1. On the Home tab, in the Paragraph group, click the **Show/Hide** button ⁋. Formatting marks appear in the document. (Remember, this button is a toggle button, so if you don't see formatting marks in your document, click the button again to select it.) This will make it easier to see AutoFormat As You Type in action.

2. Press **Ctrl+End** to position the insertion point in the blank paragraph below the last paragraph. Type **1.**, and then press **Tab**. Pressing Tab moves the insertion point to the right approximately one-half inch. The formatting mark that indicates a tab is an arrow that points to the right. The AutoCorrect Options button appears to the left of the text you typed.

3. Point to the **AutoCorrect Options** button. It changes to the same AutoCorrect Options button you saw earlier. Click the **AutoCorrect Options** button to open the menu. The second command on the menu identifies the type of automatic correction that was made; in this case, the paragraph was changed to a numbered list. On the Ribbon, you can see in the Paragraph group that the Numbering button is selected.

4. Press **Esc** to close the AutoCorrect Options menu without choosing a command. You want to create a numbered list.

5. Type **Check each student's name on the class list.** Press **Enter**. Because this text is formatted as a numbered list, the number *2* followed by a period and a tab mark automatically appear on the next line. The insertion point is blinking in the new line after the tab mark.

6. Type **On the 1st**. Press the **spacebar**. When you press the spacebar, AutoFormat As You Type changed *st* to superscript—text that is formatted much smaller than the rest of the text and raised up to the top of the line.

7. Type **day of class, check the list from the accounting office to see if the student has paid for the class.** When this line wraps, the second line is automatically indented so that it aligns with words after the tab mark in the line above it. This formatting is part of the numbered list style.

8. Press **Enter**. The next line is formatted as part of the numbered list. Type **Give any student who has not paid a green slip, and then send him or her to the office.** Press **Enter**. The fourth item in the list is created.

9. Press **Enter** again. Because you didn't type any text as part of the fourth item, the item is removed, the numbered list is ended, and the insertion point moves back to the left margin.

10. Type **If you have any questions, refer to the Instructor's page on our Web site at www.davidsdriving.biz.** Press **Enter**. A new paragraph is created and the Web page address you typed (www.davidsdriving.biz) is formatted in blue and underlined. In addition, it is changed to a hyperlink to that Web site on the Internet.

11. Position the pointer over the blue underlined text. A ScreenTip appears telling you to press Ctrl and click to follow the link (which means to jump to that Web page on the Internet). The small blue AutoCorrect box appears just below the beginning of the URL.

12. Point to the blue AutoCorrect box. The AutoCorrect Options button appears. Click the **AutoCorrect Options** button, and then click **Undo Hyperlink** on the menu. The link is removed and the text is no longer formatted as blue and underlined.

EXTRA FOR EXPERTS

To change the paragraph from a numbered list to normal text, you also can click the Normal button in the Styles group on the Home tab.

WARNING

The Web page address that you typed is not the address of a real Web page, so following the link will open a dialog box telling you that the page could not be opened.

13. On the Home tab, in the Paragraph group, click the **Show/Hide ¶** button ¶ to turn formatting marks off, and then save the document and leave it open for the next Step-by-Step.

Using Quick Parts

Building blocks are document parts that are stored and reused. *Quick Parts* are building blocks you create from frequently used text, such as a name, address, or slogan, and then save so that you can access them by clicking the Quick Parts button in the Text group on the Insert tab.

Creating and Inserting a Quick Part

To create a Quick Part, select the text that you want to save as a Quick Part. Click the Insert tab on the Ribbon, and then, in the Text group, click the Quick Parts button. The Quick Parts menu opens. If any Quick Parts are stored on your computer or in your document, they will appear at the top of this menu. On the menu, click Save Selection to Quick Part Gallery. The Create New Building Block dialog box opens, as shown in **Figure 3–5**.

Type a name for the Quick Part here

FIGURE 3–5   Create New Building Block dialog box

The first few words of the selected text appear as the default name for the Quick Part in the Name box. You can change this name if you want. Click OK to save the Quick Part. After you create a Quick Part, it appears at the top of the Quick Parts menu.

Step-by-Step 3.4

1. In the *From* line in the memo header, select your name.
2. On the Ribbon, click the **Insert** tab. In the Text group, click the **Quick Parts** button, and then click **Save Selection to Quick Part Gallery**. The Create New Building Block dialog box opens.

3. In the Name box, type **My Name** followed by your initials. You don't need to click in the box first because the text in the Name box is selected when the dialog box appears, and your typing automatically replaces the selected text.

4. Click **OK**. The dialog box closes.

5. In the first line of the second paragraph in the memo, select the text **Chantal Thomas**. Press **Delete** to delete her name.

6. On the Insert tab, in the Text group, click the **Quick Parts** button. The Quick Part you created appears at the top of the menu, similar to the one shown in **Figure 3–6**. If other *My Name* entries appear on this menu, scroll down until you see the one you created.

FIGURE 3–6
Quick Parts menu with a new Quick Part on it

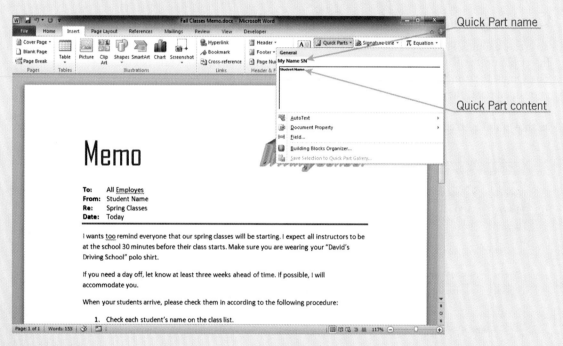

7. On the menu, click the **My Name** Quick Part that you created. The menu closes and your name appears in the document at the insertion point.

8. If there is no space between your last name and the word *know*, press the **spacebar** to insert a space.

9. Save the document and leave it open for the next Step-by-Step.

TIP

A Quick Part can consist of text several paragraphs long and it can also contain formatted text.

Deleting a Quick Part

To delete a Quick Part, you need to open the Building Blocks Organizer dialog box. To do this, on the Ribbon, click the Insert tab. In the Text group, click the Quick Parts button, and then click Building Blocks Organizer. The Building Blocks Organizer dialog box opens, similar to the one shown in **Figure 3–7**.

(handwritten notes in right margin: scroll through / displayor / scroll down => / desplacese hacia / abajo / - Trade Mark sign / - row / - compilation / - portrays)

Click a column
header to sort the
list alphabetically
by the entries in
that column

Quick Part
in the list

Preview of
the selected
building block

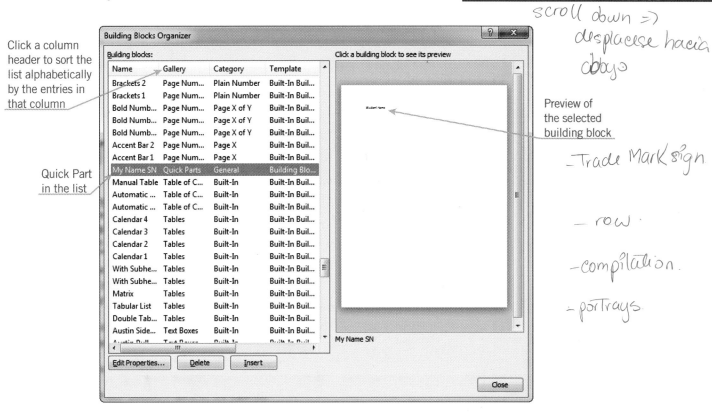

FIGURE 3–7   Building Blocks Organizer dialog box

As you see, Word comes with quite a few built-in building blocks. Building blocks are organized into galleries. By default, the list is sorted alphabetically by gallery name. You can sort the building blocks in this list by any of the column headings in the dialog box. The Quick Part you created is stored in the Quick Parts gallery. To see building blocks in the Quick Parts gallery, scroll down the list. To delete a Quick Part, select it, and then click Delete.

EXTRA FOR EXPERTS

You can use the built-in building blocks just as you used the Quick Part you created. Click a building block in the list in the Building Blocks Organizer dialog box, and then click Insert. The building block is inserted into the document.

Step-by-Step 3.5

1. On the Insert tab, in the Text group, click the **Quick Parts** button, and then click **Building Blocks Organizer**.

2. If the list of building blocks is not sorted alphabetically by Gallery name (you might see a few AutoText entries, and then two Bibliographies entries, followed by several Cover Pages entries), click the **Gallery** column header.

3. Use the scroll bar to scroll down the list until you see Quick Parts in the Gallery column. Locate the Quick Part you created. Remember its name is *My Name* followed by your initials. Click the Quick Part you created to select it.

EXTRA FOR EXPERTS

You can also click the Quick Parts button, right-click the Quick Part, and then click Organize and Delete to open the Building Blocks Organizer with that Quick Part already selected.

4. At the bottom of the dialog box, click **Delete**. A warning dialog box opens asking if you are sure you want to delete the selected building block.

5. Click **Yes**. The selected Quick Part is deleted from the list.

6. Click **Close** to close the dialog box.

7. Save the document and leave it open for the next Step-by-Step.

Using AutoComplete

AutoComplete is a feature in Word that automatically completes the spelling of days of the week and months of the year that have more than five letters in their names. After you type the first four letters, AutoComplete suggests the complete word. For example, if you type *Febr*, the word *February* appears in a ScreenTip above the insertion point. **Figure 3–8** shows an example of an AutoComplete suggestion. To insert the suggested word, press Enter, and AutoComplete automatically inserts the complete word for you. To ignore the suggested word, just keep typing.

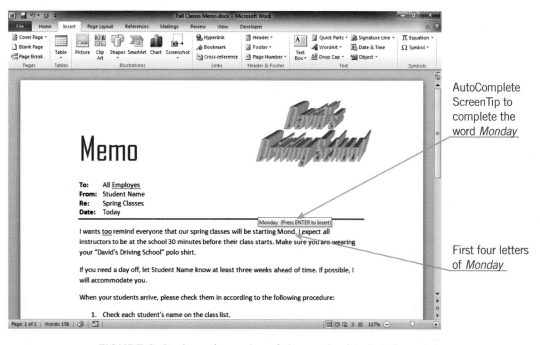

AutoComplete ScreenTip to complete the word *Monday*

First four letters of *Monday*

FIGURE 3–8   Inserting a day of the week with AutoComplete

Step-by-Step 3.6

1. In the first paragraph, at the end of the first sentence, position the insertion point between the word *starting* and the period. Press the **spacebar**.

2. Type **Mond**. A ScreenTip appears telling you to press Enter to insert *Monday*, as shown in Figure 3–8.

3. Press **Enter** to accept the AutoComplete suggestion. *Monday* appears in the document.

4. Save the document and leave it open for the next Step-by-Step.

Inserting the Date and Time

You can easily insert the current date and time into a document. To do this, on the Ribbon, click the Insert tab. Then, in the Text group, click the Date & Time button. The Date and Time dialog box opens, as shown in **Figure 3–9**. Select one of the available formats in the list. Some of the formats display only the date, and others display the date and time.

Dates and times shown are the current date and time, so your date will probably differ

Select to update the date every time the document is opened

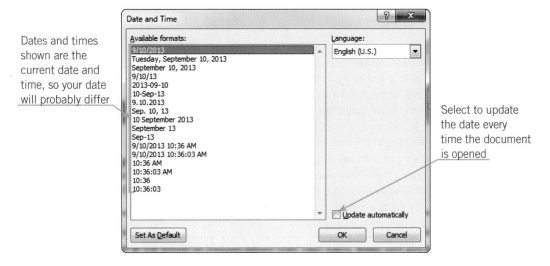

FIGURE 3–9   Date and Time dialog box

If you want to display the current date whenever you open the document, you would click the Update automatically check box to select it. For example, if you create a template or a report on a regular basis, you would probably want to have the current date displayed each time you opened the document. If you want a date inserted in the document to always show the date you inserted it, leave the Update automatically check box unselected. For example, when you create a letter or memo, you would want the date to remain unchanged for record keeping purposes.

Step-by-Step 3.7

1. In the *Date* line in the memo header, select the text **Today**, and then press **Delete**.

2. On the Insert tab, in the Text group, click the **Date & Time** button. The Date and Time dialog box opens.

3. In the Available formats box, click the third format, which shows today's date in a format similar to *September 10, 2013*.

4. If the **Update automatically** check box has a check mark in it, click it to remove the check mark. This will prevent the date from updating to the current date every time this document is opened.

5. Click **OK**. The dialog box closes and the current date is inserted in the letter.

6. Save the document and leave it open for the next Step-by-Step.

Checking Spelling and Grammar as You Type

Word has the capability to identify misspelled or misused words or incorrect grammar. ***Automatic spell checking*** flags words that might be misspelled by underlining them with a red or blue wavy line immediately after you type them. A red, wavy underline indicates Word cannot find that word in its built-in dictionary, which means the word might be misspelled. A blue, wavy underline indicates a word that might be misused. For example, if you type *We came form the store*, the word *form* would be flagged with a blue, wavy underline as a word that might be misused. Word identifies possible misusage by examining the context in which the word is used. This feature is called ***contextual spell checking***.

    Automatic grammar checking examines your document for grammatical errors. When it finds a possible error, the word, phrase, or sentence is underlined with a green, wavy line. The automatic grammar checker looks for capitalization errors, commonly confused words, misused words, passive sentences, punctuation problems, and other types of grammatical problems.

    To correct a spelling, contextual, or grammatical error that has been identified with a wavy underline, right-click the flagged word or phrase to open a shortcut menu with a list of suggestions to replace the possible error. See **Figure 3–10**. Click a suggestion on the shortcut menu to select it and replace the flagged word or phrase.

▶ VOCABULARY
automatic spell checking

contextual spell checking

automatic grammar checking

── WARNING
The automatic spell checker sometimes incorrectly identifies words as being misspelled, because the word is not in the built-in dictionary. This frequently occurs with proper names.

■ TIP
Although automatic grammar checking is a helpful tool, you still need a good working knowledge of English grammar. The grammar checker can identify a possible problem, but you must decide if the change should be made.

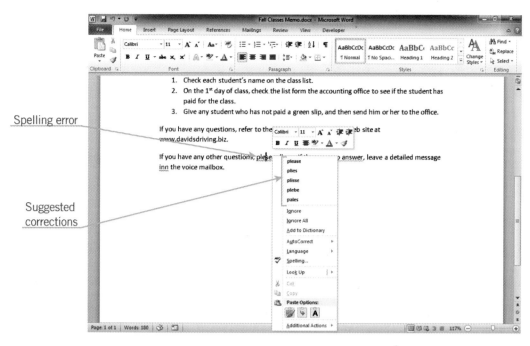

Spelling error

Suggested corrections

FIGURE 3–10   Correcting a spelling error using the shortcut menu

Automatic spelling and grammar checking can be turned on and off or adjusted in the Proofing section of the Word Options dialog box, as shown in **Figure 3–11**. The options in the spelling and grammar section of the dialog box are described in **Table 3–1**.

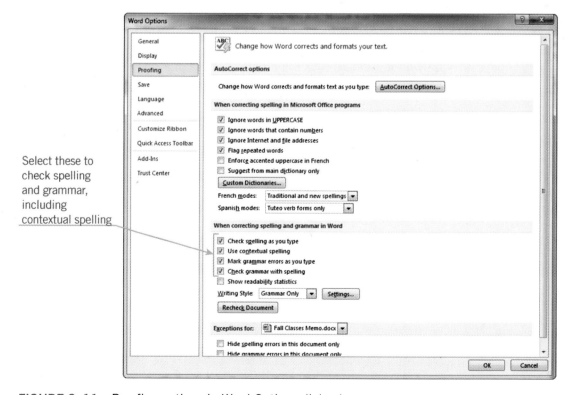

Select these to check spelling and grammar, including contextual spelling

FIGURE 3–11   Proofing options in Word Options dialog box

TABLE 3–1   Spelling and grammar options in the Word Options dialog box

OPTION	ACTION
Check spelling as you type	Flags possible misspelled words in the document with a red, wavy underline.
Use contextual spelling	When checking the document for spelling errors, flags possible misused words with a blue, wavy underline.
Mark grammar errors as you type	Flags possible grammatical errors in the document with a green, wavy underline.
Check grammar	When checking the document for spelling errors, also checks for spelling grammatical errors.
Show readability	Opens the Readability Statistics dialog box when the spelling and statistics grammar check is complete. The Readability Statistics dialog box provides information about the reading level of the document.
Writing Style	If you turn on the grammar checker, allows you to check for grammar errors only or for writing style errors, such as use of the passive voice. The default is to check for grammar only.
Settings	Opens the Grammar Settings dialog box, in which you can select the grammar and writing style rules the grammar checker uses as it checks the document.
Recheck Document	Resets the spelling and grammar checker so that words you previously chose to ignore will be flagged in the document again.

Step-by-Step 3.8

TIP

The options in the "When correcting spelling in Microsoft Office programs" section in the dialog box apply to all Microsoft Office programs installed on your computer, not just to Word.

1. On the Ribbon, click the **File** tab, and then in the navigation bar, click **Options**. In the list on the left side of the Word Options dialog box, click **Proofing**. The right side of the dialog box changes to display options for customizing the proofing tools in Word.

2. In the section labeled "When correcting spelling and grammar in Word," the first four check boxes should be selected. If any of these check boxes does not contain a check mark, click it to insert a check mark. Click **OK** to close the dialog box.

3. Press **Ctrl+End**. The insertion point moves to the end of the document.

4. Type the following sentences *exactly* as they appear here: **If you have any other questions, plese call me. If there are no answer, leave a detailed message inn the voice mailbox.** The three intentional errors are flagged by Word with wavy underlines.

5. Right-click **plese**, the word flagged with a red, wavy underline indicating a possible misspelled word. (Remember, right-click means to position the mouse pointer over the word or words specified, and then click the *right* mouse button.) A shortcut menu opens.

6. With the left mouse button, click **please** on the shortcut menu. The incorrect spelling is replaced with the correct spelling, and the red, wavy underline disappears.

7. Right-click anywhere on the words **are no answer**. This phrase is flagged with a green, wavy underline indicating a possible grammatical error. (If the green, wavy underline is not showing, click in a different paragraph, and then click in the sentence that you typed.)

8. On the shortcut menu that opens, click **is no answer**. This is the correct phrase to use in this instance. The incorrect phrase is replaced with the correct phrase, and the green, wavy underline disappears.

9. Right-click **inn**, the word flagged with a blue, wavy underline indicating that it might be used incorrectly in this context.

10. On the shortcut menu that opens, click **in**. The incorrectly used word is replaced with the correct word, and the blue, wavy underline disappears.

11. Save the document and leave it open for the next Step-by-Step.

EXTRA FOR EXPERTS

When you right-click a grammar error, you can click Grammar on the shortcut menu to learn more about the grammar error that has been identified.

Using the Spelling and Grammar Checker

In addition to checking your spelling and grammar as you type, you can use the Spelling and Grammar dialog box to check a document's spelling and grammar after you finish typing. You can check an entire document or a selected portion of a document. To do this, on the Ribbon, click the Review tab. Then, in the Proofing group, click the Spelling & Grammar button. The Spelling and Grammar dialog box opens, displaying the first flagged error identified in the document.

The options in the Spelling and Grammar dialog box change depending on the nature of the current error. When a spelling error is detected, the Spelling and Grammar dialog box appears similar to the one shown in **Figure 3–12**. When a contextual spelling error is detected, the dialog box that appears is the same as the one shown in Figure 3–12, but only the Ignore Once and Change commands are available. When a grammar error is identified, the Spelling and Grammar dialog box appears similar to the one shown in **Figure 3–13**.

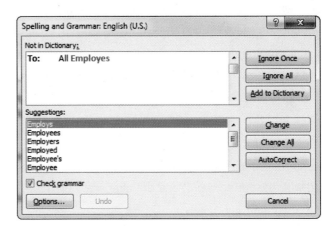

FIGURE 3–12   Spelling error flagged in the Spelling and Grammar dialog box

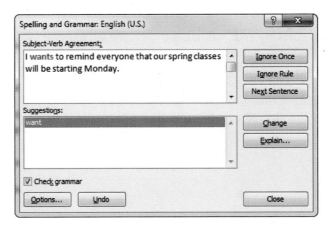

FIGURE 3–13   Grammatical error flagged in the Spelling and Grammar dialog box

When an error is found, it is highlighted in the document and listed in the top box in the dialog box. Suggestions for correcting the error are listed in the bottom box. For some grammar errors, only a description of the type of error appears in the bottom box.

You can click in the document and correct the error, click in the top box in the dialog box and correct the error, or click a suggestion in the Suggestions box to correct the error. If you click in the document to correct the error, the Ignore Once command in the dialog box changes to Resume. If you correct the error by clicking in the top box in the dialog box, the Ignore Once command changes to Undo Edit. When you are finished working in the document, click in the dialog box, and then click Resume. **Table 3–2** and **Table 3–3** explain the options in the Spelling and Grammar dialog box.

 TIP

If a word appears twice in a row, the second word will be underlined with a red, wavy underline. To delete the repeated word, click Delete Repeated Word on the shortcut menu or, in the Spelling and Grammar dialog box, click Delete (which replaces Change).

TABLE 3–2 Spelling and Grammar dialog box commands for spelling errors

COMMAND	ACTION
Ignore Once	Leaves the word in the document unchanged and jumps to the next flagged error; changes to Resume if you click in the document to correct the error; and changes to Undo Edit if you correct a change in the top box.
Ignore All	Leaves all instances of the word unchanged in the document and jumps to the next flagged error.
Add to Dictionary	Leaves all instances of the word unchanged in the document, adds the word to the built-in dictionary, and jumps to the next flagged error.
Change/Delete	The Change command changes the flagged word to the selected suggestion or to the correction you type in the top box in the dialog box, and then jumps to the next flagged error. The Delete command appears when a word appears twice in a row; click it to delete the repeated word.
Change All	Changes all instances of the flagged word in the document to the selected suggestion or to the correction you type in the top box in the dialog box, and then jumps to the next flagged error.
AutoCorrect	Changes the flagged word to the selected suggestion, adds the word and its correction to the AutoCorrect list, and jumps to the next flagged error.
Options	Opens the Proofing section in the Word Options dialog box so you can change default spelling and grammar check settings.
Undo/Undo Edit	Reverses the last decision you made in the dialog box.
Cancel/Close	Before you make a decision on the first spelling change, Cancel stops the spelling check. After you make a decision on the first error, it changes to Close, and clicking it stops the spelling and grammar check.

TABLE 3–3   Spelling and Grammar dialog box commands for grammar errors

COMMAND	ACTION
Ignore Once	Leaves the flagged error untouched and jumps to the next flagged error; changes to Resume if you click in the document to correct the error; and changes to Undo Edit if you correct a change in the top box.
Ignore Rule	Leaves all instances of errors that violate the identified grammar rule untouched and jumps to the next flagged error.
Next Sentence	Leaves the flagged error untouched or changes the flagged error to the correction you type in the top box in the dialog box, and then jumps to the next flagged error.
Change	Changes the flagged error to the selected suggestion or to the correction you type in the top box in the dialog box, and then jumps to the next flagged error.
Explain	Opens a Word Help window with an explanation of the grammar or style rule being applied.
Options	Opens the Proofing section in the Word Options dialog box to allow you to change default spelling and grammar check settings.
Undo/Undo Edit	Reverses the last decision you made in the dialog box.
Cancel/Close	Before you make a decision on the first grammar change, Cancel stops the grammar check. After you make a decision on the first error, it changes to Close, and clicking it stops the spelling and grammar check.

Step-by-Step 3.9

1. Press **Ctrl+Home**. This ensures that the spelling and grammar check starts from the beginning of the document.

2. On the Ribbon, click the **Review** tab. The Ribbon changes to display the commands on the Review tab.

3. In the Proofing group, click the **Spelling & Grammar** button. The Spelling and Grammar dialog box opens. The first error it finds in the document, *Employes*, is highlighted in the document and appears in red in the Not in Dictionary box in the dialog box. The Suggestions box at the bottom of the dialog box contains several possible alternatives for the flagged word.

4. In the Suggestions box, click **Employees**, and then click **Change**. The word is corrected in the document, and the next possible error is flagged.

5. If your first or last name is selected as the next error, click **Ignore All**, and then watch as the next error is flagged. It finds the misused word *too*.

6. Click in the box at the top of the dialog box, and then use the arrow keys to position the insertion point after the word *too*. Press the **Backspace** key to delete the second *o*.

7. Click **Change**. Word replaces the misused word and continues checking. The next error, a Subject-Verb Agreement grammatical error in the first sentence, *wants*, is highlighted.

> **TIP**
>
> To check only spelling in the document, click the Check grammar check box in the Spelling and Grammar dialog box to deselect it, or, in the Proofing section of the Word Options dialog box, click the Check grammar with spelling check box to deselect it.

8. In the Suggestions box, make sure **want** is selected, and then click **Change**. If you made any typing errors, additional words might be high-lighted next in the dialog box. If this happens, use the commands in the dialog box to correct these errors. When the spelling and grammar check is finished, the Spelling and Grammar dialog box closes and a dialog box opens telling you that the spelling and grammar check is complete.

9. Click **OK**. The dialog box closes. The insertion point returns to the beginning of the document.

10. Save the document and leave it open for the next Step-by-Step.

Using the Thesaurus

The *Thesaurus* is a useful feature for finding a synonym (a word with a similar mean-ing) for a word in your document. For some words, the Thesaurus also lists antonyms, or words with opposite meanings. You can use the Thesaurus to find the exact word to express your message or to avoid using the same word repeatedly in a document.

To use the Thesaurus, select the word you want to look up. On the Ribbon, click the Review tab. Then, in the Proofing group, click the Thesaurus button. The Research task pane opens on the right side of the window, as shown in **Figure 3–14**. The word you selected in the document appears in the top box, and *Thesaurus: English (U.S.)* appears in the second box. A list of synonyms and antonyms appears in the third box. The main entries in the list are bold. To replace the selected text, point to a word under-neath a main entry, click the arrow that appears, and then click Insert. If you click a word underneath a main entry, that word is looked up in the Thesaurus for you.

▶ **VOCABULARY**
Thesaurus

⬛ **EXTRA FOR EXPERTS**

You can also look up a word in the Thesaurus or dictionary by right-clicking a selected word and choosing Synonyms on the shortcut menu.

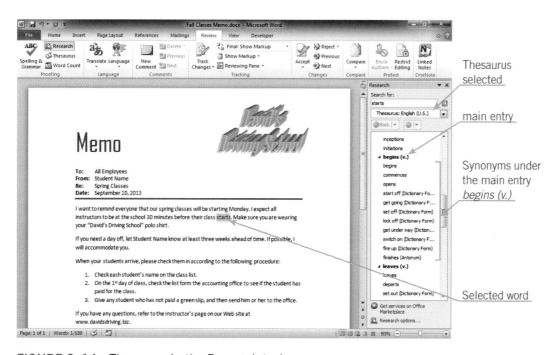

FIGURE 3–14   Thesaurus in the Research task pane

EXTRA FOR EXPERTS

To look up the definition of a word, select the word, click the Thesaurus button to open the Research task pane, click the arrow next to the second box (the one that contains *Thesaurus: English (U.S.)*), and then click Encarta Dictionary: English (North America).

If you select a plural noun or a verb in a form other than its base form (the infinitive form), a list of related words appears in the list in the task pane. For example, if you select the word *walked* in the sentence *he walked to the park*, the Research task pane would display the word *walk* under the heading "Related Words" in the task pane. You click the correct related word in the list, and the task pane changes to show the related word in the top box and its synonyms in the third box. If this happens, make sure you edit the word you insert in the document so it is in the same form as the original word.

Step-by-Step 3.10

1. In the first paragraph in the body of the memo, select the word **starts** at the end of the second sentence.

2. On the Review tab, in the Proofing group, click the **Thesaurus** button. The Research task pane opens on the right side of the window with Thesaurus: English (U.S.) in the second box. The task pane displays a list of words organized under main entries.

3. Scroll down the list until you see the main entry *begins (v.)*.

4. Under the main entry, point to the first synonym, **begins**, click the **arrow** that appears, and then click **Insert**. The word *begins* replaces *starts* in the document.

5. In the task pane title bar, click the **Close** button to close the task pane.

6. Save the document and leave it open for the next Step-by-Step.

WARNING

If you click the word in the task pane instead of clicking the arrow, the word you clicked is looked up in the thesaurus and a new set of results appears. Close the task pane, and then repeat the steps.

Inserting Symbols

At times, you may need to use a letter or symbol that is not on the keyboard. For example, you might want to insert a symbol used in a foreign language, such as the tilde over the *n* in Spanish (ñ), or a currency symbol such as the euro symbol (€) for currency in the European Union.

To insert a symbol, on the Ribbon, click the Insert tab. Then, in the Symbols group, click the Symbol button. Commonly used symbols appear on the menu. See **Figure 3–15**. To insert a symbol located on the menu, click it. If you don't see the symbol you want on the menu, click More Symbols to open the Symbol dialog box, as shown in **Figure 3–16**.

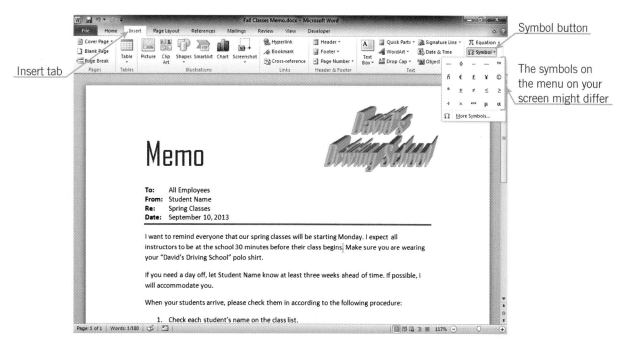

FIGURE 3–15   Symbols on the Symbol menu

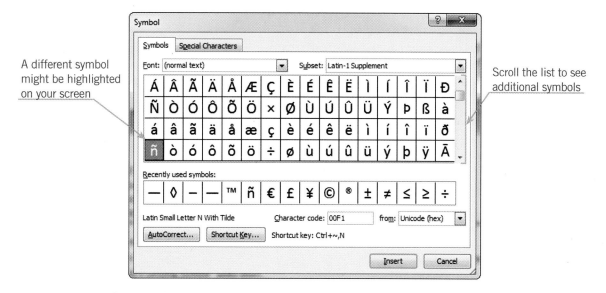

FIGURE 3–16   Symbol dialog box

Click the symbol you want in the dialog box, and then click Insert. The symbol you selected appears in the document. You then need to click Close to close the dialog box. If the symbol you inserted from the dialog box was not on the Symbol menu, it will replace one of the other symbols on the menu to make it easier for you to insert it again.

Step-by-Step 3.11

1. In the last line of the first paragraph in the body of the memo, position the insertion point between the *l* in *School* and the quotation marks.

2. On the Ribbon, click the **Insert** tab. In the Symbols group, click the **Symbol** button to open the Symbols menu. See Figure 3–15. Position the pointer on top of several of the symbols in the menu to see the ScreenTip identifying each of them.

3. Position the pointer over ™. This is the trademark symbol. The ScreenTip identifies it as TRADE MARK SIGN. (If you don't see the trademark symbol on the menu, click **More Symbols** to open the Symbol dialog box. In the Symbol dialog box, drag the scroll box to the bottom of the scroll bar, scroll up a few rows until you see the trademark symbol, click the trademark symbol, click **Insert**, and then click **Close**.)

4. Click ™. The menu closes and the trademark symbol is inserted into the document at the insertion point.

5. Save, print, and close the document.

SUMMARY

In this lesson, you learned:

- AutoCorrect automatically corrects common capitalization and spelling errors as you type. The AutoFormat As You Type feature automatically applies built-in formats to text as you type.

- You can create Quick Parts to store frequently used text so you don't have to retype the text each time. Quick Parts are a type of building block.

- AutoComplete automatically completes the spelling of days of the week and months with more than five letters in their names.

- You can automatically insert the date and time in a document using the Date & Time button.

- Automatic spell checking identifies misspelled words and words that are not in Word's dictionary by underlining them with a red, wavy underline immediately after you type them.

- Contextual spell checking identifies words that might be used incorrectly by underlining them with a blue, wavy line.

- Automatic grammar checking identifies grammatical errors by underlining the word, phrase, or sentence with a green, wavy line.

- The Spelling and Grammar dialog box contains options that allow you to check the spelling and grammar of words, make changes, and add words to your own custom dictionary.

- You can use the Thesaurus to find a synonym for a word in your document. For some words, the Thesaurus also lists antonyms.

- You can insert symbols and special characters not found on the keyboard using the Symbol button on the Insert tab.

VOCABULARY REVIEW

Define the following terms:

AutoComplete
AutoCorrect
AutoFormat As You Type
automatic grammar checking

automatic spell checking
building block
contextual spell checking

format
Quick Part
Thesaurus

REVIEW QUESTIONS

FILL IN THE BLANK

Complete the following sentences by writing the correct word or words in the blanks provided.

1. The _____ feature corrects common capitalization, spelling, grammar, and typing errors as you type.

2. All document parts that are stored and reused are called _____.

3. A blue, wavy underline in a document indicates a possible _____ error.

4. A green, wavy underline in a document indicates a possible _____ error.

5. To check the entire document for spelling and grammar errors, use the _____ dialog box.

MATCHING

Match the correct term in Column 2 to its description in Column 1.

Column 1

___B___ 1. A building block of text frequently use.

___E___ 2. Changes fractions and numbers as you type, such as 3/4 to ¾.

___C___ 3. Corrects common capitalization, typing, spelling, and grammatical errors when you press Enter or the spacebar.

___D___ 4. Identifies possible grammatical errors with green wavy underlines.

___A___ 5. Displays synonyms for a selected word.

Column 2

A. Thesaurus

B. Quick Part

C. AutoCorrect

D. Automatic grammar checking

E. AutoFormat As You Type

TRUE / FALSE

Circle T if the statement is true or F if the statement is false.

(T) F   **1.** To insert letters, symbols, and characters not found on the keyboard, you use the Symbol button in the Symbols group on the Insert tab.

(T) F   **2.** To accept an AutoComplete suggestion, you press the spacebar.

T (F)   **3.** You cannot add or delete entries from the AutoCorrect list.

(T) F   **4.** The AutoFormat As You Type feature automatically applies built-in formats to text as you type.

(T) F   **5.** You can right-click a word or phrase with a colored, wavy line under it and then select a correction from a list of suggestions.

■ PROJECTS

If you have a SAM 2010 user profile, your instructor may have assigned an autogradable version of the indicated project. If so, log into the SAM 2010 Web site at *www.cengage.com/sam2010* to download the instruction and start files.

PROJECT 3–1

1. Open the **Minutes.docx** document from the drive and folder where your Data Files are stored. Save the document as **Club Minutes** followed by your initials.

2. Check the document's spelling and grammar, and correct any errors.

3. Near the top of the document, insert the current date in the blank paragraph beneath *Minutes of the Business Meeting* in the format *Thursday, March 21, 2013*. Do not update the date automatically.

4. Insert your name at the beginning of the list of members who attended the meeting, and then create an AutoCorrect entry for your name.

5. In the second to last paragraph, position the insertion point between *recognized* and *as*. Use the AutoCorrect feature to insert your name. Insert any necessary spaces or delete extra spaces.

6. In the last sentence in the Old Business paragraph, find a synonym for the word *aim* that makes sense in context.

7. In the last sentence in the first New Business paragraph, find a synonym for the word *arrange* that makes sense in context.

8. At the end of the Announcements paragraph, type **The next meeting will be held on the 24th of April.**

9. Delete the AutoCorrect entry you added.

10. Save, print, and close the document.

SAM PROJECT 3–2

1. Open the **Lancaster Memo.docx** document from the drive and folder where your Data Files are stored. Save the document as **Lancaster Voting Memo** followed by your initials.

2. Turn on formatting marks, and then position the insertion point after the tab mark in the *From* line in the memo header.

3. Type **Dinah Muñoz**. (If the letter *ñ* is not on the Symbol menu, open the Symbol dialog box. Make sure the scroll box is at the top of the list, and then click the down scroll arrow eight times to see the row containing the character.)

4. Insert the current date after the tab mark in the *Date:* line in the format that looks like 9/29/13. Do not update the date automatically.

5. In the body of the memo, position the insertion point after the word *for* at the end of the first sentence. Use the AutoComplete and AutoFormat As You Type features to insert the text **September 31ˢᵗ**. Insert any necessary spaces. (*Hint*: You will need to press the spacebar after typing the date, and then remove the extra space before the period.)

6. Create a Quick Part named **Chamber** from the text *Chamber of Commerce* in the second sentence of the first paragraph. Insert the Chamber Quick Part at the end of the *To* line in the memo header.

7. Use the AutoFormat As You Type feature to create the following numbered list after the second paragraph in the body of the memo:

   1. **G. W. Carter Elementary School**
   2. **Kennedy Middle School**
   3. **Lancaster High School**

8. Use the Thesaurus to replace the word *personal* in the last paragraph with a word that makes sense in context.

9. Delete the Chamber Quick Part.

10. Correct the spelling and grammatical errors in the document.

11. Jump to the end of the document, press Enter twice, and then type your name.

12. Turn off formatting marks, and then save, print, and close the document.

PROJECT 3–3

1. Open the **Museum.docx** document from the drive and folder where your Data Files are stored. Save the document as **Museum Visit** followed by your initials.

2. Use the Thesaurus to change as many words as you can without changing the meaning of the text.

3. Jump to the end of the document, press Enter twice, and then type your name.

4. Save, print, and close the document.

PROJECT 3–4

1. Open the **Application.docx** document from the drive and folder where your Data Files are stored. Save the document as **Application Letter** followed by your initials.

2. Insert the current date in the format *September 29, 2013* in the blank paragraph above the inside address. Set the date to update automatically.

3. In the third paragraph in the body of the letter, position the insertion point in front of the last sentence (just before *These*), and then type the following sentence. (If you don't see the symbols on the Symbol menu, open the Symbol dialog box, click the Subset arrow, and then click Greek and Coptic to jump to the Greek alphabet.)

   I have also been active on campus, holding various leadership positions in the service organization Omega Delta Psi ($\Omega\Delta\Psi$).

4. In the last line of the document, replace *Sarah Summers* with your name.

5. Check the document's spelling and grammar, and correct any errors.

6. Save, print, and close the document.

■ CRITICAL THINKING

ACTIVITY 3–1

It is important for students to begin to develop a personal portfolio for employment before they graduate from high school or college. A personal portfolio contains a resume, well-written application letters, a list of references, and a list of achievements. Write an application letter for a job that interests you. Team up with a few classmates, and then edit and critique each other's application letters. Be careful to provide constructive criticism.

ACTIVITY 3–3

Word has many helpful editing features. Some Word features are more helpful as you type your text, and some are more useful after you have finished typing. Make one list of the Word features you would use as you type a document, and then make another list of Word features you would use after you finished typing the document. If a feature can be listed in both lists, decide when it is the most useful.

ACTIVITY 3–2

You are the regional vice president for Candlelight Time, a chain of candle stores. A new store will be opening soon, and you need to type a letter to potential customers announcing the grand opening and offering three free scented candles to the first 100 customers. Make the letter at least three paragraphs long. Use any helpful automatic features. Insert the current date (set it to update automatically), and then check the spelling and grammar.

LESSON 4

Formatting Text

■ OBJECTIVES

Upon completion of this lesson, you should be able to:

- Change the font.
- Change the size, color, and style of text.
- Use different underline styles and font effects and highlight text.
- Copy formatting using the Format Painter.
- Understand styles and apply Quick Styles.
- Change the theme.
- Create new Quick Styles.
- Clear formatting.

■ VOCABULARY

attribute

color palette

font

font effect

font size

font style

Format Painter

point

Quick Style

style

text effect

theme

Formatting Text

Once you have typed text in a document, you can format the text to change its appearance and make an impact on the reader.

In this lesson, you will learn how to change the appearance, size, color of text, and how to apply several formats at once using styles. You will learn how to copy formats and clear formatting. You will also learn how to change a document's theme and how to modify and create new styles.

To change the format of text, you must first select the text you want to change. If you are changing the format of a single paragraph, the insertion point must be located somewhere in that paragraph. If you are changing the format of multiple paragraphs, you must select at least part of each paragraph you want to format. You can also change the format before you start typing, and all the text you type from then on will have the new format applied until you change to another format.

Changing the Font

Designs of type are called *fonts*. Just as clothing comes in different designs, fonts have different designs. For example, the font used for this text is Times LT Std Roman and the font used for the blue *Changing the Font* heading above is Futura Std Medium.

Like clothing, fonts can be dressy or casual. When you are creating a document, you should consider what kind of impression you want the text to make. Do you want your document to look dressy and formal? Or do you want it to look casual and informal? Using the fonts shown in **Figure 4–1** would result in very different looking documents.

This font is called Calibri.

This font is called Times New Roman.

This font is called Arial.

This font is called Broadway.

𝔗𝔥𝔦𝔰 𝔣𝔬𝔫𝔱 𝔦𝔰 𝔠𝔞𝔩𝔩𝔢𝔡 𝔒𝔩𝔡 𝔈𝔫𝔤𝔩𝔦𝔰𝔥 𝔗𝔢𝔵𝔱 𝔐𝔗.

This font is called Comic Sans MS.

This font is called Lucida Handwriting.

FIGURE 4–1   Examples of different fonts

To change the font, locate the Font group on the Home tab on the Ribbon. Click the arrow next to the Font box, as shown in **Figure 4–2**, and then scroll to the font of your choice. If you have selected text in the document first, you can point to each font to use Live Preview, the Microsoft Office feature that enables you to watch the selected text change in the document without actually making the change. When you find the font you want, click it. The menu closes and the new font is applied to the selected text.

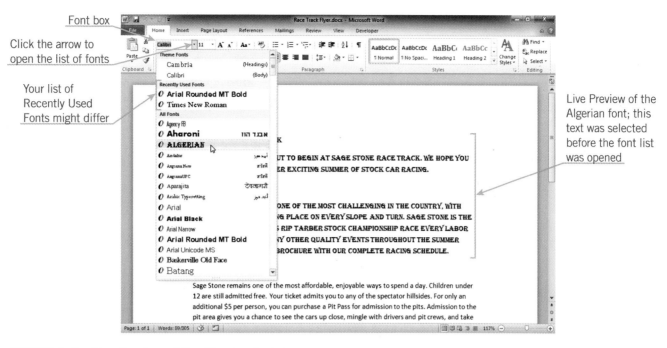

Font box

Click the arrow to
open the list of fonts

Your list of
Recently Used
Fonts might differ

Live Preview of the
Algerian font; this
text was selected
before the font list
was opened

FIGURE 4–2 Live Preview of the Algerian font

You can change the font of text already in the document by selecting it first, and then choosing a new font. To change the font of text not yet typed, first choose the font, and then type the text. The new font will be applied until you change to another font.

Step-by-Step 4.1

1. Open the **Flyer.docx** document from the drive and folder where your Data Files are stored. Save the document as **Race Track Flyer** followed by your initials.

2. On the Home tab, in the Editing group, click the **Select** button, and then click **Select All**. All the text in the document is selected.

3. On the Home tab, in the Font group, click the **arrow** next to the Font box Calibri (Body). The list of fonts opens. The font currently applied to the selected text, Calibri, is listed in the Font box and is selected at the top of the list.

4. Point to **Algerian** (but don't click it). The Live Preview feature changes the selected text in the document to the Algerian font so you can see what it would look like.

5. Point to a few other fonts in the list and watch how the Live Preview feature changes the selected text.

6. Click a blank area of the document. The Font list closes and the font of the selected text stays the same.

7. In the paragraph below the heading *Sage Stone Race Track*, in the first line of text, select the text **Sage Stone Race Track**.
8. In the Font group, click the **arrow** next to the Font box `Calibri (Body)`. Click **Arial Rounded MT Bold**. The Font list closes and the selected text is changed to Arial Rounded MT Bold.
9. Click a blank area of the document to deselect the text.
10. Save the document and leave it open for the next Step-by-Step.

Changing Font Attributes

Once you have decided on a font, you can change its *attributes*, or how it looks. For example, you can change the size of the font or change its style by making the font bold, italic, or underlined. You can also add color and apply special effects.

Changing Font Size

Font size is determined by measuring the height of characters in units called *points*. Standard font sizes for text are 10, 11, and 12 points. Font sizes for headings are usually larger. For example, this text is 10 points, and the blue *Changing Font Attributes* heading above is 18 points. The higher the point size, the larger the characters. **Figure 4–3** illustrates the Calibri font in different sizes. You can change font size by using the Font Size box on the Formatting toolbar or on the Mini toolbar.

This is 10-point Calibri.

This is 11-point Calibri.

This is 12-point Calibri.

This is 16-point Calibri.

This is 20-point Calibri.

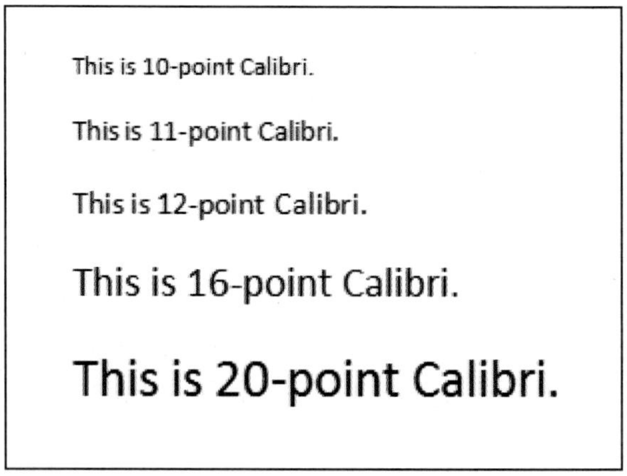

FIGURE 4–3   Examples of font sizes

Step-by-Step 4.2

1. In the paragraph below the heading *Sage Stone Race Track*, in the first line of text, select **Sage Stone Race Track**.

2. On the Home tab, in the Font group, look at the Font Size box [11 ▾]. The selected text is 11 points. See **Figure 4–4**.

Font Size box

Font group

Selected text

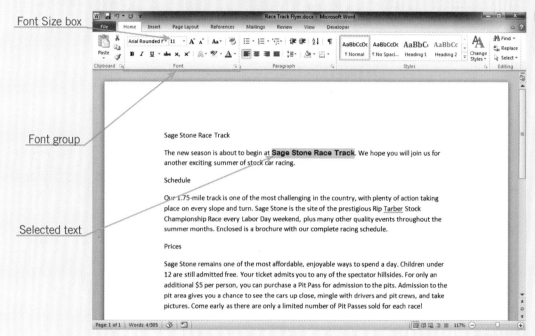

FIGURE 4–4
Font size of selected text

3. In the paragraph below the heading *Sage Stone Race Track*, select the second line of text, and then look at the Font Size box [11 ▾]. This text is also 11 points. Although these characters look smaller than *Sage Stone Race Track* in the first line of this paragraph, all of the text in the document is 11 points.

4. Scroll to the bottom of the document, and then select all the text in the last paragraph (*We can't wait to see you!*).

5. Click the **arrow** next to the Font Size box [11 ▾]. A list of font sizes appears.

6. Click **16**. The Font Size list closes, and the selected text is changed to 16 points.

7. Deselect the text.

8. Save the document and leave it open for the next Step-by-Step.

TIP

Point size tells you the size of text relative to text in other point sizes in the same font. But, 11-point text in one font might be larger or smaller than 11-point text in another font.

EXTRA FOR EXPERTS

If you want to use a font size that is not on the Font Size list, type the point size directly in the Font Size box, and then press Enter.

Changing the Color of Text

You can change the color of text to make it stand out or to add interest to a document. To change the color of text, click the arrow next to the Font Color button in the Font group on the Home tab. This opens a gallery that includes the *color palette*, a coordinated set of colors available for use in the document. See **Figure 4–5**.

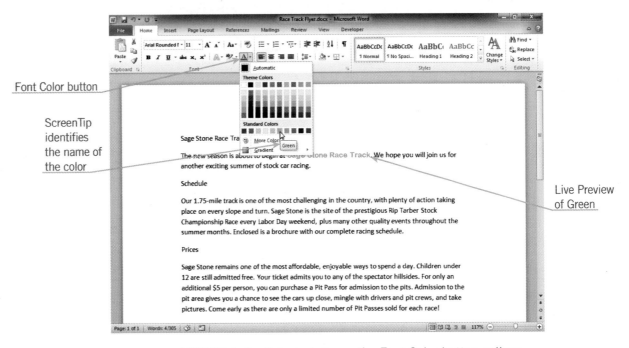

Font Color button

ScreenTip identifies the name of the color

Live Preview of Green

FIGURE 4–5   Color palette on the Font Color button gallery

The gallery has four sections. The top section contains the Automatic color for the current text; this is usually black. The middle section contains the color palette of Theme Colors, which are colors specifically designed to work with the current document. The bottom section contains the palette of Standard Colors, which are colors that are always available. Finally, the More Colors command below the color palette, opens the Colors dialog box in which you can choose many more colors.

The colors in the palette all have names. You can see the names by pointing to each color to see its ScreenTip, as shown in Figure 4–5. The Standard Colors have simple names, such as Red, Yellow, and Light Green. The Theme Colors have more complex names that identify the color, shade, and other information.

Step-by-Step 4.3

1. In the bulleted list at the end of the document, in the second bulleted item, select **recycle**.

2. On the Home tab, in the Font group, click the **arrow** next to the Font Color button [A▾]. A gallery containing the color palette opens.

3. In the Standard Colors row, click the **Green** color. The color palette closes and the selected text is now green.

4. Press **Ctrl+Home** to jump back to the beginning of the document, and then in the paragraph below the heading *Sage Stone Race Track*, select the text **Sage Stone Race Track** again. (This is the text you formatted with the Arial Rounded MT font.)

5. On the Home tab, in the Font group, click the **arrow** next to the Font Color button ![A], and then in the first row under Theme Colors, click the **Olive Green, Accent 3** color. The color palette closes and the color you selected is applied to the selected text.

6. Deselect the text.

7. Save the document and leave it open for the next Step-by-Step.

Changing Font Style

Font style is a formatting feature you can apply to a font to change its appearance. Common font styles are bold, italic, and underlining. These styles can be applied to any font. **Figure 4–6** illustrates these styles applied to the Calibri font.

This text is bold.

This text is italic.

<u>This text is underlined.</u>

<u>This text is bold, italic, and underlined.</u>

FIGURE 4–6 Examples of font styles

The easiest way to change the font style is to select the text, and then click the Bold, Italic, or Underline buttons in the Font group on the Home tab. The Bold and Italic buttons are also available on the Mini toolbar. All three of the style commands are toggle commands, so to turn a style off, you click the button again.

Changing Underline Style and Color

When you underline text, you can underline with one line or change the style to multiple lines, dotted lines, dashed lines, or another style. You can also change the color of the underline. To change to another underline style or color, click the arrow next to the Underline button. See **Figure 4–7**.

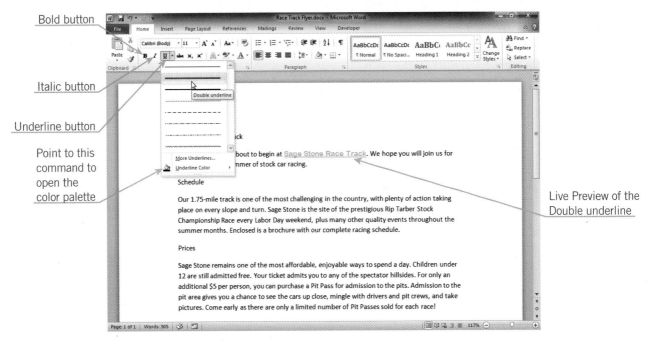

Bold button

Italic button

Underline button

Point to this command to open the color palette

Live Preview of the Double underline

FIGURE 4–7   Underline menu to choose underline style and color

You can click one of the styles on the menu, or click More Underlines to open the Font dialog box. In the Font dialog box, click the Underline style arrow, and then scroll down the list to see additional underline styles. To change the color of the underline, click the arrow next to the Underline button, and then point to Underline Color. This opens the same palette of colors available when you click the Font Color button arrow.

Step-by-Step 4.4

1. Select the text **Sage Stone Race Track** once more in the paragraph below the heading *Sage Stone Race Track*.

2. On the Home tab, in the Font group, click the **Bold** button **B**. The selected text becomes bold. The Bold button is orange to indicate that it is toggled on selected and bold formatting is turned on.

3. In the fourth paragraph (the paragraph under "Schedule"), at the end of the second line, select the text **Rip Tarber Stock Championship Race**.

4. In the Font group, click the **Italic** button **I**. The selected text is italicized and the Italic button is selected.

WARNING

Remember that you create a new paragraph every time you press Enter, so a paragraph can be a single line or even one word.

5. Press **Ctrl+End** to jump to the end of the document. In the bulleted list, in the second bulleted item, select the green text **recycle**. In the Font group, click the **Underline** button ⊔. Deselect the text. The text *recycle* is underlined.

6. Select **recycle** again. In the Font group, click the **Underline** button ⊔. The selected text is no longer underlined.

7. With *recycle* still selected, in the Font group, click the **arrow** next to the Underline button ⊔ ▾. The Underline menu opens. Click the **Double underline**. The selected text is underlined with a double underline.

8. In the Font group, click the **arrow** next to the Underline button ⊔ ▾. Point to **Underline Color**. A gallery containing the color palette opens.

9. Under Standard Colors, click the **Blue** color. The color palette closes and the color of the double underline changes to blue.

10. Deselect the text.

11. Save the document and leave it open for the next Step-by-Step.

Changing Text Effects

Text effects, sometimes called *font effects*, are similar to font styles and can help enhance or clarify text. To apply a text effect—such as, strikethrough, subscript, or superscript—to selected text, click the button corresponding to that effect in the Font group on the Home tab. Many more text effects are available on the Text Effects button gallery and menu shown in **Figure 4–8**. Like font styles, font effects are toggle commands—a font effect is either turned on or off.

VOCABULARY
text effects
font effects

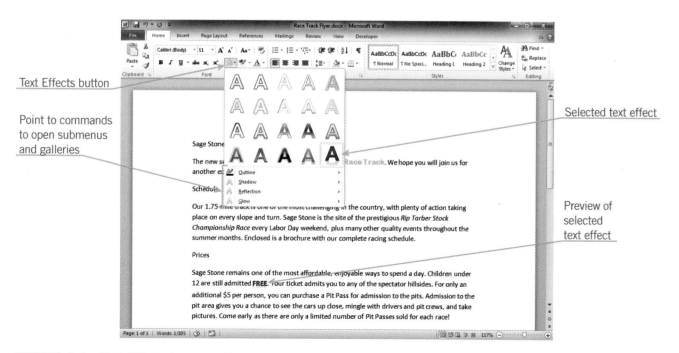

FIGURE 4–8 Text Effects button gallery and menu

Step-by-Step 4.5

1. In the sixth paragraph (the paragraph under *Prices*), in the second line, select the text **free**.

2. On the Home tab, in the Font group, click the **Text Effects** button. The Text Effects gallery and menu opens.

3. Point to a few of the effects to see the Live Preview.

4. Click the **Gradient Fill – Purple, Accent 4, Reflection** effect (the last effect in the last row). See Figure 4–8. The text is formatted so it is all uppercase, purple, and has a reflection.

5. On the Home tab, in the Font group, click the **Text Effects** button again. In the menu, point to **Reflection**. A submenu showing a gallery of reflection options appears.

6. In the gallery, click the **No Reflection** effect (in the first row under No Reflection). The reflection effect is removed from the selected text.

7. Deselect the text. Save the document and leave it open for the next Step-by-Step.

📼 EXTRA FOR EXPERTS

Another way to apply font styles and text effects is to click the Font Dialog Box Launcher to open the Font dialog box.

Highlighting Text

When you read a paper document, you sometimes use a highlighting marker to draw attention to an important part of the document. You can highlight text in a Word document for the same effect. To highlight text, click the arrow next to the Text Highlight Color button in the Font group on the Home tab. A gallery of colors opens. Click one of the colors.

If text is selected in the document, the text becomes highlighted with the color you chose. If no text is selected, the pointer changes to the Highlight pointer, an I-beam pointer with a marker on it, when you position it on top of text in the document. You can drag the pointer over any text you want to highlight. See **Figure 4–9**. When you are finished, click the Text Highlight Color button again to toggle this command off.

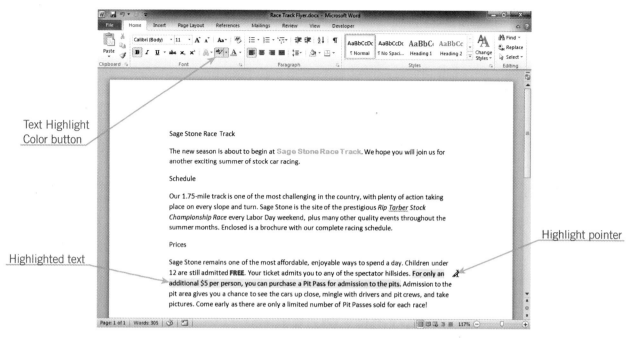

FIGURE 4-9   Text highlighted with the Highlight pointer

Text Highlight
Color button

Highlighted text

Highlight pointer

If text is highlighted and you want to remove the highlight, select the highlighted text, and then click the Text Highlight Button. If you'd rather drag over each selection of highlighted text to "erase" the highlighting, you can click the arrow next to the Text Highlight Color button, and then click No Color. The pointer changes to the Highlight pointer, and when you drag over highlighted text, you remove the highlight.

Step-by-Step 4.6

1. On the Home tab, in the Font group, locate the **Text Highlight Color** button ⬚. The colored bar near the bottom of the button indicates the current highlighter color.

2. Click the **arrow** next to the Text Highlight Color button ⬚. A gallery of colors opens. Click the **Yellow** box (even if the button already indicates that the current color is yellow). The Text Highlight Color gallery closes. The colored bar on the Text Highlight Color button is yellow to reflect the color you chose, and the button is colored orange to indicate that it is selected.

3. Move the pointer so it is positioned anywhere on top of text. The pointer changes to the Highlight pointer ⬚.

4. In the sixth paragraph (the paragraph under *Prices*), near the end of the second line, position the pointer in front of the fourth sentence (in front of the word *For*). Click and drag to select the entire sentence (finishing at *admission to the pits.*), releasing the mouse button when you have selected the whole sentence. The fourth sentence is highlighted with yellow. See Figure 4-9.

5. In the Font group, click the **Text Highlight Color** button 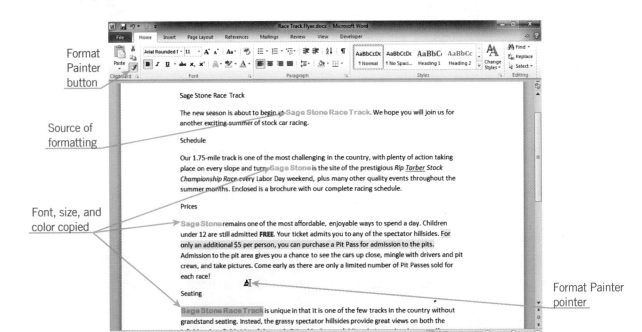. The button is no longer selected, and the pointer returns to normal.

6. In the same paragraph, select the last sentence (it starts with *Come early*).

7. In the Font group, click the **arrow** next to the Text Highlight Color button. Click the **Bright Green** color. The selected text is highlighted with bright green. The pointer does not change to the Highlighter pointer.

8. Select the green highlighted sentence.

9. In the Font group, click the **arrow** next to the Text Highlight Color button. Click **No Color**. The highlighting is removed from the selected text.

10. Save the document and leave it open for the next Step-by Step.

Copying Formatting

Often you will spend time formatting text and then find that you need the same format in another part of the document. You can copy the format of selected text to other text by using the *Format Painter*. To access the Format Painter, click the Format Painter button in the Clipboard group on the Home tab or on the Mini toolbar.

To use the Format Painter, select the text with the format you want to copy, and then click the Format Painter button. When you move the pointer over text, it changes to the Format Painter pointer, which is the I-beam pointer with a paintbrush to its left. Drag the Format Painter tool across the text you want to format. The text changes to the copied format. If you want to copy the format to more than one block of text, double-click the Format Painter button. The button will remain selected and the Format Painter stays active until you click the button again to deselect it. See **Figure 4–10**.

▶ **VOCABULARY**
Format Painter

TIP

You can also press Esc to turn off the Highlighter or the Format Painter.

FIGURE 4–10   Text after using Format Painter

Step-by-Step 4.7

1. In the paragraph below the heading *Sage Stone Race Track*, select the green **Sage Stone Race Track**. Remember, this text is formatted with the Arial Rounded MT Bold font, and you added the bold font style and changed the color to Olive Green.

2. On the Home tab, in the Clipboard group, click the **Format Painter** button. The Format Painter button is selected. Move the pointer so it is on top of any text in the document. The pointer changes to the Format Painter pointer.

3. In the fourth paragraph (under *Schedule*), in the second line, drag across the text **Sage Stone**. The text is formatted with the same formats as the text in the second paragraph.

4. Move the pointer on top of the text. It is the normal pointer again. The Format Painter button is no longer selected.

5. With *Sage Stone* still selected, in the Clipboard group, double-click the **Format Painter** button.

6. In the sixth paragraph (the paragraph under *Prices*), drag across **Sage Stone**. The copied format is copied to the text.

7. Move the pointer on top of the text to see that the Format Painter pointer is still active. The Format Painter button is still selected.

8. In the eighth paragraph (under *Seating*), drag across **Sage Stone Race Track**. The formatting is applied to the selected text, as shown in Figure 4–10.

9. Press **Ctrl+End** to jump to the end of the document. In the last bulleted item, drag across **Sage Stone**. The format is copied again.

10. In the Clipboard group, click the **Format Painter** button. The button is no longer selected and the pointer returns to normal.

11. Save your changes to the document and leave it open for the next Step-by-Step.

Understanding Styles

In Word, a *style* is a set of formatting options that have been named and saved. Character styles affect only selected text; paragraph styles affect entire paragraphs.

Using styles can save time and add consistency to a document. For example, if you are working on a long document, such as a research paper that contains headings, you would want to format the headings to stand out from the regular (the Normal) text. You could do this manually by selecting each heading, changing the font size, and applying font styles, such as bold. You might also change the color of the headings. If your document contained many headings, you would need to do this

▶ **VOCABULARY**
style

for each heading, or use the Format Painter to copy the format to each heading. If you changed your mind about the look of the headings, for example, if you decide to use red text instead of bold purple text, you would need to change each heading again.

If you used a style to format your headings, the style could define this type of heading as 14-point bold, purple text. You could then apply that style with the click of the mouse to each heading. If you changed your mind and wanted the headings in red, you could change the style definition to format the text as red instead of purple, and the headings formatted with that style would change red to reflect the new definition.

Applying Quick Styles

A *Quick Style* is a style that is available by clicking a button in the Styles group on the Home tab. If you want to see the additional Quick Styles available in the Quick Styles gallery, click the up or down arrows to scroll the gallery, or click the More button in the Styles group to open the Styles gallery. See **Figure 4–11**.

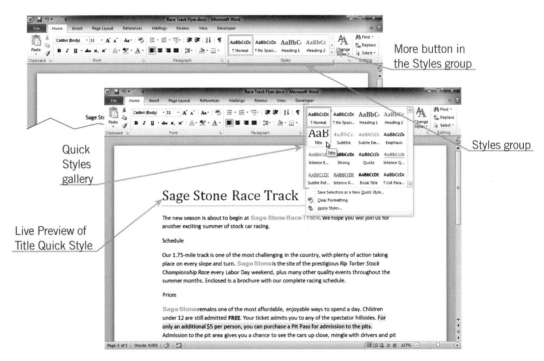

FIGURE 4–11   Quick Styles gallery

When the Quick Styles gallery is open, you can point to a Quick Style to see a Live Preview of the formatting in the document. The default style for text is the Normal Quick Style. It is used for ordinary text.

> **TIP**
>
> If you apply a style to the current paragraph and then press Enter, the new paragraph that you create has the same style as the original paragraph.

> ▶ **VOCABULARY**
>
> **Quick Style**

> **TIP**
>
> If you use the Format Painter to copy formatting from text that has a style applied to it, the style is copied to the new text.

Step-by-Step 4.8

1. Scroll to see the beginning of the document, and then click anywhere in the first line of text. On the Home tab, locate the Styles group. The Normal style has a yellow box around it indicating that it is selected.

2. In the Styles group, click the **More** button. The Quick Styles gallery opens.

3. In the second row, first column, click the **Title** style. Refer back to Figure 4–11. The Quick Styles gallery closes and the Title Quick Style is applied to the current paragraph. The text is formatted with the font, color, and size defined by the Title Quick Style. The Title Quick Style also includes a light blue horizontal line under the paragraph.

4. Select the heading **Schedule**. In the Styles group, click the **More** button to open the Quick Styles gallery. In the first row, third column, click the **Heading 1** style. The Heading 1 Quick Style is applied to the paragraph. In addition to changing the text to medium-blue 14-point Cambria, the Heading 1 Quick Style removed the extra space after the paragraph.

5. Apply the **Heading 1** Quick Style to the **Prices** and **Seating** headings.

6. In the paragraph under the Schedule heading, select the italicized text **Rip Tarber Stock Championship Race**.

7. In the Styles group, click the **More** button. Locate the style with the name *Intense E...*, and then point to it. The ScreenTip labels this style *Intense Emphasis*. Click the **Intense Emphasis** style. The italic formatting you applied earlier is removed and the formats associated with the Intense Emphasis Quick Style are applied. The selected text is now light blue, bold, and italic.

> **WARNING**
>
> When you apply a Quick Style, any manual formatting that you've already applied to the text is overridden by the Quick Style formats (except highlighting).

8. Select the yellow-highlighted sentence. Open the Styles gallery. In the second row, last column, click the **Emphasis** style. The text is formatted with the Emphasis Quick Style, which is the Normal style plus italics.

9. Deselect the text. Note that the highlighting was not removed when you applied the Quick Style. Highlighting can be part of a style definition, but manual highlighting is not removed when you apply a different style.

10. Save the document and leave it open for the next Step-by-Step.

Changing Themes

A *theme* is a coordinated set of fonts, styles, and colors. The theme determines the default font, the color of headings formatted using the Heading Quick Styles, and other features of the document. To see the available themes, click the Page Layout tab, and then, in the Themes group, click the Themes button. A gallery of themes

> **VOCABULARY**
> theme

opens, as shown in **Figure 4–12**. Word comes with 40 built-in themes. They are arranged in alphabetical order except that the default theme, the Office theme, appears first.

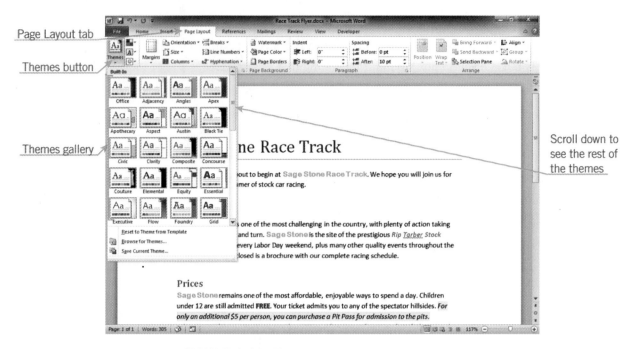

FIGURE 4–12 Themes gallery

The definitions of Quick Styles are tied to the themes. For example, in the previous section, the text that you formatted with the Heading 1 Quick Style appeared in bold, medium blue, 14-point Cambria. If you changed to the Apex theme, text formatted with the Heading 1 Quick Style would change to bold, yellow-brown, 14-point Lucida Sans. If you changed to the Verve theme, the Heading 1 text would change to bold, dark pink, 14-point Century Gothic.

The fonts used in a document are tied to the theme as well. Text formatted with the Normal style and other text tied to that style use the font labeled "(Body)" in the Font list on the Font button. Text formatted with heading styles use the font labeled "(Headings)" in the Font list.

Step-by-Step 4.9

TIP

Point to the Themes button on the Page Layout tab to see a ScreenTip that identifies the current theme.

1. On the Ribbon, click the **Page Layout** tab. In the Themes group, click the **Themes** button. The Themes gallery opens. The Office theme is the default theme for new documents and is the current theme. You might see orange highlighting on the Office theme in the Themes gallery.

2. In the first row, third column, point to the **Angles** theme. Live Preview shows the changes to the document; the title changes to black text, the headings change to gray, and the *FREE* text you formatted with using the effect on the Text Effects button gallery changes to green. In addition, the fonts change to Franklin Gothic Medium for the headings and Franklin Gothic Book for the rest of the text.

3. Point to several other theme buttons, and watch the Live Preview to see each change.

4. In the third row, third column, click the **Composite** theme. The Themes gallery closes and the Composite theme is applied to the document.

5. Save the document and leave it open for the next Step-by Step.

Redefining an Existing Quick Style

What if none of the Quick Styles formats the text exactly the way you want it to look? You can create your own style. The easiest way to create your own style is to format text with an existing Quick Style, and then make changes until you are satisfied with the final look. To redefine an existing Quick Style, select the formatted text you want to use as the style, right-click the Quick Style you want to redefine to open a shortcut menu, and then click the Update command on the shortcut menu. In the example shown in **Figure 4–13**, you would click Update Intense Emphasis to Match Selection. The selected text doesn't change, but the Quick Style is redefined to match it. The redefined Quick Style is available only in the current document.

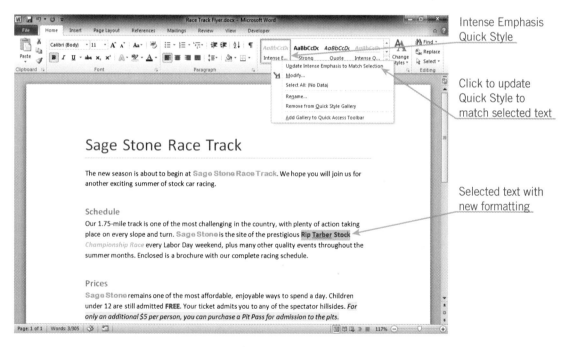

FIGURE 4–13   Redefining a Quick Style

Step-by-Step 4.10

1. In the paragraph under the Schedule heading, select the text **Rip Tarber Stock**. (Do not select *Championship Race*.)

2. On the Ribbon, click the **Home** tab. In the Font group, click the **arrow** next to the Font Color button ⒶⒷ. In the color palette, note the red box around the Lime color in the top row under Theme Colors. This is the color of the selected text.

3. In the last row of the color palette under Theme Colors, in the second to last column, click the **Orange, Accent 5, Darker 50%** color.

4. In the Font group, click the **Italic** button 𝐼 to deselect it.

5. In the Font group, click the **arrow** next to the Font Size box ⌈11 ▾⌉, and then click **12**. The selected text is changed to 12-point, dark orange, bold text that is not italicized.

6. In the Styles group, click the **More** button. Right-click the **Intense Emphasis** style. A shortcut menu opens. You're going to redefine the Intense Emphasis style. As you do the next step, keep an eye on the rest of the phrase that is formatted with the Intense Emphasis style—*Championship Race*.

7. On the shortcut menu, click **Update Intense Emphasis to Match Selection**. The Quick Styles gallery closes. The selected text retains the formatting you applied, and the Intense Emphasis style is redefined to match the formatting of the selected text. This means that *Championship Race* is now 12-point dark orange and is no longer italicized.

8. Save the document and leave it open for the next Step-by-Step.

Creating a New Quick Style

You can also create a brand new Quick Style. Again, the easiest way to do this is to first format text with the font, style, and any other characteristics that you want. To name your style and add it to the Quick Styles gallery, open the Quick Styles gallery, and then click Save Selection as a New Quick Style on the menu at the bottom of the gallery. This opens the Create New Style from Formatting dialog box. Type a name for your new Quick Style in the Name box, as shown in **Figure 4–14**. The new Quick Style is available only in your document.

> **EXTRA FOR EXPERTS**
>
> To make a redefined or new Quick Style available to other documents, right-click the Quick Style in the Styles group, click Modify on the shortcut menu to open the Modify Style dialog box, and then click the New documents based on this template option button.

Name for new Quick Style

FIGURE 4–14   Create New Style from Formatting dialog box

Step-by-Step 4.11

1. Select all of the text in the first paragraph in the document under the title.

2. In the Font group, click the **Text Effects** button [A], and then point to **Outline**. The color palette for the Composite theme appears.

3. In the second column under Theme Colors, click the **Black, Text 1, Lighter 35%** color (in the third row). The gallery closes and the selected text is formatted with a dark gray outline effect.

4. With the first paragraph still selected, in the Styles group, click the **More** button. On the menu below the gallery, click **Save Selection as a New Quick Style**.

5. In the Create New Style from Formatting dialog box, type **Important** in the Name box, as shown in Figure 4–14. Click **OK**. The dialog box closes. The new Quick Style appears in the first position in the Styles group. If you don't see the new style, click the up arrow in the Styles gallery as many times as needed to scroll up and display the first row in the gallery on the Ribbon.

6. Scroll down to the end of the document, and then select the last paragraph.

7. In the Styles group, click the **up scroll arrow** twice, and then click the **Important** style. The new Quick Style is applied to all of the text in the last paragraph.

8. Save the document and leave it open for the next Step-by-Step.

Clearing Formatting

You can use the Clear Formatting command to remove manual formatting and styles. To do this, first select the formatted text to be cleared. You can then click the Clear Formatting button in the Font group on the Home tab. Or, you can open the Quick Styles gallery, and then click Clear Formatting on the menu at the bottom of the gallery. See **Figure 4–15**. When you remove a style, the Normal Quick Style is automatically applied.

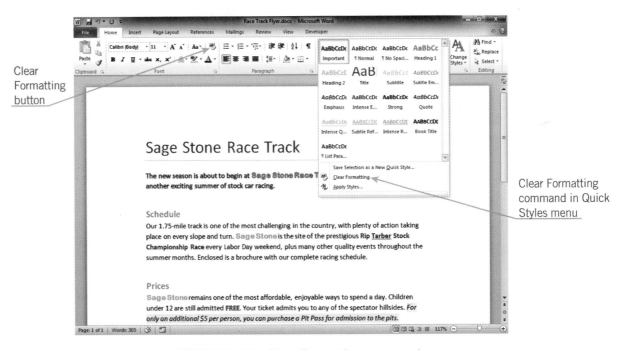

FIGURE 4–15   Clear Formatting command

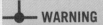

Step-by-Step 4.12

> **WARNING**
>
> To apply or clear a paragraph style, the insertion point can be located anywhere in the paragraph. To apply or clear a character style, all of the text that you want to affect must be selected.

1. If necessary, click anywhere in the last paragraph in the document.

2. In the Font group, click the **Clear Formatting** button 🔲. The Important Quick Style is removed from the current paragraph, and the Normal style button in the Styles gallery is selected.

3. In the second item in the bulleted list, select the word **recycle**.

4. In the Styles group, click the **More** button. At the bottom of the Quick Styles gallery, click **Clear Formatting**. The color and double underline is removed from the selected word.

5. Click after the last word in the document (after *We can't wait to see you!*). Press **Tab** three times, and then type your name.

6. Save, print, and close the document.

SUMMARY

In this lesson, you learned:

- Fonts are designs of type that can be used to change the appearance of a document.

- Font size is measured in points. The higher the point size, the larger the characters.

- Common font styles are bold, italic, and underline. These styles can be applied to any font. You can change the color and style of underlines.

- The look of text can be changed by changing its color and adding text effects.

- Highlighting can be used to emphasize important text.

- The Format Painter copies the format and style of blocks of text.

- Styles are predefined sets of formatting options that save time and add consistency to a document. A Quick Style appears in the Styles gallery on the Home tab.

- A theme is a coordinated set of fonts, styles, and colors. When you change the theme, all text that has a Quick Style applied to it, including the Normal Quick Style, changes to the fonts, colors, and styles in the new theme.

- You can create new Quick Styles by redefining existing Quick Styles or by creating an entirely new Quick Style.

- The Clear Formatting command clears all formatting and styles from selected text.

VOCABULARY REVIEW

Define the following terms:

attribute	font size	Quick Style
color palette	font style	style
font	Format Painter	text effect
font effect	point	theme

REVIEW QUESTIONS

TRUE / FALSE

Circle T if the statement is true or F if the statement is false.

T (F)   1.   Highlighting text has the same effect as using the Italic button.

(T) F   2.   A point is the unit of measurement for fonts.

(T) F   3.   A font attribute is its name.

T   F   4.   When you change the document theme, you change only the colors used for text.

T   (F)   5.   You can create a new Quick Style, but you cannot change the definition of an existing Quick Style.

WRITTEN QUESTIONS

Write a brief answer to each of the following questions.

1. What does the Format Painter do?

2. What are three common font styles?

3. What is the color palette in a document?

4. Why would you use a style?

5. What is a Quick Style?

FILL IN THE BLANK

Complete the following sentences by writing the correct word or words in the blanks provided.

1. The design of type is called the _____.

2. A(n) _____ is a set of formatting options that have been named and saved.

3. A(n) _____ is a coordinated set of fonts, styles, and colors.

4. Text that does not have any other Quick Style applied to it is actually formatted with the _____ Quick Style.

5. The _____ command clears manual formatting and styles.

■ PROJECTS

If you have a SAM 2010 user profile, your instructor may have assigned an autogradable version of the indicated project. If so, log into the SAM 2010 Web site at *www.cengage.com/sam2010* to download the instruction and start files.

PROJECT 4–1

1. Open the **Certificate.docx** Data File. Save the document as **Employee Certificate** followed by your initials.

2. Change all text to 20-point Castellar. If the font is not available, choose another one.

3. Apply the Gradient Fill - Purple, Accent 4, Reflection text effect.

4. Change the color of all the text to the Light Blue standard color.

5. Remove the Reflection text effect, and then add the Blue, 8 pt glow, Accent color 1 glow effect. (*Hint:* Click the Text Effects button, and then point to Glow.)

6. Select the first paragraph and change its size to 36 points.

7. Create a new Quick Style named **Certificate Heading** based on the first paragraph.

8. Change *Joe Harrington* to 36-point Edwardian Script ITC. Replace *Joe Harrington* with your name.

9. Preview the document. Save, print, and close the document.

✓ *SAM* PROJECT 4–2

1. Open the **Handbook.docx** Data File. Save the document as **Employee Handbook** followed by your initials.

2. In a new paragraph after the last paragraph, type the following: **This Data File had the theme applied.** Click immediately before *theme* in the sentence you just typed. Identify the current theme, and then type its name. Press the Spacebar.

3. Select all the text and clear the formatting.

4. Apply the Heading 1 Quick Style to the first line of text, *Employee Handbook*, and then change the font size to 22 points.

5. Add a Wavy underline to the first line of text using the same color as the text.

6. Create a new Quick Style called Handbook Title based on the first line of text.

7. Apply the Heading 2 Quick Style to the other four headings in the document.

8. Apply the Subtle Emphasis Quick Style to the last line in the document (the line you typed).

9. Change the theme to Adjacency. Go to the end of the document, create a new paragraph, and then type **It now has the Adjacency theme applied.** Create another new paragraph, and then type your name.

10. Select the heading *Regular Attendance*. Change the font size to 16 points. Change the color to Gray-50%, Accent 4 (in the first row under Theme Colors in the color palette).

11. Redefine the Heading 2 Quick Style to match the *Regular Attendance* heading.

12. In the paragraph under the *Confidential Information* heading, italicize the word *Never* in the third line.

13. Preview the document. Save, print, and close the document.

✓ PROJECT 4–3

1. Open the **Checking Account.docx** Data File. Save the document as **Checking Account Info** followed by your initials.

2. Apply the Title Quick Style to the title *New Checking Account*.

3. Apply the Heading 2 style to the three headings in the document.

4. Near the bottom of the document, highlight all four lines of the address with Gray-25% from the Text Highlight Color palette.

5. In the last line, format the phone number with bold formatting.

6. Change the theme to Horizon.

7. In the last paragraph of the document, replace *the Customer Service Department* with your name. Highlight your name with yellow.

8. Preview the document. Save, print, and close the document.

√PROJECT 4–4

1. Open the **Poster.docx** Data File. Save the document as **Break Room Poster** followed by your initials.

2. Apply the Title Quick Style to the first line of text.

3. Change the second line of text so it is 16 points, and has an Offset Right shadow effect. (*Hint:* Click the Text Effects button, and then point to Shadow.)

4. Change the theme to Opulent.

5. Change the color of the second line of text to Pink, Text 2 (in the first row under Theme Colors in the color palette).

6. Use the Format Painter to copy the style of the second line of text to the seventh line of text (*How can I build good relationships with my co-workers?*).

7. Apply the List Paragraph Quick Style to the four lines of text under both headings.

8. Change the font size of the four lines of text under both headings to 14 points.

9. Jump to the end of the document, and then type your name. Format your name with italics.

10. Preview the document. Save, print, and close the document.

√PROJECT 4–5

1. Open the **Golf Tournament 2.docx** Data File. Save the document as **Formatted Tournament Notice** followed by your initials.

2. Choose a different theme. Be sure your choice is appropriate for a golf tournament information sheet and that the colors go with the colors in the image at the top of the sheet.

3. In the four lines at the bottom of the sheet, change the format of the word in front of the colon to a different font and color, and then add a style or text effect. (Use the same formatting for each of the four words.) Format all four lines in a larger text size.

4. Underline the title. Use the style and color of your choice, but do not underline with the same color as the title text and do not use the single underline style.

5. Apply a Perspective Shadow effect to the title.

6. In the third line under the title, replace Robert Shade with your name. Format your name with a Quick Style that looks attractive.

7. Preview the document. Save, print, and close the document.

■ CRITICAL THINKING

ACTIVITY 4–1

Create a certificate honoring a person in an organization to which you belong.

ACTIVITY 4–2

You work for a photo lab. In addition to film developing, the lab also offers reprints, enlargements, slides, black-and-white prints, copies and restorations, posters, and passport photos. Your manager wants to include a list of services available with each customer's order, and he asks you to create it. List each service, how much it costs, and how much time it takes to complete. Choose an appropriate theme, and make effective use of Quick Styles, fonts, font sizes and style, colors, and effects. Print and close the document.

ACTIVITY 4–3

Hidden text is text formatted with the text effect "Hidden." You can only access this formatting if you open the Font dialog box by clicking the Font Dialog Box Launcher. Hidden text can be useful if you want to insert text in a document that won't print by default. But what if you forgot that you included hidden text in a file you sent to someone? Use Help to find out how to remove hidden data from a document, and then describe what you learned.

LESSON 5

Formatting Paragraphs and Documents

■ OBJECTIVES

Upon completion of this lesson, you should be able to:

■ Show and hide the ruler.

■ Set the margins of a document.

■ Align text and adjust paragraph indents.

■ Adjust line and paragraph spacing.

■ Change vertical alignment.

■ Set and modify tab stops.

■ Create and modify bulleted, numbered, and outline numbered lists.

■ Organize a document in Outline view.

■ VOCABULARY

alignment

bullet

center

first-line indent

hanging indent

indent

inside margin (gutter margin)

justify

leader

left-align

margin

mirrored margin

multilevel list

negative indent (outdent)

outline numbered list

outside margin

right-align

tab stop (tab)

vertical alignment

Formatting Paragraphs and Documents

Just as you apply formatting to text, you can also use Word features to format paragraphs and entire documents. Formatting presents a consistent and attractive style throughout a document, allowing readers to understand your message more easily.

In this lesson, you will learn how to use the ruler, and set margins. You will also learn how to align paragraphs, adjust paragraph indents and line spacing. Next, you will learn how to change the spacing before and after paragraphs, change the vertical alignment of a paragraph, adjust tab stops, and create lists. Finally, you will learn how to use Outline view.

Viewing the Ruler

Word provides rulers along the top and left margins to help you as you format your documents. The ruler is hidden by default. To display it, you can click the View Ruler button located at the top of the vertical scroll bar on the right side of the window. You can also click the View tab on the Ribbon, and then, in the Show group, click the Ruler check box.

Setting Margins

▶ **VOCABULARY**

margin

Margins are the blank areas around the top, bottom, and sides of a page. Word sets predefined, or default, margin settings, which you can keep or change. To change margin settings, click the Page Layout tab on the Ribbon, and then in the Page Setup group, click the Margins button. You can choose from one of the preset margin settings, as shown in **Figure 5–1**, or you can click Custom Margins at the bottom to open the Margins tab of the Page Setup dialog box, as shown in **Figure 5–2**.

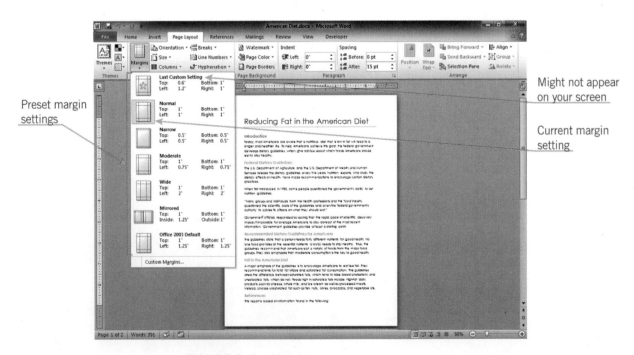

FIGURE 5–1   Margins menu

Margins tab

Margins section

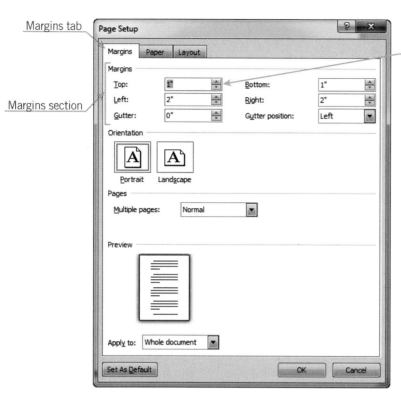

Click arrows to change measurement one-tenth of an inch at a time

▶ **VOCABULARY**
mirrored margin
inside margin (gutter margin)
outside margin

FIGURE 5–2   Margins tab in the Page Setup dialog box

Step-by-Step 5.1

1. Open the **Diet.docx** document from the drive and folder where your Data Files are stored. Save the document as **American Diet** followed by your initials.

2. If the ruler is not displayed below the Ribbon, above the vertical scroll bar, click the **View Ruler** button 🔲 to display the ruler.

3. On the Ribbon, click the **View** tab. In the Zoom group, click the **One Page** button. Note that the current margins are one inch on all sides.

4. On the Ribbon, click the **Page Layout** tab. In the Page Setup group, click the **Margins** button. The current margin, Normal, is selected. See Figure 5–1.

5. Click **Wide**. The left and right margins increase to two inches.

6. In the Page Setup group, click the **Margins** button. Wide is selected on the menu. Click **Custom Margins** at the bottom of the menu. The Page Setup dialog box opens with the Margins tab on top. See Figure 5–2.

7. In the Top box, click the **down arrow** three times to change the number to 0.7".

8. Press **Tab**. The value in the Bottom box is selected. Type **.7**.

📇 **EXTRA FOR EXPERTS**
___

Pages in books and magazines are often formatted with **mirrored margins**. The **inside margins** (also called the **gutter margins**) are the margins closest to the inside of the page, near the binding. The **outside margins** are the margins closest to the edge of the page.

9. Click **OK**. The dialog box closes and the top and bottom margins are changed.

10. In the Page Setup group, click the **Margins** button again. Notice that **Last Custom Setting** is selected at the top of the menu and that the settings match the custom settings you chose. Click a blank area of the document window to close the Margins menu without changing the current setting.

11. On the Ribbon, click the **View** tab, and then in the Zoom group, click **Page Width**.

12. Save the document and leave it open for the next Step-by-Step.

Aligning Text

▶ VOCABULARY

alignment

left-align

center

right-align

justify

Alignment refers to the position of text between the margins. As **Figure 5–3** shows, you can *left-align*, *center*, *right-align*, or *justify* text. Left-aligned and justified are the two most commonly used alignments in documents. For invitations, titles, and headings, text is often center-aligned. Page numbers and dates are often right aligned.

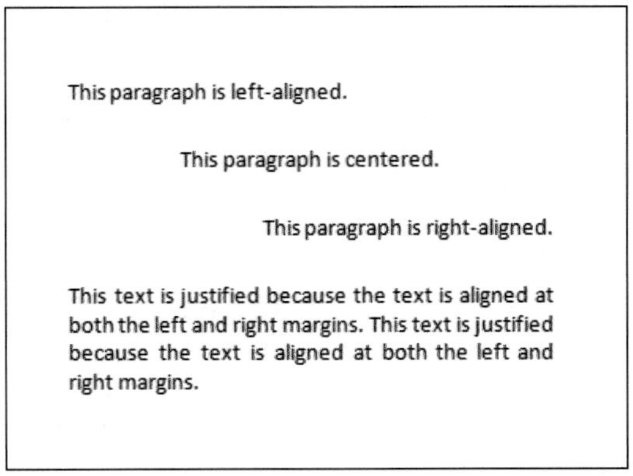

> This paragraph is left-aligned.
>
> This paragraph is centered.
>
> This paragraph is right-aligned.
>
> This text is justified because the text is aligned at both the left and right margins. This text is justified because the text is aligned at both the left and right margins.

FIGURE 5–3   Examples of different text alignments

To align text, you click one of the Alignment buttons in the Paragraph group on the Home tab, as shown in **Figure 5–4**. Alignment settings affect the current paragraph or currently selected paragraph.

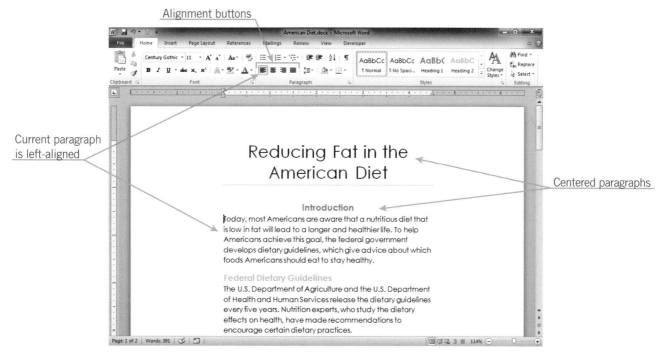

FIGURE 5–4 Alignment buttons

Step-by-Step 5.2

1. If necessary, click anywhere in the title at the beginning of the document.

2. On the Ribbon, click the **Home** tab. In the Paragraph group, notice that the Align Text Left button is selected. Only one alignment button can be selected at a time.

3. In the Paragraph group, click the **Center** button. The title is centered.

4. Click anywhere in the *Introduction* heading. In the Paragraph group, click the **Center** button.

5. Click anywhere in the third paragraph under the *Federal Dietary Guidelines* heading (it starts with *"Many groups and individuals"*). In the Paragraph group, click the **Justify** button. The paragraph is justified.

6. Press **Ctrl+End**. The insertion point moves to the end of the document.

7. Select the last two paragraphs (*Prepared by Roberta Sanchez*). In the Paragraph group, click the **Align Text Right** button. The last two paragraphs are right-aligned.

8. Save the document and leave it open for the next Step-by-Step.

> **TIP**
>
> You can also click the Center button on the Mini toolbar.

Changing Indents

An *indent* is the space between text and a document's margin. You can indent text either from the left margin, from the right margin, or from both margins. You can also indent only the first line of a paragraph or all the lines in a paragraph *except* the first line.

Indenting Entire Paragraphs

To quickly change the indent of an entire paragraph one-half inch at a time, click the Increase Indent or Decrease Indent buttons in the Paragraph group on the Home tab.

To change the indent by different amounts, you can drag the Left and Right Indent markers on the ruler. To change the left indent, drag the Left Indent marker, which is the small rectangle at the bottom of the icon at the left margin. Note, however, that the entire icon will move when you drag it. See **Figure 5–5**. Indenting from both margins sets off paragraphs from the main body of text. You might use this type of indent for long quotations.

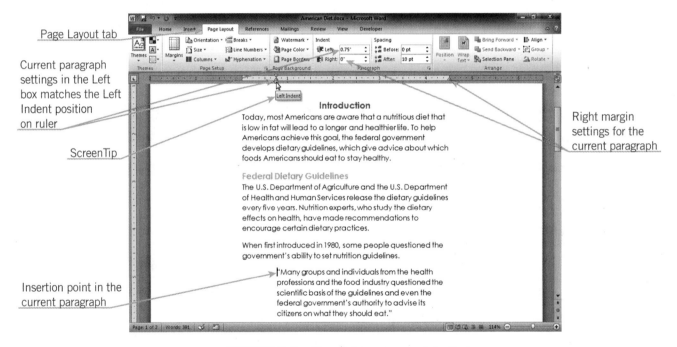

FIGURE 5–5   Examining paragraph indents

You can also change the left and right indents by clicking the Page Layout tab, and then setting the exact measurement of the indents in the Left and Right boxes in the Paragraph group, as shown in Figure 5–5.

Step-by-Step 5.3

1. Scroll up in the document, and then position the insertion point in the third paragraph under the *Federal Dietary Guidelines* section (it starts with *"Many groups and individuals*).

2. In the Paragraph group, click the **Increase Indent** button ⊞ twice. The entire paragraph indents one inch, and the Indent marker on the left end of the ruler moves to the one-inch mark on the ruler.

3. In the Paragraph group, click the **Decrease Indent** button ⊞. The paragraph indent moves back to the one-half-inch mark.

4. On the ruler, position the pointer on top of the **rectangle** ☐ at the bottom of the Left Indent marker so that the Left Indent ScreenTip appears.

5. Drag the **Left Indent marker** ☐ to the three-quarter-inch mark on the ruler, as shown in Figure 5–5. The paragraph indents another quarter of an inch.

6. On the ruler, drag the **Right Indent marker** △ to the left to the 4-inch mark. The paragraph with the quote is indented three-quarters of an inch from the left margin and one-half inch from the right margin.

7. Save the document and leave it open for the next Step-by-Step.

Setting a First-Line Indent

A *first-line indent* is just what it sounds like—only the first line of a paragraph is indented. You are familiar with this because it is the usual format for paragraphs set in type in books, newspapers, and magazines. To indent the first line of a paragraph, you can drag the First Line Indent marker on the ruler, as shown in **Figure 5–6**. After you set a first-line indent in one paragraph, all subsequent paragraphs you type will have the same first-line indent.

▶ **VOCABULARY**
first-line indent

TIP

It's better to set first-line indents than to use Tab because each time you press Enter, the new paragraph will automatically have a first-line indent.

First-line indent set for the selected paragraphs

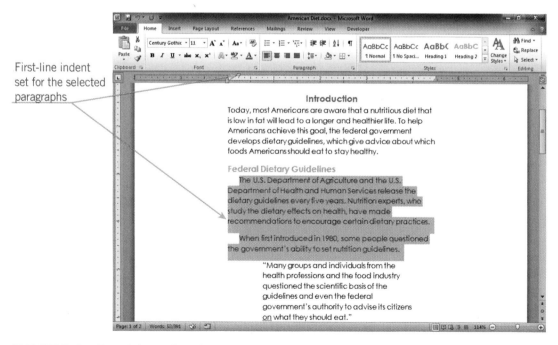

FIGURE 5–6   Examining a first-line indent

Step-by-Step 5.4

1. Select the first two paragraphs under the *Federal Dietary Guidelines* heading.

2. On the ruler, position the pointer over the **top triangle** 🔻 on the Left Indent marker so that the First Line Indent ScreenTip appears.

3. Drag the **First Line Indent marker** 🔻 to the one-quarter-inch mark on the ruler. The first line of the two selected paragraphs is indented one-quarter inch. See Figure 5–6.

4. Select the paragraph above the *Recommended Dietary Guidelines for Americans* heading. Press and hold **Ctrl**. Use the mouse to select the paragraphs under the *Recommended Dietary Guidelines for Americans* and the *Fat in the American Diet* headings. Release **Ctrl**. The three paragraphs are selected.

5. On the ruler, drag the **First Line Indent marker** 🔻 to the one-quarter-inch mark. The first line of the three selected paragraphs is indented one-quarter inch. Click a blank area of the document to deselect the text.

6. Save the document and leave it open for the next Step-by-Step.

Setting a Hanging Indent

You can also create *hanging indents* in which the first full line of text is not indented but the following lines are, as shown in **Figure 5–7**. To set a hanging indent, drag the Hanging Indent marker on the ruler to the right of the First Line Indent marker. Hanging indents appear commonly in lists and documents such as glossaries and bibliographies.

Hanging Indent marker

Paragraphs with a hanging indent applied

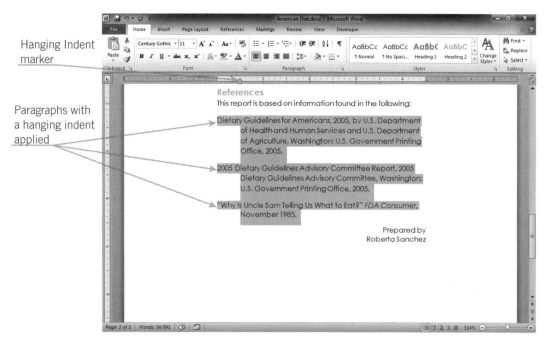

FIGURE 5–7 Examining a hanging indent

Step-by-Step 5.5

1. Select the three paragraphs above the *Prepared by* line.

2. On the ruler, position the pointer over the **bottom triangle** on the Left Indent marker so that the Hanging Indent ScreenTip appears.

3. Drag the **Hanging Indent marker** to the one-half-inch mark. All the lines except for the first line of the three selected paragraphs are indented one-half inch. See Figure 5–7.

4. Save the document and leave it open for the next Step-by-Step.

> **WARNING**
>
> If the wrong triangle moves, release the mouse button, and then try again.

Using the Paragraph Dialog Box to Set Indents

You can set indents on the Indents and Spacing tab in the Paragraph dialog box. You can open the Paragraph dialog box both from the Home tab and from the Page Layout tab by clicking the Paragraph Dialog Box Launcher in the Paragraph group. See **Figure 5–8**.

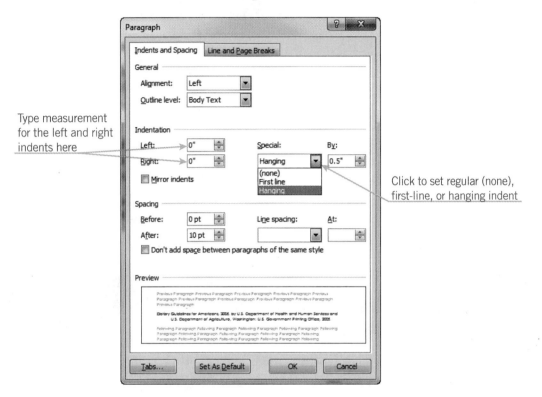

Type measurement for the left and right indents here

Click to set regular (none), first-line, or hanging indent

FIGURE 5–8   Paragraph dialog box

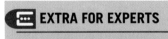
In the Indentation section on the Indents and Spacing tab, type measurements in the Left and Right boxes to change the left and right indents. This is similar to using the Left and Right boxes in the Paragraph group on the Page Layout tab. To set a first-line or hanging indent, click the Special arrow, choose the type of indent you want, and then adjust the measurement in the By box.

Adjusting Line Spacing

You can adjust line spacing in a document, which is the amount of space between lines of text. Single-spaced text has no extra space between each line; double-spaced text has an extra line of space between each line of text. You might be surprised to learn that the default setting in a Word document is 1.15 lines, not single spaced. The little bit of extra space makes text easier to read on the screen. See **Figure 5–9** for examples of different spacing.

The line spacing in this paragraph is 1.0 lines. This means the paragraph is single-spaced.

The line spacing in this paragraph is 1.15 lines This is the default line spacing for the Normal Quick Style.

The line spacing in this paragraph is 1.5 lines. This is another common line spacing.

The line spacing in this paragraph is 2.0 lines. This means the paragraph is double-spaced.

FIGURE 5–9 Different line spacing

To change line spacing, you can click the Line and Paragraph Spacing button in the Paragraph group on the Home tab, and then choose a new line spacing option on the menu.

Step-by-Step 5.6

1. Press **Ctrl+Home**, and then click anywhere in the paragraph under the *Introduction* heading. Notice that the Normal Quick Style button is selected in the Styles group on the Home tab.

2. On the Home tab, in the Paragraph group, click the **Line and Paragraph Spacing** button ⬇️≡▾. A check mark appears next to 1.15, the current line spacing, as shown in **Figure 5–10**. The 1.15 line spacing is part of the Normal Quick Style definition.

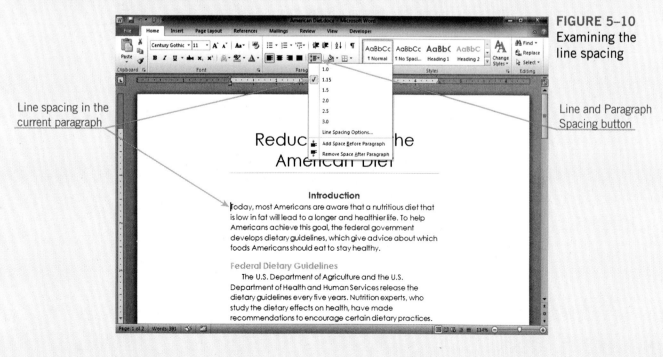

FIGURE 5–10
Examining the line spacing

Line spacing in the current paragraph

Line and Paragraph Spacing button

3. Click a blank area of the document to close the menu without making a selection.

4. Click anywhere in the title. In the Styles group, click the **down arrow** to scroll the gallery down one row. Notice that the Title Quick Style button is selected.

5. In the Paragraph group, click the **Line and Paragraph Spacing** button again. The line spacing for the title is 1.0 (single-spaced). Single spacing is part of the Title Quick Style definition. Click a blank area of the document to close the menu.

6. Press **Ctrl+A**. All the text in the document is selected. In the Paragraph group, click the **Line and Paragraph Spacing** button. Click **1.0**. All the text in the document is now single-spaced.

7. Save the document and leave it open for the next Step-by-Step.

Adjusting Paragraph Spacing

Another way to increase the readability of a page is to modify the paragraph spacing—the amount of space between paragraphs. You've seen this already because the default in Word is to add 10 points of space after each paragraph, and you used the Remove Space After Paragraph command on the Line and Paragraph Spacing menu to remove the space after the paragraphs in the letter you worked on in Lesson 2. Often heading styles include space before or after the heading paragraph as part of the style definition. For example, in this book, the format of the *Step-by-Step* headings include 30 points of space above them, and the format of the blue headings, such as the *Adjusting Paragraph Spacing* heading above, includes 42 points of space before and 10 points of space after. If you want to precisely adjust the space before or after a paragraph, you can use the Before and After boxes in the Paragraph group on the Page Layout tab. See **Figure 5–11**.

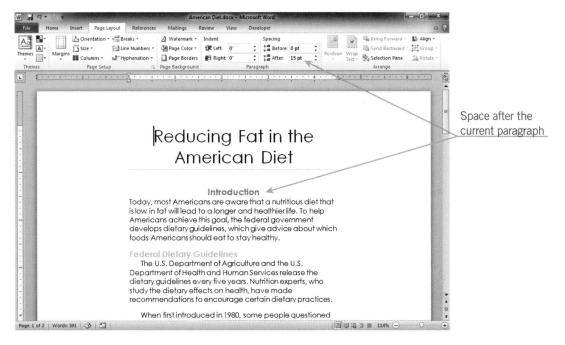

FIGURE 5-11 Examining the paragraph spacing

Step-by-Step 5.7

1. Click anywhere in the paragraph under the *Introduction* heading.

2. On the Ribbon, click the **Page Layout** tab. Locate the Spacing section in the Paragraph group, and notice that 10 pt appears in the After box. This is the default for the Normal Quick Style.

3. Click anywhere in the title, which is formatted with the Title Quick Style. The value in the After box changes to 15 pt.

4. Click anywhere in the *Introduction* heading. This paragraph is formatted with the Heading 1 Quick Style. The value in the Before box changes to 24 pt and the value in the After box changes to 0 pt.

5. Click anywhere in the *Federal Dietary Guidelines* heading. This is formatted with the Heading 2 Quick Style, which has 10 pt before and 0 pt after the paragraph.

6. In the Paragraph group, click the **up arrow** next to the Before box twice to change the value to 18 pt.

7. If necessary, scroll down in the document so that you can see both the *Federal Dietary Guidelines* and the *Recommended Dietary Guidelines for Americans* headings. The *Recommended Dietary Guidelines for Americans* heading is also formatted with the Heading 2 Quick Style, as are the other two headings in the document.

8. On the Ribbon, click the **Home** tab. Make sure the insertion point is still in the *Federal Dietary Guidelines* heading.

9. In the Styles group, right-click the **Heading 2** style button, and then click **Update Heading 2 to Match Selection**. Each paragraph formatted with the Heading 2 style is modified so that there are 18 points of space before it.

10. Click in the third paragraph under the *Federal Dietary Guidelines* heading (the paragraph that is indented from both the right and left margins). On the Ribbon, click the **Page Layout** tab. Change the space before and after the paragraph to **12 points**.

11. Press **Ctrl+End**. Select **Roberta Sanchez**, and then type your name.

12. Save, print, and close the document, but leave Word open for the next Step-by-Step.

Changing Vertical Alignment

Vertical alignment refers to positioning text between the top and bottom margins of a document. You can align text with the top of the page, center the text, distribute the text equally between the top and bottom margins (justify), or align the text with the bottom of the page. To vertically align text, select the text, click the Page Setup Dialog Box Launcher on the Page Layout tab, and then click the Layout tab in the Page Setup dialog box, which is shown in **Figure 5–12**. In the Page section, click the arrow next to the Vertical alignment box and choose Top, Center, Justified, or Bottom.

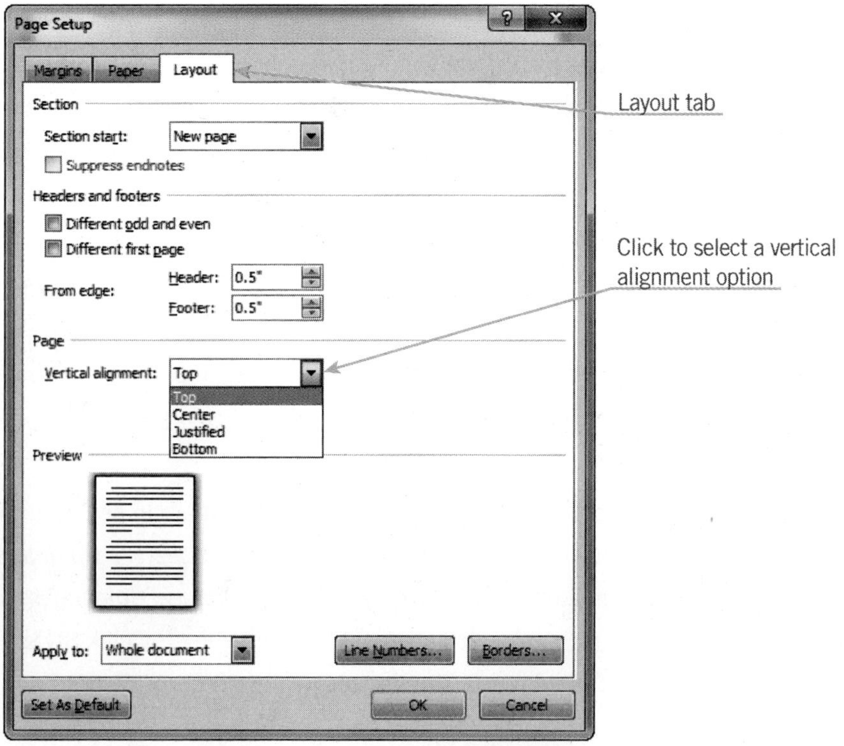

FIGURE 5–12   Layout tab in the Page Setup dialog box

Step-by-Step 5.8

1. Create a new Word document. Save the document as **American Diet Title Page** followed by your initials.

2. Type your name, and then press **Enter**. Type the following:

   Health and Nutrition 101
   Reducing Fat in the American Diet

3. On the Ribbon, click the **View** tab. In the Zoom group, click the **One Page** button.

4. Select all the text. On the Ribbon, click the **Home** tab. In the Font group, click the **arrow** next to the Font Size button 11 , and then click **20**.

5. In the Paragraph group, click the **Center** button . Deselect the text.

6. On the Ribbon, click the **Page Layout** tab. In the Themes group, click the **Themes** button, and then click **Austin**. This is the same theme that is used in the American Diet document.

7. In the Page Setup group, click the **Page Setup Dialog Box Launcher**. The Page Setup dialog box opens with the Margins tab on top.

8. At the top of the dialog box, click the **Layout** tab. The dialog box changes to show the commands on the Layout tab.

9. In the Page section, click the **arrow** next to the Vertical alignment box. See Figure 5–12.

10. Click **Center**. Click **OK**. The dialog box closes and the text is centered vertically on the page.

11. Save, print, and close the document, but leave Word open for the next Step-by-Step.

Understanding Tab Stops

Tab stops, or *tabs*, mark the place where the insertion point will stop when you press Tab. Tab stops are useful for creating tables or aligning numbered items. In Word, default tab stops are set every half inch and are left-aligned. Text alignment can be

▶ **VOCABULARY**
tab stop (tab)

set with left, right, center, or decimal tab stops. **Figure 5–13** shows examples of some of these tab stops. (You'll learn about the dotted leader in the next section.) **Table 5–1** describes each of the tab stops.

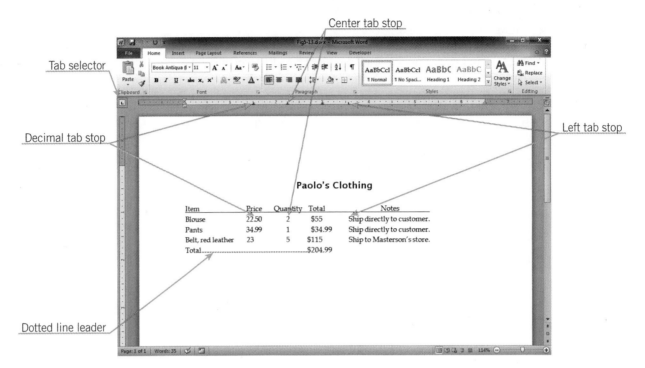

FIGURE 5–13   Types of tabs

TABLE 5–1   Tab stops

TAB	TAB NAME	FUNCTION
⌞	Left Tab	Left-aligns selected text at the point indicated on the horizontal ruler. This is the default tab.
⌟	Right Tab	Right-aligns selected text at the point indicated on the horizontal ruler. This is useful for aligning page numbers in a table of contents.
⊥	Center Tab	Centers selected text at the point indicated on the horizontal ruler. This is used with titles and announcements.
⊥•	Decimal Tab	Aligns selected text on the decimal point at the point indicated on the horizontal ruler. This is helpful when preparing price lists, invoices, and menus.

Setting, Modifying, and Clearing Tab Stops

To set a tab stop, select the paragraph, and then click the ruler at the location you want to set the tab. A tab stop marker appears on the ruler at the location you clicked. If you want to insert a tab stop other than a left tab stop, click the tab selector at the far left of the ruler. Each time you click, the tab selector changes to another type of tab—left, right, center, or decimal. When you insert a tab stop, all of the default tab stops before that tab stop marker are erased. To move a tab stop, drag the tab stop marker to a new location on the ruler. To remove a tab, drag the marker off the ruler.

> **TIP**
>
> The tab selector has additional options—Bar, First Line Indent, and Hanging Indent. Keep clicking the tab selector to return to the Left Tab icon.

> **EXTRA FOR EXPERTS**
>
> The Bar Tab is not a tab stop. It inserts a vertical line in the paragraph.

Step-by-Step 5.9

1. Open the **NADA Memo.docx** document from the drive and folder where your Data Files are stored. Save the document as **NADA Office Supplies Memo** followed by your initials.

2. If paragraph marks are not displayed, in the Paragraph group on the Home tab, click the **Show/Hide ¶** button ¶. If the ruler is not displayed, on the Ribbon, click the **View** tab. In the Show group, click the **Ruler** check box to select it. Notice that there are tab marks in each line in the memo header. The tab marks position the text after the tab mark at the next default tab stop. For all the lines except the *From* line, this is one-half inch. Because the text *From:* extends to the one-half-inch mark, the text after the tab mark is moved to the next default tab stop, one inch.

3. In the memo header, select all four paragraphs (from *To* through *Date*).

4. Locate the **tab selector** to the left of the ruler below the Ribbon. If it is not displaying the Left Tab icon └, click it as many times as necessary to display the Left Tab icon.

5. On the ruler, click the **three-quarter-inch mark**. A Left Tab marker is inserted on the ruler. In the selected paragraphs, the text after the tab mark moves over to left-align at the tab marker you inserted.

6. Scroll down until you can see all the items in the list below the paragraph in the body of the memo (from *Inkjet printer* through *Total*). Select all of the items in the list. The items in the first column are left-aligned at the one-half-inch mark, the first default tab stop. The items in the second column appear at the next available default tab stop in that line.

7. To the left of the ruler, click the **tab selector** twice. It changes to the Right Tab icon ┘.

> **TIP**
>
> Position the pointer over the tab selector or the tab stop marker on the ruler to see a ScreenTip labeling the type of tab.

8. On the ruler, click the **3½-inch mark**. The first column in the list right-aligns at 3½ inches. You wanted the prices to right-align.

9. Click the **tab selector** five times to return to the Left Tab icon [L]. On the ruler, click the **one-half-inch mark**. The first column in the list again left-aligns at one-half inch on the ruler, and the second column in the list right-aligns at the 3½-inch mark on the ruler. The price of the second item, *Surge protector*, doesn't have a decimal point, so the dollar amount doesn't align with the other dollar amounts.

10. On the ruler at the 3½-inch mark, drag the **Right Tab stop marker** [⌐] off the ruler. The tab stop marker disappears and the prices shift left to align at the next default tab stop marker.

11. Click the **tab selector** three times. It changes to the Decimal Tab icon [⊥].

12. On the ruler, click the **3½-inch mark**. The dollar amounts align on the decimal point, as shown in **Figure 5–14**. (The dollar amount for the second item in the list doesn't have a decimal point, but it is understood that it is the same as *29.00*.)

FIGURE 5–14
Left and decimal tab stops set for the selected list

Left tab stop

Decimal tab stop

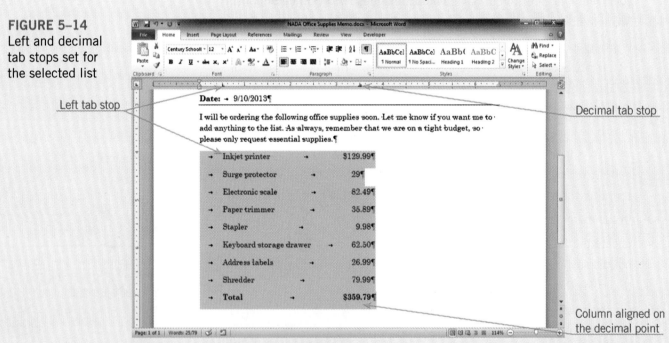

Column aligned on the decimal point

13. Save the document and leave it open for the next Step-by-Step.

Setting Leaders

▶ **VOCABULARY**
leader

Leaders are solid, dotted, or dashed lines that fill the blank space before a tab setting. Leaders are often used in tables of contents. To insert a leader, open the Tabs dialog box, as shown in **Figure 5–15**. To do this, double-click a tab stop marker on the ruler, or on the Home or Page Layout tabs, click the Paragraph Dialog Box Launcher, and then click Tabs in the Paragraph dialog box. In the Tab Stop Position list, click the tab stop to which you want to apply the leader. Then, in the Leader section, click the option button next to the leader you want to use. If you want to set leaders for more than one tab stop, click Set, and then select the next tab stop and the leader you want to set. If you are finished, you can simply click OK.

TIP

In the Tabs dialog box, click a tab to select it, and then click Clear to remove that tab stop. Click Clear All to remove all the tabs in the current paragraph.

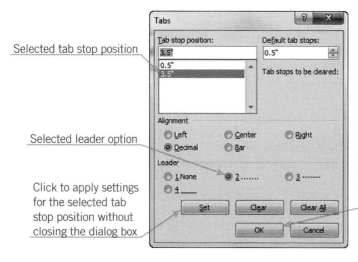

Selected tab stop position

Selected leader option

Click to apply settings for the selected tab stop position without closing the dialog box

Click to apply the settings for the selected tab stop position and close the dialog box

FIGURE 5–15   Tabs dialog box

Step-by-Step 5.10

1. Make sure the list under the first paragraph in the body of the memo is still selected.

2. On the ruler, double-click the **tab stop marker** at the 3½-inch-mark. The Tabs dialog box opens. You want to set a leader in front of the tab at the 3½-inch mark. (If the Page Setup dialog box opened instead, click Cancel and try again. If you inserted a new tab stop marker on the ruler, drag it off the ruler, and then try again.)

3. In the Tab stop position list, click **3.5"**. The value is selected.

4. In the Leader section, click the **2 ....** option button. You are setting the leader for only one tab stop, so you do not need to click Set. See Figure 5–15.

5. Click **OK**. The dialog box closes and dotted leaders are inserted in front of the items aligned at the 3½-inch mark.

6. In the *To* line in the memo header, position the insertion point after the tab mark. Type your name.

7. Save, print, and close the document, but leave Word open for the next Step-by-Step.

Using Bulleted and Numbered Lists

Sometimes you may want to create a bulleted or numbered list in a document. A numbered list is useful when items appear sequentially, such as instructions. A bulleted list often is used when the order of items does not matter. A *bullet* is any small character that appears before an item. Small, solid circles are often used as bullets, but other symbols and icons, as well as pictures, may serve as bullets.

Creating Bulleted and Numbered Lists

You have already used the AutoFormat As You Type feature to create a numbered list. Another way to create a numbered list as you type is to create a new paragraph, and then, in the Paragraph group on the Home tab, click the Numbering button. Likewise, to create a bulleted list as you type, click the Bullets button in the Paragraph group.

When you are finished adding items to the list, press Enter twice. Pressing it the first time inserts a new bulleted or numbered item. When you press Enter a second time without typing anything, the AutoFormat As You Type feature assumes you are finished with the list and changes the new paragraph to a Normal paragraph. You can also click the Bullets or Numbering button in the Paragraph group to turn the feature off, or if the next paragraph is formatted with the Normal style, you can click the Normal style button in the Quick Styles gallery.

You can also change a list that you already typed to a bulleted or numbered list by selecting all the items in the list, and then clicking either the Bullets or Numbering button in the Paragraph group.

TIP

You can also click the Bullets button on the Mini toolbar.

Step-by-Step 5.11

1. Open the **Diet Guidelines.docx** document from the drive and folder where your Data Files are stored. Save the document as **American Diet Guidelines** followed by your initials.

2. Select the two paragraphs in the first indented list.

3. On the Home tab, in the Paragraph group, click the **Numbering** button ⊞. Numbers are inserted in front of each item, and the extra space after each paragraph is removed.

4. In the list, click at the end of the first line (after *healthy weight*). Press **Enter**. A new numbered item 2 is created. Type **Be physically active each day**. See **Figure 5–16**.

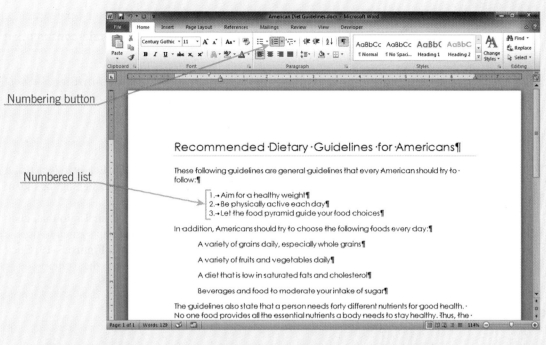

FIGURE 5–16
Numbered list

Numbering button

Numbered list

5. Select all the items in the second indented list. On the Home tab, in the Paragraph group, click the **Bullets** button ⊞. The paragraphs are changed to a bulleted list.

6. Click after the last item in the list (after *sugar*). Press **Enter**. A new bulleted item is created. Type **Food with less salt**. See **Figure 5–17**.

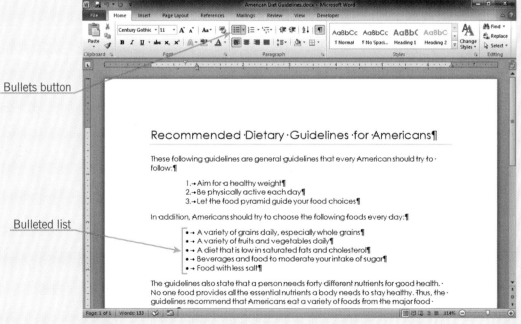

FIGURE 5–17
Bulleted list

Bullets button

Bulleted list

7. Press **Enter**. A new bulleted item is created.

8. Press **Enter** again. The bullet is removed and a new blank paragraph is created. Type **These guidelines emphasize that moderate consumption is the key to good health.**

9. Save the document and leave it open for the next Step-by-Step.

Customizing Bulleted and Numbered Lists

You can customize bulleted and numbered lists. Lists are automatically indented and formatted with a hanging indent. You can change the indents by dragging the indent markers on the ruler.

You can also customize the bullets and the numbers in a list. To do this, click the arrow next to the Bullets or Numbering button in the Paragraph group to open a gallery of bullet or number styles, as shown in **Figure 5–18** and **Figure 5–19**. Click a different style in the gallery to change the bullets or numbers to that style.

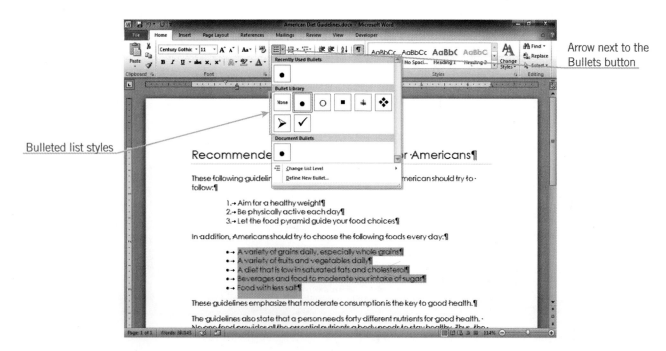

FIGURE 5–18   Bullets gallery

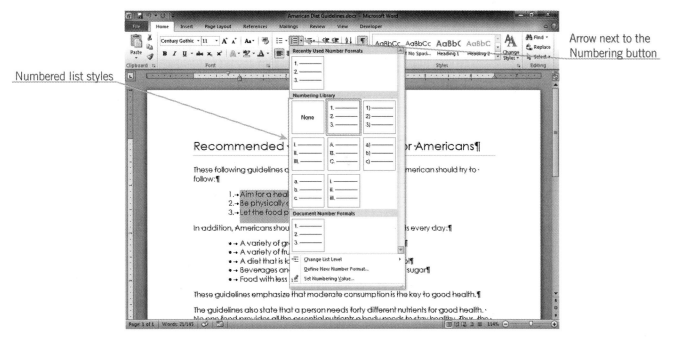

Numbered list styles

Arrow next to the Numbering button

FIGURE 5–19   Numbering gallery

Step-by-Step 5.12

1. Select the three numbered list items. (The numbers themselves will not be selected.)

2. On the Home tab, in the Paragraph group, click the **arrow** next to the Numbering button.

3. Click the uppercase Roman numerals style. The numbers in the list change to Roman numerals.

4. On the ruler, drag the **Left Indent marker** to the 1¼-inch mark. Notice that the other indent markers followed the Left Indent marker to keep the indents set the same distance apart. The indents change so that the numbers are aligned at the one-inch mark and the text after the numbers aligns at the 1¼-inch mark.

5. Select the bulleted list. (The bullets will not be selected.)

6. On the Home tab, in the Paragraph group, click the **arrow** next to the Bullets button.

7. Click the arrow pointing to the right and shaded half black and half white. The bullets in the list change to right-pointing arrows.

8. On the ruler, drag the **Left Indent marker** to the 1¼-inch mark.

9. Press **Ctrl+End**, press **Enter**, and then type your name.

10. Save, print, and close the document, but leave Word open for the next Step-by-Step.

Creating a Multilevel List

A *multilevel list* is a list with two or more levels of bullets or numbering. A numbered multilevel list is sometimes called an *outline numbered list*. An easy way to create a multilevel list is to use the Multilevel List button in the Paragraph group on the Home tab. When you click it, a gallery of multilevel list styles opens, as shown in **Figure 5–20**. Click the style you want to use, and then start typing the list.

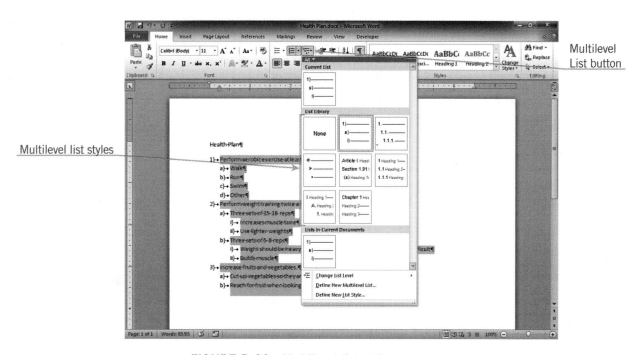

FIGURE 5–20   Multilevel list styles

To create the next item in the list, press Enter. You can change the newly inserted item to a lower-level in one of three ways: (1) press Tab; (2) click the Increase Indent button in the Paragraph group; or (3) click the Multilevel List button, point to Change List Level, and then select the level you want in the submenu that opens. Likewise, you can move an item up a level from an indented level in one of three ways: (1) press Shift+Tab, (2) click the Decrease Indent button, or (3) use the Change List Level submenu.

You can also create multilevel lists in an ordinary bulleted or numbered list using the same methods to change levels, but it's easier to choose the exact format you want when you use the Multilevel List button.

Step-by-Step 5.13

1. Create a new Word document. Save it as **Health Plan** followed by your initials.

2. Type **Health Plan**, and then press **Enter**.

3. On the Home tab, in the Paragraph group, click the **Multilevel List** button ⊞. In the gallery, click the list style that uses Arabic numbers (*1.*) as the first level, lowercase letters (*a.*) as the second level, and lowercase Roman numerals (*i.*) as the third level. The numbers and letters should be followed by a close parenthesis.

4. Type **Perform aerobic exercise at least three times a week.**, and then press **Enter**. A second item at the first level is created.

5. On the Home tab, in the Paragraph group, click the **Increase Indent** button ⊞. The paragraph is changed to a second-level item.

6. Type the following, pressing **Enter** after you type each item:

   Walk

   Run

   Swim

   Other

7. If you didn't press **Enter** after entering the last item, press it now. In the Paragraph group, click the **Decrease Indent** button ⊞. The current paragraph is changed to a first-level item.

8. Type **Perform weight training twice a week.**, and then press **Enter**. Press **Tab**. The new item is changed to a second-level item.

9. Type **Three sets of 15–18 reps**, and then press **Enter**. Press **Tab**. The item is changed to a third-level item.

10. Type **Increases muscle tone**, and then press **Enter**. Type **Use lighter weights**, and then press **Enter**.

11. Press **Shift+Tab**. The blank item is changed to a second-level item.

12. Type the rest of the items in the list, as shown below:

    b.   **Three sets of 5–8 reps**

         i.   **Weight should be heavy enough that the last rep in each set is very difficult**

         ii. **Builds muscle**

    3.   **Increase fruits and vegetables.**

    a.   **Cut up vegetables so they are easy to grab when looking for a snack**

    b.   **Reach for fruit when looking for something sweet**

13. At the top of the vertical scroll bar, click the **View Ruler** button ⊞ to hide the ruler.

14. At the top of the document, position the insertion point at the end of the first line (*Health Plan*), press **Enter**, and then type your name.

15. Save, print, and close the document, but leave Word open for the next Step-by-Step.

Organizing a Document in Outline View

In Outline view, you can type topic headings and subheadings for a document. You could use a multilevel list to do this, but when you use Outline view, you can switch to Normal view and the headings are all set up for you. To switch to Outline view, click the View tab on the Ribbon, and then in the Document Views group, click the Outline button. You can also click the Outline button to the left of the Zoom slider at the bottom-right of the document window.

When you switch to Outline view, a new tab, the Outlining tab, appears as the active tab on the Ribbon to the left of the Home tab. A round symbol with the minus sign in it appears in the document, as shown in **Figure 5–21**. When you type a heading, the text appears to the right of the circle. The minus sign indicates that there are no subheadings or body text below the heading. A plus sign in the circle before a heading indicates that there are subheadings or body text below the heading.

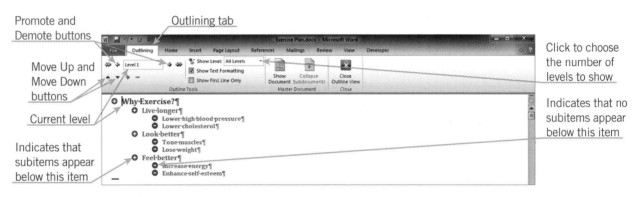

FIGURE 5–21   Text in Outline view

Creating an Outline

When you switch to Outline view in a blank document, the first line of the document is ready for you to type the first heading. Word formats this heading with the Heading 1 style. When you press Enter, a new Level 1 heading, formatted with the Heading 1 style, is created. As with bulleted and numbered lists, if you press the Tab key, you create a Level 2 heading. In Outline view, you can also click the Demote button in the Outline Tools group to demote the text to Level 2. Likewise, if you want to change a heading from a lower level to a higher level, you can press the Shift+Tab keys or click the Promote button.

Step-by-Step 5.14

1. Create a new Word document. Save the document as **Exercise Plan** followed by your initials.

2. On the Ribbon, click the **View** tab. In the Document Views group, click the **Outline** button. The Outlining tab appears on the Ribbon to the left of the Home tab and is the active tab. The insertion point is blinking next to a circle containing a minus sign. In the Outline Tools group on the Outlining tab, the level is identified as Level 1 in the Outline Level box.

3. Type **Why Exercise?**. Press **Enter**. A new Level 1 paragraph is created.

4. In the Outline Tools group, click the **Demote** button ⬜ to indent the paragraph to Level 2. The Outline Level box indicates that the item is a Level 2 item.

5. Type **Live longer**. Press **Enter**, and then press **Tab**. The next item indents more to become a Level 3 item.

6. Type **Lower high blood pressure**, and then press **Enter**. Type **Lower cholesterol**, and then press **Enter**.

7. In the Outline Tools group, click the **Promote** button ⬜. The blank paragraph moves up to become a Level 2 item.

8. Type the following:

   Feel better

      Enhance self-esteem

9. If you didn't press **Enter** after typing the last item, press it now. Press **Shift+Tab**. The blank item moves up a level to Level 2.

10. Type the following:

   Look better

      Lose weight

      Tone muscles

      Increase energy

11. Save the document and leave it open for the next Step-by-Step.

Modifying an Outline

Once you have typed an outline, you can easily modify it. You can drag a heading to a different position in the outline by dragging the circle with the plus or minus sign in it. You can also click the Move Up and Move Down buttons in the Outline Tools group. When you move a heading, all the subordinate text underneath it moves too. To make it easier to reorganize the outline, you can click the Expand or Collapse buttons in the Outline Tools group or you can click the arrow next to the Show Level box in the Outline Tools group to view only the headings you want.

Closing Outline View

If you want to add text to your document below the headings you create in Outline view, it's easier to work in Print Layout view. To close Outline view, you click the Close Outline View button in the Close group on the Outlining tab.

Step-by-Step 5.15

1. On the Outlining tab, in the Outline Tools group, click the **arrow** next to the Show Level box. Click **Level 2**. The outline changes to display only the Level 1 and Level 2 items.

2. Double-click the **plus sign** ⊕ next to *Feel better*. The item expands to display the subitems below it.

3. In the Outline Tools group, click the **arrow** next to the Show Level box. Click **All Levels**. All the levels are shown in the document again.

4. In the subitems under *Look better*, position the pointer on top of the **minus sign** ⊖ next to *Increase energy*. Press and hold the left mouse button and start dragging the minus sign up the list. As you drag, the pointer changes to a double-headed arrow ⇕ and a horizontal line appears. Drag until the line is above *Enhance self-esteem* and below *Feel better*. Release the mouse button. The *Increase energy* item is repositioned as the first subheading under *Feel better*.

5. Click the **minus sign** ⊖ next to *Lose weight*. The item is selected.

6. In the Outline Tools group, click the **Move Down** button ▼. The item moves down one line so it is the second Level 3 item in the *Look better* section.

7. Click the **plus sign** ⊕ next to the *Look better* heading. The item and its subitems are selected.

8. In the Outline Tools group, click the **Move Up** button ▲ three times. The item and its subitems move up above the *Feel better* item.

9. Insert a new Level 1 heading at the end of the document, and then type your name.

10. In the Close group, click the **Close Outline View** button. Outline view closes and you are returned to Print Layout view. You can see that the headings are formatted with the Headings Quick Styles. (You might need to scroll up.)

11. Switch back to Outline view. Hide the formatting marks.

12. Save, print, and close the document.

TIP

You can also click the Expand button in the Outline Tools group to expand an item.

TIP

The outline symbols on the screen in Outline view show you the document's structure. They will not appear when you print.

EXTRA FOR EXPERTS

To print only the headings (outline) of a document, switch to Outline view, display the level of headings you want to print, and then print the document.

SUMMARY

In this lesson, you learned:

- You can show and hide the ruler to suit your working style by clicking the View Ruler button at the top of the vertical scroll bar, or by clicking the View tab, and then selecting the Ruler check box in the Show/Hide group.

- Margins are the blank areas around the top, bottom, and sides of a page. You can change the margin settings by clicking the Margins button in the Page Setup group on the Page Layout tab.

- You can align text by clicking one of the alignment buttons in the Paragraph group on the Home tab.

- You can indent text either from the left margin, from the right margin, or from both margins. You can also set first-line and hanging indents.

- You can change the line spacing of text from the default of 1.15 lines to 1.0 (single-spaced), 2.0 (double-spaced), or greater. You can change the paragraph spacing by changing the measurements in the Before and After boxes in the Paragraph group on the Page Layout tab.

- You can change the vertical alignment of text by opening the Page Setup dialog box, clicking the Layout tab, and selecting an alignment option from the Vertical alignment list in the Page section.

- Text alignment can be set with left, right, centered, or decimal tabs. Leaders can be used with any kind of tab.

- You can use the Bullets or Numbering buttons in the Paragraph group on the Home tab to create bulleted or numbered lists. To change the appearance of a list, click the arrow next to the Bullets or Numbering button to choose a different bullet or numbering style.

- You can use the Multilevel list button in the Paragraph group on the Home tab to create a list with a hierarchical structure.

- You can work in Outline view to set up the outline of a document.

VOCABULARY REVIEW

Define the following terms:

alignment	justify	negative indent (outdent)
bullet	leader	outline numbered list
center	left-align	outside margin
first-line indent	margin	right-align
hanging indent	mirrored margin	tab stop (tab)
indent	multilevel list	vertical alignment
inside margin (gutter margin)		

REVIEW QUESTIONS

TRUE / FALSE

Circle T if the statement is true or F if the statement is false.

T F   1.   Documents are normally left-aligned or justified.

T F   2.   Line spacing is the amount of space between paragraphs.

T F   3.   Double-spaced text has a full blank line between each line of text.

T F   4.   You can change the bullet used for bulleted lists.

T F   5.   The only way to change an indent is to use the Indent markers on the ruler.

MULTIPLE CHOICE

Select the best response for the following statements.

1. Which of the following margins can you customize in a document?

   A. Top and bottom
   B. Right and left
   C. Top, bottom, right, and left
   D. You cannot customize margins in a document.

2. When you change the vertical alignment of text, you change the position of text between:

   A. two sentences
   B. all margins
   C. the left and right margins
   D. the top and bottom margins

3. The small rectangle marker below the two triangle markers at the left edge of the ruler indicates the:

   A. left indent marker
   B. first-line indent marker
   C. hanging indent marker
   D. decrease indent marker

4. Text can be aligned using all of the following types of tab stops except:

   A. decimal
   B. right
   C. center
   D. justified

5. In Outline view, which button do you click to move an item up to a higher level?

   A. Plus
   B. Promote
   C. Demote
   D. Expand

FILL IN THE BLANK

Complete the following sentences by writing the correct word or words in the blanks provided.

1. The blank areas around the top, bottom, and sides of a page are the _____.

2. A(n) _____ indents the lines that follow the first full line of text.

3. The position of text between the margins is called the _____.

4. _____ mark where the insertion point will stop when you press Tab.

5. In _____ view, you can type topic headings and subheadings for a document.

■ PROJECTS

If you have a SAM 2010 user profile, your instructor may have assigned an autogradable version of the indicated project. If so, log into the SAM 2010 Web site at *www.cengage.com/sam2010* to download the instruction and start files.

PROJECT 5–1

1. Open the **Poster 2.docx** document from the drive and folder where your Data Files are stored. Save the document as **Break Room Poster 2** followed by your initials.

2. Center the title.

3. Change the line spacing of the four items after each heading to 1.5 lines.

4. Change the four items under each heading into a bulleted list. Use any bullet symbol except the solid, round bullet symbol.

5. Press Ctrl+End, and then create a new paragraph that is not part of the second bulleted list. Type your name, press Tab, and then insert the current date. Display the ruler, if necessary, and then use a tab stop to right-align the date at the 6½-inch mark. (*Hint*: You'll have to click to position the tab stop near the 6½-inch mark on the ruler, and then drag the tab stop on top of the Right Indent marker.)

6. Vertically center the text on the page.

7. Hide the ruler, and then save, print, and close the document.

dotted. dashed. indentation..... leader
→hanging   Paragraph

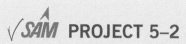 **PROJECT 5-2**

1. Open the **Shipping.docx** document from the drive and folder where your Data Files are stored. Save the document as **Overnight Shipping** followed by your initials.

2. Center the heading *Overnight Shipping*.

3. Change the spacing of the paragraph under the heading so that there are 6 points of space before it and 18 points of space after it.

4. Indent the first line of the paragraph under the *Overnight Shipping* heading one-quarter inch.

5. Single space the paragraph under the heading.

6. Jump to the end of the document, and then press Enter. Change the spacing before and after this paragraph to zero, and then change the first-line indent to zero (that is, remove the first line indent).

7. In the new paragraph, set left tabs at **1.75** inches, **3** inches, and **4.75** inches.

8. Type the headings **Company**, **Cost**, **Weight Limit**, and **Delivery Time**, using tabs to separate the four columns. Underline the headings without underlining the spaces between the headings.

9. Press Enter. In the new paragraph, remove all of the tabs from the ruler and turn off underlining.

10. Set a decimal tab at **2** inches.

11. Set a center tab at **3.5** inches.

12. Set a right tab at **5.63** inches (the tick mark on the ruler between the 5½- and 5¾-inch marks).

13. Open the Tabs dialog box. In turn, select each of the measurements in the Tab stop position list, click the 2 .... option button, and then click Set. Click OK to close the dialog box after all three of the tab stops have been formatted with the dotted line leader.

14. Using the tabs you just set, type the following information:

Zippy	$20.50	2 lbs.	10:00 a.m.
Lightning	$15.75	1 lb., 4 oz.	1:00 p.m.
Speed Air	$11.95	none	3:00 p.m.
Pronto	$10.99	10 oz.	12:30 p.m.

15. Create a new paragraph at the end of the document with 42 points of space before it. Type your name.

16. Save, print, and close the document.

- customs margins
- gutter margin on Page Layout
- Mirrored margins to abc
different. odd pages

√ PROJECT 5–3

1. Create a new Word document. Save it as **Resume for Jeffrey** followed by your initials.

2. Set all margins at 1.2 inches.

3. Type the resume shown in **Figure 5–22**. Use alignment commands, indenting, and tabs to format the text. The theme is the Office theme with the default font and font size. The name at the top is 14 points. All the text is single spaced. The text is centered vertically on the page. The final resume should not contain any blank paragraphs (in other words, adjust the paragraph spacing as needed).

4. Preview the document.

5. Insert a new paragraph at the end of the document, type **Prepared by** followed by your name. Right-align this paragraph.

6. Save, print, and close the document.

√ PROJECT 5–5

1. Open the **Interview 2.docx** document from the drive and folder where your Data Files are stored . Save the document as **Interview Preparation Tips** followed by your initials.

2. Change all the text except the title to double-spaced. Change the space after all the paragraphs except the title to 24 points.

3. Center the title. Justify the rest of the text.

4. Indent the first line of all the paragraphs except the title ¼ inch.

5. At the end of the second paragraph, position the insertion point after the colon after the words *such as*. Insert a new paragraph and then type the following as a bulleted list. Use a bullet character of your choice.

   Names and addresses of former employers

   Names and addresses of references

   Social Security card

   A copy of your resume

   School records

6. Create a new paragraph at the end of the document, right-align it, and then type your name.

7. Save, print, and close the document.

√ PROJECT 5–4

1. Open the **Invitation.docx** document from the drive and folder where your Data Files are stored. Save the document as **Wedding Invitation** followed by your initials.

2. Change the font of all the text to 24-point, bold Vivaldi. (If this font is not available, choose another font.) Change the color to Black, Text 1, Lighter 25%.

3. Center all the text vertically and horizontally on the page.

4. Create a new paragraph at the end of the document. Change the font to 11-point Calibri, not bold. Format the paragraph so that there are 36 points of space before it and 10 points after it. Type your name.

5. Save, print, and close the document.

JEFFREY WEBSTER
5524 Grand View Road
Clearwater, FL 33759-9047
727-555-9613

GOAL   An entry-level administrative assistant position with an opportunity for advancement.

WORK EXPERIENCE

<u>Assistant to the Sales Manager</u>, Four Winds Sales, Clearwater, Florida
September 2011 to present
Duties: Use computer to enter data, greet visitors, and answer telephone.

<u>Recreation Assistant</u>, Clearwater Summer Sports Camp
Summer, 2011
Duties: Taught soccer to third and fourth graders.

<u>Cashier (Part-time)</u>, Classics Videos, Clearwater, Florida
October 2010 to May 2011
Duties: Assisted customers and operated cash register.

EDUCATION

Prescott Junior College, Clearwater, Florida
September 2011 to present
Business Subjects: Accounting, Office Administration, Word, Excel, PowerPoint, and
Access

West High School, Clearwater, Florida
Graduated May 31, 2008
Grade Point Average: 3.5

EXTRACURRICULAR ACTIVITIES

Secretary, Future Business Leaders of America
National Honor Society
Varsity Soccer team
Quill and Scroll, Journalism Honor Society

Habitat for Humanity
Friends of the Library

REFERENCES

Furnished upon request.

FIGURE 5–22

PROJECT 5–6

1. Create a new Word document. Save it as **Agenda** followed by your initials.

2. Set the top margin to two inches and the bottom, left, and right margins to one inch.

3. Type the agenda shown in **Figure 5–23**. Format all the paragraphs in the list so there is no space before or after them. Format the third paragraph in the heading (it starts with *7:00 p.m.*) so there are 48 points of space after it. All the lines are single spaced, and the font color of all the text is black.

4. Insert a new paragraph at the end of the document. Deselect the Multilevel List button. Format the new paragraph with 36 points of space above it, and then type your name.

5. Save, print, and close the document.

PROJECT 5–7

1. Create a new Word document. Save it as **Government** followed by your initials.

2. In Outline view, type the list shown below.

3. Change the Senators item so that it is a Level 2 item with subitems, and then move it so that it is the first item under *Legislative Branch*.

4. Press Ctrl+Home. Type **U.S. Federal Government** as a new Level 1 heading. Insert your name as a new Level 2 heading.

5. Save, print, and close the document.

Executive Branch
   President
      Elected by Electoral College
      Term - Four years
Judicial Branch
   Supreme Court Justices
      Appointed by President
      Term - Life
Senators
   Elected by Direct Vote - Statewide
   Term - Six Years
Legislative Branch
   Representatives
      Elected by Direct Vote - Congressional District
      Term - Two Years

CRITICAL THINKING

ACTIVITY 5–1

Create your own resume using the format of the resume in Project 5-3. Trade your resume with a classmate. Edit each other's resume, and then make corrections to your resume if you feel they are warranted.

ACTIVITY 5–3

Use Help to learn how to change a single-level list into a multilevel list style. Create a new Word document and describe the process.

ACTIVITY 5–2

Make a bulleted list of your three favorite songs, three favorite books, and three favorite movies. Choose a different bullet symbol for each list by clicking Define New Bullet on the Bullets menu, and then click Symbol in the Define New Bullet dialog box. Click the arrow next to the Font box at the top of the dialog box, and then click one of the Wingdings fonts. Search for just the right bullet character for each list.

LANCASTER INDEPENDENT SCHOOL DISTRICT
Agenda for Board of Trustees Meeting
7:00 p.m., Monday, April 22, 2013

I.   Verify quorum
II.   Approve minutes for March 25, 2013 meeting
III. Approve the Tax Report for January, 2013
IV.   Committee Reports
    A.   Curriculum
    B.   Textbooks
    C.   Construction
    D.   Building Maintenance
V.   Old Business
    A.   Maintenance Contracts
    B.   Cafeteria
VI.   New Business
    A.   Recognition of students participating in School Clean-up Week
    B.   Short-term Borrowing
VII. Next Meeting, Monday, May 20, 2013

FIGURE 5-23

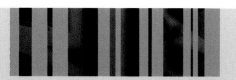

LESSON 6

Working with Graphics

■ OBJECTIVES

Upon completion of this lesson, you should be able to:

- Create and balance columns.
- Add borders and shading.
- Insert clip art and pictures.
- Insert, resize, and move inline and floating objects.
- Recolor graphics.
- Draw and modify shapes.
- Add text and callouts to drawings.
- Create and modify SmartArt and WordArt.

■ VOCABULARY

aspect ratio

callout

chart

clip art

crop

diagram

floating object

graphic

inline object

keyword

object

pull quote

rotation handle

selection rectangle

sidebar

sizing handle

SmartArt

text box

WordArt

Working with Graphics

You can enhance documents by adding graphics. ***Graphics*** are pictures that help illustrate the meaning of the text and make the page more attractive. You can add predefined shapes, diagrams, and charts as well as photographs and drawings. You can also use the drawing tools in Word to create your own graphics and add them to your documents.

Creating Columns

Sometimes a document can be more effective if the text is formatted in multiple columns. A newsletter is an example of a document that often has two or more columns. Columns are easy to create in Word. You click the Page Layout tab on the Ribbon, and then, in the Page Setup group, click the Columns button. The Columns menu opens, as shown in **Figure 6–1**.

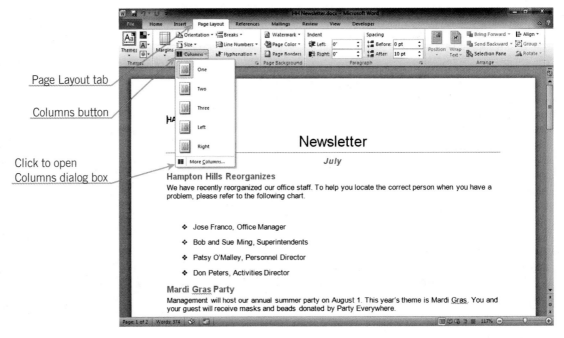

Page Layout tab

Columns button

Click to open
Columns dialog box

FIGURE 6–1   Columns menu

You can choose one, two, or three columns of equal width. You can also choose Left or Right, which creates two columns with either the left or the right column a little less than half the size of the other column. If none of these options suits you, you can click More Columns at the bottom of the Columns menu to open the Columns dialog box. See **Figure 6–2**. In this dialog box, you can create columns of custom widths, or you can add a vertical line between columns. You can also click the Apply to arrow and choose to apply the columns to the whole document (the default) or from the location of the insertion point to the end of the document.

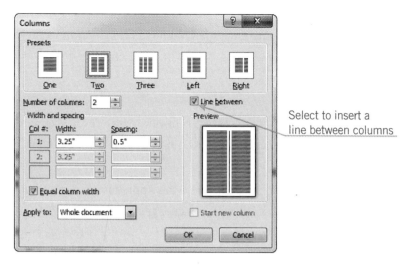

FIGURE 6–2   Columns dialog box

After you create columns, you might need to change the point at which a new column starts. You can do this using either of two methods. First, you can automatically create columns that are the same length. This is called balancing columns. To do this, click at the end of the columns you want to balance, click the Page Layout tab, and then, in the Page Setup group, click the Breaks button. On the menu that opens, click Continuous. Second, you can insert a column break to force a column to start at the point where you insert the break. To do this, position the insertion point immediately in front of the text you want to start the next column. In the Page Setup group on the Page Layout tab, click the Breaks button, and then click Column.

Step-by-Step 6.1

1. Open the **Newsletter.docx** document from the drive and folder where your Data Files are stored. Save the document as **HH Newsletter** followed by your initials.

2. On the Ribbon, click the **Page Layout** tab. In the Page Setup group, click the **Columns** button. The Columns menu opens as shown in Figure 6–1. On the menu, click **Two**. The entire document is formatted in two columns. But you want the newsletter title and date to be centered across the page, not placed in the first column.

3. On the Quick Access Toolbar, click the **Undo** button. The document returns to its original format.

4. Position the insertion point before the *H* in the *Hampton Hills Reorganizes* heading. You want everything after this point to be formatted in two columns and everything before this point to remain formatted as one column.

5. In the Page Setup group, click the **Columns** button, and then click **More Columns**. The Columns dialog box opens. Notice that the Preview section shows one column.

6. In the Presets section at the top of the dialog box, click **Two**. Click the **Line between** check box to insert a check mark. The Preview section changes to show two columns with a line between the columns. Refer back to Figure 6–2.

7. At the bottom of the dialog box, click the **Apply to** arrow, and then click **This point forward**. The Preview box changes to reflect this setting.

8. Click **OK**. The dialog box closes, all the text in the document from the first heading to the end is formatted in two columns, and a line appears between the two columns.

9. On the Ribbon, click the **View** tab. In the Zoom group, click the **One Page** button. The document appears in One Page view.

10. At the bottom of the second column, click immediately after the last period after the last word in the column, *month*. On the Ribbon, click the **Page Layout** tab. In the Page Setup group, click the **Breaks** button, and then click **Continuous**. Some of the text in the first column shifts to the second column and the two columns are now the same length.

11. On the Ribbon, click the **Home** tab. In the Paragraph group, click the **Show/Hide ¶** ⟦¶⟧ button to display formatting marks. Notice at the top of the document, after *July*, a double dotted line and the words *Section Break (Continuous)* appear. This is the point in the document at which the two-column format starts. At the bottom of the second column, a double dotted line appears. This is the continuous break you inserted.

12. In the Paragraph group, click the **Show/Hide ¶** ⟦¶⟧ button again to hide the formatting marks. Save your changes to the document. Leave it open for the next Step-by-Step.

> **TIP**
>
> To format only part of the document in columns without opening the Columns dialog box, select the paragraphs you want to format in columns. Then, click the Columns button in the Page Setup group on the Page Layout tab, and use any of the commands on this menu.

Adding Borders and Shading to Paragraphs

Borders around a paragraph draw the reader's attention to the paragraph. You can specify whether the border appears on all four sides (like a box), on two sides, or on only one side of the paragraph. You can also specify the border style, for example, whether the border consists of a single or a double line, is thick or thin, or includes a shadow or a 3-D effect.

To add a border, first select the text around which you want the border to appear. On the Home tab on the Ribbon, click the arrow next to the Borders button in the Paragraph group. A menu of border choices opens, as shown in **Figure 6–3**. You can click a command on the menu to add a border. Note that you can then click the arrow next to the Borders button again and click another command to add a second border to the selected text. For example, if you wanted to add a border above and below a paragraph, you would click Bottom Border on the menu, open the menu again, and then click Top Border. If you opened the menu again, both commands would be selected. Note that the icon for the Borders button and the exact name of the ScreenTip changes to reflect the most recent choices made.

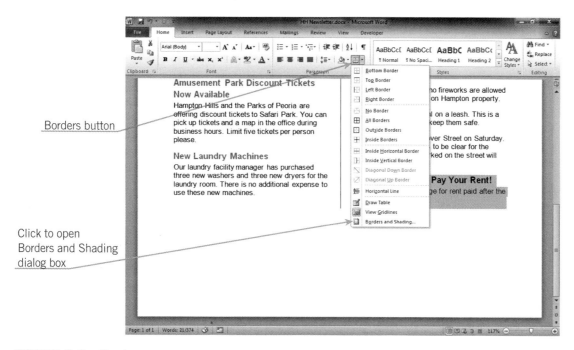

FIGURE 6–3   Borders menu

If you want to change the border style, you need to click Borders and Shading on the menu to open the Borders and Shading dialog box. In the dialog box, click the Borders tab if it is not the top tab. See **Figure 6–4**. Here you can specify the border setting, style, color, and width of the border line. To insert or remove borders, you click the sides of the paragraph preview on the right.

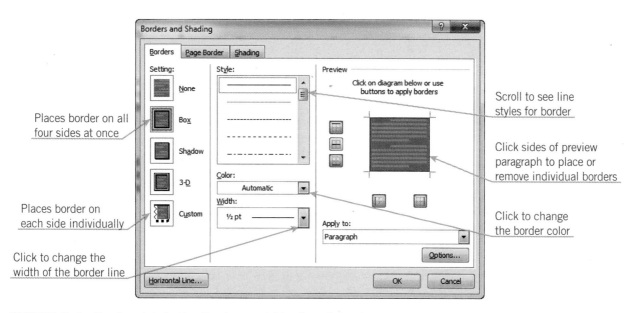

FIGURE 6–4   Borders tab in the Borders and Shading dialog box

You can also add shading or patterns to a paragraph or lines of text to emphasize the text. To do this, select the text you want to shade. In the Paragraph group on the Home tab, click the arrow beside the Shading button, and then click a color in the palette that opens.

To add a pattern, open the Borders and Shading dialog box, and then click the Shading tab, as shown in **Figure 6–5**. You can click the Fill arrow to choose a shading color from the same palette available on the Shading button. To add a pattern, click the Style arrow to choose a style or pattern for the shading (a percentage of the selected color, dots, or stripes), and then click the Color arrow to choose a color for the pattern. The Preview box shows you a sample of what your shading choices will look like.

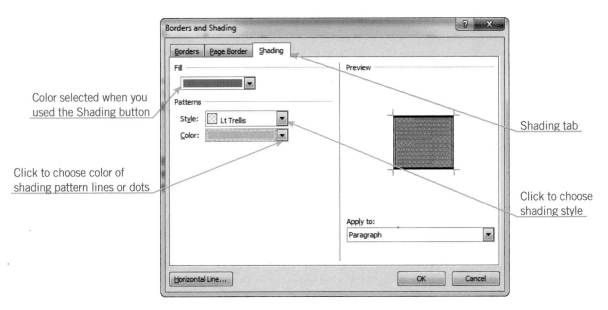

FIGURE 6–5   Shading tab in the Borders and Shading dialog box

Step-by-Step 6.2

1. Click the **View** tab, and then in the Zoom group, click the **Page Width** button. At the bottom of the page, select the heading **Don't Forget to Pay Your Rent!** and the sentence below it.

2. On the Ribbon, click the **Home** tab. In the Paragraph group, click the **arrow** next to the Borders button ⊞ ▾. The Borders menu opens. (Refer back to Figure 6–3.) Notice that none of the border commands are selected on the menu. Click **Outside Borders**. The menu closes and borders are added on all four sides of the selected text.

3. In the Paragraph group, click the **arrow** next to the Shading button. In the palette, click the **Dark Blue, Text 2, Lighter 40%** box (fourth row, fourth column). The selected paragraphs are shaded with a medium blue color.

4. In the Paragraph group, click the **arrow** next to the Borders button. Notice that the top four commands as well as the Outside Borders command are selected on the menu. At the bottom of the menu, click **Borders and Shading**. The Borders and Shading dialog box opens, with the Borders tab on top. Refer back to Figure 6–4. In the Setting section on the left, the Box button is selected. On the right, the Preview section shows the borders on all four sides of the paragraph.

5. In the center column in the dialog box, click the **Width** arrow, and then click **2 ¼ pt**. Because the Box button is selected, all four borders are changed to 2¼ points wide.

6. In the Setting section, click the **Custom** button. When the Custom button is selected, you need to click a border in the Preview section to apply the new border.

7. In the Style list, click the **down scroll arrow** twice, and then click the **double line** at the bottom of the list. In the Preview section, click the **left**, and then the **right** border. The borders you clicked change to double lines.

8. Click the **Shading** tab. Notice that the color in the Fill box is the same color you chose when you used the Shading button.

9. Click the **Style** arrow, scroll down to the bottom of the list, and then click **Lt Trellis**. The Preview section shows a trellis pattern.

10. Click the **Color** arrow, and then click the **White, Background 1, Darker 15%** box (third row, first column). Now the trellis pattern is much lighter.

11. Click **OK**. The selected paragraphs are formatted with the borders, shading, and pattern you chose.

12. Save your changes to the document. Leave it open for the next Step-by-Step.

Adding Borders and Shading to Pages

Just as you can add borders to paragraphs, you can add borders and shading to entire pages. To do this, click the Page Layout tab on the Ribbon, and then, in the Page Background group, click the Page Borders button. This opens the Borders and Shading dialog box with the Page Border tab on top, as shown in **Figure 6–6**. This is the same Borders and Shading dialog box you opened to add borders and shading to paragraphs. Everything is the same except the default in the Apply to box is Whole document, and there is an additional box at the bottom of the middle section of the dialog box. This is the Art box, from which you can choose graphics to use as a border. As with a paragraph, you can add page borders to any or all sides of a page.

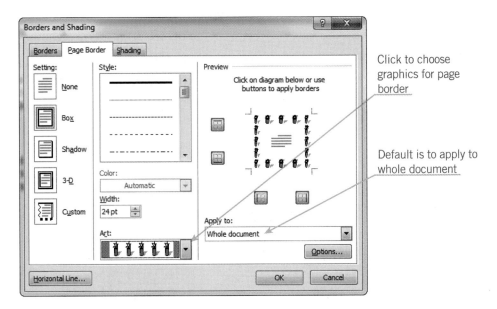

FIGURE 6–6   Page Border tab in the Borders and Shading dialog box

To add shading to an entire page, in the Page Background group on the Page Layout tab, click the Page Color button. The palette of theme colors opens. Click a color in the palette. The entire page is shaded with that color.

Step-by-Step 6.3

1. Switch to One Page view.

2. On the Ribbon, click the **Page Layout** tab. In the Page Background group, click the **Page Borders** button. The Borders and Shading dialog box opens, with the Page Border tab selected.

3. At the bottom of the middle section of the dialog box, click the **Art** arrow. Scroll down the list until you see the row of **red firecrackers**, and then click it. The Preview section changes to show a border of red firecrackers around the edge of the page.

4. Click **OK**. The dialog box closes and the firecracker border appears around the page.

5. In the Page Background group, click the **Page Color** button. In the color palette, click the **Red, Accent 2, Lighter 80%** square (second row, sixth column). The page is shaded with a light red color.

6. Save your changes to the document. Leave it open for the next Step-by-Step.

Understanding Objects

An **object** is anything that can be manipulated as a whole, such as clip art or another graphic that you insert in a document. You can insert, modify, resize, reposition, and delete objects in documents. You can cut, copy, and paste objects the same way you do text, using either the Cut, Copy, and Paste commands or by dragging and dropping the selected object.

VOCABULARY

object

clip art

keywords

Inserting Clip Art

Graphics that are already drawn or photographed and available for use in documents are called **clip art**. To insert clip art, click the Insert tab, and then, in the Illustrations group, click the Clip Art button. This opens the Clip Art task pane to the right of the document window. See **Figure 6–7**. In the Search for box, type a word or words that describe the type of clip art you want to insert. These words are called **keywords**. By default, Word searches all clip art on your computer as well as on Microsoft Office Online, a Web site maintained by Microsoft that stores thousands of pieces of clip art. When Word finds clip art that matches the keywords you typed, it displays the images in the task pane. You can scroll to view the images and click the one you want. Word inserts the clip art at the insertion point in your document.

TIP

The term *clip art* refers not only to drawn images, but also to photographs, video clips, and sound files. To restrict your search to specific types of clip art, click the Results should be arrow in the Clip Art task pane, and then select the check boxes next to the type of clip art you want.

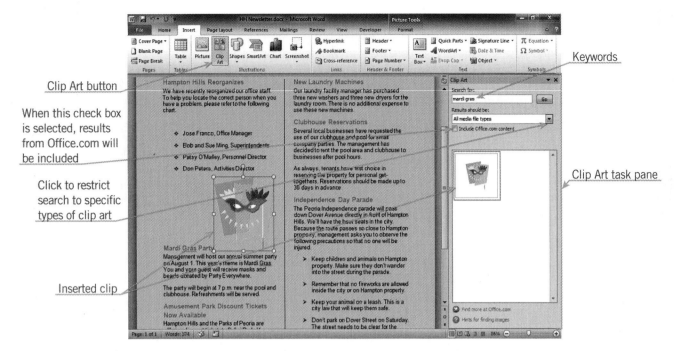

Clip Art button

When this check box is selected, results from Office.com will be included

Click to restrict search to specific types of clip art

Inserted clip

Keywords

Clip Art task pane

FIGURE 6–7   Inserting clip art

Step-by-Step 6.4

1. Click the **View** tab, and then in the Zoom group, click **Page Width**. Scroll up so that you can see the heading *Mardi Gras Party* in the first column.

2. In the first column, position the insertion point after the word *Party* in the heading *Mardi Gras Party*. On the Ribbon, click the **Insert** tab. In the Illustrations group, click the **Clip Art** button. The Clip Art task pane appears to the right of the document window.

3. At the top of the Clip Art task pane, click in the **Search for** box and select the text in the box if there is any. Type **mardi gras**, and then click **Go**. Clips relating to Mardi Gras appear in the task pane. Refer back to Figure 6–7. (Note: If you are connected to the Internet and if the Include Office.com content check box is selected, you will see more results in the task pane.)

4. In the task pane, point to the clip of a mask on top of colored panels. An arrow appears on the right side of the clip and a ScreenTip listing key words that describe the clip and other information about the clip appears.

5. Click the **arrow**, and then on the menu, click **Insert**. The clip is inserted in the document.

6. In the document window, position the insertion point immediately after the heading *Independence Day Parade*.

7. In the task pane, replace the text in the Search for box with **flag**. You need to find a photograph of a flag.

8. Click the **Results should be** arrow. Click the **All media types** check box to deselect it, and then click the **Photographs** check box to select it. The Photographs check box should be the only check box with a check mark in it. Click the **Results should be** arrow to close the menu. To find a clip art photograph of a flag, you need to search Office.com.

9. Click the **Include Office.com content** check box to select it if it is not already selected, and then click **Go**. Clip art photographs of flags appear in the task pane. (Note: If you are not connected to the Internet, delete the text in the Search for box, and then click Go. Choose any one of the photographs to insert in place of the flag.)

10. In the task pane, scroll down until you see photos of American flags. Point to one, click the **arrow** on the clip, and then click **Insert**. The clip art photo of the flag is inserted into the document.

11. In the title bar of the Clip Art task pane, click the **Close** button ❎. The task pane closes. Save the document and leave it open for the next Step-by-Step.

TIP

You can also simply click a clip in the Clip Art task pane to insert it into the document.

TIP

You can press Enter instead of clicking Go in the task pane to search for clips matching the keywords.

Selecting an Object

To manipulate or modify an object, you must select it first. To select an object, position the pointer over the object, and then click. A box with small circles at the corners and small squares on each side appears around the object, as shown in **Figure 6–8**. The box appears when the object is selected and is called the ***selection rectangle***. The squares and circles are called ***sizing handles***; you drag the sizing handles to resize the object. The green circle is the ***rotation handle***; you can drag it to rotate the object. To deselect an object, click a blank area of the document window, just as you would to deselect selected text.

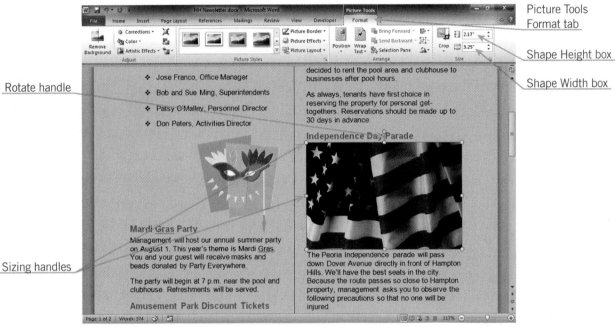

FIGURE 6–8　Selected picture

When you select a clip art image, the Picture Tools Format tab appears, as shown in Figure 6–8. Remember, contextual tabs contain commands that are available only when a particular type of object is selected. For example, after you insert clip art, you can change its height and width or recolor it. These commands appear on the Picture Tools Format tab because you cannot perform either of these actions on regular text.

Resizing an Object

Once an object has been inserted, you can resize it to fit better on the page. To resize an object, first select it, and then drag a sizing handle. When you position the pointer directly on top of one of the sizing handles, it changes to a two-headed arrow. Drag the handle inward or outward to make the object smaller or larger.

The relationship of the object's height to its width is called the ***aspect ratio***. If you drag a corner sizing handle (one of the circles), you change the size of the object without changing the aspect ratio; in other words, you change the object's height and width proportionately. If you drag a side sizing handle (one of the squares), you change the size of the object without maintaining the aspect ratio. You can also change the size of an object by selecting it, clicking the Picture Tools Format tab, and then adjusting either of the measurements in the Size group. The default is to maintain the aspect ratio, so if you change the measurement in one box, the measurement in the other box adjusts automatically.

Step-by-Step 6.5

1. If the clip art of the flag is not selected, click to select it. If the rulers are not displayed on your screen, at the top of the vertical scroll bar, click the **View Ruler** button 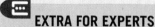 so that the rulers are displayed.

2. Using the ruler as a guide, drag the **upper-right sizing handle** on the flag until the faint outline of the clip indicates that it is approximately two inches tall.

3. Click the clip art of the mask.

4. On the Ribbon, click the **Format** tab under Picture Tools, if necessary. In the Size group, click the **up arrow** in the Shape Width box (the bottom box) as many times as necessary until the measurement in the box is **2"**. Note that the measurement in the Shape Height box changed as well.

5. In the Size group, click in the **Shape Height** box (the top box). The measurement is selected. Type **1.15**, and then press **Enter**. The height of the clip is changed to 1.15 inches, and the width automatically changed to one inch. Now both clips are resized smaller. See **Figure 6–9**.

> **EXTRA FOR EXPERTS**
>
> If you don't want part of a graphic to appear in the document, you can **crop** off (cut off) the part you don't want. Select the graphic, click the Format tab, and then, in the Size group, click the Crop button to change the pointer to the Crop pointer. Drag a sizing handle on the graphic toward the center of the graphic until the indicator box that appears includes only the section of the graphic you want to use. Click the Crop button again to turn off this feature.

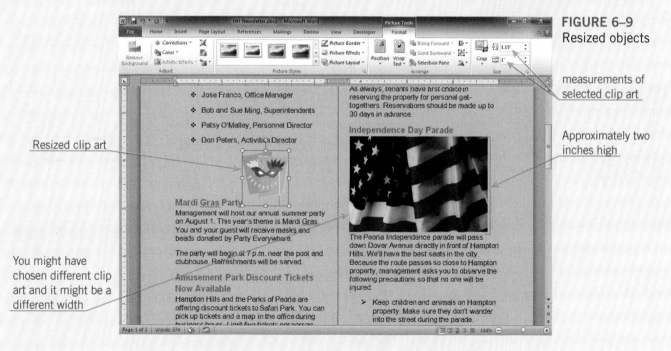

FIGURE 6–9
Resized objects

measurements of selected clip art

Approximately two inches high

Resized clip art

You might have chosen different clip art and it might be a different width

6. Save the document and leave it open for the next Step-by-Step.

Repositioning and Removing an Inline Object

VOCABULARY
inline object

When you insert an object, it is inserted as an *inline object* in the text, which means it is treated as if it were a character in the line of text. You can apply paragraph formatting commands to the paragraph that contains the inline object; for example, you can use the Align commands to change its alignment or set a specific amount of space before or after the paragraph. If you want to move or copy an inline object to another line in the document, click it to select it, and then use drag-and-drop or the Cut, Copy, and Paste commands to move or copy it, just as you would with text. If you want to delete an object, select it, and then press the Delete or the Backspace key, again, just as you would with text.

Step-by-Step 6.6

1. In the second column, click the picture of the flag to select it.

2. On the Ribbon, click the **Home** tab. In the Paragraph group, click the **Center** button. The flag and the heading above it are centered in the column. Why did the heading become centered as well as the selected clip art of the flag?

3. In the Paragraph group, click the **Show/Hide ¶** button. Because there is a paragraph mark after the flag but not after the heading, the flag is in the same paragraph as the heading, so any paragraph formatting you apply to the inline clip art of the flag also applies to the heading.

4. In the Paragraph group, click the **Align Text Left** button. The paragraph, including the heading, is again left-aligned.

5. In the first column, click the clip art of the mask to select it. Position the pointer directly on top of the selected object. The pointer changes to the Move pointer.

6. Drag the selected image down until the indicator line is between the period at the end of the first paragraph under the *Mardi Gras Party* heading and the paragraph mark, as shown in **Figure 6–10**, and then release the mouse button. The image is moved to the end of the first paragraph.

TIP

Just as you do with text, if you want to copy rather than move an object using drag-and-drop, press and hold Ctrl while you drag the object.

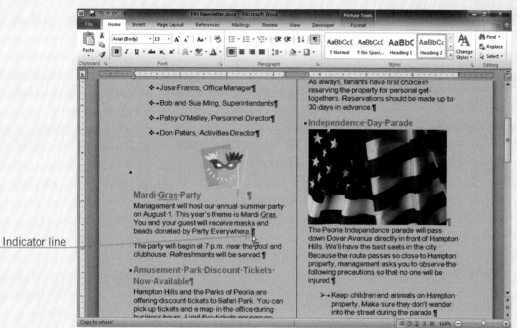

FIGURE 6–10
Moving an object

Indicator line

7.   Save the document and leave it open for the next Step-by-Step.

Wrapping Text Around an Object

To save space and make a document look more professional, you may want to wrap text around an object. To do this, you need to change the inline object to a ***floating object***, an object that acts as if it were sitting in a separate layer on the page. You can drag a floating object anywhere on the page. To do this, click the contextual Format tab, and then in the Arrange group, click the Wrap Text button to open a menu of wrapping options, as shown in **Figure 6–11**. **Table 6–1** describes these options.

▶ VOCABULARY
floating object

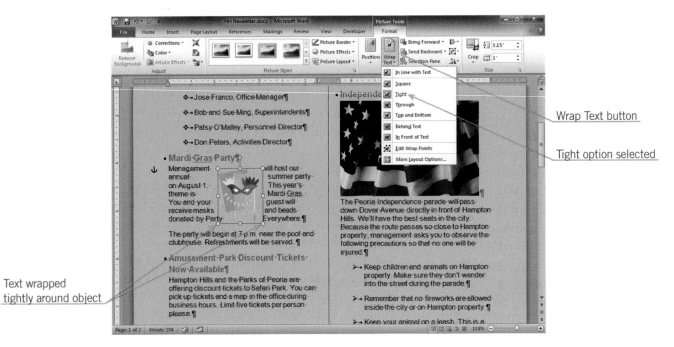

FIGURE 6–11   Wrapping text around an object

TABLE 6–1   Text wrapping commands

COMMAND	ACTION
In Line with Text	Changes a floating object to an inline object
Square	Wraps text around top, bottom, and both sides of an object
Tight	Wraps text around all sides of an object no matter what shape the object is
Through	Wraps text around all sides of an object—no matter what shape the object is—more tightly than the Tight command
Top and Bottom	Wraps text around the top and bottom of an object and leaves the space on either side of the object empty
Behind Text	Places the object behind the text
In Front of Text	Places the object in front of (on top of) the text
Edit Wrap Points	Displays small squares around the perimeter of an object, which you can drag to change the perimeter for objects wrapped with the Tight or the Through option
More Layout Options	Opens the Layout dialog box with the Text Wrapping tab on top, displaying options for adjusting the distance between the text and the sides of the object

To change the object to a floating object that is positioned in a predetermined location on the page (centered in the top, middle, or bottom, one of the corners, or in the middle of the left or right side), on the Format tab in the Arrange group, click the Position button, and then click one of the options in the gallery under With Text Wrapping. See **Figure 6–12**.

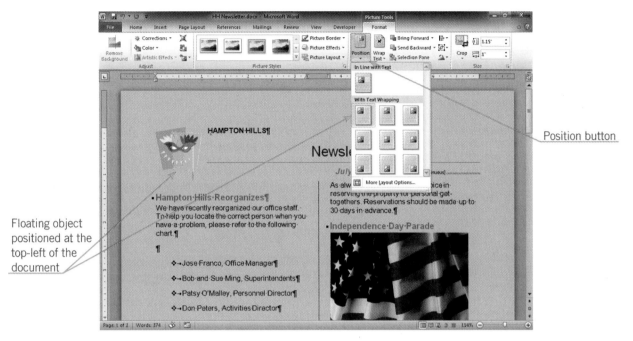

Position button

Floating object positioned at the top-left of the document

FIGURE 6–12 Positioning text in a predetermined position using the Position button

Step-by-Step 6.7

1. If the clip art of the mask is not already selected, click it.

2. On the Ribbon, click the **Picture Tools Format** tab. In the Arrange group, click the **Wrap Text** button, and then click **Tight**. The text in the first column under the *Mardi Gras Party* heading shifts and wraps around the clip art.

3. Drag the clip art up to approximately center it in the first paragraph under the *Mardi Gras Party* heading so that all the text in that paragraph wraps around the clip art. Refer to Figure 6–11.

4. In the second column, click the clip art of the flag. On the Ribbon, click the **Picture Tools Format** tab. In the Arrange group, click the **Wrap Text** button, and then click **Behind Text**. Deselect the picture. The text in the second column flows on top of the picture.

5. Click anywhere on the heading **Independence Day Parade**. The insertion point is placed in the paragraph on top of the picture; the picture does not become selected. You might be able to click directly on the flag, but sometimes when you send an image behind text, it is impossible to select it simply by clicking.

6. In the Editing group on the Home tab, click the **Select** button, and then click **Select Objects**. Click directly on the heading **Independence Day Parade**. This time, the picture is selected. When the Select Objects option is selected, you can select only objects on a page; you cannot select text.

7. Drag the selected picture so that the top of the image is just at the top of the *Independence Day Parade* heading. On the selected picture, drag the **bottom middle** and the **right sizing handles** until the picture is as wide and as tall as all the text under the Independence Day Parade heading. See **Figure 6–13**.

FIGURE 6–13
Clip art
behind text

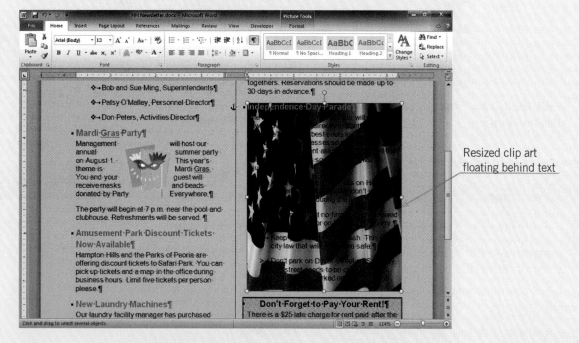

Resized clip art
floating behind text

8. In the Editing group, click the **Select** button, and then click **Select Objects**. Now you will be able to select text again.

9. Save the document and leave it open for the next Step-by-Step.

Recoloring Pictures

Sometimes you need to adjust the color of an image. You can change the brightness or contrast, or recolor an image all in one shade or with a washout (very light) style. To do this, click the contextual Format tab. In the Adjust group, click the Corrections button, and then click a button to adjust the settings. The Corrections gallery is shown in **Figure 6–14**. Also in the Adjust group, you can click the Color button, and then click a style to recolor the image all in one shade. See **Figure 6–15**.

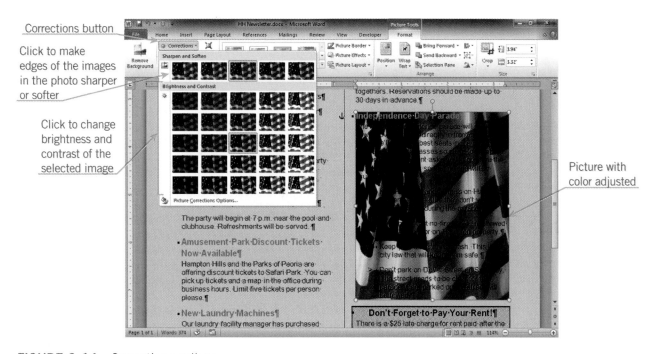

FIGURE 6–14   Corrections gallery

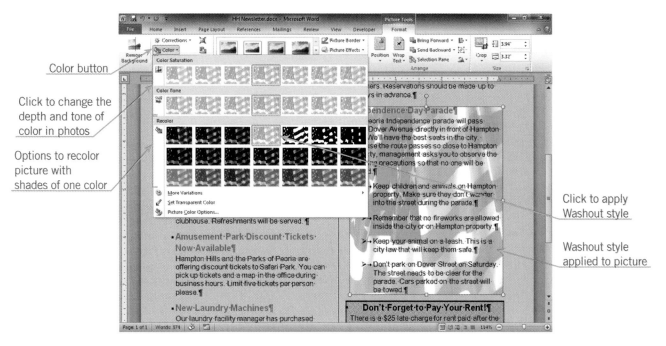

FIGURE 6–15   Color gallery

Step-by-Step 6.8

1. In the second column, select the picture of the flag, if necessary.

2. On the Ribbon, click the **Picture Tools Format** tab. In the Adjust group, click the **Corrections** button.

3. In the Sharpen and Soften section, point to the first style, and watch the Live Preview of the picture. Point to the last style in the Sharpen and Soften section, and watch the Live Preview again.

4. In the Brightness and Contrast section, point to the first style in the last row and watch the Live Preview of the picture. Point to the last style in the last row, and watch the Live Preview again. Press **Esc** to close the menu without selecting a command.

5. In the Adjust group, click the **Color** button. In the Color Saturation section, point to several of the styles to see the effect on the image. In the Color Tone section, point to several of the styles to see the effect.

6. In the Recolor section, point to several of the styles to see the effect on the picture.

7. In the first row under Recolor, click the **Washout** style (fourth style in the row). The picture is recolored in the Washout style, and the text is now readable on top of the image.

8. Save the document and leave it open. You will not use it in the next Step-by-Step, but you will use it later.

Inserting Pictures

In Word, pictures are graphic files stored on your computer. To insert a picture in a document, click the Insert tab, and then in the Illustrations group, click the Picture button to open the Insert Picture dialog box. See **Figure 6–16**. This dialog box is similar to the Open and the Save As dialog boxes. You can navigate to the folder that contains the picture you want to insert, click the file, and then click Insert. The picture is inserted as an inline object at the location of the insertion point. You can then change the object to a floating object if you want, as well as resize and reposition it, in the same manner as clip art.

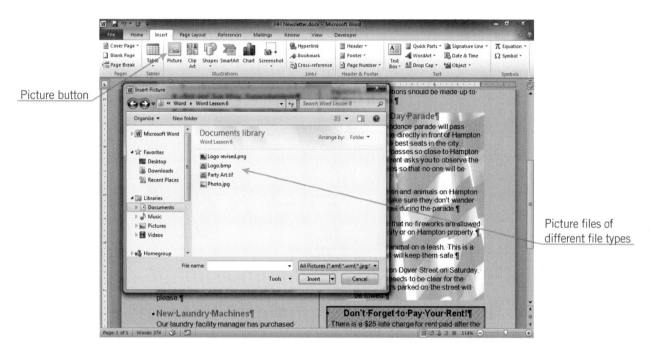

Picture button

Picture files of different file types

FIGURE 6–16   Insert Picture dialog box

Adding Shapes

Word provides tools for you to create your own graphic images. To access these tools, click the Insert tab, and then, in the Illustrations group, click the Shapes button to open a menu of choices. See **Figure 6–17**. **Table 6–2** summarizes the types of drawing tools available on the menu.

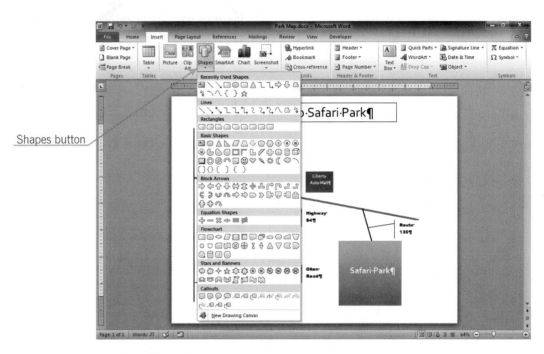

Shapes button

FIGURE 6–17   Shapes gallery

TABLE 6–2   Types of drawing tools

CATEGORY	DESCRIPTION
Lines	Draw straight or curved lines
Rectangles	Draw rectangles with different corner styles
Basic Shapes	Draw many basic shapes, including rectangles, ovals, triangles, and several more interesting shapes, such as a smiley face and a lightning bolt
Block Arrows	Draw various forms of block arrows
Equation Shapes	Draw shapes used in mathematical equations
Flowchart	Draw shapes used to create a flow chart
Stars and Banners	Draw star and banner shapes
Callouts	Draw boxes with lines that point to something to highlight or "call out" the item being pointed to

Drawing Shapes

To draw a shape, click the shape you want to draw on the menu. The pointer changes to the crosshairs pointer. Drag the pointer on the document to draw the shape. Drawn shapes are inserted as floating objects by default. As with clip art objects, you can cut, copy, and paste drawn shapes as well as move and resize them.

Step-by-Step 6.9

1. Create a new, blank Word document. Save it as **Park Map** followed by your initials. Study the map in **Figure 6–18**. You will be drawing a map similar to this one.

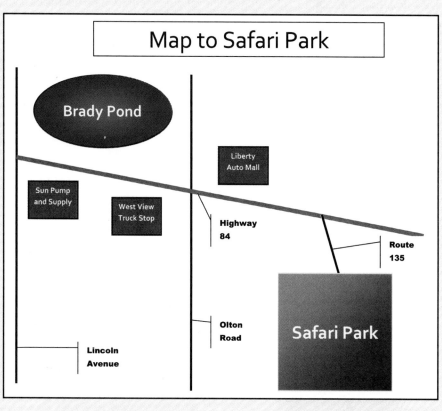

FIGURE 6–18
Map created with drawn shapes

TIP

To draw a square instead of a rectangle, a circle instead of an oval, or an equilateral triangle instead of an isosceles triangle, press and hold Shift while you drag to draw the shape.

2. If formatting marks are showing, in the Paragraph group, click the **Show/Hide ¶** button to hide them. If the ruler is not visible, at the top of the vertical scroll bar, click the **View Ruler** button to display the rulers. On the Ribbon, click the **Page Layout** tab. In the Page Setup group, click the **Orientation** button, and then click **Landscape**. On the Ribbon, click the **View** tab. In the Zoom group, click the **One Page** button. You're ready to draw the map now.

3. On the Ribbon, click the **Insert** tab. In the Illustrations group, click the **Shapes** button. The Shapes menu opens.

4. Under Basic Shapes on the menu, click the **Oval** button (second button in the top row under Basic Shapes). The mouse pointer changes to $+$.

5. Position the pointer on the blinking insertion point, press and hold the mouse button, and then drag to draw an oval approximately 3 inches wide and 1½ inches high. When the oval is approximately the same size as the pond shown in Figure 6–18, release the mouse button. The Drawing Tools Format tab is active on the Ribbon.

6. On the Ribbon, click the **Insert** tab. In the Illustrations group, click the **Shapes** button, and then under Lines, click the **Line** button (first button under Lines).

7. Position the pointer just above and about one-half inch to the left of the oval. Press and hold Shift, and then drag to draw a line down to the 6½-inch mark on the vertical ruler. Release the mouse button when your line is positioned similar to *Lincoln Avenue* in Figure 6–18.

8. Click the line you drew to select it. On the Ribbon, click the **Home** tab. In the Clipboard group, click the **Copy** button 📋, and then click the **Paste** button. A copy of the line appears in the document. Drag the line to position it to the right of the circle you drew, similar to *Olton Road* in Figure 6–18.

9. Use the **Line** button to create the road that is colored red on the map and the road labeled *Route 135*.

10. Use the **Rectangle** button under Rectangles on the Shapes menu (first shape under Rectangles) to draw the rectangle labeled *Sun Pump and Supply* in Figure 6–18. Copy the rectangle twice, and then place one copy in the position labeled *West View Truck Stop* on the map and the other copy in the position labeled *Liberty Auto Mall* on the map.

11. Click the **Rectangle** button again, press and hold **Shift**, and then draw the square labeled *Safari Park* on the map. Pressing Shift at the same time you drag creates a square.

12. Compare your document to the map shown in Figure 6–18. You have drawn the basic shapes for the map. Resize and reposition any shapes as needed to make your drawing match the map as closely as possible. You will add color and style to these shapes in the next Step-by-Step. (Ignore the labels that identify the street names.)

13. Save the document and leave it open for the next Step-by-Step.

Adding Color and Style to Drawings

Color adds life to your drawings. Word has tools that you can use to fill objects with color and change the color of lines. To change the color, select the object you want to fill or the line you want to change, and then click the Drawing Tools Format tab. This tab contains the same Arrange group of commands as on the Picture Tools Format tab as well as additional commands for working with a drawn object.

To fill the object with a different color, use the Shape Fill button on the Drawing Tools Format tab (see **Figure 6–19**). To change the line or outline color of a drawing, use the Shape Outline button on the Drawing Tools Format tab (see **Figure 6–20**). These buttons are similar to the Font Color button. You can click the arrow next to either of these buttons to open the color palette, or you can click the button itself to quickly apply the color that appears in the bar at the bottom of the button.

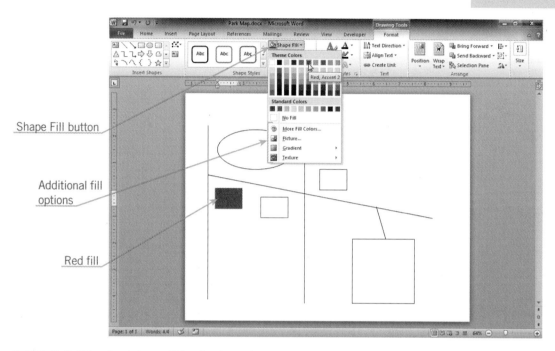

FIGURE 6–19   Applying a fill color to a shape

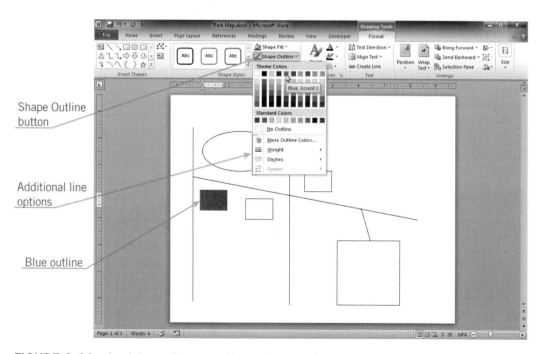

FIGURE 6–20   Applying a line or outline color to a shape

You can also use the Shape Styles gallery to add color to your drawings. To open the Shape Styles gallery, in the Shape Styles group, click the More button. See **Figure 6–21**. The gallery provides various options for quickly formatting your shapes with styles and colors associated with the current theme.

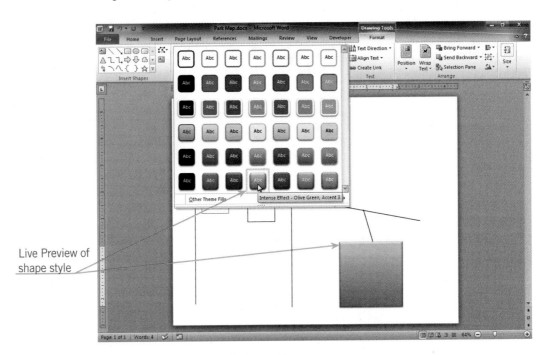

Live Preview of shape style

FIGURE 6–21   Shape Styles gallery

Finally, you can also change the line weight, or thickness, of lines or shape outlines in your drawing. To do this, select the object. In the Shape Styles group, click the Shape Outline button, and then point to Weight on the menu. A submenu of line thicknesses measured in points opens. See **Figure 6–22**. Click the line weight you want to use.

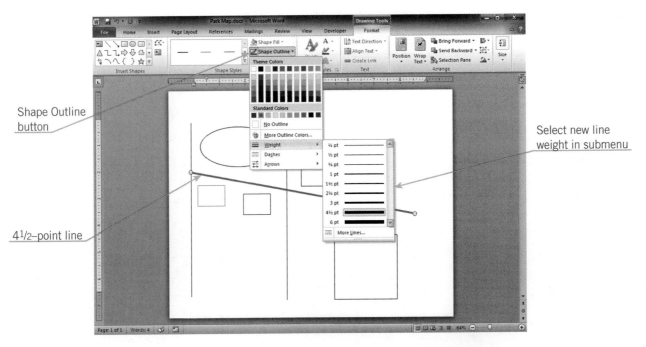

Shape Outline button

Select new line weight in submenu

4 1/2–point line

FIGURE 6–22   Changing a shape's line thickness

Step-by-Step 6.10

1. Click the **line** in the drawing that slants diagonally from the left edge of the page to the lower-right to select it.

2. If necessary, on the Ribbon, click the **Drawing Tools Format** tab. In the Shape Styles group, click the **arrow** next to the Shape Outline button. In the palette under Standard Colors, click the **Red** box. The selected line is recolored red.

3. Click one of the three rectangles in the drawing. In the Shape Styles group, click the **arrow** next to the Shape Fill button. In the palette under Theme Colors, click the **Red, Accent 2** box (first row, sixth column). The selected rectangle is filled with a dark red color.

4. With the same rectangle selected, in the Shape Styles group, click the **arrow** next to the Shape Outline button. In the palette under Theme Colors, click the **Blue, Accent 1** box (first row, fifth column). The outline color is changed to blue.

5. With the same rectangle selected, on the Ribbon, click the **Home** tab. In the Clipboard group, double-click the **Format Painter** button 🖌. Click the two other rectangles in the drawing. Press **Esc** to deselect the Format Painter button. All three rectangles are formatted the same way.

6. Select the oval in the drawing. Click the **Drawing Tools Format** tab. In the Shape Styles group, click the **More** button. The gallery of Shape Styles opens. Below the gallery, point to **Other Theme Fills**, and then click **Style 11** box (the third style in the last row). The oval is formatted with the selected style.

7. Select the square in the drawing. In the Shape Styles group, click the **More** button, and then click the **Moderate Effect – Olive Green, Accent 3** style (second to last row, fourth column). The square is formatted with the selected style. Notice that this style includes a small shadow below the shape.

8. On the **Format** tab, in the Shape Styles group, click the **Shape Effects** button. Point to **Shadow**, and then under No Shadow, click the **No Shadow** style. The shadow effect is removed from the shape.

9. Click the **red diagonal line** in the drawing. In the Shape Styles group, click the **arrow** next to the Shape Outline button, point to **Weight**, and then click **4½ pt**. The weight of the red line is now 4½ points.

10. Click one of the other lines in the drawing, press and hold **Shift**, and then click the other two lines to select all three of them. Change the weight of the selected lines to **2¼ points**.

11. Select all three maroon rectangles, and then change the weight of the outline to **1½ points**.

12. Save the document and leave it open for the next Step-by-Step.

Adding Text to Your Drawings

Often your drawings will require labels. Word provides several ways to add text to a drawing. The easiest way is to click an object, and then start typing. You can format your text as usual.

Another way to add text to your drawing is to insert text boxes. A ***text box*** is a shape specifically designed to hold text. To add a text box, click the Insert tab, and then, in the Illustrations group, click the Shapes button. Click the Text Box button in the Basic Shapes section of the menu. Or, on the Insert tab, in the Text group, click the Text Box button, and then click Draw Text Box. The pointer changes to the cross-hair pointer. Position the pointer where you want the text box to appear, and then click and drag to create a text box. An insertion point appears inside the text box so you can type the text you want. Text within a text box can be formatted in the same way you format ordinary text in a document.

A text box can be treated like any other object. You can format, resize, or change the position of a text box using the commands on the Text Box Tools Format tab that appears when you select the text box.

Step-by-Step 6.11

1. Click the oval, and then type **Brady Pond**.

2. Click the dotted line border of the shape so that the border changes to a solid line. Click the **Home** tab on the Ribbon. Format the text as bold, white, 24-point Corbel. The default is for the text to be centered in the shape. You can check this.

3. Click the **Drawing Tools Format** tab, and then in the Text group, click the **Align Text** button. Notice on the menu that Middle is selected.

4. Add the following text to the three maroon rectangles, using Figure 6–18 as a guide: **Sun Pump and Supply**, **West View Truck Stop**, and **Liberty Auto Mall**. Format the text in each text box as bold, white, 12-point Corbel, and then center it horizontally and vertically in the text boxes.

5. Add the text **Safari Park** to the large square. Change the style to **No Spacing**. Format the text as bold, white, 28-point Corbel, and then center it horizontally and vertically in the text box.

6. On the Ribbon, click the **Insert** tab. In the Illustrations group, click the **Shapes** button. Under Basic Shapes, click the **Text Box** button (first row, first column under Basic Shapes). In the document, click at the top, above the drawing. A square text box appears with the insertion point inside it.

7. Type **Map to Safari Park**.

8. Drag the **right, middle sizing handle** to the right until the text box is approximately six inches wide. Format the text as 36-point Corbel, and then center it in the text box.

9. Drag the **bottom, middle sizing handle** of the text box up to resize the text box so it is approximately one-half inch high.

10. Position the pointer on the edge of the text box so that it changes to ⬚, and then drag the text box to center it between the left and right margins.

11. On the Ribbon, click the **Insert** tab, if necessary. In the Text group, click the **Text Box** button. The Text Box gallery opens. At the bottom of the gallery, click **Draw Text Box**. Click in the document below the map, and then, in the text box that appears, type your name.

12. If necessary, resize the text box so that your name fits on one line. Reposition the text box so it appears in the lower-left corner of the map.

13. Save the document and leave it open for the next Step-by-Step.

Adding Callouts to Your Drawings

A *callout* is a special type of label in a drawing that consists of a text box with an attached line to point to a detail in the drawing. Many of the figures in this book have callouts identifying items on the screen. To add a callout, click one of the callout buttons on the Shapes menu, and then type the callout text in the callout shape.

EXTRA FOR EXPERTS

To quickly create a text box from existing text, select the text, click the Text Box button in the Text group on the Insert tab, and then click Draw Text Box. The selected text is removed from the document and placed inside the text box.

VOCABULARY
callout

Step-by-Step 6.12

1. On the Ribbon, click the **Insert** tab. In the Illustrations group, click the **Shapes** button. Under Callouts, click the **Line Callout 1 (Accent Bar)** button (first row under Callouts, fifth button from the right).

2. To create a label for Highway 84, click to the right of the center line below the red diagonal line, as shown on the map in Figure 6–18. A callout appears on the map, with the insertion point inside the text box.

EXTRA FOR EXPERTS

To add an arrow to the end of a callout line (or any other drawn line), click the Format tab. In the Shape Styles group, click the Shape Outline button, point to Arrows, and then click the style of arrow you want to add.

3. Type **Highway 84**. Format the text as **12-point Arial Black**, change the font color to **Black, Text 1**, and then change the shape fill to **No Fill**. (Make sure you format the text.)

4. Repeat Steps 2 and 3 to insert the callouts for **Lincoln Avenue**, **Olton Road**, and **Route 135** as shown on the map.

5. Compare your map to Figure 6–18. Make adjustments as needed.

6. Save, print, and close the document.

Creating Diagrams and Charts with SmartArt

▶ **VOCABULARY**
diagram
chart
SmartArt

EXTRA FOR EXPERTS

To change a SmartArt graphic to another shape, click the More button in the Layouts group on the SmartArtTools Design tab, and then click More Layouts to open the Choose a SmartArt Graphic dialog box again.

Diagrams and *charts* are visual representations of data. They organize information in illustrations so readers can better understand relationships among data. In Word, you can insert diagrams and charts quickly using predesigned drawings called *SmartArt*. You can create many types of diagrams using SmartArt, including List, Process, Cycle, Hierarchy, Relationship, Matrix, Pyramid, and Picture. Organization Charts, a common chart in business, are hierarchical charts.

To create a SmartArt graphic, click the Insert tab, and then, in the Illustrations group, click the SmartArt button. The Choose a SmartArt Graphic dialog box opens, as shown in **Figure 6–23**. You can click a category in the list on the left to narrow the available choices in the middle pane in the dialog box. To insert a SmartArt graphic, click the one you want in the pane in the middle of the dialog box, and then click OK. The graphic appears in the document with a border around it, and two SmartArt Tools tabs—Design and Format—appear on the Ribbon. You can use the commands on these tabs to add elements (shapes) and text to a diagram and to change its size and color.

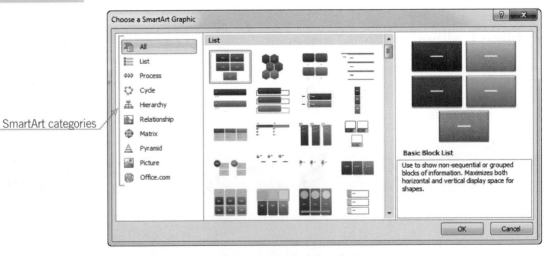

FIGURE 6–23   Choose a SmartArt Graphic dialog box

Step-by-Step 6.13

1. If the **HH Newsletter.docx** document that you worked on earlier in this lesson is not open, open it now. If formatting marks are not visible, display them. Press **Ctrl+Home** to jump to the top of the document.

2. In the first column in the newsletter, click in the blank paragraph above the bulleted list. On the Ribbon, click the **Insert** tab. In the Illustrations group, click the **SmartArt** button. The Choose a SmartArt Graphic dialog box opens.

3. In the category list on the left side of the dialog box, click **Hierarchy**. The middle section of the dialog box changes to display only charts that show hierarchical relationships. In the middle section of the dialog box, click the **Organization Chart** style (first row, first column). Click **OK**. An organization chart appears in the document as an inline object at the insertion point.

4. Save the document and leave it open for the next Step-by-Step.

Add Text to a SmartArt Graphic

When you create a SmartArt graphic, placeholder text appears in each shape. To insert text in a SmartArt graphic, click in each box in the graphic and start typing. The text you type replaces the placeholder text.

Step-by-Step 6.14

1. Click in the top box in the organization chart. The placeholder text disappears and the insertion point blinks in the box.

2. Type **Jose Franco**. The placeholder text is replaced with your text. Press **Enter**. Type **Office Manager**. Notice that the font size adjusted automatically as you typed so that all the text fits in the box.

3. Replace the text in the three boxes in the third row in the chart with the names and titles in the last three bullets in the bulleted list under the chart. Make sure you press Enter before typing the job titles.

4. Select the four names and titles in the bulleted list below the chart, and then delete them. You will have one extra box in the SmartArt graphic.

5. Save the document and leave it open for the next Step-by-Step.

> **TIP**
>
> You can click the Text pane control on the left side of the SmartArt graphic's border or the Text Pane button in the Create Graphic group to open the Text pane, which displays the text of the SmartArt graphic as a bulleted list. You can add items to the list in the Text pane as you would to a bulleted list in a document.

Modify a SmartArt Graphic

You can resize SmartArt graphics as you would resize any object. Instead of squares or circles, the sizing handles on a SmartArt graphic are three dots at each corner and in the middle of the sides of the selection rectangle. You can change a SmartArt graphic from an inline object to a floating object. You can also add an outline and a colored fill to the entire graphic.

In addition, you can change the look and structure of a SmartArt graphic by using some of the many commands available on the SmartArt Tools contextual tabs. On the Design tab (see **Figure 6–24**), you can add, move, or remove shapes to and from the diagram by using commands in the Create Graphic group. To change the layout of the graphic, click the More button in the Layouts group to display all the available layouts in the Layouts gallery. You can change the color scheme of the diagram by clicking the Change Colors button in the SmartArt Styles group. Or, you can change the style of the SmartArt, including choosing a 3-D look, by clicking the More button in the SmartArt Styles group to display the SmartArt Styles gallery.

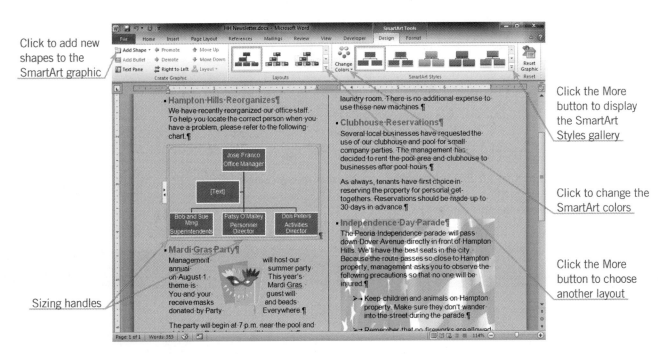

FIGURE 6–24   Modifying SmartArt

Step-by-Step 6.15

1. In the organization chart, click the edge of the box in the second row. If a dashed line appears around the edge of the box, click the edge again to change it to a solid line. Press **Delete**. The box is deleted and the chart now contains only two rows of boxes.

2. Click the **Patsy O'Malley** box. On the Ribbon, click the **SmartArt Tools Design** tab, if necessary. In the Create Graphic group, click the **arrow** next to the Add Shape button.

3. On the menu, click **Add Shape Below**. A box appears in the chart below the Patsy O'Malley box. Type **Rosa Mendez**, press **Enter**, and then type **Assistant**.

4. On the Design tab, in the Layouts group, click the **More** button. Click the **Horizontal Organization Chart** style (third row, second column). The chart changes to the horizontal style.

5. In the SmartArt Styles group, click the **Change Colors** button. Under Accent 2 in the gallery, click **Colored Fill – Accent 2** (second style from the left). The chart colors change to dark red.

6. In the SmartArt Styles group, click the **More** button. Under Best Match for Document in the gallery, click **Intense Effect** (last style in the row under Best Match for Document). The chart style changes so that boxes have some shading.

7. Save the document and leave it open for the next Step-by-Step.

Creating WordArt

WordArt is stylized text that is formatted and placed in a text box. To create WordArt, click the Insert tab, and then, in the Text group, click the WordArt button. A gallery of WordArt styles opens, as shown in **Figure 6–25**. Click one, and a text box appears. if you select text before you click the WordArt button, the text you selected appears in the text box; otherwise *Your text here* appears in the text box, and you can type the text you want to use as the WordArt text.

▶ **VOCABULARY**
WordArt

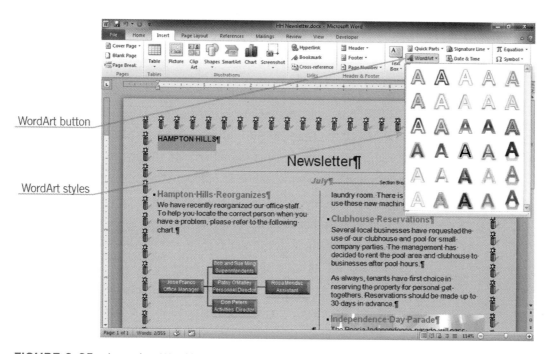

FIGURE 6–25   Inserting WordArt

You can change the WordArt style, color, and outline color by clicking the appropriate buttons in the WordArt Styles group on the Drawing Tools Format tab. See **Figure 6–26**. In addition, you can click the Text Effects button in the same group, and then apply shadow, reflection, glow, bevel, and 3-D effects. You can also use the Text Effects button to change the shape of the WordArt by selecting an option on the Transform submenu. As with any other object, you can drag the sizing handles or use the boxes in the Size group on the Format tab to resize WordArt.

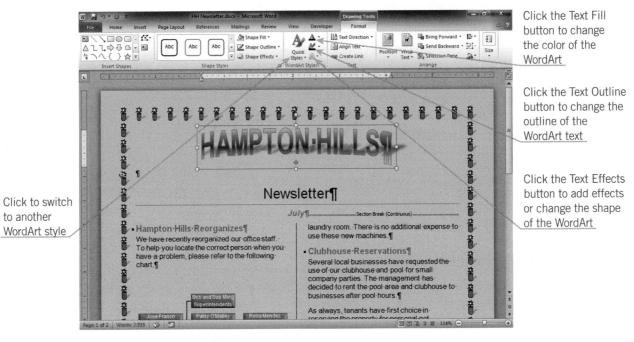

Click to switch to another WordArt style

Click the Text Fill button to change the color of the WordArt

Click the Text Outline button to change the outline of the WordArt text

Click the Text Effects button to add effects or change the shape of the WordArt

FIGURE 6–26 Modifying WordArt

Step-by-Step 6.16

1. Scroll to the top of the document, if necessary. Select **HAMPTON HILLS**. Do not select the paragraph mark.

2. On the Ribbon, click the **Insert** tab. In the Text group, click the **WordArt** button. Click the **Gradient Fill – Blue, Accent 1** style (third row, fourth column). The selected text is formatted with the style you selected, and the Drawing Tools Format tab is selected on the Ribbon.

3. In the WordArt Styles group on the Drawing Tools Format tab, click the **Text Effects** button [A▾]. Point to **Shadow**. Click the **Perspective Diagonal Upper Right** style (middle style in the row under Perspective). A shadow is added to the text.

4. In the WordArt Styles group, click the **Text Effects** button [A▾]. At the bottom of the menu, point to **Transform**. In the Warp section, click the **Can Up** style (fourth row under Warp, third column). The WordArt changes shape.

5. In the Arrange group, click the **Wrap Text** button. Click **Top and Bottom**. The text box is changed to a floating object and the newsletter text moves below the WordArt.

6. In the Arrange group, click the **Align** button [icon], and then click **Align Center**. The WordArt title is centered between the left and right margins. See Figure 6–26.

7. On the Ribbon, click the **View** tab. In the Zoom group, click the **One Page** button. You need to adjust the SmartArt graphic so that the newsletter still fits on one page.

8. On the SmartArt graphic, drag the **bottom middle sizing handle** up a little. The scroll box in the vertical scroll bar disappears and you see a blank paragraph at the bottom of the first column. The newsletter fits on one page again. Compare your document to **Figure 6–27**, and make any adjustments necessary.

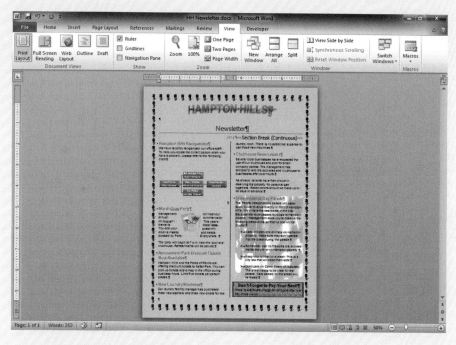

FIGURE 6–27
Completed newsletter document

9. Press **Ctrl+End** to jump to the blank paragraph at the end of the document, and then type your name.

10. Hide formatting marks and the ruler. Save, print, and close the document.

SUMMARY

In this lesson, you learned:

- Graphics add interest to documents.

- You can format all or part of a document in multiple columns.

- You can add borders and shading to selected text to emphasize it. You can also add a page border and shading to the entire page.

- An object is anything that can be manipulated as a whole. An inline object is inserted as if it were a character in a line of text. A floating object acts as if it is sitting in a separate layer on the page.

- You can insert clip art and resize and recolor it to fit your document. You can also insert and resize pictures in a document.

- You can draw shapes in a document. Drawn objects can be resized, moved, and colored.

- You can add text to drawn shapes or create a text box shape. Text boxes can be formatted, resized, or moved just like other drawn objects.

- Callouts are special text boxes that have a line attached to them to point to specific items in a document.

- Charts and diagrams organize your data in a manner that illustrates relationships among data. You can use SmartArt to add charts and diagrams to documents. You can change the structure and look of SmartArt.

- You can insert WordArt to create stylized text objects. As with other objects, you can resize, reposition, and format WordArt.

■ VOCABULARY REVIEW

Define the following terms:

aspect ratio	graphic	selection rectangle
callout	inline object	sidebar
chart	keyword	sizing handle
clip art	object	SmartArt
crop	pull quote	text box
diagram	rotation handle	WordArt
floating object		

REVIEW QUESTIONS

FILL IN THE BLANK

Complete the following sentences by writing the correct word or words in the blanks provided.

1. Choose the _____ tab on the Ribbon to add clip art, pictures, shapes, and WordArt to a document.

2. To automatically balance columns, insert a(n) _____ section break.

3. When text wraps around an object, the object is called a(n) _____ object.

4. Words that you use to search for clip art are _____.

5. The _____ is the relationship of an object's height to its width.

TRUE / FALSE

Circle T if the statement is true or F if the statement is false.

T F **1.** You must carefully choose the type of SmartArt to create because you cannot change it to another type later.

T F **2.** You can add a border to paragraphs, but you cannot add a border to a page.

T F **3.** Borders can be placed on all four sides of a selected paragraph.

T F **4.** Objects that you insert in a document can be placed only in a line of text in a paragraph.

T F **5.** To find an appropriate piece of clip art, you must scroll through an alphabetized list of all the available clip art.

MATCHING

Match the correct term in Column 2 to its description in Column 1.

Column 1

_____ 1. Pictures that help illustrate the document and make the page more attractive

_____ 2. Anything that can be manipulated as a whole

_____ 3. An object that is inserted as if it were a character in the line of text

_____ 4. Squares and circles on a selected object that you drag to resize the object

_____ 5. Visual representation of data

Column 2

A. Diagram or chart

B. Object

C. Graphics

D. Inline object

E. Sizing handles

PROJECTS

If you have a SAM 2010 user profile, your instructor may have assigned an autogradable version of the indicated project. If so, log into the SAM 2010 Web site at *www.cengage.com/sam2010* to download the instruction and start files.

PROJECT 6–1

1. Open the **Shelter.docx** document from the drive and folder where your Data Files are stored. Save the document as **Shelter News** followed by your initials.

2. Format the text in the document below the phone number as two columns. Do not add a line between the two columns.

3. Center the headings in the columns.

4. Balance the columns.

5. Near the bottom of the first column, apply a 2¼-point border at the top and the bottom of the paragraph that contains *Thank you for your help!*. Change the color of the border to Tan, Accent 2, Darker 50%. Add shading using the Tan, Accent 2, Lighter 40% theme color and add a 10% pattern, changing the color of the pattern to White, Background 1, Darker 15%.

6. At the top of the second column, insert clip art of a person and a dog. Try using the keyword **pet** or **dog**. Use a photograph or an illustration.

7. Change the clip art to a floating object so that the text wraps tightly around it, and then resize it to approximately one-inch by one-inch. (If it is impossible to resize the clip art you chose to this size, click the Crop button in the Size group on the Format tab, and then drag one of the sizing handles on the side of the clip to crop off a portion of the clip so that the final size is close to one-inch by one-inch.) Position the clip art in the middle of the paragraph at the top of the second column.

8. At the top of the newsletter, change *Plains Animal Shelter* to WordArt. Use the Fill – Gold, Text 2, Outline – Background 2 style (the first style in the first row). Add a Tan, 8 pt glow, Accent color 2 glow text effect, and then use the Transform effect to change the WordArt to the Square effect in the Warp section.

9. Change the WordArt to a floating object and wrap the text around the top and bottom of the object.

10. View the document in One Page view. If necessary, adjust the clip art so that the entire newsletter fits on one page.

11. Insert a text box near the lower-left corner of the document. Type your name, and then resize the text box so your name fits on one line. Fill the text box with Yellow.

12. Save, print, and close the document.

SAM PROJECT 6–2

1. Create the poster shown in **Figure 6–28** using what you have learned in this lesson. The theme used is Clarity. Refer to the instructions shown in the figure.

2. Insert a text box near the upper-right corner of the document. Type your name in the text box. Change the border of the text box so it is 4½ points wide.

3. Save the document as **Garage Sale** followed by your initials.

4. Print and close the document.

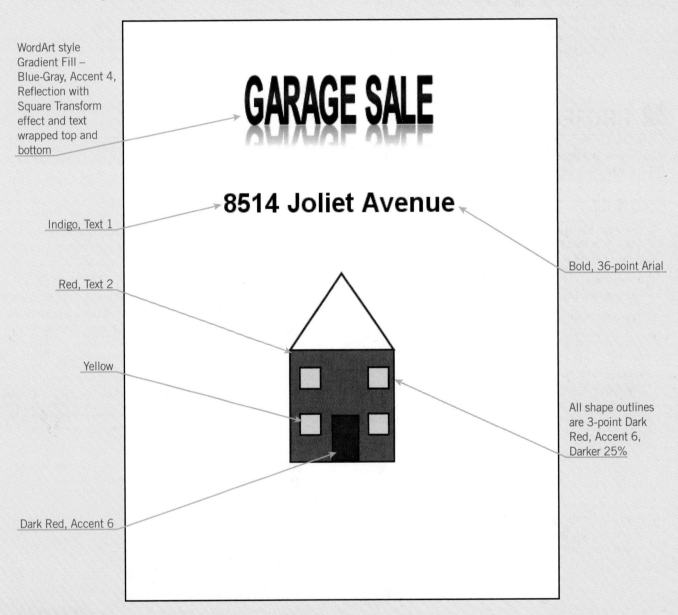

WordArt style Gradient Fill – Blue-Gray, Accent 4, Reflection with Square Transform effect and text wrapped top and bottom

Indigo, Text 1

Red, Text 2

Yellow

Dark Red, Accent 6

Bold, 36-point Arial

All shape outlines are 3-point Dark Red, Accent 6, Darker 25%

FIGURE 6–28

PROJECT 6–3

1. Open the **Invitation2.docx** document from the drive and folder where your Data Files are stored. Save the document as **Holiday Invitation** followed by your initials.

2. Insert clip art with a holiday theme above the text. Resize and align the graphic to fit the document.

3. Change the text to a color, font, and size of your choice. The entire document should fit on one page.

4. Apply an appropriate page border and page color.

5. Insert a text box near the lower-right corner of the document. Type your name, and then resize the text box so that your name fits on one line. Format the text as bold, 12-point Calibri. Fill the text box with red.

6. Save, print, and close the document.

PROJECT 6–4

1. Open the **Memo2.docx** Data File from the drive and folder where your Data Files are stored. Save the document as **Org Chart Memo** followed by your initials.

2. At the top of the document, change the color of *New World Marketing, Inc.* to Blue, Accent 2, Darker 25%. Change the color of the heading *MEMORANDUM* to the same color.

3. Add a border below *MEMORANDUM*. Choose a line style that has one thick line and one thin line on either side of the thick line. Apply the same color to the line as you used for *MEMORANDUM*.

4. At the top of the document, insert clip art. Use the keyword **world** to find an image of the earth.

5. Change the object to a floating object using the Behind Text wrapping option, and then resize it so it is approximately the same height as the header information at the top of the document (from the company name through the Web site address).

6. Change the object so that it appears behind the text. Recolor it or change the brightness or contrast so that the text is visible on top of the object.

7. At the end of the document, insert an organization chart using a SmartArt graphic.

8. Modify the organization chart and insert text so it matches the chart shown in Figure 6–29. The color is the Primary Theme Color Dark 2 Fill; the SmartArt style is Intense Effect under Best Match for Document; and the Layout style is Half Circle Organization Chart.

9. Add a callout in any style pointing to Rosa Molina's box. Type **Rosa was promoted to District Manager last week** as the text of the callout.

10. In the *From* line in the memo header, replace *Vera Thomas* with your name.

11. Save, print, and close your document.

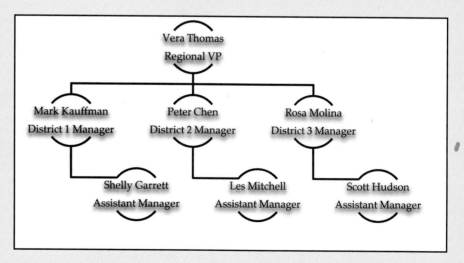

FIGURE 6–29

CRITICAL THINKING

ACTIVITY 6–1

You are having a birthday party for your friend. Create an invitation using clip art, borders, and shading. Use the drawing tools to create a map from your school to your house.

ACTIVITY 6–3

Use the Help system to find out how to insert a chart in a document. Create a new document, and insert a pie chart. Close the Excel window that opens, and then change the style to one that uses shades of all one color.

ACTIVITY 6–2

With a classmate, create a newsletter about your class. Decide on a name for the newsletter, what information should be included, a page design, and attractive clip art. Have the class vote for their favorite.

Estimated Time: 2 hours

LESSON 7

Working with Documents

■ OBJECTIVES

Upon completion of this lesson, you should be able to:

- Insert page breaks, headers, footers, and page numbers.
- Understand content controls.
- Modify document properties.
- Insert predesigned cover pages.
- Create a section with formatting that differs from other sections.
- Use the Research tool.
- Insert, modify, and format tables.
- Sort text.

■ VOCABULARY

cell

content control

footer

gridline

header

orphan

page break

property

section

sort

table

widow

As you work with longer documents, you can make the content clearer by creating pages and inserting information at the tops and bottoms of pages to identify the content, author, date, page number, and so on. Word also provides tools that help you insert content and conduct research online. You can also create tables of information.

Inserting Page Breaks

In a multipage document, Word determines the place to end one page and begin the next. The place where one page ends and another begins is called a *page break*. Word automatically inserts page breaks where they are needed, but you can insert a page break manually. For example, you might want to do this to prevent an automatic page break from separating a heading from the text that follows, or you might want to start a new section of a document on a new page.

To insert a page break manually, click the Insert tab on the Ribbon, and then in the Pages group, click the Page Break button. You can also execute this command on the Page Layout tab—in the Page Setup group, click the Breaks button, and then click Page. Finally, you can also use the keyboard to insert a page break by pressing Ctrl+Enter. If formatting marks are displayed, a manual page break appears immediately after the last line of text on the page. It is indicated by a dotted line with the words *Page Break* in the middle of the line, as shown in **Figure 7–1**. To delete manual page breaks, select the page break line, and then press Backspace or Delete.

EXTRA FOR EXPERTS

Similar to a manual page break, you can also insert a manual line break to create a new line without creating a new paragraph. To do this, position the insertion point at the location in the line where you want the line to break, and then press Shift+Enter.

Page Break button on Insert tab

Manual page break

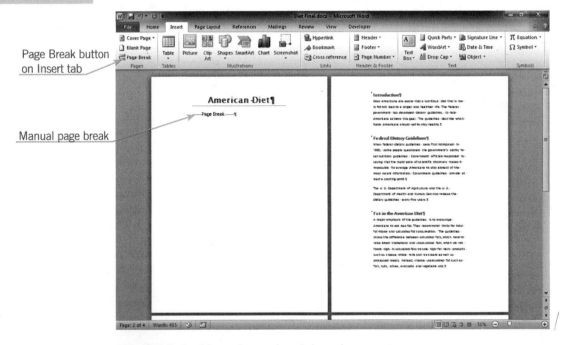

FIGURE 7–1 Manual page break in a document

Step-by-Step 7.1

1. Open the **Diet2.docx** from the drive and folder where your Data Files are stored. Save the document as **Diet Final** followed by your initials.

2. Display formatting marks. Position the insertion point at the beginning of the *Introduction* heading.

3. On the Ribbon, click the **Insert** tab. In the Pages group, click the **Page Break** button. A page break is inserted, and the document scrolls down so that the insertion point is blinking at the top of the new page 2. You created a new cover page for the document.

4. Scroll up so that you can see the text near the top of page 1. The manual page break is indicated by a dotted line below the last line of text on the page with the words *Page Break* in the middle of it.

5. Scroll down to page 4 in the document. Position the insertion point at the beginning of the heading *References*. Insert a page break.

6. Save your changes and leave the document open for the next Step-by-Step.

> **TIP**
>
> When you insert manual page breaks, you should try to avoid creating widows and orphans. A **widow** is when the first line of a paragraph appears at the bottom of a page; an **orphan** is when the last line of a paragraph appears at the top of a page. Widows and orphans are avoided when automatic page breaks are inserted.

The style definition for headings can include a setting to keep the heading on the same page as the first line in the next paragraph. You can also specify that there is always a manual page break before a heading. To change these settings, in the Paragraph group on the Home tab or the Page Layout tab, click the Paragraph Dialog Box Launcher, and then click the Line and Page Breaks tab in the Paragraph dialog box. The settings are at the top in the Pagination section.

> **▶ VOCABULARY**
>
> **widow**
>
> **orphan**
>
> **content control**

Understanding Content Controls

Many predesigned elements in Word contain **content controls**, which are special placeholders designed to contain a specific type of text, such as a date or the page number. When you click a content control, the entire control is selected and a title tab appears at the top or to the left of the control. See **Figure 7–2**. The title tab can identify the type of information that appears in the control.

Title tab on content control with title of content control

Title tab on content control with no title

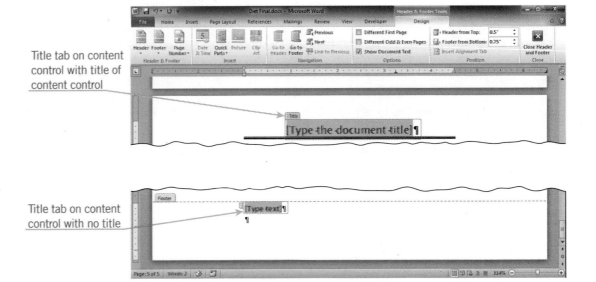

FIGURE 7–2   Content controls

For most controls, you simply start typing, and the text you type replaces the placeholder text. For some controls, an arrow appears when you click the control, and you click the arrow to choose an item from a list or a date from a calendar. Sometimes the content control is removed when you enter text, and sometimes the content control remains in the document (although only the contents of the control will appear in the printed document). If you decide you don't want to use a content control, you can delete it. Click the title tab to select the entire control, and then press Delete or Backspace.

Inserting Headers, Footers, and Page Numbers

Headers and footers allow you to include the same information, such as your name and the page number, on each page of a document. A *header* is text that is printed at the top of each page. A *footer* is text that is printed at the bottom of each page. **Figure 7–3** shows both a header and a footer.

▶ **VOCABULARY**
header
footer

Header

Footer

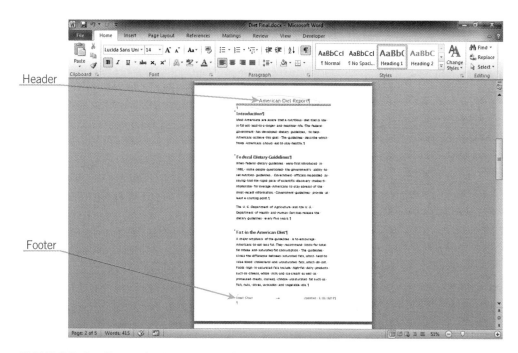

FIGURE 7-3   Page with header and footer

Inserting and Modifying Headers and Footers

Insert headers and footers by clicking the Insert tab, and then clicking the Header or Footer button in the Header & Footer group. When you click either of these buttons, a gallery of predesigned headers or footers opens, as shown in **Figure 7–4**. At the top of the list, two Blank styles are listed, and then additional styles are listed alphabetically. Each header and footer contains content controls.

Header button

Footer button

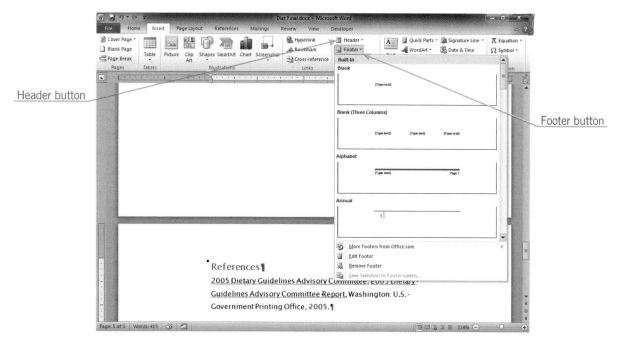

FIGURE 7-4   Footer gallery

When the header or footer area is active, the Header & Footer Tools Design tab appears on the Ribbon, as shown in **Figure 7–5**. This tab contains buttons you can use to insert elements such as the date, time, and page numbers. Other buttons allow you to set formatting options. In the Options group, you can select the Different First Page check box to remove the header and footer from the first page of the document.

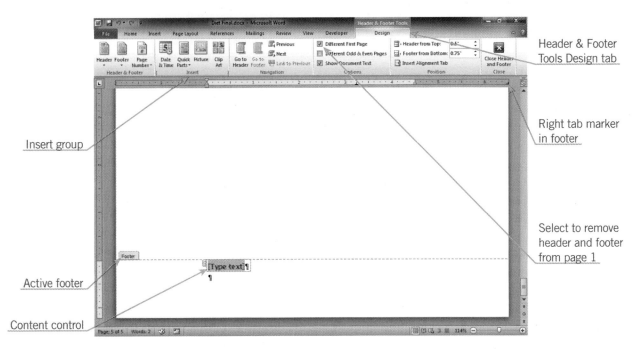

FIGURE 7–5   Footer with selected placeholder text

Step-by-Step 7.2

1. Display the rulers, if necessary.

2. On the Insert tab, in the Header & Footer group, click the **Footer** button. A gallery of footer styles appears. Refer back to Figure 7–4. Click **Blank**. The footer section appears at the bottom of the current page with placeholder text at the left margin. Refer back to Figure 7–5. Notice that the footer contains a center tab marker at the 3¼-inch mark on the ruler and a right tab marker at the 6½-inch mark. The Header & Footer Tools Design tab appears on the Ribbon and is the active tab. The content control in the footer is selected, ready for you to enter text.

3. In the footer section in the document, type your name. The text you type replaces the placeholder text in the content control. In this case, the content control is deleted as soon as you start typing.

4. On the ruler, drag the **right tab marker** positioned at the 6½-inch mark to the left so that it is directly on top of the right margin marker. Press **Tab** twice. The insertion point is at the right margin in the footer.

TIP

To remove a header or footer, click the Header or Footer button on the Insert tab or the Header & Footer Tools Design tab, and then click Remove Header or Remove Footer.

5. On the Design tab, in the Insert group, click the **Date & Time** button. In the Date and Time dialog box, deselect the **Update automatically** check box, if necessary, and then click **OK**. The current date is inserted in the footer in the format 5/25/2013.

6. On the Design tab, in the Header & Footer group, click the **Header** button, and then click the **Alphabet** style. The header section at the top of the page comes into view. The Alphabet style header with placeholder text is centered in the header. It includes a brown horizontal graphic line. A blue border appears around the placeholder text and a title tab appears at the top, identifying this as a Title content control, that is, a content control that contains the document title.

7. Type **American Diet Report**. The text you type replaces the placeholder text, but the content control stays in the document. See **Figure 7–6**.

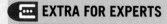

EXTRA FOR EXPERTS

You can insert an empty header and footer with no content controls. In the Header & Footer group on the Insert tab, click the Header or Footer button, and then click Edit Header or Edit Footer on the menu.

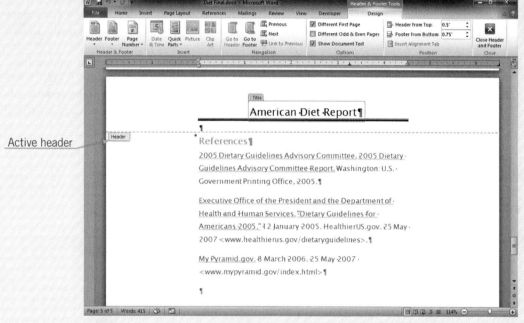

FIGURE 7–6
Header with text entered in Title content control

Active header

8. With the headers and footers still active, scroll up in the document so that you can see the top of page 2 and the bottom of page 1. Click in the header on page 2. On the Design tab, in the Options group, click the **Different First Page** check box, and then scroll up again so that you can see the bottom of page 1. The footer no longer appears on the first page of the document.

9. Scroll to the top of page 1. The header does not appear on the first page.

10. Scroll back down so you can see the insertion point in the header at the top of page 2. On the Design tab, in the Navigation group, click the **Go to Footer** button. The footer on page 2 comes into view with the insertion point blinking at the beginning of the line.

11. Position the insertion point in front of the date. Type **Updated:**, and then press the **spacebar**.

12. Double-click the document window above the footer section. The section of the document that was active before you started working on the header and footer (page 5) jumps into view. The headers and footers appear faded, and the insertion point is blinking in the document window. (If you clicked somewhere in the document before you started working on the header and footer, the current page will be different.)

13. Save your changes and leave the document open for the next Step-by-Step.

Inserting Page Numbers

Page numbers are included in some of the header and footer styles. If you choose a header or footer style that does not include page numbers, or if you want to insert page numbers without inserting anything else in a header or footer, you can use the Page Number button in the Header & Footer group on the Insert tab or on the Header & Footer Tools Design tab. A menu opens with choices for you to insert page numbers at the top or the bottom of the page, in the margin, or at the current position. When you point to any of these options, a gallery of choices appears. If you choose Top of Page or Bottom of Page, you automatically create a header or footer with only the page number as content. See **Figure 7-7**. If a header or footer already exists, the page number style you choose replaces it.

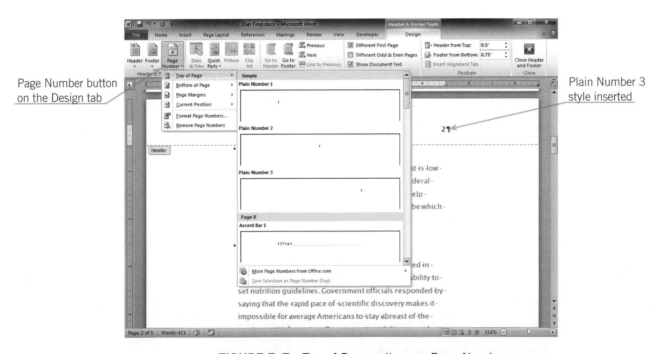

Page Number button on the Design tab

Plain Number 3 style inserted

FIGURE 7-7   Top of Page gallery on Page Number menu

If you want to insert the page number in an existing header or footer, first position the insertion point in the header or footer at the location where you want the page number to appear. Click the Page Number button, point to Current Position, and then choose a style.

Step-by-Step 7.3

1. Scroll so that you can see the top of page 2. Double-click anywhere in the header on page 2. The header becomes active and the insertion point blinks at the beginning of the content control.

2. On the Design tab, in the Header & Footer group, click the **Page Number** button, point to **Top of Page**, and then click **Plain Number 3**. Instead of adding the page number near the right margin, the page number header replaced the header you created.

3. On the Quick Access Toolbar, click the **Undo** button . The header you created reappears.

4. On the ruler, drag the **right tab marker** positioned at the 6½-inch mark to the left so that it is directly on top of the right margin marker. Drag the **center tab marker** positioned at the 3¼-inch mark off the ruler to remove it. Press **End**, and then press the **right arrow key**. The insertion point is positioned between the content control and the paragraph mark. Press **Tab**. The insertion point is positioned at the right margin.

5. In the Header & Footer group, click the **Page Number** button. Point to **Current Position**, and then click **Plain Number**. The page number appears at the location of the insertion point, formatted in the same style as the rest of the header text.

6. On the Design tab, in the Close group, click the **Close Header and Footer** button.

7. Save your changes and leave the document open for the next Step-by-Step.

TIP

To hide the margins and space between pages in a document, move the insertion point to the top of the page until it changes to a button with double arrows, and then double-click. To show the space again, position the insertion point on the top of the line between pages so that it changes, and then double-click.

Modifying Document Properties

When you save a file, identifying information about the file is saved along with it, such as the author's name and the date the file was created. This information is known as the file **properties**.

To view or add properties to a document, click the File tab, and then click Info. The properties appear in the right pane in Backstage view, as shown in **Figure 7–8**.

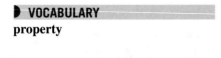

VOCABULARY
property

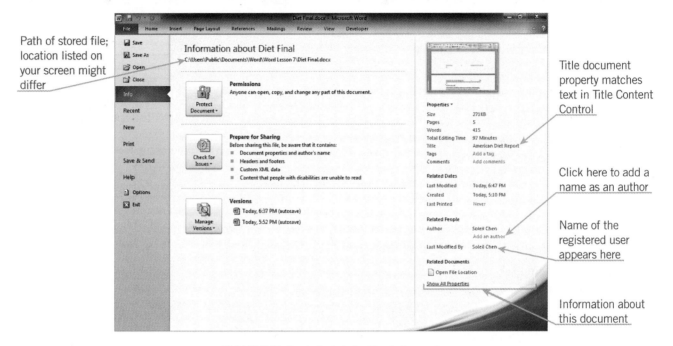

Path of stored file; location listed on your screen might differ

Title document property matches text in Title Content Control

Click here to add a name as an author

Name of the registered user appears here

Information about this document

FIGURE 7–8   Info tab in Backstage view

Content controls can be linked to document properties so that they pick up and display the information stored as a document property. For example, if a content control is tied to the Title document property, it displays the information stored in the Title box in the Properties section of the Info tab in Backstage view. The connection works both ways, so that if you change the Title in the content control, the change appears in the Title box in the Properties section and in every other Title content control in the document.

Step-by-Step 7.4

1. If necessary, scroll up so you can see the header at the top of page 2. Click the **File** tab, and then in the navigation bar, click **Info**, if it is not already selected. The document properties appear in the right pane in Backstage view. Refer back to Figure 7–8. Notice that *American Diet Report*, the title you typed in the Title content control in the header, appears as the Title property.

2. Click anywhere on *American Diet Report* next to Title, and then select **American Diet Report**. Type **Reducing Fat in the American Diet**. Click a blank area in Backstage view. The text in the Title content control in the header on page 2 also changed to the text you just typed.

3. On the Ribbon, click the **File** tab. Backstage view closes and your document appears again. Notice that the title in the header is changed to the new title you typed in Backstage view.

4. Click the **File** tab. Backstage view appears again with the Info tab selected.

5. Under Related People in the Backstage view, click **Add an author**. The placeholder text disappears and a box appears with the insertion point in it. Type your name in the box.

6. Right-click **Soleil Chen**. On the shortcut menu, click **Remove Person**. Now your name is the only name listed as the author of the document.

7. At the top of the right pane, click **Properties**, and then click **Advanced Properties**. The Diet Final.docx Properties dialog box opens. Click the **Summary** tab. See **Figure 7–9**.

Summary tab

Your name will appear here

FIGURE 7–9
Summary tab in Diet Final.docx Properties dialog box

8. If there is any text in the Company box, select it. Type your school name in the Company box. Click **OK**.

9. Click the **Home** tab. Backstage view closes.

10. Save your changes and leave the document open for the next Step-by-Step.

Inserting a Cover Page

You can quickly create a cover page for your document by inserting one of the many predesigned cover pages available with Word. To insert a predesigned cover page, click the Insert tab, and then, in the Pages group, click the Cover Page button. A gallery of cover pages opens, as shown in **Figure 7–10**.

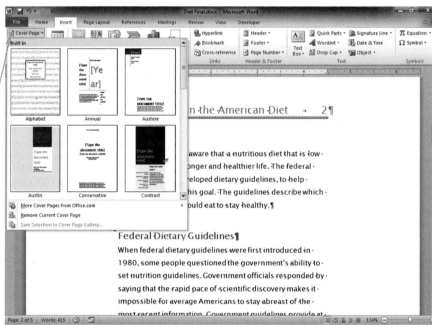

Cover Page button

FIGURE 7–10   Cover Page gallery

The cover pages contain content controls, as shown in **Figure 7–11**. As with the content controls that appear in headers and footers, you can use them or delete them, and then insert your own content.

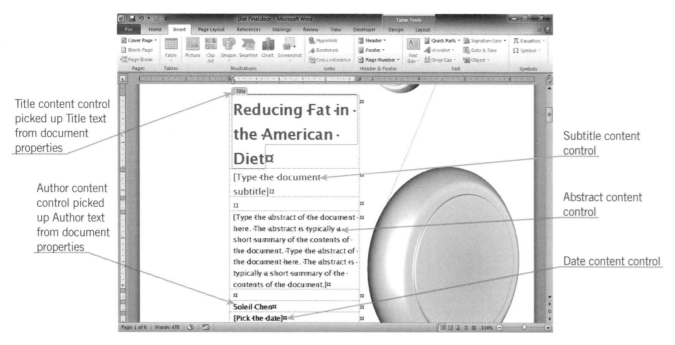

Title content control picked up Title text from document properties

Author content control picked up Author text from document properties

Subtitle content control

Abstract content control

Date content control

FIGURE 7–11   Mod cover page with information from document properties

Step-by-Step 7.5

1. On the Ribbon, click the **Insert** tab. In the Pages group, click the **Cover Page** button. In the gallery, scroll down until you see Mod, and then click **Mod**. A cover page is inserted at the beginning of the document.

2. Scroll up to see the title tab on the content control containing *Reducing Fat in the American Diet*. The word *Title* in the title tab identifies this as a content control that picked up the title from the document properties.

3. Click anywhere on your name. The word *Author* identifies this as a content control that picked up the author from the document properties.

4. Click the placeholder that says *Type the document subtitle*. Click the **Subtitle** title tab. The title tab darkens. Press **Delete**. The content control is deleted.

5. Delete the content control that contains the placeholder text *Type the abstract... .*

6. Scroll down to the bottom of the cover page, and then click the placeholder that says *Pick the date*. The Date title tab appears, and an arrow appears to the right of the control.

7. Click the **arrow**. A calendar appears displaying the current month and year with today's date in a red box. See **Figure 7–12**.

FIGURE 7–12
Selecting a date with a Date content control

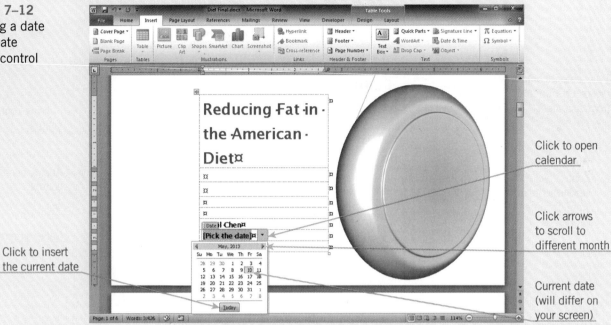

Click to open calendar

Click arrows to scroll to different month

Click to insert the current date

Current date (will differ on your screen)

8. Click tomorrow's date in the calendar. Tomorrow's date appears in the document. (If you need to scroll to the next month, click the arrow to the right of the month name.)

9. Scroll down, if necessary, so that you can see the text and the page break on page 2. You don't need the temporary cover page any more.

10. On page 2, select **American Diet**, the paragraph mark at the end of the line, the Page Break formatting mark, and the paragraph mark at the end of the line. Press **Delete**. The text on the page and the page break are deleted, removing the entire page from the document. The first page in the document is numbered page 1 instead of page 2. This is because, like the cover of a book, the cover page is not included in the page count.

11. Save your changes and leave the document open for the next Step-by-Step.

Creating New Sections

You can divide a document into two or more sections. A **section** is a part of a document where you can create a different layout from the rest of the document. For example, you might want to format only part of a page with columns, as you did in Lesson 6. You can also have different headers and footers, page numbers, margins, orientation, and other formatting features in different sections.

To create a new section, click the Page Layout tab, and then in the Page Setup group, click the Breaks button. A menu of choices for inserting breaks appears, as shown in **Figure 7–13**. The bottom half of the menu lists types of section breaks. To start the new section on the next page, choose Next Page. To start the new section on the same page, choose Continuous. To start the new section break on the next even-numbered or odd-numbered page, choose Even Page or Odd Page.

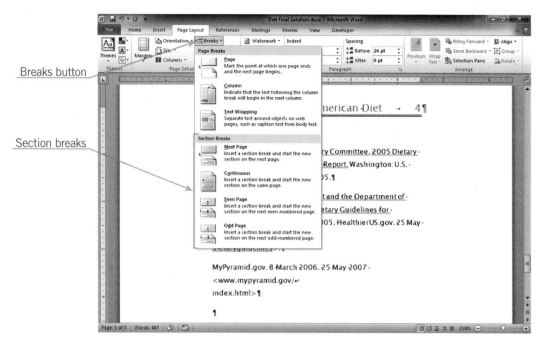

FIGURE 7–13   Breaks menu

When formatting marks are displayed, a section break is indicated by a double dotted line across the page with the words *Section Break* in the middle, as shown in **Figure 7–14**. To delete a section break, select the section break line, and then press Delete or Backspace.

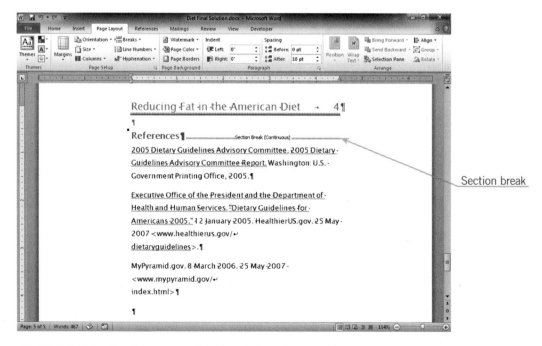

FIGURE 7–14   Continuous section break in a document

Step-by-Step 7.6

1. Go to the last page in the document. Position the insertion point in front of *2005 Dietary Guidelines Advisory Committee* in the first reference.

2. On the Ribbon, click the **Page Layout** tab. In the Page Setup group, click the **Breaks** button. Under Section Breaks, click **Continuous**. Because formatting marks are displayed, you can see that a continuous section break was inserted.

3. In the Page Setup group, click the **Columns** button, and then click **Two**. The current section is formatted in two columns. If the section break were not there, the entire document would have been formatted in two columns. You want to force the third reference to move to the top of the second column.

4. Position the insertion point in front of the third reference, *MyPyramid.gov*. In the Page Setup group, click the **Breaks** button, and then under Page Breaks, click **Column**. A column break is inserted below the last line in the *Executive Office of the President* reference.

5. Save your changes and leave the document open for the next Step-by-Step.

EXTRA FOR EXPERTS

Turn on the Mini Translator by clicking the Translate button in the Language group on the Review tab, and then clicking Mini Translator. Select the language to translate to by clicking the Translate button, and then clicking Choose Translation language.

Using the Research Tool

Word provides online access to a dictionary, thesaurus, and other resources to help you research information. You need an Internet connection for all research resources except the dictionary, thesaurus, and some features of the translation tool. To use the Research tool, click the Review tab on the Ribbon. In the Proofing group, click the Research button. The Research task pane opens to the right of the document window. Type a word or phrase that describes the topic to be researched in the Search for box, and then click the arrow in the box below the Search for box to select the reference that you want to use. The search executes and the results appear in the task pane. See **Figure 7–15**. If the reference you want to use already appears in the Search for box, you can click the Start searching button to execute the search.

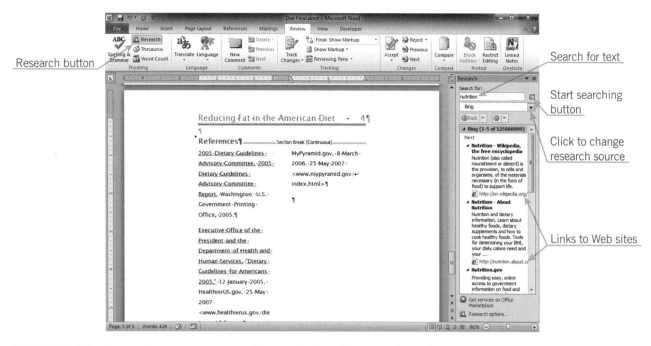

Research button

Search for text

Start searching button

Click to change research source

Links to Web sites

FIGURE 7-15   Research task pane open with results from Bing search engine

Step-by-Step 7.7

1. On the Ribbon, click the **Review** tab. In the Proofing group, click the **Research** button. The Research task pane opens to the right of the document window.

2. In the Research task pane, select all the text in the Search for box if there is any, or simply click in the Search for box if it is empty. Type **nutrition**.

3. Click the **arrow** next to the box below the Search for box. Click **Bing**. If the search doesn't start, click the Start searching button . The search starts and, after a moment, results appear in the task pane. This is a shortcut to using the Bing search engine in a browser. (*Note*: If you are not connected to the Internet, you will not get any results. Read the rest of the steps in this section and only complete Steps 7 through 10.)

4. Scroll down and look for the result *Nutrition.gov*. Click the link at the bottom of that result. Your browser starts, and the Nutrition.gov home page appears in the browser window. (If you don't see your browser window, look on the taskbar. The taskbar button for your browser should be blinking or appear orange. Click the browser taskbar button. If more than one button for your browser appears on the taskbar, click the orange button.)

5. Look in the Address bar at the top of the browser window. The address is very long, but to send someone to this home page, all you need is the part that starts with *www* and ends with *.gov*.—www.nutrition.gov.

> **TIP**
>
> If you need to translate a word or phrase, select Translation in the All Reference Books list.

6. In the upper-right corner of the browser window, click the **Close** button . The browser window closes, and the Diet Final document appears again. (If another browser window is open, click its Close button.)

7. In the document, go to page 2 (numbered page 1 in the header). In the paragraph under the *Fat in the American Diet* heading, position the insertion point at the end of the last sentence between the period and the paragraph mark. Press **spacebar**.

8. Type **For more information, go to www.nutrition.gov.**

9. In the Research task pane title bar, click the **Close** button ☒.

10. Save your changes and leave the document open for the next Step-by-Step.

Creating Tables

A *table* is an arrangement of text or numbers in rows and columns, similar to a spreadsheet. Tables are useful for organizing information. The intersection of a row and column is called a *cell*. Tables are sometimes easier to use than trying to align text with tabs.

Inserting a Table

To create a table, click the Insert tab, and then, in the Tables group, click the Table button. A menu opens with a grid in the top portion. As you move the pointer over the grid, the outline of the cells in the grid changes to orange, and the label at the top of the menu indicates the dimensions of the table. As you drag, the table appears in the document behind the grid. See **Figure 7–16**. Click when the grid and the label indicate the number of rows and columns you want to create. A table is inserted at the location of the insertion point. To enter text in a table, click in a cell, and then type. To move to the next cell to the right, press Tab or click in the cell. To move back one cell, press Shift+Tab.

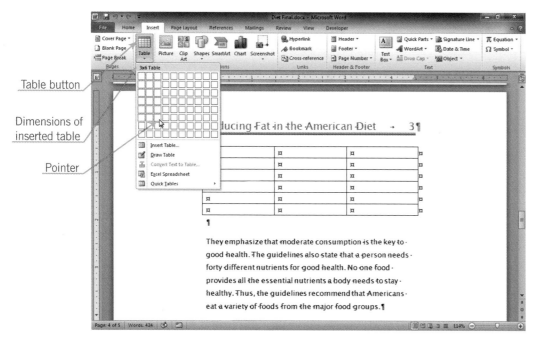

FIGURE 7–16   Inserting a table

Step-by-Step 7.8

1. Go to page 4 in the document (numbered page 3 in the header). Position the insertion point in the empty paragraph at the top of the page, above the paragraph that starts *They emphasize that.*

2. On the Ribbon, click the **Insert** tab. In the Tables group, click the **Table** button. A menu opens with a grid at the top of it. Insert Table appears above the top of the grid.

3. Without clicking the mouse button, drag the pointer over the grid. As you drag, the boxes in the grid change from black to orange outlines, and the text above the grid changes to the number of columns and rows you have selected.

4. Point to the cell that creates a **3×6 Table**, and then click. The menu closes and a table with three columns and six rows is inserted in the document. The insertion point is blinking in the first cell in the table.

5. Type **Food Groups**. The text you type appears in the first cell in the table. Press **Tab**. The insertion point moves to the next cell to the right.

6. Type **Daily Recommendations**, and then press **Tab** twice. The insertion point moves to the second cell in the first column.

7. Type the rest of the data in the table as shown in **Figure 7–17**. Leave the third column blank.

FIGURE 7–17
Data in table

Food Groups¤	Daily · Recommendations¤	¤	¤
Grains¤	3 oz whole grains¤	¤	¤
Vegetables¤	2 to 3 cups¤	¤	¤
Fruits¤	1–1/2 to 2 cups¤	¤	¤
Oils¤	5 to 7 teaspoons¤	¤	¤
Milk¤	3 cups¤	¤	¤

8. Click in the last cell in the table. Press **Tab**. A new row is created at the bottom of the table.

9. Type **Meat & beans**. Press **Tab**. Type **5 to 6-1/2 oz**.

10. Save your changes and leave the document open for the next Step-by-Step.

Modifying the Table Structure

You can modify the structure of a table by using commands on the Table Tools Layout tab on the Ribbon. To insert a row, click a cell in the table, and then in the Rows & Columns group, click the Insert Above or Insert Below button, depending on where you want the row to appear in relation to the insertion point. To insert a column, click the Insert Left or Insert Right button. To delete a row or column, position the insertion point in the row or column you want to delete. In the Rows & Columns group, click the Delete button, and then click the appropriate command to delete cells, columns, rows, or the entire table.

You can change the width of columns and the height of rows. Position the pointer on top of a gridline in the table so that it changes to a double-headed arrow. Drag the border line to resize the column or the row.

You can split cells to transform one column or row into two or more. You can merge cells to create one large cell out of several small cells. To merge cells, select the cells, and then click the Merge Cells button in the Merge group on the Table Tools Layout tab. To split cells, select a cell or cells, and then click the Split Cells button to open the Split Cells dialog box. Specify the number of columns and rows you want to create from the selected cell or cells, and then click OK. If the result is not what you expected, undo your change, open the Split Cells dialog box again, and then click the Merge cells before split check box.

Step-by-Step 7.9

1. Position the insertion point in any cell in the last column of the table. On the Ribbon, click the **Table Tools Layout** tab, if necessary. In the Rows & Columns group, click the **Delete** button. Click **Delete Columns**. The current column is deleted.

2. Position the insertion point in any cell in the first row of the table. In the Rows & Columns group, click the **Insert Above** button. A new row is inserted above the row containing the insertion point.

3. Click in the first cell in the new row. Type **USDA Food Pyramid Guidelines**.

4. Position the pointer over the column divider between the two columns. The pointer changes to a double-headed arrow ⁺‖⁺. Press and hold the mouse button, and then drag the column divider to the left until the left column is approximately 1¼ inches wide.

5. Drag the right border of the table to the right until the right column is approximately two inches wide and Daily Recommendations fits on one line in the cell.

6. Drag to select the two cells in the top row. On the Layout tab, in the Merge group, click the **Merge Cells** button. The two cells are merged into one cell. See **Figure 7–18**.

> **TIP**
>
> To select an entire row, click to the left of the row (outside the table). To select an entire column, position your pointer just above the column so that the pointer changes to a downward-pointing arrow, and then click.

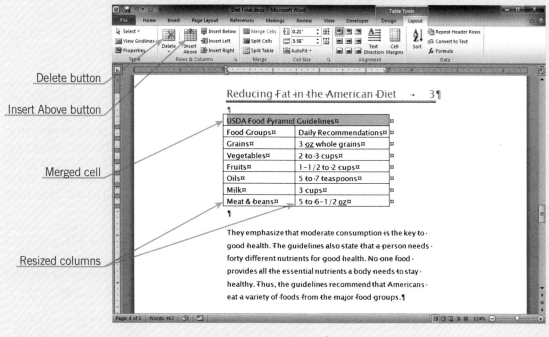

FIGURE 7–18
Modified table

7. Save your changes and leave the document open for the next Step-by-Step.

Formatting Tables

The easiest way to format a table is to use one of the many predesigned formats in the Table Styles group on the Table Tools Design tab. See **Figure 7–19**. If you want to treat the first and last rows or the first and last columns differently from the rest of the rows and columns in the table, you can select the Header Row, Total Row, First Column, and Last Column check boxes in the Table Style Options group on the Table Tools Design tab. To add shading to every other row or every other column, select the Banded Rows or Banded Columns check boxes in the same group.

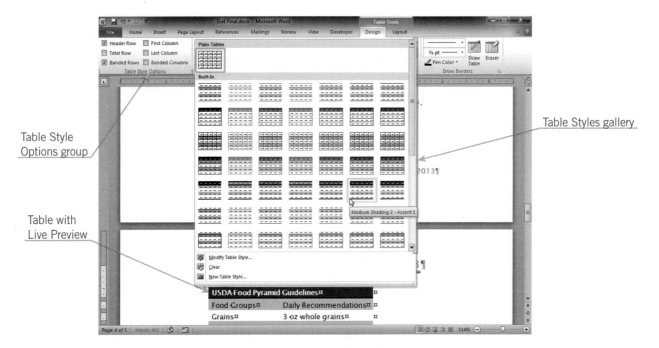

FIGURE 7–19   Live Preview of a table style

TIP

You can quickly access table commands for working with tables by right-clicking anywhere on the table to open a shortcut menu.

▶ **VOCABULARY**
gridline

You can manually format text in a table as you would format any text in a document. You can select the entire table by positioning the pointer on top of the table and then clicking the table move handle that appears above the upper-left corner of the table. Then you can position the table on the page by clicking an alignment button in the Paragraph group on the Home tab. You can also change the color of the table lines and the fill color of the cells by using the Shading and Borders buttons in the Table Styles group on the Table Tools Design tab. To change the alignment of text in a cell, click one of the alignment buttons in the Alignment group on the Table Tools Layout tab.

When you add color to borders, you need to make sure you are trying to format border lines, not table gridlines. Border lines are visible lines that print when you print your document. When a table is created, the *gridlines* form the structure of the table, the outline of the rows and columns. To make sure the table prints the way you expect, turn off the gridlines by checking the Gridlines button on the View tab.

Step-by-Step 7.10

1. Click anywhere in the table. On the Ribbon, click the **Table Tools Design** tab. In the Table Style Options group, notice that the Header Row, First Column, and Banded Rows check boxes are selected.

2. On the Design tab, in the Table Styles group, click the **More** button, and then in the gallery, click the **Medium Shading 2 – Accent 5** style (fifth row, second to last column under Built-In). The gallery closes and the table is reformatted with that style.

3. In the Table Style Options group, click the **First Column** check box to deselect it. The shading and bold formatting is removed from the first column.

4. Click in the first row of the table. On the Ribbon, click the **Table Tools Layout** tab. In the Alignment group, click the **Align Center** button ▤. The text in the top row is centered in the cell.

5. Select all the text in the second row of the table. On the Ribbon, click the **Home** tab. In the Font group, click the **Bold** button **B**. The text in the second row is bold, and *Daily Recommendations* might wrap to two lines.

6. If *Daily Recommendations* is now on two lines, click in the table to position the insertion point without selecting any text. Drag the right border of the table to the right just enough so that *Daily Recommendations* fits on one line again.

7. Position the pointer over the table. The table move handle ⊞ appears above the upper-left corner of the table. Position the pointer over the table move handle ⊞ so that the pointer changes to a four-headed arrow ✛, and then click the **table move handle** ⊞. The entire table is selected.

8. On the Home tab, in the Paragraph group, click the **Center** button ▤. The table is centered on the page. Click anywhere in the table to deselect it and keep the table active.

TIP

You can double-click the right border of a column to automatically resize the column to accommodate the width of the longest entry in the column.

TIP

Using the table move handle, you can drag a table anywhere in a document.

9. On the Ribbon, click the **Table Tools Layout** tab. In the Table group, locate the View Gridlines button and determine if it is selected. If it is selected, it will be orange. See **Figure 7–20**. If it is selected, you will see a dotted gridline between the two columns in the table.

FIGURE 7–20
Formatted table with gridlines visible

View Gridlines button (selected)

Gridline

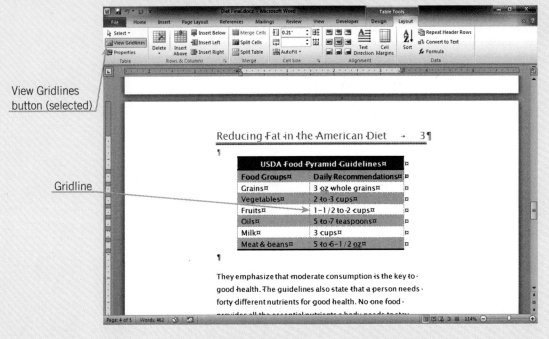

10. If the View Gridlines button is selected, click the **View Gridlines** button to deselect it. The dotted gridline between the two columns in the table disappears.

11. Drag to select all the rows in the table except the first row. On the Ribbon, click the **Table Tools Design** tab. In the Table Styles group, click the **arrow** next to the Borders button. Click **Inside Vertical Border**. A vertical line appears between the first and second columns in the table.

12. Save your changes and leave the document open for the next Step-by-Step.

Converting Text into Tables

You can convert text you have already typed into a table. Select the text you want to convert to a table. On the Insert tab on the Ribbon, click the Table button in the Tables group, and then click Convert Text to Table on the menu. The Convert Text to Table dialog box opens. Word converts the text to a table by creating columns from text separated by a comma or a tab, and by creating rows from text separated by a paragraph marker.

Sorting Text

Sorting arranges a list of words in ascending order (*a* to *z*) or in descending order (*z* to *a*). Sorting can also arrange a list of numbers in ascending order (smallest to largest) or descending order (largest to smallest). Sorting is useful for putting lists of names or terms in alphabetical order.

To sort text in a table, click anywhere in the table, click the Table Tools Layout tab, and then in the Data group, click the Sort button. The Sort dialog box opens, as shown in **Figure 7–21**. In this dialog box, you can choose the options for the sort.

▶ **VOCABULARY**

sort

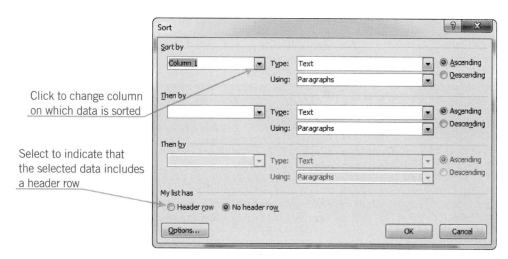

Click to change column on which data is sorted

Select to indicate that the selected data includes a header row

FIGURE 7–21   Sort dialog box

EXTRA FOR EXPERTS

If the table contains numbers, click the Type arrow in the Sort dialog box, and then click Number to sort the table numerically. Otherwise, it will sort the data using the first digit only, so that 10 would come before 2.

Step-by-Step 7.11

1. If necessary, drag to select all the rows in the table except the first row with USDA Food Pyramid Guidelines, and then click the **Table Tools Layout** tab.

2. In the Data group, click the **Sort** button. The Sort dialog box opens.

3. Make sure **Column 1** appears in the Sort by box. Make sure that the **Ascending** option button at the top of the dialog box is selected. The table will be sorted in alphabetical order by the values in the first column.

TIP

You can also sort a list that is not organized in a table. Select the list, and then, in the Paragraph group on the Home tab, click the Sort button.

WARNING

If a thick border line appears in the middle of the table, reapply the Medium Shading 2 – Accent 5 table style, add the vertical border between rows 2 through 8, and then center the table horizontally.

4. At the bottom of the dialog box, click the **Header row** option button. This will exclude the first row of the selected rows from being included in the sort.

5. Click **OK**. The dialog box closes and the data in the table is sorted in alphabetical order by the data in the first column.

6. Deselect the table. Turn off the rulers and hide formatting marks.

7. Save, print, and then close the document.

SUMMARY

In this lesson, you learned:

- Word automatically inserts page breaks where they are necessary. You also can insert page breaks manually.

- Content controls are special placeholders designed to contain a specific type of text. When you insert text, some content controls remain in the document and some are deleted.

- Headers appear at the top of every page in the document; footers appear at the bottom of every page. The Header & Footer Tools Design tab appears when a header or footer is active.

- You can insert page numbers in the header or footer area. The page number style can replace a header or footer, or you can use the Current Position command to insert a page number at the location of the insertion point.

- You can modify file properties in Backstage view. Some types of content controls are linked to document properties.

- You can insert a predesigned cover page with content controls by clicking the Cover Page button in the Pages group on the Insert tab.

- To create different page layouts within one document, divide the document into sections.

- The Research tool allows you to access the Internet to explore different sources for information.

- Tables show data in columns and rows. You can modify tables by adding and removing rows and columns and merging and splitting cells. You can format a table with styles as well as use manual formatting. You can convert text into a table with the Convert Text to Table command.

- You can sort text in a document alphabetically or numerically in ascending or descending order.

VOCABULARY REVIEW

Define the following terms:

cell	header	section
content control	orphan	sort
footer	page break	table
gridline	property	widow

REVIEW QUESTIONS

MULTIPLE CHOICE

Select the best response for the following statements.

1. When formatting marks are displayed, a manual page break is indicated in the document by a:

   A.   series of dashes.

   B.   thick horizontal line.

   C.   dotted line with the words Page Break in the middle of the line.

   D.   row of paragraph marks with the words Page Break in the middle of the line.

2. To modify the document properties, you need to display the:

   A.   Summary dialog box.

   B.   Backstage view.

   C.   Properties task pane.

   D.   Document dialog box.

3. A part of a document that is formatted with a different page layout than the rest of the document is called a(n):

   A.   auto-orientation.

   B.   table.

   C.   section.

   D.   manual break.

4. To find information on the Web using a variety of sources, what button do you click in the Proofing group on the Review tab?

   A.   Proof

   B.   Encyclopedia

   C.   Research

   D.   Web

5. What is the intersection of a row and column in a table called?

   A.   box

   B.   cell

   C.   grid

   D.   content control

FILL IN THE BLANK

Complete the following sentences by writing the correct word or words in the blanks provided.

1. Text that is printed at the top of each page is called a(n) _____ .

2. Document or file _____ are identifying information about the file, such as the author's name and the date the file was created, that is saved along with the file.

3. To combine two or more cells into one, use the _____ command.

4. If a list of words is sorted alphabetically, it is listed in _____ order.

5. _____ form the structure of a table.

TRUE / FALSE

Circle T if the statement is true or F if the statement is false.

T   F   **1.**   The place where one page ends and another begins is called section break.

T   F   **2.**   Content controls are special placeholders designed to contain a specific type of information, such as a date or the page number.

T   F   **3.**   The only place you can insert page numbers in a document is in the header.

T   F   **4.**   Some content controls are linked to specific document properties.

T   F   **5.**   When you insert a section break, the text after the section break always appears on the same page as the section break.

◼ PROJECTS

If you have a SAM 2010 user profile, your instructor may have assigned an autogradable version of the indicated project. If so, log into the SAM 2010 Web site at *www.cengage.com/sam2010* to download the instruction and start files.

PROJECT 7–1

1. Open the **Guidelines.docx** Data File from the drive and folder where you store your Data Files. Save the document as **Correspondence Guidelines** followed by your initials.

2. Create a header using the Annual style. Type **Guidelines** in the Title content control, and use the Date content control to insert the current year. (*Hint:* Just click the Today button.)

3. Insert the Stacks footer. Do not replace the placeholder text.

4. Do not display the header or footer on the first page of the document.

5. Open the Info tab in Backstage view. Add your name as the author, and then delete the current author. Add your school as the Company name. Change the title to **Guidelines for Correspondence**. Close Backstage view and verify that the Title property is displayed in the header and that the Company name property is displayed in the footer.

6. Position the insertion point to the right of the content control in the footer, and then press Tab. Insert the Accent Bar 2 page number style at the current position.

7. On page 1, insert a page break before the *Check Spelling* heading.

8. Select the words *commonly misspelled words* in the *Check Spelling* section. Open the Research pane to find other lists of commonly misspelled words. Change the source for the research to Bing.

9. If you are connected to the Internet, open the Web page associated with one of the search results. Click in the Address bar at the top of the window to select the entire Web address. Right-click the selected address, and then click Copy on the shortcut menu. Close the browser window. Position the insertion point before the period at the end of the second sentence in the paragraph under the *Check Spelling* heading. Press the spacebar, type (and then paste the contents of the Clipboard which contains the Web site address. Type) and then close the Research task pane. (If you do not have access to the Internet, skip this step.)

10. Add the following words to the list of misspelled words: **laboratory**, **beginning**, **maintenance**, **cooperate**, and **friend**. Use the Sort button in the Paragraph group on the Home tab to sort the list in ascending order.

11. Insert a continuous section break before the spelling list. Format the second section (the one containing the spelling list) in three columns. Insert another continuous section break after the spelling list, and then format the last section of the document in one column.

12. Save, print, and close the document.

PROJECT 7–2

1. Open the **References.docx** Data File from the drive and folder where you store your Data Files. Save it as **References Formatted** followed by your initials.

2. Convert the text in the document into a table with two columns.

3. Use the Merge cells command to merge each cell containing a person's name with the two cells below it. Merge the three cells containing each address into one cell.

4. Enter the last row of information as shown in the table in **Figure 7–22**—the row containing *Wayne Parks*. Don't be concerned with the formatting yet.

References	
Dr. John Dugan, Chairperson	State University Department of Computer Science Santa Fe, NM 87501
Selma Hernandez, President	Sierra Computer Consultants 1734 Water Street Santa Fe, NM 87505
Wayne Parks	Parks Electronics 8755 Arbor, Suite A Santa Fe, NM 87509

FIGURE 7–22

5. Format the table as shown in Figure 7–22. The table style is Medium Grid 3 – Accent 2. The text in the first row is 14 points. Notice that the names of the references in the first column are in bold, but the titles of the references are not. This means the first column is not formatted differently from the rest of the table; you need to format the names and titles manually. Also note that the first row is just tall enough to fit the text.

6. Resize the columns to the widths shown in Figure 7–22.

7. Change the name *Wayne Parks* to your name. Save your changes, and then print (but do not close) the document.

8. Select the entire table. On the Design tab, use the Shading and Borders buttons to remove the shading and the borders. The text in the first row is formatted in white, so it looks like there's nothing there. Change the color of the text in the first row to black. Save the revised document as **References Unformatted** followed by your initials.

9. Delete the first row in the document. If the new first row was reformatted as white text, select it, and then change the color of the text in the new first row to black. If necessary, correct the bold formatting in the first row.

10. Insert any style cover page you want. Use the content controls on the cover page or use the Info tab in Backstage view to insert **References** as the Title property and your name as the Author. (Make sure you delete any other author names.) If the cover page includes a Date content control, insert the current date. Delete all other content controls in the cover page.

11. Save, print, and close the document.

PROJECT 7–3

1. Open the **Sales.docx** Data File from the drive and folder where you store your Data Files. Save the document as **Sales Leaders** followed by your initials.

2. Insert a new row at the top of the table. Type the following headings: **Name,** (skip the second column), **Region, Manager**, and **Year–to-Date Sales**.

3. Merge the cell containing *Name* and the cell to its right. Merge each of the cells containing first and last names so that each person's name appears in one cell. Remove the paragraph mark after each first name, and then insert a space between the first and last names.

4. Widen the fourth column so that *Year-to-Date Sales* fits on one line.

5. Format the table with the Colorful List - Accent 6 style. Add special formatting for the header row, and use banded columns.

6. Sort the table by year-to-date sales in descending order.

7. Center the table horizontally. Center the column headings and everything in the last column.

8. In the memo header, replace *All Employees* in the To line with your name.

9. Save, print, and close the document.

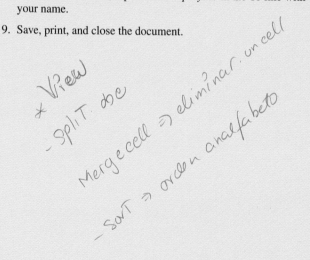

CRITICAL THINKING

ACTIVITY 7–1

Using a table without borders, create your own list of references for your personal portfolio for employment.

ACTIVITY 7–3

You own a small company that sells used CDs and DVDs. To increase sales, you decide to develop a presence on the Web. To do this, you need to register a Web site address with a domain name registrar. Most registrars also offer to host your Web site, which means they store all the files that make up your Web site on a computer so that anyone using the Web can access your site.

Use the Internet to locate at least three registrars. (Try going to **www.internic.net** to find a list of registrars.)

Create a table in Word to compare the data you find on the Internet regarding each registrar company's services provided, cost per month (per service, if available), and any convenience factors such as setup or installation requirements, fees, and customer service. Which company or companies offer the best package or services for your company?

After you have determined which registrar would be able to best serve your needs, think of a possible Web site address for your company, and then use the registrar's search function to see if that Web site address is available. If the Web site address you want to register is already taken with *.com* as the top-level domain (the last three or four letters of a Web site address), try other top-level domains such as *.biz, .net*, or *.name*.

ACTIVITY 7–2

Use Help to learn how to insert a formula to add a column of numbers in a table. Use a formula to add the Year-to-Date Sales column in the Sales Leaders.docx document that you worked on in Project 7–3.

LESSON 8

Increasing Efficiency Using Word

■ OBJECTIVES

Upon completion of this lesson, you should be able to:

- Use and create templates.
- Use mail merge.
- Create and print envelopes and labels.
- Insert, view, edit, and print comments.
- Track changes.
- Accept and reject changes and delete comments.
- Combine different versions of a document.
- Customize Word.

■ VOCABULARY

data source

mail merge

main document

merge field

template

Track Changes

workgroup collaboration

Word provides many tools and customization that you can use to increase your efficiency when using the program. For example, you can create and use templates to help you create consistent looking documents that contain the correct information. You can merge a list of addresses with a form letter to create personalized form letters. You can also ask other people to review your documents and make changes and suggestions using features that display the changes as colored text and the suggestions in balloons. Finally, you can customize many options in Word to take advantage of the way you work.

Using Templates

Suppose you are a sales representative, and you must file a report each week that summarizes your sales and the new contacts you have made. Parts of this report will be the same each week, such as the format and the headings. Re-creating the document each week would be time consuming. You can solve this problem by creating a template in Word or using an existing Word template for documents that you create frequently.

A ***template*** is a file that contains the basic elements of a document, such as page and paragraph formatting, fonts, and text. You can customize the template to create a new document that is similar to but slightly different from the original. For example, a report template for a sales representative would save all formatting, font choices, and text that does not change, allowing you to fill in only the new information each week.

▶ **VOCABULARY**
template

Using an Installed Template

Word contains many templates you can use to create documents. Some templates are installed on your computer, and others are available on the Microsoft Office Online Web site. To use an installed Word template, click the File tab, and then in the navigation bar, click New. In the Available Templates list, click Sample Templates. The middle pane in the dialog box changes to show all the templates installed on your computer. You can scroll down to see the various templates installed. See **Figure 8–1**.

Sample templates are the templates installed on this computer

Preview shows the selected template

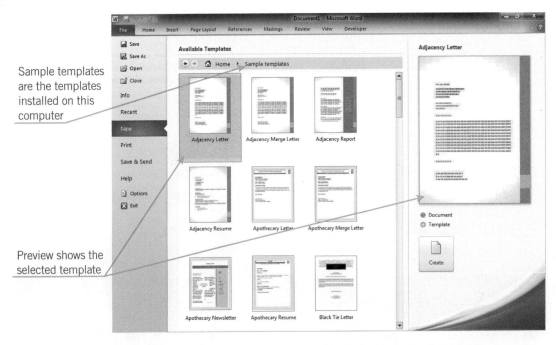

FIGURE 8–1   Sample templates on the New tab in Backstage view

To create a new document based on one of the templates, click it, and then in the right pane, click the Create button. Word opens a new blank document with the settings and text specified by the template already in place. As with any new document, the file name in the title bar is *Document* followed by a number. Replace the data in the template with your own data and save it.

> **TIP**
>
> To create a document based on a template from Office.com, click one of the categories under Office.com Templates in the center of the New tab, click a category folder as needed, select a template, and then click the Download button.

Step-by-Step 8.1

1. Start Word. On the Ribbon, click the **File** tab, and then in the navigation bar, click **New**. The New tab appears in Backstage view.

2. In the center under Available Templates, click **Sample templates**. The installed templates appear. Scroll down and then click the **Origin Fax** icon. The preview on the right shows the Origin Fax template.

3. In the right pane, make sure the **Document** option button is selected, and then click the **Create** button. The Origin Fax template appears on your screen as a new, unsaved document. Note that the title in the title bar is *Document* followed by a number, like all new documents.

> **WARNING**
>
> If the Template option button is selected, the file that you open will be a template file type, not a document file type.

4. On the Quick Access Toolbar, click the **Save** button 💾. Navigate to the drive and folder where you save your files. Replace the text in the File name box with **Bank Fax** followed by your initials, and then click **Save**.

5. At the top of the document, on the right, click **[Pick a date]**. This is a date content control. Click the **arrow** to the right of the content control. Click **Today**.

6. Next to *From*, if placeholder text appears in the content control, click **[Type the sender name]**, and then type your name. If a name already appears in that location, select the name, and then type your name.

7. Next to *Phone* under *From*, click the placeholder text **[Type the sender phone number]**, and then type **(914) 555-7534**.

8. Next to *Fax* under *From*, replace the placeholder text **[Type the sender fax number]** with **(914) 555-6409**, and replace the placeholder text **[Type the sender company name]** with **White Plains National Bank**.

9. To the right of *To*, replace **[Type the recipient name]** with **Wyatt Brown**.

10. In the *To* section, replace **[Type the recipient phone number]** with **(914) 555-6430**, replace **[Type the recipient fax number]** with **(914) 555-6432**, and then replace **[Type the recipient company name]** with **Graphic Designers**.

11. Under *Comments*, click **[Type comments]** and then type:

   I reviewed the first draft of the checking account pamphlet and added my comments to the draft. Please revise the pamphlet by next Thursday. Thank you.

12. Save your changes. Print and close the document, but do not exit Word.

Creating a Template

You can create a customized template by modifying an existing template or document. To create a template, you need to save the document as a template. Click the File tab, in the navigation bar, click Save As, click the Save as type arrow, and then click Word Template (*.dotx). Type a file name in the File name box, and then click Save. Your document will be saved as a template in the current folder.

Step-by-Step 8.2

1. Create a new, blank document.

2. Type the following:

   White Plains National Bank

   309 Third Street

   White Plains, NY 10610

   (9.14) 555-7534

   www.whiteplainsnationalbank.com

3. Press **Enter** twice. Type **<Replace with current date>**. Press **Enter** again.

4. Change the theme to **Grid**. Change the style of the first five paragraphs to **No Spacing**, and then center those paragraphs.

5. Change the paragraph spacing of the *<Replace with current date>* paragraph so that it has 36 points of space before it and 10 points of space after it.

6. Right-click the Web site address at the top of the document, and then on the shortcut menu, click **Remove Hyperlink**.

7. Format the first line in the document as **14-point Copperplate Gothic Bold**. Change the font size of the rest of the lines in the header to **12 points**.

8. Position the insertion point in front of the word *White* in the first line of the header, and then search for clip art using the keyword **bank**. Insert a clip of a piggy bank. If you can't find that clip, use another appropriate clip. If you do not have access to Office.com, try the search using the keyword *money* instead, and use the clip with the dollar sign. Close the Clip Art task pane when you are finished.

9. Proportionately resize the image so that at least one side is one inch.

10. With the image still selected, on the Ribbon, click the **Picture Tools Format** tab, if necessary. In the Arrange group, click the **Position** button, and then click the first icon in the first row under With Text Wrapping. The image changes to a floating graphic and moves to the top-left corner of the document. Deselect the image. See **Figure 8–2**.

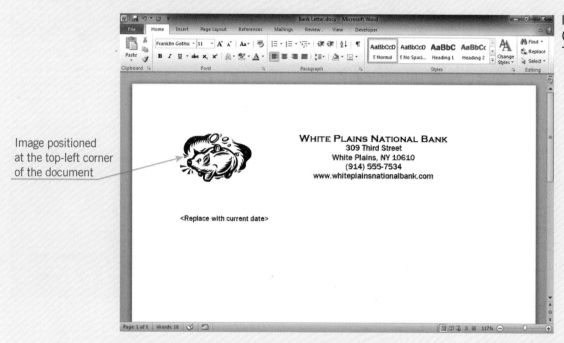

Image positioned at the top-left corner of the document

FIGURE 8–2
Completed Bank Template document

11. Add your name in the paragraph below the date placeholder.

12. Click the **File** tab, and then in the navigation bar, click **Save As**. In the Save As dialog box, click the **Save as type** arrow, and then click **Word Template (.dotx)**.

13. Select the text in the File name box, and then type **Bank Template** followed by your initials. Click **Save**.

14. Close the file, but do not exit Word.

EXTRA FOR EXPERTS

To store your templates so that others can easily locate them, in the Save As dialog box, click Templates in the navigation pane, and then save the template in that folder. To access these templates, in the New tab in Backstage view, click My templates, and then select the template in the New dialog box that opens.

Creating a Document Using a Custom Template

You can use the template you created as many times as needed. To create a new document based on your template, open the New tab in Backstage view. Under Available Templates, click New from existing. The New from Existing Document dialog box opens, as shown in **Figure 8–3**.

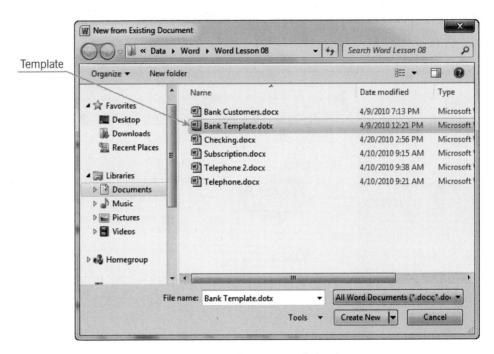

Template

FIGURE 8–3   New from Existing Document dialog box

The files shown in the dialog box are both template and document files. Click the template or document you want to use, and then click Create New. A new document opens with all the text and formatting from the template or document you selected. As with the new document you created from the installed template, the file name in the title bar is *Document* followed by a number. After you make changes to this document, you can save the document as you normally would.

Step-by-Step 8.3

1. Click the **File** tab, and then in the navigation bar, click **New**. The New tab appears in Backstage view. Under Available Templates, click **New from existing**. The New from Existing Document dialog box opens. Notice that the command button on the left in the lower-right corner of the dialog box is Open.

2. Locate the folder in which you saved the Bank Template file. Click **Bank Template.dotx**. The Open button changes to Create New. Click **Create New**. The template opens as a new document.

3. Save the document as **Bank Letter** followed by your initials.

4. Position the insertion point at the beginning of the line containing your name, and then press **Enter** to insert a blank paragraph between the *<Replace with current date>* line and your name.

5. Open the **Checking.docx** file from the drive and folder where your Data Files are stored. Select all the text in the document, and then copy it to the Clipboard. Close the Checking.docx document.

6. Select your name in the Bank Letter document. In the Clipboard group on the Home tab, click the **Paste** button.

7. On the right end of the status bar, click the number to the left of the Zoom slider to open the Zoom dialog box. In the Percent box, select the value, and then type **77**. Click **OK**. Scroll down so that you can see the entire letter on the screen. Your screen should match **Figure 8–4**.

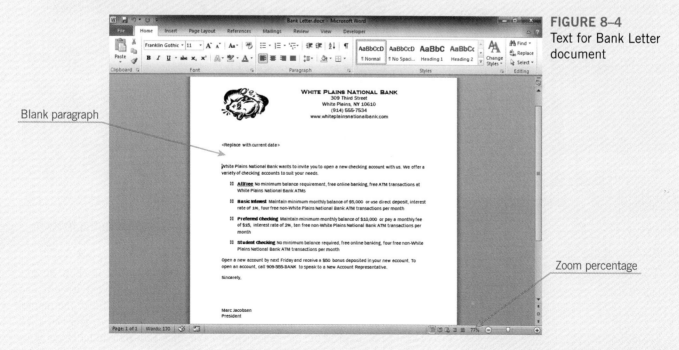

FIGURE 8–4
Text for Bank Letter document

Blank paragraph

Zoom percentage

8. On the Ribbon, click the **View** tab, and then in the Zoom group, click the **Page Width** button.

9. Save your changes, and leave the document open for the next Step-by-Step.

Using Mail Merge

▶ **VOCABULARY**

mail merge

main document

data source

merge fields

Mail merge combines a document with information that personalizes the document. For example, you might send a letter to each member of a professional organization. In each letter, the text is the same but the names of the recipients are different. For example, a letter may begin *Dear Mr. Montgomery* or *Dear Ms. Jansen*. The document with the information that does not change is called the ***main document***. The *data source* is the file containing the information that varies in each document.

To perform a mail merge, you use the commands on the Mailings tab on the Ribbon. You start by clicking the Start Mail Merge button in the Start Mail Merge group, and then clicking the type of mail merge you want to do. The most common type is a letter. The second step is to choose the data source by clicking the Select Recipients button in the Start Mail Merge group. Next, you need to insert merge fields. ***Merge fields*** are placeholders that are replaced with data from the data source when you perform the merge. See **Figure 8–5**.

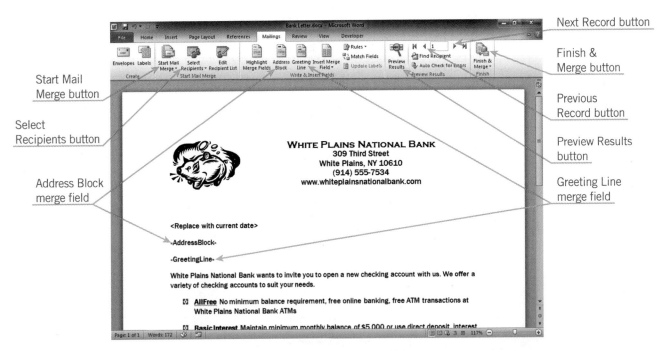

FIGURE 8–5   Merge fields inserted using the Mailings tab on the Ribbon

After you have inserted all the merge fields, you can click the Preview Results button in the Preview Results group. You can then click the Next Record and Previous Record buttons to scroll through the results preview. To finish the merge, click the Finish & Merge button in the Finish group. On the menu, you can click Print Documents to print the merged documents or click Edit Individual Documents to create a new document consisting of all the merged documents.

Step-by-Step 8.4

1. Open the **Bank Customers.docx** file from the drive and folder where your Data Files are stored. This file contains a table with a list of names and addresses. This is the data source for the merge. Notice that each person's title, first name, and last name are in separate columns. Close this file.

2. On the Ribbon, click the **Mailings** tab. In the Start Mail Merge group, click the **Start Mail Merge** button. Click **Letters**. The current document is identified as a letter you will merge with a data source. Notice that none of the buttons in the Write & Insert Fields, Preview Results, or Finish groups are available.

3. In the Start Mail Merge group, click the **Select Recipients** button. Click **Use Existing List**. The Select Data Source dialog box opens. This dialog box is similar to the Open dialog box.

4. Navigate to the drive and folder where you store your Data Files. Click **Bank Customers.docx**, and then click **Open**. Now the rest of the buttons on the Mailings tab are available.

5. Position the insertion point in the blank paragraph below the date placeholder text. First, you need to insert the Address Block merge field, which will be replaced with the inside address in the letter. In the Write & Insert Fields group, click the **Address Block** button. The Insert Address Block dialog box opens.

6. If necessary, in the list on the left, scroll down and then click the **Mr. Joshua Randall Jr.** name format, as shown in **Figure 8–6**.

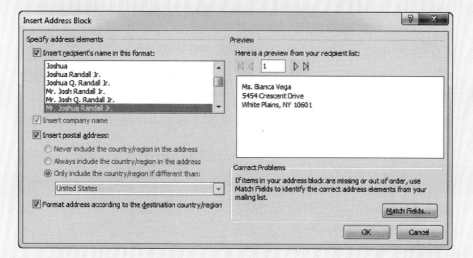

FIGURE 8–6
Insert Address Block dialog box

FIGURE 8–7
Insert Greeting Line dialog box

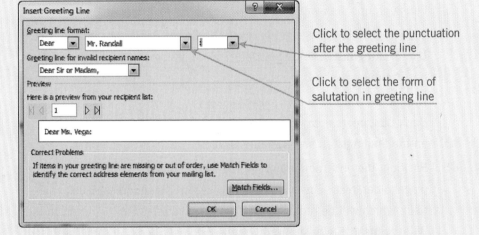

Click to select the punctuation after the greeting line

Click to select the form of salutation in greeting line

7. Click **OK**. The Address Block merge field is inserted in the document.

8. Press **Enter**. In the Write & Insert Fields group, click the **Greeting Line** button. The Insert Greeting Line dialog box opens.

9. If necessary, click the **arrow** next to the middle box in the row under Greeting line format, and then click **Mr. Randall** in the list. Click the **arrow** next to the comma (next to the rightmost box), and then click **:** (the colon). See **Figure 8–7**.

10. Click **OK**. The Greeting Line merge field is inserted in the document.

11. On the Mailings tab, in the Preview Results group, click the **Preview Results** button. The merge fields in the document are replaced with data in the first row in your data source (Bianca Vega's information). Notice that each line in the inside address has extra space after it. This is not normal formatting for the inside address.

12. In the Preview Results group, click the **Preview Results** button. The preview turns off and you see the merge fields again.

13. Click anywhere in the line containing the Address Block merge field, and then change the style to **No Spacing**. The blank line below the Address Block merge field disappears. Position the insertion point at the end of the Address Block line, and then press **Enter**. This inserts a single blank line (a paragraph formatted with the No Spacing style) between the last line of the inside address and the salutation.

14. On the Ribbon, click the **Mailings** tab, and then, in the Preview Results group, click the **Preview Results** button. Bianca Vega's information appears in the letter properly formatted. In the Preview Results group, to the right of the number 1, click the **Next Record** button ▶. The data from the recipient in the second row in the table in the data source (George Corrigan) appears in the document.

15. Replace the date placeholder text with the current date in the form June 27, 2013.

16. On the Ribbon, click the **Mailings** tab. In the Finish group, click the **Finish & Merge** button, and then click **Print Documents**. The Merge to Printer dialog box opens, in which you can specify the records you want to print. Click the **Current record** option button. This tells Word to print only the current letter (the letter addressed to George Corrigan) rather than all three letters. Click **OK**. The Print dialog box opens.

17. Click **OK**. The Print dialog box closes and the current letter prints.

18. In the Preview Results group, click the **Preview Results** button to display the merge fields again. In the Finish group, click the **Finish & Merge** button, and then click **Edit Individual Documents**. The Merge to New Document dialog box opens. Click the **All** option button, if necessary, and then click **OK**. A new document opens with the temporary name "Letters" followed by a number. This document contains one letter for each of the recipients listed in the data source.

19. Save the document as **Bank New Customer Letters** followed by your initials. Close the document. Close the Bank Letter document, and when the dialog box opens asking if you want to save changes, click **Don't Save**. Do not exit Word.

EXTRA FOR EXPERTS

You can insert customized information in the body of the letter. Add the data to the data source, and then use the Insert Merge Field button on the Mailings tab to insert the custom data.

Creating and Printing Envelopes

Addressing envelopes is easy using Word. Click the Mailings tab on the Ribbon. In the Create group, click the Envelopes button to open the Envelopes and Labels dialog box with the Envelopes tab on top, as shown in **Figure 8–8**.

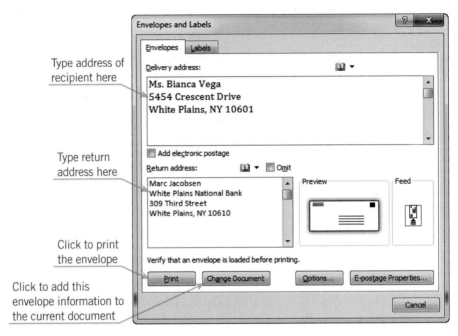

FIGURE 8–8   Envelopes tab in the Envelopes and Labels dialog box

If you select an address (such as the inside address in a letter) before you open the dialog box, the address appears in the Delivery address box in the dialog box, although you can replace the text in the address box with any address you like. If there is any text in the Return address box, select it, and then type your own name and address. To print the envelope, insert an envelope in your printer, and then click Print. To see the envelope layout before you print, click Add to Document. The envelope appears at the top of the current document, as shown in **Figure 8–9**. Then you can print the envelope as you would any document.

Envelopes button

Your name appears here

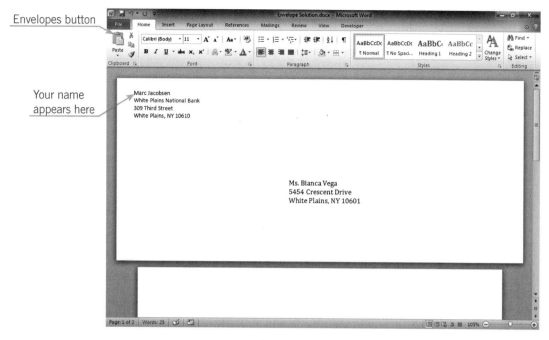

FIGURE 8–9   Completed envelope

Step-by-Step 8.5

1. Create a new, blank Word document.

2. On the Ribbon, click the **Mailings** tab. In the Create group, click the **Envelopes** button. The Envelopes and Labels dialog box opens with the Envelopes tab on top.

3. In the Delivery address box, type the following:

   Ms. Bianca Vega

   5454 Crescent Drive

   White Plains, NY 10601

4. Click in the **Return address** box, type your name, and then type the following address:

   White Plains National Bank

   309 Third Street

   White Plains, NY 10610

> **TIP**
>
> You can also perform a mail merge with a data source to print envelopes and labels. In the Start Mail Merge group on the Mailings tab, click the Start Mail Merge button, and then click Envelopes or Labels.

> **EXTRA FOR EXPERTS**
>
> To change the envelope size from the standard business-sized envelope, click Options on the Envelopes tab in the Envelopes and Labels dialog box.

5. Click **Add to Document**. A dialog box opens asking if you want to save the return address as the default return address. Click **No**. The dialog box closes and the setup of the document is changed to an envelope with the addresses you typed in the correct locations.

6. If you have an envelope, insert it into the printer; otherwise you can print on plain paper. Print the document.

7. Save the document as **Envelope** followed by your initials.

8. Close the document, but do not exit Word.

Creating and Printing Labels

Creating labels is similar to creating envelopes. On the Mailings tab, click the Labels button in the Create group. The Envelopes and Labels dialog box opens with the Labels tab on top, as shown in **Figure 8–10**.

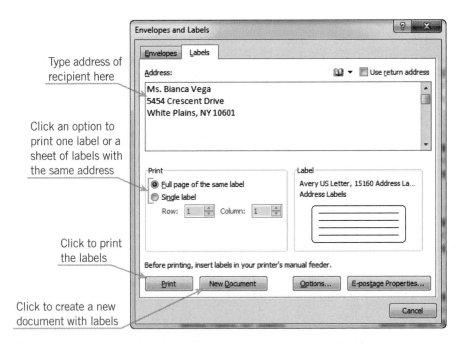

FIGURE 8–10   Labels tab in the Envelopes and Labels dialog box

Type the address you want to appear on the labels. The default is to print a full page of the same label. If you want to print just one label, in the Print section, click the Single label option button.

The dimensions of the label are listed in the Label section. To print the labels, insert a sheet of labels in your printer, and then click Print. To see the layout of the labels before you print, click New Document. A new document opens with the labels, as shown in **Figure 8–11**. Then you can format and print the document as you would any document.

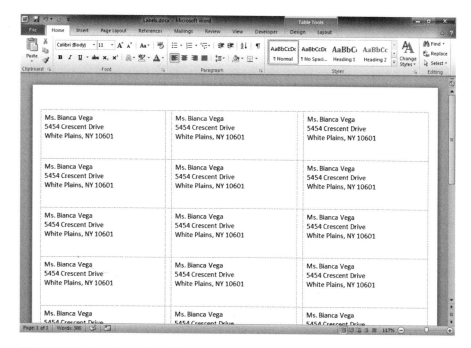

FIGURE 8–11   Completed Labels document

To choose a label type other than the one listed, click Options on the Label tab in the Envelopes and Labels dialog box. The Label Options dialog box opens. You can buy labels at an office supply store. Click the Label vendors arrow, and then click the manufacturer of the labels you purchased. Scroll down the Product number list, and then click the product number of the labels you bought (it will be on the box of labels).

Step-by-Step 8.6

1. Create a new, blank Word document.

2. On the Ribbon, click the **Mailings** tab. In the Create group, click the **Labels** button. The Envelopes and Labels dialog box opens with the Labels tab on top.

3. In the Address box, type your name and the following address. Notice that the address is inserted with either the No Spacing or the Normal style applied.

   5454 Crescent Drive

   White Plains, NY 10601

4. In the Print section, make sure the **Full page of the same label** option button is selected.

5. Click **Options** to open the Label Options dialog box, and then click the **Label vendors** arrow. A list of label manufacturers opens. Each manufacturer sells labels of different sizes. If you have labels that you bought at an office supply store, you could click the name of the manufacturer of your labels, and then, in the Product number list, scroll down if necessary and click the product number of your labels. For now, you'll print on ordinary paper.

6. Click **Avery US Letter** in the Label vendors list, scroll down the Product number list until you see 15160, and then click **15160 Address Labels**. The Label information on the right indicates that the document will be set up for mailing labels one inch high and 2.63 inches wide on 8.5" x 11" paper.

7. Click **OK**. The Label Options dialog closes. Click **New Document**. The Envelopes and Labels dialog box closes and a document opens with the name and address you typed inserted into cells in a table. Dotted lines indicate the borders of the table.

8. Save the document as **Labels** followed by your initials. Print the document.

9. Close the document, but do not exit Word.

Collaborating with a Workgroup Using Comments and Tracked Changes

The process of working together in teams, sharing comments, and exchanging ideas for a common purpose is called *workgroup collaboration*. When you work in groups, the tasks are often divided among the team members. The team meets to review each other's work, comment on it, and suggest changes.

Word provides several ways team members can collaborate. Team members can circulate a document and add comments to the document. Each member can also make changes to the document and have those changes tracked so that it is easy for the owner of the document to see suggested insertions, deletions, and moved text.

Changing the User Name

When you make certain changes to a document, Word identifies the changes with the user name. To change the user name that appears for these changes, you need to open the Word Options dialog box. Click the File tab, and then in the navigation bar, click Options. The Word Options dialog box opens with General selected in the list on the left, as shown in **Figure 8–12**.

General options
are displayed

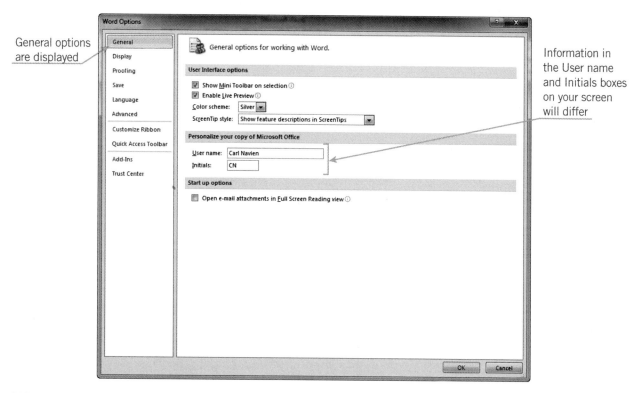

Information in
the User name
and Initials boxes
on your screen
will differ

FIGURE 8–12   Word Options dialog box with General selected

Under Personalize your copy of Microsoft Office, the User name and Initials boxes appear. You can change the name and initials in these boxes. When you are finished, click OK to close the dialog box and save your changes.

Using Comments

One way you can collaborate with others is to send a document out for review. Each person who reviews the document can insert comments in the document. To insert a comment, either position the pointer or select the text about which you wish to comment. On the Ribbon, click the Review tab, and then in the Comments group, click the New Comment button. A comment balloon appears to the right of the text. The comment balloon is connected to the text by a line. The initials from the General section of the Word Options dialog box and the comment number appear in the comment balloon. If you position the pointer on top of the comment balloon or the highlighted text in the document, the name of the person who made the comment as well as the date and time the comment was made appear in a ScreenTip, as shown in **Figure 8–13**. If you send the same version of the document to another person for review and that person inserts comments, their comments appear in a different color.

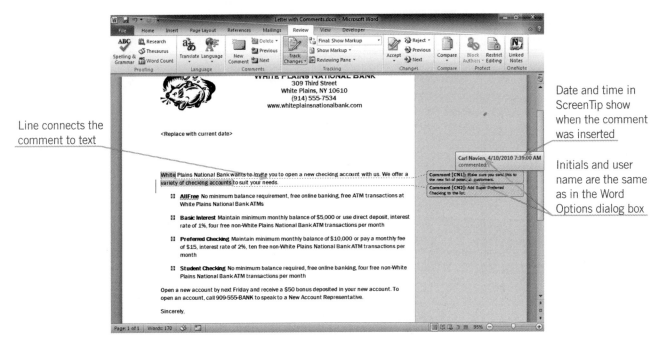

FIGURE 8–13   Comments in a document

After you have inserted your comments in a document, you can go back and make changes to them. To move from comment to comment, click the Next or Previous button in the Comments group on the Review tab. To edit a comment, click inside the comment balloon, and then make your changes.

Step-by-Step 8.7

1. Open the **Bank Letter.docx** file that you created earlier in this lesson. Save it as **Letter with Comments** followed by your initials. Change the zoom to **Page Width**.

2. Click the **File** tab, and then in the navigation bar, click **Options**. The Word Options dialog box opens with General selected in the list on the left. Write down the name and initials that appear in the User name and Initials boxes.

3. Select all the text in the User name box, and then type **Carl Navien**. Select the text in the Initials box, and then type **CN**. Click **OK**. The dialog box closes.

4. Position the insertion point at the beginning of the first paragraph in the body of the letter. On the Ribbon, click the **Review** tab. In the Comments group, click the **New Comment** button. The first word in the paragraph is highlighted in color and a comment balloon appears off to the right. The initials CN appear in the balloon, and the insertion point is blinking in the balloon.

5. Type **Make sure you send this to the list of potential customers.**

6. In the second sentence of the first paragraph in the body of the letter, select the phrase **variety of checking accounts**. In the Comments group, click the **New Comment** button. The phrase you selected is highlighted with your comment color, and another comment balloon appears.

7. In the comment balloon, type **Add Super Preferred Checking to the list.**

8. Click in the first comment balloon. Position the insertion point immediately in front of the word *list*. Type **new**, and then press the **spacebar**.

9. Click the **File** tab, and then in the navigation bar, click **Options**. Change the name in the User name box to **Stefanie E. Riposa**. Change the initials in the Initials box to **SER**. Click **OK**.

10. In the second item in the bulleted list (the *Basic Interest* item), select the word **four**. On the Review tab, in the Comments group, click the **New Comment** button. A new comment is inserted with Stefanie's initials and in a color different from the color used for Carl's comments. Type **This is now three transactions per month**. See **Figure 8–14**.

FIGURE 8–14
Document with comments from two people

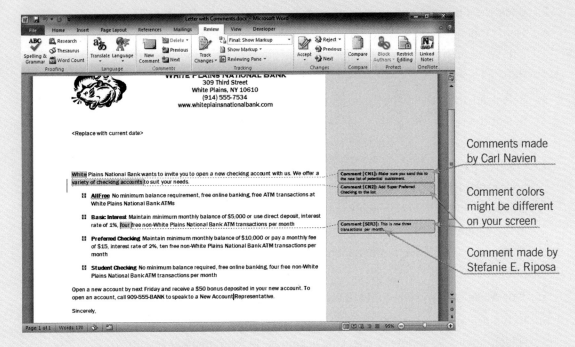

11. Position the pointer over the first comment. A ScreenTip appears identifying Carl Navien as the person who inserted the comment. The date and time the comment was inserted also appear in the ScreenTip.

12. Position the pointer over the last comment in the document. The ScreenTip identifies Stefanie E. Riposa as the author of this comment.

13. Save the document. Leave it open for the next Step-by-Step.

Tracking Changes

▶ **VOCABULARY**
Track Changes

Word provides a tool called **Track Changes** that keeps a record of any changes you or a reviewer makes in a document. If you turn this feature on, any changes made are marked in the document. Text that you insert is underlined and colored with the same color as your comments. Text you delete is put into a Deleted balloon similar to a comment balloon.

If you move text and it is at least a sentence long, the text you cut is marked with a Moved balloon. The pasted text is also marked with a Moved balloon and appears in green with a green double underline. Both Moved balloons have a Go button in them. You can click the Go button to jump back and forth between the cut and paste locations. The two Moved balloons associated with the first moved selection both have the number 1 in them. If you move a second selection, the two Moved balloons for the second move will have the number 2 in them.

You can position the pointer on top of inserted, deleted, or moved text, and as with comments, a ScreenTip identifies the person who made the change and the date and time the change was made.

To turn on the Track Changes feature, click the Review tab on the Ribbon, and then, in the Tracking group, click the Track Changes button.

⊞ EXTRA FOR EXPERTS

To show the document with all the changes, in the Tracking group, click the Final Showing Markup arrow, and then click Final. The insertions appear as normal text, and the Moved and Deleted balloons are removed.

Step-by-Step 8.8

1. On the Review tab, in the Tracking group, click the **Track Changes** button to turn on the Track Changes feature.

2. In the first item in the bulleted list (the *AllFree* item), delete the phrase **free online banking,**. Make sure you delete the comma and the space after the comma. A Deleted balloon appears to the right of the document, showing the deleted text. As with the comment balloons, a line connects the balloon to the location of the deleted text in the document. The line and the outline of the balloon are the same color as Stefanie Riposa's comment. (*Note*: If the deleted text appears with a line through it instead of in a Deleted balloon, in the Tracking group, click the **Show Markup** button, point to **Balloons**, and then click **Show Revisions in Balloons**.)

3. In the last paragraph at the bottom of the letter, select **New Account**, and then type **Customer Service**. Note that the new text is underlined and shown in the color of Stefanie's comment.

WARNING

If the Moved balloons do not appear, click the Review tab, click the arrow on the Track Changes button in the Tracking group, click Change Tracking Options, click the Use Balloons (Print and Web Layout) arrow in the Balloons section, click Always, and then click OK.

4. In the last paragraph, select the first sentence. (It starts with *Open a new account*.) Use drag-and-drop or the Cut and Paste commands to move the selected sentence to the end of the first paragraph. The moved text appears in green with a double underline, and a Moved balloon with a Go button appears next to the moved text and next to the paragraph where the text was located before you moved it. The two Moved balloons both have the number 1 in them. See **Figure 8–15**.

FIGURE 8–15
Document with tracked changes

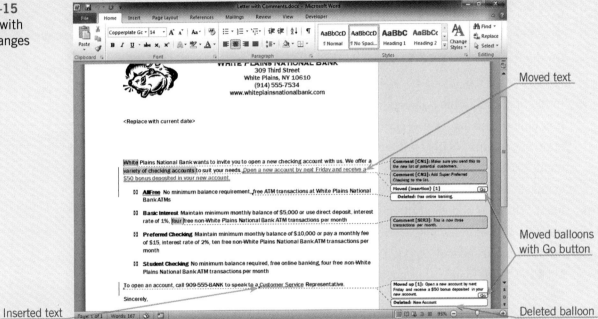

5. In the Moved balloon next to the first paragraph, click **Go**. The other Moved balloon associated with this Moved balloon is selected.

6. Click the **File** tab, and then in the navigation bar, click **Options**. Select the text in the User name box, and then replace it with the original name that you wrote down when you first opened the Word Options dialog box. Select the text in the Initials box, and then replace it with the original initials. Click **OK**.

7. Save the document, and leave it open for the next Step-by-Step.

Accepting and Rejecting Changes and Deleting Comments

Now that the changes have been made to the document, you have an opportunity to either accept or reject them. To accept or reject a change in the document, click the text that has been changed to select it, and then click the Accept or Reject button in the Changes group on the Review tab. The change is accepted or rejected, and the insertion point jumps to the next change in the document. If you don't want to jump to the next change in the document, click the arrow below the Accept or Reject button, and then click Accept Change or Reject Change.

Step-by-Step 8.9

1. Move the insertion point to the beginning of the document. On The Review tab, in the Comments group, click the **Next** button. The first comment in the document, Carl Navien's first comment, is selected. This comment is a reminder to send the letter to the new list of potential customers, so it would be helpful to leave it in the letter.

2. In the Comments group, click the **Next** button. The next comment is selected. You'll add the information requested after deleting the comment. In the Comments group, click the **Delete** button. The comment is deleted.

3. In the document, click after the last word in the *Preferred Checking* bullet (after *month*). Press **Enter**. Type **Super Preferred Checking**. Press **Ctrl+B** to turn off the automatic bold formatting that was picked up from the previous item in the list. Press the **spacebar** twice. Type **Maintain minimum monthly balance of $25,000 or pay a monthly fee of $25, interest rate of 2.5%, free transactions at all ATMs**. Because you changed the User name and Initials back to their originals, the inserted text appears in a third color.

4. Press the **left arrow key** to position the insertion point in the new bulleted item. In the Changes group, click the **Accept** button. The inserted text is accepted and changes to the normal black color, and the next change, the Moved balloon, is selected.

5. In the Changes group, click the **arrow** below the **Accept button**, and then click **Accept Change**. Both Moved balloons disappear, and the green underlined moved text in the first paragraph changes to black. The insertion point stays at the location of the Moved balloon that was selected.

6. In the Comments group, click the **Next** button. A dialog box opens asking if you want to start searching from the beginning of the document. Click **Yes**. The first comment is selected again.

7. In the Comments group, click the **Next** button to select the second comment in the document, Stefanie's comment. In the Comments group, click the **Delete** button. In the Tracking group, click the **Track Changes** button to turn off the Track Changes feature. In the Basic Interest bullet, replace the word *four* with **three**.

TIP

To delete all comments in a document, in the Comments group, click the arrow next to the Delete button, and then click Delete All Comments in Document.

TIP

To reject a tracked change, in the Changes group, click the Reject button or click the arrow next to the Reject button, and then click Reject Change.

8. In the Changes group, click the **Next** button. The deletion *New Account* is selected. In the Changes group, click the **Accept** button. Click the **Accept** button again to accept the insertion of *Customer Service*. In the dialog box, click **Yes** to continue searching from the beginning of the document. The CN1 comment is highlighted again.

9. In the Changes group, click the **Next** button. The space between the second and third sentences in the first paragraph is highlighted. When you moved the sentence, Word automatically inserted the space. The space wasn't accepted when you accepted the Moved text because the inserted space wasn't part of the moved text.

10. In the Changes group, click the **arrow** below the Accept button, and then click **Accept All Changes in Document**. The inserted space and the deletion in the bulleted list are accepted.

11. Save the document as **Letter with Changes Accepted** followed by your initials. Leave it open for the next Step-by-Step.

Print Comments and Tracked Changes

You can print a document with comments and tracked changes. To do this, click the File tab, and then in the navigation bar, click Print. In the Settings list click the Print All Pages button, and verify that Print Markup on the menu at the bottom of the list has a check mark next to it.

Step-by-Step 8.10

1. Click the **File** tab, and then in the navigation bar, click **Print**. The Print tab appears in Backstage view.

2. In the Settings list, click the **Print All Pages** button. Make sure **Print Markup** has a check mark next to it. Click the **Print All Pages** button again to close the menu without making a selection.

3. Click the **Print** button. The document prints with the comment.

4. Delete the comment in the document.

5. Save the document as **Final Bank Letter** followed by your initials. Leave the document open for the next Step-by-Step.

Combine Different Versions of a Document

The Compare and Combine commands are useful ways to see differences between documents. Suppose you send your document to several colleagues for review. They return their copies with changes and suggested revisions. Using the Compare or Combine command, you can merge their comments and changes into one document for easy review.

To combine documents, click the Review tab on the Ribbon. In the Compare group, click the Compare button. On the menu that opens, click Combine. The Combine Documents dialog box opens. The dialog box can display many or few options. The command button in the lower-left corner of the dialog box is *More* when no options are displayed in the dialog box, and *Less* when the dialog box is expanded. **Figure 8–16** shows the expanded dialog box.

Click to select documents from a list of recently opened documents

Button changes to the More button when the bottom part of the dialog box isn't visible

Combined document will be created in a new document

Click to open a dialog box and browse for documents

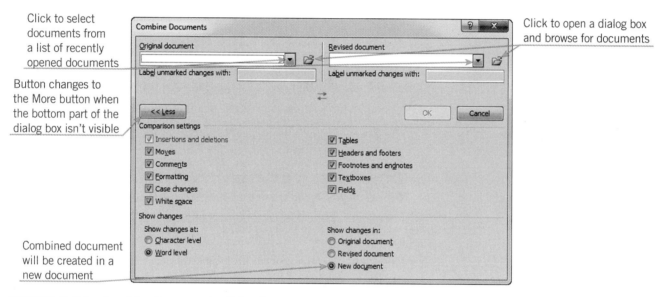

FIGURE 8–16   Combine Documents dialog box

Click the Original document arrow to display a list of recently opened documents or click the Browse button in the dialog box to use a dialog box similar to the Open dialog box to locate the original document. Click the original document in the list or double-click it in the Browse dialog box. Do the same in the Revised document section. The name that appears in the Label unmarked changes with box below the Original document box is the name that was in the User name box in the Word Options dialog box when the document was saved.

When you click OK, the dialog box closes, and a new document is created with the changes from the revised document marked. You can then choose to view just the combined document or view the combined document along with the original, the revised, or both the original and revised documents in a pane to the right of the combined document with the Revision pane open to the left. You should always look over the combined document carefully because the results might not be what you expect.

EXTRA FOR EXPERTS

To compare two documents side by side, close any other open documents. On the Ribbon, click the View tab, and then in the Window group, click the View Side by Side button. The two documents appear side by side, and when you scroll in one window, the other window scrolls as well. To scroll each window independently, click the Window button in either window, and then click Synchronous Scrolling to deselect it.

Step-by-Step 8.11

1. On the Review tab, in the Compare group, click the **Compare** button, and then click **Combine**. The Combine Documents dialog box opens. If the More button appears instead of the Less button, click **More** to expand the dialog box.

2. Click the **Original document** arrow. Locate and click **Bank Letter.docx**.

3. Click the **Revised document** arrow. Locate and click **Final Bank Letter. docx**. Notice that the New document option button is selected under Show changes in at the bottom of the dialog box.

4. Click **OK**. A new document with *Combine Result* in the document window title bar, followed by a number, opens.

5. In the Compare group, click the Compare button, point to **Show Source Documents**, and then click **Show Both** (even if it's already selected). The document window is divided into four panes. The combined document appears in the middle pane in the window. On the right, the original document appears at the top and the revised document appears on the bottom. The Revision pane appears on the left.

6. Scroll through the combined document in the middle pane. Note that the changes made to create the Final Bank Letter document are indicated in the combined document. The author of the changes is the name that currently appears in the Word Options dialog box.

7 Save the document as **Combined Bank Letter** followed by your initials. Print the document showing markup, and then close the document. Close the Final Bank Letter document.

> **TIP**
>
> If the document you want to compare or combine is not in the list, click the Browse button (the folder icon) to the right of the Original document or Revised document arrow.

Handwritten notes:

- Review
  - Reviewing Pane / vertical Pane
  - Review Accept ·· All changes to edit.

- Mailings → Start Mail Merge
  labels
  - Product number.

- Select recipient
  Use existing list

- address block
  update labels
  Review Results

- Mailings
  Review Results 1 - 2
- Mailings. finish Merge
  Print doc.

- Review
  New Comment
- Review
  delete comment
- ʺ Track changes.
  Track ʺ changes feature
  is active.

Customizing Word

You can customize many features of Word by using the Word Options dialog box. You have already used this dialog box when you checked the spelling and grammar settings and when you changed the user name and initials.

To customize Word, click the File tab, and then click Options. The Word Options dialog box displays different options and commands depending on the category selected in the list on the left. The options that appear when General is selected are some of the most common options for customizing Word, including the User name and Initials boxes. The options that appear when Display is selected (see **Figure 8–17**) affect how the document looks on the screen and when printed.

Display options
are displayed

Word Options

General
Display
Proofing
Save
Language
Advanced
Customize Ribbon
Quick Access Toolbar
Add-Ins
Trust Center

Change how document content is displayed on the screen and when printed.

Page display options

☑ Show white space between pages in Print Layout view ⓘ
☑ Show highlighter marks ⓘ
☑ Show document tooltips on hover

Always show these formatting marks on the screen

☐ Tab characters   →
☐ Spaces   ⋯
☐ Paragraph marks   ¶
☐ Hidden text
☐ Optional hyphens   ¬
☐ Object anchors   ⚓
☐ Show all formatting marks

Printing options

☑ Print drawings created in Word ⓘ
☐ Print background colors and images
☐ Print document properties
☐ Print hidden text
☐ Update fields before printing
☐ Update linked data before printing

OK   Cancel

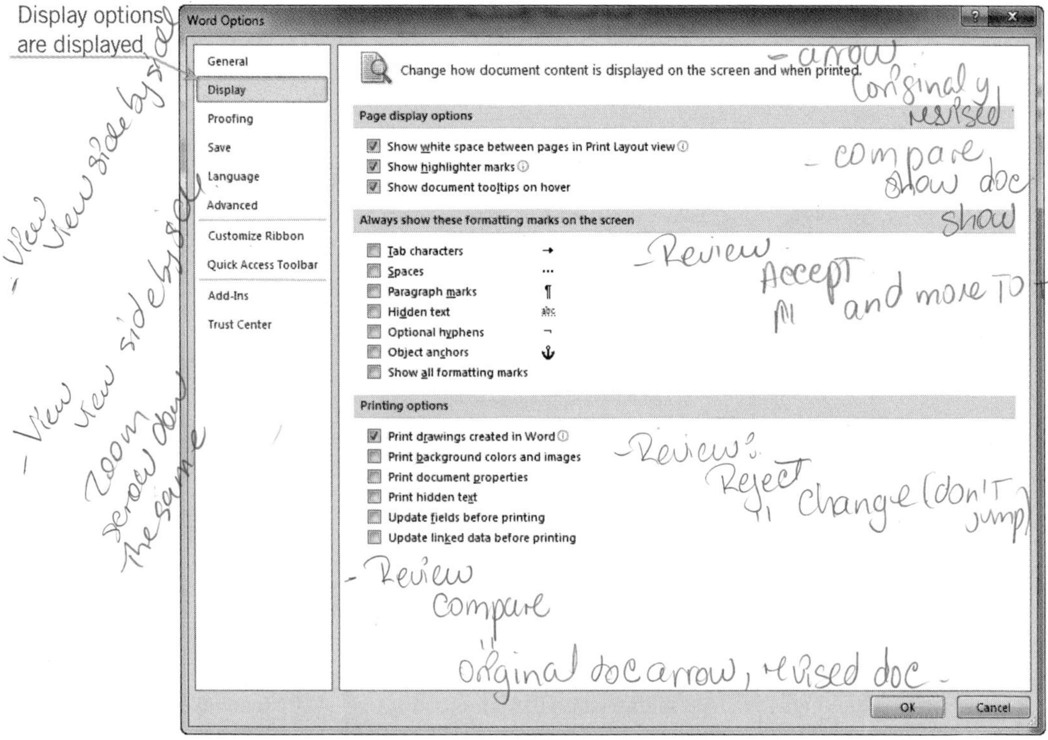

FIGURE 8–17   Word Options dialog box with Display selected

The Proofing options (see **Figure 8–18**) affect the spelling and grammar checker. You can also open the AutoCorrect dialog box when Proofing is selected in the list on the left.

Proofing options displayed

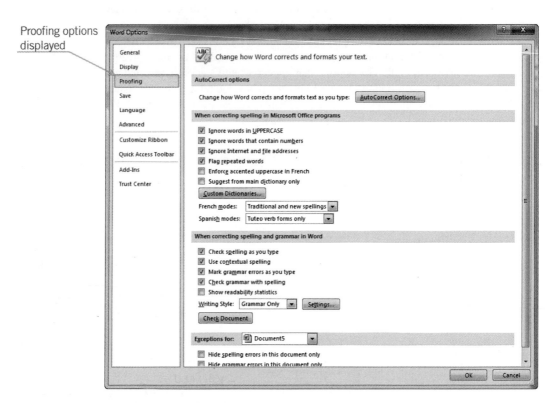

FIGURE 8–18 Word Options dialog box with Proofing selected

Clicking Save in the list on the left (see **Figure 8–19**) changes the dialog box so that you can change default save locations and behaviors. You can click Language in the list on the left to change the default language from English to another language. Clicking Advanced in the list on the left (see **Figure 8–20**) changes the dialog box so that it shows several categories of advanced options.

Save options
displayed

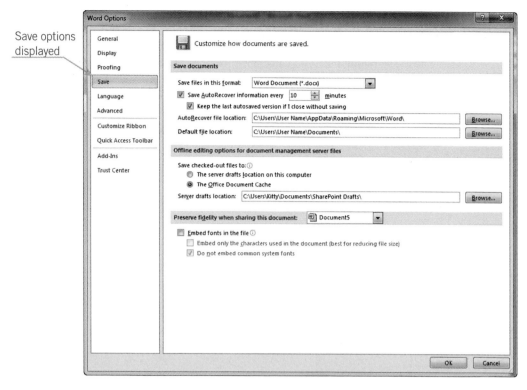

FIGURE 8–19 Word Options dialog box with Save selected

Advanced
options displayed

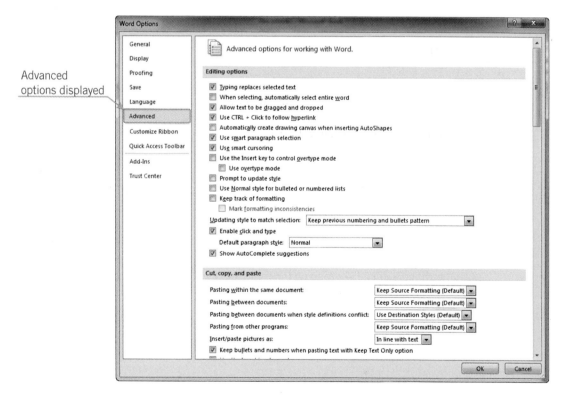

FIGURE 8–20 Word Options dialog box with Advanced selected

Finally, there are two options for customizing Word. You can customize the Ribbon and you can customize the Quick Access Toolbar. To do this, click Customize Ribbon or click Quick Access toolbar in the list on the left of the Word Options dialog box. The dialog box with Customize Ribbon selected is shown in **Figure 8–21**. The dialog box looks similar when Quick Access Toolbar is selected.

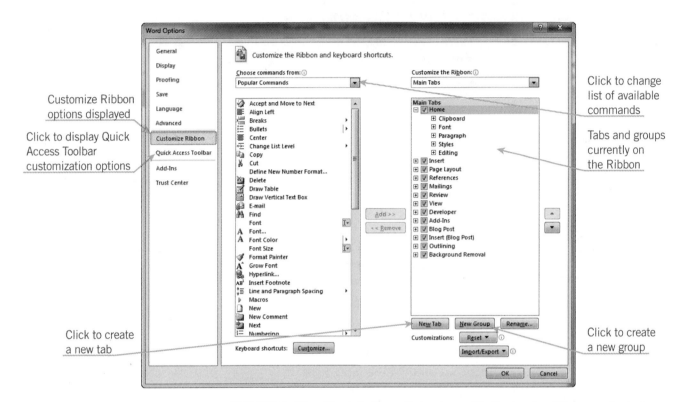

FIGURE 8–21 Word Options dialog box with Customize Ribbon selected

The tabs currently on the Ribbon are shown in the list on the right in the order they appear on the Ribbon. (For the Quick Access Toolbar, the list shows the commands on the toolbar.) The list on the left shows the commands available in Word. To filter the commands in this list, click the Choose commands from arrow at the top of the list, and then click a category of commands. The default is the set of Popular Commands. You can also choose to list all the commands and commands not in the Ribbon. The commands appear alphabetically in the list. To add a command to a group on a tab on the Ribbon or to the Quick Access Toolbar, in the list on the left, click the command you want to add. If you are adding the command to a group on the Ribbon, click the group on the right, and then click Add. To remove a command from a group or the toolbar, click the command in the list on the right, and then click Remove.

You can also create new tabs and new groups on the Ribbon. To create a new tab, click New Tab below the list on the right to create a new tab in that list. Likewise, click New Group to create a new group on the selected tab.

SUMMARY

In this lesson, you learned:

- Templates allow you to save the format, font choices, and text of commonly produced documents. You can use installed templates, templates available on Microsoft Office Online, or you can create your own.

- Mail merge lets you insert changing information into a standard document.

- You can quickly create envelopes and labels in Word.

- When working in a group, suggesting changes to a document is easily done by inserting comments, which are labeled with the person's name and the date and time the comment was made.

- Changes made by each person can be identified and labeled by using the Track Changes feature.

- You can accept or reject tracked changes and delete comments.

- You can print a document with tracked changes and comments, or you can print the document without the comments and as if all the tracked changes were accepted.

- You can combine documents with comments and changes into one document for easy review.

- You can customize Word by changing the options in the Word Options dialog box.

VOCABULARY REVIEW

Define the following terms:

data source	merge field	Track Changes
mail merge	template	workgroup collaboration
main document		

REVIEW QUESTIONS

WRITTEN QUESTIONS

Write a brief answer to each of the following questions.

1. How does using a template to create documents increase your efficiency?

2. Describe *workgroup collaboration*.

3. How does Word indicate each of the following when the Tracked Changes feature is turned on?
   a. Inserted text

b. Deleted text

c. Moved text

4. Under what circumstances would you use Mail Merge?

5. What name appears in the ScreenTip associated with a comment?

TRUE / FALSE

Circle T if the statement is true or F if the statement is false.

T   F   **1.** A template file can be used only once.

T   F   **2.** If you want to create a sheet of labels with different names and addresses on each label, you should use the Labels button on the Mailings tab.

T   F   **3.** Comments automatically show the name of the person typing the comment, regardless of the text in the User name box on the General tab in the Word Options dialog box.

T   F   **4.** ScreenTips for comment balloons identify the date and time the comment was made.

T   F   **5.** You can print comments.

MATCHING

Match the correct term in Column 2 to its description in Column 1.

Column 1

_____ 1. The file in a mail merge that contains the information that varies in each document

_____ 2. The process of combining a document with information that personalizes it

_____ 3. A file that contains the basic elements of a document, such as page and paragraph formatting, fonts, and text

_____ 4. The document in a mail merge that contains the information that does not change

_____ 5. A placeholder in a main document that is replaced with data from the data source when you perform a mail merge

Column 2

A. Main document

B. Data source

C. Merge field

D. Template

E. Mail merge

■ PROJECTS

If you have a SAM 2010 user profile, your instructor may have assigned an autogradable version of the indicated project. If so, log into the SAM 2010 Web site at *www.cengage.com/sam2010* to download the instruction and start files.

PROJECT 8-1

1. Create a new document based on the installed template **Adjacency Resume**. Save the document as **My Resume** followed by your initials.

2. Replace the name at the top of the document with your name, if necessary. Replace the appropriate placeholders with your address, phone number, and email address. (Note that some of the placeholder text in this template does not automatically select when you click the placeholder, therefore you need to drag to select it.)

3. Delete the date placeholder.

4. If you have a Web site, type the Web site address in the *Type your website* placeholder; otherwise, type **www .websiteplaceholder.com**. Press the spacebar after typing the Web site address. Remove the hyperlink formatting from the Web site address.

5. Below the *Education* heading, replace the placeholder with the name of your school.

6. Save, print, and close the document.

SÁM PROJECT 8-2

1. Open the **Subscription** Data File. Save the document as a template named **Journal Subscription** followed by your initials.

2. Create a new blank document. Save it as **Journal Addresses** followed by your initials. Create a table with seven columns and four rows. Type as the column names **First Name**, **Last Name**, **Company**, **Address**, **City**, **State**, and **Zip**. Enter the following data in the appropriate columns in table:

Barry Hodges
Pillar Shipping Company
1908 Queens Street
Los Angeles, CA 90025

David Norris
Unisource Marketing, Inc.
6421 Douglas Road
Coral Gables, FL 33134

Charlotte Smith
Accent Wireless
717 Pacific Parkway
Honolulu, HI 96813

3. Save and close the document.

4. Insert the current date in the appropriate position in the Journal Subscription template. Change the letter to a mail merge letter, and then select the Journal Addresses document as the recipient list. Insert the Address Block merge field with the recipient's name in the format *Joshua Randall Jr.* Insert the Greeting Line merge field with the greeting in the format *Dear Joshua,*. Adjust the spacing for the Address Block field.

5. In the closing, replace *Alan Dunn* with your name. Save your changes and close the document.

6. Create a new document based on the Journal Subscription template. When the dialog box opens asking if you want to continue using data from the database *Journal Addresses.docx*, click the Yes button.

7. Preview the results of the merge. Scroll through the three documents. Print the third document (the letter addressed to Charlotte Smith). Merge the documents in a new document, and then save the merged document as **Merged Journal Letters** followed by your initials. Close the document. Close the Journal Subscription document without saving changes.

8. Create a new document, and then create and print an envelope for Barry Hodges. Use your name and address as the return address. Save it as **Hodges Envelope**, and then print and close the document.

9. Create and print a sheet of labels with Barry Hodges's information. In the labels document, replace the name in the first cell with your name. Adjust the paragraph spacing, if necessary. Save it as **Hodges Labels**. Print and close the document.

PROJECT 8–3

1. Open the **Telephone.docx** Data File. Save the document as **Telephone Etiquette** followed by your initials.

2. Turn on the Tracked Changes feature. Change the User name and Initials in the Word Options dialog box to your own.

3. Click at the end of the first numbered item, after the text *Answer the telephone promptly*. Insert the following as a comment: **Add a note to answer the phone after the first ring.**

4. In the third sentence in the third item, delete the words **using** and **terms**.

5. In item 5, delete the last sentence. (Make sure you do not delete the paragraph mark.)

6. Move the sixth item under *Answering the Telephone* so it is the third item under *Taking Messages*. Change its number accordingly.

7. In the second item under *Taking Messages*, add the prefix **pre** to the word *determined*.

8. In a blank paragraph at the end of the document, type your name.

9. Print the document showing changes and comments.

10. Turn the Track Changes feature off. Change the User name and Initials in the Word Options dialog box back to their original values.

11. Save and close the document.

PROJECT 8–4

1. Open the **Telephone 2.docx** Data File. Save it as **Telephone Etiquette 2** followed by your initials.

2. Turn on the Tracked Changes feature. Change the User name and Initials in the Word Options dialog box to your own.

3. Make the changes suggested in the two comments.

4. Delete the comments.

5. In a blank paragraph at the end of the document, type your name.

6. Accept the changes in the first numbered item. Reject the changes in the third numbered item. Accept the rest of the changes in the document.

7. Save, print, and close the document, but do not exit Word.

8. Use the Combine command to combine the **Telephone 2.docx** Data File with the **Telephone Etiquette 2.docx** file you created. Show both documents.

9. Save the combined document as **Telephone Combined**. Print the document showing the changes and comments. Close the document.

◼ CRITICAL THINKING

ACTIVITY 8–1

Write an application letter for a job that interests you. Save the document on a USB drive or other removable media and give it to a classmate. Have your classmate use Track Changes to add comments and propose changes. Review your classmate's suggestions, and accept or reject the changes and delete the comments.

ACTIVITY 8–2

Create a letterhead for an organization to which you belong. Save it as a template.

ACTIVITY 8–3

It is career week at your school, which gives students an opportunity to explore possible careers. Your faculty advisor asks you to prepare a list of jobs that interest you. Next, follow the steps outlined below.

1. Set up appointments with at least two people who currently are working in the field(s) that interest you.

2. Interview each person. Ask leading questions, such as:
   a. Why did you choose this career?
   b. What did you have to do to prepare for this career?
   c. What work habits did you have to form to succeed in your job?

Listen attentively to the answers. Make sure you take notes as well. Before leaving the interview, read back your responses to the person you are interviewing to make sure you captured the appropriate information.

3. Write a report in a Word document explaining the job responsibilities of the people you interviewed and disclose whether you would consider a career in that field.

4. Present your findings to the class.

UNIT REVIEW

Introduction to Microsoft Word

 REVIEW QUESTIONS

MATCHING

Match the correct term in Column 2 to its description in Column 1.

Column 1

_____ 1. Feature that lets you copy the format of selected text to other text

_____ 2. Feature that corrects common capitalization, spelling, grammar, and typing errors as you type

_____ 3. Text printed at the top of each page

_____ 4. Building block you create from frequently used text

_____ 5. File that contains formatting with text you can customize

Column 2

A. Quick Part

B. footer

C. hanging indent

D. AutoCorrect

E. Format Painter

F. template

G. header

WRITTEN QUESTIONS

Write a brief answer to the following questions.

1. What does the Undo command do?

2. How do you align text? What are the four text alignment positions?

3. Describe how to redefine an existing Quick Style, and then describe how to create a new Quick Style.

4. How do you automatically balance columns?

5. What is the difference between the system Clipboard and the Office Clipboard?

TRUE / FALSE

Circle T if the statement is true or F if the statement is false.

T   F   **1.**   The blank areas around the top, bottom, and sides of a page are called indents.

T   F   **2.**   Graphics help illustrate the meaning of the text and make the page more attractive.

T   F   **3.**   Content controls are special placeholders designed to contain a specific type of text, such as a date or the page number.

T   F   **4.**   A style is a coordinated set of fonts and colors applied to an entire document.

T   F   **5.**   Contextual spell checking is the process of identifying possible misusage by examining the context in which the word is used.

■ PROJECTS

PROJECT WD 1

1. Open the file **Properties.docx** from the drive and folder where your Data Files are stored.

2. Save the document as **Island West Properties** followed by your initials.

3. Check the document for spelling and grammar errors. Make corrections as needed.

4. Find the word *Property* and replace it with **Properties** each time it occurs in the document.

5. Move the heading *How do I get more information?* and the paragraph that follows to the end of the document.

6. Use the Find command to locate the word *excellent*, and then replace it with a synonym that makes sense in context.

7. Change the theme to Austin.

8. Select the first heading, *Are You in the Market for a New Home?*, and change its color to Olive Green, Accent 4, Darker 50%, then update the Heading 1 style so that it reflects this change.

9. Change the orientation to landscape.

10. Add an appropriate page border and page color.

11. Center align the text vertically on the page.

12. Change the title to 36 points, centered. Change the font of the title to one of your choice. Change the color to one that coordinates with the page border.

13. Change each of the headings to the Heading 1 Quick Style.

14. Indent the last paragraph one inch on each side.

15. Create a 3-point border around the last paragraph. Change the color of the border and paragraph shading to colors that match the page border.

16. Add your name in a blank paragraph under the paragraph with the border around it. Preview the document. Save, print, and close the document.

PROJECT WD 2

1. Open the file **Tenses.docx** from the drive and folder where your Data Files are stored. Save the document as **Verb Tenses** followed by your initials.

2. Apply any appropriate Quick Style to the title except for the Heading 1 Quick Style, and then, if necessary, center it and apply bold formatting. Change the font size to 28.

3. Select all the text in the document, set a left tab marker at the 1½-inch mark on the ruler, and then set a right tab marker at the 4¾-inch mark.

4. Modify the right tab so that there is a dotted line leader in front of it.

5. Format the *Present* heading so it is 18 points, Dark Blue, Text 2, Lighter 40%, centered, and bold.

6. Change the paragraph spacing before the *Present* heading to 12 points.

7. Redefine the Heading 1 Quick Style to match the style of the heading you just formatted, and then apply the new Heading 1 Quick Style to the other two headings.

8. Insert a formatted header that contains a date content control, and then insert a footer that has a content control that contains the company name. Add your name as the Company name in the document properties. Select the current date in the Date content control in the header. Delete any other content controls (including the page number) that appear in the header or footer.

9. Center the text vertically on the page.

10. Preview the document. Save, print, and close the document.

PROJECT WD 3

1. Open the file **Bagels.docx** from the drive and folder where your Data Files are stored.

2. Save the document as **Bagel Mania** followed by your initials.

3. Change the theme to Clarity, change the size of all the text to 14 points, and change the color of all the text to Dark Red, Accent 6, Darker 25%.

4. Format the title *Bagel Mania* with the Title Quick Style. Center the title, change it to 24-point Arial Black, and add a shadow font effect. Define a new Quick Style named Bagel Title based on this formatting.

5. Center the subtitle *"The Best Bagels in Town"*. Change the subtitle to Arial Black, 16-point, bold, and italic.

6. Indent the first line of the first paragraph under the subtitle one-half inch.

7. Change the list of bagels (from *Rye* to *Cinnamon-Raisin*) to a bulleted list, and then sort the list in alphabetical order. Make all the text in the list bold.

8. Format the list of bagels in three columns. The rest of the document should remain one column.

9. Format the *Breakfast Bagels* heading with the Heading 1 Quick Style. Add a double underline in the same color as the text. Redefine the Heading 1 Quick Style based on this formatting.

10. Apply the redefined Heading 1 Quick Style to the *Lunch Bagels* heading.

11. Change the left margin of the entire document to 1.25 inches, and the right margin to .75 inches.

12. Change the items in the breakfast and lunch bagel lists to numbered lists.

13. Change the line spacing of the paragraph under the subtitle to single-spacing and the types of bagels list to 1.5 lines.

14. Format the last line, *Come again!*, as 18-point, bold, italic Arial.

15. Add your name in 10-point type in a new line at the end of the document. Save, preview, and print the document, and then close the document.

PROJECT WD 4

1. Open a new Word document. Switch to Outline View.

2. Type the outline shown in **Figure UR–1**. (Note that the zoom in the figure is set at 120% zoom so that you can more easily read the text.)

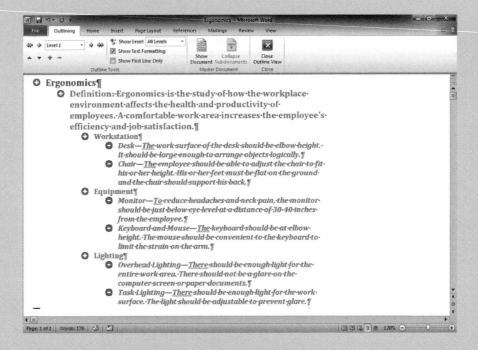

FIGURE UR–1

3. Collapse the outline to show only the heading levels 1-3.

4. Rearrange the Level 2 headings so that they are in the following order: *Equipment*, *Lighting*, *Workstation*.

5. Expand the outline.

6. Move the *Chair* heading (and its text) above the *Desk* heading.

7. Add your name in a new blank Level 1 paragraph at the end of the document. Save the document in Outline view as **Ergonomics** followed by your initials.

8. Preview the document. Print and close the document.

PROJECT WD 5

1. Open a new Word document. Create letterhead for Star Financial Group, as shown in **Figure UR–2**.

WordArt Style
Fill – Orange,
Accent 6, Warm
Matte Bevel with
Half Reflection,
touching effect

Use different
clip art if you
can't find this one

550 CORNELL STREET
INDIANAPOLIS, IN 46202
(317) 555-0991

12-point
Engravers MT

FIGURE UR–2

2. Save the document as a Word Template named **Star Template** followed by your initials.

3. Insert four blank paragraphs below the letterhead. Insert the current date so that it is updated automatically.

4. Press Enter twice, type **Sincerely,** press Enter three times, and then type your name. Save this as a Quick Part named **Closing** in the template only.

5. Save your changes. Close the file.

6. Create a new document based on the **Star Template** that you created.

7. After the date, press Enter three times. Type the letter shown in **Figure UR–3.**

This is to let you know that I have recently joined the professionals at the Star Financial Group. I am happy to be working with such a highly regarded company.

I would like to set up a meeting with you to discuss the type of services I can provide. This brief visit will not obligate you in any way, and it could result in an exchange of worthwhile ideas regarding your general financial strategy.

I plan to call you within the next few days to arrange an appointment at your convenience. Thank you for your consideration.

FIGURE UR–3

8. In a new paragraph below the body of the letter, insert four blank lines at the end of the letter. Insert the Closing Quick Part that you created.

9. Save the document as a Word document named **Star Letter** followed by your initials.

10. Create a new document. Create a table and type the following names as the contact list. Include columns for the title, first name, last name, address, city, state, and zip code. Format the table with a table style (choose any style you like). Save the contact list as **Star Contacts** followed by your initials, and then close the file.

Mr. Adam McGuire
717 Oakridge Avenue
Indianapolis, IN 46225

Ms. Sandra Novak
5506 Douglas Street
Indianapolis, IN 46216

Mr. Michael Lombardi
1908 Cameron Road
Indianapolis, IN 46206

11. Use the mail merge process to merge the Star Letter document with the Star Contacts data source. Use the recipient's title in the greeting line. Complete the merge to a new document, and then print the letter to Adam McGuire.

12. Save the document as **Star Merge** followed by your initials, and then close the document. Close the Star Letter document without saving changes.

13. Create an envelope in a new document addressed to Adam McGuire for the letter using your address as the return address. Save it as **Star Envelope** followed by your initials, and then print and close the document.

PROJECT WD 6

1. Open the file **Recycling.docx** from the drive and folder where your Data Files are stored. Save the document as **Recycling Flyer** followed by your initials.

2. Format all the text in the document as a multilevel list. Indent items so they make sense.

3. Switch to the theme of your choice. Add **Recycling** as the document title, and format it appropriately.

4. Add the title you typed in Step 3 as the Title document property. Add your name as an Author document property, and delete the placeholder *Your Name* author property.

5. Insert one of the Cubicles footers, type **Sage Stone Race Track** in the Company name content control, and then delete the empty content control in the footer. Insert one of the Cubicles headers. Delete the empty content control in the header.

6. Save, print, and close the document.

PROJECT WD 7

You need to have access to the Internet and Office.com in order to complete this project.

1. Open the New tab in Backstage view, click Greeting cards under Office.com Templates, and then click the category folders and scroll through the greeting card templates.

2. To see a preview of a template, click it to select it, and then look at the preview in the pane on the right.

3. When you find a greeting card you like, select it, and then click Download. The template appears in a new document window.

4. Replace the placeholder text with your own text.

5. If you don't like the colors used, adjust the text and page background colors.

6. Add clip art if you like. Resize and reposition the clip art to fit nicely on the page. Change it to a floating object if necessary.

7. Add your name in a text box in an appropriate place in the card. Use a font that looks like script (handwriting).

8. Save the document with a name of your choice, and then print and close it.

■ SIMULATION

You work at the Java Internet Café, which has been open only a few months. The café serves coffee, other beverages, and pastries, and offers Internet access. Seven computers are set up on tables along the north side of the store. Customers can come in, have a cup of coffee and a muffin, and explore the World Wide Web.

Because of your Microsoft Office experience, your manager asks you to create and revise many of the business's documents.

JOB WD 1

Some customers at Java Internet Café do not have much experience using computers or accessing the Internet. Your manager asks you to create a poster with definitions of the most common terms users encounter while surfing the Internet. The poster will hang near each computer.

1. Open the file **Internet.docx** from the drive and folder where your Data Files are stored. Save it as **Internet Terms** followed by your initials.

2. Create the poster shown in **Figure UR–4**. Use the Trek theme.

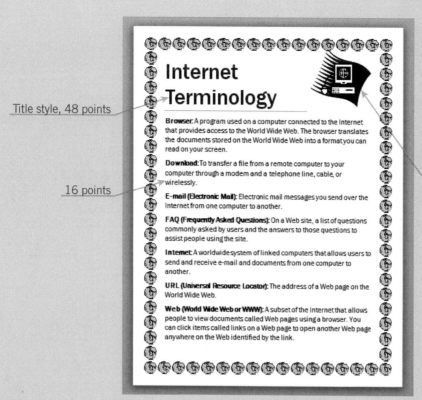

Title style, 48 points

16 points

Clip art is recolored with Black and White: 75%

FIGURE UR–4

3. Add your name in a text box at the bottom of the document. Save your changes.

4. Print and close the document.

JOB WD 2

Many customers become curious when they see computers through the window of the coffee shop. The café servers are often too busy to explain the concept to customers entering the store. Your manager asks you to revise the menu to include a short description of the café. These menus will be printed and placed near the entrance.

1. Open the **Menu.docx** Data File. Save the document as **Java Menu** followed by your initials.

2. Jump to the end of the document, and then type the following text:

> **Java Internet Café offers customers computers with high-speed Internet access as well as free Wi-Fi. Each of our computers has a special interface for new users to help you get started exploring the World Wide Web. You have heard about it; now you need to try it! Ask your server to help you get started.**

3. Change the font of the paragraph you just typed to Corbel, 11 point.

4. Change the left and right margins to 1½ inches.

5. Insert a new paragraph, and then type the title **Menu**.

6. Format *Menu* with the Title Quick Style.

7. Center the title.

8. Change the bottom border to the style that is a long dashed line followed by a short dashed line, change the color to Lavender, Accent 3, Darker 50%, and change the width to 1½ points. (*Hint*: Don't forget to reapply the border to the preview.)

9. Redefine the Title Quick Style to reflect the modified format.

10. Save, print, and close the document.

ADVANCED

MICROSOFT WORD UNIT

LESSON 9

Enhancing Documents

■ OBJECTIVES

Upon completion of this lesson, you should be able to:

- Modify the document background color and effects.
- Apply shading and borders to text, paragraphs, and pages.
- Create a watermark.
- Format drop caps.
- Create a sidebar and a pull quote using text boxes.
- Repeat text box contents on multiple pages.
- Change the orientation of text in text boxes.
- Modify and create document themes.

■ VOCABULARY

chain

drop cap

gradient fill

pull quote

sans serif fonts

serif fonts

serifs

sidebar

story

watermark

Word offers several features that you can use to add visual interest to your documents, as well as make them more useful. You can use these features to emphasize the content in newsletters and flyers, and you can also create sophisticated and professional-looking documents such as formal invitations.

Formatting Document Backgrounds

You can make the appearance of documents more interesting by modifying the page background. The colors and special effects can be added to the entire document, or to sections within the document. The formats you apply will depend on how you plan to distribute the document. Color highlights and shading are most effective when the recipient of the document reviews the document online or on a color printout. If the document is to be printed in black and white, light colors and shading patterns work best.

Modifying the Document Background Color and Effects

Changing the page background in a document can make the document easier to read, especially if the document is going to be published as a Web page, posted online, or attached to an e-mail message. Several formats are available, including gradients, textures, and patterns. A *gradient fill* is a gradual blending together of two or more fill colors. You can use built-in gradient fills, or you can create your own. You can also use pictures for the page background.

A page background looks great on the screen, but when you print the document, the page background colors and effects will not print. Saving the document in PDF or XPS format also saves the background effects, and they will print. However, sometimes the background effects change when the file is converted to PDF or XPS format, and the backgrounds don't look the same as they do in Word. And, depending on the printer, any border area around the background might not print.

▶ **VOCABULARY**
gradient fill

Step-by-Step 9.1

1. Launch Word and then open the **Plastic** file from the drive and folder where your Data Files are stored. Save the document as **Enhanced Plastic 1**, followed by your initials.

2. On the Ribbon, click the **Page Layout** tab. In the Page Background group, click the **Page Color** button.

3. Move the mouse pointer over the color options to see live previews of the options. Then, under Theme Colors, in the second row of colors, fifth column, click the **Blue, Accent 1, Lighter 80%** color. The page is filled with a background color.

4. Click the **Page Color** button again, then click **More Colors** to open the Colors dialog box shown in **Figure 9–1**. Because you already applied a background color, the Custom tab appears, and you can customize the setting.

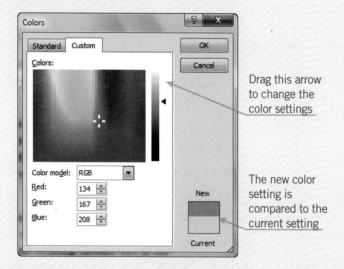

FIGURE 9–1
Colors dialog box

Drag this arrow to change the color settings

The new color setting is compared to the current setting

5. Drag the arrow to the right of the vertical bar to change the color. Notice as you drag the arrow, the new and current colors both show at the bottom of the dialog box, so you can compare the colors. Also, as you drag the arrow, you will see that the number references for the RGB (Red, Green, Blue) settings change.

6. Click the **Standard** tab and then click a light blue color in the middle of the diagram. Compare the new and current colors at the bottom of the dialog box. When you are satisfied with the new color choice, click **OK** to apply the change to the background color.

7. Click the **File** tab and then click **Print**. Notice that the background color you applied does not show in Print Preview. The page color background will not print. Click the **File** tab to close the Print Preview.

EXTRA FOR EXPERTS

If you know the exact RGB settings, you can manually change them. You can also click the Color model list arrow and select HSL (Hue, Saturation, Luminosity) to view and change those settings.

8. In the Page Background group, click the **Page Color** button, and then click **Fill Effects**. The Fill Effects dialog box shown in **Figure 9–2** opens. On the Gradient tab, under Colors, click the **Preset** option and then click the **Preset colors** list arrow. Click some of the options to view the built-in gradient fills.

FIGURE 9–2
Fill Effects dialog box

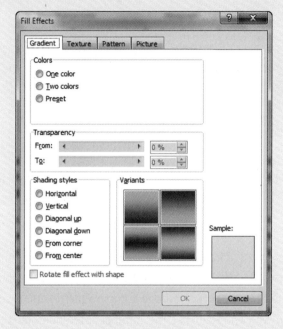

9. Under Colors, click the **Two colors** option. Leave the color setting in the Color 1 box as is. Click the **Color 2** list arrow and select a darker blue color.

10. Under Shading styles, click the **Diagonal down** option, and then under Variants, click each of the four samples. Each time you click a different variant, the Sample in the dialog box will reflect the change. Click the variant in the lower-right corner, then click **OK** to apply the custom gradient fill.

11. Click the **Page Color** button, click **Fill Effects**, and then click the **Pattern** tab. Under Pattern, click any one of the options. Click the **Foreground** list arrow, and select a dark blue color. Click the **Background** list arrow, and select a light blue color. Notice that the Sample previews your selections. Click **OK** to replace the two-color gradient background with the new customized patterns background.

12. Click the **Page Color** button, click **Fill Effects**, and then click the **Picture** tab. Click **Select Picture** to open the Select Picture dialog box. Navigate to the Data Files, select the file **Recycling Symbol.jpg**, click **Insert**, and then click **OK**. Several images of the picture appear in the background.

13. Click the **Page Color** button, click **Fill Effects**, and then click the **Texture** tab. Scroll down to view the options. Click the texture in the fourth row, third column. The texture name *Parchment* will appear in the text box just below the options. Click **OK**. The picture background is replaced with the new texture background.

14. Save the changes, and keep the document open for the next Step-by-Step.

Applying Shading and Borders to Text, Paragraphs, and Pages

You can set apart sections of a document by applying shading and borders. You can add shading and borders to an entire page, to a paragraph or group of paragraphs, and to a letter, word, or group of words. Border options include many line styles and colors as well as a variety of graphics. A page border is a section format, and the border prints on all pages in the section formatted with a page border. The border can be formatted for any or all sides of each page in a document, for pages in a section, for the first page only, or for all pages except the first page.

Step-by-Step 9.2

1. If necessary, open **Enhanced Plastic 1** from your solution files. Save the document as **Enhanced Plastic 2**, followed by your initials.

2. Click anywhere within the title *Recycled Plastic is Fantastic!*. Click the **Home** tab, and in the Paragraph group, click the **Shading** button arrow ![shading icon] to open a menu containing the color palette. Select a tan (light brown) color. The shading is applied to the entire paragraph. Triple-click the title to select the entire paragraph, and then increase the font size to **36** point.

3. Position the insertion point at the end of the document and type your first and last names, press **spacebar**, and then enter the current date. Select your first and last names, and then click the **Shading** button ![shading icon] to apply the same tan color you applied to the title paragraph. The shading is applied only to the selected text.

4. Click anywhere within the third paragraph of text that begins *PET (PETE)*. Click the **Shading** button arrow again to open the color palette. Under Theme Colors, select an olive green color.

> **TIP**
>
> To apply shading to multiple paragraphs, select all the paragraphs before choosing a color.

5. Click anywhere within the title, then click the **Borders** button arrow 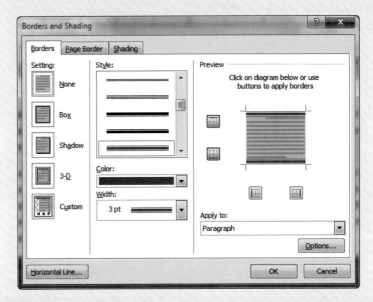. At the bottom of the menu, click **Borders and Shading** to open the dialog box shown in **Figure 9–3**. The settings in the dialog box will vary depending on the formats recently applied.

FIGURE 9–3
Borders tab in the Borders and
Shading dialog box

6. Select the border settings:
   a. Under Style, scroll down and select the style with three lines, as shown in Figure 9–3. (The middle line is thick, and the top and bottom lines are thin.)
   b. Under Color, select a dark olive green color.
   c. If necessary, under Width, select **3 pt**.
7. Select where the border will be applied:
   a. Under Setting, click the **None** setting to clear all settings.
   b. In the Preview pane, click at the top of the sample paragraph in the diagram. A new border line will appear above the paragraph.
   c. Click at the bottom of the sample paragraph to apply a border line below the paragraph.
   d. Click **OK**.
8. Click the **Borders** button arrow and then click **Borders and Shading** to reopen the dialog box. Under Color, select a dark tan (brown) color. Notice that the colors in the Preview pane are still green. Click the top and bottom borders in the diagram to update the color settings. Then click **OK** to apply the new format.
9. At the end of the document, select the current date that you entered. Click the **Borders** button arrow, and then click **Outside Borders**. The most recent border settings (style, color, and weight) are applied to all sides of the selected text. Click **Undo**.

10. With the date still selected, click the **Borders** button arrow. Then click **Borders and Shading** to reopen the dialog box. All the default settings appear. Under Setting, click the **Box** setting, then click **OK**. The new border style is applied to the selected text.

11. Click the **Page Layout** tab, and in the Page Background group, click the **Page Borders** button to open the Borders and Shading dialog box. If necessary, click the **Page Border** tab in the dialog box. Under Setting, click the **Box** setting. Under Color, select the dark tan (brown) color you chose for the title paragraph border. Under Art, scroll down about halfway through the list and select the border shown in **Figure 9–4**. Change the width to **30 pt**. When your dialog box settings match those in Figure 9–4, click **OK**.

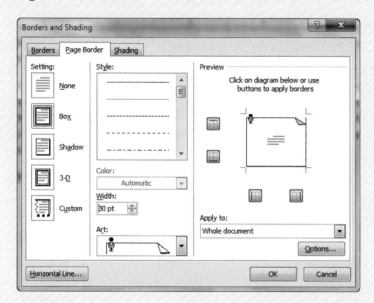

FIGURE 9–4
Page Border tab in the Borders and Shading dialog box

12. On the Page Layout tab, in the Page Setup group, click the **Dialog Box Launcher** to open the Page Setup dialog box. Click the **Layout** tab. Under Page, click the **Vertical alignment** list arrow, select **Center**, and then click **OK**. The document content is centered vertically on the page.

13. Click the **File** tab and then click **Print**. Note that the borders and the shading will print, but the texture background will not print. Click the **File** tab to close Print Preview.

14. Save the changes and keep the document open for the next Step-by-Step.

Creating a Watermark

A *watermark* is a ghost image that appears behind the content of a document. Watermarks traditionally have been used to print logos or text, such as *CONFIDENTIAL*, on company stationery. A watermark can be created from text or a graphic and printed in the background of a document. A watermark image can

▶ **VOCABULARY**
watermark

also be created by impressing text or a graphic image in the paper when the paper is manufactured. An impressed watermark is visible when the paper is held to the light.

Word offers several options for creating watermarks in documents that are to be distributed in hard copies and onscreen. To see a watermark in a Word document on screen, you must view the document in Print Preview or in Print Layout or Full Screen Reading view. The watermark will appear in the printed document.

When you create a watermark, the formats for the text or image are stored within the header and footer panes. Therefore, to edit a watermark (resize, recolor, reposition, and so on), you must access the watermark content in the header or footer. This does not mean, though, that a watermark must appear at the top or bottom of the page. A watermark can be positioned anywhere on the document page.

Step-by-Step 9.3

1. If necessary, open **Enhanced Plastic 2** from your solution files. Save the document as **Enhanced Plastic 3**, followed by your initials.

2. Click the **View** tab. In the Zoom group, click the **One Page** button.

3. Click the **Page Layout** tab, and in the Page Background group, click the **Watermark** button to show the built-in watermark options. Under Confidential, click the **DO NOT COPY 1** watermark. Then switch to Full Screen Reading view to clearly see the watermark in the document. Close Full Screen Reading view.

4. On the Page Layout tab, click the **Watermark** button again, and this time click **Custom Watermark** to open the Printed Watermark dialog box shown in **Figure 9–5**.

WARNING

The screen resolution settings affect the Full Screen Reading view. If your screen resolution is set low, the watermark image may not appear in Full Screen Reading view.

FIGURE 9–5
Printed Watermark dialog box

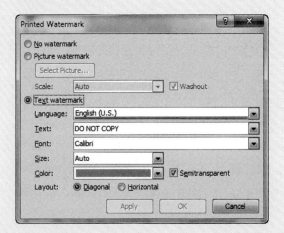

5. If necessary, click to enable the **Text watermark** option. Click the **Text** list arrow, scroll down, and select **TOP SECRET**. Click **Apply**. The dialog box remains open, and the watermark text changes. Select the text in the Text box and type **Eco Friends** to create your own custom text. Then change the text formats as follows:

   Font: **Cambria**

   Size: **48**

   Color: a dark olive green

   Layout: **Diagonal**

6. Click **Apply**. The dialog box remains open. If necessary, reposition the dialog box so you can see the watermark in the document. Change the size to **72**, click **Apply**, and then click **Close**.

7. Double-click in the margin area above the document title to open the header pane. On the Header & Footer Tools Design tab, in the Options group, click **Show Document Text** to disable the option. This will make it easier for you to work with the watermark image.

8. In the body of the document, move the mouse pointer over the watermark text, and when the pointer changes to a four-headed arrow, click to select the image. The image is selected when you see eight object handles around the text. Drag the watermark text upward and to the left so that the watermark is positioned in the upper-left corner on the page.

9. A watermark is created as a WordArt graphic, so when you select the watermark object, the Ribbon adapts. Click the **WordArt Tools Format** tab. In the Word Art Styles group, click the **WordArt Shape Fill** button arrow and select a light olive green color. Then click the **WordArt Shape Outline** button arrow and select a slightly darker color.

10. Click the **Header & Footer Tools Design** tab, then click the **Close Header and Footer** button. Click the **File** tab, then click **Print** to preview the document as it will print.

11. Click the **Page Layout** tab, and in the Page Background group, click the **Watermark** button and then click **Custom Watermark**.

12. Click to enable the **Picture watermark** option, then click **Select Picture** to open the Insert Picture dialog box. Navigate to the data files, select the file **Recycling symbol.jpg**, and click **Insert**. Click **Apply** and then click **Close**.

13. The white background in the picture covers the texture format. On the Page Layout tab, in the Page Background group, click the **Page Color** button, and then click **No Color**. Then click anywhere in the third paragraph. Click the **Home** tab. In the Paragraph group, click the **Shading** button arrow and then click **No Color**.

14. Save the changes and leave the document open for the next Step-by-Step.

> **TIP**
>
> When you create the watermark, it is anchored in the header pane. When you reposition the watermark image, the anchor may move to the footer pane. So, if you cannot access the image through the header pane, try opening the footer pane.

Formatting Drop Caps

A ***drop cap*** is a letter or word at the beginning of a paragraph that is larger than the rest of the text. Drop caps are used to draw attention to the content, such as the beginning of a magazine article or the beginning of a chapter in a book. The drop cap format can be added to the first letter in the first word of a paragraph, or it can be added to the entire first word. You can position a drop cap to appear in the paragraph or in the margin. However, a drop cap cannot be positioned in the margin when the text is formatted in columns.

Step-by-Step 9.4

1. If necessary, open **Enhanced Plastic 3** from your solution files. Save the document as **Enhanced Plastic 4**, followed by your initials.

2. Position the insertion point anywhere in the first paragraph of text, which begins with *The promise*. Click the **Insert** tab. In the Text group, click the **Drop Cap** button. Position the mouse pointer over the **Dropped** option. A live preview of the format will show in the document.

3. Position the mouse pointer over the **In margin** option, and a new live preview shows the first letter of the paragraph formatted in the margin to the left.

4. Go back up in the list and click the **Dropped** option. The first letter in the paragraph is formatted as a drop cap with the default settings, positioned in the upper-left corner of the paragraph.

5. Position the insertion point in the second paragraph of text, and click the **Repeat** button on the Quick Access Toolbar (or press **F4**) to repeat the drop cap edit.

6. With the insertion point still positioned in the second paragraph, click the **Drop Cap** button, and then click **None** to remove the drop cap format. Then position the insertion point in the first paragraph and click the **Repeat** button on the Quick Access Toolbar (or press **F4**) to repeat the edit.

7. Select the first word *The* in the first paragraph of text. Click the **Drop Cap** button, and then click **Drop Cap Options** to open the Drop Cap dialog box shown in **Figure 9–6**.

FIGURE 9–6
Drop Cap dialog box

8. Change the settings for the drop cap format:

   a. Under Position, select the **Dropped** option.

   b. Under Options, click the **Font** list arrow, scroll down, and then select **Baskerville Old Face**.

   c. In the Lines to drop setting, click the **down arrow** once to change the setting to **2**. This setting specifies the height of the drop cap in lines of text.

   d. Leave the Distance from text setting as is. This setting controls the amount of space between the drop cap and that text that follows it.

9. When the settings match those shown in Figure 9–6, click **OK**. The entire word is formatted as a drop cap in a frame in the upper-left corner of the paragraph.

10. In the drop cap frame, select just the letter *h*. Using the Mini toolbar, change the font size to **26** point. Then, select the letter *e* in the drop cap frame, and change the font size to **20** point.

11. Save the changes and close the document.

Formatting Text Boxes

Many types of documents include special sections of text relating to the subject matter that are formatted differently from the rest of the document. For example, newsletters and magazine articles often include sections that summarize the contents of the article, highlight specific text, and draw the reader's attention to specific content.

You can use text boxes to position these special sections of text and to apply various formats, such as shading, font styles, line fills, and shadows. You can adjust the text box size so that the content fits, and you can change the alignment of text inside the text box.

Creating a Sidebar

A *sidebar* is distinct, supplemental text added to a document such as a magazine or newspaper article to highlight the main text. For example, a sidebar can be used

▶ **VOCABULARY**
sidebar

to list the names of officers in a club newsletter, or it can be used to summarize the contents of a magazine article. Sidebars are usually formatted in a boxed area with effects to draw the reader's attention. If the sidebar content is extensive, you can link text boxes so the content can continue on another page.

Sidebars are formatted in text boxes, so they can be positioned anywhere on the pages. The Text Box gallery in Word's Building Blocks Organizer provides several preformatted text boxes, especially designed for sidebars. Of course, you can modify these built-in text box formats to fit your needs.

The text contained within a text box is called a *story*. When you create a link between two or more text boxes, you create a *chain*, which is a series of links that lets the story flow from one text box to the next, enabling you to continue the story elsewhere in the document. The chain can move either forward or backward, and one document can contain several stories, each with a chain of links. However, all the linked text boxes must be contained in the same document. When linking text boxes, the new box that you are adding to the chain must be empty.

VOCABULARY

story

chain

Step-by-Step 9.5

1. Open the **Get Fit** file from the drive and folder where your Data Files are stored. Save the document as **Enhanced Get Fit 1**, followed by your initials.

2. Position the insertion point in the second paragraph of text. Click the **Insert** tab. In the Text group, click the **Quick Parts** button, and then click **Building Blocks Organizer** to open the Building Blocks Organizer dialog box shown in **Figure 9–7**.

FIGURE 9–7
Building Blocks Organizer
dialog box

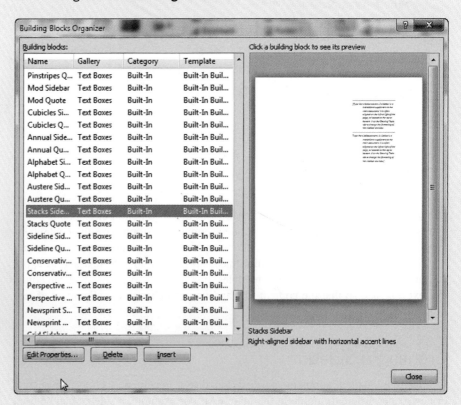

3. Scroll down to the Text Boxes gallery, and in the Name column, click **Stacks Sidebar** (near the end of the list). Click **Insert**, and the preformatted text box is inserted in the document. The text box is already formatted for text wrapping.

4. The text box should be selected, and the Drawing Tools Format tab should show on the Ribbon. If necessary, click the Size button to the right of the Arrange group to show the options in the Size group. In the Size group, change the Height setting to **3.25"**. Drag the text box to reposition it in the lower-left corner of the page, next to the last two paragraphs in the section under the heading *Eat Smart*. (*Hint*: Point to a border of the text box. When the mouse pointer changes to a four-headed arrow, drag the text box.)

5. Click the placeholder in the text box and then type **Power-Packed Foods**. Press **Enter**. Each time you press Enter in the text box placeholder, Word automatically formats a line to divide the paragraphs.

6. Continue to enter the sidebar content by typing the following text.

   Asparagus - High in B vitamins; also a good source of Vitamins A and C and iron.

   Bananas - High in fiber, low in sodium, and fat-free; a good source of Vitamins B6 and C and potassium.

7. Position the insertion point in the first paragraph on the second page of the document. Insert a **Stacks Sidebar** text box. If necessary, click anywhere in the text box to select the placeholder. Press **Delete**. To link text boxes, the text box must be empty.

8. Select the text box on the first page. On the **Drawing Tools Format** tab in the Text group, click the **Create Link** button. The mouse pointer changes to an upright pitcher 🝐.

9. Scroll to the second page and position the mouse pointer over the new text box. The mouse pointer changes to a pouring pitcher 🝐. Click to add the text box to the chain. Now the text from the previous text box in the chain can flow into this text box.

10. Position the insertion point at the end of the text in the text box on the first page. Press **Enter** and type the following. As you enter the new text, it will flow to the text box on the second page.

Broccoli – Ounce for ounce, twice as much Vitamin C as oranges; low in sodium; a great source of potassium, calcium, and fiber.

Brussels sprouts - An excellent source of Vitamin C and iron; rich in Vitamin B and potassium.

Carrots - Rich in potassium and calcium; more Vitamin A than any other vegetable.

Citrus fruits - A prime source of Vitamin C, fiber, and potassium; low in calories and sodium-free.

Lima beans - High in iron, B vitamins, and calcium; excellent source of potassium.

Spinach - Low in sodium and fat, and cholesterol-free; a great source of iron, calcium, potassium, and Vitamin A.

Strawberries - Naturally sweet and sodium-free; an excellent source of Vitamin C and fiber.

Sweet potatoes - Second only to carrots as a source of Vitamin A; also very high in Vitamin C.

11. Select the heading in the sidebar text box on the first page. Right-click and, using the Mini toolbar, change the font size to **12** point and center the line of text. Then select all the remaining text in that text box and change the font size to **11** point. You'll notice that some of the newly formatted text flows to the next text box. Select all the text in the text box on the second page and change the font size to **11** point.

12. Select the text box on the first page. The Drawing Tools Format tab appears on the Ribbon. Click the tab to show the groups and commands. Format the fill color and border:

    a. In the Shape Styles group, click the **Shape Fill** button arrow and then click the **Blue, Accent 1** color.

    b. Select all the text in the sidebar text box, right-click and, on the Mini toolbar, change the font color to **White**.

    c. In the Shape Styles group, click the **Shape Outline** button arrow and select the **Olive Green, Accent 3** color. Click the **Shape Outline** button arrow again, and change the border weight to **2 ¼** point.

    d. Click anywhere in the text box on the second page, and apply the same fill and border formats as the text box on the first page.

    e. Select all the text in the second text box. Using the Mini toolbar, change the font color to **White**.

13. Select the text box on the first page. Drag the sizing handles on the top or bottom of the text box to adjust the size of the text box on the first

---

TIP

To remove the link between text boxes, select the text box from which the text is flowing and then click the Break Link button in the Text group on the Drawing Tools Format tab.

page so that all the information about the first three foods (asparagus, bananas, and broccoli) appears in that text box. Then adjust the size of the second text box to eliminate extra blank space at the bottom.

14. Save the changes, and leave the document open for the next Step-by-Step.

Creating a Pull Quote

A *pull quote* is a line or phrase excerpted from the main text and used to draw attention. Pull quotes are often used in magazine and newsletter articles to highlight specific text included within the article. A pull quote is usually positioned on the same page and close to where it is referenced. The pull quote text is often formatted in a different font style, size, or color to add emphasis.

　Like sidebars, pull quotes are formatted in text boxes. Word's Building Blocks Organizer also provides several preformatted text boxes that are especially designed for pull quotes. After inserting the building block, you can enter the pull quote text. If you are pulling a lot of text for the pull quote, you can copy the text in the document and then paste the content into the pull quote text box.

▶ **VOCABULARY**
pull quote

Step-by-Step 9.6

1. If necessary, open **Enhanced Get Fit 1** from your solution files. Save the document as **Enhanced Get Fit 2**, followed by your initials.

2. Position the insertion point in the first paragraph under the heading *Eat Smart* to anchor the pull quote text box to this paragraph.

3. Click the **Insert** tab. In the Text group, click the **Quick Parts** button, and then click **Building Blocks Organizer**.

4. Scroll down to the Text Boxes gallery, and in the Name column, select **Sticky Quote**. Click **Insert**, and the preformatted text box is inserted in the document. The text box is already formatted for text wrapping.

5. The text box should be selected, and the Drawing Tools Format tab should show on the Ribbon. If necessary, click the **Size** button to expand the Size group. Change the height to **1.5"** and the width to **2"**.

6. Drag the text box to reposition it. Align the text box in the middle of the paragraph beginning with *Experts agree*, with the right side of the text box aligned with the right margin.

7. Click the placeholder in the text box and type the following:

   Nutritionists recommend that not more than 30 percent of the total daily calories you consume come from fat.

8. Select the pull quote text box. The Drawing Tools Format tab shows on the Ribbon. In the Shape Styles group, click the **Shape Fill** button arrow and select the **Blue, Accent 1, Lighter 40%** color.

9. Save the changes and leave the document open for the next Step-by-Step.

◀ **TIP**

To select the text box, position the mouse pointer over the object border. When the pointer changes to a four-headed arrow, click and drag the box to reposition it.

Repeating Text Box Contents and Changing the Text Direction

You can repeat text box contents on every page of a document or section of a document by inserting a text box item in a header or footer and positioning the text box where you want the contents to print.

The default setting for text boxes is to show the text in a horizontal orientation. However, you can easily change the text format to a vertical orientation. For example, you may want to print a title in the left margin on each page of a document. You can format the text to read from bottom to top or from top to bottom.

Step-by-Step 9.7

1. If necessary, open **Enhanced Get Fit 2** from your solution files. Save the document as **Enhanced Get Fit 3**, followed by your initials.

2. Click the **View** tab, and in the Zoom group, click the **One Page** button.

3. Double-click in the margin at the top of the document to access the header pane. The Ribbon will adapt and show the Header & Footer Tools Design tab.

4. Click the **Insert** tab. In the Text group, click the **Text Box** button and then select the **Simple Text Box** option. A text box with a placeholder for a quote is inserted, and the text box is anchored in the header pane.

5. If necessary, click the placeholder in the text box. Type **Healthy Living**. Word automatically adjusts the height of the text box.

6. Click the **Header & Footer Tools Design** tab, then click the **Close Header and Footer** button. Scroll down to the second and third pages, and you'll see that the text box also appears in the header on those pages. Press **Ctrl+Home** to return to the top of the document.

7. Double-click in the top margin of the document to access the header pane. Select the text box, and then click the **Drawing Tools Format** tab on the Ribbon. In the Text group, click the **Text Direction** button, and then click **Rotate all text 90°**.

8. Drag the text box down to the document and position it in the right margin, about halfway down the page. (*Hint*: Click a text box border. When the pointer changes to a four-headed arrow, drag the box to reposition it.)

9. Triple-click inside the text box to select all the text. You may see only a shading color and no text, or you may see no color at all. Use the Mini toolbar to increase the font size to **26** point. The size of the text box will adjust, and you still probably won't be able to see the text.

10. Click a border on the text box to select it, and then drag a handle at the top or bottom of the box to make the box taller so that the text fits on one line in the text box.

11. Triple-click in the text box again to select all the text. Use the Mini toolbar to change the font color to **Blue, Accent 1**, to match the blue fill in the sidebar text box.

12. With the text box still selected, click the **Drawing Tools Format** tab. In the Shape Styles group, click the **Shape Outline** button arrow, then click **No Outline**.

13. Double-click anywhere in the body of the document to close the header pane. Your page should now look similar to the one shown in **Figure 9–8**.

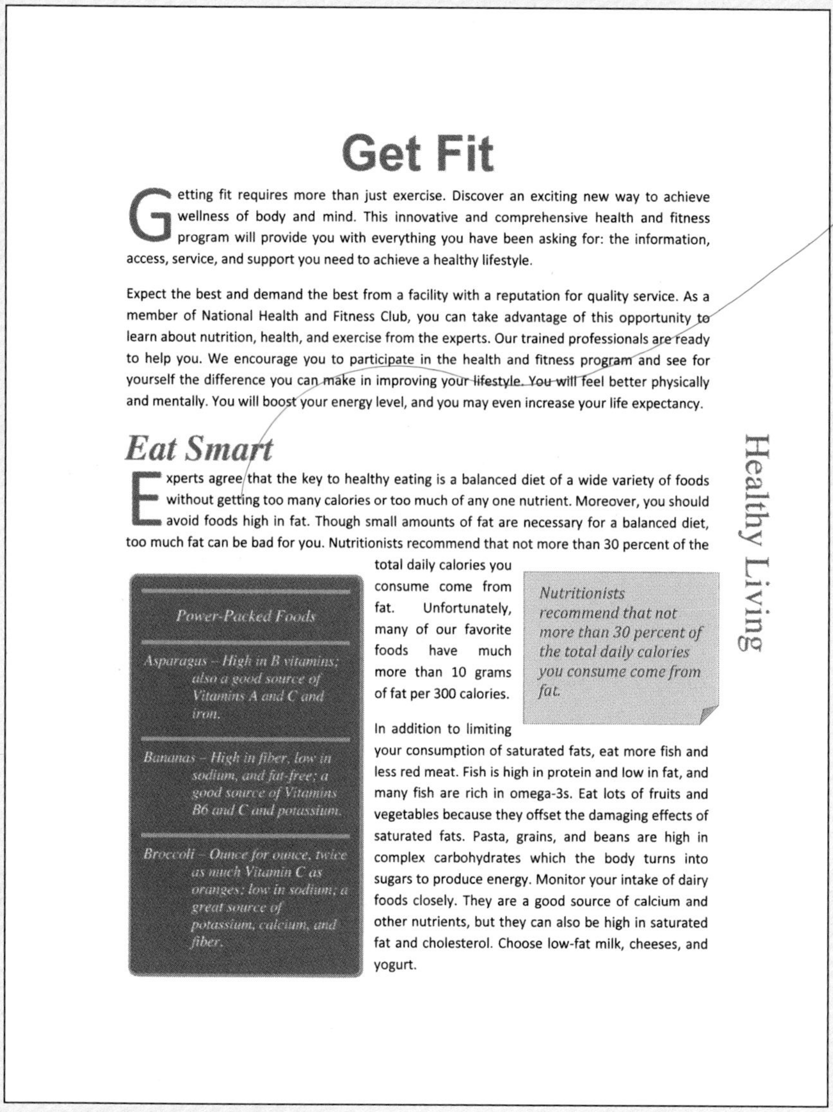

FIGURE 9–8
Enhanced Get Fit 3 document

Get Fit

Getting fit requires more than just exercise. Discover an exciting new way to achieve wellness of body and mind. This innovative and comprehensive health and fitness program will provide you with everything you have been asking for: the information, access, service, and support you need to achieve a healthy lifestyle.

Expect the best and demand the best from a facility with a reputation for quality service. As a member of National Health and Fitness Club, you can take advantage of this opportunity to learn about nutrition, health, and exercise from the experts. Our trained professionals are ready to help you. We encourage you to participate in the health and fitness program and see for yourself the difference you can make in improving your lifestyle. You will feel better physically and mentally. You will boost your energy level, and you may even increase your life expectancy.

Eat Smart

Experts agree that the key to healthy eating is a balanced diet of a wide variety of foods without getting too many calories or too much of any one nutrient. Moreover, you should avoid foods high in fat. Though small amounts of fat are necessary for a balanced diet, too much fat can be bad for you. Nutritionists recommend that not more than 30 percent of the total daily calories you consume come from fat. Unfortunately, many of our favorite foods have much more than 10 grams of fat per 300 calories.

Power-Packed Foods

Asparagus – High in B vitamins; also a good source of Vitamins A and C and iron.

Bananas – High in fiber, low in sodium, and fat-free; a good source of Vitamins B6 and C and potassium.

Broccoli – Ounce for ounce, twice as much Vitamin C as oranges; low in sodium; a great source of potassium, calcium, and fiber.

Nutritionists recommend that not more than 30 percent of the total daily calories you consume come from fat.

In addition to limiting your consumption of saturated fats, eat more fish and less red meat. Fish is high in protein and low in fat, and many fish are rich in omega-3s. Eat lots of fruits and vegetables because they offset the damaging effects of saturated fats. Pasta, grains, and beans are high in complex carbohydrates which the body turns into sugars to produce energy. Monitor your intake of dairy foods closely. They are a good source of calcium and other nutrients, but they can also be high in saturated fat and cholesterol. Choose low-fat milk, cheeses, and yogurt.

Healthy Living

14. Save the changes, and keep the document open for the next Step-by-Step.

Modifying Document Themes

Themes help you quickly change the appearance of a document and make it look professional. Word provides many built-in themes, and each has a specific look and feel. You can consistently apply formats to multiple documents because the same themes are also available in Excel and PowerPoint. For example, you can use the same theme to format a report in Word, a chart in an Excel spreadsheet, and slides in a PowerPoint presentation.

When you apply a theme, the new formats show up in headings, charts, picture borders, and tables. If you don't find a built-in theme that fits your needs, you can find additional themes online, you can modify the existing themes, or you can create your own themes. Office 2010 provides many built-in themes, and each theme defines three document elements: colors, fonts, and effects.

Several research studies and extensive discussions have been conducted to determine if the typeface can make text easier to read. *Serif fonts* have *serifs* (small lines or curls) at the ends of characters. The serifs are an embellishment for the font character. Some argue that the serifs help guide the eye along a line of text and connect the characters in a word. *Sans serif fonts* do not include the serifs, and some believe that sans serif typefaces are more difficult to read. Typically, sans serif fonts are used for headings and captions, and serif fonts are used for large blocks of text. Many people think serif fonts are easier to read on screen, but the research is still inconclusive. **Table 9–1** lists commonly used serif and sans serif fonts.

▶ VOCABULARY

serif fonts

serifs

sans serif fonts

TABLE 9–1   Commonly used serif and sans serif fonts

SERIF FONTS	SANS SERIF FONTS
Cambria	Arial
Courier	Calibri
Garamond	Franklin Gothic
Georgia	Helvetica
Rockwell	Trebuchet MS
Times New Roman	Verdana

Step-by-Step 9.8

1. If necessary, open **Enhanced Get Fit 3** from your solution files. Save the document as **Enhanced Get Fit 4**, followed by your initials.

2. Change the zoom to **35%**, so you can view all three pages in the document side by side.

3. Click the **Page Layout** tab. In the Themes group, click the **Themes** button to show the available built-in themes. The current theme for the document is the default, *Office*.

4. Slowly move the mouse pointer over several of the options. Notice in the live previews that the formats in the headings, text boxes, and table change. Not only do the colors change, but the flow of text is sometimes rearranged because the font styles and sizes change.

5. Select the **Grid** theme. Click the pull quote text box. Then click the Drawing Tools Format tab, and in the Shape Styles group, click the **Shape Fill** button arrow and change the fill color to a darker tan. Your edit affected the document, but no changes were made to the theme settings. When you apply this theme to another document, the fill color will show the lighter tan.

6. Click the **Page Layout** tab. In the Themes group, click the **Theme Colors** button. The Theme Colors gallery opens. At the bottom of the list, click **Create New Theme Colors**. The Create New Theme Colors dialog box shown in **Figure 9–9** opens. A theme has a combination of twelve colors: four colors for body text and backgrounds, six accent colors for headings and tables, and two colors for new and used hyperlinks.

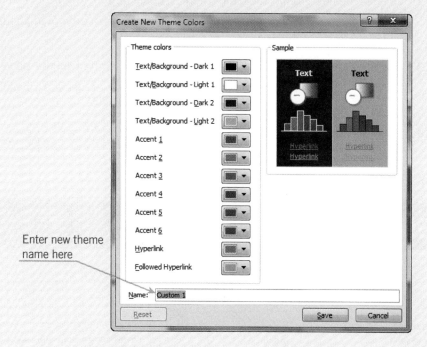

FIGURE 9–9
Create New Theme Colors
dialog box

Enter new theme name here

7. Click the **Accent 1** list arrow and then select a darker tan color. Notice that the Name box shows a proposed new theme name, such as *Custom 1*. Enter your first and last name followed by the number 1. Click **Save**. The changes are updated in the document, and the revised theme is saved under a new theme name.

8. In the Themes group, click the **Theme Fonts** button ⒜⁻. The Theme Fonts gallery opens. Scroll down and click the **Flow** option. The font changes are reflected in the document, but the theme settings are not altered.

9. In the Themes group, click the **Theme Effects** button ◉⁻. The Theme Effects gallery opens. Click the **Concourse** option. You will notice a slight difference in the effects for the SmartArt object on the third page. Twenty effects are available for themes, including shadows, lines, and 3D.

10. In the Themes group, click the **Themes** button. At the bottom of the menu, click **Save Current Theme**. The Save Current Theme dialog box opens. In the File name box, enter your first and last name followed by the number 1. Click **Save**.

11. Click the **Themes** button again. Your new theme appears at the top of the list under the heading *Custom*. Right-click your custom theme and then click **Delete**. When prompted about deleting the theme, click **Yes**.

12. In the Themes group, click the **Themes Color** button. Right click the custom theme with your name, then click **Delete**. When prompted about deleting the theme colors, click **Yes**.

13. With the theme changes, the content may have shifted in the document. Review each page, and adjust the text flow as needed so that content layout looks good.

14. Save the changes and close the document.

SUMMARY

In this lesson, you learned:

- Changing document backgrounds can enhance the appearance of a document and make the document easier to read.

- Shading and borders enable you to set apart sections of a document.

- Watermarks are often used to print logos or text on company stationery. A watermark can be created from text or a graphic and formatted to appear behind the document content, or the image can be impressed in the paper when the paper is manufactured.

- Drop caps are used to draw attention to the content in a document.

- Sidebars and pull quotes are used to highlight content in a document. Several Quick Parts are available to help you quickly create professional text boxes to format these features.

- You can repeat text box contents on every page or section of a document by inserting a text box in a header or footer.

- You can change the direction of text in a text box so that the text reads from top to bottom or from bottom to top.

- You can override formats within the many built-in themes for a single document, or you can modify the formats and then save the changes using a new theme name.

polish to your document.   *standard 3colors*   *shading*

VOCABULARY REVIEW

Define the following terms:

chain

drop cap

gradient fill

pull quote

sans serif fonts

serif fonts

serifs

sidebar

story

watermark

REVIEW QUESTIONS

TRUE / FALSE

Circle T if the statement is true or F if the statement is false.

T   F   **1.**   The drop cap format can be added to only the first letter of a word.

T   F   **2.**   Even though document background colors will not print, a document background texture or pattern will print.

T   F   **3.**   All linked text boxes must be in the same document.

T   F   **4.**   Changing the background color in a document can make it easier to read if the document is going to be distributed online.

T   F   **5.**   Watermark formats are stored in the header and footer panes.

FILL IN THE BLANK

Complete the following sentences by writing the correct word or words in the blanks provided.

1. A(n) _____ is a ghost image that appears behind the document content.

2. The _____ is the content in a text box.

3. When two or more text boxes are connected, it is referred to as a(n) _____.

4. The lines or curls added to the ends of font characters are referred to as _____.

5. _____ fonts are often used to format headings and captions.

MULTIPLE CHOICE

Select the best response for the following statements.

1. If a document is to be printed in black and white, _____.

    A.   light colors and shading patterns are most effective

    B.   gradients and textures are most effective

    C.   color highlights are most effective

    D.   background colors are most effective

2. Shading can be applied to _____.

    A.   an entire page

    B.   a paragraph or a group of paragraphs

    C.   a letter, a word, or a group of words

    D.   all of the above

3. Themes define three elements in a document: _____.

    A.   colors, fonts, and page layout

    B.   colors, fonts, and effects

    C.   fonts, margins, and page layout

    D.   colors, page backgrounds, and patterns

4. Borders can be applied to any or all sides of _____.

    A.   a page or a section

    B.   only the first page of a document

    C.   all pages except the first page of a document

    D.   all of the above

5. A sidebar _____.

    A.   is used to format headings and captions

    B.   emphasizes a passage from a document, such as a magazine article

    C.   is supplemental text added to a magazine or newspaper article

    D.   none of the above

■ PROJECTS

If you have a SAM 2010 user profile, your instructor may have assigned an autogradable version of the indicated project. If so, log into the SAM 2010 Web site at *www.cengage.com/sam2010* to download the instruction and start files.

PROJECT 9–1

The company you work for has asked you to format a banquet invitation that is to be distributed online. It is a formal banquet, so you need to create a classy, professional-looking document. The primary color in the company logo is burgundy, but you do not have to use that color.

1. Open the **Invitation** file from the drive and folder where your Data Files are stored. Save the document as **Enhanced Invitation**, followed by your initials. This file includes all the information that needs to be included on the invitation.

2. Format the document to create an attractive one-page invitation. Consider applying the following formats: backgrounds, page borders, paragraph borders and shading, font styles, font colors, and paragraph alignment. (You do not have to use all of those formats.) Adjust the spacing between lines of text as needed.

3. Format the document so it is centered vertically on the page.

4. Save the changes and close the document.

SAM PROJECT 9–2

Your boss asked you to format content for a flyer that will be distributed in the local community. To be effective, the flyer needs to be attractive and easy to read.

1. Open the **Trees** file from the drive and folder where your Data Files are stored. Save the document as **Enhanced Trees**, followed by your initials.

2. Center the title and change the font style and font size so that the title is much bigger, but not so big that it wraps to a second line.

3. Change the title to a serif font. (*Hint*: See Table 9–1.)

4. Format a box border around the title text, using a line style and color of your choice. Then add a shade to the paragraph, using a color that complements the border color. If necessary, change the font color of the title text so it complements the shading and border.

5. Format the first word in the first paragraph as a drop cap, using the dropped option. Adjust the number of drop lines to **2** and change the distance from the text to **.2"**. Change the drop cap font to a font style of your choice (a serif font is recommended), and then change the font color so it complements the colors in the title.

6. Repeat the drop cap formats for the first word in each of the two remaining paragraphs.

7. Format the last paragraph with an outline border, using a border style and color of your choice.

8. This document needs approval before it is published and distributed, so you need to make sure anyone who sees it knows that it is a draft copy. Choose a text watermark from the built-in options, or create your own custom watermark.

9. Position the watermark near the bottom of the document, and apply a shape outline to make the watermark more noticeable.

10. Save the changes and close the document.

PROJECT 9–3

1. Open the **Lead Out** file from the drive and folder where your Data Files are stored. Save the document as **Enhanced Lead Out 1**, followed by your initials.

2. Click anywhere in the second paragraph and insert the Motion Sidebar text box from the Building Blocks Organizer.

3. Format the sidebar text box so the height is 3.5" and the width is 2". Position the text box in the lower-right corner of the first page.

4. Copy the text box to the Clipboard, click anywhere in the middle of the second page of the document, and paste the text box.

5. Link the text box on the first page so the text will flow to the text box on the second page. Be sure to delete the content in the text box placeholder before you create the link.

6. Cut the entire first paragraph to the Clipboard, then paste the text in the sidebar text box. The story will flow to the second text box.

7. Deselect the text boxes, then select the text box on the second page and adjust the height so it is big enough to show the entire story. Position the text box in the upper-left corner of the second page, and if necessary, adjust the font size and font color.

8. Click in the first sentence of the second paragraph under the heading *Health Risks*. Open the Building Blocks Organizer and insert the Exposure Quote text box. Format the text box size so that it is approximately 1" high and 2" wide.

9. Position the text box where it fits best near the heading *Health Risks*. Type the following excerpt in the text box. Adjust the text box size if necessary so that all the pull quote text fits. If necessary, adjust the font size and font color.

Lead poisoning is the most common environmental illness in children.

10. At the end of the document, select the heading *Prevention of Lead Poisoning* and all of the bulleted items below the heading. Apply a paragraph shading and an outside border that complements the color theme for the sidebars and the pull quote.

11. Apply a border to the title at the top of the document using a border setting, style, and color of your choice. If desired, add a shading format to the title. If necessary, or if it makes the document attractive, adjust the font size and font color.

12. Check to make sure all the text in the sidebar text boxes and the pull quote text box are visible. If necessary, adjust the height of the text boxes. Check the flow of text from one page to the next. Make sure the headings stay with the first paragraph below them, and make line spacing adjustments as needed to keep content together so that it is easier to read.

13. Save the changes, and leave the document open for the next project.

PROJECT 9–4

1. If necessary, open **Enhanced Lead Out 1** from your solution files. Save the document as **Enhanced Lead Out 2**, followed by your initials.

2. Change the margin settings to 1" top and bottom and 1.25" left and right.

3. Format a text box in the header pane so it will appear on every page. In the text box, type **HEALTH WATCH**. Change the font size to 28 point and change the font color to one that fits in with the current theme colors.

4. Change the text orientation so that the text reads from bottom to top, then resize the text box to show all of the text. The width of the text box should be no more than .7".

5. Position the text box about halfway down the page in the left margin. Remove the outline from the text box shape.

6. Apply a new theme to the document.

7. Modify one or more color formats in the document, such as changing shading to a darker color. Do not make any changes to an existing theme, and do not create a new theme.

8. Check to make sure all the text in the sidebar text boxes and the pull quote text box are visible. If necessary, adjust the height of the text box. Check the flow of text from one page to the next. Make sure the headings stay with the first paragraph below them, and make line spacing adjustments as needed to keep content together so that it is easier to read. Also check that the *Health Watch* text box is visible on all pages.

9. Save the changes and close the document.

▮ CRITICAL THINKING

ACTIVITY 9–1

Open a new blank document. Type **=rand(2,2)** and then press Enter to create some sample text. Select the first paragraph of text and apply a serif font. Then select the second paragraph of text and apply a sans serif font. (*Hint*: See Table 9–1.) If necessary, increase the font sizes of both paragraphs of text so you can compare the ends of the characters. Describe the differences you see in the two types of fonts. Also comment on which font type you prefer and whether you find one font type easier to read than the other.

ACTIVITY 9–2

Word provides shortcuts that enable you to insert a horizontal line by typing only a few characters. The horizontal lines are automatically formatted for page width. Search the Help screens to learn about these shortcuts. When you find the information, practice the shortcuts, then make a list of the shortcuts and describe how to insert the horizontal lines with just a few taps on the keyboard. Include a few sentences about which shortcut you like most, and describe when you would find that shortcut useful.

LESSON 10

Working with Templates and Styles

■ OBJECTIVES

Upon completion of this lesson, you should be able to:

- Create a custom document template.
- Create a new document based on a document template.
- Attach a template to a document and make a template global.
- Apply and change styles.
- Create and modify styles.
- Copy, edit, and delete styles.
- Reveal and clear formats.
- Use a template to share building blocks.

■ VOCABULARY

boilerplate text

document template

global template

Normal template

style

style sheet

template

When you open a new blank document, do you ever think about all the predefined formats that are part of the document? It is easy to take for granted the default settings that affect the page layout, margin settings, paragraph spacing, and font styles. As you work with a document, you often change those default settings. You can predefine your own set of formats to help you save time and effort and ensure consistency when formatting your documents.

Working with Templates

► VOCABULARY

template

document template

global template

Normal template

boilerplate text

Every Microsoft Word document is based on a ***template***, a file that affects the basic structure of a document and contains document settings such as fonts, line spacing, margins, and page layout. Using templates increases the speed and efficiency of your work since you do not need to spend time formatting page layouts and font formats. Templates also help you maintain consistency in the documents you create.

Word has two basic types of templates. A ***document template*** contains document settings, content, and styles that are available only to documents based on that template. A ***global template*** contains document settings that are available to all documents. Word's default global template is the ***Normal template*** (Normal.dotm), and it shares styles with all open documents. To run Word, you must have a Normal template. If the Normal template is deleted, Word will create a new one using the factory defaults.

You can create additional global templates so that you can store customized styles, formats, and AutoText, and then make them available to all documents. Although you can only use one document template to create a document, you can use multiple global templates. For example, you can open a document that is based on the global template Normal, and then you can also access the styles and formats in another global template.

TIP

Depending on your Word installation, many document templates may already be installed, but if you can't find what you need, hundreds more are available at the Microsoft Web site.

EXTRA FOR EXPERTS

The default location for saving templates varies depending on the version of Word. You can see (and modify) the default location from the File tab. Click Options, and in the Word Options dialog box that opens, click Advanced. Scroll to the end of the Advanced options list, and under General, click File Locations. In the File Locations dialog box, under File types, click User templates. The location is indicated to the right.

Creating a Custom Document Template

Microsoft provides a variety of document templates to help you quickly create a new document, such as a resume, brochure, fax cover sheet, or business cards. A document template can include headers and footers, AutoText, pictures and graphics, styles and themes, and more. Standard text that is reusable in documents, such as contracts and correspondence, is referred to as ***boilerplate text***. At any time, you can edit the template contents.

If you frequently create a particular document, such as an agenda for monthly meetings, you can make a customized document template and then use that template each time you need to prepare an agenda. You can make a customized document template by opening a blank document or by modifying an existing document or an existing template.

Step-by-Step 10.1

1. Launch Word and then open the **Agenda** file from the drive and folder where your Data Files are stored. Note that the document is already formatted and contains boilerplate text and graphics that can be used in future documents.

2. Click the **File** tab, and then click **Save As** to open a Save As dialog box similar to the one shown in **Figure 10–1**.

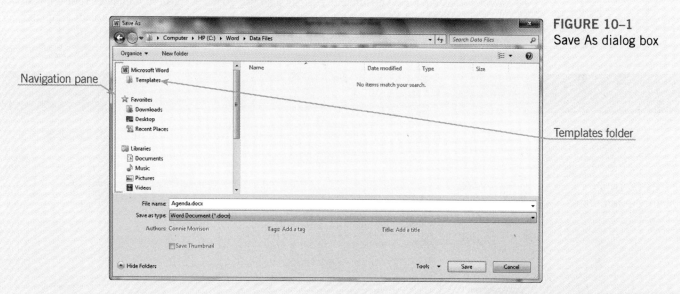

Navigation pane

Templates folder

FIGURE 10–1
Save As dialog box

3. In the File name box, change the filename to **Agenda Template**, followed by your initials. In the Save as type box, select **Word Template (*.dotx)**.

4. Navigate to the folder where you save your solution files, and then click **Save** to save the template file in that folder.

5. In the Paragraph group, click the **Show/Hide ¶** button ¶ to show non-printing characters in the document.

6. Make the following changes to the template, taking care not to change the formatting:

    a. In the lower-right corner of the document heading, replace the date *October 14, 2014* with **Date**.

    b. In the column to the right of *PLEDGE OF ALLEGIANCE*, delete *Eagle Scout Eric Chapman*.

    c. Under *APPROVAL OF MINUTES*, delete the date *September 16, 2014*.

    d. Under *OPEN ISSUES*, in the left column, delete the two entries of text, but be sure to leave all formatting symbols. This will maintain the formats and make it easy for you to create new entries for future documents.

    e. In the right column under *OPEN ISSUES*, delete the two occurrences of *Patrick Carmody*.

    f. Under *NEW BUSINESS*, in the left column, delete the one entry of text, but leave the nonprinting formatting symbol. In the right column, delete *Superintendent Brad Jones*.

7. Save the changes and close the document.

⊞ EXTRA FOR EXPERTS

If the template contains macros (which you will learn about in Lesson 16), you would select the Word Macro-Enabled Template (*.dotm) file type.

Creating a New Document Using a Custom Template

Just as you use the installed templates and those available at www.office.com to create a new document, you can also use your new custom template. Your template won't include any field placeholders like those provided in the Microsoft templates, but you will still be able to create a new document quickly and efficiently.

Step-by-Step 10.2

1. Click the **File** tab, and then click **New**. Available templates appear in a screen similar to the one shown in **Figure 10–2**.

FIGURE 10–2
Available templates

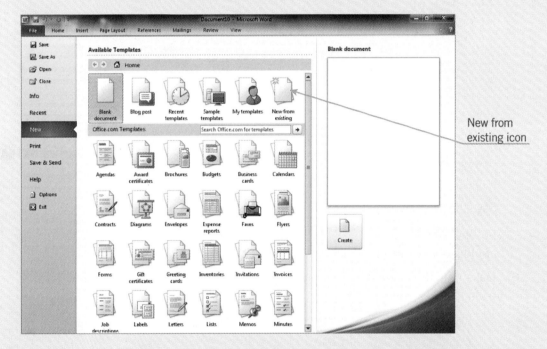

New from existing icon

2. In the Home section, click the **Sample templates** icon and review the types of document templates available. Above the first row of sample templates, click **Home** to return to the Available Templates.

3. Click the **New from existing** icon. Navigate to the folder where you save your solution files and then click **Agenda Template.dotx**. Click **Create New**. A new document opens and shows the template boilerplate text.

4. Click the **File** tab, click **Save As**, and navigate to the folder where you save your solution files. Name the document **November Agenda**, followed by your initials. Click **Save**. Note that the file is saved as a new document and the template is no longer open, so as you make changes, the changes will be saved to the document and not to the template.

5. In the lower-right corner of the heading, replace *Date* with *November 18, 2014*.

6. Click in the column to the right of *PLEDGE OF ALLEGIANCE* and type **Eagle Scout Aidan Rivera**.

7. Under *APPROVAL OF MINUTES*, position the insertion point after the word *of* and type the date **October 14, 2014**.

8. In the left column under *OPEN ISSUES*, position the insertion point to the right of the tab symbol. Type **Dunham Road, street lighting**. Delete the ¶ symbol and the tab symbol because you do not need to use the blank line below.

9. Click in the right column next to *Dunham Road, street lighting* and type **Ethan Brzezinski**. Delete the ¶ symbol to remove the blank line below.

10. Under *NEW BUSINESS*, in the left column, type **Interlocal agreement with Wilson Township for ambulance service**. Click in the right column and type **Les Hanes**.

11. Save the changes and then close the document.

Creating a Personal Template

By default, Word stores styles and building blocks in the Normal template. All users of the computer have access to the Normal template. Because you may share a computer with learners in other classes, you will create a personal template so you can store the new styles and building blocks that you create in this lesson. That way you can also copy the template and use it on other computers.

TECHNOLOGY TIMELINE

Before electric typewriters and computers, manual typewriters were used to create formal documents. The manual typewriters used monospaced fonts (also referred to as fixed-width fonts), so all characters were the exact same width. For example, the amount of horizontal space provided for the letter *i* was the same as the amount of horizontal space provided for the letter *w*. It was common practice to create two blank spaces at the end of a sentence because the extra blank space made it easier to see the break between sentences. Today's word-processing applications include proportional fonts, which means the character widths vary depending on the shape of the characters. Proportional fonts are easier to read because there is no excess blank space between characters. Also, the blank spaces between sentences are more obvious, so you need only enter one blank space between sentences.

Although proportional fonts are easier to read, monospaced fonts have not vanished. They are especially useful when aligning text in columns. Computer programmers use monospaced fonts to increase the readability of source code.

Step-by-Step 10.3

1. Open a new blank document.

2. Click the **File** tab, and then click **Options.** In the left pane of the Word Options dialog box, click **Advanced**. Scroll down to the Save section shown in **Figure 10–3**.

FIGURE 10–3
Save options in the Advanced options for working with Word

Option to prompt before saving

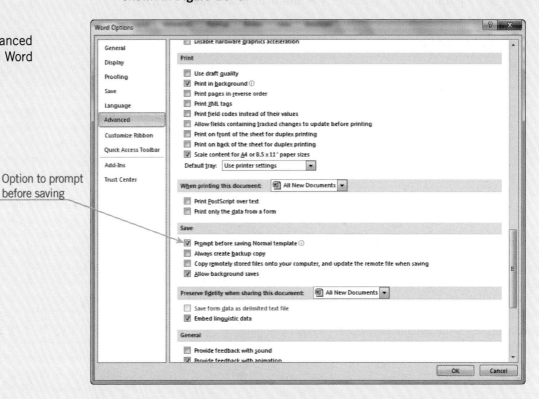

3. If necessary, enable the **Prompt before saving Normal template** option, and then click **OK**. Turning on this prompt will prevent you from accidentally saving changes to the Normal template, and Word will also prompt you to save changes to your personal template.

4. Click the **File** tab, and then click **Save As** to open the Save As dialog box. Navigate to the folder where you save your solution files.

5. In the File name box, type your first and last names, type **Template**, and then type your initials.

6. In the Save as type box, select **Word Template (*.dotx)**.

7. Click **Save**. Your personal template contains all the styles provided in the Normal template, and you can add additional styles to the template.

8. Close the template.

WARNING

If prompted to save changes to the global Normal template upon exiting Word, click No.

Attaching a Template and Making a Template Global

By default, Word attaches the Normal template to a new blank document. If you want to use styles or formats from a different template, you can attach additional templates to the document. When you attach a template to a document, it gives you access to the styles in the newly attached template. The styles in the attached template are only available to that one document.

   You can make the template temporarily global to all open documents and all new documents that you create during the Word session. However, when you restart Word, the template will no longer be global. To make a template permanently global, you can store it in Word's startup folder, and then the template will be loaded as an add-in every time you start Word. Do not save any global templates on a classroom computer unless you have permission.

> **EXTRA FOR EXPERTS**
>
> If you move the document or template to a different folder or to a different computer, the attachment between the document and the template will be broken. The existing styles and formats in the document will not change, but unless you reattach the template or make the template global, you will not be able to apply additional formats and styles from the template.

Step-by-Step 10.4

1. Open the **Pharmacy** file from the drive and folder where your Data Files are stored. In the folder where you save your solution files, save the document as **Pharmacy 1**, followed by your initials.

2. Click the **File** tab, and then click **Options**. In the left pane in the Word Options dialog box, click **Add-Ins**. The Word Options screen opens with information and options for Add-ins, as shown in **Figure 10–4**.

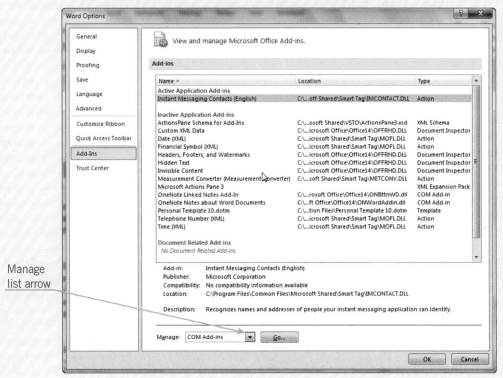

Manage list arrow

FIGURE 10–4
Information and options to manage Microsoft Office Add-ins

3. Click the **Manage** list arrow, click **Templates**, and then click **Go**. The Templates and Add-ins dialog box shown in **Figure 10–5** opens, and the Normal template name appears in the Document template box.

FIGURE 10–5
Templates and Add-ins dialog box

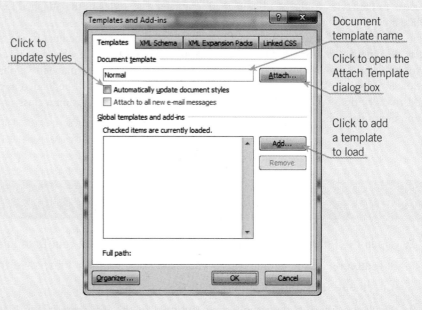

4. Click **Attach** to open the Attach Template dialog box shown in **Figure 10–6**. Your folders and filenames may differ.

FIGURE 10–6
Attach Template dialog box

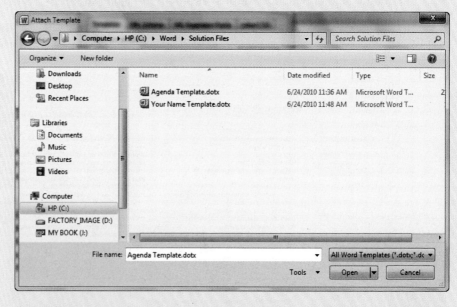

5. Navigate to the folder where you save your solution files. Select your personal template and then click **Open**. Now the name of your personal template will appear in the Document template box in the Templates and Add-ins dialog box.

6. Under Global templates and add-ins, click **Add**. Navigate to your solutions folder, select your personal template, and then click **OK**.

7. Under *Checked items are currently loaded*, your personal template now appears in the list. Make sure the check box next to your personal template file is enabled. Click **OK**.

8. Leave the document open for the next Step-by-Step.

Working with Styles

A *style* is a set of predefined formats you can apply to characters, paragraphs, tables, and numbered and bulleted lists. When you apply a style, you apply a whole group of formats in one simple step. For example, instead of taking multiple steps to change the font, font size, font color, and alignment for heading text, you can achieve the same results in one step by applying a title style. When a paragraph is moved or copied, the styles are moved or copied with the text and they do not need to be reapplied.

By applying styles to text, you can make sure that parts of your document, such as headings, are formatted consistently throughout the document. Styles are included in templates, and several styles are available in the Normal template. You can also create your own styles. When you save the styles in a template, they are available when the template is attached to a document. By saving styles in a template, you can ensure formatting consistency across multiple documents.

> **VOCABULARY**
> **style**

Applying and Changing the Formatting of Styles

To apply a new style, you must identify the text or content you want to format. When applying a paragraph format, you need only position the insertion point anywhere within the paragraph. However, when applying a character format, you must select all of the text to which you want to apply the style.

You can modify a style by changing one or more of the style formats. For example, after applying a heading style, you can select the text and change the font size. The other formats will remain unchanged. When you modify a style in a document, the changes are applied only to the current selected content, and the settings for the original style are not affected. When a paragraph is moved or copied within a document, the text retains the style.

When working with styles, you can open the Styles pane, which lists the styles available in the template that is attached to the document. An alternative to opening the Styles pane is to open the Apply Styles pane. The Apply Styles pane is smaller and shows only the current style, but you can scroll through all the available styles and apply, update, and modify them.

Step-by-Step 10.5

1. If necessary, open the **Pharmacy 1** document from your solution files.

2. On the Home tab, in the Styles group, click the **Dialog Box Launcher** to open the Styles pane shown in **Figure 10–7**.

FIGURE 10–7
Styles pane

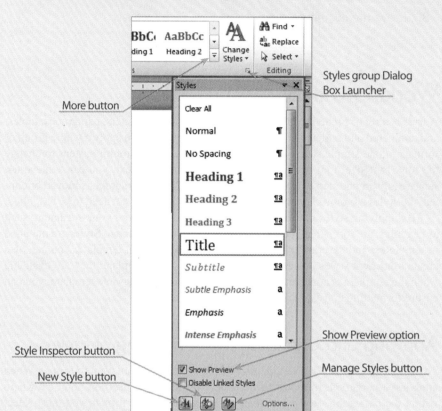

3. Note that the styles listed in the Styles pane are the same as the styles available in the Styles group on the Home tab. If necessary, enable the option **Show Preview** to see what the styles look like in the Styles pane.

4. If necessary, click anywhere within the title *Pharmacy*. Note that in the Styles pane (and also in the Styles gallery on the Ribbon), the style *Title* is selected, indicating that the style is applied.

5. Select the title text and change the font size to **24** point. Then, change the font color to a dark red or burgundy color. Change the paragraph alignment to **Center**.

6. Deselect the text, and then position the insertion point anywhere in the title *Pharmacy*. Reapply the Title style by clicking **Title** in the Styles pane. Even though you changed the formats where the style was applied in the document, the Title style settings were not changed.

7. Click the **More** button in the Styles group (see Figure 10–7), and then click **Apply Styles** to open the Apply Styles pane, shown in **Figure 10–8**. The style name Title appears in the Style Name box.

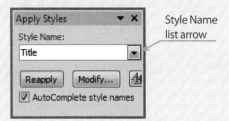

Style Name
list arrow

FIGURE 10–8
Apply Styles pane

8. Click the title bar of the Apply Styles pane and drag the pane to the left side of the document. You can reposition the pane anywhere on the screen. (If you drag the pane to the edge of the window, it will expand. Drag the pane back toward the center of the screen to reduce its size.)

9. Triple-click anywhere in the paragraph under the title *Pharmacy* to select the entire paragraph.

10. Click the **Style Name** list arrow in the Apply Styles pane. Scroll down and select the style **Intense Emphasis**. Because the style is a character format, it is applied to only the selected characters.

11. Click anywhere within the heading *Course of Study*. Apply the style **Heading 2**. The new style replaces the original style. Because the style contains both paragraph and character settings, all the formats were applied to the entire heading paragraph.

12. Save the changes and leave the document open for the next Step-by-Step.

Creating Styles Based on Formatted Text

You can create your own styles for characters, paragraphs, tables, and lists. You can quickly create a style based on formatted text. In this course, you will store the custom styles that you create in your personal template so that you do not alter the Normal template.

Step-by-Step 10.6

1. If necessary, open **Pharmacy 1** from your solution files. Save the document as **Pharmacy 2**, followed by your initials. Your personal template is already attached to the document, and if you did not close Word, the template is still temporarily global.

2. If necessary, open the **Styles** pane. (*Hint*: On the Home tab, in the Styles group, click the Dialog Box Launcher.) If necessary, open the **Apply Styles** pane. (*Hint*: On the Home tab, in the Styles group, click the More button.)

3. Select all the text in the document title. Change the font color to **Red, Accent 2**.

4. With the text still selected, at the bottom of the Styles pane, click the **New Style** button ⊞. The Create New Style from Formatting dialog box opens, as shown in **Figure 10–9**.

FIGURE 10–9
Create New Style from Formatting dialog box

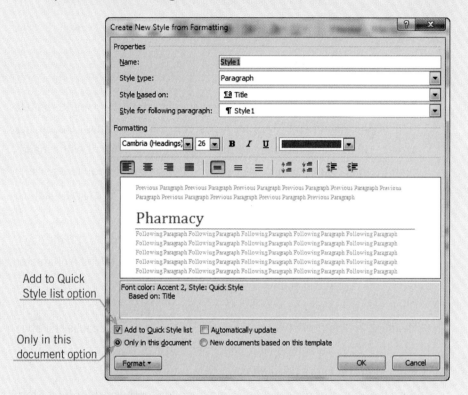

Add to Quick Style list option

Only in this document option

5. In the Name box, replace *Style1* with **Title1**, followed by your initials.

6. Leave the Style type and Style based on settings as is. Make sure the options **Add to Quick Style list** and **Only in this document** are enabled.

7. Click **OK** to save the new style and close the dialog box. The new style appears in the Styles gallery on the Ribbon, in the Styles pane, and in the Apply Styles pane.

8. Close the Apply Styles pane.

9. Save the changes and leave the document open for the next Step-by-Step.

Creating Styles Using Commands and Existing Styles

You can also create a style using formatting commands, or you can base a style on an existing style. When you base a new style on an existing style, the new style inherits the characteristics of the existing style. This can save you a lot of time when creating a new style.

Step-by-Step 10.7

1. If necessary, open **Pharmacy 2** from your solution files. Save the document as **Pharmacy 3**, followed by your initials. If necessary, open the **Styles** pane.

2. Position the insertion point in the heading *Introduction*. Click the **New Style** button in the Styles pane to open the Create New Style from Formatting dialog box.

3. In the Name box, replace *Style1* with **Side Heading 1**, followed by your initials. In the Style type box, leave the setting *Paragraph* as is.

4. Click the **Style based on** list arrow, scroll to the top, and then click **(no style)**. This will allow you to create the style without using previous format settings.

5. In the Style for following paragraph box, select **Normal**. The paragraph immediately following this style will have the Normal character and paragraph formats.

6. Define the character and paragraph formats for the new style:

   a. Click **Format** in the lower-left corner of the dialog box, and then click **Font**. If necessary, click the **Font** tab.

   b. Change the font to **Calibri**, and change the point size to **16** point. Change the font color to **Dark Blue, Text 2, Darker 25%**, and then click **OK**.

   c. Click **Format** and then click **Paragraph**. If necessary, click the **Indents and Spacing** tab, and then under Spacing, set Before to **6 pt** and After to **6 pt**.

   d. Click **OK** twice to close both dialog boxes.

7. Using the Styles pane, apply your new **Side Heading 1** style to the headings *Education*, *Licenses*, *Opportunities*, *Benefits*, and *Conclusion*.

8 Position the insertion point anywhere in the heading *Course of Study*. Apply your new **Side Heading 1** style.

9. In the Styles pane, click the **New Style** button to open the Create New Style from Formatting dialog box. In the Name box, replace *Style 1* with **Side Heading 2**, followed by your initials.

10. In the Create New Style from Formatting dialog box, leave the Style type and the Style based on settings as is. You will create the new style settings based on the Side Heading 1 style you just created.

11. In the Formatting section, change the font size to **14** point and also click the **Italic** button. Click **OK** to close the dialog box.

> **TIP**
>
> You must set capitalization options in the Font dialog box if you want them to be part of the style.

12. Using the Styles pane, apply your new **Side Heading 2** style to the headings *Internships, Residencies, and Fellowships* and *Skills*.

13. Save the changes and leave the document open for the next Step-by-Step.

Copying Styles from Other Templates or Documents

Styles can also be moved between templates and documents. You can show the styles for documents and templates in panes side by side, and then you can copy the styles from one pane to the other. You can copy styles from a document to a template, and from a template to a document. You can also copy styles between two templates or between two documents.

Step-by-Step 10.8

1. If necessary, open **Pharmacy 3** from your solution files. If necessary, open the **Styles** pane.

2. At the bottom of the Styles pane, click the **Manage Styles** button ⬛. The Manage Styles dialog box opens, as shown in **Figure 10–10**.

FIGURE 10–10
Manage Styles dialog box

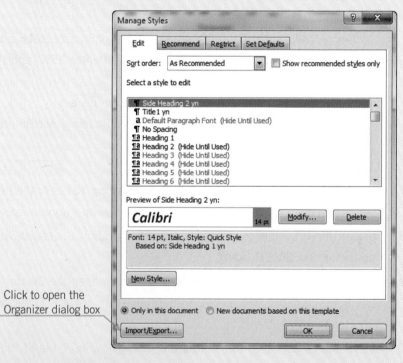

Click to open the
Organizer dialog box

3. Click **Import/Export** to open the Organizer dialog box shown in **Figure 10–11**. Note that the styles in the Normal template appear on the right, and your new styles are not available in the Normal template. However, if you scroll down through the list on the left, you will see that your new styles are stored in the document.

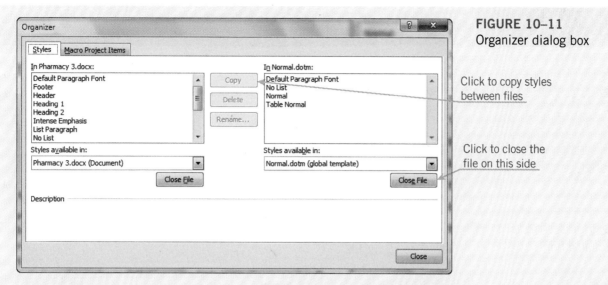

FIGURE 10–11
Organizer dialog box

Click to copy styles between files

Click to close the file on this side

4. On the right, under the Styles available in box for the Normal.dotm template, click **Close File**. The list of Normal template styles is removed from the pane.

5. Click **Open File**. In the navigation pane of the Open dialog box, navigate to the folder where you save your solution files, select your personal template, and then click **Open**. The styles available in your personal template now appear on the right.

6. In the Pharmacy 3.docx style list on the left, click your new style **Side Heading 1** (followed by your initials). Then click **Copy** to copy the style to your personal template.

7. Scroll down to show the remainder of the style list for Pharmacy 3.docx. Select your new **Side Heading 2** (followed by your initials). Hold down **Ctrl** and then click your new style **Title1** (followed by your initials). Click **Copy** to copy both styles to your personal template.

8. Click **Close** to close the dialog box. Now when you attach your personal template to a document, these three new styles will be available.

9. Leave the document open for the next Step-by-Step. (If you close the document, you will be prompted to save the changes to your personal template. Click Save.)

Editing and Deleting Styles

After you create a style, you can easily modify it. You can change the style name and/or the formatting options. You can also remove styles from a template.

Step-by-Step 10.9

1. If necessary, open **Pharmacy 3** from your solution files. Save the document as **Pharmacy 4**, followed by your initials. Click Yes if prompted to save changes to the document template. If necessary, open the **Styles** pane.

2. Position the insertion point in the title *Pharmacy*. In the Styles pane, point to the style name **Title1** (followed by your initials) and then click the **list arrow** that appears next to the style name. In the menu that opens, click **Modify** to open the Modify Style dialog box shown in **Figure 10–12**.

FIGURE 10–12
Modify Style dialog box

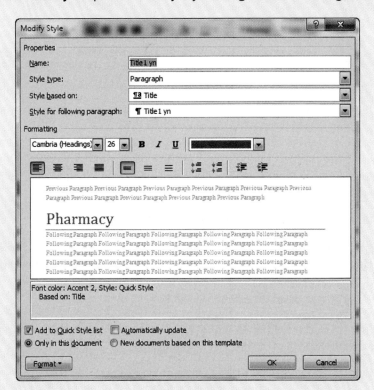

3. In the lower-left corner of the dialog box, click **Format** and then click **Font**. In the Font dialog box, under Effects, enable the **All caps** option. Click **OK** to close the Font dialog box.

4. In the Name box of the Modify Style dialog box, change the style name to **Title2**, followed by your initials, and then click **OK**. All the characters in the title are now formatted in all caps.

5. In the Styles pane, click the **Manage Styles** button to open the Manage Styles dialog box. Click **Import/Export** to open the Organizer dialog box. On the right side, click **Close File** to close the Normal global template. Then click **Open File** and navigate to and select your personal template file. Click **Open**.

6. In the Pharmacy 4 document styles list on the left, scroll down and select your new style **Title2** (followed by your initials). Click **Copy** to save the style to your personal template.

7. You can also easily delete styles from a template. In the list of styles on the right, select the **Title2** style. Click **Delete**. When prompted to delete the style, click **Yes**. Deleting the style from the template does not affect the style stored in the document. Close the Organizer dialog box.

8. Save the changes to the document, and if prompted to save changes to the document template, click Yes. Leave the document open for the next Step-by-Step.

Revealing and Clearing Formats

A *style sheet* is a list of all styles that are used in a document or available in a template. Style sheets are automatically saved with each Word document. Therefore, if you open the document on a different computer, the style sheet is automatically loaded and the styles you applied are still available.

Many people prefer to show the descriptions of the styles and formats as they work with documents. The Style Inspector pane shows the currently applied paragraph- and text-level formatting, and it offers options for creating a new style or modifying the currently applied style. For more detail, you can open the Reveal Formatting pane to show paragraph settings including alignment, indentation, spacing, and tabs. This enables the user to verify the existing formats and quickly edit the formats if desired.

You can easily remove some or all styles from formatted content and restore the content to the Normal document style by using the Clear All option on the Styles pane or the Style Inspector pane.

> **VOCABULARY**
> style sheet

EXTRA FOR EXPERTS

To print a list of all the styles used in a document (including a description of each style), click the File tab and then click Print. Under Settings, click Print All Pages. Under Document Properties, click Styles, and then click the Print button at the top of the center pane.

Step-by-Step 10.10

1. If necessary, open **Pharmacy 4** from your solution files. If necessary, open the **Styles** pane.

2. Position the insertion point in the title. Click the **Style Inspector** button 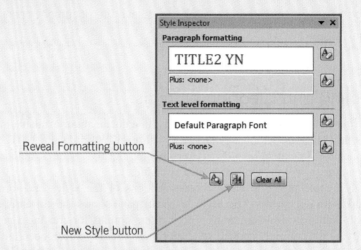 at the bottom of the Styles pane. The Style Inspector pane opens and displays the styles for the current paragraph, as shown in **Figure 10–13**.

FIGURE 10–13
Style Inspector pane

Reveal Formatting button

New Style button

3. Click the title bar in the Style Inspector pane and drag the pane to position it away from where you are working in the document window. Position the mouse pointer over the buttons in the pane to view the ScreenTip and see the options available.

4. Position the insertion point in the first paragraph below the title. Note that the information in the Style Inspector pane changes.

5. Click the **Reveal Formatting** button at the bottom of the Style Inspector pane. A new pane similar to the one shown in **Figure 10–14** opens in the upper-right corner of the document window. (You may have to move or close the Styles pane to see the Reveal Formatting pane.)

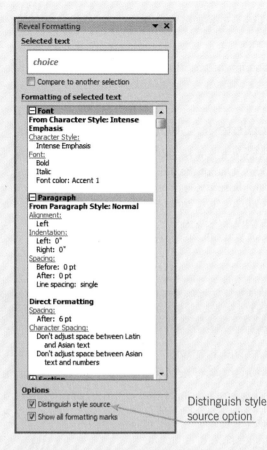

FIGURE 10–14
Reveal Formatting pane

Distinguish style
source option

6. In the Reveal Formatting pane, under Options, enable the **Distinguish style source** option. Notice that the pane now shows information about the source of the style, and you can determine whether the style is based on another style source.

7. Close the Reveal Formatting pane.

8. Click anywhere in the title. In the Style Inspector pane, click **Clear All**. The paragraph and character formats are removed, and the paragraph is now formatted with the default Normal style.

9. Click the **Undo** button to restore all the paragraph and character formats. Close the Style Inspector pane. If necessary, show the **Styles** pane.

10. Select any word in the first paragraph below the title. In the Styles pane, scroll to the top of the list of styles and click **Clear All**. Only the current word is affected because the Intense Emphasis style that is applied to this paragraph is a character style. To remove the style from the entire paragraph, you would need to first select the entire paragraph.

11. Click the **Undo** button to restore the character formats.

12. In the document window, select the entire document. In the Styles pane, click **Clear All** in the task pane. All the style formats are removed, and the entire document is formatted with the Normal style.

> **TIP**
>
> To quickly remove styles, select the text and then press the shortcut key combination Ctrl+Shift+N.

13. Click the **Undo** button to restore all the styles in the document. Close the Styles pane.

14. Close the document and the application without saving any changes.

Using a Template to Share Building Blocks

In a team environment, it can be useful for everyone to use the same styles and settings in documents. One of the advantages of using templates is that it makes it easy for you to share those styles and settings. For example, if you create your own building blocks, you can store them in your personal template, and then you can share the template with others. To share the template, you can distribute the file to all team members, or you can save the file in a central location, such as on a shared network drive.

Step-by-Step 10.11

1. Launch Word and then open the **Quick Parts** file from the drive and folder where your Data Files are stored. Note that the document contains boilerplate text and graphics that can be used in future documents.

2. Since this is a new Word session, you need to attach your personal template and make sure it is global.

   a. Click the **File** tab, click **Options**, and then, in the Word Options dialog box, click **Add-Ins**.

   b. Click the **Manage** list arrow, click **Templates**, and then click **Go**.

   c. Click **Attach**, open your solutions folder and select your personal template, and then click **Open**.

   d. If necessary, under Global templates and add-ins, add your personal template to the list. Make sure there is a check mark to the left of the filename, and then click **OK**.

3. Triple-click in the first paragraph to select the entire paragraph.

4. Click the **Insert** tab. In the Text group, click the **Quick Parts** button, and then click **Save Selection to Quick Part Gallery**. The Create New Building Block dialog box opens, similar to the one shown in **Figure 10–15**.

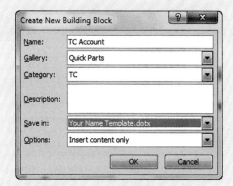

FIGURE 10–15
Create New Building Block
dialog box

5. In the Name box, type **TC Account**. Leave the Gallery setting as *Quick Parts*.

6. Click the **Category** list arrow and then click **Create New Category**. In the Create New Category dialog box, type **TC**. Click **OK**.

7. Click the **Save in** list arrow and select your personal template. When the options in your dialog box match those in Figure 10–15, click **OK** to save the building block to your personal template.

8. Click anywhere on the company logo to select it. Click the **Quick Parts** button and then click **Save Selection to Quick Part Gallery**.

9. In the Name box, type **TC Logo**. Click the **Category** list arrow and then select **TC**.

10. Click the **Save in** list arrow and then click your personal template. Then, click **OK**.

11. Close the document, but do not close Word. When prompted to save the changes to the document, click **Don't Save**. Then when prompted to save changes to your personal template, click **Save**.

12. Open a new blank document. Click the **Insert** tab. In the Text group, click the **Quick Parts** button. You should see the two new building blocks you created and stored in the TC category. Scroll down if necessary.

13. Click the **TC Logo** building block to insert it in the document.

14. Close the document without saving the changes, and then close Word.

TIP

If you do not see the building blocks you just created, your personal template may not be global. Repeat Step 2 above.

SUMMARY

In this lesson, you learned:

- You can create a customized document template by opening a blank document or by modifying an existing document or an existing template.

- When you attach a template to a document, you have access to the styles and building blocks stored in the template. When you make a template temporarily global to all open documents, the template is available to all new documents you work with during that Word session.

- Word's Normal template provides many styles, but you can create your own styles. Using styles helps you format documents consistently.

- You can change document formats by applying new styles. When you override style formats in a document, the changes apply only to the selected content, but the original style settings are unaffected.

- Styles can be copied from documents to templates, and vice versa.

- Revealing formats enables you to view them as you work with a document. You can see the style information in the Style Inspector pane. More details about the style settings are provided in the Reveal Formatting pane.

- The Clear All option on the Styles pane and the Style Inspector pane enables you to remove applied styles quickly and restore the document text to the Normal style.

- Templates make it easy for you to share styles and building blocks with others.

■ VOCABULARY REVIEW

Define the following terms:

boilerplate text
document template
global template

Normal template
style

style sheet
template

■ REVIEW QUESTIONS

TRUE / FALSE

Circle T if the statement is true or F if the statement is false.

T   F   **1.**   If the Normal template is deleted, Word will automatically create a new template using the factory defaults.

T   F   **2.**   A style can contain both paragraph and character formats.

T   F   **3.**   You must save all template files in the Microsoft Word Templates folder.

T   F   **4.**   When a paragraph is moved or copied, you must reapply the style.

T   F   **5.**   When you clear a style in a document, the text is formatted with the Normal style.

FILL IN THE BLANK

Complete the following sentences by writing the correct word or words in the blanks provided.

1. A(n) _____ is a set of predefined formats you can apply to characters, paragraphs, tables, and numbered and bulleted lists.

2. The _____ is Word's default global template.

3. Standard text that is reusable in various documents is referred to as _____.

4. A(n) _____ is a file that affects the basic structure of a document and contains document settings.

5. A(n) _____ is a list of all styles that are used in a document or available in a template.

WRITTEN QUESTIONS

Write a brief answer to the following questions.

1. List ten examples of document templates that Word provides.

2. Describe how to change the Word settings so that you do not accidently save changes to the Normal template.

3. Describe how to attach a template to a document.

4. Describe how to make a template global.

5. Describe how to copy styles from a document to a template file.

◼ PROJECTS

If you have a SAM 2010 user profile, your instructor may have assigned an autogradable version of the indicated project. If so, log into the SAM 2010 Web site at *www.cengage.com/sam2010* to download the instruction and start files.

PROJECT 10–1

1. Launch Word and open the **Certificate** file from the drive and folder where your Data Files are stored.

2. Save the document as a template in your solutions folder. Name the template **Certificate Template**, followed by your initials.

3. Remove the variable text from the template:
   a. Select the name *Elizabeth H. Kasper* and type **Name**.
   b. Select *25* and type **XX**.

4. Leave the rest of the boilerplate text. Save the changes and close the template file.

5. Open a new document based on the new certificate template you just created. Save the document to your solutions folder as **Weber Certificate**, followed by your initials.

6. Enter the variable data:
   a. Replace *Name* with **Alexander E. Weber**.
   b. Replace *XX* with **30**.

7. Save the changes and close the document.

SAM PROJECT 10–2

1. Open the **Flyer** file from the drive and folder where your Data Files are stored. Save the document as **Final Flyer**, followed by your initials.

2. Position the insertion point in the paragraph that begins *Hours*. Create a new style by defining the formats:
   a. Name the style Hours.
   b. Set the style type for Paragraph, and base the style on no other style.
   c. Set the style format for the following paragraph to the Normal style.
   d. Change the font style to Georgia, change the font size to 14 point, and change the font effects to Small caps.
   e. Apply the style only in the current document.

3. Select the text *WINTER INVITE*. Change the font color to a dark red to match the star in the logo.

4. With *WINTER INVITE* still selected, create a new style using the existing formats:
   a. Name the style Action Heading.
   b. Format the style type setting for Character.
   c. Save the style only in the current document. Do not add the new style to the Quick Style list.

5. In the Styles pane, click the Manage Styles button. Click Import/Export to open the Organizer dialog box. Then open your personal template file in the right pane.

6. Copy the two new styles (*Action Heading* and *Hours*) from the Final Flyer document to your personal template. Save the changes to your personal template.

7. Save the changes and close the document.

8. Open **Events** from the Data Files and save the document as **Final Events**, followed by your initials.

9. Attach your personal template to the document, and make the template global. Also enable the option to automatically update document styles.

10. Apply the Action Heading style to the text *UPCOMING EVENTS*.

11. Format the list of upcoming events with a 1/2" left indent.

12. Save the changes and close the document.

PROJECT 10–3

1. Open the **Waste** file from the drive and folder where your Data Files are stored. Save the document as **Final Waste**, followed by your initials.

2. Open the Styles pane and clear all the styles in the title and the headings.

3. Select the title text and apply the Title style.

4. From the Styles pane, open the Modify Style dialog box to modify the Title style. With the title text still selected, increase the font size to 16 point and change the font style to Georgia. Also, change the font color to Olive green, Accent 3, Darker 50%.

5. Apply the Subtitle style to the first heading *REDUCE WASTE*.

6. From the Styles pane, open the Modify Styles dialog box to modify the Subtitle style. Change the font color to Olive green, Accent 3, Darker 50%, and add the bold format.

7. Use the Styles pane to apply the modified Subtitle style to the remaining headings in the document: *CONVERT WASTE*, *RECYCLE IN BUSINESS*, *RECYCLE ALUMINUM*, and *RECYCLE PLASTICS*.

8. Save the changes and close the document.

PROJECT 10–4

1. Open the **LCCU Building Blocks** file from the drive and folder where your Data Files are stored.

2. If necessary, make your personal template file global. Also, check the Word settings to make sure that you will be prompted before any changes are made to the Normal template.

3. Select the first paragraph and save the text in the Quick Parts gallery:
   a. Name the building block Privacy.
   b. Leave the Gallery setting as Quick Parts.
   c. Create a new category LCCU and save the building block in the new category.
   d. Save the new building block in your personal template.

4. Select the second paragraph and save the text as a building block in the Quick Parts gallery. Name the building block Cards, and save it to the Quick Parts gallery in the LCCU category. Be sure to save the building block in your personal template.

5. Select the third paragraph and save the text as a building block in the Quick Parts gallery. Name the building block Report,

and save it to the Quick Parts gallery in the LCCU category. Be sure to save the building block in your personal template.

6. Close the LCCU Building Blocks document, without saving any changes. If prompted to save the changes to your personal template, click **Save**.

7. Open the file **Credit Letter** from the Data Files. Save the document as **Updated Credit Letter**, followed by your initials.

8. Position the insertion point in front of the second paragraph in the body of the letter. Insert the building block **Cards**.

9. Position the insertion point at the end of the letter. First insert the building block Privacy. Press Enter, and then insert the building block Report.

10. Correct any spacing issues between paragraphs.

11. Save the changes and close the document. (If you close Word, click **Save** when prompted to save the changes to your personal template.)

■ CRITICAL THINKING

ACTIVITY 10–1

One of the installed templates provided in Word 2010 is the Blog post template. To learn more about creating a blog post in Word, go to the Microsoft Web site and search the keywords *blogging with Word*. After you have explored Word's blogging features, open a new Word document and write a brief summary describing the advantages of using the Blog post template. Also, comment on whether you feel the Blog post template will be useful to you now or in the future. Cite the sources of your information by including the URLs for the Web pages where you found the most useful information.

ACTIVITY 10–2

If you are sharing files with users who have older versions of Word software, you can save a Word .docx file as a Word 97–2003 document (with a .doc extension). When converting documents to the older format, you often lose some of the features. For example, some formats and graphics become static and you are unable to edit them. Search the Help screens and gather information about whether styles can be successfully converted to the older version and whether or not you can open Word 2010 templates using 97–2003 versions of Word. Write a brief summary of your findings.

Estimated Time: 2 hours

LESSON 11

Customizing Tables and Creating Charts

■ OBJECTIVES

Upon completion of this lesson, you should be able to:

- Rearrange the rows and columns in a table.
- Sort table data.
- Adjust column and row spacing, modify table styles, and split a table.
- Draw a table and split table cells.
- Change text alignment in table cells and align a table.
- Calculate sums and create other formulas in a table.
- Embed worksheet data into, or link worksheet data to, a Word document.
- Create and modify a chart.

■ VOCABULARY

caption

destination file

embedded object

gridlines

import

linked object

source file

Tables are very effective for organizing and presenting data. Word offers some powerful features to help you customize the table layout and design. And to illustrate data, you can quickly and easily create charts.

Rearranging Table Contents

After a table is created, you often need to rearrange the contents. You can move, copy, and paste the contents in a table the same way you move, copy, and paste text in a document.

Step-by-Step 11.1

1. Launch Word and then open the **Accounts Receivable** file from the drive and folder where your Data Files are stored. Save the document as **Balances Due 1**, followed by your initials.

2. Position the mouse pointer above the column heading *Balance Due*. When the pointer changes to a down arrow, click to select all cells in the column. Then click the **Cut** button (or press **Ctrl+X**). Position the insertion point anywhere in the heading *Date Due* above the first column. Click the **Paste** button (or press **Ctrl+V**). The *Balance Due* column is inserted to the left of the *Date Due* column.

3. Select the *Balance Due* column and then drag the mouse to the left to select the *Date Due* column. Then drag the selected columns to the right until the mouse pointer is positioned anywhere in the *Customer* heading cell, then release the mouse button to drop the two selected columns to the right of the *Customer* column.

4. In the middle of the table, select the three rows that show a due date of *12-15*. Position the insertion point to the left of the *R. Johnson* row. When the pointer changes to a right-pointing arrow, click to select all the cells in the row and then drag the pointer down to include the *W. Diaz* and *C. Featherhold* rows.

5. Click the **Table Tools Layout** tab. In the Rows & Columns group, click the **Insert Below** button. Three new rows are inserted below the selected rows.

6. Enter the following new data in the *Customer* and the *Balance Due* columns.

   Jonathon Latham   15,678.11

   Caroline Johnson   10,009.85

   Wendy Evans   12,433.66

7. Select the **12-14** due date in the third column, just below the new table rows. Copy the content to the Clipboard, and then click each of the empty cells in the *Date Due* column and paste the due date in each of those cells.

WARNING

If you select a range of cells by dragging across the cells (instead of selecting the entire row by clicking to the left of the first cell in the row), when you paste the selected data in another cell range, it will replace the existing data. So, be sure you select the entire row when you want to move data.

8. Select the bottom row (W. Grisham) and then cut the row to the Clipboard. Position the insertion point anywhere in the *Abby Johnson* cell just below the *Customer* heading, and then paste the row. The entire *W. Grisham* row is moved to a new position above the row where the insertion point is positioned.

9. Select the last two rows in the table (E. Diaz and A. Perez). With the rows selected, position the mouse pointer over the first selected cell. Press **Esc** to hide the Mini toolbar, and then drag the selected rows to the top of the table. When the insertion point is positioned anywhere in the *Jessi Smith* cell near the top of the *Customer* column, release the mouse button to drop the selected rows in the new position. The two rows are inserted above the *Jessi Smith* row.

10. Save the changes and leave the document open for the next Step-by-Step.

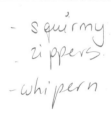

TIP

If you dropped the rows in the wrong location, click the Undo button and try the move again.

Sorting Table Contents

To reorder the contents of a table, you can use the Sort feature. You can choose to sort a single column without rearranging the data for the remaining columns, or you can sort all the data based on a specified column. Sorts can be based on as many as three criteria in multiple columns. Furthermore, you can sort by multiple words contained within a single table column. For example, if the column contains both first and last names, you can sort by either the last name or the first name.

[handwritten margin notes: - squirmy / zippers / - whipern]

Step-by-Step 11.2

1. If necessary, open the **Balances Due 1** file from your solution files. Save the document as **Balances Due 2**, followed by your initials.

2. To sort only the data in the first column of the table:

   a. Select the first column in the table. Note that the first data row shows the customer *Weston Grisham*. The account balance is *2,802.11* and the due date is *12-04*.

b. Click the **Home** tab, and in the Paragraph group, click the **Sort** button ⬛ to open the dialog box shown in **Figure 11–1**. Your dialog box settings will be different.

FIGURE 11–1
Sort dialog box

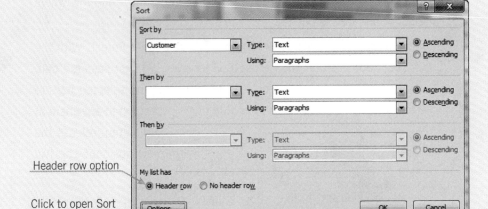

Header row option

Click to open Sort
Options dialog box

c. Under My list has, enable the **Header row** option. When this option is enabled, Word does not include the table column headings in the sort. Make sure your settings match those in Figure 11–1.

d. Click **Options** to open the Sort Options dialog box shown in **Figure 11–2**.

FIGURE 11–2
Sort Options dialog box

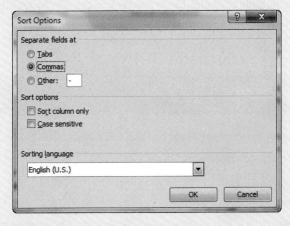

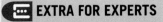 **EXTRA FOR EXPERTS**

When turned on, the Case sensitive option sorts text so words beginning with the same letter are arranged so that lowercase letters appear before uppercase letters.

e. Under Sort options, enable the **Sort column only** option, and then click **OK**.

f. Click **OK** in the Sort dialog box. The first column data is sorted in alphabetical order by first name, but the data in the other two columns did not sort.

3. Because the data is no longer accurate, click the **Undo** button to undo the sort.

4. To sort by multiple words within a single column:

a. Click anywhere in the table to deselect the first column. Then, drag the mouse pointer over all the cells with customer names to select those cells. (Do not select the column heading *Customer*.)

b. Click the **Sort** button. Under My list has, make sure the **No header row** option is enabled. If necessary, in the Sort by box, select **Column 1**, and in the first Type box, select **Text**. Also, make sure the **Ascending** option is enabled.

c. Click the **Options** button. In the Sort Options dialog box, under Separate fields at, enable the **Other** option.

d. Click and drag the mouse pointer across the **Other** text box to select the contents (even if the box appears blank). If any content is in the text box from a previous sort, such as a blank space or a hyphen, the content will be highlighted in blue. Press the **spacebar** to enter a blank space.

e. Under Sort options, disable the **Sort column only** option. This will ensure that all the data in a row will stay together. Then click **OK**.

f. In the Sort dialog box, click the **list arrow** to the right of the first Using box, and then click **Word 2**, as shown in **Figure 11–3**.

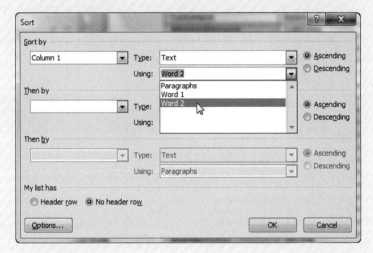

FIGURE 11–3
Using options in the Sort dialog box

g. Under the first Then by, select **Column 1**, and for the Using box, click **Word 1**. Click **OK**. The table content is sorted first based on the second word (or last name) in the first column. Then the content is sorted by the first word in the first column, and all the data remains intact.

5. To sort the table content based on criteria from multiple columns:

a. Click anywhere in the table to deselect the table cells. Then click the **Sort** button.

b. Under My list has, enable the **Header row** option.

c. Under Sort by, select **Date Due**. The Type setting will automatically change to *Date*. To the right of the Type setting, make sure the **Ascending** option is enabled.

d. Under the first Then by, click **Balance Due**. The Type setting will automatically change to *Number*. To the right of the Type setting, enable the **Descending** option.

e. Click **OK**. The rows are rearranged, first by the due date and then by the balance due. For accounts with the same due dates, the account with the highest balance due appears first in the order.

6. Click anywhere inside the table to deselect the rows.

7. Save the changes and leave the document open for the next Step-by-Step.

Modifying Table Structure and Formats

Word offers some powerful features to help you customize the layout and design for your tables. Not only can the layout and design make a table look professional, but using the right layout and design can also make the table easier to read.

Adjusting Column and Row Spacing

Generally, when you need to adjust the width of a column, you can simply drag a column border. But Word offers several other ways for you to automatically control column width. In certain instances, you may want rows or columns to be spaced evenly throughout the table. In the following steps, you will experiment with features that give you more control over column and row spacing.

Step-by-Step 11.3

1. If necessary, open the **Balances Due 2** file from your solution files. Save the document as **Past Due Accounts 1**, followed by your initials. If the ruler is not displayed above your document, click the View tab and in the Show group, select Ruler.

2. Select the **Customer** column. On the left side of the Ruler, click the **tab selector** until the Left Tab icon ⌊ displays. Then click 1/4-inch to the right of the margin on the Ruler to set a left-aligned tab stop, as shown in **Figure 11–4**.

FIGURE 11–4
Left-aligned tab stop on the Ruler

3. Position the insertion point after *Emanuel Diaz* in the second row. Press **Enter** to create a second line in the cell. Then hold down **Ctrl** and press **Tab** to create a paragraph indent inside the cell. Then type the company name **A-1 Construction**.

4. Repeat Step 4 to add company names below the following customer names. The text will automatically wrap as needed to fit within the cell.

Weston Grisham   **Grisham Construction**

Abby Johnson   **ADCO Foundations**

Jonathon Latham   **Latham-Guenther Developers**

Robert Johnson   **R & S Builders**

5. Position the mouse pointer over the right border for the *Customer* column. When the pointer changes to a horizontal double-headed arrow, hold down the **Alt** key and drag the right column border. As you drag the column border, the column size displays on the horizontal ruler just below the Ribbon. Set the column width at **2.16"**.

6. Select the first row. Position the mouse pointer over the bottom border of the first row. When the pointer changes to a vertical double-headed arrow, hold down the **Alt** key and drag the border down to increase the height of the row. As you drag the row border, the row height displays on the vertical ruler at the left side of the document window. Set the row height to **0.5"**.

7. Select the second, third, and fourth rows (E. Diaz, S. Smith, and S. Diaz) in the table. Click the **Table Tools Layout** tab. In the Cell Size group, click the **Distribute Rows** button ⊞. The height for all the selected rows is adjusted so that they are the same height.

8. Select all the rows in the table except for the first row, and then click the **Distribute Rows** button to evenly adjust the height of all the rows in the table except the first row.

9. Select all three columns in the table. In the Cell Size group, click the **Distribute Columns** button ⊞. The width of the table remains the same, but the column widths are automatically adjusted to equal width.

10. Position the insertion point anywhere within the table. In the Cell Size group, click the **AutoFit** button, and then click **AutoFit Contents**. The column widths adjust to the longest line in each column.

11. Select the *Date Due* column. In the Rows & Columns group, click the **Insert Right** button. Click in the first row of the new column and type **Late Fee**. The width of the new column automatically adjusts to show all of the new text.

12. With the insertion point anywhere within the table, click the **AutoFit** button and then click **AutoFit Window**. The widths of the columns widen, and the table fills the document window and extends from the left margin to the right margin. This is the default setting that is applied when you first create a table in a document. Click the **Undo** list arrow and then click **Insert Column Right** to switch the table to its previous size and remove the new column.

TIP

You can double-click the right border of a column to resize a column quickly to accommodate the longest entry in the column. In some tables, however, you may have to narrow one or more columns before you can double-click to widen another.

13. Position the insertion point anywhere in the table. Click the **AutoFit** button, and then click **Fixed Column Width**. You will not see any changes in the column widths. Position the insertion point in the *Date Due* column, and then insert a new column to the right. The new column is the exact same width as the *Date Due* column. Type the heading **Late Fee**.

14. Save the changes and leave the document open for the next Step-by-Step.

Modifying Table Styles and Creating a New Table Style

In most cases, the default ½-point single-line border will be appropriate for the tables you create. However, sometimes you might want to customize the border and add shading to some or all of the table cells to make the content easier to read. Word offers many built-in table styles that are already formatted with borders, shading, and color. The six table style options are described in **Table 11–1**. You can easily toggle these style options on and off.

TABLE 11–1   Descriptions of table style options

OPTION	RESULT
Header Row	The first row is given special formatting, which is good for highlighting the column headings.
Total Row	The last row is given special formatting.
Banded Rows	Odd rows are formatted differently than even rows; for example, all the even rows have shading, which makes it easier to read the table contents.
First Column	The first column is given special formatting.
Last Column	The last column is given special formatting.
Banded Columns	Odd and even columns are formatted differently.

▶ **VOCABULARY**

gridlines

caption

As you apply and modify table styles, you may choose to remove some or all cell borders. So that you can tell where the table cells begin and end, you can display the table *gridlines*, the lines that distinguish the cell boundaries. Although gridlines are visible on your screen, they do not print. When you apply a cell border, the gridlines for the cell are no longer visible.

Most tables include captions, especially when more than one table appears in a document. A *caption* is a label that identifies or describes an illustration, a table, or a picture. You can easily add captions to tables, and if you choose to add numbers to the table captions, Word will automatically update the table numbers for you.

Step-by-Step 11.4

1. If necessary, open the **Past Due Accounts 1** file from your solution files. Save the document as **Past Due Accounts 2**, followed by your initials.

2. Position the insertion point anywhere within the table. Click the **Table Tools Design** tab. In the Table Styles group, click the **More** button to show the gallery of built-in table styles. If necessary, scroll to the bottom and, in the last row, click the **Colorful Grid – Accent 1** table style.

3. To view the cell borders as you work with the table, click the **Table Tools Layout** tab. In the Table group, click the **View Gridlines** button to toggle the option on to show the cell borders.

4. Click the **Table Tools Design** tab. Explore the options in the Table Style Options group, as follows:

   a. Click the **Header Row** option to toggle the setting off. The shading format in the first row changes, and the header row is formatted with the same shading as all the other rows in the table. Click the **Header Row** option again to toggle the setting back on.

   b. Click the **Banded Rows** option to toggle the setting off. The shading format is the same for all rows in columns 2, 3, and 4.

   c. Click the **First Column** option to toggle the setting off. The shading format in the first column changes, and the column does not stand out as much. Click the **First Column** option again to toggle the setting back on.

   d. Click the **Last Column** option. The shading format in the last column is now the same as in the first column. Click the **Last Column** option again to toggle the setting off.

   e. Click the **Banded Columns** option. The shading format changes for the second and fourth columns.

5. Create a new table style by modifying an existing style:

    a. In the Table Styles group, click the **More** button. Click **Modify Table Style** to open the dialog box shown in **Figure 11–5**. Your dialog box settings will be different.

FIGURE 11–5
Modify Style dialog box

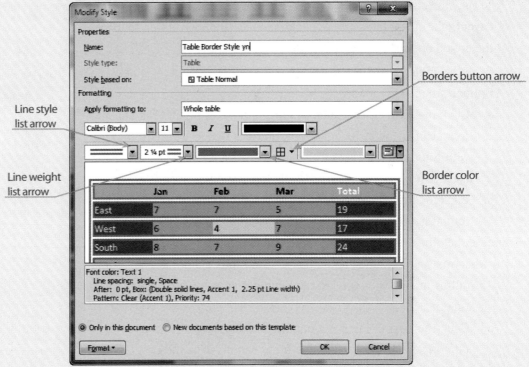

b. In the Name box, replace the current style name with **Table Border Style**, followed by your initials.

c. Click the **Line Style** list arrow and then click the first double-line style (the 7th line style).

d. Click the **Line Weight** list arrow and then select **2 ¼ pt**.

e. Click the **Border Color** list arrow and then select the **Blue, Accent 1** theme color.

f. Click the **Borders** button arrow and then select **Outside Borders**. Your sample preview should look like the preview in Figure 11–5. Adjust the border settings if necessary.

g. Make sure the **Only in this document** option is enabled, and then click **OK**. The new table style is added to the Table Styles gallery.

6. In the Table Styles group, click the **More** button. If necessary, scroll to the top of the Table Styles gallery. Under Custom, you will see the new table style you created. Position the mouse pointer over the new table to show the style name. Click anywhere in the document window to close the Table Styles gallery.

EXTRA FOR EXPERTS

If you enable the option *New documents based on this Template*, the new style will be saved to the attached template and available for future documents.

7. With the insertion point positioned anywhere in the table, click the **References** tab. In the Captions group, click the **Insert Caption** button to open the Caption dialog box shown in **Figure 11–6**.

8. Click the **Label** list arrow to view the built-in labels: *Equation*, *Figure*, and *Table*. Click the arrow again to avoid making any changes. Click the **Position** list arrow, and then click **Below selected item**. Click **OK**. The caption *Table 1* is inserted below the table.

9. Click the **Insert Caption** button, and then click **AutoCaption** to open the AutoCaption dialog box, as shown in **Figure 11–7**. Under Add caption when inserting, scroll down and enable the **Microsoft Word Table** option. Click **OK**.

TIP

To customize the caption text, click New Label in the Caption dialog box and then enter text for the label.

10. Double-click below the *Table 1* caption to insert a new paragraph. Press **Ctrl+Enter** to insert a page break.

11. Insert a new table with 8 rows and 4 columns. Notice that the caption *Table 2* automatically appears below the table.

12. Apply your new custom table style to the new table.

13. Save the changes and leave the document open for the next Step-by-Step. If you are ending your Word session, follow Step 13 in Step-by-Step 11.5, to turn off the AutoCaption feature.

Splitting a Table

Sometimes the contents in a table grow and the number of table rows grows. Often a big table won't fit on one page, and when the table wraps to the next page, it does not include header rows. Or maybe you decide you want to divide the table content into two or more separate tables. Word provides features that can help you format long tables.

Step-by-Step 11.5

1. If necessary, open the **Past Due Accounts 2** file from your solution files. If necessary, enable the **AutoCaption** feature. (See Step-by-Step 11.4, Step 9.)

2. Select all of Table 1. (*Hint*: Click the **Table Select** button ⊞ at the upper-left corner of the table.) Then copy the table to the Clipboard.

3. Open a new blank document and paste the table. The caption *Table 1* appears below the table because you enabled the AutoCaption setting. Save the new document as **Past Due Accounts 3**, followed by your initials.

4. Position the insertion point in front of the word *Customer* in the first cell at the top of the table. Press **Enter** twice to insert two blank lines above the table.

5. Switch to the Past Due Accounts 2 document. Select Table 2 and copy it to the Clipboard. Then switch to the Past Due Accounts 3 document. Position the insertion point in the first blank paragraph at the top of the document, and then paste the second table at this location. The new table is labeled *Table 1*, and the second table is now labeled *Table 2*.

6. Scroll down to the end of the second table. You will see that the table has wrapped to the next page. Position the insertion point in the first row of Table 2. Click the **Table Tools Layout** tab. In the Table group, click the **Properties** button. Click the **Row** tab to access the options, as shown in **Figure 11–8**.

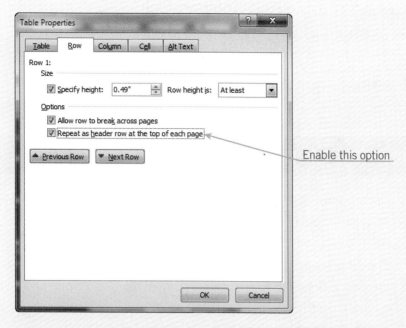

FIGURE 11–8
Row tab in the Table Properties
dialog box

7. Enable the **Repeat as header row at the top of each page** option. Click **OK**. The header row for Table 2 now appears at the top of the table, and it also appears above the first row of the table on the second page.

8. Scroll back to Table 2 on the first page. Position the insertion point in the *Abby Johnson* cell. On the Table Tools Layout tab, in the Merge group, click the **Split Table** button. Notice that the header row is not repeated in the second table (instead, the *Abby Johnson* row is formatted as a header), and the first table does not have a caption.

9. Position the insertion point anywhere in what is now the second table in the document. Click the **References** tab. In the Captions group, click the **Insert Caption** button. Leave the settings as they are in the dialog box, and click **OK**. The new table is labeled *Table 2*, and the caption for the table below changes to *Table 3*.

10. With the insertion point after the caption *Table 2*, enter a blank space and then type **- 30 days past due**. Position the insertion point after the caption *Table 3*. Enter a blank space and then type **- 15 days past due**.

11. Select the header row in Table 2 and copy it to the Clipboard. Then position the insertion point at the beginning of the first cell in Table 3 and paste the contents. The new header row appears at the top of Table 3.

12. Scroll down to see the rest of Table 3 on the next page. The header row also appears at the top of the table on the next page, because the header row you pasted was formatted to repeat the header row.

13. Turn off the AutoCaption feature. Click the **References** tab, and in the Captions group, click the **Insert Caption** button. In the Caption dialog box, click **AutoCaption**, disable the **Microsoft Word Table** option, and click **OK**.

14. Save the changes and close both documents.

Drawing a Table and Splitting Cells

The Draw Table tool allows you to use a pen pointer to draw a table boundary just the size you want, and then draw column and row lines within the boundary, creating cells of various sizes.

Splitting a cell converts a single table cell into multiple cells. You can split a cell into two or more rows and/or into two or more columns.

Step-by-Step 11.6

1. Open a new blank document and save the document as **Products 1**, followed by your initials. If necessary, click the **View** tab, and in the Show group, enable the **Ruler** option.

2. Click the **Insert** tab. In the Tables group, click the **Table** button and then click **Draw Table**. The mouse pointer changes to a pen ✐ and, if the document is displayed in Draft or Outline view, Word automatically changes to Print Layout view.

3. Use the Draw Table tool to create the table shown in **Figure 11–9**. Follow these simple steps:

FIGURE 11–9
Table grid for Step 3

a. Position the pointer at the left edge of the screen. Click and drag down and to the right as if you were using the Rectangle drawing tool. Use the rulers at the top and left edges of the window to estimate the size. Release when the table (box) is approximately 5 inches wide by 4 inches high.

TIP

If the pointer does not show the Draw Table pen, click the Table Tools Design tab and, in the Draw Borders group, click the Draw Table button.

b. If the new table border is a double line, the formats for the border style you created earlier in the lesson are still active. On the Table Tools Design tab, in the Draw Borders group, change the Line Style to a single line, the Line Weight to 1/2 pt, and the Pen Color to Automatic.

c. Position the Draw Table tool near the top border of the table, at about the ½-inch mark on the horizontal ruler. Then click and drag the tool down to create the first vertical line. Word completes the line for you and automatically makes it straight.

d. Position the Draw Table tool near the top border of the table, at about the 3½-inch mark on the horizontal ruler. Click and drag the tool down to create the second vertical line.

e. Position the Draw Table tool near the first vertical line, at about the 1¼-inch mark on the vertical ruler. Click and drag the tool to the right to create the first horizontal line. Draw a second horizontal line at about the 2¾-inch mark on the vertical ruler.

f. Press **Esc** to toggle off the Draw Table pen.

4. Position the insertion point in the second column of the first row. Click the **Table Tools Layout** tab. In the Merge group, click the **Split Cells** button to open the dialog box shown in **Figure 11–10**. Your dialog box settings will be different.

FIGURE 11–10
Split Cells dialog box

5. Change the number of columns to **1**, and change the number of rows to **4**. Click **OK**.

6. Position the insertion point in the second column of the second row. Split the cells by changing the number of columns to **1** and the number of rows to **3**.

7. Position the insertion point in the second column of the third row. Split the cells by changing the number of columns to **1** and the number of rows to **4**.

8. Position the insertion point anywhere in the top row. In the Rows & Columns group, click the **Insert Above** button.

9. Your table should look like the one shown in **Figure 11–11**. Click the **Table Tools Design** tab, and in the Draw Borders group, click the **Eraser** button. The mouse pointer changes to an eraser ✎. Click the cell borders identified in Figure 11–11, and the targeted borders are removed.

FIGURE 11–11
Table grid for Step 9

Erase these borders

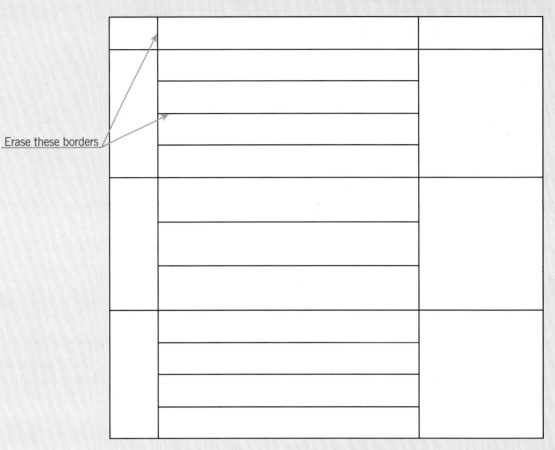

10. Click the **Eraser** button to toggle off the Table Eraser tool. Select all but the first row in the second column. Click the **Table Tools Layout** tab. In the Cell Size group, click the **Distribute Rows** button.

11. Complete the table by entering the data shown in **Figure 11–12**.

Product		Recycled Material
Indoor	Glass tiles	Glass
	Flooring	
	Counter tops	
Attire	Jewelry	Plastic
	T-shirts	
	Jackets	
Outdoor	Motor oil	Rubber
	Playground surfaces	
	Asphalt road repair	
	Roofing	

FIGURE 11–12
Table data for Step 11

12. Save the changes and leave the document open for the next Step-by-Step.

Changing Alignment and Rotating Text

Text can be aligned within a cell in a number of different ways. Word provides several settings for both horizontal and vertical alignment of the contents within a cell. You can also change the direction of text in a table cell by rotating the text.

Not only can you change the alignment of the content within a cell, but you can also change the alignment of the table, which affects where the table is positioned on the page. You can reposition the table anywhere in the document by dragging the table to a new location. You can also change the table alignment settings so the position of the table is relative to a paragraph, the margin, or the page.

Step-by-Step 11.7

1. If necessary, open the **Products 1** file from your solution files. Save the document as **Products 2**, followed by your initials.

2. Select the **Product** and **Recycled Material** cells. If necessary, click the Table Tools Layout tab. In the Alignment group, click the **Align Center** button 🔲, as shown in **Figure 11–13**.

FIGURE 11–13
Options in the Alignment group
on the Table Tools Layout tab

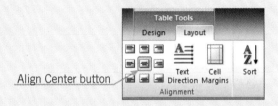

Align Center button

3. Select the **Glass**, **Plastic**, and **Rubber** cells, and then click the **Repeat** button on the Quick Access Toolbar to repeat the edit. Then select the **Indoor**, **Attire**, and **Outdoor** cells and repeat the edit.

4. Position the insertion point in the *Indoor* cell. In the Alignment group, click the **Text Direction** button twice to rotate the text so it can be read from the bottom to the top. The Text Direction button changes to show an image of rotated text. Also, the direction of the alignment option buttons changes.

5. Select the **Attire** cell and then click the **Repeat** button twice. Select the **Outdoor** cell and repeat the rotations.

6. Select the **Product** and **Recycled Material** cells. Click the **Table Tools Design** tab. In the Table Styles group, click the **Shading** button arrow and then select the **Orange, Accent 6, Darker 50%** color. With the cells still selected, change the font color to **White**.

7. Click anywhere in the *Indoor* cell. Click the **Shading** button arrow and then select the **Orange, Accent 6, Lighter 80%** color. Then repeat the edit in the *Glass tiles*, *Flooring*, *Counter tops*, and *Glass* cells.

8. Click anywhere in the *Attire* cell and apply the **Orange, Accent 6, Lighter 60%** color. Then repeat the edit for all the cells in the same row.

9. Click anywhere in the *Outdoor* cell and apply the **Orange, Accent 6, Lighter 40%** color. Then repeat the edit for all the cells in the same row.

10. Click the **View** tab, and in the Zoom group, click the **One Page** button. Point to the upper-left corner of the table. When the Table Move Handle appears, click the handle and drag the table down to the bottom of the page.

11. Click the **Table Tools Layout** tab. In the Table group, click the **Properties** button. If necessary, click the **Table** tab to open the Table Properties dialog box shown in **Figure 11–14**.

FIGURE 11–14
Table Properties dialog box

12. Under Alignment, click the **Center** option. Under Text wrapping, click the **Around** option. Then click **Positioning** to open the Table Positioning dialog box shown in **Figure 11–15**. Your dialog box settings will be different.

FIGURE 11–15
Table Positioning dialog box

13. Under Vertical Position, change the setting to **0**. Make any other necessary changes so your settings match those in Figure 11–15. Click **OK** twice to close the dialog boxes. The table is repositioned near the top of the document.

14. Save the changes and close the document.

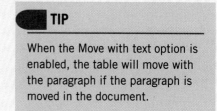

TIP

When the Move with text option is enabled, the table will move with the paragraph if the paragraph is moved in the document.

Using Quick Tables

If you want to create a professional-looking table, but you don't have time to fuss with the table structure and the table styles, you can use a Quick Table. Word provides several table templates, including calendars. Choose a table that provides the structure and style you need, and then replace the boilerplate text with your own content.

Step-by-Step 11.8

1. Open a new blank document. Save the document as **Sales Report 1**, followed by your initials. If necessary, click the **View** tab and change the zoom to 100%.

2. Click the **Insert** tab. Click the **Table** button and then point to **Quick Tables**. The Built-In dialog box opens. Scroll down to view the Tabular List and With Subheads quick tables, as shown in **Figure 11–16**.

FIGURE 11–16
Built-In quick tables

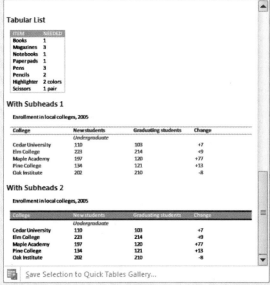

3. Select the **With Subheads 2** quick table. A new table with boilerplate text is inserted in the document. Notice the table has a custom caption.

4. Delete the text above the table, and then replace the boilerplate column headings with the following:

Sales Representative **April** **May** **June**

5. Delete the words *Undergraduate* and *Graduate*.

6. Replace the boilerplate text in rows 3 through 7 with the following data. Row 2 will have no data. The *June* column will not have data, so delete the boilerplate text in that column.

Mari Colace	**51,342**	**62,005**
Michelle Fracassa	**48,254**	**49,807**
Jeff Guetle	**57,654**	**58,009**
Rita Homminga	**62,350**	**63,242**
William Jamison	**41,078**	**43,209**

7. Select rows 8–13 (all remaining rows except the *Total* row). Right-click the selected rows, and then click **Delete Rows**.

8. Leave the word *Total* in the last row of Column 1, but delete the numbers in Columns 2, 3, and 4.

9. Select and delete the caption.

10. Save the changes and leave the document open for the next Step-by-Step.

Performing Math Calculations

Word provides a calculation feature that enables you to add numbers in text and in tables. To perform a calculation in a table, position the insertion point in the cell where the result (such as a total) is to appear, and then enter a formula. You can also specify number formats or choose a function from the list of frequently used functions in Word.

Calculating Sums in Tables

When calculating sums in a table, Word provides an easy shortcut to total the columns and/or rows. You can calculate a sum by inputting a SUM formula using the Formula button. The SUM formula adds numbers in cells above the cell containing the insertion point or in cells to the left of the cell containing the insertion point.

After creating formulas to perform calculations, you may discover that you need to change the data in the cells. Word does not automatically update calculations as does a spreadsheet program such as Excel. However, Word does provide a shortcut that enables you to recalculate an entire table quickly. When you use the Formula button, Word inserts hidden fields for each total. To recalculate, you simply select the cells containing those fields and update the fields.

Step-by-Step 11.9

1. If necessary, open the **Sales Report 1** file from your solution files. Save the document as **Sales Report 2**, followed by your initials.

2. Insert a new column to the right of the *June* column. (*Hint*: Position the insertion point in the *June* column, and then click the **Table Tools Layout** tab. In the Rows and Columns group, click the **Insert Right** button.) Add the column heading **Total**.

3. Calculate the total for the *Mari Colace* row:

   a. Position the insertion point in the last cell in the *Mari Colace* row.

   b. Click the **Table Tools Layout** tab. In the Data group, click the **Formula** button. The Formula dialog box opens with the proposed formula =SUM(LEFT), as shown in **Figure 11–17**.

FIGURE 11–17
Formula dialog box

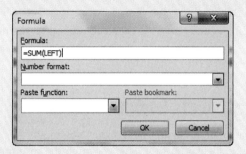

   c. Click **OK** to accept the proposed formula. The result (sum) of *113,347* is automatically inserted in the active cell.

4. To quickly insert the same formula in the other cells of the *Total* column, click in each cell and then click the **Repeat** button on the Quick Access Toolbar (or use the shortcut keys **Ctrl+Y**). Do not insert a formula for the *Total* row.

5. Calculate the total of the *April* column:

   a. Position the insertion point in the last cell in the *April* column.

   b. Click the **Formula** button. Word proposes the formula =SUM(ABOVE).

   c. Click **OK**. The total *260,678* is inserted in the active cell.

6. Repeat the formula to calculate the total for the *May*, *June*, and *Total* columns. Even though the *June* column has no numbers, you can still enter the formula for the column total. The result will be *0*.

7. Enter the following amounts in the *June* column:

Colace	**69,804**
Fracassa	**73,168**
Guetle	**92,544**
Homminga	**79,007**
Jamison	**47,996**

WARNING

When it is possible to add from either direction, the SUM formula may not choose the direction you want. Therefore, always check the accuracy of the result when using the SUM formula or any formula from the Formula button.

8. Select the entire table. Note that the current result in the *Total* column is *536,950*.

9. Press **F9**, the Update Field key. All sums are automatically recalculated. Click anywhere in the table to deselect the rows. Note that the new result in the *Total* column is now *899,469*.

10. Save the changes and leave the document open for the next Step-by-Step.

Creating Other Formulas in a Table

You can also perform other complex math calculations in tables, such as subtracting, multiplying, dividing, averaging, and calculating a percentage. For calculations, Word assigns letters to columns and numbers to rows, as in an Excel worksheet. Cells are named for their intersecting rows and columns. For example, A2 would be the intersection of the first column (A) and the second row (2); B3 would be the intersection of the second column (B) and third row (3); and so on.

Some basic symbols for operators in a formula are described in **Table 11–2**. Word also calculates results for functions such as AVERAGE, COUNT, MIN, and MAX by referencing the table cells. To learn about the operators and the available functions, search the Help screens for the keywords *formula*, *field*, *codes*, *operators*, and *functions*.

TABLE 11–2   Symbols for operators in formulas

SYMBOLS	OPERATORS
plus sign (+)	addition
hyphen (-)	subtraction
asterisk (*)	multiplication
forward slash (/)	division

Step-by-Step 11.10

1. If necessary, open the **Sales Report 2** file from your solution files. Save the document as **Sales Report 3**, followed by your initials.

2. Insert a new column between the *June* and *Total* columns. Type the heading **Average Sales.**

3. Calculate the average sales for Mari Colace:

   a. Position the insertion point in the *Average Sales* column for the *Mari Colace* row.

   b. Click the **Formula** button.

   c. Word proposes the formula =SUM(LEFT). If you accepted this formula, the results would be the sum of the *April*, *May*, and *June* amounts.

    d.   In the Formula text box, delete the proposed formula. To create your own formula, type **=(B3+C3+D3)/3**. This formula instructs Word to first add the amounts in the third row of Columns B, C, and D and then to divide that sum by 3 to find the average.

    e.   Under Number format, click the **list arrow** and select **#,##0**.

    f.   Click **OK**. The result *61,050* appears in the active cell.

4.   You cannot use the Repeat Formula command because the cell references must change for each row. Create a new formula for row 4 **=(B4+C4+D4)/3**, following the actions in Step 3. Don't forget to change the number format to **#,##0**.

5.   You can calculate averages quickly by pasting in a predefined function. Click cell **E5** (the Average Sales column for Jeff Guetle). Click the **Formula** button.

6.   In the Formula text box, delete all except the equal sign in the proposed formula. Under Paste function, click the **list arrow** and then click **AVERAGE**.

7.   The insertion point is positioned between the two parentheses in the Formula text box. Type **B5:D5**. This formula instructs Word to calculate the average of the amounts in cells B5 through D5.

8.   Change the number format to **#,##0**, and then click **OK**. The result *69,402* is inserted in the active cell.

9.   Create formulas to calculate the average sales for the remaining two sales reps.

10.   Click in the last cell in the *Average Sales* column. Enter a formula to calculate the average for cells E3:E7, in the same format as the rest of the data.

11.   Save the changes and close the document.

> **TIP**
>
> If the formula does not produce any results, check to make sure that the equal sign precedes the word AVERAGE in the formula.

Integrating Word and Excel

You have seen that Word tables can become fairly sophisticated. However, at times you might need a more complex table, or you may wish to include Excel data or an Excel chart in a Word document. If you want the additional functionality of an Excel worksheet, you can insert an Excel worksheet into your Word document. If you want your Word document to include data that is already in an Excel worksheet, you do not need to retype all the data. You can ***import*** the data, which means you bring the data into a document from another compatible application. To import Excel data into a Word document, you can copy and paste worksheet data, or you can integrate the worksheet into the Word document as a linked or embedded object.

▶ **VOCABULARY**
import

Inserting an Excel Worksheet in a Word Document

The easiest way to create a complex table in which you can calculate and instantly recalculate and update numbers in your Word document is to insert an Excel worksheet into your Word document. Then you have access to all of the data formatting and calculation options from Excel, and you also have access to all Word features.

Step-by-Step 11.11

1. Open a new blank document and save the document as **Purchase Order**, followed by your initials.

2. Click the **Insert** tab. In the Tables group, click the **Table** button, and then click **Excel Spreadsheet**. A worksheet is inserted in the document, and the Excel Ribbon replaces the Word Ribbon.

3. Enter the data below in the worksheet cells.

Item #	Qty.	Price
11-356	4	29.99
11-358	1	54.99
11-067	2	37.59
Total		

4. Click anywhere outside the worksheet. The worksheet data appears in an embedded table, and the Word Ribbon appears.

5. Double-click the table, and the Excel Ribbon appears again.

6. Click cell **C5**. On the Excel Home tab, in the Editing group, click the **Sum** button Σ to calculate the total for cells C2:C4 and then press **Enter**.

7. Click anywhere outside of the worksheet.

8. Save the changes and close the document.

Copying Worksheet Data into a Word Document

The simplest way to import Excel data is to copy it in Excel and then paste it into a Word document. When copied and pasted into a Word document, the worksheet data is converted to a table. Then, you can edit and format the data as you would any other Word table data.

Step-by-Step 11.12

1. Open the **Rates** file from the drive and folder where your Data Files are stored. Save the document as **New Rates**, followed by your initials.

2. Launch Excel, navigate to the Data Files folder, and open the file **Rates.xlsx**.

3. Select the range **A1:D4**. (*Hint*: Click in cell A1, then drag the mouse pointer to the right and down to cell D4.)

4. Click the **Copy** button (or press **Ctrl+C**) to copy the worksheet data to the Clipboard.

5. Switch to the Word document. Position the insertion point in the blank paragraph after the paragraph of text. Click the **Paste** button (or press **Ctrl+V**) to paste the worksheet data.

6. Select the entire table. Click the **Table Tools Layout** tab. In the Cell Size group, click the **AutoFit** button and then click **AutoFit Contents**.

7. Click the **Table Tools Design** tab, and then apply a table style of your choosing.

8. Save the changes, and then close the Word document and the Excel document. Leave both applications open.

Embedding and Linking a Worksheet in a Word Document

▶ VOCABULARY
source file

destination file

embedded object

linked object

If the Excel data you would like to include in your Word document is going to be updated regularly, you can import the worksheet data into your Word file as either an embedded object or a linked object. When importing data from one application to another, the document file from which you are transferring data is called the *source file*. The document to which you are transferring the data is called the *destination file*. For example, you can import sales data from an Excel worksheet (the source file) into a report created in Word (the destination file) and have access to the most recent data.

    An *embedded object* becomes part of the destination file and can be edited in the destination file. For example, if you embed worksheet cells for the sales data into a Word document, you can double-click the cells and then use Excel commands to modify the sales data. To save file space in the destination file, you can choose to insert the source file as a linked object. A *linked object* is inserted as a static object and accesses data stored in the source file, so you cannot update the linked data in the destination file. However, if the destination file is open when the data is modified in the source file, the data is automatically updated in the destination file. If the destination file is not open when the source file is updated, the next time you open the destination file, a dialog box will open, prompting you to update the document with the data from the linked file. If the source file has been renamed or moved to a new location, the data will not be updated when you reopen the destination file.

▨ EXTRA FOR EXPERTS

Another way to embed or to link worksheet data into a document is to use the Object command on the Insert tab. This command enables you to create a new object, or to link or embed an object that already exists in an earlier version of Excel.

Step-by-Step 11.13

1. In Word, open a new blank document and save it as **Monthly Sales 1**, followed by your initials.

2. In Excel, navigate to the Data Files folder and open the file **Sales.xlsx**. Save the worksheet as **Regional Sales**, followed by your initials.

3. Select the range **A1:E7**. Then click the **Copy** button (or press **Ctrl+C**) to copy the data to the Clipboard.

4. Switch to the Word document. Position the insertion point at the beginning of the document. On the Home tab, in the Clipboard group, click the **Paste** button arrow and then click **Paste Special**.

5. The Paste option is enabled. Under As, select **Microsoft Excel Worksheet Object**. Click **OK**. The selected cells from the worksheet are inserted in the document.

6. Press **Enter** two times. Then click the **Paste** button arrow again, click **Paste Special**, and this time enable the **Paste link** option. Under As, select **Microsoft Excel Worksheet Object** and then click **OK**. The worksheet appears in the Word document again, but this time it is not embedded. All the data is still stored in the Excel file.

7. Switch to the Excel worksheet. Press **Esc** and then enter the following numbers for June:

   138,911

   145,001

   133,041

   149,210

8. Save the changes to the Regional Sales Excel worksheet, and then switch to the Word document. Notice that the linked table is updated with the June data. However, the embedded worksheet does not include the June data.

9. Save the changes to the Word document, and close the document.

10. Switch the Excel worksheet. Use the Sum button to calculate the totals in the *TOTAL* column and the *TOTAL* row. Save the changes, and then close the worksheet and exit Excel.

11. Open your **Monthly Sales 1** Word document. When prompted to update, click **Yes**. Note that the linked table is updated, even though the Excel spreadsheet file is not open.

12. Save the Monthly Sales 1 document as **Monthly Sales 2**, followed by your initials.

13. To break the link, right-click the second (linked) Word table, point to **Linked Worksheet Object**, and then click **Links**. In the Links dialog box, click **Break Link**. When prompted to break the link, click **Yes**. Now when the worksheet data is updated, the Word table will not be updated.

14. Save the changes and close the Word document.

Creating Charts

Charts provide a visual display of data and often make the material easier to understand. Word enables you to convert table data into colorful three-dimensional charts. Word offers several options for chart types, including column, bar, line, and pie. In addition, you can change the elements used to format a chart. For example, you can insert a title for the chart or the axes, you can add labels for the data, and you can change the font and location of the chart's legend.

When you use the Insert Chart feature, a sample chart is embedded in the Word document and an Excel worksheet opens. You replace the sample data in the worksheet with the data you want to appear in the chart, and as you enter new data in the worksheet, the embedded chart is updated. After closing the worksheet, you can still update the chart data at any time by right-clicking the chart and then clicking Edit Data.

If you do not have Excel installed on the computer, obviously an Excel worksheet will not open. However, an associated datasheet will open with the chart, and you can enter your own data in the datasheet.

Step-by-Step 11.14

1. Open a new blank document and save it as **Fourth Quarter Sales**, followed by your initials.

2. Click the **Insert** tab. In the Illustrations group, click the **Chart** button to open the Insert Chart dialog box, similar to the one shown in **Figure 11–18**.

FIGURE 11–18
Insert Chart dialog box

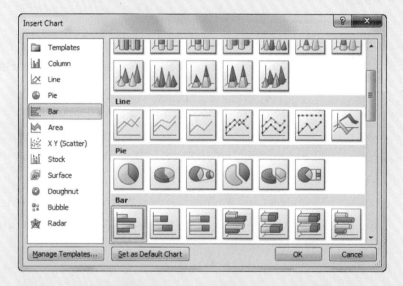

3. In the left pane, select **Bar**. In the right pane, under Bar, click the first option in the first row, **Clustered Bar**. (*Hint:* Position the mouse pointer over the options to see a ScreenTip with the chart name.) Then click **OK**. Word inserts a sample chart in the document and then opens an Excel worksheet in a new window. The applications appear side by side.

4. In the Excel worksheet, replace the sample data with the data below. The chart in Word is linked to the worksheet, so as you enter the data in the worksheet, the chart is automatically updated. (If you don't have Excel installed on your computer, enter the data in the datasheet.)

Sales Representative	October	November	December	Total
Colace, M.	36,443	42,775	45,982	
Fracassa, M.	43,907	44,168	46,561	
Guetle, J.	38,856	40,125	42,213	
Homminga, R.	41,006	21,766	53,447	
Jamison, W.	37,226	51,112	44,487	

5. Use the **Sum** button to calculate the totals in the *Total* column. Note that the SUM formula references table column headings instead of cells. Make sure only data in Columns B, C, and D are included in the SUM formula.

6. Change the chart type:
   a. In the Word document, click anywhere within the chart to select it. (*Hint*: When the chart is selected, the drawing canvas border appears around the chart.)
   b. On the Chart Tools Design tab, in the Type group, click the **Change Chart Type** button. The Change Chart Type dialog box opens.
   c. Under Column, click the second option in the second row, **Stacked Cylinder**. Click **OK**. The chart in the Word document adapts to the style change.

7. In the worksheet, click anywhere outside the range border. Then point to the lower-right corner of the range border. When the mouse pointer changes to a double-headed arrow , drag the border to the left one column to exclude the Total column from the selected range. Now that the monthly figures are stacked, it is not necessary to include the total data.

8. In the Word document, click the **Chart Tools Layout** tab. In the Labels group, click the **Chart Title** button and then click **Above Chart**. A text box with *Chart Title* is inserted above the chart. Select the text *Chart Title* and replace the text with **Fourth Quarter Sales**.

9. In the Labels group, click the **Axis Titles** button, point to **Primary Horizontal Axis Title**, and then click **Title Below Axis**. A new text box is inserted below the chart. Change *Axis Title* to **Sales Representatives**.

10. In the Labels group, click the **Axis Titles** button, point to **Primary Vertical Axis Title**, and then click **Rotated Title**. Replace *Axis Title* with **Sales Volume**. Then, in the Labels group, click the **Legend** button and click **Show Legend at Right**. The legend labels are inserted on the right side of the chart.

11. Save the Excel worksheet as **Quarterly Sales**, followed by your initials. Close the worksheet and exit Excel.

12. In the Word document, if necessary, click the **Chart Tools Layout** tab. In the Labels group, click the **Data Table** button and then click **Show Data Table with Legend Keys**. The data table appears below the chart.

13. Position the mouse pointer over the middle handle at the bottom border of the drawing canvas. When the pointer changes to a double-headed arrow, drag the border down to resize the chart and table to a height of 5½". Then drag the text box for the horizontal axis label to reposition the label below the chart.

14. Save the changes to the Word document, and then close the document.

SUMMARY

In this lesson, you learned:

- To rearrange table contents, you can copy and paste data, drag and drop rows and columns, and sort data.

- Word offers several ways for you to control column and row spacing.

- Sorting can be based on as many as three criteria at a time, and when sorting a single column, the data in the other table columns is not reordered.

- If a table gets too big and cannot fit on a page, you can repeat the header rows when the table wraps to the next page. Or, you can split the table content into separate tables.

- The Draw Table tool and the Draw Eraser tool enable you to create custom tables with cells of various sizes.

- Word provides several options for aligning text within a table cell, and you can also specify the alignment of the entire table.

- The Formula button enables you to perform math calculations in tables, such as adding, subtracting, multiplying, dividing, and averaging.

- You can insert data from an Excel worksheet into a Word document and then edit and format the data in the Word document.

- You can easily create charts in Word using an Excel worksheet to enter the chart data.

■ VOCABULARY REVIEW

Define the following terms:

caption
destination file
embedded object

gridlines
import

linked object
source file

REVIEW QUESTIONS

TRUE / FALSE

Circle T if the statement is true or F if the statement is false.

T   F   **1.**   When copied and pasted into a Word document, Excel worksheet data is converted to a table.

T   F   **2.**   When you open a Word document with linked data in an Excel worksheet, the worksheet must also be open to update the table data.

T   F   **3.**   Gridlines appear in a printed document.

T   F   **4.**   You can move rows and columns in a table the same way you move text in a document.

T   F   **5.**   A linked object saves file space.

FILL IN THE BLANK

Complete the following sentences by writing the correct word or words in the blanks provided.

1. A(n) _____ is a label that describes an illustration, table, or picture.

2. When you link an object, you create a connection between the destination file and the _____.

3. A(n) _____ file becomes part of the destination file.

4. When you _____ data, you bring data into a document from another compatible application.

5. When adjusting column widths, if you want the table to fill the document window and extend from the left margin to the right margin, click the AutoFit button and choose the _____ option.

WRITTEN QUESTIONS

Write a brief answer to the following questions.

1. If you want to create a professional-looking table but you don't have a lot of time, describe the fastest way to create the table.

2. Describe how to rotate text in a table cell.

3. Describe how to quickly recalculate formulas after updating data in a Word table.

4. Explain how the Banded Rows or Banded Columns options affect the formatting of table styles.

5. What symbols can you use as operators in formulas for addition, subtraction, multiplication, and division?

■ PROJECTS

If you have a SAM 2010 user profile, your instructor may have assigned an autogradable version of the indicated project. If so, log into the SAM 2010 Web site at *www.cengage.com/sam2010* to download the instruction and start files.

PROJECT 11–1 *

1. Open the Employee file from the drive and folder where your Data Files are stored. Save the document as **Employee Data 1**, followed by your initials.

2. Insert a new paragraph above the table and enter the title **COMPANY EMPLOYEES**. Center the title.

3. Change the order of the columns so that the columns appear in the following order from left to right: *Name, Department, Title,* and *Date Hired*.

4. Sort by department in ascending order, and then by the date hired in ascending order.

5. Save the changes to the document. Then save the document as **Employee Data 2**, followed by your initials.

6. Near the top of the marketing department, for the employee *Pfeifer*, change the department to **Human Resources** and change the title to **Assistant Director**. Then move the row up in the table so that it is positioned before employee *Foster-Hale* in the Human Resources department.

7. Enter the following new employees in the table so they appear at the end of the Legal department employees. Complete the row data. All three new employees are in the Legal department, and their job title is Paralegal. They were all hired on 11-12-2013.

   Giroux, Jason
   Morris, Adam
   Torres, Tracey

8. Create a custom caption below the table. For the caption text, type **Current Employees**. Edit the caption by removing the number "1" at the end.

9. Format the header row to repeat at the top of the second page.

10. Select all the employee names in the first column, but do not select the column headings. Sort the table data based on the last and then the first names of the employees. (*Hint*: Open the Sort dialog box and then open the Sort Options dialog box. Under Separate fields at, select Commas and click OK. Then in the Sort dialog box, select a Sort by of Column 1 with Field 1 in the Using box, and a Then by of Column 1 with Field 2 in the Using box.)

11. Save the changes to the document, and then save the document as **Employee Data 3**, followed by your initials.

12. Remove the caption below the table. Click in the table and then sort the table content in ascending alphabetical order based on the *Department* column.

13. Split the table so that each department is in a separate table. Then copy and paste the header row into each of the new tables.

14. Save the changes and close the document.

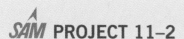 **PROJECT 11–2**

1. Open a new blank document and save it as **Payroll**, followed by your initials.

2. Create the table shown in **Figure 11–19**.

3. Insert formulas to calculate the earnings for each employee by multiplying the regular hours times the hourly rate. Apply the **$#,##0.00** format for the results.

4. Insert formulas to calculate the sums for the *Regular Hours* and *Earnings* columns.

5. Insert a new row at the end of the table. In the first column, type **AVERAGE**.

6. Insert a formula to calculate the average for rows 2 through 7 in the *Regular Hours* column. Apply the **#,##0.00** format for the results.

7. AutoFit the table to the contents.

8. Apply a table style to make the data easier to read. Modify the table style borders and shading to customize the style, and then save the modified table style as Payroll Table Style, followed by your initials. When you save the new style, be sure to enable the Only in this document option.

9. Save the changes and close the document.

Employee	Regular Hours	Hourly Rate	Earnings
Beintez, L.	40	14.00	
Daniel, K.	36	15.50	
Huang, M.	39.5	12.50	
O'Neil, A.	40	16.00	
Parker, N.	34.5	14.00	
Kennedy, N.	40	12.50	
TOTAL			

FIGURE 11–19 Table data for Project 11–2

PROJECT 11–3

1. Open a new blank document and save it as **Recycling Rate**, followed by your initials.

2. Use the Draw Table tool to create the table shown in **Figure 11–20**. The table is approximately 6 inches wide by 3 inches high.

3. Add shading and border formats to enhance the appearance of the table and make it easier to read.

4. Save the changes to the document.

5. Open the Green Bucket file from the folder where your Data Files are stored. Save the document as **Green Bucket Letter**, followed by your initials.

6. Switch to the Recycling Rate document and copy the table to the Clipboard.

7. Switch to the Green Bucket Letter document. Position the insertion point at the beginning of the paragraph below the bulleted list, and then paste the table.

8. AutoFit the table to the contents.

9. Format the table so that it is aligned at the right side of the paragraph and the text wraps around the paragraph. (*Hint:* Open the Table Properties dialog box. Under Alignment, select Right, and under Text wrapping, select Around.)

10. Save the changes and close both documents.

Recycling Rate			
PET	Soft drink bottles	55%	59%
	Vegetable oil bottles	15%	24%
HDPE	Milk jugs	33%	40%
	Bleach and laundry detergent bottles	19%	27%

FIGURE 11–20 Table data for Project 11–3

PROJECT 11-4

1. Open a new blank document and save it as **New Members**, followed by your initials.

2. Use a Quick Table to create the table shown in **Figure 11-21**. Modify the table structure as needed so it has the right number of columns and rows, and then replace the boilerplate text with the data shown in Figure 11-21.

3. Select the table and change the font to Calibri, 14 point.

4. Adjust the column widths to AutoFit the contents.

5. Save the changes and close the document.

Member #	Last Name	First Name	Address	ZIP
24561	Sautter	Arthur	6443 West Brandt	44904-2304
24562	Cole	George	1102 South Elm	44906-3941
24563	Takamoto	Li	256 North Diamond	44904-2855
24564	Dierks	Barbara	650 Wayne	44904-3027
24565	Fitzpatrick	Lorraine	747 Lenox Avenue	44906-0462
24566	Barry	David	162 North Murray	44906-3609
24567	Tolzmann	Agnes	202 Third Street	44906-2742

FIGURE 11-21   Table data for Project 11-4

PROJECT 11-5

1. Open a new blank document and save it as **First Quarter Report**, followed by your initials.

2. Launch Excel, navigate to the Data Files folder, and open the file Expenses.xlsx. Save the worksheet as **First Quarter Expenses**, followed by your initials.

3. Select the range A1:D9 and copy the data to the Clipboard.

4. Switch to the Word document, and paste the worksheet data into the document as a linked Microsoft Excel Worksheet Object.

5. Switch to the Excel worksheet and enter the following expense data in the *March* column:

4250
995
250
421
1992

6. Save the changes to the worksheet.

7. Switch to the Word document. Save the changes, and then close the document.

8. In the Excel worksheet, edit the Miscellaneous Expense for March so that it shows 429 instead of *421*.

9. Save the changes to the worksheet, and then close Excel.

10. In Word, open the First Quarter Report.docx document. When prompted, click Yes to update the linked data.

11. Save the changes and close the document.

PROJECT 11-6

1. Open a new blank document and save it as **Country Requests**, followed by your initials.

2. Insert a column chart.

3. In the Excel worksheet, replace the boilerplate text in Columns A–C with the following data. Delete the boilerplate data in Column D, and adjust the range border to include only the information shown in **Figure 11-22**.

Country	Year One	Year Two
Austria	85	144
Germany	110	175
Italy	98	143
Switzerland	78	133

4. Save the worksheet as **Countries**, followed by your initials.

5. Switch to the Word document, and create the chart title **Requests by Country** above the chart.

6. Insert a vertical axis title on the left side of the chart, and change the axis title to **# of Requests**. The text should be rotated so you can read it from bottom to top.

7. If necessary, show the legend at the right.

8. Save the changes to the Word document, and then close both the Word document and the Excel worksheet. Exit both applications.

FIGURE 11-22   Table data for Project 11-6

CRITICAL THINKING

ACTIVITY 11–1

Create a formula to calculate the number of items in the first column in **Figure 11–23**. Note that the first row is a header row. To find information in the Help screens, search for the keywords *formula functions*.

Item#	Qty. in Stock
11-4508	542
29-545	10
33-090	54
33-091	98

FIGURE 11–23   Data for Activity 11-1

ACTIVITY 11–2

You create a newsletter each month in Word. The newsletter includes an update on the status of a fundraiser project. Data on the fundraising progress is provided in a table. You have several options for creating the newsletter table each month. Describe how you would create the table, and explain whether you would embed or link the data and why.

LESSON 12

Creating Mail Merge Documents

■ OBJECTIVES

Upon completion of this lesson, you should be able to:

- Identify a main document and a data source.
- Insert merge fields into the main document.
- Preview, merge, and print merged documents.
- Create a new data source.
- Edit, sort, and filter data source records.
- Prepare mail merge documents for mass mailing labels and envelopes.
- Create a main document for mass e-mails.
- Use mail merge features to create catalogs and directories.

■ VOCABULARY

data source

field

field name

filter

MAPI (Messaging Application Programming Interface)

main document

merge field

record

switch

ADVANCED   Microsoft Word Unit

Word's mail merge feature enables you to personalize and customize letters, envelopes, labels, and e-mail messages for group or mass mailings. You can also use mail merge features to create a single document, such as a catalog or a membership directory.

Creating Mail Merge Documents

The merge process combines boilerplate text with variable information, such as names and addresses. To begin the process, you must identify a main document and a data source. The *main document* is a file that contains the boilerplate text and formats that remain constant during the merge process, such as the body of a letter or the standard text for a catalog. The *data source* is a collection of variable information to be used in a merge. In the merge process, the variable information from the data source is merged into the main document. For example, the data source can be an Outlook file with contacts' names and addresses that can be merged into a letter. Another example of a data source is an Excel worksheet or an Access database that contains product data that can be merged into a catalog.

Identifying the Main Document and the Data Source

The first step in the merge process is to select the main document type. The options available include letters, e-mail messages, envelopes, labels, or a directory.

The second step is to select the starting (or main) document. You can use the current document, or you can start from a template or an existing document.

The third step in the mail merge process is to select the recipients. You must first locate or create the data source. The data source stores information in a *field*, which is one or more characters that create a piece of information, such as a first name, last name, or telephone number. The *field name* is a label that identifies a field in a data source. When you identify a Word table or an Excel spreadsheet as the data source, Word uses the column headings for the field names. A *record* is a group of related fields, or a single field, treated as a unit in a data source, such as all the contact information for one individual. Once you identify the data source, you then identify the recipients (or records) you want to include in the merge.

If you are inexperienced at creating merges, you will find that the Mail Merge Wizard feature makes the process very easy. The wizard guides you through six basic steps to complete the merge process. Step-by-Steps 12.1, 12.2, and 12.3 cover the six steps for the Mail Merge Wizard. If you are unable to complete all six wizard steps in one session, you can save the changes to the main document and continue with the remaining steps later. Word will retain the data source and field information, and when you reopen the main document, you can continue the merge process at the point where you stopped.

Step-by-Step 12.1

1. Launch Word and open the **Orders** file from the drive and folder where your Data Files are stored. Save the document as **Orders Data Source**, followed by your initials, and close the document.

2. Open the **Order Confirmation** file from the drive and folder where your Data Files are stored. Save the document as **Order Confirmation Main Document**, followed by your initials.

3. Review the document, and you will notice that the letter is incomplete—it has no inside address or salutation. These elements will be determined by the variable information in a data source. The letters *XX* in the first paragraph of the body of the letter indicate locations where you will insert fields to merge additional variable information.

4. Click the **Mailings** tab. In the Start Mail Merge group, click the **Start Mail Merge** button, and then click **Step-by-Step Mail Merge Wizard**. The Mail Merge task pane shown in **Figure 12–1** opens. You can drag the Mail Merge task pane to reposition it on the screen.

FIGURE 12–1
Step 1 of 6 in the Mail Merge
task pane

5. If necessary, under Select document type, enable the **Letters** option. At the bottom of the task pane, click **Next: Starting document**. Under Select starting document, the option Use the current document is already enabled.

6. At the bottom of the task pane, click **Next: Select recipients**. Under Select recipients, the option Use an existing list is already enabled.

7. Under Use an existing list, click **Browse**. The Select Data Source dialog box opens. Navigate to your solutions folder, select the file **Orders Data Source**, and then click **Open**.

8. The Mail Merge Recipients dialog box shown in **Figure 12–2** opens. Notice that a check mark appears to the left of each record in the second column of the data source.

FIGURE 12–2
Mail Merge Recipients
dialog box

Header row

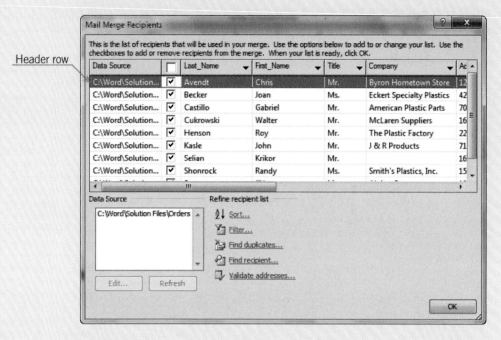

9. Click the **check box** to the right of *Data Source* in the header row. A check mark is added to the box. Click the **check box** again, and all the check marks are removed. Deselecting all the records is useful when the list is extensive and you want to include only a few records in the merge.

10. Click the same **check box** again. All the records are again selected and all the recipients will be included in the merge.

11. Click the **check box** to the left of the last name *Cukrowski*. The check mark is removed, which means the record will be excluded from the merge.

12. Click the **check box** next to *Cukrowski* again to include the record in the merge. This method of adding/removing recipients to and from the merge is most useful when the list of records is short.

13. Click **OK** in the Mail Merge Recipients dialog box to close it.

14. Leave the main document and the Mail Merge task pane open for the next Step-by-Step.

Inserting Merge Fields into the Main Document

The fourth step in the merge process is to add merge fields to the main document. The *merge field* is a placeholder in the main document that instructs Word to find and insert the corresponding information from the data source. The merge field shows the field name surrounded by chevrons (e.g., *«LastName»*), which helps to distinguish the field from the regular text. Word simplifies the process of inserting merge fields by providing composite fields that group a number of fields together. For example, Word provides a preformatted address block with fields for the recipient's title, name, and address. You can use these composite fields to save time, and you can customize them as needed.

▶ **VOCABULARY**
merge field

Step-by-Step 12.2

1. If necessary, open the **Order Confirmation Main Document** file from your solution files. Because the data source file is already linked to the main document, you will be prompted to place data from the data source. Click Yes.

2. If necessary, click the **Mailings** tab, click the **Start Mail Merge** button, and then click **Step by Step Mail Merge Wizard**. At the bottom of the Mail Merge task pane, if necessary, advance to Step 3 of 6.

3. At the bottom of the Mail Merge task pane, click **Next: Write your letter**.

4. If the nonprinting formatting characters are not visible, click the Home tab, toggle on the Show/Hide ¶ button, and then return to the Mailings tab. Position the insertion point in the second blank paragraph below the date line.

5. In the Mail Merge task pane, under Write your letter, click **Address block**. The Insert Address Block dialog box opens, as shown in **Figure 12–3**. Because the record for Walter Cukrowski was selected in the data source, a preview of that address appears in the preview pane of the dialog box.

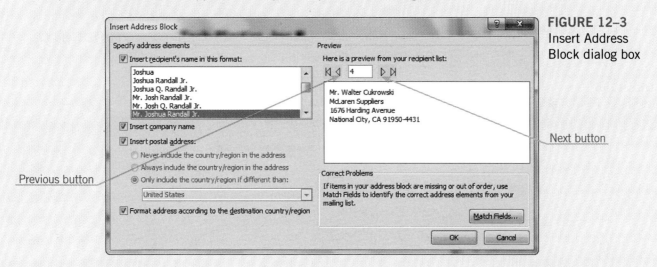

FIGURE 12–3
Insert Address Block dialog box

6. In the Preview section, click the **Previous** and **Next** arrows to view the proposed address blocks for the other records in the data source.

7. Click **OK** to accept the proposed recipient information in the address block. The merge field *«AddressBlock»* is inserted in the main document.

8. In the Write & Insert Fields group on the Ribbon, click the **Highlight Merge Fields** button. In addition to the chevrons, the highlight will make it easy to quickly identify the merge fields in the document.

9. Press **Enter** twice. Then click **Greeting line** in the Mail Merge task pane to open the Insert Greeting Line dialog box shown in **Figure 12–4**. If the greeting line is formatted to read Dear *«FirstName»* and the merged record doesn't include a first name, Word will automatically insert "Dear Sir or Madam" instead.

TIP

If the merge fields appear inside braces { } instead of chevrons « », Word is displaying field codes instead of merge fields. Right-click the field codes inside the braces, and then click Toggle Field Codes on the shortcut menu.

FIGURE 12–4
Insert Greeting
Line dialog box

Text inserted if merged record doesn't include field data

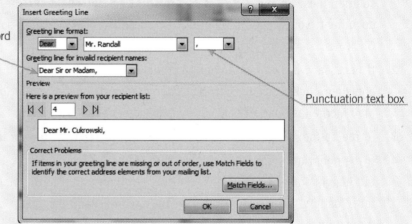

Punctuation text box

10. Click the **list arrow** in the Punctuation text box, and select **:** (a colon). Click **OK**. The GreetingLine merge field is inserted into the main document.

11. Delete **XX** after the # sign in the first sentence of the first paragraph. With the insertion point positioned just to the right of the # sign, click **More items** in the Mail Merge task pane. The Insert Merge Field dialog box opens, as shown in **Figure 12–5**.

FIGURE 12–5
Insert Merge Field dialog box

12. Under Fields, select **Order**, and then click **Insert**. The merge field *«Order»* is inserted in the main document. Click **Close** in the Insert Merge Field dialog box.

13. Delete the next occurrence of **XX** in the same paragraph and repeat Step 12, inserting the **Total_Amount** field.

14. Save the changes to the main document, and leave the document and the Mail Merge task pane open for the next Step-by-Step.

Previewing, Merging, and Printing the Merged Documents

The fifth step in the process allows you to preview the merged data in the main document. If you are not satisfied with the preview results, you can click the Previous link at the bottom of the Mail Merge task pane to go back to Step 4 and edit the main document.

The sixth and final step in the process is to complete the merge. You can send the merged results directly to the printer, with options to print some or all of the merged records. Or, you can choose to save the merged results in a new document. The benefit of creating a new document is that you can print this document later, as you would any other Word document. For example, if you merged data to create labels or envelopes for a bulk mailing, you can save the merged results and then use the document in the future to print another set of labels or envelopes. You can also edit the results in the new document without altering the main document or the data source. For example, you can personalize the greeting line in one of several merged letters.

Step-by-Step 12.3

1. If necessary, open the **Order Confirmation Main Document** file from your solution files. And, if necessary, open the **Mail Merge** task pane to Step 4 of 6.

2. Click **Next: Preview your letters** at the bottom of the Mail Merge task pane. The main document is updated and shows the letter with a merged record. The merge fields are replaced with the variable data for Walter Cukrowski.

3. In the task pane, under Preview your letters, click the **Previous** button ⟨⟨ to view the merged letter to Recipient 3 (Castillo). Click the **Next** button ⟩⟩ twice to view the letter to Recipient 5 (Henson). Go to the letter addressed to Mr. Krikor Selian (Recipient 7).

> **TIP**
>
> If a merged document shows unexpected spaces or punctuation, you may have typed unnecessary spaces or punctuation in the data source records. Click *Previous: Write your letter* at the bottom of the task pane to return to Step 4. Make any necessary corrections to the data source, then click *Next: Complete the merge.*

4. To quickly locate a specific record, click **Find a recipient** in the Mail Merge pane. The Find in Field dialog box opens, as shown in **Figure 12–6**.

FIGURE 12–6
Find in Field dialog box

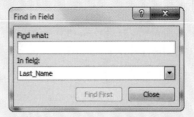

5. In the Find What box, type **J & R Products**. Click the **In Field** list arrow, and then click **Company**. Click **Find first**. When prompted to continue searching at the beginning of the database, click **Yes**. The merged document to John Kasle at J & R Products is displayed. Click **Close**.

6. In the task pane, under Make changes, click **Exclude this recipient**. The merged document is deleted, and the merged document for Krikor Selian is displayed.

7. Click **Next**: **Complete the merge** to show the final step in the process. Under Merge, click **Edit individual letters**. In the Merge to New Document dialog box, select the **Current record** option, then click **OK**. Word opens a new document titled *Letters1*. The new document contains only the merged letter for Krikor Selian.

8. In the greeting line, select **Mr. Selian** and then type **Krikor**. This makes the greeting less formal, which is appropriate when you know the recipient personally.

9. Save the new document as **Selian Letter**, followed by your initials. Close the document. The main document and the Mail Merge task pane should still be open, and the Selian letter is still part of the merged results.

10. At the bottom of the task pane, click **Previous: Preview your letters**. With the original Selian letter in the document window, click **Exclude this recipient** because you have saved a customized version of the letter as a separate document.

11. At the bottom of the task pane, click **Next: Complete the merge**. Under Merge, click **Print**. In the Merge to Printer dialog box, select **From** and then type **5** in both text boxes. Click **OK**. A Print dialog box opens. If you choose to print, only the merged letter for the specified record will print. Click **Cancel** in the Print dialog box.

12. Click **Edit individual letters**. In the Merge to New Document dialog box, select the **All** option, and then click **OK**. A new document, *Letters2*, opens. Save the new document as **Merged Order Confirmations**, followed by your initials.

13. Click the **File** tab and then click **Print**. The merged document appears in the Preview pane. You can view all seven pages of merged letters by clicking the Next and Previous buttons, using the vertical scroll bar on the right, or moving the wheel on the mouse.

14. Close the merged document. Close the main document, and when prompted to save the changes, click **Save**.

Creating and Editing Data Sources

As you have learned, the data source used for a mail merge can be created in a variety of applications. If the data source does not already exist, you can use the Mail Merge feature to help guide you through the process of creating a new data source. During the mail merge process, you can also edit and organize the records.

Creating a Data Source Using the Mail Merge Feature

Your first step in creating a data source is to identify the field names to be used. Although fields do not need to be in a particular order in the data source, for convenience, you may want to arrange the list so the fields are in an order that will make entering the data more expedient. Multiple merge documents can share the same data source. Some of the merge documents will use more fields than others. Therefore, when creating a data source, you must be sure to include all possible fields so the data can be used for a variety of merge documents.

Now that you are familiar with the mail merge process, you do not have to use the Wizard to guide you. Instead, you can use the buttons on the Mailings tab to complete the process. The advantage of using the Ribbon is that more options are available. When using the buttons on the Ribbon, you must perform the same basic tasks that you complete for all other merged documents. The buttons are arranged in a sequence that corresponds with the steps in the Mail Merge Wizard.

Step-by-Step 12.4

1. Open a new blank Word document.
2. Click the **Mailings** tab. In the Start Mail Merge group, click the **Start Mail Merge** button, and then click **Letters**.

3. In the Start Mail Merge group, click the **Select Recipients** button, and then click **Type New List**. The New Address List dialog box shown in **Figure 12–7** opens and shows common field names for addresses, which are frequently used in merged letters.

FIGURE 12–7
New Address List dialog box

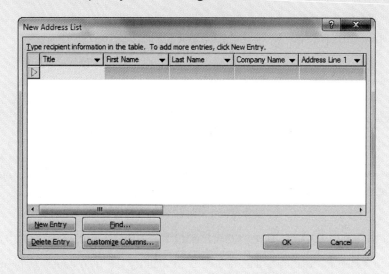

4. Click **Customize Columns** at the bottom of the dialog box to open the Customize Address List dialog box shown in **Figure 12–8**.

FIGURE 12–8
Customize Address List dialog box

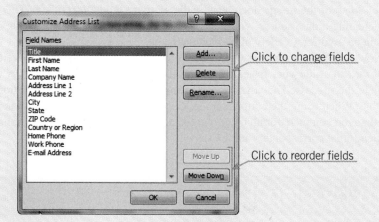

5. Under Field Names, click **Company Name**, and then click **Delete** in the dialog box. When prompted to confirm the deletion, click **Yes**. Delete the following field names: **Address Line 2**, **Country or Region**, and **Work Phone**.

6. Click the field name **Address Line 1**, and then click **Rename**. In the To box, type **Address**, and then click **OK**.

7. Click the field name **E-mail Address**, and then click **Move Up** once to rearrange the order of the field names.

8. In the dialog box, click **Add**. In the Add Field dialog box, type **Contribution**, and then click **OK**. Click **Move Down** to make *Contribution* the last field name in the list. Click **OK** to close the dialog box.

9. The New Address List dialog box should still be open. Type the following data in the appropriate fields, pressing **Tab** to advance to the next field. To show more fields, enlarge the dialog box by dragging the dialog box borders.

    Title: **Mrs.**

    First Name: **Patsy**

    Last Name: **Stump**

    Address: **2237 Pinehurst Court**

    City: **Sterling Hts.**

    State: **MI**

    ZIP Code: **48310-7106**

    E-mail Address: **pstump@gateway.xyz**

    Home Phone: **248-555-8907**

    Contribution: **$500**

10. Click **New Entry** (or you can press Tab) to show a new row for the next record. Enter each of the following records. Do not be concerned when information such as contributions or e-mail addresses is not available. Just leave the fields blank.

Mr. Matt Caulfield
2650 Biddle Street
Wyandotte, MI 48192-5235
mc34@tools.xyz
734-555-8976

Mr. Lane Sumners
15420 Meyer Avenue
Allen Park, MI 48101-2690
313-555-2323
$250

Ms. E. Moya
23761 Edward Street
Dearborn, MI 48128-1276
313-555-8767

Ms. Eloisa Moya
23761 Edward Street
Dearborn, MI 48128-1276
moya331@tir.xyz
313-555-8767
$750

Ms. Sharon Miller
6644 Norwood Avenue
Allen Park, MI 48101-2439
samiller@cool.xyz
313-555-9087
$100

11. Click **OK** to close the New Address List dialog box. The Save Address List dialog box opens. Navigate to your solution folder, and in the File name box, type **Membership Contacts Data Source**, followed by your initials. Note in the Save as type box that the document type is Microsoft Office Address Lists. Click **Save**.

12. Close the document without saving changes.

Editing Data Source Records

As you work in the mail merge process, you can edit or delete existing entries and add new entries in the data source. If the data source is saved in an Access table, you can edit the data source in the Mail Merge Recipients dialog box by clicking the Edit button. However, if the data source was created in a Word table or in an Excel spreadsheet, the Edit button may not be available. When you close the Mail Merge Recipients dialog box, the data source is updated automatically to reflect the changes you made.

You should always check to make sure the fields in the data source correspond to the merge fields you have selected for the main document. The Match Fields command helps you identify fields from your data source that correspond with the required field. You should also check to make sure you do not have duplicate records.

Step-by-Step 12.5

1. Open the **Donation Letter** file from the drive and folder where your Data Files are stored. Save the document as **Donation Letter Main Document**, followed by your initials.

2. Click the **Mailings** tab. In the Start Mail Merge group, click the **Start Mail Merge** button, and then click **Letters**.

3. In the Start Mail Merge group, click the **Select Recipients** button, and then click **Use Existing List**. Navigate to and open your solution file **Membership Contacts Data Source**.

4. In the Start Mail Merge group, click the **Edit Recipient List** button. The Mail Merge Recipients dialog box opens, as shown in **Figure 12–9**.

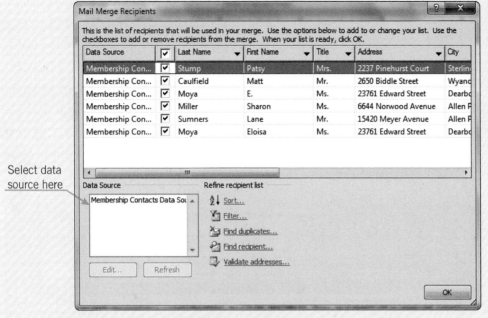

FIGURE 12–9
Mail Merge Recipients dialog box

5. Under Data Source, select **Membership Contacts Data Source**. Click the **Edit** button. The Edit Data Source dialog box opens, as shown in **Figure 12–10**.

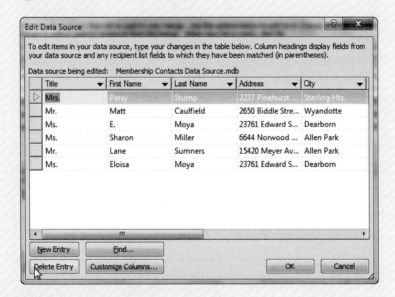

FIGURE 12–10
Edit Data Source dialog box

6. Select the record for **Sharon Miller**, and then scroll to the right end of the record to show the Contribution field. Change the contribution amount to **$900**.

7. Scroll back to the left. In the first record, *Patsy Stump*, change the last name to **Marquez**.

8. Click **OK** to close the dialog box. When prompted to save the changes to the recipient list and the data source, click **Yes**. The Mail Merge Recipients dialog box is still open. Notice that the records in the dialog box reflect the changes you just made.

9. Click **Find duplicates**. The Find Duplicates dialog box shown in **Figure 12–11** opens, identifying two records with similar data. Deselect the first record, and then click **OK** to close the dialog box. The first Moya record will not be included in the merge. Click **OK** again to close the Mail Merge Recipients dialog box.

FIGURE 12–11
Find Duplicates dialog box

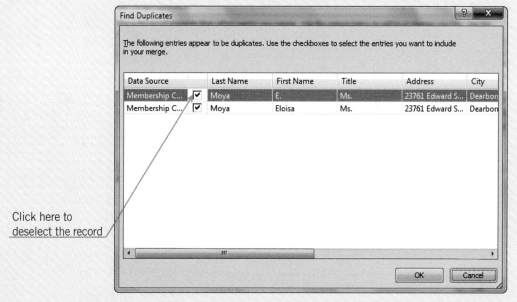

Click here to deselect the record

10. In the main document, delete the first set of XXs under the date line. Leave the insertion point positioned in the blank line. In the Write & Insert Fields group, click the **Address Block** button. The Insert Address Block dialog box opens.

11. In the Correct Problems section, click **Match Fields**. The Match Fields dialog box shown in **Figure 12–12** opens. Notice that the *Address* field in the data source is matched to the *Address 1* field in the Address Block. Word automatically matched the fields, but when necessary, you can manually match a field by clicking the list arrow and selecting a field name. Click **OK** twice to close the dialog boxes.

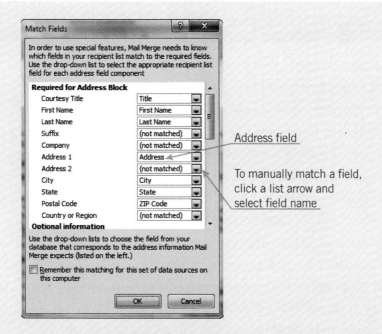

FIGURE 12–12
Match Fields dialog box

12. In the main document, delete the next occurrence of XX. In the Write &
    Insert Fields group, click the **Greeting Line** button. Change the punctua-
    tion to a colon, and then click **OK**.

13. Save the changes to the main document and leave it open for the next
    Step-by-Step.

Sorting and Filtering Data Source Records

If you want the merged documents to be organized in alphabetic or numeric order,
you can sort the data source records before completing the merge. The records can
be sorted in ascending or descending order by up to three fields in the records. For
example, businesses can get a discount on postage rates by presorting the envelopes
by postal code. By sorting the records before completing the merge, the envelopes
will printed in the required order.

A *filter* screens records by identifying criteria that must be met before the
records are included in a merge. Suppose, for example, you want to merge records
only for people who live in the state of Michigan. To add additional criteria to the filter, you can use the And operator. For example, you might want to merge all records
of individuals who live in the city of Dearborn and have the last name Smith. Only
records that meet all three of these conditions will be merged. You can use the Or
operator to filter for two different conditions. For example, you can specify a merge
for records where the person lives in Bay City or Saginaw. This filter would merge
all records for both cities.

▶ **VOCABULARY**
filter

Step-by-Step 12.6

1. If necessary, open the **Donation Letter Main Document** file from your solution files. When prompted to place data from the data source file, click **Yes**.

2. In the Start Mail Merge group on the Mailings tab, click the **Edit Recipient List** button. The Mail Merge Recipients dialog box opens. Resize the dialog box to show all the fields, or as many fields as possible.

3. Click the **Last Name** column heading. The records are sorted in ascending alphabetic order by last name. Click the **Last Name** column heading again. The records are sorted in descending alphabetic order by last name.

4. If necessary, scroll to the right to view the E-mail Address field. Click the **list arrow** in the E-mail Address column heading, and then select **(Blanks)**. The E. Moya and Lane Sumners records, which have blank e-mail address fields, are displayed. Notice that the list arrow in the E-mail Address column heading changes color to indicate that the field has been filtered.

5. After you specify filter options for a data source, the options remain in effect until you change them. To remove the filter options, click the **list arrow** in the E-mail Address column heading, and then select **(All)** to show all the records in the E-mail Address field.

6. If necessary, scroll to the left to show the *City* field. Click the **list arrow** in the City column heading, and then select **Allen Park**. Only records of those contacts living in Allen Park are displayed. Click the **list arrow** in the City column heading, and then select **(All)** to show all the records again.

7. Click the **list arrow** in the City column heading, and then select **(Advanced...)**. The Filter and Sort dialog box opens.

8. Filter the records using multiple criteria:

   a. In the first row, click the **list arrow** in the Field box, and then select **City**.

   b. Make sure Equal to appears in the Comparison box.

   c. In the Compare to text box, type **Allen Park**.

   d. In the first text box of the second row, *And* should already be selected.

   e. In the second row, click the **list arrow** in the Field box, scroll down, and then select **Contribution**. Click the **list arrow** in the Comparison box, and then select **Greater than or equal**. In the Compare to text box, type **$500**.

f. The filter criteria should match that shown in **Figure 12–13**.

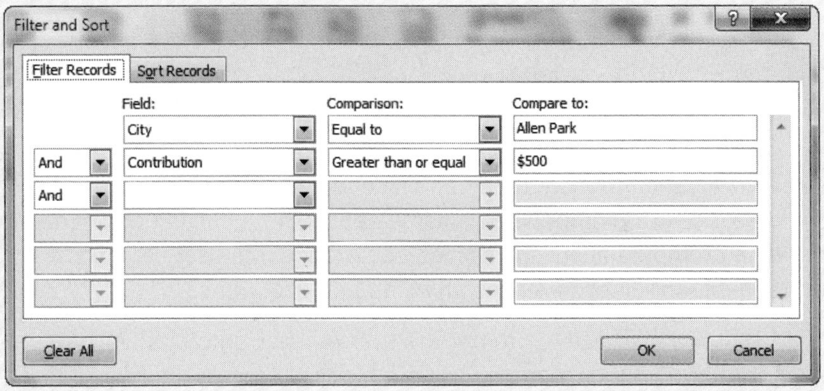

FIGURE 12–13
Filter and Sort dialog box

9. Click **OK** to close the Filter and Sort dialog box. The record for Sharon Miller is the only record that meets both criteria.

10. Click the **list arrow** in any column heading, and then select **(Advanced…)**. The Filter and Sort dialog box reopens. Click **Clear All** to remove all filters, and then click **OK**. All of the records should appear again in the Mail Merge Recipients dialog box.

11. Click **OK** to close the Mail Merge Recipients dialog box.

12. Save the changes to the main document, and leave it open for the next Step-by-Step.

Inserting Fields with Conditions

The Rules button provides special fields that set conditions for performing an action during the merge process. When you insert these special fields in a main document, you set parameters that Word uses to make a decision. For example, you can insert a rule in the main document for adding a paragraph of text under certain conditions. During the merge process, Word compares the specified field criteria to the merged field data. If the referenced merged field data meets the specified criteria, Word includes the additional paragraph in the merged letter. On the other hand, if the merged field data does not meet the specified field criteria, the additional paragraph does not appear in the merged letter for that record.

Table 12–1 describes each of the field rules.

TABLE 12–1   Field rules

RULE NAME	DESCRIPTION OF THE RULE
Ask	Instructs Word to show a message to prompt the user to respond. Use this field to repeat the same information in more than one place in a document. For example, you can set a rule to show a prompt when a name appears in a document for the second time. When prompted about the second occurrence, the user can choose to use only the first name for all occurrences after the first occurrence.
Fill in	Instructs Word to show a message to prompt the user to insert information. Use this field to insert information only once. For example, you can set the rule so that Word will prompt the user to enter the current date.
If...Then...Else...	Instructs Word to take action for set conditions. For example, if the merged record data includes a specified postal code, the letter will include a sentence about the location of a store.
Merge Record #	Instructs Word to insert the ordinal position of the merged data record, which reflects any sorting or filtering before the merge. For example, you can set a rule such that an applicant's entry number will appear in the document.
Merge Sequence #	Instructs Word to count the number of records in the merged document. The number is not visible in the merged document until the merge is completed. For example, the main document includes a sentence about the number of individuals attending an event. When the merge is completed, the number in the sentence will reflect the number of merged records.
Next Record	Instructs Word to insert the next data record into the current document without starting a new document. For example, this field is used when Word creates a full page of labels so that multiple records appear on the same page.
Next Record If	Instructs Word to determine whether the next data record should be merged into the current document or into a new document. For example, if two contacts have the same last name and address, both names can be inserted in the same document to eliminate mailing the same letter twice to the same address.
Set Bookmark	Instructs Word to refer to specific information stored in a bookmark. For example, the date for an event may appear several times throughout the document. Each occurrence of the date in the letter is cross-referenced to the bookmark. If the date changes, you simply change the content in the bookmark field and then all occurrences of the date in the document will be updated.
Skip Record If	Instructs Word to exclude records from the merge if conditions are not met. For example, if the contact has an out-of-state address, the record is not included in the merge.

Step-by-Step 12.7

1. If necessary, open the **Donation Letter Main Document** file from your solution files. When prompted to place data from the data source file, click **Yes**.

2. Position the insertion point in front of the second sentence in the first paragraph of the body of the letter. In the Write & Insert Fields group on the Mailings tab, click the **Rules** button, and then click **If…Then…Else…**. The Insert Word Field: IF dialog box opens, as shown in **Figure 12–14**.

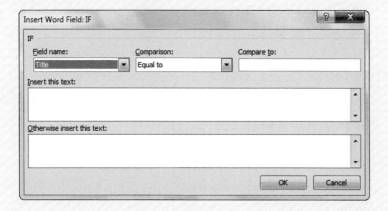

FIGURE 12–14
Insert Word Field: IF dialog box

3. Click the **Field name** list arrow, scroll down, and then select **Contribution**.

4. Click the **Comparison** list arrow, then select **Greater than or equal**.

5. In the Compare to text box, type **$500**.

6. In the Insert this text box, type **Your donation is very generous.**, and then press the **spacebar** to create a blank space after the sentence. Leave the next text box empty. Click **OK**.

7. In the Preview Results group, click the **Preview Results** button. Use the Next Record and Previous Record buttons, shown in **Figure 12–15**, to navigate through the merged documents. You will see that the merged documents for Recipients 2, 4, and 5 include the extra sentence. Recipient 3 does not appear in the preview because that record was not included in the merge.

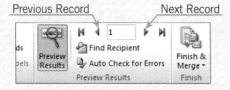

FIGURE 12–15
Preview Results group on the Mailings tab

8. Go to a letter containing the new sentence (Recipients 2, 4, or 5). Notice that the font style and size for the additional sentence does not match the font or format for the rest of the paragraph. Select the first paragraph, then right-click to open the Mini toolbar. Change the font style to **Calibri** and the font size to **11** point.

9. Click the **Next Record** and **Previous Record** buttons. The variable text should now match the boilerplate text in all letters. Click the **Preview Results** button to toggle off the preview.

10. In the Finish group, click the **Finish & Merge** button, and then click **Edit Individual Documents**. If necessary, select the **All** option in the Merge to New Document dialog box. Click **OK**.

11. A new document (such as *Letters3*) is opened. Save the new merged document as **Merged Donation Letters**, followed by your initials.

12. Click the **File** tab and then click **Print** to view the merged document in Preview pane. Navigate through all the pages in the document to view all five letters. At this point you could print one or all of the merged letters.

13. Close the merged document and the main document. When prompted to save the changes to the main document, click **Save**.

Preparing Mailing Labels and Envelopes

The processes for merging data to create envelopes and labels are similar to those used for creating mail merge letters. As with other merges, you can use data from an existing data source or you can create a new data source. Just as you can edit individual letters and print letters for selected records, you can edit individual labels or envelopes for selected records.

Preparing Mailing Labels

Label options include more than just mailing labels. You can also merge records to create labels for name badges, business cards, postcards, folder labels, and more. When you select the Labels document type, Word automatically inserts the Next Record field rule, which propagates the first label to the other labels on the same page.

You can preview the merged records before you print. You may want to print a sample of labels on plain paper to compare the plain sheet sample with the sheet of labels. Then you can check to see if you need to position the sheet of labels differently in the printer or if you need to adjust your main document settings (margins, page length, and column width).

TIP

Note that the Envelopes and Labels buttons in the Create group are used only for individual envelopes or labels. These buttons are not used in mail merge documents.

Step-by-Step 12.8

1. Open the **Customers** file from the drive and folder where your Data Files are stored. Save the document as **Customers Data Source**, followed by your initials, and then close the document.

2. Open a new blank Word document and save it as **Customer Labels Main Document**, followed by your initials.

3. Click the **Mailings** tab. In the Start Mail Merge group, click the **Start Mail Merge** button, and then select **Labels**. The Label Options dialog box opens, as shown in **Figure 12–16**. The options shown in the dialog box vary depending on the type of printer you use.

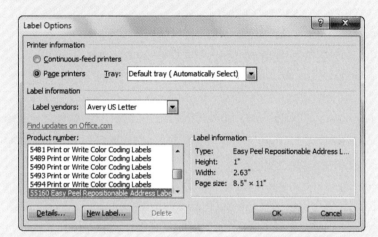

FIGURE 12–16
Label Options dialog box

4. Under Printer information, make sure the **Page printers** option is enabled. Under Label information, in the Label vendors box, select **Avery US Letter**. Under Product number, select **55160 Easy Peel Repositionable Address Labels**. A description of the label height and width is provided at the right.

5. Make sure your settings match those shown in Figure 12–16 (your Tray information may differ), and then click **OK**. If the gridlines for your label placement in the document are not visible, click the Table Tools Layout tab, and in the Table group, click the View Gridlines button, then click the Mailings tab.

6. In the Start Mail Merge group, click the **Select Recipients** button. Click **Use Existing List**, navigate to the folder where you save your solution files, select **Customers Data Source**, then click **Open**. The first label is still blank, but the other labels contain the merge field *Next Record*.

> **TIP**
>
> Labels come in a variety of sizes. Be sure to use the correct product number in the Label Options dialog box. The product number is generally provided on the label package.

7. The insertion point should be positioned in the first label. In the Write & Insert Fields group, click the **Address Block** button to open the Insert Address Block dialog box. Use the Next and Previous buttons in the Preview pane to view the data source addresses. You'll see that Recipients 3 and 11 require more than four lines; there won't be enough space to print all the lines on these labels. Return to Recipient 1 and click **Cancel**.

8. Format the address fields manually:

   a. In the Write & Insert Fields group, click the **Insert Merge Field** button arrow. Click **Title**. The merge field is entered in the first label. Press the **spacebar** to enter a blank space after the merge field.

   b. Click the **Insert Merge Field** button arrow, click **FirstName**, and then press the **spacebar**.

   c. Insert the **LastName** field, and then press **Enter**.

   d. Insert the **Company** field, and then press **Enter**.

   e. Insert the **Address1** field, and then press the **spacebar**. Insert the **Address2** field, and then press **Enter**.

   f. Insert the **City** field, type , (a comma), and then press the **spacebar**. Insert the **State** field, press the **spacebar**, and then insert the **PostalCode** field.

9. Select all the merge fields in the first label. Right-click to open the Mini toolbar, and then change the font size to **10** point. With the merge fields still selected, click the **Home** tab. In the Paragraph group, click the **Line and Paragraph Spacing** button and then click **Remove Space Before Paragraph**.

10. Click the **Mailings** tab. In the Write & Insert Fields group, click the **Update Labels** button to propagate the address fields for each label on the sheet. Word inserts the merge fields, with the 10-point font format, on all the other labels in the document. Do not be concerned that the first line of merge fields wraps to the next line.

11. In the Preview Results group, click the **Preview Results** button to view the merged data. You will notice that many of the labels on the page are blank, because the data source did not contain enough records to fill the page of labels. Click the **Preview Results** button again to toggle off the feature.

12. In the Finish group, click the **Finish & Merge** button, and then click **Edit Individual Documents**. Confirm that the All option is selected, then click **OK**. All records are merged into a single document.

13. Save the new merged labels document as **Merged Customer Labels**, followed by your initials. Click the **File** tab, and then click **Print** to view the document in the Preview pane.

14. Close the merged document, and then close the main document. When prompted to save the changes to the main document, click **Save**.

Preparing Envelopes Using the Mail Merge Feature

You can also use the Mail Merge feature to prepare addressed envelopes for a group or mass mailing. The process for preparing envelopes is very similar to the process you just completed to create mailing labels. However, instead of specifying label options, you specify options for the envelope size. You must also set the printing options to indicate how the envelopes are fed into the printer. Word will automatically insert a return address derived from the user information stored on your computer. You can replace this return address with a new one, or you can delete the return address if you are using envelopes with preprinted return addresses.

Step-by-Step 12.9

1. Open the **Clients** file from the drive and folder where your Data Files are stored. Save the document as **Clients Data Source**, followed by your initials, and then close the document.

2. Open a new blank Word document, and save it as **Client Envelopes Main Document**, followed by your initials. If necessary, toggle on **Show/Hide ¶** to display nonprinting formatting characters.

3. Click the **Mailings** tab. In the Start Mail Merge group, click the **Start Mail Merge** button, and then click **Envelopes**. The Envelope Options dialog box opens, as shown in **Figure 12–17**.

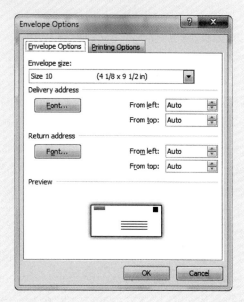

FIGURE 12–17
Envelope Options tab in the Envelope Options dialog box

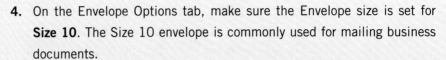

4. On the Envelope Options tab, make sure the Envelope size is set for **Size 10**. The Size 10 envelope is commonly used for mailing business documents.

5. Click the **Printing Options** tab to display options similar to those shown in **Figure 12–18**. Options vary depending on the type of printer you use. This tab includes feed method settings, which are dependent on your currently selected printer. Under Feed method, Word suggests how to place the envelope in the tray. Click **OK** to close the dialog box. The document changes to landscape orientation.

FIGURE 12–18
Printing Options tab in the
Envelope Options dialog box

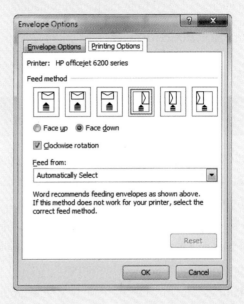

6. In the Start Mail Merge group, click the **Select Recipients** button, and then click **Use Existing List**. Navigate to and select your solution file **Clients Data Source**. Click **Open**.

7. Click near the paragraph mark in the middle of the envelope where you want the delivery address to appear. A cross-hatched border appears to indicate a preformatted text box.

8. In the Write & Insert Fields group, click the **Address Block** button. Click **OK**, and the AddressBlock merge field is inserted in the text box.

9. If necessary, show the nonprinting formatting characters. Click in the first blank paragraph in the upper-left corner. Type the following return address:
MAPPS Investments
259 Madison Avenue
New York, NY 10016-2401

10. In the Preview Results group, click the **Preview Results** button to view the merged data. Navigate through the merged documents, and then click the **Preview Results** button again to close the preview.

11. In the Start Mail Merge group, click the **Edit Recipient List** button. In the Mail Merge Recipients dialog box, under Refine recipient list, click **Find duplicates**. Uncheck one of the records for *Garverich*, then click **OK** twice to close both dialog boxes.

12. In the Finish group, click the **Finish & Merge** button, and then click **Edit Individual Documents**. Confirm that the All option is selected, then click **OK**. All records are merged into a single document.

13. Save the new merged envelopes document as **Merged Client Envelopes**, followed by your initials. Scroll down through the document and you will see that one page has been created for each record.

14. Close the new merged document and main document. When prompted to save the changes to the main document, click **Yes**.

Creating a Main Document for Mass E-Mails

The merge feature also enables you to create group or mass mailings for personalized e-mail messages. You can use Outlook or another MAPI-compliant e-mail program. *MAPI (Messaging Application Programming Interface)* is a Windows programming interface that provides applications with a standard way to communicate when sending e-mail. This interface enables Word to share information during the merge process with one of the many MAPI-compliant e-mail programs.

For the data source, you can use the contact information in your e-mail program, and in some cases, such as a customer or client list, the list of recipients may already be saved in a contacts subfolder. You can also access data files in Word, Excel, or Access, which are all MAPI-compliant.

The merge process for sending e-mails is similar to that for creating a merged letter. After you finalize the e-mail message in the main document, however, you send the messages using your e-mail program instead of printing the merged results.

To create a mass e-mail merge, you must use the same versions of Outlook and Word, such as Outlook 2010 and Word 2010. Also note that you cannot designate a recipient in the Cc line in the e-mail header, and you cannot attach files to the message.

> ▶ **VOCABULARY**
> **MAPI (Messaging Application Programming Interface)**

Step-by-Step 12.10

1. Open the **Orders Shipped** file from the drive and folder where your Data Files are stored. Save the document as **Orders Shipped Data Source**, followed by your initials, and then close the document.

2. Open the **Shipped Message** file from the drive and folder where your Data Files are stored. Save the document as **Shipped Message Main Document**, followed by your initials. If necessary, toggle on **Show/Hide ¶** to display nonprinting formatting characters.

3. Click the **Mailings** tab. In the Start Mail Merge group, click the **Start Mail Merge** button, and then click **E-mail Messages**. The document view changes to Web Layout view.

4. Click the **Select Recipients** button, and then click **Use Existing List**. Navigate to and select your solution file **Orders Shipped Data Source**. Click **Open**.

5. Click the **Edit Recipient List** button. Scroll to the right to show the last column, *Shipped*. Click the **list arrow** in the Shipped column heading, and then click **Yes**. Click **OK** to close the dialog box.

6. With the insertion point in the first blank paragraph of the document, click the **Greeting Line** button in the Write & Insert Fields group. Click **OK** to accept the settings.

7. Delete the **XX**s in the second sentence of the message. Click the **Inset Merge Field** button arrow, and then click **Order**. The Order field is inserted following the # sign.

8. In the Preview Results group, click the **Preview Results** button. Review some of the messages to make sure the greeting line looks appropriate and the product number is inserted correctly. Click the **Preview Results** button again to close the preview.

9. In the Finish group, click the **Finish & Merge** button, and then click **Send E-mail Messages**. The Merge to E-mail dialog box opens, as shown in **Figure 12–19**.

FIGURE 12–19
Merge to E-mail dialog box

10. If necessary, click the **list arrow** in the To box and then select **Email_Address**. In the Subject line text box, type **Your order has shipped!**.

11. The next step would be to click OK, which would send all the e-mails in your default e-mail program. Instead, click **Cancel**.

12. Click the **Finish & Merge** button, and then click **Edit Individual Documents**. Click **OK** to accept that all records will be merged.

13. Scroll down through the document. You will see the message repeated several times, and each message is formatted on its own page with a Next Page section break. So that your instructor can see that you have completed all the steps, save the document as **Merged Shipped Messages**, followed by your initials.

14. Close the merged document and the main document. When prompted to save the changes to the main document, click **Save**.

Creating Catalogs and Directories

The merge feature is also convenient for creating a catalog or a price list. For example, a company may release a product price list at the beginning of each month. If the product information is stored in a data source, the information can easily be updated and merged into a Directory type main document.

Before the merge, you can edit a directory main document and data source in the same way you edit main documents and data sources for other types of merges. You can update the data source records, add or delete records, and sort and filter the records.

When you apply formats to the merge fields in the main document, the formats are applied to the variable data when the records are merged. Another way to format merged data is to add a formatting switch to the field code. A *switch* is a special instruction that modifies a field result. For example, if the data source includes the price of a product (55.95), but the information does not include dollar signs, you can create a switch to control the number format. The following is a merge field with a switch to add the dollar sign and the number format: { Price \# $#,###.00 }. In this switch, *Price* refers to the name of the field; \# indicates the switch is to format numbers; $ is the character to be added in front of the field results; #, ### specifies the maximum number of digits; and .00 indicates the decimal place and the number of digits to follow the decimal.

Table 12–2 shows a few more switches that are commonly used. You can find additional switches by searching the keywords "field codes" in the Word Help screens, and then looking for a specific field name, such as *Date*. Then you can see if switches are available for that field.

▶ **VOCABULARY**
switch

TABLE 12–2 Common switches

SWITCH	TYPE	EXAMPLES	DESCRIPTION OF THE SWITCH
*	Capitalization	{ State * Upper }	The results for the field *State* will display all letters capitalized.
\@	Date/Time	{ Date \@, "dddd, MMMM d" } { Time \@, "hh:mm AM/PM" }	The results for the field *Date* will display in the format *Monday, April 11*. The results for the field *Time* will display in the format *10:30 AM*.
\#	Number	{ Phone \# ###'-' ###'-'#### }	The results for the field *Phone* will display with hyphens.
\p	Path	{ Filename \p }	The results for the field *Filename* will display the file location, or path, after the filename.

Step-by-Step 12.11

1. Open the **Products** file from the drive and folder where your Data Files are stored. Save the document as **Products Data Source**, followed by your initials, and then close the document.

2. Open the **Catalog** file from the drive and folder where your Data Files are stored. Save the document as **Catalog Main Document**, followed by your initials. If necessary, toggle on **Show/Hide ¶** to display nonprinting formatting characters.

3. Click the **Mailings** tab. In the Start Mail Merge group, click the **Start Mail Merge** button and then select **Directory**.

4. Click the **Select Recipients** button, and then click **Use Existing List**. Navigate to and select your solution file **Products Data Source**, and then click **Open**.

5. Click the **Edit Recipient List** button. Under Data Source, click the data source filename, **Products Data Source**, and then click **Edit**. The Data Form dialog box opens, as shown in **Figure 12–20**.

FIGURE 12–20
Data Form dialog box

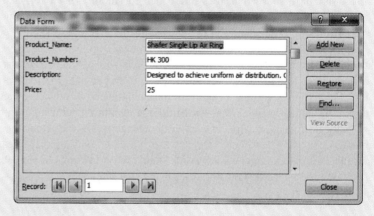

6. Click **Find**. Drag the Find in Field dialog box that opens so you can see the Data Form dialog box. In the **Find what** text box, type **Shafer**, and then click **Find First**. Click **Find Next** to go to the next occurrence.

7. The *Shafer Internal Bubble Cooling System, IBC 150* appears in the Data Form dialog box. Close the Find in Field dialog box.

8. In the Data Form dialog box, change the price from *495* to **575**. Click **Close**, and then click **OK** to close the Mail Merge Recipients dialog box.

9. Insert the merge fields into the main document:

   a. Position the insertion point in the main document after *Item #:* and press the **spacebar**.

   b. In the Write & Insert Fields group, click the **Insert Merge Field** button arrow, and then click **Product_Number**.

    c. Position the insertion point after *Product:*. Press the **spacebar** and insert the merge field **Product_Name**.

    d. Position the insertion point in the blank paragraph just below *Product:*. Insert the merge field **Description**.

    e. Position the insertion point in the main document after *List Price:*. Press the **spacebar** and insert the merge field **Price**.

10. Right-click the **Price** field, and then click **Edit Field**. The Field dialog box opens. In the lower-left corner, click **Field Codes**. The dialog box changes to display the options shown in **Figure 12–21**.

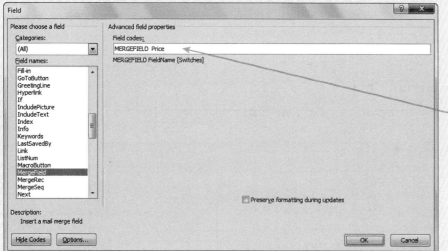

FIGURE 12–21
Field code options in the Field dialog box

Enter switch here

11. Click to the right of *Price* in the Field codes text box and type **\# $#,###.00**. Then click **OK**.

12. In the Preview Results group, click the **Preview Results** button. A $ appears before each price, and the numbers are formatted with commas and decimals. Click the **Preview Results** button again to toggle off the feature.

13. In the Finish group, click the **Finish & Merge** button, and then click **Edit Individual Documents**. Click **OK** to merge all the records to a new document. Save the new merged document as **Merged Product Catalog**, followed by your initials.

14. Close the merged document, and then close the main document. When prompted to save changes to the data source file, click **Yes**. When prompted to save the changes to the main document, click **Save**.

SUMMARY

In this lesson, you learned:

- You can use the mail merge feature to create personalized and customized form letters, mailing labels, and envelopes.

- The mail merge process involves combining a main document with variable information from a data source.

- To create the main document, you can use the current document, or you can start from a template or an existing document.

- For the variable data, you can use an existing data source or you can create a new data source.

- You insert fields into the main document to merge the variable data from the data source.

- Data records can be sorted and edited before you merge them with a main document, and you can apply rules to the fields, which set parameters for the variable content.

- You can preview merge results before you complete a merge, and you can edit individual merged records.

- You can use the mail merge process to personalize an e-mail message to be sent to multiple recipients.

- You can use the mail merge process to create catalogs and directories.

■ VOCABULARY REVIEW

Define the following terms:

data source
field
field names
filter

MAPI (Messaging Application
 Programming Interface)
main document

merge fields
record
switch

■ REVIEW QUESTIONS

TRUE / FALSE

Circle T if the statement is true or F if the statement is false.

T   F   1.   If the data source does not already exist, you can create a new data source during the merge process.

T   F   2.   When the merge process is completed for a letter document type, you can choose to print all letters, the letter for the current record, or the letters for a range of records.

T   F   3.   The Ribbon provides more options for the mail merge process than the Mail Merge Wizard.

T   F   4.   Fields must be arranged in a specific order in the data source before the records can be merged into the main document.

T   F   5.   During the mail merge process, you can update and add or delete records.

MATCHING

Match the correct term in Column 2 to its description in Column 1.

Column 1

_____ 1. one or more characters that create a piece of information

_____ 2. a collection of variable information to be used in a merge

_____ 3. a label identifying a field

_____ 4. a placeholder in the main document

_____ 5. a group of related fields

Column 2

A.   record

B.   field name

C.   main document

D.   field

E.   data source

F.   filter

G.   merge field

MULTIPLE CHOICE

Select the best response for the following statements.

1. The mail merge feature enables you to personalize and customize _____ for mass mailings.

   A.   letters

   B.   e-mail messages

   C.   envelopes and labels

   D.   all of the above

2. The _____ contains the variable information used in the merge process.

   A.   field name

   B.   main document

   C.   merge field

   D.   data source

3. The _____ command helps you identify fields from your data source that correspond with the required field.

   A.   Match Fields

   B.   Highlight Merge Fields

   C.   Auto Check for Errors

   D.   Find Recipient

4. The _____ button provides special fields that set conditions for performing an action during the merge process.

   A.   Address Block

   B.   Select Recipients

   C.   Rules

   D.   Insert Merge Field

5. The _____ rule instructs Word to show a message to prompt the user to insert information.

   A.   If...Else...

   B.   Fill in

   C.   Next Record If

   D.   Set Bookmark

■ PROJECTS

If you have a SAM 2010 user profile, your instructor may have assigned an autogradable version of the indicated project. If so, log into the SAM 2010 Web site at *www.cengage.com/sam2010* to download the instruction and start files.

√ PROJECT 12–1

1. Open the **Sponsors Letter** file from the drive and folder where your Data Files are stored. Save the document as **Sponsors Letter Main Document**, followed by your initials.

2. Begin the merge process and create a merge document for letters. The current document is the main document.

3. Create a new data source with the following field names: **Title, First Name, Last Name, Company Name, Address, City, State,** and **ZIP Code**.

4. Enter the following records in the data source:
   Mr. Erik Stein
   Shannon Auto Sales
   954 West State Street
   Trenton, OH 45067-9690

   Mrs. Jennifer O'Brian
   Time for You
   3569 Radabaugh Road
   Trenton, OH 45067-2046

   Ms. Patti Ruiz
   Trenton Heating & Cooling
   5301 Kennedy Road
   Trenton, OH 45067-9436

   Dr. Barry Grossman
   McCormick Health Center
   607 Wayne Madison Road
   Trenton, OH 45067-9665

5. Save the data source as **Sponsors Data Source**, followed by your initials.

6. Complete the letter by inserting the appropriate fields for the inside address and the greeting. This letter will be printed on stationery that includes the Chamber name and address at the top of the page.

7. Add one more record to the data source:
   Mrs. Becky Laws
   Trenton Grocery and Pharmacy
   519 Holland Drive
   Trenton, OH 45067-9704

8. Sort the records in ascending order by the company name.

9. Preview the merged documents, and merge all the records to a new document. Save the new document as **Merged Sponsors Letters**, followed by your initials.

10. In Backstage view, preview how the Merged Sponsors Letters document will print.

11. Close the merged document and the main document. Save the changes to the main document.

√ ŚAM PROJECT 12–2

1. Open the **Account Holders** file from the drive and folder where your Data Files are stored. Save the file as **Account Holders Data Source**, followed by your initials. This data source contains account balance data that is updated daily. Close the data source file.

2. Open the **Overdraft Letter** file from the folder where your Data Files are stored. Save the document as **Overdraft Letter Main Document**, followed by your initials.

3. Begin the merge process by identifying the document type as **Letters**. Identify the data source as **Account Holders Data Source**.

4. Insert fields for the recipient's address and fields for the greeting line. Use appropriate punctuation in the greeting line.

5. In the first paragraph, insert fields for the account number and the current account balance. Edit the Account_Balance merge field by adding the switch **\# -$#,###.00**. This will format the field results so that a minus sign and a $ will appear in front of the number data.

6. Edit the data source. Add the title **Ms.** for Recipient 2, and add the title **Mr.** for Recipient 7.

7. Filter the records using the data in the Account_Balance field. In the Comparison box, select Less than. In the Compare to text box, type **0** (the number zero).

8. Preview the results. Go back and edit steps if necessary. Then complete the merge. You should have five merged letters. Save the merged letters as a single new document, and name the document **Merged Overdraft Letters**, followed by your initials.

9. Close the merged document and the main document. Save the changes to the data source and to the main document.

10. Open a new Word document and create mailing labels for the Avery US letter, **55160 Easy Peel Repositionable Address Labels**. Save the document as **Overdraft Labels Main Document**, followed by your initials.

11. Select the recipients from the **Account Holders Data Source**. You will need to repeat Step 7 above to filter the records.

12. Insert the Address Block in the first label, and then update the labels to propagate the fields for the remaining labels. Preview the merged results. You should have five labels.

13. Save the merged labels as a single new document, and name the document **Merged Overdraft Labels**, followed by your initials.

14. Close the new merged document, and then close the main document. Save the changes to the main document.

Saturday | Sunday.
9:00am 2:00p.m.

PROJECT 12–3

1. Open the **Prospects** file from the drive and folder where your Data Files are stored. Save the file as **Prospects Data Source**, followed by your initials. Close the data source file.

2. Open a new blank Word document, and save the document as **Prospects Envelopes Main Document**, followed by your initials.

3. Start the process to create envelopes for a mass mailing. Accept the default Size 10 setting for the envelope size.

4. Select the data source Prospects Data Source.

5. Exclude the record for Brad Jackson from the merge.

6. In the first paragraph, enter the following return address:
New England Medical Association
Two Federal Street
Boston, MA 02110-2012

7. Insert the address fields in the preformatted text box. Format the fields so that the Address1 and Address2 data appear on the same line, separated with a blank space. Change the font size to 14 point.

8. Preview the merged envelopes and make any necessary corrections.

9. Complete the merge and saved the merged envelopes as the document **Merged Prospects Envelopes**, followed by your initials.

10. Close the merged document and the main document. Save the changes to the main document.

PROJECT 12–5

1. Open the **Courses** file from the drive and folder where your Data Files are stored. Save the document as **Courses Data Source**, followed by your initials. This data source contains information about all the community education course offerings. Close the document.

2. Open the **Course Catalog** file from the drive and folder where your Data Files are stored. Save the document as **Courses Catalog Main Document**, followed by your initials.

3. Begin the merge process to create a directory. Use the current document, and identify the file **Courses Data Source** as the data source.

4. Insert the merge fields in the main document as follows:
   a. Delete the first occurrence of xxx, and insert the **Course_Name** field.
   b. Delete the second occurrence of xxx, and insert the **Description** field.
   c. After *Class Begins*, replace xxx with the **Date_Beginning** field.
   d. After *Days*, replace xxx with the **Days** field.
   e. After *# of Times Class Meets*, replace xxx with the **Sessions** field.
   f. After Fee, replace xxx with the **Fee** field.

PROJECT 12–4

1. Open the **Staff** file from the drive and folder where your Data Files are stored. Save the document as **Staff Data Source**, followed by your initials, and then close the document.

2. Open a new blank Word document, and then start the mail merge process by creating an e-mail message. Save the document as **Staff E-mail Main Document**, followed by your initials.

3. Identify the data source as **Staff Data Source**.

4. Edit the data source by adding the following new staff member:
John Georgakopalous
Physician
j_georgakopalous@fhc.xyz

5. Insert the First_Name field at the beginning of the document, and then type a comma after the merge field. Press Enter and type the following message.
The staff meeting has been rescheduled for Thursday at 7:30 a.m.

6. Press Enter and type your initials.

7. Preview the merged results and make any necessary changes. Do not send the e-mail messages. Instead, save the merged results to a new document. Save the new document as **Merged Staff Messages**, followed by your initials.

8. Close the merged document and the main document. Save the changes to the data source and to the main document.

5. Filter the records for all classes offered at the Western campus for the spring term, which begins 3/26. (*Hint*: Filter the Location field for records equal to Western Campus and the Date Beginning field for records Greater than or equal to 3/26.)

6. Sort the records in ascending alphabetic order by Course Name.

7. Preview the merged results. Twelve courses should appear in the catalog.

8. Complete the merge process by saving the merged results as a new document.

9. Insert the following title at the top of the new document: **WESTERN CAMPUS SPRING COURSE OFFERINGS**. Center and bold the title, and change the font size to **16 point**.

10. Save the new merged document as **Merged Spring Courses Catalog**, followed by your initials.

11. In Backstage view, preview how the catalog pages will print.

12. Close the merged document and the main document. Save the changes to the main document.

■ CRITICAL THINKING

ACTIVITY 12–1

Click the File tab, and then click New. Under Office.com Templates, click the Letters folder. Search Office.com for a business thank you letter template. Download the template file and then open it. Explain how this template file would save you time when creating a mass mailing.

ACTIVITY 12–2

Henry works for a large distribution company. His company recently printed custom-sized address labels with preprinted information that included the company's address and logo. Henry is setting up the main document to print new mailing labels, but he cannot find a label in the Product Number box that matches the dimensions and layout of the new address labels. How can Henry create custom labels for the merge process? Use the Help feature and search for the keywords "set up labels" to find the answer.

prompts box
wrap up lecture

✓ Mailing ; envelopes

✓ Mailing ; Start mail merg ; step by step ; next: starting doc. (default option select recipient (specify the merge doc: template).

first merge.
Mail Merge ; Browse. (specify the merge data source).

✓ Mailings; select recip.; type new list. (create and save a mail merge data source).

✓ Mailing ; edit recip. list; data source; edit;
✓   "   ;   "   ; (select records to merge)

✓ Mailings; start mail merge; labels; select recip.; use existing list; Address block; update labels (30 per page, preview results. (create mailing labels using an existing data source.

✓ Mailings; edit recip. list
✓   "   ;   "   ; (filter records in a data source).
✗   "   ; rules; files name, Title. change If (Insert an If merge field)
✓   "   ; preview results-f next record. (preview a mail merge)
✓   "   ; finish Merge ; print doc; (print merged from letters)

✓ mail merge; more items (Insert a merge field
write four letter.

✓ Mail Merge Complete the merge; print; (merge the doc with the data source).

LESSON 13

Sharing Documents

■ OBJECTIVES

Upon completion of this lesson, you should be able to:

- Track changes and add comments.
- Merge revisions from multiple documents.
- Review and accept or reject changes.
- Compare documents.
- Restrict access to a document.
- Inspect documents to prepare for electronic distribution.
- Attach a digital signature to a document.
- Upload files to the Web.

■ VOCABULARY

case-sensitive

comment

digital signature

document workspace site

encryption

markup

metadata

Portable Document Format (PDF)

read-only document

revision bar

XML Paper Specification (XPS)

Many team members are often involved in the development of a document. If you collaborate with others to create or edit a document, Word offers many features that will help you and your teammates make the development process easier and more efficient.

Revising Documents

Team members commonly collaborate to develop a document. Often the document is reviewed by several individuals before the final version is prepared. As team members review the document, they edit the content, add new content, change formats, and share their thoughts. Word offers many features that make it easy for workgroups to track the changes, add comments, and compare revisions.

Tracking Changes in a Document

The Track Changes feature enables you to review suggested changes and feedback from reviewers. Word uses revision marks to indicate changes such as insertions, deletions, and formatting changes. Reviewers can also provide feedback in annotations without changing the content in the document. These revision marks and annotations that Word places in a document are called *markup*.

When the Track Changes feature is toggled on, edits and annotations appear as the changes are made. The revisions are easy to recognize because the edits appear in different font colors and with strikethrough and underline effects, and annotations appear in the document margin. In addition, a vertical line referred to as a *revision bar* appears in the left margin and indicates a tracked change or comment related to the paragraph. Tracked changes can appear on the screen and in printed documents.

Word assigns a different markup color for up to eight reviewers. For example, one reviewer's edits appear in red and another reviewer's edits appear in blue. Using a unique color for each reviewer helps to distinguish the revisions that each reviewer contributes. If the more than eight reviewers edit the document, Word reuses the colors.

Each user can customize the Track Changes feature by enabling options and/or specifying specific colors. For example, you can choose to change the settings so that all moved text appears in yellow and all format changes appear in green. You can also choose to show formatting changes in the right or left margins.

▶ **VOCABULARY**

markup

revision bar

Step-by-Step 13.1

1. Launch Word and open the **Board Minutes** file from the drive and folder where your Data Files are stored. Save the document as **Revised Board Minutes 1,** followed by your initials.

2. Click the **Review** tab. In the Tracking group, click the **Track Changes** button arrow and then click **Change User Name**. The Word Options dialog box opens, as shown in **Figure 13–1.**

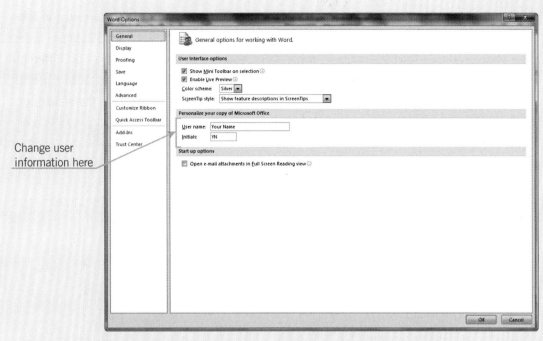

FIGURE 13–1
Word Options
dialog box

Change user
information here

3. Make note of the User name and the Initials text boxes. Then change
    the User name to **Reviewer A**, and change the Initials to **RA**. Click **OK** to
    accept the changes and close the dialog box.

4. In the Tracking group, click the **Track Changes** button arrow, and then click **Change Tracking Options**. The Track Changes Options dialog box opens, as shown in **Figure 13–2**. Your settings may be different. Compare your settings, and if necessary make changes so they match the settings shown in the figure. Then click **OK** to close the dialog box.

FIGURE 13–2
Track Changes Options dialog box

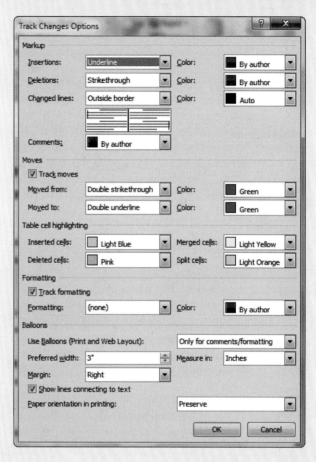

TIP

You can also use the shortcut keys Ctrl+Shift+E to toggle on and off the Track Changes feature.

FIGURE 13–3
Tracking group on the Review tab

5. Click the upper half of the **Track Changes** button to toggle on the feature. The feature is on when the button has an orange highlight, as shown in **Figure 13–3**.

Orange highlight indicates feature is toggled on

6. In the document, under the heading *ROLL CALL*, delete the second occurrence of *Janice Stork* and the comma and blank space following the name. The deleted text remains in the document, but it now appears in a different font color with a strikethrough effect. The revision bar in the left margin of the document indicates the lines of text that contain revisions.

7. In the document, under the heading *APPROVAL OF MINUTES FROM LAST MEETING*, position the insertion point at the end of the sentence. Press the **spacebar** and type **The minutes were approved as read.**. The new text is identified with an underline, and it also appears in the same font color as the deleted text above.

8. Scroll down to the heading *NEW BUSINESS*, select the three paragraphs beginning with *Finance*, *Production*, and *Sales*. Then click the **Home** tab, and in the Paragraph group, click the **Bullets** button. Deselect the text.

9. If necessary, scroll up to view the first selected paragraph. Notice that the document window adjusts to show both the text and the markup area (the shaded column on the right) using the same page orientation. Balloons appear in the markup area and describe the format changes. The color of the balloon borders matches the color for the markup related to the current reviewer.

10. Position the mouse pointer over a balloon in the markup area. A ScreenTip appears showing the user name *Reviewer A*, the current date and time, and a description of the format change.

11. Position the mouse pointer over the text connected to the balloon, and the same ScreenTip appears.

12. Scroll up to the heading *ROLL CALL*. Position the mouse pointer over the deleted text. The information about the reviewer and the date and time is displayed in a ScreenTip. The deleted text also is shown in the ScreenTip.

13. Save the changes and leave the document open for the next Step-by-Step. (If you are ending your Word session, click the **Track Changes** button arrow, click **Change User Name**, and restore the user name and initials to what you noted in Step 3 above.)

> **TIP**
>
> If the reviewer information does not appear in a ScreenTip, click the File tab, and then click Options. In the Word Options dialog box, click Display. Under Page display options, enable the Show document tooltips on hover option.

Adding Comments to a Document

A *comment* is an annotation that is added within a document by the author or reviewer. Comments provide an easy way for reviewers to share their ideas and suggestions without changing the content of the document. Word automatically assigns numbers to comments as they are inserted in the document. The numbers are sequential, regardless of the user name.

Like revision marks, comments can appear on the screen and in printed documents. Comments can be formatted to appear in balloons in the markup area, and you can also view the comments in ScreenTips above selected text in the document. You can insert comments even when the Track Changes feature is toggled off.

The Reviewing Pane offers an alternate way to show markup and provides a summary of tracked changes. You can work with the pane open, and you can choose to position the pane at the left side of the document or at the bottom of the screen.

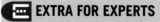

> **VOCABULARY**
> **comment**

> **EXTRA FOR EXPERTS**
>
> If you have a Tablet PC, you can create handwritten notes in a comment balloon or in the Reviewing Pane.

Step-by-Step 13.2

1. If necessary, open the **Revised Board Minutes 1** file from your solution files. Save the document as **Revised Board Minutes 2,** followed by your initials.

2. Click the **Review** tab. Click the **Track Changes** button arrow, and then click **Change User Name**. Change the User name to **Reviewer B** and change the Initials to **RB,** and then click **OK**.

3. In the document, under the heading *OLD BUSINESS*, in the second paragraph, position the insertion point after the amount *$1,375,000,* press the **spacebar,** and then type **higher**. The inserted text appears in a different color to indicate a new reviewer.

4. Select the amount **$1,375,000**. On the Review tab, in the Comments group, click the **New Comment** button. The selected text is shaded, and a new balloon, formatted in the new color, appears in the right margin with the reviewer initials and the number 1. Type **Should this be $1,372,000?**.

5. Click anywhere outside the balloon to deselect it. To edit the comment, click the balloon to make it active again. Position the insertion point after the word *Should* and type **n't**.

6. On the Review tab, in the Tracking group, click the **Reviewing Pane** button arrow and then click **Reviewing Pane Vertical**. The Reviewing Pane opens on the left side of the document, as shown in **Figure 13–4**. If you do not see the markup summary details at the top of the Reviewing Pane, click the **Detailed Summary** button so that your Reviewing Pane matches Figure 13–4.

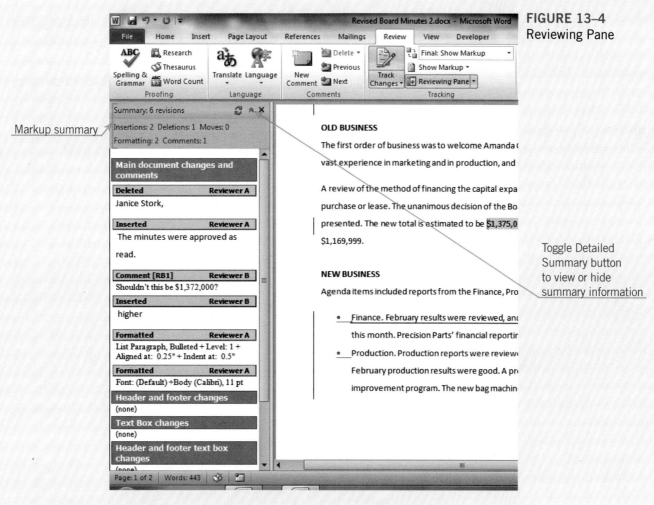

FIGURE 13–4
Reviewing Pane

Markup summary

Toggle Detailed
Summary button
to view or hide
summary information

7. In the Reviewing Pane, click the text of the insertion made by Reviewer B. Delete the blank space and the word *higher*. As you edit the tracked change in the Reviewing Pane, the edit is updated in the document window. When you finish deleting all of the inserted text, the tracked change is removed from the Reviewing Pane.

8. On the Review tab, in the Tracking group, click the **Reviewing Pane** button arrow and then click **Reviewing Pane Horizontal**. The Reviewing Pane is moved to the bottom of the screen. Click the **Close** button in the upper-right corner of the pane.

9. On the Review tab, in the Tracking group, click the **Track Changes** button arrow and then click **Change Tracking Options**. Under Balloons, in the list box next to *Use Balloons (Print and Web Layout)*, click the **list arrow** and then select **Never**, as shown in **Figure 13–5**. Click **OK** to apply the changes and close the dialog box.

FIGURE 13–5
Track Changes Options dialog box

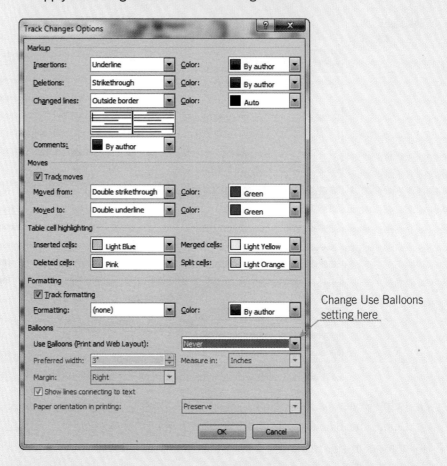

Change Use Balloons setting here

10. In the document, under the heading *ROLL CALL*, select the name **Rufenacht** at the end of the paragraph. On the Review tab, in the Comments group, click the **New Comment** button. A new comment box opens in the Reviewing Pane at the bottom of the screen. In the comment box, type **Make sure name is spelled correctly.**, and then click the **Close** button to close the pane. The reviewer's initials and the number 1 appear in brackets to the right of the selected word, and the comment will appear in a ScreenTip. The other comment, which appears below this comment, is now number 2.

11. Under the heading *ROLL CALL*, select the entire last sentence. Drag and drop the sentence to position it at the top of the document. When the text is moved or copied, the comment stays with the text. (If the text is deleted, the comment is also deleted.)

12. Notice, too, that the new position of the text appears with an underline to show it is new text. The text in the original position appears with a strikethrough effect to show it has been deleted. Click the **Undo** button to undo the edit.

13. On the Review tab, in the Tracking group, click the **Show Markup** button and then point to **Balloons**. In the menu that opens, enable the **Show Only Comments and Formatting in Balloons** option. Then click the **Track Changes** button arrow and click **Change User Name**. Restore the user name and initials to what you noted in Step 3 of Step-by-Step 13.1, above. Click **OK**.

14. Save the changes and leave the document open for the next Step-by-Step.

Showing and Hiding Markup

Word does not limit the number of reviewers for a document. When multiple reviewers add comments and make revisions to the document, it can be difficult to read the content and visualize the effect of all the revisions. You can choose from several options to control the markup that is shown in a document. For example, you can show markup for only specified types of edits or for specific reviewers. Even though the markup does not appear on the screen, it remains in the document until you accept or reject the changes.

If the markup shows on your screen when you send the document to the printer, then the markup will also appear in the printed document. If you want the document to print without the markup, you must first hide the markup.

Step-by-Step 13.3

1. If necessary, open the **Revised Board Minutes 2** file from your solution files. Save the document as **Revised Board Minutes 3,** followed by your initials.

2. If necessary, click the **Review** tab. In the Tracking group, click the **Show Markup** button. In the menu that opens, all markup types that are set to show in the document are indicated with check marks.

3. Point to **Reviewers** to show the names of the reviewers and their associated colors, as shown in **Figure 13–6**. The default setting will show all reviewer comments and changes in the document.

FIGURE 13–6
Show Markup options with the
names of the reviewers

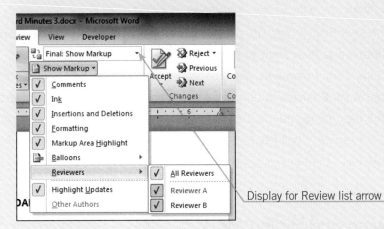

Display for Review list arrow

4. Click **Reviewer A** to uncheck the reviewer name. Now only markup made by Reviewer B will be shown in the document. However, even though the markup will not be visible, Reviewer A's changes are still saved in the document.

5. Click the **Show Markup** button, point to **Reviewers**, and then click **All Reviewers** to show changes for all reviewers.

6. Click the **Show Markup** button, and then click **Formatting** to uncheck the option. Under the heading *NEW BUSINESS*, the balloons describing the bullet format are no longer shown in the document. However, the bullets are shown as inserted characters.

7. Click the **Show Markup** button, and then click **Formatting** to enable the option again.

8. In the Tracking group, next to the list box containing the setting *Final: Show Markup*, click the **Display for Review** list arrow, as indicated in Figure 13–6, and then click **Final**. The document is shown on the screen with all the revisions accepted and the comments hidden. The markup has not been accepted or removed from the document; it just doesn't appear on the screen.

9. Click the **Display for Review** list arrow again, and then click **Final: Show Markup**.

10. Click the **File** tab, and then click **Print**. The Print preview pane confirms that the revision marks and the comments will print. The document is reduced in size so that the comments can be printed on the same page.

11. In the center pane, under Settings, click **Print All Pages** to open a menu with the options shown in **Figure 13–7**. Notice that the option Print Markup is selected. This is the default setting.

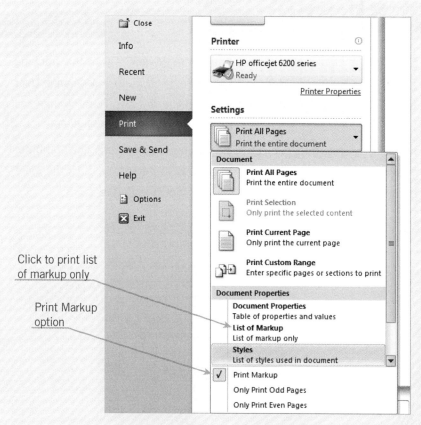

FIGURE 13–7
Document Properties
printing options

Click to print list
of markup only

Print Markup
option

12. Under Document Properties, click **List of Markup**. The menu closes. If you were to click the Print button, the document would not print; only the information in the Reviewing Pane would print.

13. Under Settings, click **List of Markup**. Click **Print All Pages** to restore the default setting, and then click the **Home** tab to close the print options.

14. Close the document without saving any changes.

Combining Revisions from Multiple Documents

Sometimes reviewers will make changes to their own copy of the same document, creating different versions of the document. Word lets you combine all the changes into one document. You can merge all the changes into the original document, or you can create a new document to show the combined revisions. Once combined, changes from each reviewer will appear in a unique color to differentiate the changes made by each reviewer. Reviewer identity is also revealed in a ScreenTip that shows above revision marks.

Step-by-Step 13.4

1. Open a new blank document and click the **Review** tab. In the Tracking group, click the **Track Changes** button arrow and then click **Change User Name**. Make note of the user name and the initials. Then change the User name to **Reviewer C** and change the Initials to **RC**. Click **OK**.

2. In the Compare group, click the **Compare** button and then click **Combine**. The Combine Documents dialog box opens. If necessary, click the **More** button to reveal the comparison options shown in **Figure 13–8**.

FIGURE 13–8
Combine Documents
dialog box

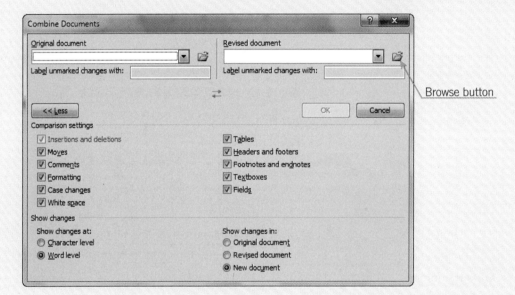

3. Click the **Original document** list arrow. Recently opened documents appear in the list. Scroll down and click **Revised Board Minutes 3**.

4. Click the **Browse** button [icon] next to the Revised document list box. Navigate to the Data Files folder, select **Board Minutes RD**, and then click **Open**. Click **OK**.

5. A prompt appears stating that only one set of formatting changes can be merged. Make sure the Revised Board Minutes 3 document is selected and then click **Continue with Merge**. A new combined document opens showing the revisions from both documents.

6. If, in addition to the new combined document, the original document (Revised Board Minutes 3) and the revised document (Board Minutes RD) also appear, and the Reviewing Pane is open, skip to step 7. If not, then in the Tracking group, click the **Reviewing Pane** button to open the Reviewing Pane. In the Compare group, click the **Compare** button, point to **Show Source Documents**, and then click **Show Both**.

7. Scroll through the new document or the Reviewing Pane. You will see revisions from Reviewers A, B, and D.

8. The combined document is the active document. Save the combined document to your solutions folder as **Revised Board Minutes 4**, followed by your initials. Close the document. The Revised Board Minutes 3 and Board Minutes RD document windows also close.

9. In a new blank document, on the Review tab, in the Compare group, click the **Compare** button, and then click **Combine**.

10. In the Original document list box, select **Revised Board Minutes 4**. Next to the Revised document list box, click **Browse**. Navigate to the Data Files folder, select **Board Minutes RE**, and click **Open**. Click **OK**. Then click **Continue with Merge**.

11. If necessary, click the **Reviewing Pane** button in the Tracking group to show the Reviewing Pane. Scroll through the Reviewing Pane and you will see changes from five reviewers.

12. Close the Reviewing Pane. Save the new combined document to your solutions folder as **Revised Board Minutes 5**, followed by your initials.

13. Close the Revised Board Minutes 5 document. If the Revised Board Minutes 4 and Board Minutes RE documents are open, they will close, too. Click the **Track Changes** button arrow, click **Change User Name**, and restore the user name and initials to what you noted in Step 1 above.

Reviewing Revisions

The next step is to review the revisions and decide whether to accept or reject the proposed changes. Buttons on the Ribbon make it easy to navigate to revisions and comments. You can accept or reject the changes individually, or you can accept several or all changes at once. And you can easily remove the comments.

EXTRA FOR EXPERTS

You can also navigate to the next comment by clicking the Select Browse Object button on the vertical scroll bar and then clicking Browse by Comment. To go to a specific reviewer's comments, double-click the page number on the status bar. The Go To tab in the Find and Replace dialog box will open. Under Go to what, select Comment and then under Enter reviewer's name, select the reviewer. Click Next or Previous to move to that reviewer's comments.

Step-by-Step 13.5

1. Open the **Revised Board Minutes 5** file from your solution files. Save the document as **Final Board Minutes**, followed by your initials.

2. Position the insertion point at the top of the document. Click the **Review** tab. In the Comments group, click the **Next Comment** button. The first comment in the document is highlighted. Click the **Next Comment** button again to move to the second comment in the document. The Next Comment button moves the insertion point only to comments in the document.

3. Position the insertion point at the top of the document. On the Review tab, in the Changes group, click the **Next Change** button. The first comment is highlighted. Click the **Next Change** button again. The first revision showing deleted text is highlighted. The Next Change button moves the insertion point to the next tracked change or comment.

4. On the Review tab, in the Changes group, click the **Accept** button arrow, and then click **Accept and Move to Next**. The text *Janice Stork* is removed, and the next change in the document, a comment, is highlighted.

5. In the last sentence under the heading *APPROVAL OF MINUTES FROM LAST MEETING*, right-click anywhere in the new text and then click **Accept Change**. The change is accepted, but the next change is not highlighted. Choosing the Accept Change option is useful when you want to review the accepted changes before you move on to the next change.

6. In the Changes group, click the **Next Change** button. Under *OLD BUSINESS*, the first change in the set of numbers is highlighted. Click the upper half of the **Accept** button. The change is accepted and the next change, a deletion, is highlighted.

7. Click the **Next Change** button two times. The three bulleted items under the heading *NEW BUSINESS* are highlighted, and the balloon describing the format changes is highlighted. In the Changes group, click the **Reject** button arrow, and then click **Reject Change**. The bullet formats are removed. Click the **Undo** button. Deselect the paragraphs.

8. Show the Reviewing Pane. In the Reviewing Pane, delete the text for the first comment. (*Hint*: You cannot delete the ending paragraph mark.) Note that deleting all the text in the Reviewing Pane or in a comment balloon does not remove the comment mark in the document pane. You must delete the comment mark in the document pane to remove a comment.

9. The insertion point is in the comment box in the Reviewing Pane. The comment balloon is highlighted in the margin area. In the Comments group, click the **Delete Comment** button. The comment is removed from the margin area and from the Reviewing Pane.

10. In the document pane, scroll down and over, if necessary, and select the first paragraph with the bullet format. Right-click the selected paragraph and click **Accept Change**. All the selected changes are accepted.

11. If necessary, scroll to the bottom of the Reviewing Pane. Under Header and footer changes, click the Page number insertion by Reviewer E. Right-click the title bar for the change, and then click **Reject Insertion**. Click anywhere in the document pane.

12. In the Changes group, click the **Accept** button arrow and then click **Accept All Changes in Document**. All remaining changes in the document are accepted, but the comments are not removed. In the Tracking group, click the upper half of the **Track Changes** button to toggle off the feature.

13. In the Comments group, click the **Delete** button arrow, and then click **Delete All Comments in Document**. All comments are removed from the document. Close the Reviewing Pane.

14. Save the changes and close the document.

Comparing Documents

Sometimes you might want to compare the current version of a document with another version of the same document. For example, if a team member edited a copy of your document, but did not track the changes, you could compare the team member's version with a current version to review the edits. To compare the two documents, you can open the revised document and the original document and view them side by side.

If the documents you are comparing are long, it would be very time consuming to compare everything in both documents in order to identify the differences. The Compare feature in Word offers a simpler way to identify the differences. When you use the Compare feature, nothing will change in either of the documents you are comparing. The differences in the two documents will appear as tracked changes in a new third document. If either of the compared documents contains tracked changes, those changes are accepted before the documents are compared.

Step-by-Step 13.6

1. Open two blank documents. Then open the **Emergency Contacts 1** file from the drive and folder where your Data Files are stored. If necessary, maximize the document window and use the zoom controls to set the zoom level to 100%.

2. Open the **Emergency Contacts 2** file from the drive and folder where your Data Files are stored. Make sure the document window is maximized and the zoom level is set to 100%.

3. The Emergency Contacts 2 document should be the active document. Click the **View** tab. In the Window group, click the **View Side by Side** button. The Compare Side by Side dialog box opens, showing all the open files except the active document. (If only two Word documents are open, this dialog box will not open.)

4. Click the filename **Emergency Contacts 1**, and then click **OK**. The two documents appear side by side on the screen.

5. In the Emergency Contacts 2 document window on the left, drag the vertical scroll bar up and down. As you scroll through the document on the left, the page in the window on the right will also move.

6. Switch to the Emergency Contacts 1 document window on the right, and then click the **View** tab. If necessary, click the **Window** button to expand the Window group to access the group buttons, as shown in **Figure 13–9**. Note that both the View Side by Side and Synchronous Scrolling buttons are highlighted. Click the **Synchronous Scrolling** button to toggle off the feature. Then drag the vertical scroll bar in the window on the right and in the window on the left. The documents are no longer synchronized.

FIGURE 13–9
Window group on the View tab

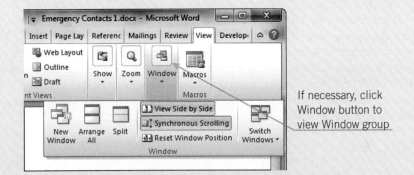

7. If necessary, expand the Window group in the document in the right pane. Click the **View Side by Side** button. The documents are no longer shown side by side. The Emergency Contacts 1 document should be the active document.

8. Switch to the Emergency Contacts 2 document. Click the **Review** tab. In the Compare group, click the **Compare** button, and then click **Compare**. The Compare Documents dialog box, which is very similar to the Combine Documents dialog box, opens.

9. Click the **Original document** list arrow and select **Emergency Contacts 1**. Then click the **Revised document** list arrow and select **Emergency Contacts 2**. Click **OK**. A compared document with merged tracked changes opens. The original document (Emergency Contacts 1) and the revised document (Emergency Contacts 2) are also still open. If it is not open, show the Reviewing Pane.

10. Save the merged results document as **Final Emergency Contacts**, followed by your initials. Close the Emergency Contacts 1 and Emergency Contacts 2 documents.

11. In the Final Emergency Contacts document window, click the **Review** tab, if necessary. In the Changes group, click the **Accept** button arrow and then click **Accept All Changes in Document**.

12. Save the changes to the Final Emergency Contacts document, and then close the document and any other open documents.

Preparing Documents for Electronic Distribution

The majority of the information we work with is now generated by electronic files. Instead of printing documents, it is common to exchange information using electronic files. When sharing files, you may want to consider saving the document as a read-only document. Users are able to open and read a *read-only document*, but they are not able to save any changes to the document. To save changes, users will need to save the file in a different folder or use a different filename. When you use the Mark as Final command, you imply that the status of the document is final. Word saves the file as a read-only document, but the content is not secure. If a user wants to make edits, they can easily toggle off the Mark as Final feature.

> ▶ VOCABULARY
> **read-only document**

You can also protect a document by setting controls to restrict access, allowing only specified individuals to open the document. And for those individuals who are able to open the document, you can restrict formatting and edits.

Before distributing a document, you might want to ensure that the document is compatible with other platforms and Word versions. You also might want to prevent others from seeing some of the properties, such as personal information and document statistics. To help validate the authenticity of a document, you can embed a digital ID into the document. You can also personalize a document by adding your signature in a digital format.

Restricting Access

To restrict access to a document, you can assign a password to it so that only users who know the password can open the document. To secure additional protection, you can encrypt the document so that it is unreadable without a password. *Encryption* is a standard method for encoding data. When assigning passwords in Word, you can use up to 15 characters in any combination of letters, numerals, spaces, and symbols. A strong password has at least eight characters in a combination of text, numbers, and symbols. The password is *case-sensitive*, which means that when entering a password to open a document, the upper and lower casing of the letters must be identical to the casing of the letters in the assigned password. If the casing of the letters differs, the file will not open.

> **VOCABULARY**
> **encryption**
> **case-sensitive**

⎯⎮⎯ WARNING

If you forget a password, you cannot access a document. Write down passwords and keep them in a secure location, or use a password management application.

Step-by-Step 13.7

1. Open the **Employee Evaluation** file from the drive and folder where your Data Files are stored. Save the document as **Restricted Employee Evaluation 1**, followed by your initials.

2. Click the **File** tab, and in the center pane, click the **Protect Document** button. Click **Mark as Final**, and then click **OK** when prompted to confirm that the document will be marked as final. Click **OK** again, and the document is saved as a read-only document.

3. Click the **Home** tab. Notice that a yellow bar appears at the top of the window and the Mark as Final icon appears in the status bar. In the yellow bar at the top of the window, click **Edit Anyway**. You have just toggled off the Mark as Final feature, and the yellow bar no longer appears at the top of the document. You can make changes to the document.

4. Click the **File** tab, click the **Protect Document** button, and then click **Encrypt with Password**. In the Password text box, type **aem1116PS!** and then click **OK**. Type the password again and click **OK**. The document is encrypted, and users will need to enter that password to open the document.

5. Close the document. When prompted to save changes to the document, click **Save**. Reopen the document **Restricted Employee Evaluation 1** from your solution files. When prompted, type the password **aem1116PS!** and then click **OK**.

6. Save the document as **Restricted Employee Evaluation 2**, followed by your initials. Even though the filename has changed, the encryption still applies. Close the document. Then reopen the document. When prompted to enter a password, type **aem1116PS!** and then click **OK**.

7. To remove the encryption, click the **File** tab. Notice in the center pane, next to the Protect Document button, a Permission note appears indicating that a password is required. Click **Save As**. The Save As dialog box opens. At the bottom of the dialog box, next to Save, click **Tools** and then click **General Options**. The General Options dialog box opens, as shown in **Figure 13–10**.

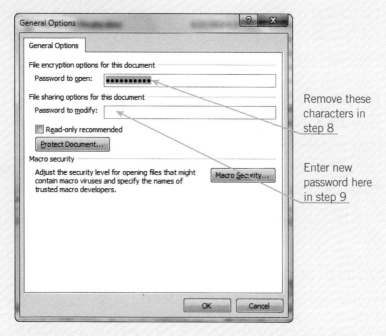

FIGURE 13–10
General Options dialog box

8. Remove all the characters in the Password to open text box. Click **OK** and then click **Save**. Close the document and then reopen it. The encryption is removed and the document opens without a password.

9. Click the **File** tab and then click **Save As**. Click **Tools** and then click **General Options**. In the Password to modify text box, type **CAM#54mxA+**. Click **OK**. When prompted, reenter the password. Click **OK** to close the General Options dialog box. Click **Save** to save the changes and close the Save As dialog box, and then close the document.

10. Reopen the **Restricted Employee Evaluation 2** document from your solution files. In the Password dialog box, click the option to **Read Only**. Notice that the document title in the title bar includes *[Read-Only]*. Click the **File** tab. Notice the Read-Only note in the center pane next to the Save As button. Although you can edit the document, you will not be able to save the changes without assigning a new filename or a new path. Close the document.

11. Reopen the **Restricted Employee Evaluation 2** document from your solution files. When prompted to open as read only again, click **No**. Then when prompted to enter a password, type **CAM#54mxA+** and then click **OK**. The document opens and the read-only feature is disabled so you can save changes to the document.

12. Position the insertion point to the right of *Date:* in the second row of the table in the right column. Click the **Insert** tab. In the Text group, click the **Date & Time** button. Select the XX/XX/XX format and enable the option **Update automatically**. Click **OK**. Save the changes to the document.

13. Remove the password. Click the **File** tab, and then click **Save As**. Click **Tools** and then click **General Options**. Delete the password characters, and then click **OK**.

14. In the File name box, change the filename to **Restricted Employee Evaluation 3**, followed by your initials. Click **Save** and leave the document open for the next Step-by-Step.

Restricting Formatting and Editing

When sharing documents, you want others to be able to open, read, and even edit a document, but you might want to restrict the areas in the document that they can change. You can designate certain parts of the document to be unrestricted but grant permission for specific individuals only to modify other restricted sections.

Step-by-Step 13.8

1. If necessary, open the **Restricted Employee Evaluation 3** file from your solution files.

2. Click the **Review** tab. In the Protect group, click the **Restrict Editing** button. The Restrict Formatting and Editing task pane opens.

3. Under Editing restrictions, click to enable the option **Allow only this type of editing in the document**. Exceptions options now appear in the task pane, as shown in **Figure 13–11**. These options enable you to make exceptions and allow specified reviewers to edit all or part of the document.

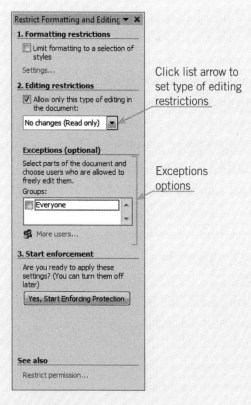

Click list arrow to
set type of editing
restrictions

Exceptions
options

FIGURE 13–11
Restrict Formatting and Editing
task pane

4. Under Editing restrictions, the current setting is *No changes (Read only)*. Click the **list arrow** in the setting box, and then click **Tracked changes**. Notice that the Exceptions options no longer appear. Users can make changes and add comments throughout the entire document.

5. Under Editing restrictions, click the **list arrow**, and then click **Comments**. The Exceptions are again available. You can specify reviewers and limit their access to the document.

6. Under Editing restrictions, click the **list arrow**, and then click **Filling in forms**. The exceptions are not available, and users cannot track changes or add comments.

7. Under Editing restrictions, click the **list arrow**, and then click **No changes (Read only)**.

8. Select the row with the heading *ACHIEVEMENTS, ACCOMPLISHMENTS, AND RESPONSIBILITIES*. Hold down **Shift** and then click anywhere in the row below the selected heading. In the task pane, under Exceptions (optional), enable the **Everyone** option.

9. Select the row with the heading *STRENGTHS AND AREAS FOR DEVELOPMENT*. Hold down **Shift** and then click anywhere in the blank row below *GOALS AND OBJECTIVES FOR NEXT EVALUATION PERIOD*. In the task pane, enable the **Everyone** option.

10. Click some of the other rows in the table. Note that as you click some of the other rows, the check mark does not appear next to the Everyone option. The option is only available in the rows you selected; users can edit only those rows in the document.

11. Under Start enforcement, click **Yes, Start Enforcing Protection**. In the first password text box, type the password **99$a*61820***. Reenter the password in the second password text box. Click **OK**. Users cannot change these settings unless they have the password. The areas in the document that can be edited by everyone are highlighted with a light yellow color.

12. Close the document. When prompted to save the changes, click **Save**. Reopen the **Restricted Employee Evaluation 3** document from your solution files.

13. Type the following data in the form:

    a. In the row under the heading *ACHIEVEMENTS, ACCOMPLISHMENTS, AND RESPONSIBILITIES*, position the insertion point at the end of the third paragraph.

    b. Press **Enter** and then type the following paragraph:
    Started a safety training program and developed a new recordkeeping system so that accidents and work-related injuries are documented and recorded accurately.

    c. In the blank row under the heading *CAREER DEVELOPMENT PLAN*, type the following three paragraphs:
    Complete requirements to attain certification in production and inventory management.
    Gain more experience to advance to the position of Senior Production Manager.
    Interested in working at an international plant.

14. Save the changes and close the document.

> **TIP**
>
> To remove the restriction from a document, click the Stop Protection button at the bottom of the Restrict Formatting and Editing task pane. You will need to enter the password to complete the task.

Inspecting the Document

The Backstage view offers several features to help you prepare for the distribution of your Word documents. In the right pane of the Info options, you will see a summary of document properties. The properties listed include when the document was created, the document size, the number of pages, and when the document was last modified. To aid in searching for documents, you can add additional information to the document properties, such as the subject matter and keywords in the document. Protecting a document, however, also means protecting your personal information. *Metadata*—data that describes other data—is stored in the files that you create. Some of the metadata contains personal information that you might not want others to see. For example, the properties in Word documents include information about the author, the date and time the document was created, and the last person who modified the document.

▶ **VOCABULARY**
metadata

The Inspect Document command checks the file for personal information, such as names and dates. For example, you may have hidden the markup to review the file, and you've forgotten that the document still contains comments and tracked changes. The markup includes a lot of personal information, including the reviewer name, date, and time for each revision and comment. Headers and footers also contain personal information, such as company names, addresses, and dates. Completing an inspection before sharing a document will help you search the document for this type of information, and then you can decide if you want to remove some of the personal data.

You can also quickly check for compatibility to determine if some features in the document are not supported by earlier versions of Word. This check is especially useful when you are sharing documents with users who are working with previous versions of Word.

Step-by-Step 13.9

1. Open the **Completed Employee Evaluation** file from the drive and folder where your Data Files are stored. In the password dialog box, type **jck@554E5** and click **OK**. Save the document as **Final Employee Evaluation**, followed by your initials. Note that the document has a header and two comments from Reviewer C.

2. In the first cell of the second row, position the insertion point in front of *Zurla*, type **James**, and press the **spacebar**. In the cell below, position the insertion point in front of *Schroeder*, type **R.**, and then press the **spacebar**. Save the changes to the document.

3. Click the **File** tab. The properties for the document appear on the right pane. The properties include information about the document size, number of pages, number of words, personal information such as the author, when the document was last modified, and the total editing time.

4. To update the information, click **Properties** at the top of the right pane, and then click **Show Document Panel**. The Document Properties panel opens, as shown in **Figure 13–12**. Your Location setting will be different.

Click here to show
Advanced Properties

FIGURE 13–12
Document Properties panel

5. Click the **Title** text box, and then type **Adam Zurla**. In the Subject text box, type **Employee Evaluation**. In the Keywords text box, type **achievements**, **accomplishments**, **responsibilities**, **evaluation**, **strengths**, **goals**. Save the changes to the document.

6. At the top of the Document Properties panel, click **Document Properties** and then click **Advanced Properties**. The Properties dialog box for this document opens.

7. Click the **Statistics** tab. Notice that this includes information about when the document was created, the number of times the document has been revised, and the total editing time. Click **OK** to close the dialog box. Then click the **Close** button in the upper-right corner of the Document Properties panel.

8. Save the changes to the document. Then save the document as **Confidential Employee Evaluation**, followed by your initials.

9. Click the **File** tab. In the center pane, click the **Check for Issues** button, and then click **Inspect Document**. The Document Inspector dialog box shown in **Figure 13–13** opens, showing features that can be inspected.

FIGURE 13–13
Document Inspector dialog box

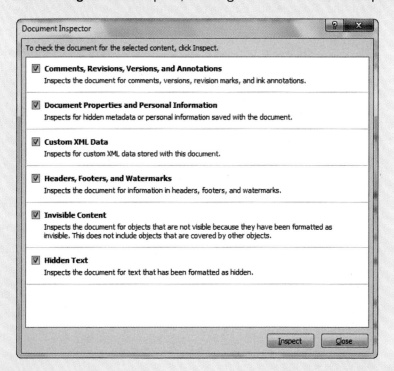

10. At the bottom of the dialog box, click **Inspect**. Word inspects the document and displays the results. You do not want to remove the comments from the document, so ignore the first Remove All button. In the Document Properties and Personal Information section, click **Remove All**. In the Headers, Footers, and Watermarks section, click **Remove All**. Close the Document Inspector dialog box.

11. Close the document, saving the changes. Then reopen the document. In the Password dialog box, type **jck@554E5** and click **OK**. Notice that the header has been removed from the document.

12. Notice, too, that the initials in the comment balloons have been replaced with *A1* and *A2*. Position the mouse pointer over the comment. The name of the reviewer is now *Author*, and there is no date or time. Because the personal information was removed from the document, the comments are now anonymous.

13. Click the **File** tab. Notice in the right pane that all the personal information has been removed from the properties. In the right pane, click **Properties** and then click **Advanced Properties**. Much of the data in the Statistics tab is still available, but the name of the last user to access the file and the total editing time has been removed. Click **OK** to close the dialog box.

14. In the center pane, click the **Check for Issues** button and then click **Check Compatibility**. The Microsoft Word Compatibility Checker dialog box opens and indicates that no issues were found. Close the dialog box. Save the changes, close the document, and then exit Word.

Attaching a Digital Signature

A *digital signature* is an attachment to a file or e-mail message that certifies that the infor mation in the file is authentic and safe. The digital signature is embedded in the document, and although it is not visible, recipients of the document can see that the document has been digitally signed. Signed files are marked as final and remain signed until the file is changed. If the document is edited, the signature is removed. You can embed multiple digital signatures in the same document.

Digital signatures are easy to create using the SelfCert.exe tool. However, when you use this program, you create a self-signed digital certificate, which does not verify your identity and, therefore, is appropriate only for personal use. The SelfCert.exe tool is used in this lesson to demonstrate how to attach a digital signature to a document. If you need an authenticated certificate, you must secure a service from a third-party vendor. Several commercial certification authority services are compatible with Office applications.

▶ **VOCABULARY**
digital signature

Step-by-Step 13.10

To complete this Step-by-Step, the SelfCert.exe file must be installed.

1. Click the **Start** button on the taskbar and navigate to the folder where the Windows file SelfCert.exe is saved. The file is usually found in the c:\Program Files\Microsoft Office\Office14 folder. If necessary, use the Search feature to locate the file. Double-click the filename **SelfCert.exe**.

2. The Create Digital Certificate dialog box opens. Read the instructions, then type your first and last names and click **OK**.

3. A message box appears indicating that a new certificate has been successfully created. Click **OK**. If necessary, close the Search dialog box.

4. Launch Word and open the **Confidential Employee Evaluation** file from your solution files. In the Password dialog box, type **jck@554E5** and click **OK**. Save the document as **Certified Employee Evaluation**, followed by your initials.

5. Click the **File** tab. In the center pane, click the **Protect Document** button, and then click **Add a Digital Signature**. A message box appears explaining that Microsoft does not warrant a digital signature's legal enforceability. Click **OK**. The Sign dialog box opens, as shown in **Figure 13–14**. Your settings may be different.

FIGURE 13–14
Sign dialog box

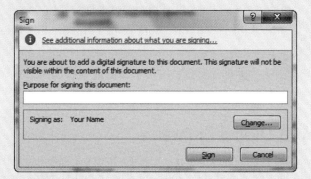

6. Click **See additional information about what you are signing**. The Additional Information dialog box shows more information that is being saved with the document. Click **OK**.

7. In the Sign dialog box, under Purpose for signing this document, type **To confirm the validity of the information in this document.**.

8. If your name does not appear after Signing as, click **Change**, select your certificate, and then click **OK**. Click **Sign**. If a message box appears indicating that the certificate cannot be verified, click **Yes**. (This is because it is a self-signed certificate.) A message box opens confirming that the signature has been successfully saved with the document. If any changes are made to the document, the signature will be invalid. Click **OK**.

9. An Invalid Signatures warning appears in the center pane, as shown in **Figure 13–15**. The signature is invalid because it is a self-signed certificate and the certificate was not issued by a trusted certificate authority.

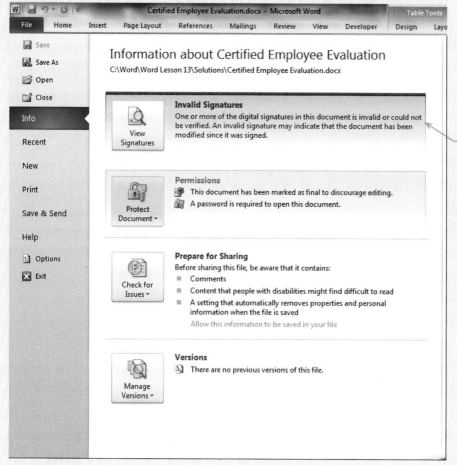

FIGURE 13–15
Invalid Signatures warning

10. Click the **View Signatures** button to the left of the warning note to open the Signatures pane. You can have multiple signatures attached to a document. Point to your signature in the pane, and then click the **list arrow** to the right of your signature. A menu of options for the selected signature opens, as shown in **Figure 13–16**. Your settings may look different.

FIGURE 13–16
Signatures pane showing options for a signature

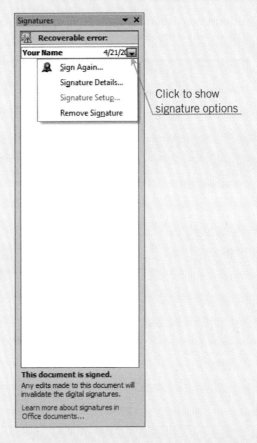

11. Click **Signature Details**. The dialog box shown in **Figure 13–17** opens.

FIGURE 13–17
Signature Details dialog box

12. Click the link **Click here to trust this user's identify**. The signature is now valid. Close the Signature Details dialog box.

13. A yellow bar at the top of the document window shows that the document has been marked as final. The Signatures icon  appears in the status bar and indicates that the document contains a signature.

14. The signature was automatically saved with the document. Close the document.

Creating a Signature Line

Word offers a feature that enables you to create a signature line in documents. The signature line looks like a typical signature placeholder, but it is actually more than just a placeholder. The signature line specifies information about the intended signer, and you can even provide instructions for the signer. When the signer receives the document, he or she can choose how to add their signature. If the signer receives an electronic copy of the document, they can choose to type a signature, insert a digital image of his or her signature, or write a signature using the inking feature on a Tablet PC. When a digital image of a signature is added to the document, a digital signature is added simultaneously to authenticate the identity of the signer. As is true with all digitally signed documents, the document will become read-only to prevent edits to the content.

Step-by-Step 13.11

1. Open the **Bill of Sale** file from the drive and folder where your Data Files are stored. Save the document as **Final Bill of Sale**, followed by your initials.

2. Position the insertion point at the end of the document. Click the **Insert** tab. In the Text group, click the **Signature Line** button. A dialog box opens showing a disclaimer stating that Microsoft cannot warrant the legal enforceability of a digital signature. Click **OK** to open the Signature Setup dialog box, as shown in **Figure 13–18**.

FIGURE 13–18
Signature Setup dialog box

3. In the first text box, type **Trevor Jones**. In the second text box, type **Seller**. Under Instructions to the signer, edit the text to read "Before signing this document, verify that the **dollar amount and the model number are** correct." Note that the option to show the sign date in the signature line is enabled. Click **OK**. The signature placeholder is inserted.

4. Press **Enter**. In the Text group, click the **Signature Line** button. Click **OK** to accept the disclaimer statement. The Signature Setup dialog box opens.

5. In the first text box, type **Jared Mancini**. In the second text box, type **Buyer**. Then enable the option **Allow the signer to add comments in the Sign dialog**. Click **OK**. A second signature placeholder is inserted.

6. Save the changes to the document. Close the document and reopen it. Note that a yellow bar at the top of the document indicates that the document needs to be signed. When the receiver opens the document, this note will prompt them to sign the document.

7. Save the document as **Signed Bill of Sale**, followed by your initials.

8. Right-click the first signature placeholder, and then in the shortcut menu, click **Sign**. Click **OK** to accept the disclaimer. The Sign dialog box opens, as shown in **Figure 13–19**.

FIGURE 13–19
Sign dialog box

Type name
or select an image

Attached digital
signature

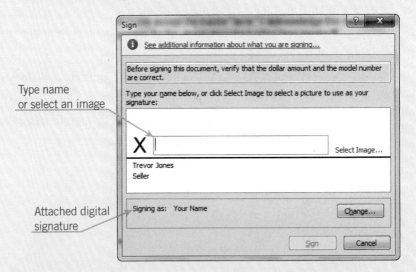

9. Note that the instructions at the top of the dialog box include the note you edited telling the signer to verify the dollar amount and model number. You can type your name in the box or select an image. Also note that your digital signature is automatically attached. If a digital signature for Trevor Jones was available on file, you could click Change and select that signature.

10. Click the link **Select Image**. Navigate to the drive and folder where your Data Files are stored. Select the filename **Jones.jpg** and then click **Select**. The digital image of the signature is inserted in the placeholder.

11. Click **Sign** and then click **OK** to confirm the signature. The digital image and the current date are both included in the signature placeholder.

12. Right-click the second signature placeholder, and then click **Sign**. Click **OK**, and in the Sign dialog box, type **Jared Mancini**. Click **Sign**, and then click **OK**. The typed signature and the current date are added to the signature placeholder.

13. Note that a yellow bar at the top of the document indicates that the document is marked as final. Close the document. The signatures have already been automatically saved. Leave Word open for the next Step-by-Step.

Sending Documents

Now that the document is protected, it is ready for distribution. You have several options for sending the document. You can send the file via e-mail or in a fax message. Obviously, to send the file via e-mail, you must have a network or Internet connection, and you must have sufficient bandwidth (the speed of data transfer) for transferring the file. Publishing to a blog is another alternative.

If you know the recipient of the file is working with a previous version of Office, you can convert the document to an earlier version of Word. If you're not sure what applications, platforms, or operating systems the recipient is using, you should consider saving the document in PDF or XPS format. The *Portable Document Format (PDF)* was created by Adobe Systems in 1993. Microsoft first offered the *XML Paper Specification (XPS)* format in Office 2007. Both the PDF and XPS document formats are designed to preserve the visual appearance and layout of each page and enable fast viewing and printing. PDF and XPS formats are especially useful for resumes, newsletters, and forms such as applications and invoices, because you can trust that when the receiver opens the document it will look and print exactly as intended.

 VOCABULARY

Portable Document Format (PDF)

XML Paper Specification (XPS)

WARNING

A computer must be properly configured to send or receive and open documents in PDF and XPS formats. If your computer is unable to use these formats, you can download a free add-in from Microsoft.

Step-by-Step 13.12

1. Open the **Certified Employee Evaluation** file from your solution files. The password is **jck@554E5**.

2. Click the **File** tab, and then click **Save and Send**. In the center pane, click **Create PDF/XPS Document**, and then, in the right pane, click the **Create PDF/XPS** button. The Publish as PDF or XPS dialog box opens.

3. In the File name box, the same filename appears, but the document extension is changed to .pdf or .xps. If necessary, click the **Save as type** box, and then click XPS Document (*.xps).

4. Click **Publish**. When prompted to save in a format other than a Word document, click **Yes**. The document is no longer password protected.

5. The document opens in XPS format in Internet Explorer, your default browser, or the XPS Viewer. Drag across some text to select it, then press **Delete**. Because the XPS format is a read-only format, you cannot edit the document. Close the browser or viewer.

6. Click the **File** tab. Click **Save and Send**, and then, in the center pane, click **Change File Type**. The available document file types appear in the right pane. In the pane at the left, click **Close** to close the Certified Employee Evaluation document.

7. Open the **Final Board Minutes** document from your solution files. Click the **File** tab, and then click **Save and Send**. If necessary, click **Send Using E-mail** in the center pane. Then, in the right pane, click the **Send as Attachment** button. If Outlook is your default e-mail application, a new message window will open. If a different e-mail application is set as the default, a new message window will open in that application.

8. Note that the document is already attached to the e-mail message. At this point you would complete the header information and type a message. Close the message document window without saving any changes.

9. Click the **File** tab, and then click **Save and Send**. In the right pane, click the **Send as PDF** button. The document is attached to the e-mail message. Note that the filename extension is .pdf; when the e-mail process is completed, a PDF formatted version of the file will be attached. Close the message document window without saving any changes.

10. Click the **File** tab, and then click **Save and Send**. In the center pane, click **Publish as Blog Post**, and then, in the right pane, click the **Publish as Blog Post** button. A new document opens with a new Ribbon that shows blog features. If prompted to register a blog account, click Register Later.

11. The document content is formatted and ready to be published on the Web. At this point you would type a blog post title and publish the blog. Close the new document without saving the changes.

12. Leave the Final Board Minutes document open for the next Step-by-Step.

Storing, Accessing, and Sharing Documents

Word also enables you to upload and access documents online so that you can share files with others. You can upload documents to a ***document workspace site***, which is a Web site that provides a central location for storing and sharing files. Documents are stored in a library. Access to the documents can be controlled using encryption, so that users must know the password to gain access to the library or to open folders or files.

Microsoft Windows SharePoint Services provides a document workspace site that enables a business to customize document storage and handling. Documents can be stored and updated, information about document status is provided, and employees can access the files remotely, enabling team members to collaborate and work together in real time. You need authorization to publish or access files at a SharePoint site, so introducing and showing SharePoint features is beyond the scope of this lesson.

Microsoft also offers SkyDrive, a free Windows Live service that provides password-protected online storage. You can assign passwords to control who has access to your files. To access SkyDrive, you must have a Windows Live account. The following Step-by-Step will guide you in setting up a personal SkyDrive account.

▶ **VOCABULARY**
document workspace site

Step-by-Step 13.13

1. If necessary, open the **Final Board Minutes** file from your solution files.

2. Click the **File** tab, and then click **Save and Send.** In the center pane, click **Save to Web**.

3. If you have a Windows Live ID, click the **Sign-In** button, and then enter your ID (e-mail address) and password and click **OK**. (If you do not have an account, click the link to sign up for Windows Live and follow the directions to create a new account.)

4. If necessary, under Personal Folders, click the **My Documents** folder to select it. Then click the **Save As** button. The Save As dialog box opens. Note that the path where the file will be stored shows a Windows Live network address.

5. You do not need to change the filename, so leave everything as is and click **Save**.

6. Close the Final Board Minutes document. The document has been uploaded to the server.

7. Using your Web browser, go to *http://skydrive.live.com*. If necessary, sign in. Open the My Documents folder, and then click the **Final Board Minutes** document.

8. Click the document icon to view the document in the Word WebApp.

9. If you want full access to the Word features as you edit the document, you can open the document in Word. Above the document window, click the option **Open in Word**. If a prompt appears asking if you trust the source, click **OK**. The document will open in Word on your computer. Close the document and exit Word on your computer.

10. In your browser, click **sign out** in the upper-right corner to sign out of Windows Live. Close your browser.

EXTRA FOR EXPERTS

When you click Download, you can choose to save the file. When you save the file, it is saved in the default Download folder on your computer.

SUMMARY

In this lesson, you learned:

- Tracked changes can appear in up to eight different colors, which helps distinguish changes made by multiple reviewers.

- Reviewers can provide feedback on a document without changing the content by adding comments.

- You can control the markup that shows on the screen or prints in a document.

- Comments can be edited in the markup balloons or in the Reviewing Pane.

- Revisions from multiple documents can be combined into a single document.

- You can accept or reject changes individually in documents, or you can accept or reject some or all changes at the same time.

- To compare documents, you can view them side by side, or you can use the Compare feature, which enables you to show the differences between the two documents using tracked changes in a new document.

- Access to a document can be restricted by assigning a password.

- Before sharing a document, it is good practice to inspect it so that you can control what others see.

- Word offers several options for distributing documents electronically, including e-mail, blogs, and document workspaces.

VOCABULARY REVIEW

Define the following terms:

case-sensitive

comment

digital signature

document workspace site

encryption

markup

metadata

Portable Document Format (PDF)

read-only document

revision bar

XML Paper Specification (XPS)

REVIEW QUESTIONS

TRUE / FALSE

Circle T if the statement is true or F if the statement is false.

T F **1.** Deleting the comment text in the Reviewing Pane also removes the comment mark from the document pane.

T F **2.** When you attach a digital signature to a document, the document is marked as final.

T F **3.** When tracking changes, insertions are always blue with an underline effect and deletions are always red with a strikethrough effect.

T F **4.** When showing markup for tracked changes, you can choose to show only the comments in the document, or you can show only the changes for one reviewer.

T F **5.** Saving a file as a read-only document is one of the more secure ways to protect a document.

FILL IN THE BLANK

Complete the following sentences by writing the correct word or words in the blanks provided.

1. _____ is a standard method for encoding data.

2. A(n) _____ is an attachment to a file or e-mail message that certifies that the information in the file is authentic and safe.

3. The _____ appears in the left margin and indicates a tracked change related to the paragraph.

4. Data that describes other data is referred to as _____.

5. A(n) _____ is a central location for storing and sharing documents.

WRITTEN QUESTIONS

Write a brief answer to the following questions.

1. What are some of the benefits of saving a document in a PDF or XPS format?

2. Describe how to format comments so that they appear only as ScreenTips and not as balloons.

3. Describe how you can create and print a summary of all the tracked changes and comments in a document.

4. What does it mean when a password is referred to as case-sensitive?

5. How can you identify which reviewer made the changes in a document?

■ PROJECTS

If you have a SAM 2010 user profile, your instructor may have assigned an autogradable version of the indicated project. If so, log into the SAM 2010 Web site at *www.cengage.com/sam2010* to download the instruction and start files.

PROJECT 13–1

1. Open the **Sales Goal** file from the drive and folder where your Data Files are stored. Save the document as **Revised Sales Goal**, followed by your initials.

2. Toggle on the Track Changes feature. Make note of the current user name and initials and then change the user name to **Reviewer F** and change the initials to **RF**.

3. In the first paragraph, change *$500,000* to **$525,000** and change *$610,000* to **$635,000**. Also in the first paragraph, select the words **worst possible** and apply the italic format.

4. Select the entire first paragraph, and then insert the comment **Confirm these numbers.**.

5. In the second paragraph, delete the second sentence.

6. In the last paragraph, move the last sentence to the beginning of the paragraph. Adjust spacing as necessary.

7. Reset the user name and initials to the settings you noted in Step 2 above.

8. Save the changes and close the document.

SAM PROJECT 13–2

1. Open the **Will Draft 1** file from the drive and folder where your Data Files are stored. Then open the **Will Draft 2** file from the drive and folder where your Data Files are stored.

2. Compare the two documents, using Will Draft 1 as the original document. Save the new compared document as **Updated Will**, followed by your initials.

3. Review the document revisions:
   a. Accept the revision in the first paragraph.
   b. Reject the revisions in the third paragraph.
   c. In the fourth paragraph, accept all revisions.
   d. Accept the new fifth paragraph.
   e. In the sixth paragraph, reject the change from *bequeath* to *leave* and then accept the final revision in that same paragraph.

4. Toggle off the Track Changes feature. At the end of the document, replace both occurrences of ///// with the current month and year (for example, *April, 2014*).

5. Save the changes to the Updated Will document, and then close the document. Close the Will Draft 1 and Will Draft 2 documents.

New Manual? chapter 13 Lecture & Questions fecha 9/3/2015.

PROJECT 13–3

1. Open the **Job Description RA** file from the drive and folder where your Data Files are stored. Then open the **Job Description RB** file from the drive and folder where your Data Files are stored.

2. View the documents side by side with synchronized scrolling.

3. Combine the two documents into a new document, using Job Description RA as the original document. Save the new document as **Final Job Description**, followed by your initials.

4. Reject the change in the footer pane.

5. Accept all the remaining changes in the document.

6. Delete the comment.

7. Save the changes to the Final Job Description document, and then close the document. Close the Job Description RA and Job Description RB documents.

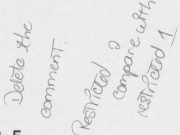

√ PROJECT 13–5

1. Open the **Challenge** file from the drive and folder where your Data Files are stored.

2. The file is encrypted. Type the password **rrw*F4#67** and click OK.

3. Remove the encryption, and then save the document with the filename **Completed Challenge**, followed by your initials.

4. Position the insertion point at the end of the document. Create a signature line. Use your own name for the signer, and type **IT Manager** for the signer title.

PROJECT 13–4

1. Open the **Consultation Call** file from the drive and folder where your Data Files are stored. Save the document as **Restricted Consultation Call**, followed by your initials.

2. In the DATE cell, insert the current date using the XX/XX/XXXX format.

3. In the TIME cell, insert the current time using the ##:## PM format.

4. Set the editing restrictions for No changes (Read only).

5. Select the row in the document for entering information about the PLAN. Then change the settings to allow all users to freely edit this section of the document.

6. Enforce the protection and enter the password ***YntPYd#134**.

7. Save the changes and close the document. Reopen the document from your solution files. Save the document as **Protected Consultation**, followed by your initials.

8. In the document, under PLAN, type **Scheduled appointment with Dr. Lis for two weeks from today at 10:20 a.m.**.

9. Save the changes to the document. Then encrypt the document using the password **20Ewb100%&**.

10. Save the changes and close the document.

5. Sign the document by typing your name in the signature placeholder. If necessary, select your digital signature to authenticate the signature line.

6. Close the document.

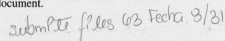

◼ CRITICAL THINKING

ACTIVITY 13–1

Mary manages an insurance office and is responsible for updating the company's office procedures manual. She needs to share the current file for the manual with her workgroup so they can read it, mark revisions, and add comments. Mary's colleagues spend much of the time working outside of the office, and she has a short window of time to get their feedback. What would be the advantages of Mary uploading the file to a SharePoint server?

ACTIVITY 13–2

Mary likes the new Word markup features because she can easily review changes and comments. However, after she combines the changes and comments from all members of the workgroup, she is overwhelmed with the markup. Mary knows how to control the markup so that all the revisions are not shown at once, but she doesn't know where to begin. What suggestions do you have for Mary to complete the task effectively and efficiently?

word97-2003

2. file; save & send; change file tyle; document file types; save (save a word 2010 doc in an earlier format.

- file, save & send, create PDF/xps doc.; publish, (save a doc. as a PDF)

- file, save & send, save to web, my doc, save as, save (save a word doc to skydrive)

- Doc library, password, (open a password protected doc)

- file, save & send, send as attachment (email a doc)

✓ file, check for issues, check compatibility, OK (run the compatibility checker)

- file, check " ", inspect doc, inspect, ~~inspect~~, close (use the doc. Inspector)

- file, check " ", add a digital signature; sign, home (create a digital signature)

- file, protect doc, mark as final, OK, OK (finalize a document).

- 2 doc thumbnails (switch between open word doc)

- suggested signer

- Insert, signature line, - " " letter, OK. (add a signature line to a doc)

✓ Review, new comment, (Insert a comment)

- Review, delete (delete a comment).

- Review, track changes, track changes (track changes in a doc).

✓ Review, reviewing pane, reviewing pane vertical (open the reviewing pane).

✓ Review, final, final show markup, show markup, reviewers, tim (display edits by a specific reviewer.

- Review, accept, accept all changes in doc (accept all changes in a doc).

✓ Review, accept, accept and move to text (accept individual changes in a doc)

✓ Review, reject, reject change, (reject changes in a doc)

- Review, compare, compare, orig doc and revised doc, (compare 2 doc).

- Review, compare, combine, " " " ", OK (combine 2 doc)

- Review, " " " ", OK, compare, show source doc, show
  both, (show source doc when comparing doc)

✓ View, view side by side,
  scroll simultaneamente (manage multiple doc with synchronous scrolling)

- View, " " " ", everyone, choose tracked changes,

- Developer; "restrict editing", ☑ allow only this type..., yes, start enforcing protection, password (protect a doc)

LESSON 14

Working with Long Documents

Handwritten notes:
- Developer, restrict editing,
Yes, start enforcing protection, password, ok,
(project parts of a form)
- Developer, restrict editing,
stop protection, password, ok,
(unprotect a form)

■ OBJECTIVES

Upon completion of this lesson, you should be able to:

- Change and organize document views and windows.
- Navigate documents, reorganize content within a document, and search for text and objects.
- Create and modify hyperlinks and bookmarks.
- Create section breaks and format columns.
- Use pagination options, hyphenation, and nonbreaking spaces to control text flow.
- Manage sources, create citations, and create a bibliography.
- Insert footnotes and endnotes.
- Determine the readability level of document content.

■ VOCABULARY

bibliography

bookmark

citation

endnote

footnote

hyphenation

incremental search

nonbreaking hyphen

nonbreaking space

optional hyphen

orphan

pagination

reference marker

section

section break

separator line

widow

works cited page

Working with long documents involves much more than formatting the page numbers. Word provides several features that help you navigate through the pages, search for content, cite sources of information, and control the text flow throughout the pages.

Working with Multiple Documents

When long documents such as reports, studies, and proposals are prepared, the information is often compiled from several different documents. Microsoft Word allows you to open multiple documents and work with all of them at the same time. The number of windows you can open depends on available system memory.

Viewing Documents and Splitting Windows

When multiple documents are open, you have several options for arranging the document windows on your screen. Some of the features are available in Windows and apply to all applications, and some of the features are available only in the Word application.

Step-by-Step 14.1

1. Launch Word. Click the **File** tab, and then click **Open**. Navigate to the drive and folder where your Data Files are stored.

2. To select a range of filenames, click the filename **Apollo 11**, hold down **Shift**, and then click **Apollo 13**. Three filenames are selected. To select another filename in the list, hold down **Ctrl** and click the filename **Moon Missions**. Click **Open**. All four documents open.

3. Point to the Word icon in the taskbar at the bottom of the screen. A thumbnail appears for each open document in the Word application, and the highlighted thumbnail indicates the active document. Move the mouse pointer over each thumbnail to preview the first page of each document. Click the **Apollo 12** thumbnail to make it the active document.

4. Position the mouse pointer over the Word icon in the taskbar, and then position the mouse pointer over the Apollo 13 thumbnail. The title bar in the thumbnail changes and now shows the Close button. Click the **Close** button in the thumbnail to close the document.

5. Right-click a blank area in the taskbar. In the shortcut menu, click **Show windows stacked**. The document windows are stacked on top of each other so that you see each of the documents. If you are running any other applications, those windows will also be stacked. Right-click the taskbar and then click **Show windows side by side**. The three documents are arranged next to each other.

6. Right-click a blank area in the taskbar and then click **Cascade windows**. The windows are arranged in a single stack so that the title bar for each document window is shown.

7. In the Apollo 12 document window, click the **View** tab. In the Window group, click the **Switch Windows** button and then click the filename **Apollo 11**. The Apollo 11 document appears on the top of the stack, and it is now the active document.

8. Click the **View** tab for any one of the document windows. In the Window group, click the **Arrange All** button. Word rearranges the documents on the screen. The three documents are stacked on top of each other; however, the arrangement will vary depending on the number of open documents.

9. Close the Moon Missions and Apollo 12 documents. Maximize the Apollo 11 document window. Scroll down through the document to view the heading *Mission Objective*.

10. If necessary, click the **View** tab. In the Window group, click the **Split** button. The mouse pointer changes and shows a horizontal line that spans the width of the window. Position the mouse pointer above the heading *Mission Objective* and then click. The document window is divided into two panes, as shown in **Figure 14–1**.

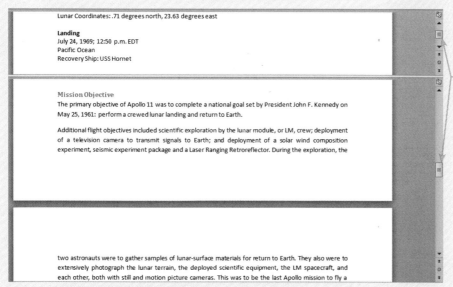

FIGURE 14–1
Document split into two panes

Vertical scrollbar
for each pane

11. Note that each pane has its own vertical scroll bars. Drag the scroll box on the vertical bars in both panes. You will see that both panes contain the same content. Splitting the document window is useful when you are working with a long document and you want to view content in two different parts of the document.

12. To reposition where the document splits, point to the horizontal line that separates the two panes. When the mouse pointer changes to a double-headed arrow, drag the scroll bar up about one inch and drop the horizontal line in a new position.

13. In the Window group, click the **Remove Split** button. The document once again appears in a single pane.

14. Close the document without saving any changes.

Copying and Pasting Content from Multiple Documents

When multiple files are open, you can copy and paste content from one document to another. You can copy up to 24 items from one or more documents to the Office Clipboard. New items are added at the top of the list in the Clipboard pane. When the number exceeds 24, the items at the bottom of the list are removed from the Clipboard. You can paste the items individually or as a group into a document. You can also insert the entire contents of a file into your document without even opening the file.

Step-by-Step 14.2

1. Open the **Apollo 11** and **Mission Highlights** files from the drive and folder where your Data Files are stored. Make the Apollo 11 document the active document, and then save it as **Apollo 11 Revised**, followed by your initials. Also, if necessary, click the **Home** tab and click the **Show/Hide ¶** button to show nonprinting formatting characters.

2. Switch to the Mission Highlights document. In the Clipboard group, click the **Dialog Box Launcher** 🔲 to open the Clipboard pane. If necessary, click the **Clear All** button to remove all contents from the Clipboard.

3. In the document window, triple-click anywhere in the first paragraph to select the entire paragraph. Copy the selected text to the Clipboard. An item displaying a portion of the new content added to the Clipboard appears at the top of the pane.

4. Scroll to the end of the document and select the last paragraph, beginning *Re-entry procedures*. Copy the selected text to the Clipboard. A new item appears at the top of the Clipboard pane.

5. Scroll to the top of the document so that you can view both the second and the fourth paragraphs. Select the second paragraph. Hold down **Ctrl** and triple-click to select the fourth paragraph. Copy the selected text to the Clipboard. The Clipboard pane now contains three items.

6. Switch to the **Apollo 11 Revised** document. Open the Clipboard pane and, if necessary, show nonprinting formatting characters. In the document, scroll down to the heading *Mission Highlights*. Position the insertion point in front of the first paragraph that begins *Two hours, 44 minutes*. In the Clipboard pane, click the item that begins *Apollo 11 launched* to paste the content into the document.

7. Press **Ctrl+End** to move to the end of the document. Scroll up and position the insertion point in the blank paragraph above the source information.

8. In the Clipboard pane, click the item that begins *Armstrong and Aldrin* to paste the content of that item into the document. Two new paragraphs are inserted in the document. In the Clipboard pane, click the item that begins *Re-entry procedures* to paste the content of that item into the document.

9. In the Clipboard pane, click the **Paste All** button. All the items in the Clipboard pane are inserted in the document. Click the **Undo** button three times to remove all three paste edits. Close the Clipboard pane.

10. Save the changes to the document. Then save the document as **Journeys to the Moon 1**, followed by your initials. Close the Mission Highlights document without saving any changes.

11. Reposition the insertion point at the end of the document, and then press **Enter**. Note that the document currently has five pages. Click the **Insert** tab. In the Text group, click the **Object** button arrow and then click **Text from File**. The Insert File dialog box opens.

12. Navigate to the drive and folder where your Data Files are stored. Select the filename **Apollo 12** and then click **Insert**. Without opening the document, all the content from the Apollo 12 document is inserted in the Journeys to the Moon 1 document at the location of the insertion point. The document now has 10 pages.

13. In the Text group, click the **Object** button arrow and then click **Text from File**. Select the filename **Apollo 13**, hold down **Ctrl** and click **Moon Missions**, and then click **Insert**. All the content from both documents is inserted in the open document. The document now has 18 pages.

14. Save your changes and leave the document open for the next Step-by-Step.

Navigating a Document

The more pages in a document, the more time consuming it is to move around in the document and find content. The Navigation Pane provides features to help you quickly navigate through a document, organize the document content, and find content and objects.

Viewing and Reorganizing the Content

Using the Navigation Pane is similar to viewing a document in Outline view. When you format document headings and subheadings using heading styles, the headings and subheadings appear in the Navigation Pane. Instead of scrolling through the document, you can quickly browse through the headings in the Navigation Pane for a quick overview of the contents, and you can use the Navigation Pane to move to a specific area in the document. Word displays up to nine levels of headings, and the subheadings are indented for easy review. If desired, you can collapse the subheadings so that only the main headings are displayed.

An alternative way to browse document contents is to view thumbnails of all the pages in the document and then click a thumbnail to quickly jump to a specific page.

Step-by-Step 14.3

1. If necessary, open the **Journeys to the Moon 1** file from your solution files. Save the document as **Journeys to the Moon 2**, followed by your initials.

2. Click the **View** tab. In the Show group, enable the **Navigation Pane** option. The Navigation Pane shown in **Figure 14–2** appears, usually at the left side of the screen. You can reposition the pane on your screen by dragging the title bar, and you can also resize the pane by dragging the borders.

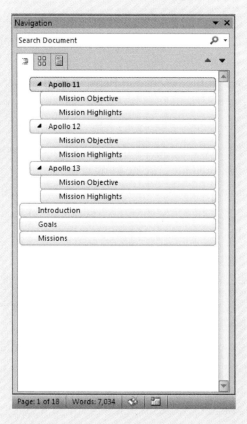

FIGURE 14–2
Navigation Pane

3. In the Navigation Pane, right-click the **Apollo 11** heading. In the short-cut menu, point to **Show Heading Levels**, and then click **Show Heading 2** to show only level one and two headings. Right-click the **Apollo 11** heading again and click **Expand All**. The Navigation Pane shows three levels of headings.

4. In the Navigation Pane, click the **Apollo 12** heading. The document window shows the page in the document where the heading appears. Scroll down to page seven and click anywhere below the heading *Mission Highlights*. Notice that the heading is highlighted in the Navigation Pane, indicating your location in the document.

5. In the Navigation Pane, click the **Goals** heading. The insertion point moves to the heading in the document window. Type **The Apollo** and press the **spacebar** to edit the heading. The heading is updated in the Navigation Pane. In the document window, click in front of the heading *Missions*, and then type **The Apollo** and press the **spacebar** to edit that heading.

6. In the Navigation Pane, right-click the **The Apollo Missions** heading. In the shortcut menu, click **Demote**. The heading is changed to a level two heading, and the Heading 2 style is applied to the heading text in the document. Right-click the **The Apollo Missions** heading again, and then click **Promote** to restore the Heading 1 level and style.

7. In the Navigation Pane, under the Apollo 13 heading, right-click the **Mission Highlights** heading. In the shortcut menu, click **New Heading After**. A new level three heading box (the same level as the heading above) appears in the Navigation Pane. Type **Summary**. The new heading appears in the Navigation Pane and in the document, and it is formatted with the Heading 3 style.

8. In the Navigation Pane, right-click the **Summary** heading. In the shortcut menu, click **Promote**. The heading is promoted to a level two. Right-click the **Summary** heading again, and then click **Promote**. The heading is now a level one heading, and the heading in the document window is formatted with the Heading 1 style.

9. In the Navigation Pane, click the **Collapse** button ◢ to the left of the Apollo 11 heading. Both of the subheadings below the heading are hidden in the Navigation Pane. Click the **Expand** arrow ▷ to the left of the Apollo 11 heading to show all the subheadings.

10. In the Navigation Pane, click and drag the **Introduction** heading to the top of the list of headings. As you drag the heading, a horizontal bar will appear. Drop the heading at the top of the list. Drag and drop the **The Apollo Goals** heading to position it after the Introduction heading. Then drag and drop the **The Apollo Missions** heading to position it after the The Apollo Goals heading.

11. In the Navigation Pane, click the **Introduction** heading. Press **Enter**. Position the insertion point in the new blank paragraph and type **Journeys to the Moon**. Click the **Home** tab, and in the Styles group, apply the **Title** style to the new paragraph.

12. A new yellow bar appears at the top of the Navigation pane. No text appears in the bar because the paragraph is not formatted with a heading style. This blank bar only appears when new content (not formatted as a heading style) is inserted in the first line of a document. Position the mouse pointer over the bar to show the ScreenTip. You can use this bar to navigate to the top of the document.

13. In the Navigation Pane, click the **Browse the pages of your document** button ⊞. Thumbnails of each page in the document appear. Click the **thumbnail** for page four. The insertion point moves to page four in the document window. Click the **Browse the headings in your document** button ▤ to show the document headings.

14. Save the changes and leave the document open for the next Step-by-Step.

Finding Text and Objects

The Navigation Pane can do more than just help you move around in a document. For example, you may want to look for specific words that appear throughout the document. The Find command can be accessed in the Navigation Pane to quickly identify all occurrences of the search words. By default, Word completes an incremental search. In an *incremental search*, as you begin typing the string of characters to search for, Word highlights the matches for the character string in the document. As the search text is augmented, the matches in the document change.

When searching for text, you may want to further define the search. For example, you may want to find matches for whole words only. You can also search for all occurrences of a specific format in the document, such as all text formatted bold and italic. Or, you may be looking for variations of text. You can use a wildcard character, a keyboard character used to represent one or more characters in a search. The character ? searches for a single character; the character * (asterisk) searches for a string of characters. For example, when the search text is *d?n*, matches will include *Dan* and *Don*. When the search text is *dan**, the matches will include *Daniel*, *Danielle*, and *Danny*. When you want to replace occurrences of matched text with new text and/or formats, you can use the Replace command.

> **▶ VOCABULARY**
> **incremental search**

Step-by-Step 14.4

1. If necessary, open the **Journeys to the Moon 2** file from your solution files. Save the document as **Journeys to the Moon 3**, followed by your initials. If necessary, show the **Navigation Pane**, and click the **Browse the headings in your document** button.

> **TIP**
>
> If the Navigation Pane is not displayed, you can use the shortcut keys Ctrl+F.

2. In the Navigation Pane, click the **Search Document** text box and type **Armstrong**. When you finish entering the search text, all the matches in the document are highlighted in the document window. The total number of matches is indicated in the Navigation Pane, as shown in **Figure 14–3**. Some of the headings are highlighted in the Navigation Pane to indicate that matches can be found in those sections of the document.

FIGURE 14–3
Navigation Pane
with matches
for Armstrong

Number of matches

Matches

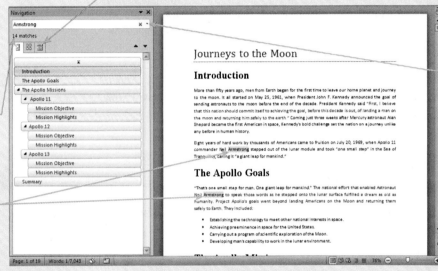

Browse the resultsfrom your
current search button

Find Options and
additional search
commands arrow

TIP

If you enter the characters slowly, you can watch the process of the incremental search. As you enter each new character, the highlights appear in both the document window and the Navigation Pane.

---

3. In the Navigation Pane, click the **The Apollo Goals** heading. Then click the **Next Search Result** button ▼. The first occurrence of the search text under the selected heading is highlighted in the document window. Click the **Previous Search Result** button ▲. The previous occurrence of the search text is highlighted.

4. In the Navigation Pane, click the **Browse the pages in your document** button ⊞. Only the pages with matches appear in the Navigation Pane.

5. In the Navigation Pane, click the **Browse the results from your current search** button ▤. Items showing some of the document content appear in the pane so you can see the occurrence of the match in the context of the document. Click the item that shows only the name *Neil Armstrong* to go to that location in the document.

6. In the Navigation Pane, on the right side of the Search Document text box, click the **Find Options and additional search commands** arrow. In the menu that opens, you can search for graphics, tables, equations, footnotes/endnotes, and comments. Under Find, click **Graphics**. Click the **Browse the pages in your document** button. Six matches are identified, and the third of those occurrences is selected in the document window.

7. Click the **Find Options and additional search commands** button. Click **Options** to open the Find Options dialog box shown in **Figure 14–4**. These options enable you to further define your search.

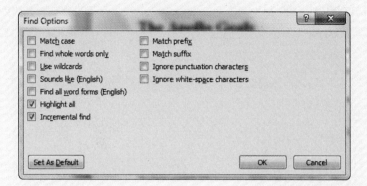

FIGURE 14–4
Find Options dialog box

8. Enable the **Find whole words only** option and click **OK**. In the Navigation Pane, click the **Browse the headings in your document** button. Under the heading *Apollo 11*, click the **Mission Objective** heading. In the Search Document text box, type **crew**. In the document window, the first match in the second paragraph under the heading is highlighted. Notice that the word *crewed* appears in the paragraph above, but it is not highlighted because the search was for whole words only.

9. Click the **Find Options and additional search commands** arrow. Click **Options**, enable the **Use wildcards** option, and then click **OK**. In the Navigation Pane, in the Search text box, type **Aldr*** and press **Enter**. Ten matches for the surname *Aldrin* are highlighted, and all occurrences are in the Apollo 11 section.

10. Click the **Find Options and additional search commands** arrow. Click **Options**, and then disable the option **Use wildcards**. Enable the **Incremental find** option and click **OK**.

11. Click the **Find Options and additional search commands** arrow. Click **Replace** to open the Find and Replace dialog box. In the Find what text box, the previous search text *Aldr** is selected. Type **ALSEP** to enter new search text. Click **More** to show more options, as shown in **Figure 14–5**.

FIGURE 14–5
More options in the Find and Replace dialog box

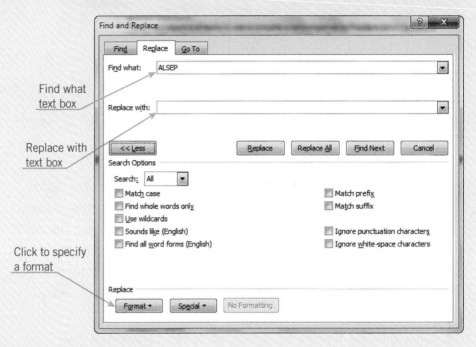

12. In the lower-left corner of the dialog box, click **Format**, and then click **Font** to open the Find Font dialog box, as shown in **Figure 14–6**. Under Font style, select **Italic** and then click **OK**. The format *Font: Italic* is displayed below the Find what text box.

TIP

As in previous Word versions, you can quickly open the Replace tab in the Find and Replace dialog box by using the shortcut keys Ctrl+H.

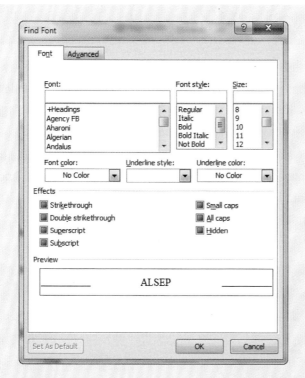

FIGURE 14–6
Find Font dialog box

13. In the Replace with box, type **ALSEP**. Click **Format**, and then click **Font**. Under Font style, click **Regular**, and then click **OK**. The format *Font: Not Bold, Not Italic* is displayed below the Replace with text box. Click **Replace All**. Eight replacements are made. Click **OK**.

14. Close the Find and Replace dialog box. Save the changes and leave the document open for the next Step-by-Step.

Creating and Modifying Hyperlinks

You can create your own navigation tools to help move around within and between your documents. You already know that a hyperlink takes you to a new location. You can use a hyperlink to move quickly to a location in your current document or to another existing document. For example, you can use a hyperlink in Word to jump to a location in another Word document, an Excel worksheet, or a PowerPoint presentation. By default, Word automatically creates a hyperlink when you type a Web or Internet address in a document.

You can select any text or object in a document, then create a hyperlink and specify the document or URL for the link. If desired, you can create ScreenTips for the hyperlinks you create.

Step-by-Step 14.5

1. If necessary, open the **Journeys to the Moon 3** file from your solution files. Save the document as **Journeys to the Moon 4**, followed by your initials. If necessary, show the Navigation Pane with headings displayed. Also, if necessary, show nonprinting formatting characters.

2. In the Navigation Pane, click the **The Apollo Missions** heading. Scroll to the second page to show the three graphics. Select the **Apollo 11** mission patch graphic. Click the **Insert** tab. In the Links group, click the **Hyperlink** button to open the Insert Hyperlink dialog box, as shown in **Figure 14–7**. Your dialog box settings will differ.

FIGURE 14–7
Insert Hyperlink dialog box

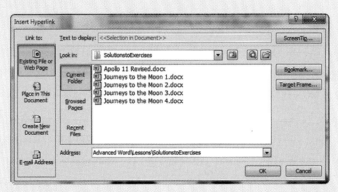

3. Under Link to, the option Existing File or Web Page is already enabled. In the Look in box, navigate to the drive and folder where your Data Files are stored. Select **Apollo 11**.

4. Click **ScreenTip** in the upper-right corner of the dialog box. The Set Hyperlink ScreenTip dialog box opens. Type **Original Apollo 11 document**. Click **OK** to save the ScreenTip, and then click **OK** to complete the hyperlink.

5. Deselect the graphic. Position the mouse pointer over the graphic to display the ScreenTip. Hold down **Ctrl** and click the **Apollo 11** graphic. The Apollo 11 document opens. Close the Apollo 11 document without saving any changes.

6. Position the insertion point in the second blank paragraph below the three graphics. On the Insert tab, in the Links group, click the **Hyperlink** button. Under Link to, the option Existing File or Web Page is already enabled. In the Address text box, type **http://www.nasa.gov**.

7. In the Text to display text box, select any text, if necessary, and then type **Get more information about the Apollo missions.**. Click **ScreenTip**, type **Learn more at NASA.gov/**, and then click **OK** twice to complete the hyperlink. The text in the document is formatted in a different color and underlined to indicate it is a hyperlink.

8. Click anywhere in the hyperlink you just created. In the Links group, click the **Hyperlink** button. Because a hyperlink is already formatted, the Edit Hyperlink dialog box opens.

9. In the Address box, position the insertion point at the end of the existing text and type **missions** to complete the URL. Click **OK** to apply the changes.

10. If you have an Internet connection and your browser is open, hold down **Ctrl** and click anywhere in the hyperlink. If the Web site is still current, the Web page should display in your browser. Close the Web page and switch to the Journeys to the Moon 4 document.

11. On page 2 of the document, right-click the **Apollo XIII** graphic, and in the shortcut menu, click **Hyperlink** to open the Insert Hyperlink dialog box. Under Link to, click the **Place in This Document** option. The document headings appear in the center pane of the dialog box. Click the **Apollo 13** heading.

12. Click **ScreenTip**. Type **Apollo 13 information**, and then click **OK** twice.

13. Deselect the graphic. Hold down **Ctrl** and click the **Apollo XIII** graphic. Page 13 appears in the document window, and the insertion point is positioned in front of the heading *Apollo 13*.

14. Save the changes to the document and leave the document open for the next Step-by-Step.

> **TIP**
>
> If the text is not automatically formatted as a hyperlink, the AutoCorrect option may be turned off. Click the File tab, click Options, and then click Proofing. Click AutoCorrect Options, and then click the AutoFormat As You Type tab. Under Replace as you type, make sure that the Internet and network paths with hyperlinks option is enabled.

Adding a Bookmark

You can also create a navigation tool by inserting a bookmark. A ***bookmark*** is an item or location in a document that you identify and name for future reference so you can jump quickly to a specific location within the same document. For example, you may want to bookmark a word, phrase, or table in a document so you can return to that location without searching for the text. The advantage of using bookmarks over using hyperlinks or the features in the Navigation Pane is that bookmarks do not have to be tied to headings.

Bookmarks can be placed anywhere within a document. To add a bookmark, you simply identify a location in a document and assign a bookmark name. Bookmark names can be up to 40 characters, must begin with a letter, and can contain numbers. Bookmark names cannot contain blank spaces. To separate words in a bookmark name, use the underscore character. If desired, you can make bookmarks visible in your document, but they will not print. You can edit, cut, copy, move, and paste items that are marked with a bookmark. Unless the content is removed from the document, the bookmark stays with the text.

> ▶ **VOCABULARY**
> **bookmark**

Step-by-Step 14.6

1. If necessary, open the **Journeys to the Moon 4** file from your solution files. Save the document as **Journeys to the Moon 5**, followed by your initials. If necessary, show the Navigation Pane, with headings displayed.

2. To show bookmarks in the document, click the **File** tab. Click **Options** and then in the Word Options dialog box, click **Advanced**. Scroll down about halfway, and under Show document content, enable the **Show bookmarks** option. Click **OK**.

3. Position the insertion point at the top of the document. In the Navigation Pane, in the Search Document text box, type **explosion**. Click the **Browse the results from your current search** button. In the document window where the first match is highlighted, select **An oxygen tank explosion on board**.

4. If necessary, click the **Insert** tab. In the Links group, click the **Bookmark** button to open the Bookmark dialog box, as shown in **Figure 14–8**. You can drag the dialog box title bar to reposition it on the page.

FIGURE 14–8
Bookmark dialog box

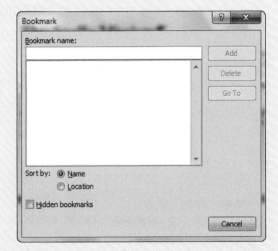

5. In the Bookmark name box, type **explosion** and then click **Add**. Deselect the text. Brackets appear before and after the bookmark text. These brackets do not print.

6. In the Navigation Pane, the Browse the results from your current search tab is still displayed, but the matches do not appear. Click the **Next Search Result** button to show the matches again, and then click the item for the last match. In the document window, position the insertion point in front of the paragraph with the highlighted search text. On the Insert tab, in the Links group, click the **Bookmark** button. In the Bookmark name box, type **explosion_cause**. Click **Add**. An I-beam appears to the left of the paragraph. The I-beam will not print.

7. On the Insert tab, in the Links group, click the **Bookmark** button. Under the Bookmark name box, two bookmarks are listed. Click the bookmark name **explosion** and then click **Go To**. The insertion point moves to the first bookmark in the document.

8. In the Bookmark dialog box, in the Bookmark name text box, position the insertion point to the right of the *explosion* text and type **_type**. Click **Add**.

9. Click the **Bookmark** button. Now three bookmarks appear in the list. Click the bookmark name **explosion** and then click **Delete**.

10. Click the bookmark name **explosion_cause** and then click **Go To**. The insertion moves to the paragraph that begins *After an intensive* near the end of the document. Close the dialog box.

11. Click the **File** tab, click **Options**, and then click **Advanced**. Under Show document content, disable the **Show bookmarks** option, and then click **OK**.

12. Even though the bookmarks are no longer visible, they still exist. In the Links group, click the **Bookmark** button, click **explosion_type**, and then click **Go To**. The first bookmarked text is selected. Close the dialog box.

13. On the vertical scroll bar in the lower-right corner of the screen, click the **Select Browse Object** button ⬚. Then click the **Go To** button →. The Go To tab in the Find and Replace dialog box opens. Under Go to what, click **Bookmark**. In the Enter bookmark name text box, the *exposure_cause* bookmark appears. To the right of the bookmark name, click the **list arrow** to see all bookmarks in the document. Click **Go To** and then close the dialog box.

14. Save the changes and leave the document open for the next Step-by-Step.

TIP

Ctrl+Shift+F5 is a shortcut for Insert Bookmark.

Controlling Text Flow

Monitoring how text flows throughout a multi-page document is important. Word provides several features so you can format text in multiple columns and also control how text flows from one page to the next.

Creating Sections and Formatting Columns

The default setting in a Word document displays all of the text in a single column, approximately six inches wide. Formatting text to display in multiple columns sometimes saves space on a page, and because the width of the line of text is smaller, the text is often easier to read. Word evenly balances the text in the columns, but you can manually control where the text ends in a column by inserting a column break.

▶ **VOCABULARY**
section

section break

A *section* is an area within a document that can have its own separate page formats. When you create a new blank document in Word, the document consists of just one section. When a document has only one section, the page formats, such as page orientation, margins, and headers and footers, apply to the entire document. The page formats are stored in a hidden, nonprinting end-of-file marker. If you want to change the page formats for only a portion of the document, you need to divide the document into multiple sections and then change the settings for the section that contains the content you want to format differently. To divide the document into multiple sections, you insert a *section break*, which divides the document into sections. The section break is indicated with a formatting mark, and all page formatting settings for the section that precedes the section break are stored in that mark. Therefore, if you delete a section break, the preceding content becomes part of the following section and assumes the formatting of that section.

Step-by-Step 14.7

1. If necessary, open the **Journeys to the Moon 5** file from your solution files. Save the document as **Journeys to the Moon 6**, followed by your initials. If necessary, show the Navigation Pane. Also, if necessary, show nonprinting formatting characters.

2. In the Navigation Pane, click the **Browse the headings in your document** button and then click the **The Apollo Goals** heading. The insertion point should be positioned in front of the heading in the document window.

3. Click the **Page Layout** tab. In the Page Setup group, click the **Breaks** button, and then, under Section Breaks, click **Continuous**. A continuous section break formatting mark appears at the end of the paragraph above the heading, as shown in **Figure 14–9**. If necessary, scroll up to see the section break. Because you selected a continuous break, the text below the section break will continue on the same page.

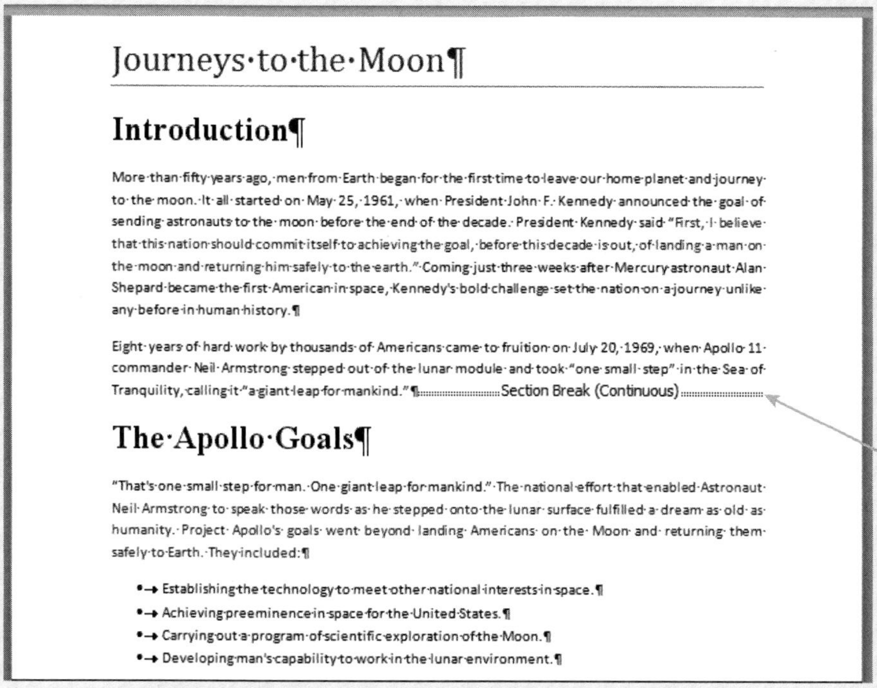

FIGURE 14–9
Continuous section break

Journeys·to·the·Moon¶

Introduction¶

More·than·fifty·years·ago,·men·from·Earth·began·for·the·first·time·to·leave·our·home·planet·and·journey·to·the·moon.·It·all·started·on·May·25,·1961,·when·President·John·F.·Kennedy·announced·the·goal·of·sending·astronauts·to·the·moon·before·the·end·of·the·decade.·President·Kennedy·said·"First,·I·believe·that·this·nation·should·commit·itself·to·achieving·the·goal,·before·this·decade·is·out,·of·landing·a·man·on·the·moon·and·returning·him·safely·to·the·earth."·Coming·just·three·weeks·after·Mercury·astronaut·Alan·Shepard·became·the·first·American·in·space,·Kennedy's·bold·challenge·set·the·nation·on·a·journey·unlike·any·before·in·human·history.¶

Eight·years·of·hard·work·by·thousands·of·Americans·came·to·fruition·on·July·20,·1969,·when·Apollo·11·commander·Neil·Armstrong·stepped·out·of·the·lunar·module·and·took·"one·small·step"·in·the·Sea·of·Tranquility,·calling·it·"a·giant·leap·for·mankind."¶·············Section·Break·(Continuous)·············

The·Apollo·Goals¶

"That's·one·small·step·for·man.·One·giant·leap·for·mankind."·The·national·effort·that·enabled·Astronaut·Neil·Armstrong·to·speak·those·words·as·he·stepped·onto·the·lunar·surface·fulfilled·a·dream·as·old·as·humanity.·Project·Apollo's·goals·went·beyond·landing·Americans·on·the·Moon·and·returning·them·safely·to·Earth.·They·included:¶

- Establishing·the·technology·to·meet·other·national·interests·in·space.¶
- Achieving·preeminence·in·space·for·the·United·States.¶
- Carrying·out·a·program·of·scientific·exploration·of·the·Moon.¶
- Developing·man's·capability·to·work·in·the·lunar·environment.¶

Continuous
section break
formatting mark

4. Make sure the insertion point is positioned somewhere below the section break. In the Page Setup group, click the **Margins** button, and then click **Narrow**. The margins for all the text below the section break change are not as wide, and the flow of text changes.

5. To remove the section break, in the document, click the **Section Break (Continuous)** formatting mark and then press **Delete**. The text above the section break is now formatted with the same margin settings as the text that was below the section break. In the Page Setup group, click the **Margins** button, and then click **Normal**.

6. In the Navigation Pane, click the **Apollo 11** heading. In the document window, under the quotation *"The Eagle has landed…,"* select the crew and backup crew member information. Be sure to include both headings and the ending paragraph mark in the selection.

7. On the Page Layout tab, in the Page Setup group, click the **Columns** button, and then click **Two**. Word automatically inserts continuous section breaks above and below the selected content, and the content is arranged in two columns.

8. In the Navigation Pane, click the **Mission Objective** heading for Apollo 11. Select the two paragraphs below the heading, including the ending paragraph mark. Click the **Columns** button, and then click **More Columns** at the bottom of the menu to open the Columns dialog box, shown in **Figure 14–10**.

FIGURE 14–10
Columns dialog box

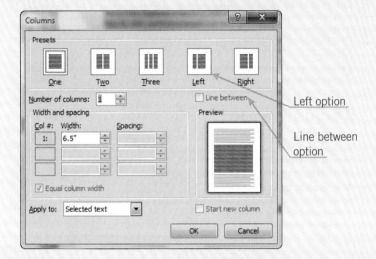

9. Under Presets, enable the **Left** option. In the Number of columns box, change the number to **3** and enable the **Line between** option. A preview of the three-column format appears in the Preview pane in the dialog box, and the column on the left is not as wide as the other two columns. Click **OK**. With the text still selected, click the **Columns** button and click **More Columns**. Change the number of columns to **2** and click **OK**. Word automatically controls the text flow so that the column lengths are balanced.

10. To create a manual column break, position the insertion point in front of the second paragraph in the left column. On the Page Layout tab, in the Page Setup group, click the **Breaks** button and then click **Column**. The text after the insertion point is moved to the top of the next column. Click the **Undo** button.

11. Position the insertion point in front of the first line of text below the heading *Mission Highlights*. Then use the vertical scroll bar (or the wheel on the mouse) to scroll down until you can see the source information for Apollo 11. Hold down **Shift** and click the mouse pointer at the end of the paragraph ending with *…July 24, 1969*. Be sure to include the paragraph marker. All the text between the two clicks is selected.

12. Click the **Columns** button, and then click **More Columns**. Enable the **Left** option, enable the **Line between** option, and then click **OK**.

13. Navigate to the Apollo 12 information. Format the list of crew and backup crew members in two even columns. Format all the content under the headings *Mission Objective* and *Mission Highlights* in two columns, using the Left option and adding a line between the columns. Navigate to the Apollo 13 information and apply the same column formats to the same content areas.

14. Save the document and leave the document open for the next Step-by-Step.

Using Pagination Options

Pagination is the system by which text and objects are manipulated to create the page layout. Just as text automatically wraps to the next line when the content extends beyond the right margin, lines in a paragraph automatically wrap to the next page. When a page fills with text and graphics, Word inserts an automatic page break so that the content will flow to the next page. Sometimes, though, the automatic page break will separate lines of text or entire paragraphs that you want to keep together. Of course, you can control the flow of text by manually inserting page breaks, but if you later edit or rearrange the content, the pagination will change and your manual adjustments may result in a page break in the wrong place. Using Word's pagination options can save you time and ensure that the text flows from one page to the next as desired.

One of Word's pagination options prevents widows and orphans. A *widow* is the last line of a multiline paragraph that is split from the other lines in the paragraph and wraps to the next page or column. An *orphan* is the first line of a multiline paragraph that is split from the other lines in the paragraph and appears at the bottom of a page or a column. When the Widow/Orphan option is enabled, a single line of text will not be separated from other lines in the same paragraph and appear on a different page. Heading styles commonly include pagination formats to prevent widows and orphans.

Other pagination options enable you to format paragraphs so that they stay together and appear on the same page. For example, when formatting document content with headings, you want to keep the headings attached to the first paragraph that follows the heading so that the heading doesn't appear by itself on a different page. And if the content includes a bulleted list, you probably don't want that list to be split between two pages.

▶ **VOCABULARY**
pagination
widow
orphan

Step-by-Step 14.8

1. If necessary, open the **Journeys to the Moon 6** file from your solution files. Save the document as **Journeys to the Moon 7**, followed by your initials. If necessary, show the Navigation Pane. Also, if necessary, show nonprinting formatting characters.

2. In the Navigation Pane, click the **Apollo 12** heading. In the document window, note the marker to the left of the heading, as shown in **Figure 14–11**. The marker indicates that a pagination format is applied to the paragraph.

FIGURE 14–11
Marker to indicate
pagination format

3. Make sure the insertion point is positioned in the heading paragraph. Click the **Home** tab. In the Paragraph group, click the **Dialog Box Launcher**. If necessary, click the **Line and Page Breaks** tab to show the dialog box settings shown in **Figure 14–12**. (You can also access this dialog box from the Page Layout tab, which is described below in Step 10.)

FIGURE 14–12
Paragraph dialog box

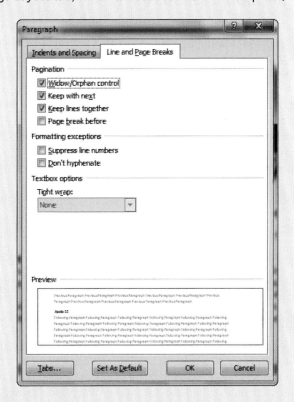

4. Note that under Pagination, the Widow/Orphan control, Keep with next, and Keep lines together options are already enabled. With these options enabled, the heading will not appear on a page by itself without the first line of the first paragraph.

5. Under Pagination, enable the **Page break before** option and click **OK**. The heading and content below the heading move to the next page. This pagination setting will ensure that the heading always begins at the top of a new page.

6. In the document window, triple-click the heading **Apollo 12** to select the entire heading, including the ending paragraph mark. In the Clipboard group, double-click the **Format Painter** button to copy the paragraph formats.

7. In the Navigation Pane, click the **Apollo 13** heading. In the document window, click anywhere in the heading **Apollo 13**. The paragraph formats are updated to include the Page break before format, and the heading and content below the heading move to the next page.

8. In the Navigation Pane, click the **Apollo 11** heading. In the document window, click anywhere in the heading **Apollo 11** to apply the paragraph formats. Even though the heading is positioned at the top of a page, applying the formats will ensure that the formatting will remain consistent. Click the **Format Painter** button (or press **Esc**) to toggle off the feature.

9. In the Navigation Pane, click the heading **The Apollo Goals**. In the document window, select the four paragraphs in the bulleted list. Be sure to include the ending paragraph mark after the fourth bulleted item.

10. Click the **Page Layout** tab, then in the Paragraph group, click the **Dialog Box Launcher**. Enable the **Keep lines together** option. If edits cause changes in the text flow, the four bulleted paragraphs will not be separated. Click **OK**.

11. Scroll down to show the three graphics on your screen. Select the entire sentence above the graphics that begins *Use the following links*. Be sure to include the ending paragraph mark.

12. On the Page Layout tab, in the Paragraph group, click the **Dialog Box Launcher**. Enable the **Keep with next** option, and then click **OK**. The selected paragraph will not be separated from the graphics because the graphics are anchored in the next paragraph.

13. In the Navigation Pane, click the **Mission Highlights** heading for Apollo 12. Depending on how the text flows in your document, this heading may be orphaned from the text that follows because the heading is followed by a section break. The heading style pagination settings are not effective because of the section break. If the heading is orphaned in your document, insert a manual page break by clicking the **Breaks** button in the Page Setup group and then clicking **Page**.

14. Save the changes to the document and leave the document open for the next Step-by-Step.

TIP

When you want to keep two or more paragraphs together using a Keep with next text flow option, do not select the last paragraph of the group (because you do not want to keep it with the next paragraph).

Using Hyphens and Nonbreaking Spaces

When a word doesn't fit within a line of text, Word automatically wraps the word to the next line. This is especially noticeable when the justified paragraph format is applied. The result usually shows a lot of white space between words in the line where the word would not fit. The *hyphenation* setting allows a word at the end of a line to split between syllables, which results in more uniform spacing so that more text will fit in a line.

An *optional hyphen* is a special formatting character used to indicate where a word can be divided. When an optional hyphen is inserted in a word, the word will not be divided and the hyphen will not print unless the word is pushed to the end of the line and the entire word will not fit on the line. If that happens, the word will be divided at the optional hyphen, the hyphen will print, and the text following the hyphen will wrap to the next line. A *nonbreaking hyphen* is a format used to indicate hyphenated words that should not be split if the hyphen falls at the end of a line. For example, if a person's last name has a hyphen, such as Smith-Conners, you can make sure the surname is not split between two lines. A *nonbreaking space* is a format used to indicate words that should not be split between lines, such as dates and measurements.

▶ **VOCABULARY**

hyphenation

optional hyphen

nonbreaking hyphen

nonbreaking space

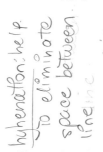

hyphenation: help to eliminate space between lines

Step-by-Step 14.9

1. If necessary, open the **Journeys to the Moon 7** file from your solution files. Save the document as **Journeys to the Moon 8**, followed by your initials. If necessary, show the Navigation Pane. Also, if necessary, show nonprinting formatting characters.

2. The document contains several white spaces in the lines of text. Hyphenating the text will help to eliminate the white spaces and also fit more text within a line. Move the insertion point to the beginning of the document. On the Page Layout tab, in the Page Setup group, click the **Hyphenation** button and then click **Manual**.

3. Word proposes the first word to hyphenate: *send-ing*. The hyphen in the word is highlighted in the upper-left corner of the document window. Note that all the characters of the word *send-ing* appear on the same line in the document. The hyphen you see is an optional hyphen, and the word will only be divided with a hyphen if all of the word doesn't fit on the line. Click **Yes**.

4. The next proposed hyphenation is *Pres-i-dent*. In the dialog box, the second hyphen is highlighted. In the upper-left corner of the document window, the hyphen appears after *Presi* and the hyphen is highlighted. Click the **left arrow** key to select the first hyphen in the dialog box. By selecting the first hyphen, you have indicated that you prefer the word to be divided after *Pres* instead of after *Presi*. Click **Yes**. Notice that the optional hyphenation in the document window now displays as *Pres-ident*.

5. Click **Cancel** to close the dialog box, and then click the **Home** tab. In the Paragraph group, click the **Show/Hide ¶** button to hide the nonprinting formatting characters. Depending on where the line of text wraps in the document, the hyphen may no longer appear in the word *President*. The hyphen is optional, and if it is not needed in this text flow, it will not appear.

6. This is a long document and hyphenating manually will take a long time. Click the **Page Layout** tab. In the Page Setup group, click the **Hyphenation** button, and then click **Hyphenation Options** to open the Hyphenation dialog box, as shown in **Figure 14–13**.

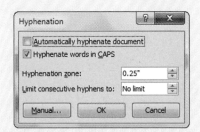

FIGURE 14–13
Hyphenation dialog box

7. Enable the **Automatically hyphenate document** option. Disable the **Hyphenate words in CAPS** option so that acronyms are not hyphenated. Click **OK**. The hyphenation feature is applied to the entire document and the text flow is readjusted. Many of the white spaces are eliminated or reduced.

8. In the Navigation Pane, click the **Apollo 13** heading. Search for *Roger*, and then click in the paragraph with the search result. Depending on the flow of text in your document, *Roger* may be hyphenated and split between lines. If Roger is not divided, and if no other words in the current paragraph are divided at the end of a line, move to the next paragraph that shows a divided word.

9. In the Paragraph group, click the **Dialog Box Launcher**. If necessary, show the Line and Page Breaks tab. Under Formatting exceptions, enable the **Don't hyphenate** option and then click **OK**. The automatic hyphenation is removed from the current paragraph. If needed, you could manually hyphenate the words in this paragraph.

10. In the Navigation pane, click the **Mission Highlights** heading for Apollo 13. Click the **Home** tab. In the Paragraph group, click the **Show/Hide ¶** button to show the nonprinting formatting characters.

11. In the first line under the heading, delete the blank space between *5* and *½*. With the insertion point positioned between the 5 and the 1, hold down **Ctrl** and **Shift** and then press the **spacebar**. A nonbreaking space is inserted, and a small circle appears between the numbers *5* and *½*. Those numbers will always appear on the same line.

TIP

To remove the hyphenation feature from multiple paragraphs, select the paragraphs before enabling the Don't hyphenate option in the Paragraph dialog box.

12. In the fifth line of the same paragraph, you will see *S-11*. Delete the hyphen. With the insertion point positioned between the *S* and *11*, hold down **Ctrl** and **Shift** and press the **hyphen** key. The nonbreaking hyphen will prohibit the *S* and *11* from being divided between lines.

13. Although a nonbreaking hyphen displays larger than a normal hyphen when nonprinting formatting characters are showing, the nonbreaking hyphen prints the same as a normal hyphen. Click the **Show/Hide ¶** button to hide the nonprinting formatting characters. The nonbreaking hyphen appears normal.

14. Save the changes to the document and leave the document open for the next Step-by-Step.

Citing Sources

▶ **VOCABULARY**
citation

A *citation* is a reference in a document that credits the source of information or other content, such as a picture or a chart, or references specific legal cases, statutes, or other authorities in legal documents. Several formal styles can be used for citing sources. Each style has its own set of rules for referencing the sources, and the style used is directed by the objective of the document. For example, the academic field customarily uses the MLA and APA styles. The Chicago style is often used in journalism and publishing. Within the document, citations are referenced either in the line of text or in a footnote or endnote, depending on the style.

Managing Sources

Citing sources in the proper format is a tedious task because there are so many rules regarding the required information and how to format it. Word offers some valuable features to help you manage your sources and make sure you use the correct capitalization, spacing, and indentation. Each time you create a new source, the source information is saved in the Current List, which is saved with the current document. You can also save the source information in a Master List on your computer, which is saved on your computer and stores sources from all your documents. Then as you work in the current document or future documents, you can easily find and access the source information you have already saved.

Step-by-Step 14.10

1. If necessary, open the **Journeys to the Moon 8** file from your solution files. Save the document as **Journeys to the Moon 9**, followed by your initials. Show nonprinting formatting characters.

2. Open the **Apollo Resources** file from the drive and folder where your Data Files are stored. The document provides a list of resources that were used to create the content for the Journeys to the Moon document.

3. In the Apollo Resources document, position the insertion point in front of the first paragraph marker. Click the **References** tab. In the Citations & Bibliography group, click the **Manage Sources** button to open the Source Manager dialog box, as shown in **Figure 14–14**. The Master List in your dialog box will be different.

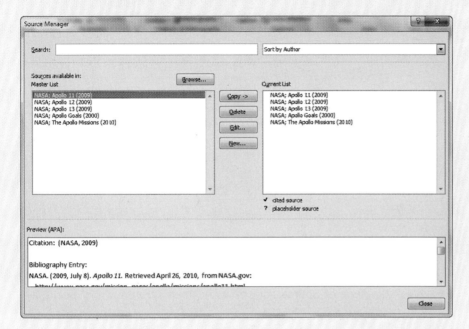

FIGURE 14–14
Source Manager dialog box

4. Select all the sources in the Current List, and then click **Copy**. The copied sources are now stored on your computer and will be available for other documents. Close the dialog box, and then close the Apollo Resources document without saving any changes.

5. In the Journeys to the Moon 9 document, click the **References** tab. In the Citations & Bibliography group, click the **Style** list arrow and then click **APA Fifth Edition**.

6. In the Citations & Bibliography group, click the **Manage Sources** button. In the Master List, select the following sources:

   NASA; Apollo 12 (2009)

   NASA; Apollo 13 (2009)

   NASA; Apollo Goals (2000)

   NASA; The Apollo Missions (2010)

7. Click **Copy** to copy the selected sources to the Current List. The sources will be saved with the current active document.

8. Click **New** to open the Create Source dialog box, as shown in **Figure 14–15**. Your dialog box settings will be different. The form guides you to enter the information you will need to create a citation and bibliography following the APA Fifth Edition style rules.

FIGURE 14–15
Create Source dialog box

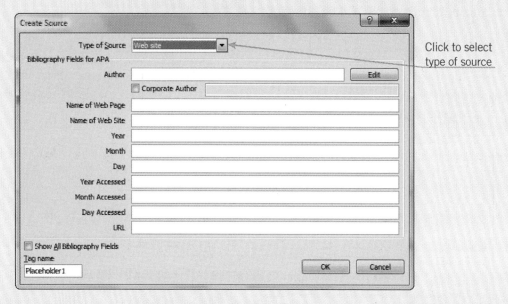

9. Click the **Type of Source** list arrow and then scroll down, if necessary, and select **Web site**. The form changes to adapt for the information required for the type of source.

10. In the Author text box, type **NASA** and then enable the **Corporate Author** option. Complete the form by entering the following source information.

    Name of Web Page: **The Apollo Program**

    Name of Web Site: **NASA.gov**

    Year: **2009**

    Month: **November**

    Day: **6**

    Year Accessed: **2010**

    Month Accessed: **April**

    Day Accessed: **26**

    URL: **http://www.nasa.gov/mission_pages/apollo/missions/index.html**

11. Proofread the information to make sure it is accurate, and then click **OK**. The new source is added to both the Master List and the Current List.

12. In the Current List, select the source **NASA; Apollo Goals (2000)**. Then click **Edit** to open the Edit Source dialog box. In the URL box, after *www*, change the period to a hyphen. Click **OK**. When prompted to save the changes in both lists, click **Yes**. Close the dialog box.

13. Save the changes and leave the document open for the next Step-by-Step.

TIP

When creating a Web source, you can save it by copying the URL in your browser and then pasting it in the Create Source dialog box.

Creating Citations

When you insert a citation in the body of the document, Word inserts a field and automatically applies a format based on the selected style. At any time you can update the fields, or you can convert the fields to static text.

Step-by-Step 14.11

1. If necessary, open the **Journeys to the Moon 9** file from your solution files. Save the document as **Journeys to the Moon 10**, followed by your initials.

2. If necessary, click the **References** tab. In the Citations & Bibliography group, make sure the selected Style is **APA Fifth Edition**.

3. Navigate to the heading *The Apollo Goals.* Position the insertion point at the end of the paragraph directly above the heading. In the Citations & Bibliography group, click the **Insert Citation** button. The sources from the Current List appear in the menu that opens. Click **NASA The Apollo Missions, (2010)**. The citation reference to NASA is automatically inserted in the document and formatted as a field.

4. Under the heading *The Apollo Goals*, position the insertion point at the end of the last bulleted item. In the Citations & Bibliography group, click the **Insert Citation** button and then click **NASA Apollo Goals, (2000)**. Scroll down to the end of The Apollo Missions information (below the patches) and delete the Source Information section.

5. In the Navigation Pane, click the **Apollo 12** heading. Scroll up to the previous page (page 7) and delete the Source Information section at the bottom of the page.

6. Position the insertion point after the last paragraph on the page and before the section break. Click the **Insert Citation** button, and then click **NASA Apollo 11, (2009)**. The citation *(NASA, 2009)* is inserted in the document.

7. Navigate to the end of the Apollo 12 information and delete the Source Information section. Position the insertion point after the last paragraph on the page (and before the section break) and insert the citation **NASA Apollo 12, (2009)**. If necessary, delete the extra paragraph marker so that there will not be a full blank page before the Apollo 13 information.

8. Navigate to the end of the Apollo 13 information at the end of the document and delete the Source Information section and the heading *Summary*. Insert a citation for **NASA Apollo 13, (2009)** at the end of the last paragraph.

TIP

Placeholder tag names are numbers assigned by default, but you can customize the placeholder tag name with whatever tag you want.

9. Navigate to the top of the document. Under the heading *Introduction*, in the first paragraph, position the insertion point after the quotation mark following the quotation by President Kennedy. Click the **Insert Citation** button and then click **Add New Placeholder**. Word proposes a name, *Placeholder 1*, for the placeholder. Click **OK**.

10. In the Citations & Bibliography group, click the **Manage Sources** button. Notice that check marks appear next to the sources you have already cited in the document. In the Current List, click **Placeholder 1** and then click **Edit**. The Edit Source dialog box opens.

11. Click the **Type of Source** list arrow. Scroll down to the bottom of the list and select **Miscellaneous**. Complete the form by entering the following source information.

    Author: **President John F. Kennedy**

    Title: **Special Message to the Congress on Urgent National Needs**

    Publication Title: **Delivered in person before a joint session of Congress**

    Year: **1961**

    Month: **May**

    Day: **25**

    City: **Washington**

    State/Province: **D.C.**

12. Click **OK**. Click the **Copy** button to save the source in the Master List. Close the dialog box. Notice that the placeholder in the document is updated to show the citation *Kennedy, 1961*.

13. To view the other citations in the document, press **F11** to move to the next field. The next citation is selected. Click the **list arrow** for the field. In the shortcut menu, click **Convert citation to static text**. The citation is no longer formatted in a field and it will not be updated if you edit the source information. Click the **Undo** button.

14. Save the changes and leave the document open for the next Step-by-Step.

TIP

To remove a citation, click the tab on the left side of the field to select the entire field, then click Delete.

Creating a Bibliography

▶ **VOCABULARY**
bibliography
works cited page

A *bibliography* is a list of source materials that are used in the preparation of a work. The bibliography, often referred to as a *works cited page*, is normally placed at the end of a document. Manually creating a bibliography is a tedious task because you must enter all the source information following a specified format. Fortunately, Word can do all that work automatically, and you can create a bibliography with a couple of clicks. Word generates the bibliography using the information stored in the Current List in the Source Manager. The format for the bibliography is based on the selected style. Placeholder citations do not appear in the bibliography. If you change citations or add and delete sources, you can quickly update the field instead of creating a new bibliography.

Step-by-Step 14.12

1. If necessary, open the **Journeys to the Moon 10** file from your solution files. Save the document as **Journeys to the Moon 11**, followed by your initials.

2. Position the insertion point at the end of the document. Click the **Page Layout** tab, and in the Page Setup group, click the **Breaks** button. Under Section Breaks, click **Next Page**. A new section is added to the document, and the new section begins on the next page.

3. With the insertion point positioned at the top of the new section, click the **References** tab. In the Citations & Bibliography group, click the **Bibliography** button, and then click **Bibliography**. A built-in bibliography appears with an alphabetical list of all the sources in the Current List. Scroll up to review the bibliography.

4. Click to position your insertion point below the bibliography and then press **Enter**. In the Citations & Bibliography group, click the **Bibliography** button again, and then click **Works Cited**.

5. Scroll up to review the *Works Cited* bibliography. Another bibliography appears, but the information is preceded with the title *Works Cited* instead of *Bibliography*. Click the **Undo** button to remove the second bibliography.

6. Click anywhere inside the bibliography content. Note that all the content is contained in a field. The content is already formatted with a hanging indent. If desired, you can edit the formats.

7. Click the **Manage Sources** button, and then click **New**. Click the **Type of Source** list arrow and then click **Book**. Complete the form by entering the following source information.

   Author: **Seamans, Robert C., Jr.**

   Title: **PROJECT APOLLO The Tough Decisions**

   Year: **2005**

   City: **Washington, D.C.**

   Publisher: **National Aeronautics and Space Administration**

8. Click **OK**, and close the Source Manager dialog box.

9. If necessary, click anywhere within the bibliography to select it. Press **F9** to update the fields in the bibliography. The new source is added to the bibliography.

10. Save the changes and leave the document open for the next Step-by-Step.

Creating Footnotes and Endnotes

Footnotes and endnotes allow you to add information to a document or cite the source of content. A *footnote* appears at the bottom of the same page where it is referenced. An *endnote* is placed along with other notes at the end of a document. Both types of notes are linked to a reference marker in the text, which is a superscript number or a custom character, such as an asterisk. The *reference marker* indicates that a note with a matching number or character is at the bottom of the page or at the end of the document. When you use numbers to reference each note, Word automatically assigns the numbers for you. If you rearrange your text or move, copy, or delete a note, Word will automatically renumber the reference marker in the document and rearrange the order of the notes.

To insert a footnote, position your insertion point in the line of text and click the Insert Footnote button. Word automatically inserts the reference marker and a separator line at the bottom of the page. The *separator line* separates the body text from the footnote area. Then you can enter the note text in the footnote area.

After you insert footnotes in a document, you can change them to endnotes and vice versa. If you have a combination of footnotes and endnotes in the same document, you can swap the notes so that the footnotes become endnotes and the endnotes become footnotes.

▶ **VOCABULARY**

footnote

endnote

reference marker

separator line

EXTRA FOR EXPERTS

If you copy text with a footnote/endnote reference, when you paste the text into a PowerPoint slide or an Excel worksheet, the note text will also display.

Step-by-Step 14.13

1. If necessary, open the **Journeys to the Moon 11** file from your solution files. Save the document as **Journeys to the Moon 12**, followed by your initials. If necessary, show the Navigation Pane.

2. In the Navigation Pane, under *Apollo 11*, click the **Mission Highlights** heading. In the document window, under the heading *Mission Highlights*, position the insertion point at the end of the first paragraph.

3. If necessary, click the **References** tab. In the Footnotes group, click the **Insert Footnote** button. The reference marker is inserted in the body of the document, and a separator line and the reference marker appear at the bottom of the page, as shown in **Figure 14–16**.

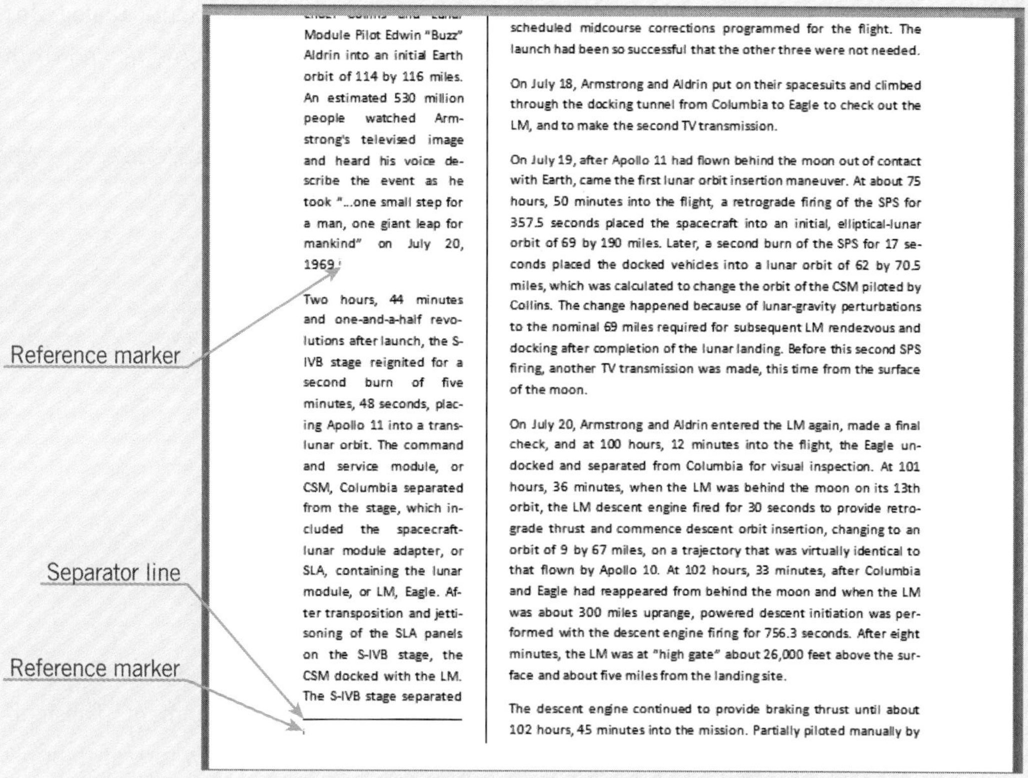

FIGURE 14–16
Footnote reference
markers

Reference marker

Separator line

Reference marker

(Figure 14-16 document text:)

Module Pilot Edwin "Buzz" Aldrin into an initial Earth orbit of 114 by 116 miles. An estimated 530 million people watched Armstrong's televised image and heard his voice describe the event as he took "...one small step for a man, one giant leap for mankind" on July 20, 1969.

Two hours, 44 minutes and one-and-a-half revolutions after launch, the S-IVB stage reignited for a second burn of five minutes, 48 seconds, placing Apollo 11 into a translunar orbit. The command and service module, or CSM, Columbia separated from the stage, which included the spacecraft-lunar module adapter, or SLA, containing the lunar module, or LM, Eagle. After transposition and jettisoning of the SLA panels on the S-IVB stage, the CSM docked with the LM. The S-IVB stage separated

scheduled midcourse corrections programmed for the flight. The launch had been so successful that the other three were not needed.

On July 18, Armstrong and Aldrin put on their spacesuits and climbed through the docking tunnel from Columbia to Eagle to check out the LM, and to make the second TV transmission.

On July 19, after Apollo 11 had flown behind the moon out of contact with Earth, came the first lunar orbit insertion maneuver. At about 75 hours, 50 minutes into the flight, a retrograde firing of the SPS for 357.5 seconds placed the spacecraft into an initial, elliptical-lunar orbit of 69 by 190 miles. Later, a second burn of the SPS for 17 seconds placed the docked vehicles into a lunar orbit of 62 by 70.5 miles, which was calculated to change the orbit of the CSM piloted by Collins. The change happened because of lunar-gravity perturbations to the nominal 69 miles required for subsequent LM rendezvous and docking after completion of the lunar landing. Before this second SPS firing, another TV transmission was made, this time from the surface of the moon.

On July 20, Armstrong and Aldrin entered the LM again, made a final check, and at 100 hours, 12 minutes into the flight, the Eagle undocked and separated from Columbia for visual inspection. At 101 hours, 36 minutes, when the LM was behind the moon on its 13th orbit, the LM descent engine fired for 30 seconds to provide retrograde thrust and commence descent orbit insertion, changing to an orbit of 9 by 67 miles, on a trajectory that was virtually identical to that flown by Apollo 10. At 102 hours, 33 minutes, after Columbia and Eagle had reappeared from behind the moon and when the LM was about 300 miles uprange, powered descent initiation was performed with the descent engine firing for 756.3 seconds. After eight minutes, the LM was at "high gate" about 26,000 feet above the surface and about five miles from the landing site.

The descent engine continued to provide braking thrust until about 102 hours, 45 minutes into the mission. Partially piloted manually by

4. Type the following text. (Because the footnote appears on the same page at the bottom of the column, some of the paragraph text in the left column will move to the top of the next column.)

   Onboard audio recordings of conversations of the crew members during the Apollo 11 mission are available at the NASA Web site. Go to NASA.gov and search for the keywords *audio recordings Apollo 11*.

5. Position the mouse pointer over the reference marker in the body of the document. The footnote text appears in a ScreenTip, so you don't need to scroll to the bottom of the page to read the note.

6. In the Navigation Pane, click the **The Apollo Missions** heading. Position the insertion point at the end of the first paragraph below the heading. In the Footnotes group, click the **Insert Footnote** button. The reference marker number 1 is inserted. Word automatically changed the other reference marker to number 2 because it appears later in the document.

7. Type the following text.

   The Lunar Sample Laboratory Facility at the Johnson Space Center is the chief repository for materials returned from the moon during the Apollo era.

TIP

Instead of clicking the Insert Footnote button, you can insert a continuously numbered footnote by pressing Alt+Ctrl+F.

8. On the References tab, in the Footnotes group, click the **Dialog Box Launcher** to open the Footnote and Endnote dialog box, as shown in **Figure 14–17**.

FIGURE 14–17
Footnote and Endnote dialog box

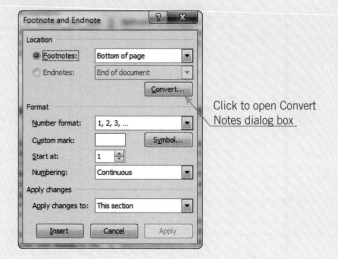

Click to open Convert
Notes dialog box

9. Click the **Number format** list arrow and then click **i, ii, iii, ...**. Click the **Apply changes to** list arrow and then click **Whole document**. The footnotes appear in different sections, so you want the new format to apply to all the sections in the document. Click **Apply**. The reference markers change to the new number format.

10. Go to page two. Position the insertion point at the end of the second paragraph. On the References tab, in the Footnotes group, click the **Dialog Box Launcher**. Under Format, in the Custom mark text box, type * (asterisk). Click **Insert**. Type **The Apollo program came to an end in December 1972.**.

11. Select the * reference marker in the document and cut the marker to the Clipboard. Scroll up to the top of the document, click to position the insertion point at the end of the first paragraph under the heading *Introduction*, and then paste the reference marker.

12. At the bottom of page one, select the first note (with an asterisk), and then press **Delete**. You can delete the note text, but you cannot delete the reference marker below the separator line. Click **OK** to close the alert box. Scroll back to the top of the page, select the * reference marker, and press **Delete**. The reference marker is removed from the body text, and the note is removed from the bottom of the page.

13. In the Footnotes group, click the **Dialog Box Launcher**. In the Footnote and Endnote dialog box, under Location, click **Convert**. In the Convert Notes dialog box, click **OK**. Close the dialog box and navigate to the end of the document. The notes appear below a separator line. Click the **Undo** button.

14. Save the changes and leave the document open for the next Step-by-Step.

Analyzing Content and Readability

Word offers yet another automated tool that will help you in the preparation of long documents. After you finish checking the spelling and grammar in your document, you can perform an analysis of the content and determine the reading level of the document. The analysis generates statistics including word count, average number of words per sentence, and the average number of characters per word. Word calculates several readability scores based on a rating of the average number of syllables per word and the number of words per sentence.

The readability levels are indicated with three scores: (1) the percentage of passive sentences; (2) the Flesch Reading Ease score; and (3) the Flesch-Kincaid Grade level score. The Flesch Reading Ease score provides a rating based on a 100-point scale; the higher the score, the easier the content is to understand. A good score to aim for is between 60 and 70 in order for most people to easily understand the document. The Flesch-Kincaid Grade Level score is a rating based on a U.S. grade level. For example, a score of 11.0 means that an eleventh grader can understand the document. Scores of at least 7.0 to 8.0 are good for most documents.

Step-by-Step 14.14

1. If necessary, open the **Journeys to the Moon 12** file from your solution files.

2. To quickly check the number of pages and word count, click the **Review** tab. In the Proofing group, click the **Word Count** button. The Word Count dialog box shown in **Figure 14–18** opens and shows the statistics for the number of pages, words, characters, paragraphs, and lines. Your statistics may differ.

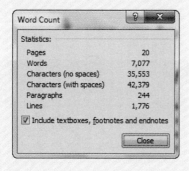

FIGURE 14–18
Word Count dialog box

3. Close the dialog box.

4. Click the **File** tab, and then click **Options**. Click **Proofing**. Under When correcting spelling and grammar in Word, enable the **Show readability statistics** option. Click **OK**.

5. To analyze the readability, move the insertion point to the beginning of the document. In the Proofing group, click the **Spelling & Grammar** button.

TIP

If you have previously completed a spelling and grammar check and ignored suggestions and rules or made corrections, you will see a message indicating that text marked with "Do not check spelling or grammar" was skipped. The skipped text is the text you already changed or ignored in a previous spell check. If you get this prompt, click OK to proceed.

6. You will need to pass through many suggested edits. Ignore all spellings and all rules. When the dialog box opens and confirms that the spelling and grammar check is complete, click **OK**. The Readability Statistics dialog box opens, as shown in **Figure 14–19**. Your statistics may differ.

FIGURE 14–19
Readability Statistics dialog box

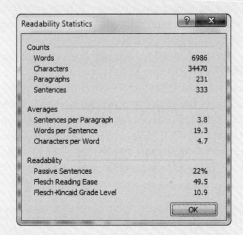

7. Press **Alt+Print Screen**. A capture of the active window is saved on the Clipboard. Click **OK** to close the dialog box.

8. Open a new blank document and press **Ctrl+V** to paste the Clipboard item in the document.

9. Save the document as **Journeys to the Moon Readability**, followed by your initials. Close the document and close the Journeys to the Moon 12 document without saving.

SUMMARY

In this lesson, you learned:

- You can open and work with several documents at the same time, and there are several ways to arrange multiple document windows to make it easy to switch between documents.

- The Navigation Pane provides several features for browsing documents, reorganizing the document content, and finding text and objects.

- Hyperlinks and bookmarks are features you can add to a document to quickly navigate within a document.

- You can divide a document into sections to apply different page layout formats to portions of the document.

- You can control text flow from one page to the next by applying pagination options.

- You can enable a hyphenation setting so that Word will automatically split long words between syllables when the entire word will not fit at the end of a line of text.

- You can control text flow from one line to the next by creating nonbreaking hyphens and nonbreaking spaces.

- Creating citations and bibliographies is made simple by using the Source Manager.

- You can also create footnotes and endnotes to cite sources, and you can easily convert footnotes to endnotes and vice versa.

- Word provides a feature that analyzes document content and determines the readability level of the document content.

VOCABULARY REVIEW

Define the following terms:

bibliography	incremental search	reference marker
bookmark	nonbreaking hyphen	section
citation	nonbreaking space	section break
endnote	optional hyphen	separator line
footnote	orphan	widow
hyphenation	pagination	works cited page

 # REVIEW QUESTIONS

TRUE / FALSE

Circle T if the statement is true or F if the statement is false.

T   F   **1.**   When you open a new blank document in Word, the document is already formatted with multiple sections.

T   F   **2.**   The Find command can be accessed in the Navigation Pane.

T   F   **3.**   The academic field customarily uses the MLA and APA styles to format citations and bibliographies.

T   F   **4.**   When you have copied 24 items to the Clipboard, you must clear the Clipboard before you can copy more items.

T   F   **5.**   Placeholder citations appear in the bibliography along with the other sources cited in the document.

MATCHING

Match the correct term in Column 2 to its description in Column 1.

Column 1

_____   1.   An area that can have its own separate page formats

_____   2.   A type of search in which the matches for the search change as the text is augmented

_____   3.   The last line of a paragraph split from the other lines in the paragraph

_____   4.   Setting that provides more uniform spacing of a line of text

_____   5.   Document element automatically generated based on the sources stored in the Current List in the Source Manager

Column 2

A.   citation

B.   incremental

C.   bibliography

D.   hyphenation

E.   orphan

F.   widow

G.   section

WRITTEN QUESTIONS

Write a brief answer to the following questions.

1. What is the advantage of using bookmarks instead of hyperlinks?

2. Describe the difference between the wildcard characters ? and *.

3. Inserting manual page breaks to control text flow is quick and easy, so why would you apply paragraph formats to keep lines of text together?

4. What is the benefit of having the bibliography formatted in a field?

5. Describe why you would insert a placeholder citation in a document.

PROJECTS

If you have a SAM 2010 user profile, your instructor may have assigned an autogradable version of the indicated project. If so, log into the SAM 2010 Web site at *www.cengage.com/sam2010* to download the instruction and start files.

PROJECT 14–1

1. Open the Lease file from the drive and folder where your Data Files are stored. Save the document as **Final Lease**, followed by your initials.

2. Change the paper size to Legal 8.5" × 14". Change the top and bottom margins to 1.0". Change the left margin to 1.5" and change the right margin to 1.0".

3. Position the insertion point in front of the first paragraph under the title LEASE AGREEMENT that begins *This Lease Agreement*. Select the text in the document, except for the title, and apply the Justify alignment format.

4. Automatically hyphenate the document.

5. At the end of the document, format the last paragraph of text, blank paragraphs, and signature lines so that all the lines stay together.

6. Create some bookmarks to help users quickly navigate to information in this contract.
   a. Search for the first occurrence of *landlord*, select the phrase *James R. Kraus, hereinafter known as the Landlord*, create a bookmark, and name the bookmark **landlord**.
   b. Search for the first occurrence of *tenant*, select the phrase *Jennifer Lynn Hamilton, hereinafter known as the Tenant*, create a bookmark, and name the bookmark **tenant**.
   c. Search for the first occurrence of *home*, select the phrase *943 Ashcreek Drive, Centerville, Ohio 45458-3333*, create a bookmark, and name the bookmark **address**.
   d. Search for the first occurrence of *rental rate*, select the phrase *a monthly rental rate of five hundred seventy-five dollars ($575)*, create a bookmark, and name the bookmark **rate**.
   e. Search for the first occurrence of *security deposit*, select the phrase *a Security Deposit of one month's rent, five hundred seventy-five dollars ($575)*, create a bookmark, and name the bookmark **deposit**.
   f. Search for the first occurrence of *late charge*, select the phrase *a late charge of fifteen dollars ($15) for every day past the due date*, create a bookmark, and name the bookmark **late_charge**.

7. Use the bookmark to go to the address in the document. Replace the hyphen in the postal code with a nonbreaking hyphen.

8. Save the changes and close the document.

SAM PROJECT 14–2

1. Open the Family Disaster Plan file from the drive and folder where your Data Files are stored. Save the document as **Family Disaster Plan**, followed by your initials. Then close the document.

2. Open the Returning Home file from the drive and folder where your Data Files are stored. Save the document as **Preparing for Natural Disasters 1**, followed by your initials.

3. Enter the following new text at the top of the document.

   PREPARING FOR NATURAL DISASTERS
   It is important that we improve the nation's ability to prepare for and respond to public health emergencies. To prepare for emergencies, you need to be aware of health threats and how to protect yourself and others. The resources below will help you prepare for natural disasters and severe weather.

   Get information about how to create a family disaster plan.

4. Apply the Title style to the first line of text.

5. Move the insertion point to the end of the document. Insert text from the following Data Files: **Extreme Heat**, **Floods**, **Landslides**, and **Tornadoes**.

6. Use the Navigation Pane to reorganize the contents. Move the *Returning Home after a Disaster* heading to the end of the document. Then move the *Extreme Heat* heading so that the Heat section follows the section on Tornadoes.

7. Format the heading *Returning Home after a Disaster* to include a page break before the heading.

8. Position the insertion point in front of the heading *Floods*. Select all the text from this point to the end of the document. With the text selected, apply a two-column format with a line between the columns.

9. Select each of the five level-one headings and apply a one-column format.

10. Automatically hyphenate the document, but do not hyphenate words in CAPS.

11. Insert a page number style of your choice in the lower-right corner of the document.

12. At the beginning of the document, select the sentence *Get information about how to create a family disaster plan*. Create a hyperlink to the file **Family Disaster Plan** in the drive and folder where your solution files are stored. Create a ScreenTip that displays **Family Disaster Plan**.

13. Save the changes and leave the document open for the next Project.

PROJECT 14–3

1. If necessary, open the **Preparing for Natural Disasters** 1 file from your solution files. Save the document as **Preparing for Natural Disasters 2**, followed by your initials.

2. Open the Natural Disasters Sources file from the drive and folder where your Data Files are stored.

3. Copy all the sources in the Current List for the Natural Disasters document to the Master List on your computer. Then close the Natural Disasters document without saving any changes.

4. Copy the following Centers for Disease Control and Prevention sources to Preparing for Natural Disasters 2 document.

   Develop a Family Disaster Plan
   Extreme Heat: A Prevention Guide to Promote Your Personal Health and Safety
   Key Facts About Flood Readiness
   Landslides and Mudslides
   Returning Home After a Disaster

5. Create the following new source for a Web site.
   Author: **Centers for Disease Control and Prevention** (Corporate Author)
   Name of Web Page: **Tornadoes: Being Prepared**
   Name of Web Site: **CDC.gov**
   Year: **2007**
   Month: **October**
   Day: **18**
   Year Accessed: **2010**
   Month Accessed: **April**
   Day Accessed: **26**
   URL: **http://emergency.cdc.gov/disasters/tornadoes/prepared.asp**

6. Edit the source Key Facts About Flood Readiness. The date for the Web page is **2009, March 27**. Update both lists.

7. Navigate to the end of the Floods section. Remove the source information. At the end of the last paragraph, insert a citation for **Key Facts About Flood Readiness**.

8. Navigate to the end of the Landslides section. Remove the source information. At the end of the last paragraph, insert a citation for **Landslides and Mudslides**.

9. Navigate to the end of the Tornadoes section. Remove the source information. At the end of the last paragraph, insert a citation for **Tornadoes: Being Prepared**.

10. Navigate to the end of the Extreme Heat section. Remove the source information. At the end of the last paragraph, insert a citation for **Extreme Heat: A Prevention Guide to Promote Your Personal Health and Safety**.

11. Navigate to the end of the Returning Home after a Disaster section. Remove the source information. At the end of the last paragraph, insert a citation for **Returning Home after a Disaster: Be Healthy and Safe**.

12. Insert a next page section break. Format the new section with a one-column format. Create a bibliography.

13. Save the changes and close the document.

PROJECT 14–4

1. Open the Soil file from the drive and folder where your Data Files are stored. Save the document as **Final Soil**, followed by your initials.

2. Select the heading *Pollution-Eating Bacteria* and apply paragraph formatting to keep the heading with the next line of text.

3. Repeat the paragraph format for the remaining four headings.

4. Select the heading *Soil Washing* and create a bookmark. Name the bookmark **soil_washing**.

5. Position the insertion point at the beginning of the second paragraph that begins *Liquids and solvents....* Insert a bookmark and name the bookmark **cleanup_costs**.

6. Use the Navigation Pane to find matches for PCBs. Insert a numbered footnote after the first occurrence. For the note, type **Polychlorinated biphenyls**.

7. Position the insertion point at the end of the third paragraph that ends *...puts people at risk*. Insert a numbered footnote. For the note, type **Direct contact and airborne migration**.

8. Click anywhere in the document. Find the acronym EPA. Insert a numbered footnote after the acronym. For the note, type **Environmental Protection Agency**.

9. Convert the footnotes to endnotes.

10. Save the changes and close the document.

■ CRITICAL THINKING

ACTIVITY 14–1

You learned in this lesson that you can change page formats for individual sections in a document. You have already practiced changing section formats for columns. The following is a list of other section formats that you can change. Pick three formats from this list and describe when and why you would change this format for only one section in a document and not the whole document.

- Margins
- Paper size or orientation
- Page borders
- Vertical alignment
- Page numbering
- Line numbering

ACTIVITY 14–2

A document is divided into three sections. The text in the first section in the document is formatted in two columns; the top and bottom margins are set to 1 inch, and the left and right margins are set to .5 inch. The text in the second section in the document is formatted in three columns; the top and bottom margins are set to .5 inch, and the left and right margins are set to 1 inch. The text in the third section in the document is formatted in one column, and the margins are all set to 1 inch. If the two section breaks are deleted, what column format and margin settings will apply?

LESSON 15

Creating Indexes and Tables of Contents, Figures, and Authorities

■ OBJECTIVES

Upon completion of this lesson, you should be able to:

■ Identify index entries and indicate a range of pages for an index entry.

■ Create an index entry for a cross-reference.

■ Generate and update an index.

■ Create a table of contents using heading styles.

■ Create a table of contents using fields.

■ Update a table of contents.

■ Insert captions and create a table of figures.

■ Create a table of authorities.

■ VOCABULARY

cross-reference

index

passim

table of authorities

table of contents

table of figures

When presented with a document of ten or more pages, readers usually like to survey the contents. They might be interested in a specific topic discussed in the document, or they might be looking for specific information referenced in the document. Lists of the topics, specific information, tables, and figures can help the reader navigate to specific areas in the document. Word provides several features to help you create these types of lists.

Creating and Updating an Index

▶ **VOCABULARY**

index

cross-reference

An *index* is an alphabetic listing of pertinent words and phrases that reference the page numbers where the related topics appear in the document. The index usually appears at the end of a document. An index is a valuable tool when it includes the right choice of entries. Index entries often include the main ideas and/or subjects of the document, various headings and subheadings, special terms, and acronyms.

The index is usually formatted with multiple levels of entries. The entries in the first level are called main entries. The entries in the second level are called subentries. Depending on the detail of the index, additional levels of subentries can be formatted.

Marking Index Entries Manually

Any word in a document can be marked (identified) as an index entry. You can mark index entries as you create the document, or after you finish writing the document. When you mark an index entry, a field is inserted at the location of the insertion point. The field is formatted as hidden text. To show these fields in the document as you work, the nonprinting formatting characters must be displayed. If you want to mark a range of pages for an index entry that spans multiple pages, you can mark a bookmark for the index entry. Because the bookmark identifies the range of text, the field for the index entry can be inserted anywhere in the document.

If the index entry is often referred to with another name or word, such as *MLA* and *Modern Language Association*, you can format a marked entry with text instead of a page number by creating a cross-reference. A **cross-reference** is a reference from one part of a document to related material in another part of the document. In an index, a cross-reference refers the reader to another index entry. Since the cross-reference does not refer to a specific page, you can insert the cross-reference field anywhere in the document. For example, you can insert a cross-reference when the need for one becomes evident as you work in the document, or you can insert all cross-references at the beginning or end of the document.

Step-by-Step 15.1

1. Open the **Apollo Missions 11-17** file from the drive and folder where your Data Files are stored. Save the document as **Apollo Missions 1**, followed by your initials.

2. If necessary, on the Home tab in the Paragraph group, click the **Show/Hide ¶** button to display nonprinting formatting characters. Also, if necessary, show the Navigation Pane.

3. Click the **File** tab, click **Options**, and then click **Display**. Under Always show these formatting marks on the screen, make sure that the Hidden text option is disabled. (If necessary, click the **check box** to remove the check mark.) Click **OK**.

4. Mark a main index entry by selecting text:

   a. In the Navigation Pane, click the **Apollo 11** heading. In the document window, select the words **Apollo 11**. (Do not include the paragraph mark in the selection.)

   b. Click the **References** tab. In the Index group, click the **Mark Entry** button. The Mark Index Entry dialog box opens, as shown in **Figure 15-1**. Notice that the selected text is displayed in the Main entry text box.

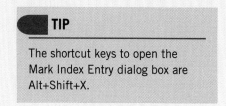

TIP

The shortcut keys to open the Mark Index Entry dialog box are Alt+Shift+X.

FIGURE 15-1
Mark Index Entry dialog box

   c. Under Page number format, enable the **Bold** and **Italic** options to format page number references in bold and italic in the index.

   d. Click **Mark**. The dialog box stays open, but the index entry field is inserted at the end of the selected text. If necessary, reposition the dialog box on the screen so you can see the field for the index entry, as shown in **Figure 15-2**.

Index entry field code   Switches indicating bold and italic formatting

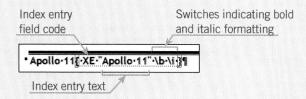

Index entry text

FIGURE 15-2
Index entry field

   e. Note the components in the field. The XE in the field stands for index entry. The index entry text is enclosed in quotation marks. A backslash (\) within the field is a switch that provides additional instructions for formatting the characters bold and italic.

5. Mark a main index entry without selecting text:

   a. In the Navigation Pane, click the **Apollo 12** heading. In the document window, position the insertion point at the end of the heading *Apollo 12*.

   b. Click the **title bar** for the Mark Index Entry dialog box. The current entry in the Main entry text box disappears. Click the **Main entry** text box and type **Apollo 12**. The Bold and Italic options should still be enabled.

   c. Click **Mark**. The index entry field is inserted in the document at the location of the insertion point.

6. Mark additional index entries:

   a. Navigate to the Apollo 13 section, and in the document window, select the **Apollo 13** heading. (Do not include the paragraph mark in the selection.)

   b. Click the **title bar** for the Mark Index Entry dialog box. The selected text appears in the Main entry text box.

   c. Click **Mark**.

   d. Repeat Steps 6a, 6b, and 6c to create index entries for the headings for the Apollo 14–17 sections.

7. Mark a subentry under a main entry:

   a. Navigate to the heading *Mission Objective* for Apollo 11.

   b. Click the **title bar** for the Mark Index Entry dialog box. Click the **Main entry** text box and type then **Apollo 11**.

   c. Position the insertion point in the Subentry text box and type **mission objective**.

   d. Click **Mark**. Note that in the XE field, the main entry text and the subentry text are separated by a colon, as shown in **Figure 15–3**.

FIGURE 15–3
Index entry field inserted into a document

Index entry field

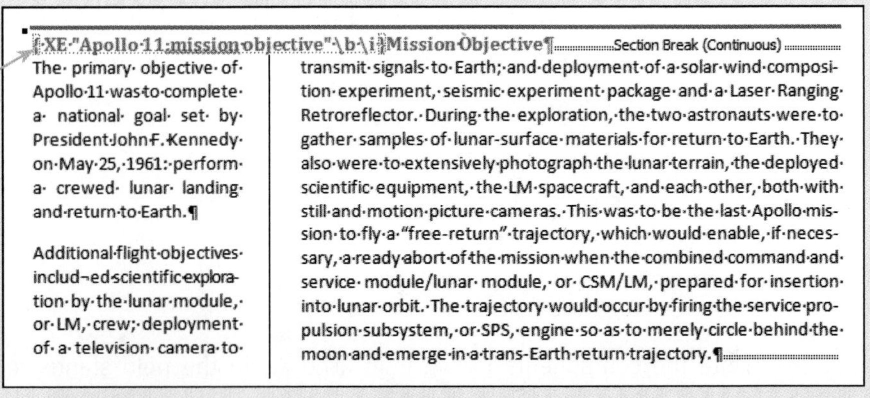

{ XE "Apollo 11:mission objective" \b \i }Mission Objective¶ ....Section Break (Continuous) ....

The· primary· objective· of· Apollo·11·was·to·complete· a· national· goal· set· by· President·John·F.·Kennedy· on·May·25,·1961:·perform· a· crewed· lunar· landing· and·return·to·Earth.¶

Additional·flight·objectives· includ¬ed·scientific·explora- tion· by· the·lunar·module,· or· LM,· crew;· deployment· of· a· television· camera· to·

transmit·signals·to·Earth;·and·deployment·of·a·solar·wind·composi- tion· experiment,· seismic· experiment· package· and· a· Laser· Ranging· Retroreflector.·During·the·exploration,·the·two·astronauts·were·to· gather·samples·of·lunar·surface·materials·for·return·to·Earth.·They· also·were·to·extensively·photograph·the·lunar·terrain,·the·deployed· scientific· equipment,· the· LM· spacecraft,· and· each· other,· both· with· still·and·motion·picture·cameras.·This·was·to·be·the·last·Apollo·mis- sion·to·fly·a·"free-return"·trajectory,·which·would·enable,·if·neces- sary,·a·ready·abort·of·the·mission·when·the·combined·command·and· service· module·/lunar· module,· or· CSM/LM,· prepared· for·insertion· into·lunar·orbit.·The·trajectory·would·occur·by·firing·the·service·pro- pulsion·subsystem,·or·SPS,·engine·so·as·to·merely·circle·behind·the· moon·and·emerge·in·a·trans-Earth·return·trajectory.¶...........

8. Repeat Steps 7a–8d to mark an additional subentry for the heading *Mission Highlights* for Apollo 11. Type **Apollo 11** as the main entry, and then type **mission highlights** for the subentry text.

9. Mark a level 3 subentry:

   a. Go to the top of the document and search for the first occurrence of *TV transmission*. It is in the Apollo 11 Mission Highlights section. In the document window, position the insertion point after the matched text.

   b. In the Mark Index Entry dialog box, type the main entry **Apollo 11**.

   c. In the Subentry text box, type **mission highlights:TV transmission**.

   d. Click **Mark**.

10. Mark an additional level 3 index subentry:

    a. Navigate to the heading *Apollo 15*, and then search for *lunar samples*. In the document window, position the insertion point after the match in the Apollo 15 section.

    b. In the Mark Index Entry dialog box, type the main entry **Apollo 15**.

    c. In the Subentry text box, type **mission highlights:lunar samples**.

    d. Click **Mark**.

11. Mark all instances of a specific word or text phrase:

    a. Move the insertion point to the top of the document and search for the first occurrence of *Neil Armstrong*. There are four matches.

    b. In the Search box, edit the search text to show only *Armstrong*. There are 14 matches and they are all in the Apollo 11 section. In the Navigation Pane, click the **Browse the results from your current search** button, and then click the first match.

    c. Click the **title bar** for the Mark Index Entry dialog box, and edit the main entry to show **Armstrong, Neil**.

    d. Click **Mark All**. An XE field is inserted after each of the 14 occurrences of the word *Armstrong*.

12. Create a bookmark to mark a range of pages:

    a. In the Navigation Pane, click the **Browse the headings in your document** button, and then click the **Apollo 17** heading. Select all the content for the Apollo 17 mission, including the heading. (The content spans across three pages.)

    b. Click the **Insert** tab. In the Links group, click the **Bookmark** button. In the Bookmark name box, type **Apollo_17** and then click **Add**.

    c. In the Mark Index Entry dialog box, if necessary, change the main entry to **Apollo 17**. In the subentry box, type **mission details**.

    d. Under Options, enable the **Page range** option.

    e. In the Bookmark text box, click the **list arrow** and select **Apollo _17**.

    f. Click **Mark**.

> **TIP**
>
> Typographical errors can affect the accuracy of your index. Proofread each index entry for which you type the entry text. If you find an error after you click Mark, position the insertion point in the field text in your document and make the necessary correction.

TIP

A bookmark name can be up to 40 characters, and it must begin with a letter. The bookmark name can contain only letters, numbers, and the underscore character; it cannot contain spaces.

13. Create a cross-reference to another index entry:

    a. Position the insertion point at the beginning of the document.

    b. In the Mark Index Entry dialog box, type the main entry **Sea of Tranquility**.

    c. Under Options, enable the **Cross-reference** option. In the Cross-reference text box, after *See*, type **lunar locations**.

    d. Click **Mark**.

14. Close the Mark Index Entry dialog box. Save the changes and then close the document.

AutoMarking Index Entries

To automatically mark entries, you must first create an Index AutoMark file to identify words to be included in the index. When you apply the AutoMark feature, Word automatically inserts codes for all occurrences of the words identified in the AutoMark file. Although AutoMarking is quick and convenient, the downside is that none of the index entries are customized.

Index entries are case sensitive, so you need to pay attention to lowercase and uppercase letters as you create index entries in the Index AutoMark file. For example, when *Crew* is capitalized in the document, it must be shown with initial caps when identifying the text to be marked. You must also make sure the capitalization is correct for main entries and subentries.

Step-by-Step 15.2

1. Open the **Index Entries** file from the drive and folder where your Data Files are stored. Save the document as **AutoMark Index Entries**, followed by your initials.

2. Note that the data in the left column identifies the words or phrases to be marked for the index. The data in the right column shows how the entries should appear in the index. Note that some of the entries include colons to distinguish subentries.

3. Note also that some of the cells at the bottom of the right column are blank. If the cell in the right column is blank, Word will create an entry exactly the same as the text in the left column.

4. Add the following additional entries in the blank cells at the end of the list.

Kennedy	**president:President John F. Kennedy**
Nixon	**president:President Richard M. Nixon**
Crew	**crew**
Backup Crew	**backup crew**

5. By default, the AutoCorrect settings enable the option to capitalize the first letter of sentences, so as you enter index entries, the first word is formatted with initial caps. Make corrections as needed so the capitalization is consistent with that shown in the right column in Step 4. Correct capitalization will avoid creating two main entries for the same word (such as *President* and *president*).

6. Save the changes and close the document.

7. Open the **Apollo Missions 1** document from your solution files and save the document as **Apollo Missions 2**, followed by your initials.

8. Click the **References** tab. In the Index group, click the **Insert Index** button to open the Index dialog box, as shown in **Figure 15–4**.

FIGURE 15–4
Index dialog box

9. Click **AutoMark**. Navigate to the drive and folder where your solution files are stored. Select the **AutoMark Index Entries** file and click **Open**.

10. Scroll through the document and you will see many new XE coded fields.

11. Save the changes and leave the document open for the next Step-by-Step.

Generating, Formatting, and Updating an Index

After all index entries have been marked, you can pull them together to create the index. This is often referred to as generating the index. You should make all changes and revisions to your document before you generate the index. If you make changes to the document after the index is created, the page number references in the index may no longer be correct; you will then need to update your index. When you update an index, you will lose any formatting you applied to the index.

Generally, you will format the index on a page by itself at the end of a document. Entries in the index are arranged in alphabetic order with letters inserted as separators to organize the list. Word offers nine built-in styles to help you format the index. An indented index displays all subentries indented below the main entry. To save space, a run-in index can be created, displaying subentries on the same line as the main entries.

The option to show nonprinting formatting characters should be disabled when you generate the index. If nonprinting characters are displayed, the hidden text (such as field codes) will be included in the pagination, which may result in incorrect page numbers in the index.

Step-by-Step 15.3

1. If necessary, open the **Apollo Missions 2** file from your solution files. Save the document as **Apollo Missions 3**, followed by your initials.

2. Position the insertion point at the end of the document, and insert a page break.

3. If necessary, click the **Home** tab. In the Paragraph group, click the **Show/Hide ¶** button to turn off the display of nonprinting formatting characters.

4. Click the **References** tab. In the Index group, click the **Insert Index** button. The Index dialog box opens.

5. Select format settings for the index:

   a. Scroll through the Print Preview pane. Note that the subentries are shown indented.

   b. To the right of Type:, enable the **Run-in** option. Scroll through the Print Preview pane. All the subentries are combined in one paragraph instead of appearing on separate lines. Enable the **Indented** option.

   c. Under the Print Preview pane, click the **Formats** list arrow and click each format to preview the available styles.

   d. In the Formats box, select **Formal**. Note that the Right align page numbers option is now enabled and a tab leader is inserted between the entry and the page number.

   e. Click **OK**. The index is inserted as a field at the position of the insertion point. Note that the page number formats are inconsistent: The AutoMark entries do not include the bold and italic formats.

6. Scroll to the top of the index and position the insertion point in front of the letter *A*. Press the **up arrow** to position the insertion point in the blank paragraph above the index.

7. Type **Index**. Without moving the insertion point, click the **Home** tab, and in the Styles group, click the **Heading 1** style.

8. In the index, note that the name of a backup crew member (Brand) is missing. If necessary, show the Navigation Pane. In the Navigation Pane, click the **Apollo 15** heading.

EXTRA FOR EXPERTS

You can modify the built-in style format *From template* by clicking the Modify button in the Index dialog box.

9. In the document window, in the Backup Crew column, select the name **Brand**. Click the **References** tab. In the Index group, click the **Mark Entry** button. The main entry box will display *Brand*. Edit the main entry to show **Brand, Vance DeVoe**. Enable the **Bold** and **Italic** options, and then click **Mark All**. Close the Mark Index Entry dialog box.

10. Click the **Home** tab. In the Paragraph group, click the **Show/Hide ¶** button to toggle off the display of nonprinting formatting characters.

11. In the Navigation Pane, click the **Index** heading. To update the index, click anywhere inside the index to select the field containing the index. Click the **References** tab, and in the Index group, click the **Update Index** button. The index is updated and now the name *Brand* appears under the letter *B*.

12. Note that when you updated the index, the heading style was removed from the title above the index. Click anywhere in the Index title. Click the **Home** tab. In the Styles group, click the **Heading 1** style.

13. Save the changes and leave the document open for the next Step-by-Step.

> **TIP**
>
> Alternatives to clicking the Update Index button: press F9, or right-click anywhere within the index and select Update Field in the shortcut menu.

Creating and Updating a Table of Contents

> ▶ **VOCABULARY**
> **table of contents**

A **table of contents** shows a sequential order of the contents contained within the document, providing an overview of the topics in a document. In Print Layout view, you can use the table of contents to quickly locate page numbers for specific information. In Web Layout view, the entries in the table of contents are formatted as hyperlinks. When you click a hyperlink, the insertion point moves to that section of the document.

Each entry in the table of contents is formatted on a separate line. The entry name is separated from the page number by a tab character. You can choose from nine built-in styles.

If you plan to include both an index and a table of contents in your final document, you should create the index first so the page numbers for the index can be included in the table of contents.

Using Heading Styles to Create a Table of Contents

A table of contents can be created based on heading styles already applied within a document. These heading styles may be built-in heading styles supplied by Word or outline-level styles assigned when you create a document in outline format. When Word's heading styles are already applied in the document, Word will recognize the styles and generate the table of contents based on the first three levels of headings.

The option to show nonprinting formatting characters should be disabled when you generate the table of contents. If nonprinting characters are displayed, the hidden text (such as field codes) will be included in the pagination. With hidden text included, page numbers in the table of contents may be inaccurate. If you edit the document after generating the table of contents, be sure to update the table of contents to ensure page numbers and headings are accurate.

Step-by-Step 15.4

1. If necessary, open the **Apollo Missions 3** file from your solution files. Save the document as **Apollo Missions 4**, followed by your initials. If necessary, turn off the display of nonprinting formatting characters. Also, if necessary, show the Navigation Pane.

2. Position the insertion point at the beginning of the document, and insert a page break. Then once again position the insertion point at the top of the document.

3. Click the **References** tab. In the Table of Contents group, click the **Table of Contents** button to open the Table of Contents gallery, as shown in **Figure 15–5**.

FIGURE 15–5
Table of Contents gallery

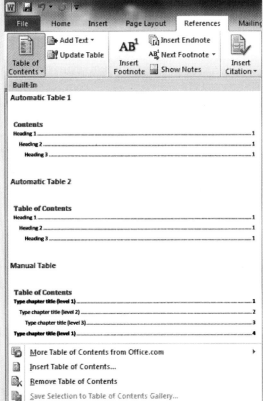

4. At the bottom of the list, click **Insert Table of Contents** to open the Table of Contents dialog box, as shown in **Figure 15–6**. Note that the dialog box provides two preview panes: Print Preview and Web Preview.

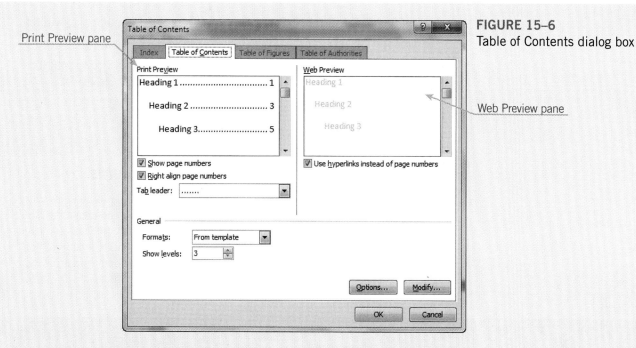

Print Preview pane

Web Preview pane

FIGURE 15–6
Table of Contents dialog box

5. Under General, click the **Formats** list arrow and preview some of the styles in both panes. Then select the **Formal** style. Because you chose the Formal style, the Right align page numbers option and the Tab leader options are enabled.

6. The document uses three levels of headings, so no other changes are necessary. Click **OK**. The table of contents is inserted as a field.

7. Position the insertion point at the top of the document, in front of the table of contents. Type **Table of Contents** and press **Enter**. Do not be concerned that the text appears in all caps. Position the insertion point anywhere in the new paragraph. Click the **Home** tab, and then in the Styles group, click the **Heading 1** style.

8. Note in the table of contents that the heading *Apollo 11* appears on page three. In the Navigation Pane, collapse the Apollo 11 heading and then drag the heading and position it in front of the Apollo 15 heading.

9. Navigate back to the top of the document. Notice that the page number for Apollo 11 did not change. Click anywhere in the table of contents field to select it. Click the **References** tab. In the Table of Contents group, click the **Update Table** button. A prompt opens and the Update page numbers only option is enabled. Click **OK**. Note that the page number is changed to 16. Also note that the heading format did not change.

10. Click the **Undo** button to restore the table of contents before the update. Click the **Undo** button again to restore the Apollo 11 heading and the related content back to its previous location in the document.

11. Save the changes to the document.

12. Position the insertion point at the beginning of the document. Switch to Web Layout view. The entries in the table of contents are displayed as hyperlinks. Hold down **Ctrl** and click one of the links to go to that location in the document.

13. Close the document.

Inserting Fields to Create a Table of Contents

If your document does not have obvious headings for every table of contents entry (or if your headings are not formatted with heading styles), you can create the table of contents using fields. The TC field is used to identify the entry (the text and page number) to appear in the table of contents. By default, Word builds a table of contents by styles. When you insert fields to identify the table of contents entries, you must change this default setting before compiling the table of contents.

Step-by-Step 15.5

1. Open the **Financial Review** file from the drive and folder where your Data Files are stored. Save the document as **Revised Financial Review**, followed by your initials.

2. On the Home tab, in the Paragraph group, toggle on the display of non-printing formatting characters so you will see the table of contents field entries as you create them. The entries will be formatted as hidden text.

3. Add a Level 1 table of contents entry in a field:

   a. Position the insertion point at the end of the heading *FINANCIAL PERFORMANCE AND SOLVENCY*. The page number will be referenced to this location.

   b. Click the **Insert** tab. In the Text group, click the **Quick Parts** button and then click **Field** to open the Field dialog box, as shown in **Figure 15–7**.

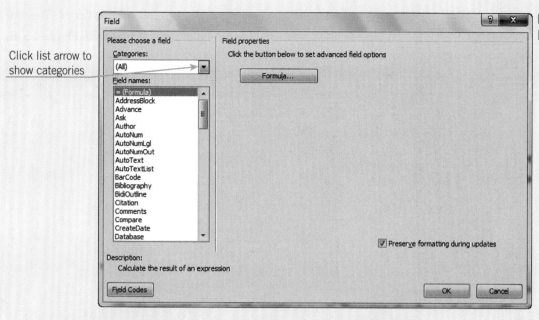

Click list arrow to show categories

FIGURE 15–7
Field dialog box

c. Click the **Categories** list arrow and then select **Index and Tables**.

d. Under Field names, select **TC** (not TOC).

e. In the center pane, under Field properties, position the insertion point in the Text entry box. Type **FINANCIAL PERFORMANCE AND SOLVENCY**.

f. Click **OK**. A field with the TC code is inserted at the location of the insertion point.

4. Position the insertion point after the heading *ACCOUNTING SYTEMS*. Repeat Steps 3b–3f to create a Level 1 table of contents entry. For the text entry, type **ACCOUNTING SYSTEMS**.

5. Add a Level 2 table of contents entry in a field:

a. Position the insertion point at the end of the heading *Chart of Accounts*. In the Text group, click the **Quick Parts** button and then click **Field**.

b. In the Field dialog box, under Field names, select **TC**. In the Text entry box, type **Chart of Accounts**.

c. Under Field options, enable the **Outline level** option, and then in the text box, type **2**.

   d. In the lower-left corner of the dialog box, click **Field Codes**. The dialog box changes to display the field codes as shown in **Figure 15–8**.

FIGURE 15–8
Field dialog box with field
codes displayed

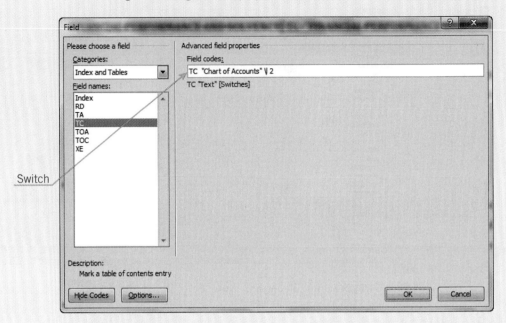

Switch

   e. The codes that Word uses to identify the table of contents entry are displayed in the Field codes box. Notice that the code includes the switch \l2.

   f. Click **Hide codes**. Click **OK**.

6. Position the insertion point at the end of the heading *General Ledger*. Repeat Steps 5a and 5b to create a Level 2 table of contents entry. In the Text entry box, type **General Ledger** and set the Outline level to **2**. Click **OK**.

7. Position the insertion point at the end of the heading *Accounts Payable*. Repeat Steps 5a and 5b to create a level 3 table of contents entry. In the Text entry box, type **Accounts Payable**. Enable the **Outline level** option, and then in the text box, type **3**. Click **OK**.

8. Position the insertion point at the end of the heading *Accounts Receivable*. Repeat Steps 5a and 5b to create a level 3 table of contents entry. In the Text entry box, type **Accounts Receivable**. Enable the **Outline level** option, and in the text box, type **3**. Click **OK**.

9. Scroll through the remaining pages of the document. You will see that fields have already been inserted for the remaining headings. Position the insertion point at the beginning of the document. Insert a page break, and then position the insertion point at the beginning of the document again (in front of the Page Break line).

10. Click the **Home** tab. In the Paragraph group, click the **Show/Hide ¶** button to turn off the display of nonprinting formatting characters.

11. Click the **References** tab. In the Table of Contents group, click the **Table of Contents** button, and then click **Insert Table of Contents**. The Table of Contents dialog box opens. In the dialog box, click **Options** to open the Table of Contents Options dialog box, as shown in **Figure 15–9**.

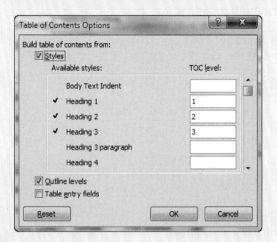

FIGURE 15–9
Table of Contents Options dialog box

12. Enable the **Table entry fields** option. Click **OK** twice to accept the changes and close the dialog boxes. The table of contents is inserted at the location of the insertion point.

13. Position the insertion point at the top of the document, in front of the table of contents field. Type **Table of Contents** and then press **Enter**. Do not be concerned if the text you entered appears in all caps. Position the insertion point anywhere within the new heading. Click the **Home** tab. In the Styles group, click the **Title** style.

14. Save the changes and close the document.

Updating a Table of Contents

If changes are made in the document after the table of contents is created, changes may also be necessary in the table of contents. If the pagination changes, the page references in the table of contents may be incorrect. If headings were edited or deleted, or new headings were added, the list of headings in the table of contents would need to be edited. Updating the table of contents is quick and easy. You simply update the field.

The page on which the table of contents appears should be numbered separately from the rest of the document. Usually, page numbers for front matter, such as a table of contents, are formatted in lowercase Roman numerals. Therefore, when you format page numbers, you need to format the table of contents page(s) in a different section so it will have its own page number formats.

Step-by-Step 15.6

1. Open the **Apollo Missions 4** file from your solution files. Save the document as **Apollo Missions 5**, followed by your initials. Toggle on the display of nonprinting formatting characters.

2. Position the insertion point in front of the Page Break line below the table of contents and press **Delete**. Then click the **Page Layout** tab. In the Page Setup group, click the **Breaks** button. Under Section Breaks, click **Next Page**.

3. Position the insertion point on the first page, anywhere above the section break. Note that the number 1 appears in the footer pane. Click the **Insert** tab. In the Header & Footer group, click the **Footer** button, and then click **Edit Footer**. The Ribbon adapts to show more features.

4. In the Header & Footer group, click the **Page Number** button, and then click **Format Page Numbers** to open the Page Number Format dialog box, as shown in **Figure 15–10**.

FIGURE 15–10
Page Number Format dialog box

Click list arrow to change number format

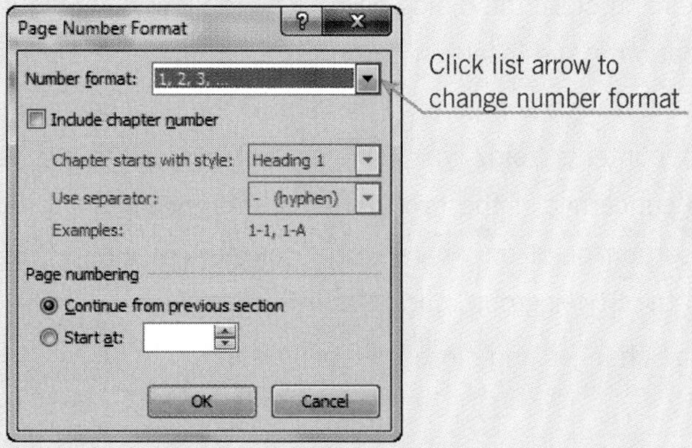

5. Click the **Number format** list arrow and then select **i, ii, iii, ...**. Click **OK**. Note that the number style changes in the document window.

6. Scroll down to the second page in the document, and then double-click in the footer pane.

7. In the Header & Footer group, click the **Page Number** button and then click **Format Page Numbers** to open the Page Number Format dialog box. Under Page numbering, enable the **Start at** option. In the text box, make sure the number 1 is displayed. Click **OK**. The number 1 appears at the bottom of the second page in the document.

8. On the Header & Footer Tools Design tab, in the Options group, enable the **Different First Page** option. With this setting enabled, a page number will not print on the first page of this section.

9. Double-click anywhere in the document window to make it active. Turn off the display of nonprinting formatting characters.

10. Navigate to the first page and click anywhere in the table of contents to select it. Click the **References** tab. In the Table of Contents group, click the **Update Table** button. When prompted to update the page numbers or to update the entire table of contents, make sure the Update page numbers only option is enabled and click **OK**. The table of contents is updated and now shows the heading *INTRODUCTION* on page 1.

11. Save the changes and close the document.

Creating a Table of Figures

A table of figures is similar to a table of contents. A ***table of figures*** provides a sequential list of all the figures (such as tables, equations, pictures, charts, graphs, and other illustrations) included in a document. This list can be very useful when a document contains several illustrations.

> ▶ **VOCABULARY**
> **table of figures**

Before you create a table of figures, the figures in your document must be formatted with captions. As you have already learned, a caption is a label that identifies a figure, and Word automatically updates the caption numbers as you add captions in the document. However, when you delete or move a caption, you must manually update the captions. The caption is not attached to the figure, so when you copy and paste a figure, make sure you include the caption in the selection.

Inserting an AutoCaption

Word offers three different options for caption labels (Equation, Figure, or Table). You can customize the caption label by changing the label name, choosing where the caption appears, and changing the format of the caption number. Word automatically assigns consecutive numbers to captions. You can enable a setting to automatically add a caption each time you insert an object (such as a table or graphic) in the document.

Step-by-Step 15.7

1. Open the **Calories** files from the drive and folder where your Data Files are stored. You do not need to save the file in your solutions folder.

2. Open the **Nutrition Facts** file from the drive and folder where your Data Files are stored. Save the document as **Revised Nutrition Facts**, followed by your initials.

3. Click the **References** tab. In the Captions group, click the **Insert Caption** button to open the Caption dialog box, as shown in **Figure 15–11**.

FIGURE 15–11
Caption dialog box

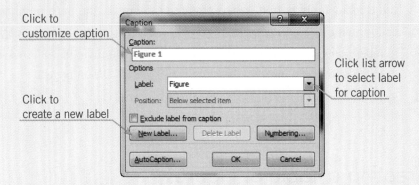

Click to customize caption

Click to create a new label

Click list arrow to select label for caption

4. Click the **Label** list arrow and then select **Table**. Note that the Caption box shows *Table 1*. Click **Numbering** to open the Caption Numbering box. Click the **Format** list arrow and then select **A,B,C…**. Click **OK**. Note that the Caption box now shows *Table A*.

5. Click **AutoCaption** to open the AutoCaption dialog box. Under Add caption when inserting, scroll down and enable the **Microsoft Word Table** option, as shown in **Figure 15–12**. (Make sure the check mark appears in the box.) Note that captions are not limited to figures and tables. With this setting enabled, Word will automatically add captions to all Word tables as they are inserted, and the setting applies to all Word documents.

FIGURE 15–12
AutoCaption dialog box

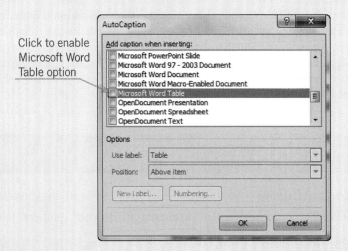

Click to enable Microsoft Word Table option

6. Under Options, the Use label box should already show **Table**. If necessary, in the Position box, select **Above item**. Click **OK**.

7. Switch to the **Calories** document and copy the first table (green/vegetables) to the Clipboard. Switch to the **Revised Nutrition Facts** document. Position the insertion point in the blank paragraph after the second paragraph in the body of the document. Paste the table.

8. Note that the caption *Table A* appears above the inserted table. Position the insertion point after the letter *A* in the caption, press the **spacebar**, and then type **Vegetable Calories**.

9. Switch to the **Calories** document. Copy the second table (blue/nuts) to the Clipboard. Switch to the **Revised Nutrition Facts** document, and then paste the table in the blank paragraph at the end of the document.

10. Note that the caption *Table B* appears above the inserted table. Edit the caption by adding **Nut Calories**.

11. Switch to the **Calories** document. Copy the third table (orange/fruits) to the Clipboard. Switch to the **Revised Nutrition Facts** document, and paste the table in the blank paragraph after the third paragraph in the body of the document.

12. Note that the caption *Table B* appears above the inserted table. Scroll down and you will see that the caption for the third table in the document was updated to show the caption *Table C*. Go back to Table B and edit the caption by adding **Fruit Calories**.

13. If necessary, click the **References** tab. In the Captions group, click the **Insert Caption** button and then click **AutoCaption** to open the AutoCaption dialog box. Disable the **Microsoft Word Table** option. Click **OK**.

14. Save the changes to the Revised Nutrition Facts document. Close both documents.

> **TIP**
>
> To copy the table to the Clipboard, point to the upper-left corner of the table and then click the Table Selector icon to select the table. Then click the Copy button (or press Ctrl+C).

Inserting a Customized Caption

If desired, you can create a new label to add to the list of labels for captions. For example, instead of referring to the figure as a table, you may want the caption to show a different label, such as Illustration or Graphic.

Step-by-Step 15.8

1. Open the **Apollo Missions 5** file from your solution files. Save the document as **Apollo Missions 6**, followed by your initials. If necessary, show the Navigation Pane and nonprinting formatting characters.

2. Navigate to the heading *Apollo 12*. Position the insertion point in the blank paragraph below the table of crew members.

3. Click the **References** tab. In the Captions group, click the **Insert Caption** button to open the Caption dialog box.

4. Under Options, click the **Label** list arrow and select **Table**. Click **Numbering**, select **1,2,3**, and then click **OK**.

5. Click the **Caption** text box. The insertion point is positioned to the right of the caption label *Table 1*. Press the **spacebar**, and then type **Apollo 12 Crew Members**. Click **OK**. The caption text is inserted at the insertion point.

6. Navigate to the heading *Apollo 11* and position the insertion point in the blank paragraph below the table of crew members. In the Captions group, click the **Insert Caption** button. In the Caption text box, press the **spacebar** and then type **Apollo 11 Crew Members**. Click **OK**. Note that the caption shows *Table 1*.

7. Navigate to the heading *Apollo 12*. Note that the caption shows *Table 2*. Word automatically adjusted the table number.

8. Navigate to each of the remaining Apollo headings (13–17) and insert a table caption under the crew information using the text *Apollo XX Crew Members* and replacing the *XX* with the appropriate mission number.

9. Navigate to the heading *Apollo 11*. Position the insertion point in the blank paragraph below the graphic of the Apollo 11 patch.

10. In the Captions group, click the **Insert Caption** button. Click **New Label** to open the New Label dialog box. Type **Illustration** and click **OK**. Note that the Caption box now shows *Illustration 1*. Click the **Label** list arrow. The new label *Illustration* appears in the list.

11. Click the **Caption** text box. Press the **spacebar** and type **Apollo 11 Mission Patch**. Click **OK**. Press **Ctrl+E** to center the caption.

12. Navigate to each of the remaining Apollo headings (12–17) and insert and center an illustration caption under the mission patch. Use the text *Apollo XX Mission Patch* and replace the *XX* with the appropriate mission number.

13. Save the changes and leave the document open for the next Step-by-Step.

Inserting a Table of Figures

Creating a table of figures is similar to creating a table of contents. One distinctive difference, though, is that the table of figures is based on captions instead of fields, so if new captions are added to the document, even though the caption numbers are automatically updated, the table of figures cannot be updated. If the document is edited, you must replace the existing table of figures with a new table.

In Print Layout view, you can use the table of figures to quickly locate a specific illustration by identifying the page number where the illustration appears. In Web Layout view, the entries in the table of figures are formatted as hyperlinks, which you can use to quickly navigate to an illustration.

You can create multiple tables of figures in the same document. For example, you can create a table of illustrations and a table of figures. There is no hidden text related to figure captions; therefore, the pagination is not affected. However, if the document includes other hidden text, you need to turn off the display of nonprinting characters before compiling the table of figures.

Step-by-Step 15.9

1. If necessary, open the **Apollo Missions 6** file from your solution files. Save the document as **Apollo Missions 7**, followed by your initials.

2. Position the insertion point at the end of the document. Insert a page break. Type **List of Tables** and press **Enter**. Toggle off the display of non-printing formatting characters.

3. Click the **References** tab. In the Captions group, click the **Insert Table of Figures** button to open the Table of Figures dialog box, as shown in **Figure 15–13**. Notice that the dialog box includes two preview panes: Print Preview and Web Preview.

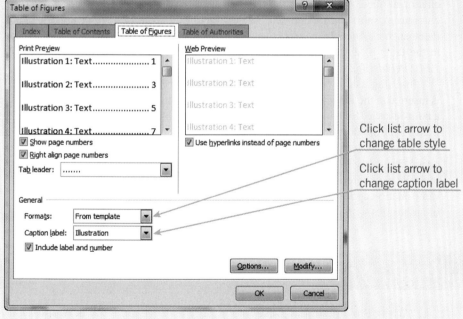

FIGURE 15–13
Table of Figures dialog box

4. Under General, click the **Formats** list arrow and select **Formal**. Click the **Caption label** list arrow and select **Table**. Click **OK**. A list of the seven tables is inserted at the location of the insertion point.

5. Press **Enter** two times. Type **List of Illustrations** and press **Enter**. Click the **Insert Table of Figures** button. In the Formats box, make sure the Formal style is selected. In the Caption label box, select **Illustration**. Click **OK**. A list of the seven illustrations is inserted at the location of the insertion point.

6. Save the changes to the document.

7. Switch to Web Layout view. Hold down **Ctrl** and click one of the links to navigate to a table or illustration. Because the width of the page is expanded in this view, the table caption does not appear below the table.

8. Close the document.

Creating a Table of Authorities

A table of authorities is often used in the legal profession. A *table of authorities* summarizes the references used in a legal document. The references might be cases, statutes, rules, or other sources. When completed, the table of authorities closely resembles a table of contents. Because of the variety of reference types, when you mark each reference, you can specify a category. Then when the table of authorities is created, the references can be organized by categories.

Before you can create a table of authorities, you must insert fields to mark the citations (references to specific legal cases, statutes, or other legal documents) in the document. You mark citations in much the same way you mark index entries. You can mark an individual reference to a citation, or you can mark all references to a citation at once. As you enter the required fields, you can create both short and long citations. A short citation indicates the text you want Word to search for in the document, such as *Johnston v. IVAC Corp.* A long citation shows the text as it will appear in the table of authorities, such as *Johnston v. IVAC Corp., 885 F.2d 1574, 1577, 12 USPQ2d 1382, 1384 (Fed. Cir. 1989).*

Inserting a table of authorities is similar to inserting a table of figures. The table is inserted at the location of the insertion point. Like tables of figures, you can choose a built-in style. Like indexes and tables of contents, a table of authorities is based on fields, so if the document is edited, the table of authorities can easily be updated.

The word *passim* is used to indicate that terms, passages, or page references occur frequently in the work cited. In Word, the default setting *Use passim* formats multiple page references on the same line in a table of authorities. For example, if the same citation appears on pages 2 and 3, the citation will appear only once in the table of authorities with a reference to both page numbers.

Step-by-Step 15.10

1. Open the **Freedman Case** file from the drive and folder where your Data Files are stored. Save the document as **Freedman Case Summary**, followed by your initials. If necessary, show nonprinting formatting characters.

2. In the first paragraph, select **Lanham Act § 43(a), 15 U.S.C. 1125(a) (1982)**. Click the **References** tab. In the Table of Authorities group, click the **Mark Citation** button to open the Mark Citation dialog box, as shown in **Figure 15–14**. Your settings may differ. Note that the text you selected in the document window appears in both the Selected text and the Short citation boxes.

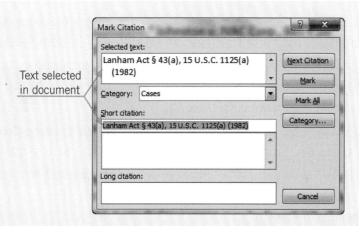

FIGURE 15–14
Mark Citation dialog box

Text selected in document

3. In the Category box, select **Statutes**. Click **Mark All**. Note that the selected text now appears in the Long Citation box, and this is how the citation will appear in the table of authorities. A TA field containing the citation text is inserted into the document. Leave the Mark Citation dialog box open. Reposition the dialog box on the screen so you can see the document window.

4. Click in the document window, and in the first paragraph, select **Minnesota Deceptive Trade Practices Act ("MDTPA"), Minn. Stat. § 325D.44**. Then click the **title bar** for the Mark Citation dialog box. *Statutes* is already selected in the Category box. Click **Mark All**.

5. In the second paragraph, select **Johnston v. IVAC Corp., 885 F.2d 1574, 1577, 12 USPQ2d 1382, 1384 (Fed. Cir. 1989)**.

6. In the Mark Citation dialog box, click the **Category** list arrow and then select **Cases**.

7. Click anywhere in the Short Citation box and then use the left arrow key to position the insertion point after the period in the word *Corp.*. Beginning with the comma, delete all characters to the right so that the short citation box displays only *Johnston v. IVAC Corp*. Then click **Mark All**. Word will search for and mark all occurrences of the short citation. Note that the full citation still appears in the Long Citation box, as shown in **Figure 15–15**.

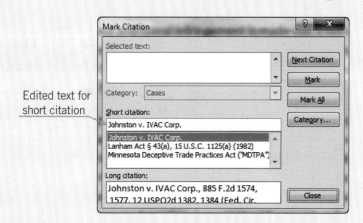

FIGURE 15–15
Mark Citation dialog box with an edited short citation

Edited text for short citation

8. At the end of the second paragraph, select **Becton Dickinson & Co. v. C.R. Bard, Inc., 922 F.2d 792, 795-96 (Fed. Cir. 1990)**. In the Mark Citation dialog box, *Cases* is already selected in the Category box. Edit the Short Citation box to show only *Becton Dickinson & Co. v. C.R. Bard, Inc.*, and then click **Mark All**.

9. At the end of the fourth paragraph, select **Wilson Sporting Goods Co. v. David Geoffrey & Assoc., 904 F. 2d 677, 683, 14 USPQ2d 1942, 1947-48 (Fed. Cir. 1990)** and create a case citation. Edit the short citation to display *Wilson Sporting Goods Co. v. David Geoffrey & Assoc.*. Then click **Mark All**.

10. Close the Mark Citation dialog box. Toggle off the display of nonprinting formatting characters.

11. Position the insertion point at the beginning of the document, and insert a page break. Again, position the insertion point at the beginning of the document. Type **Table of Authorities** and press **Enter**.

12. Click the **References** tab. In the Table of Authorities group, click the **Insert Table of Authorities** button to open the dialog box shown in **Figure 15–16**. Your settings will differ.

FIGURE 15–16
Table of Authorities dialog box

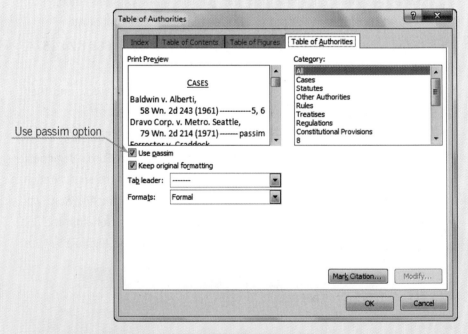

13. Under Category, make sure that **All** is selected. In the Formats box, select **Formal**. The Use passim option should be enabled. Click **OK**. The table of authorities is inserted at the location of the insertion point. Note that the *Johnston v. IVAC Corp.* case appears only once in the table of authorities and shows two page references.

14. Save the changes and close the document.

SUMMARY

In this lesson, you learned:

- To create an index, you must first mark the index entries.

- Word enables you to format bookmarks and cross-references to create customized index entries.

- If a document is revised, you can quickly update the fields in an index.

- You can use Word's heading styles or outline-level styles to create a table of contents, or you can create a table of contents using fields.

- If edits are made in the document that affect pagination or headings, the table of contents can be easily updated.

- Word's caption feature enables you to label and automatically number figures throughout a document.

- When the figures in a document include captions, you can automatically create a table of figures.

- To create a table of authorities, you must first mark the citations. Marking citations is similar to marking index entries.

VOCABULARY REVIEW

Define the following terms:

cross-reference	passim	table of contents
index	table of authorities	table of figures

REVIEW QUESTIONS

TRUE / FALSE

Circle T if the statement is true or F if the statement is false.

T F **1.** If you plan to include both an index and a table of contents in your final document, you should create the table of contents first.

T F **2.** To create a table of figures, you must apply captions to the figures.

T F **3.** To format the table of contents page numbers differently from the other pages in the document, you need to create a new section for the table of contents.

T F **4.** A cross-reference in an index is an entry followed by text instead of a page number.

T F **5.** When you delete or move captions in a document, Word automatically updates all the caption numbers in the document.

MULTIPLE CHOICE

Select the best response for the following statements.

1. When you _____, Word automatically performs an update.

   A. mark an index entry   C. apply a new heading style

   B. add a caption   D. insert a citation

2. When marking citations for a table of authorities, the _____ shows the text as it will appear in the table of authorities.

   A. long citation   C. TA field

   B. short citation   D. citation category

3. When creating a(n) _____, you can specify a category to organize the entries.

   A. index   C. table of contents

   B. table of figures   D. table of authorities

4. A(n) _____ is an alphabetical listing of pertinent words and phrases contained in a document.

   A. index   C. table of authorities

   B. table of figures   D. table of contents

5. _____ are case sensitive.

   A. Citations   C. Captions

   B. Table of contents entries   D. Index entries

WRITTEN QUESTIONS

Write a brief answer to the following questions.

1. What are the advantages to creating a table of contents based on the heading styles in a document?

2. Why would you use the run-in option when formatting an index?

3. Why would you show a table of figures in Web Layout view?

4. Why would you create a bookmark for an index entry?

5. When generating a table of figures, should the display of nonprinting formatting characters be on or off, and why?

■ PROJECTS

If you have a SAM 2010 user profile, your instructor may have assigned an autogradable version of the indicated project. If so, log into the SAM 2010 Web site at *www.cengage.com/sam2010* to download the instruction and start files.

PROJECT 15–1

1. Open the **Foreign Trade** file from the drive and folder where your Data Files are stored. Save the document as **Revised Foreign Trade**, followed by your initials.

2. Create a new label **Chart** for captions.

3. Read the content above the first chart to create an appropriate customized caption, and then, using the Chart label, insert a caption in the blank paragraph below the chart. Center the caption.

4. Using the Chart label, create and insert custom captions below the other two charts. Center the captions.

5. Insert a table of figures on a new page at the end of the document using the Simple format. Add the heading **TABLE OF FIGURES** above the table in bold and centered formatting.

6. Save, print, and close the document.

7. Exit Word. If prompted to save changes to the Normal global template, click No.

⋏SAM PROJECT 15–2

1. Launch Word and open the **Natural Disasters** file from the drive and folder where your Data Files are stored. Save the document as **Revised Natural Disasters 1**, followed by your initials.

2. Mark main index entries for each of the following phrases where they occur in the level 2 headings. Use the same capitalization shown below. Do not format the page numbers for the index entries in bold and italic.

   Floods
   Landslides
   Tornadoes
   Extreme Heat
   Wildfires

3. Navigate to the Prepare a Family Disaster Plan section. Create a subentry index entry for the heading *Create a Plan*. The main entry text should show **Family Disaster Plan**. The subentry text should show **Create a Plan**.

4. Create a second subentry for the Family Disaster Plan section. Select the **Practice Your Plan** heading. The main entry text should show **Family Disaster Plan**. The subentry text should show **Practice Your Plan**.

5. Create a cross-reference in the index. Use **mudslides** for the main entry. Use **landslides** for the cross-reference text.

6. The document already has field entries for three bookmarks. Create an index entry for each of the bookmarks:

   a. Use the main entry **Family Disaster Plan** to create an index for the bookmark **family_disaster_plan**.

   b. Use the main entry **Natural Disasters and Severe Weather** to create an index entry for the bookmark **natural_disasters_severe_weather**.

   c. Use the main entry **Returning Home After a Disaster** to create an index entry for the bookmark **returning_home**.

7. Open the **Disaster Index Entries** file from the drive and folder where your Data Files are stored. Save the document as **Updated Disaster Index Entries**, followed by your initials.

8. Add the following index entries to the list. Be sure to use the capitalization exactly as shown below. When the new entries are completed, save the changes and close the document.

Health Threats	**health threats**
Emergency Supplies	**emergency supplies**
Evacuate	**evacuate**
hazards	**hazards**
Intense Storms and Rainfall	**intense storms and rainfall**
Funnel Cloud	**funnel cloud**
American Red Cross	**American Red Cross**

9. AutoMark the index entries stored in the Updated Disaster Index Entries file.

10. Insert a page break at the end of the document. Type **INDEX** and press Enter. Apply the Heading 1 style to the new heading.

11. Position the insertion point in the blank paragraph after the heading *INDEX*. Toggle off the nonprinting formatting characters, and then generate an indented index using the Modern style.

12. Save the changes and leave the document open for the next project.

PROJECT 15–3

1. If necessary, open the **Revised Natural Disasters 1** file from your solution files. Save the document as **Revised Natural Disasters 2**, followed by your initials. Toggle on the nonprinting formatting characters.

2. Insert a Next Page section break at the beginning of the document. Position the insertion point at the top of the document. Type **Table of Contents** and then press Enter two times.

3. Select the heading and the blank paragraph below the heading. Apply the Normal style, then change the font size to 14 point and apply the bold format. With the text and blank paragraph still selected, use the Line and Paragraph Spacing button to remove the space after the paragraphs.

4. Deselect the text and position the insertion point in the blank paragraph below the new heading. Toggle off nonprinting formatting characters, and then insert a table of contents using the Distinctive style, showing 3 levels. If the table of contents does not fit on one page, click anywhere in the field to select it and then remove the space before the paragraph.

5. Use the Page Number button on the Insert tab to insert a Plain Number 3 style page number at the bottom of the first section in the document, the table of contents page. Then format the page number in the i, ii, iii number format.

6. In the next section of the document that begins with the heading *EMERGENCY PREPAREDNESS*, use the Page Number button to format the page numbers in the second section of the document. Continue to use the Plain Number 3 style, but change the number format to the 1, 2, 3 format. Set the numbers to start at 1. Then format the footer with a different first page setting so that the page number does not appear on the first page in that section.

7. Save the changes and close the document.

PROJECT 15–4

1. Open the **Fohey Case** file from the drive and folder where your Data Files are stored. Save the document as **Fohey Case Summary**, followed by your initials.

2. Locate and mark all occurrences of the following citations in the document. Notice that there are two categories of citations. For the case citations, create a short citation using the italicized text.

Statute:
17 U.S.C. § 117(a)(1)

Cases:
Universal City Studios, Inc. v. Corley, 273 F.3d 429, 438-39 (2d Cir.2001)
Aymes v. Bonelli, 47 F.3d 23, 26 (2d Cir. 1995)

3. Insert a page break at the beginning of the document, and then generate a table of authorities on a separate page at the beginning of the document, using the Distinctive style and with the Use passim option enabled.

4. Enter the heading **Table of Authorities** above the table. The heading should be centered with bold and italic formatting.

5. Save and close the document.

■ CRITICAL THINKING

ACTIVITY 15–1

In this lesson, you used hyperlinks to navigate throughout a document. Do you usually review documents online, or do you prefer to read hard copies of the document? Write a short paragraph explaining your preference for reading documents.

ACTIVITY 15–2

You need to create an index for a five-page document. What do you think would be better—creating the index entries by manually marking them or by AutoMarking the index entries? Write a short paragraph about which feature you would use to create the index entries and explain your reasoning.

LESSON 16

Working with Macros

■ OBJECTIVES

Upon completion of this lesson, you should be able to:

- Create a macro-enabled document.
- Name, store, record, and run a macro.
- Choose a macro security setting.
- Create a document template to store macros.
- Create shortcuts to run macros.
- Edit macros.
- Copy, delete, and rename macro projects.
- Add a digital signature to a macro project.

■ VOCABULARY

code

macro

macro project

VBA (Visual Basic for Applications)

virus

ADVANCED Microsoft Word Unit

As you work with documents, you most likely perform some repetitive tasks such as creating customized headers and footers or setting page margins and paper sizes. Although Word provides several features to make these tasks easy, you must still perform multiple actions to complete the tasks. In this lesson, you will learn how to turn these multiple actions into a single step.

Understanding Macros

A **macro** is a group of sequential commands and actions combined as a single command to automatically complete a task. Word provides numerous macros that are ready for you to use. For example, each time you use the building blocks to insert a page number, all the actions to create and format the header or footer are completed automatically. Creating your own macros enables you to automate repetitive tasks, such as inserting the document path and filename in a header or footer pane.

To create a macro, you record a sequence of commands and actions. As you record the macro, the actions are translated into code. **Code** is a set of instructions and data for a computer program. The code that Word creates is for **VBA (Visual Basic for Applications)**, which is a computer programming language and environment designed for use within Office and other Microsoft applications. Developers use VBA to automate processes.

Creating and Storing Macros in a Document

You can store macros in a document or in a template. Storing a macro in a document is quick and convenient, but it does have its limitations. When macros are stored in a document, the macros are only available in that document.

The following scenario helps to explain why you would create a macro for an individual document. You have a Word file that contains contact information for individuals registered to attend a conference. The contact information will later be converted and used in a database. Because commas can cause problems when converting text for the database file, users are asked to avoid using commas when entering the contact information in the Word document. However, the document is frequently updated by multiple users, and sometimes commas are included in the contact information. To save time reviewing the information and repetitively removing commas when necessary, you can create a macro to do this for you.

Creating a Macro-Enabled Document

When you store a macro in a document, the document must be saved in macro-enabled document format, which allows you to run the macro when the document is active. The default format for a Word document has the file extension .docx. The format for a macro-enabled document has the file extension .docm.

Step-by-Step 16.1

1. Open the **Registrations.docx** file from the drive and folder where your Data Files are stored.

2. Click **File** and then click **Save As**. Navigate to the folder where your solution files are stored.

3. In the File name text box, type **Updated Registrations 1**, followed by your initials. Click the **Save as type** box and select **Word Macro-Enabled Document (*.docm)**. Then click **Save**.

4. Click the **File** tab and then click **Options**. In the left pane of the Word Options dialog box, click **Advanced**. Scroll down to the Save section, as shown in **Figure 16–1**.

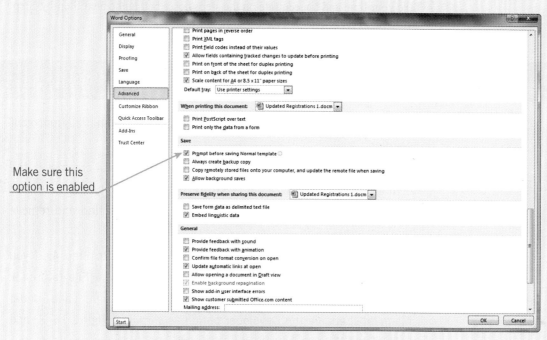

Make sure this option is enabled

FIGURE 16–1
Advanced options for working with Word

5. If necessary, enable the **Prompt before saving Normal template** option and then click **OK**. Turning on this prompt will prevent you from accidentally saving changes to the Normal template.

6. Leave the document open for the next Step-by-Step.

Naming and Storing a Macro

Before recording the sequence of commands and actions, you must name the macro and assign a location to store it. By default, Word assigns a name to each macro you create, such as *Macro1* and *Macro2*. To help identify the macro, you can create a unique name that describes the task, such as *PersonalFooter* or *table_format*. A macro name must begin with a letter and can contain up to 80 letters and numbers. The name cannot contain spaces or symbols, but you can use the underscore character.

Unless you specify a different location, Word saves macros in the Normal (*.dotm) template. You can save the macro to the normal template, the current document, or a document template.

Recording the Macro Actions

It is important that you plan the actions required to perform the task before you begin recording a macro. You can use the Undo command, but any mistakes and corrections you make as you record will be saved in the macro. You should make every effort to avoid prompts Word might display that require a response from you. For example, if you record an action to close a document, Word may ask you to save the changes to the document. To avoid this prompt, plan to save the document before closing it.

Take your time and concentrate on the steps described in the next Step-by-Step. The recording process does not have a time limit!

Step-by-Step 16.2

1. If necessary, open the **Updated Registrations 1.docm** file from your solution files.

2. Scroll through the document and identify occurrences of commas in the contact information (for a name, suffix, between the city and state, and before phone extensions). You will create a macro to find and remove these commas.

3. If the Developer tab is displayed on the Ribbon, go to Step 4. If you do not see the Developer tab on the Ribbon, click the **File** tab, click **Options**, and then click **Customize Ribbon**. In the right pane, under Main Tabs, enable the **Developer** option as shown in **Figure 16–2**, and then click **OK**.

FIGURE 16–2
Options for customizing the Ribbon and keyboard shortcuts

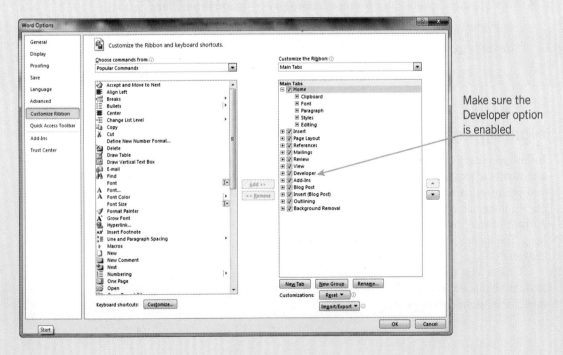

Make sure the Developer option is enabled

4. Click the **Developer** tab. In the Code group, click the **Record Macro** button to open the Record Macro dialog box, as shown in **Figure 16–3**. Note the Record Macro button 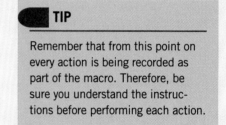 in the status bar. You can use this button as an alternative for opening the Record Macro dialog box.

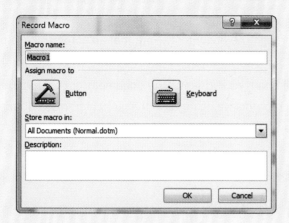

FIGURE 16–3
Record Macro dialog box

5. In the Macro name box, type **NoCommas**.

6. Click the **Store macro in** list arrow, and then select your solution file **Updated Registrations 1.docm (document)**.

7. Under Description, type **Remove commas from contact information.**.

8. Click **OK**. Note that the Stop Recording button 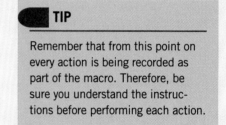 appears in the status bar and the mouse pointer changes to a pointer with a cassette tape. On the Developer tab, in the Code group, two new buttons, Stop Recording and Pause Recording, appear. See **Figure 16–4**.

> **TIP**
>
> Remember that from this point on every action is being recorded as part of the macro. Therefore, be sure you understand the instructions before performing each action.

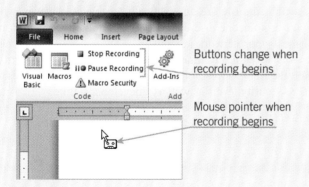

FIGURE 16–4
Code group on the Developer tab during a recording

9. Perform the actions to find and replace all commas:

   a. Press **Ctrl+H** to open the Replace tab in the Find and Replace dialog box.

   b. In the Find what box, type a single comma.

   c. Leave the Replace with box empty.

   d. Click the **More** button. If necessary, under Search Options, change the option in the Search box to **All** to ensure that the macro will always search the entire document.

  e. Click **Replace All**. A prompt appears indicating that eight replacements have been made. Click **OK**.

  f. Close the Find and Replace dialog box.

10. On the Developer tab, in the Code group, click the **Stop Recording** button.

11. Scroll through the document. Note that all commas have been removed from the contact information.

12. Save the changes and leave the document open. If you exit Word and see a prompt to save changes to the global template Normal.dotm, click Don't Save.

Running Macros

▶ **VOCABULARY**
virus

Sometimes computer viruses are stored in macros. A *virus* is a computer program designed to replicate itself, and viruses often cause damage to computer data. Once stored in a macro, the virus can be copied to the Normal.dotm template when the macro is executed. Once copied to the Normal.dotm template, the virus can be attached to all new documents and thereby cause damage to documents and the computer operating system. To counter potential corruption, Word offers several security levels for running macros.

Choosing a Macro Security Setting

When you open a Word template or load an add-in that was already installed with Word, macros within the file are automatically enabled. However, when you run a macro that you or someone else created, you should apply Word's macro security settings. Unless your network administrator enforces a security level, you can change the security level at any time. But before you choose a security level, you must understand the implications for each level. **Table 16–1** describes Word's four options for macro security levels as well as a developer setting.

TABLE 16–1   Macro security settings

MACRO SETTINGS	DESCRIPTION
Disable all macros without notification	All macros are disabled and will not function.
Disable all macros with notification	This is the default setting. A warning is displayed whenever Word encounters a macro from a source that is not on your list of trusted sources, allowing you to choose whether or not to enable the macro.
Disable all macros except digitally signed macros	Only macros that are digitally signed can be executed. If you have already trusted the source, a digitally signed macro will be executed without notification. If you have not trusted the source, you will be notified and you can choose to enable the macro and/or add the publisher as a trusted source. If the macro is not digitally signed, however, the macro is disabled without notification.
Enable all macros (not recommended; potentially dangerous code can run)	All macros run without any notification.
Trust access to the VBA project object model	Created for developers, this setting provides security by limiting access to code that is written for a VBA (Visual Basic for Applications) environment and object model.

You can also choose security settings to automatically enable macros stored in specific folders and documents or from designated publishers.

NET BUSINESS

The first widespread macro virus was Melissa. On March 26, 1999, the macro Melissa traveled to numerous computers through a Microsoft Word document attached to an e-mail message. When the receiver of the e-mail message opened the Word document, the macro was triggered. Melissa then accessed the victim's e-mail address book and sent copies of the e-mail to fifty entries in the address book. The virus spread quickly around the world. Microsoft and anti-virus computer security companies responded quickly, issuing warnings and supplying fixes to counteract the virus and minimize the impact. Despite all efforts, many corporate and government e-mail gateways were overloaded and forced to shut down because of the massive volume of e-mails. Within a week after the virus was exposed, a suspected virus writer was arrested. Melissa raised the awareness that safeguards must be in place when sharing documents. Security settings in current Microsoft Office software versions provide strong protection against macro viruses.

Step-by-Step 16.3

1. If necessary, open the **Updated Registrations 1.docm** file from your solution files.

2. Click the **File** tab and then click **Options**. In the left pane of the Word Options dialog box, click **Trust Center** to open security options. In the right pane, click **Trust Center Settings**. If necessary, click **Macro Settings** to display the options, as shown in **Figure 16–5**.

FIGURE 16–5
Trust Center Macro Settings

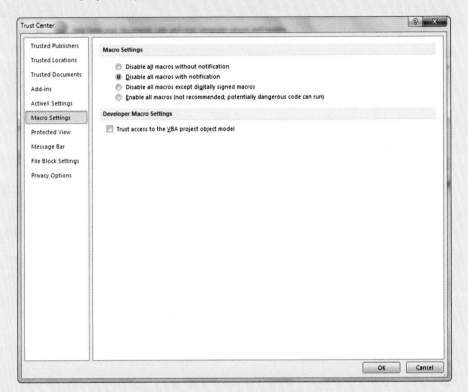

3. Make a note of the current security setting so you can reset the option to the original setting at the end of the lesson (in Step-by-Step 16.12).

4. If necessary, enable the **Disable all macros with notification** option.

5. In the left pane, click **Trusted Locations** to display the options, as shown in **Figure 16–6**.

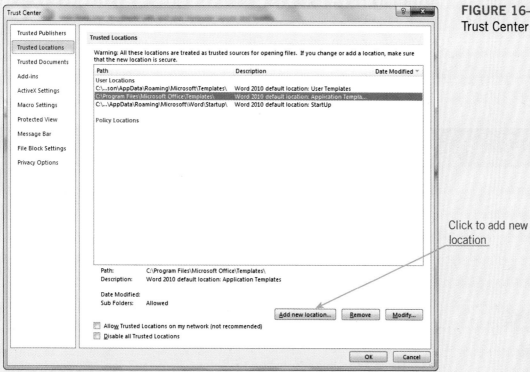

FIGURE 16–6
Trust Center Trusted Locations

6. In the lower-right corner, click **Add new location** to open the Microsoft Office Trusted Location dialog box, as shown in **Figure 16–7**. Your settings will differ.

FIGURE 16–7
Microsoft Office Trusted Location dialog box

7. Click **Browse**. Navigate to the folder where you save your solution files. Click **OK** to close the Browse dialog box.

8. The path for your solution files folder should appear in the Path text box. Click **OK** three times to close the dialog boxes.

9. Leave the document open for the next Step-by-Step. If you exit Word and see a prompt to save changes to the global template Normal.dotm, click Don't Save.

WARNING

If you are ending your Word session now, or any time before you complete the remaining Step-by-Steps in this lesson, you must restore all the settings you changed. Go to Step-by-Step 16.12 and complete all seven steps to restore the changed settings.

Running a Macro

You can run your macro by opening the Macros dialog box. (Later in the lesson, you will use shortcuts to run macros.) Before applying the macro, be sure to select the appropriate text or reposition the insertion point. For example, if the macro actions involve inserting a graphic, be sure the insertion point is positioned in the correct location.

Step-by-Step 16.4

1. If necessary, open the **Updated Registrations 1.docm** file from your solution files. Save the document as **Updated Registrations 2**, followed by your initials. Make sure the file is saved with the extension .docm.

2. If you are beginning a new Word session, click the File tab, then click Options. In the left pane, click Trust Center, and then click Trust Center Settings. For Macro Settings, make sure the option Disable all macros with notification is enabled. Make sure your solutions folder is included in the Trusted Locations list.

3. Navigate to page 2. In the first blank form, add the following contact information for a new conference registration. Use the Tab key to navigate through the form. Include the commas so you can later test the macro to remove the commas.

   Maria Sanchez

   TechKnow

   541 East 29th Street

   Oklahoma City, OK 73129

   405-555-3114, ext. 4041

   msanchez@techknow.xyz

4. On the Developer tab, in the Code group, click the **Macros** button to open the Macros dialog box, as shown in **Figure 16–8**.

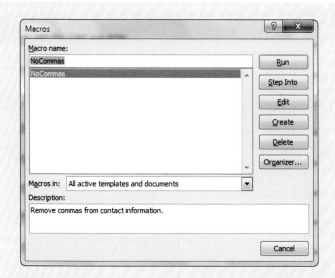

FIGURE 16–8
Macros dialog box

5. Under Macro name, only macros in all active templates and documents appear. If necessary, select **NoCommas**. Then click **Run**.

6. Note that the two commas (after Oklahoma City and before the phone extension) have been removed from the new contact information you just added.

7. Save the changes and close the document.

> **TIP**
>
> If your macro did not run correctly, go back to Step-by-Step 16.2 and repeat Steps 4–10 to re-create the macro using the same name. Answer Yes when prompted to replace the existing macro.

Creating a Document Template to Store Macros

If you want the macros that you create to be available for other documents, you should store the macros in the Normal.dotm template or in a document template. When stored in the Normal.dotm template, the macros are available to all users of the computer for all documents and at any time. When macros are stored in a document template, they are available only when the document template is global or is attached to a document. The advantage to storing macros in a document template is that you can copy the document template, share macros with others, and use the macros on other computers.

You can only attach one template to a document. As you work with a Word document, you may want to access additional macros that are available in other templates. If you make those other templates global, you can access macros available in the global templates as well as those in the attached template. Templates marked as global using the Templates and Add-ins dialog box remain global until you exit Word. When you launch Word again, the templates that were previously global will appear in the list of templates in the Templates and Add-ins dialog box, but they will not be marked as global. To make the templates in this list global again, you must check the box next to the template name.

Because you may share a classroom computer with others, you will store the macros that you create in this lesson in a document template. You already created a personal document template in Lesson 10, but it is not macro-enabled, so you cannot store macros in that template. The new personal document template you create in the next Step-by-Step will be saved in a macro-enabled format.

> **WARNING**
>
> To successfully complete the remaining Step-by-Steps and Projects, you must make sure the template and security settings are set correctly, so read the steps thoroughly and work through them diligently.

Step-by-Step 16.5

1. Open a new blank document. If you are beginning a new Word session, click the File tab, and then click Options. In the left pane, click Trust Center, and then click Trust Center Settings. For Macro Settings, make sure the option Disable all macros with notification is enabled. Click Trusted Locations and make sure your solutions folder is included in the Trusted Locations list. Close all dialog boxes.

2. Click the **Developer** tab. In the Templates group, click the **Document Template** button to open the Templates and Add-ins dialog box.

3. Under Global templates, select and remove all templates listed. When all global templates are removed from the list, click **OK**.

4. Click the **File** tab and then click **Save As** to open the Save As dialog box. Navigate to the folder where your solution files are stored.

5. In the File name box, type **Personal Template 2**, followed by your initials.

6. In the Save as type box, select **Word Macro-Enabled Template (*.dotm)**. Click **Save**. Your personal template contains all the macros provided in the Normal.dotm template, and you can add your own macros to the template.

7. Close the Personal Template 2 document template.

8. Open the **Updated Registrations 2.docm** file from your solution files, and save it as **Updated Registrations 3**, followed by your initials. Make sure the file is saved with the extension .docm.

9. Click the **Developer** tab. In the Templates group, click the **Document Template** button to open the Templates and Add-ins dialog box, as shown in **Figure 16–9**. Your settings may differ.

FIGURE 16–9
Templates and Add-ins dialog box

10. Click **Attach** and then navigate to the folder where you save your solution files. Select your **Personal Template 2** document template, and then click **Open**.

11. Under Checked items, click **Add**. Navigate to and select your **Personal Template 2** document template, and then click **OK**. Click **OK** to close the Templates and Add-ins dialog box. Your Personal Template 2 document will be global during this Word session.

12. Save the changes and close the document.

EXTRA FOR EXPERTS

If you don't attach your personal template to a document, you will still have access to the macros if the template is global. The advantage of attaching the template is that you know the macros will be available when you reopen the document in the future.

Creating and Deleting Macro Shortcuts

You have the option to assign a keyboard shortcut or a button to a macro. You cannot assign a shortcut key combination and a button at the same time, but you can create a second shortcut after the macro is recorded, which you will learn how to do in Step-by-Step 16.8. If you no longer use a macro, you can delete the shortcut.

Creating a Macro with a Keyboard Shortcut

When you create a keyboard shortcut, you must choose a key combination that is not already assigned to other commands or functions. If the key combination is already assigned to another command or function, Word will display a message indicating that those keys have already been assigned.

EXTRA FOR EXPERTS

To print a list of the key assignments saved in a document or template, open the document or template. Click the File tab, click Print, and then under Settings, click the first list arrow (usually shows Print All Pages). Under Document Properties, select Key Assignments and then click Print.

Step-by-Step 16.6

1. Open the **Personal Template 2.dotm** document template from your solution files.

2. If you are beginning a new Word session, click the File tab, and then click Options. In the left pane, click Trust Center, and then click Trust Center Settings. For Macro Settings, make sure the option Disable all macros with notification is enabled. Make sure your solutions folder is included in the Trusted Locations list.

3. Click the **Developer** tab. Create a new macro:
   a. In the Code group, click the **Record Macro** button.
   b. In the Macro name text box, type **Path_Filename_Header**.
   c. Click the **Store macro in** list arrow, and then select **Documents Based On Personal Template 2.dotm**.
   d. In the Description text box, type **Insert path and filename in a header.**.

TIP

If an error message appears indicating that the macro could not be created, close the template and save any changes, if prompted. Reopen the template file, and continue.

4. Assign a keyboard shortcut to the macro:

    a. Under Assign macro to, click the **Keyboard** icon. The Customize Keyboard dialog box opens, as shown in **Figure 16–10**.

FIGURE 16–10
Customize Keyboard dialog box

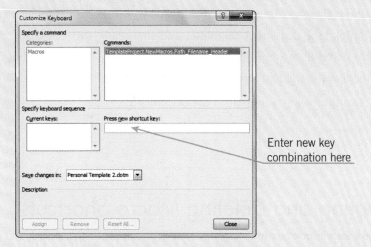

Enter new key combination here

b. The insertion point is positioned in the Press new shortcut key box. Press and hold the **Alt** key and then press the number **9**. (If Word tells you that the Alt+9 key combination is already assigned, choose another similar combination.)

c. If necessary, click the **Save changes in** list arrow and then select your Personal Template 2.dotm document template.

d. Click **Assign** and then click **Close**.

5. Perform the actions to insert the path and filename in a header:

    a. Click the **Insert** tab. In the Header & Footer group, click the **Header** button. At the bottom of the menu, click **Edit Header**. The insertion point moves to the header pane.

    b. On the Header & Footer Tools Design tab, in the Insert group, click the **Quick Parts** button and then click **Field** to open the Field dialog box, as shown in **Figure 16–11**.

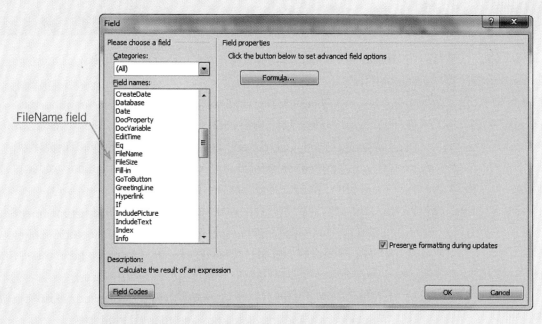

FIGURE 16-11
Field dialog box

FileName field

c.   Under Field names, scroll down and select **FileName**. The dialog box adapts to show more options. In the center pane, under Format, select **Lowercase**. In the pane on the right, under Field options, enable the **Add path to filename** option. Then click **OK**.

d.   In the Close group, click the **Close Header and Footer** button.

6.   Click the **Developer** tab. In the Code group, click the **Stop Recording** button.

7.   Close the document template. When prompted to save changes, click **Save**.

8.   Open the **Updated Registrations 3.docm** file from your solution files.

9.   Press and hold **Alt** and press **9**. The new header, showing the path and filename, is inserted in the header pane and appears on all three pages of the document.

10. Save the changes and close the document.

Creating a Macro with a Button Shortcut

When you create a button shortcut for a macro, the new button is added to the Quick Access Toolbar.

When recording a macro, you can use the mouse to choose commands and click buttons, but you cannot record mouse movements within the document window. For example, you cannot click the mouse to position an insertion point or drag to select text. Instead, you must use keystrokes to complete these actions. So when planning the steps for the macro you should also consider the keyboard shortcuts you can use to navigate through the document. If you are interrupted during the recording process, you can temporarily stop recording and then resume recording at a later time.

Step-by-Step 16.7

1. Open your **Personal Template 2.dotm** document template from your solution files.

2. If you are beginning a new Word session, click the File tab, and then click Options. In the left pane, click Trust Center, and then click Trust Center Settings. For Macro Settings, make sure the option Disable all macros with notification is enabled. Make sure your solutions folder is included in the Trusted Locations list.

3. Click the **Developer** tab, and in the Templates group, click the **Document Template** button to open the Templates and Add-ins dialog box. Under Global templates and add-ins, Personal Template 2 should be in the list with a check mark. Do one of the following:

    a. If the Personal Template 2 is in the list and checked, close the Templates and Add-ins dialog box and then go to Step 4.

    b. If the Personal Template 2 template is in the list but it is not checked, select the check box to make the template global. Click **OK**. Save and close the document template. Then reopen the document template and confirm that the Personal Template 2 template is global. Close the Templates and Add-ins dialog box and leave the Personal Template 2 document template open.

    c. If the template does not appear in the list, click **Add**, navigate to your solutions folder, select **Personal Template 2**, and click **OK**. Make sure the Personal Template 2 is checked. Click **OK**. Save and close the document template. Reopen the document template and confirm that the Personal Template 2 template is global. Close the Templates and Add-ins dialog box and leave the Personal Template 2 document template open.

4. Create a new macro:

    a. In the Code group, click the **Record Macro** button.

    b. In the Macro name text box, type **LegalFormat**.

    c. Click the **Store macro in** list arrow and select **Documents Based On Personal Template 2.dotm**.

    d. In the Description text box, type **Margin and paper size formats for legal documents.**.

    e. Under Assign macro to, click the **Button** icon to open the Word Options for customizing the Quick Access Toolbar, as shown in **Figure 16–12**. Your settings may differ.

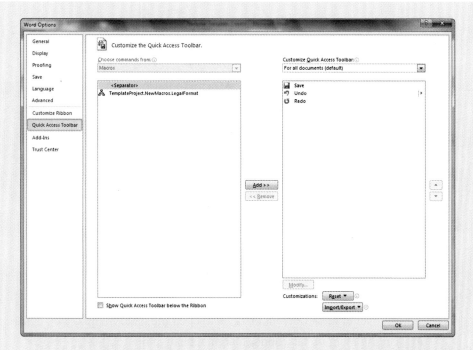

FIGURE 16–12
Options for customizing the Quick Access Toolbar

    f. In the left pane, select the macro name **TemplateProject. NewMacros.LegalFormat**. Click **Add** to add the new button to the Quick Access Toolbar. Click **OK** to close the dialog box.

5. Note that a new button appears on your Quick Access Toolbar. Position the mouse pointer over the button to display the ScreenTip.

6. Record the following steps to format margins and paper size:

    a. Press and hold the **Ctrl** key and then press **Home** to make sure the insertion point is positioned at the top of the document.

    b. Click the **Page Layout** tab. In the Page Setup group, click the **Size** button and then click **Legal 8.5" × 14"**.

    c. In the Page Setup group, click the **Margins** button. At the bottom of the menu, click **Custom Margins** to open the Page Setup dialog box.

    d. On the Margins tab, under Margins, set the margins as follows: top: **2"**; bottom: **1"**; left: **1.5"**; and right: **0.75"**.

    e. Click **OK.**

7. Click the **Developer** tab. In the Code group, click the **Pause Recording** button. At this point you can open new documents, scroll through the active document, or just take a break before continuing to record actions for the macro.

8. In the Code group, click the **Resume Recorder** button to continue recording.

9. Record the following steps to create a section break and change the margin settings in the new section:

   a. Press and hold the **Ctrl** key and then press **G**. Under Enter page number, type **2** and then click **Go To** to move to the top of the second page in the document. (However, the insertion point does not move because there is no second page in this document template.) In the Find and Replace dialog box, click **Close**.

   b. Click the **Page Layout** tab. In the Page Setup group, click the **Breaks** button. Under Section Breaks, click **Continuous**.

   c. Press and hold the **Ctrl** key and then press the **down arrow** to move the insertion point down one paragraph to ensure that you are in the second section of the document. (The insertion point does not move in this document.)

   d. In the Page Setup group, click the **Margins** button. At the bottom of the menu, click **Custom Margins** to open the Page Setup dialog box.

   e. On the Margins tab, under Margins, change the top margin to **1.5"**. The other margin settings should be okay as is: bottom: 1"; left: 1.5"; and right: .75".

   f. At the bottom of the dialog box, under Preview, make sure the Apply to setting shows **This section**. Then click **OK**.

   g. Click the **Developer** tab. In the Code group, click the **Stop Recording** button.

10. Close the document template. When prompted to save the changes, click **Save**.

11. Open the **Investment Club.docx** file from the drive and folder where your Data Files are stored. Save the document as **Investment Club Agreement 1**, followed by your initials. Make sure the file is saved with the extension .docx.

12. On the Quick Access Toolbar, click the **TemplateProject.NewMacros. LegalFormat** button. Because your Personal Template 2 document template is global, the macro is available.

13. Scroll through the document and make sure the margin settings for the first page and all subsequent pages look accurate. The first page should have a top margin of 2" and all remaining pages in the document should have a top margin of 1.5".

14. Save the changes and close the document.

WARNING

If you are ending your Word session now, or any time before you complete the remaining Step-by-Steps in this lesson, you must restore all the settings you changed. Go to Step-by-Step 16.12 and complete all seven steps to restore the changed settings.

Creating and Deleting Shortcuts for Existing Macros

Perhaps when you created a macro you did not create a shortcut, or maybe you created a keyboard shortcut and now you want to create a button for the macro. You can easily create shortcuts for existing macros, and you can customize the button icons.

Step-by-Step 16.8

1. Open your **Personal Template 2.dotm** document template.

2. Click the **File** tab, then click **Options**. In the left pane, click **Quick Access Toolbar**. Under Choose commands from, click the **list arrow** and then click **Macros**. A list of all macros appears.

3. Click the **TemplateProject.NewMacros.Path_Filename_Header** macro, and then click **Add**. A new button appears on the Quick Access Toolbar.

4. At the bottom of the right pane, click **Modify** to open the Modify Button dialog box, as shown in **Figure 16–13**.

Click this graphic

FIGURE 16–13
Modify Button dialog box

5. Click the last button in the first row to select the folder icon for the button, and then click **OK**. Note that the button for the Quick Access Toolbar is updated in the dialog box.

6. In the left pane, click **Customize Ribbon**. Below the center pane, next to Keyboard shortcuts, click **Customize** to open the Customize Keyboard dialog box.

7. Under Categories, scroll to the bottom of the list and select **Macros**. The dialog box options change and the available macros are displayed. Under Macros, select the **Path_Filename_Header** macro to show the dialog box shown in **Figure 16–14**. The keys already assigned appear in the Current keys list. Your settings may differ.

FIGURE 16–14
Customize Keyboard dialog box showing available macros and assigned keys

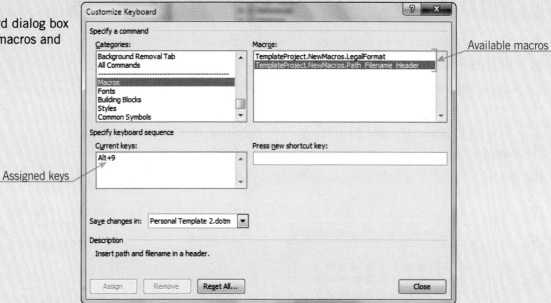

8. Click in the **Press new shortcut key** box. Press and hold the **Alt** key and then press the number **6**. (If Word tells you that the Alt+6 key combination is already assigned, choose another similar combination.)

9. Make sure the Save changes in setting shows your **Personal Template 2.dotm** document template. Click **Assign** and then click **Close**. Click **OK** to close the Word Options dialog box.

10. Right-click the **TemplateProject.NewMacros.LegalFormat** button on the Quick Access Toolbar, then click **Remove from Quick Access Toolbar**.

11. Click the **File** tab and then click **Options**. In the left pane, click **Customize Ribbon**. At the bottom, next to Keyboard shortcuts, click **Customize** to open the Customize Keyboard dialog box. Under Categories, scroll down and click **Macros**, and then, under Macros, click the **Path_Filename_Header** macro.

12. Under Specify keyboard sequence, in the Current keys box, select **Alt+6**. At the bottom of the dialog box, click **Remove**.

13. Close the dialog box and click **OK** to close the Word Options dialog box.

14. Save the changes and close the document template.

Editing Macros

Generally the easiest way to change a macro is to record it again. When you create a new macro using an existing macro name, Word will prompt you to replace the existing macro with the new recording. However, if the macro is complex and the changes you want to make are minor (such as changing one margin setting or changing the macro name), you should consider editing the macro code. Each instruction you recorded in the macro appears in Visual Basic code.

You can edit the code in the Visual Basic Editor (VBE) window. Even if you're not familiar with VBA code, you will most likely recognize some of the code information and be able to edit some parts of the code. The first line of a macro code begins with the word *Sub*, which is then followed by the name of the macro. If you included a description when you created the macro, the description appears below the Sub line. The last line of the macro code shows *End Sub*.

> **TIP**
>
> You can use the VBA Help feature to learn more about the code information.

Step-by-Step 16.9

1. Open your **Personal Template 2.dotm** document template.

2. If you are beginning a new Word session, click the File tab, click Options, click Trust Center, and then click Trust Center Settings. For Macro Settings, make sure the option Disable all macros with notification is enabled. Make sure your solutions folder is included in the Trusted Locations list.

3. Click the **Developer** tab, and in the Code group, click the **Macros** button to open the Macros dialog box, as shown in **Figure 16–15**. Even though you deleted the new button from the Quick Access Toolbar, the LegalFormat macro is still stored in your personal template.

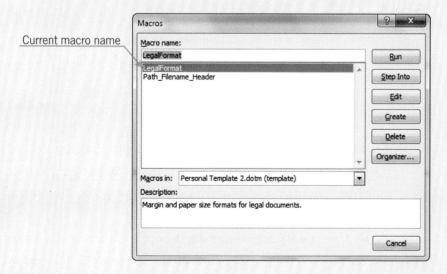

Current macro name

FIGURE 16–15
Macros dialog box

4. Under Macros, if necessary, select **LegalFormat**. Click **Edit**. The VBA window and the Visual Basic Editor (VBE) open, as shown in **Figure 16–16**. The code in your Visual Basic Editor window may be a little different.

FIGURE 16–16
Microsoft Visual
Basic Editor in
the VBA window

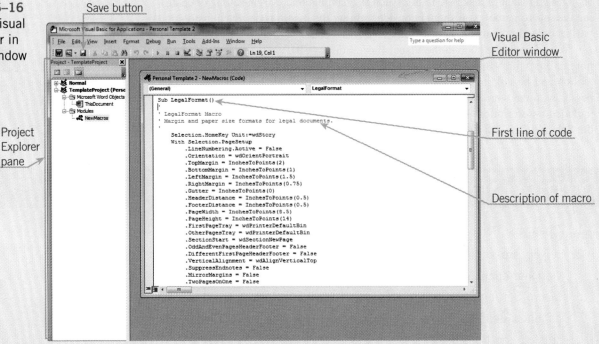

Save button

Visual Basic
Editor window

First line of code

Description of macro

Project
Explorer
pane

5. At the top of the Visual Basics Editor window, rename the macro by changing the first line of code. Edit the line so it reads **Sub Legal_Formats ()**.

6. Scroll down to the second occurrence of *End With*. Seven lines below that point, in the line reading *RightMargin = InchesToPoints (0.75)*, change the 0.75 to **1**.

7. Scroll down to view two more occurrences of *End With*. Nine lines below that point, in the line reading *RightMargin = InchesToPoints (0.75)*, change the 0.75 to **1**.

8. At the top of the window, on the VBA standard toolbar, click the **Save** button ⊞ to save the changes to the macro code. Click **File** and then click **Close and Return to Microsoft Word** to close the VBA application.

9. On the Developer tab, in the Code group, click the **Macros** button. Note that the macro name is now shown as *Legal_Formats*. Close the Macros dialog box, and then close the document template.

10. Open the **Investment Club Agreement 1.docx** file from your solution files. Save the document as **Investment Club Agreement 2**, followed by your initials. Make sure the file is saved with the extension .docx.

11. Click the **Developer** tab. In the Templates group, click the **Document Template** button, click **Attach**, navigate to and select your **Personal Template 2** document template, click **Open**, and then click **OK**.

12. In the Code group, click the **Macros** button. *Legal_Formats* should already be selected. Click **Run**.

13. Scroll through the document to confirm that the right margin on all pages is adjusted to 1".

14. Save the changes and close the document.

Copying, Deleting, and Renaming Macro Projects

When macros are stored in a document or in a template, they are stored as a collection in a ***macro project***. The default name for the macro project is *NewMacros*. You can rename a macro project, which helps you keep your macros organized.

> ▶ **VOCABULARY**
> **macro project**

To make the macros available to other documents and other users, you can copy a macro project to the Normal (default) template or to another document template. Options in the Organizer dialog box enable you to copy, delete, and rename only projects. You cannot copy or rename individual macros using the Organizer options. When you no longer want to use a macro, you can open the Macros dialog box and remove the macro from the macro project.

Step-by-Step 16.10

1. Open the **Personal Template 2.dotm** document template from your solution files.

2. Click the **Developer** tab. In the Code group, click the **Macros** button to open the Macros dialog box.

3. Click **Organizer**, and if necessary, click the **Macro Project Items** tab to open the Organizer dialog box, as shown in **Figure 16–17**.

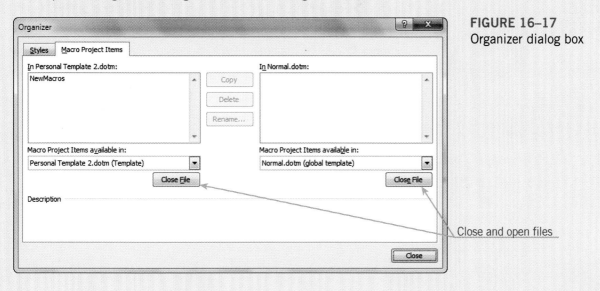

FIGURE 16–17
Organizer dialog box

4. In the left pane, the NewMacros project group in your Personal Template 2 document template appears. Select **NewMacros**.

5. To rename the project group, click **Rename**. In the Rename dialog box, type **Lesson16** and then click **OK**.

6. In the left pane, under Macro Project Items available in, click **Close File**. Then click **Open File** and navigate to the folder where your solution files are stored.

7. In the lower-right corner of the Open dialog box, click the **File type** box and select **All Files (*.*)**. Select **Updated Registrations 3.docm** and then click **Open**. The left pane changes to show the NewMacros project group in the Updated Registrations 3.docm macro-enabled document.

8. In the pane on the right, under Macro Project Items available in, click **Close File**. Then click **Open File** and navigate to the folder where your solution files are stored. Select your **Personal Template 2.dotm** document template and then click **Open**.

9. In the left pane, *NewMacros* should already be selected. Click **Copy**. The NewMacros group is copied to the document template. Close the Organizer dialog box.

10. On the Developer tab, in the Code group, click the **Macros** button. Notice that the NoCommas macro is now available in the document template.

11. Close the Macros dialog box. Save the changes to the document template.

12. Open the **Updated Registrations 3.docm** document from your solution files. Save the document as **Updated Registrations 4**, followed by your initials. Make sure the file is saved with the extension .docm.

13. Click the **Developer** tab. In the Code group, click the **Macros** button. Select the macro **Project.NewMacros.NoCommas** and then click **Delete**. When prompted to confirm deletion of the macro, click **Yes**. The macro is no longer stored in the document, but as you can see, the macro is still stored in the document template as TemplateProject.NewMacros.NoCommas.

14. Close the Macros dialog box. Save the changes and close the document. Close the Personal Template 2 document template, and leave Word open for the next Step-by-Step.

Signing a Macro Project

If you plan to share your macros with others, signing the macro project by adding a digital signature will enable users who run the macro to identify its creator and be assured that the macro has not been altered. Earlier in this lesson, Table 16–1 provided descriptions for several macro security settings. Depending on the security settings, users may not be able to open a document with macros unless the macro project or template is signed.

Signing a macro template or project is similar to signing a Word document. You can use the digital signature you created in Lesson 13. If the valid digital certificate is on your computer, the project is re-signed when you make changes to the macro code. However, if another user edits the code after the project is signed, the digital signature becomes invalid.

Step-by-Step 16.11

1. To view the digital signatures on your computer:
   a. Launch Internet Explorer.
   b. Click the **Tools** button and then click **Internet Options**.
   c. In the Internet Options dialog box, click the **Content** tab. Under Certificates, click **Certificates**. A list of digital signatures available on your computer appears. Check to see if the digital signature you created in Lesson 13 is in the list.
   d. Close both dialog boxes and then close Internet Explorer.
   e. If your personal signature was not in the list, go to Step 2. If your personal signature was in the list, go to Step 3.

2. To create a new digital certificate:
   a. On the taskbar, click the **Start** button, click **All Programs**, click **Microsoft Office**, click **Microsoft Office 2010 Tools**, and then click **Digital Certificate for VBA Projects**.
   b. In the Create Digital Certificate dialog box, in the Your certificate's name box, enter your first and last names.
   c. Click **OK** twice to close the dialog boxes.

3. Attach a digital signature to your document template:
   a. Open the **Personal Template 2** file from your solution files.
   b. Click the **Developer** tab. In the Code group, click the **Visual Basic** button. If you do not see the Project Explorer pane (as shown in Figure 16–16) with the heading *Project – TemplateProject*, click **View** and then click **Project Explorer**.

c.   In the Project Explorer pane, select **TemplateProject (Personal Template 2)**. Click **Tools** and then click **Digital Signature** to open the Digital Signature dialog box, as shown in **Figure 16–18**.

FIGURE 16–18
Digital Signature dialog box

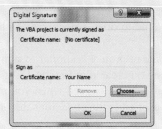

d.   If your digital signature does not appear under Sign as, click **Choose**. In the Windows Security dialog box, select your certificate and then click **OK**.

e.   Your digital signature should now appear below Sign as. Click **OK** to close the Digital Signature box.

f.   Click the **Save** button on the toolbar at the top of the application window, then close the VBA application and return to the Word document.

4.   Close the Personal Template 2 document template.

Restoring Settings

Even if you don't share your computer with others, it's good practice to review the settings you have customized before ending a Word session. For example, if you don't want the changes to affect future documents, it is easier to restore the original settings before exiting Word. That way you don't need to remember to change the settings when you start a new Word session. In this lesson, you made changes to the security settings and global templates. The following steps will help you restore those settings before you end a Word session.

Step-by-Step 16.12

1.   Click the **File** tab and then click **Options**. In the left pane, click **Trust Center**. Click **Trust Center Settings**.

2.   Click **Macro Settings**, and if necessary, reset the default setting to the original setting noted in Step-by-Step 16.3, Step 3.

3.   Click **Trusted Locations**, and if necessary, remove your solutions folder from the list. Click **OK** twice to close the dialog boxes.

4. If you added new macro buttons to the Quick Access Toolbar, right-click each of the buttons on the toolbar and then select **Remove from Quick Access Toolbar**.

5. Click the **Developer** tab. In the Templates group, click the **Document Template** button to open the Templates and Add-ins dialog box. Under Global templates and add-ins, remove your personal templates from the list.

6. If the Developer tab did not appear in the Ribbon when you began the lesson (see Step-by-Step 16.2, Step 3), click the **File** tab and then click **Options**. In the left pane, click **Customize Ribbon**. In the right pane, under Main Tabs, uncheck the **Developer** tab name to hide the Developer tab, and then click **OK**.

7. Exit Word. If prompted to save changes to the global Normal.dotm template, click **Don't Save**.

SUMMARY

In this lesson you learned:

- You can store a macro in a document or in a template. When stored in a document, macros are only available for that document.

- When you create a macro, you record the sequence of actions necessary to perform a task.

- Word enforces a security level for running macros. Depending on the security level, you may need to enable macros when you open a document.

- To make macros available for other documents, you can store them in the normal template or in a document template.

- To create shortcuts to run a macro, you can assign a shortcut key combination or you can add a new button to the Quick Access Toolbar.

- To run a macro, you can use the Macros dialog box or a keyboard or button shortcut.

- When you want to change a macro, you can re-record it or you can edit it in the Microsoft Visual Basic Editor.

- You can copy macro projects to make them available to other documents and users. When you no longer need a macro, you can delete it from the macro project.

- You can rename macro project groups to help organize your macros.

- When sharing macros with others, you should sign the macro project by adding a digital signature.

■ VOCABULARY REVIEW

Define the following terms:

code

macro

macro project

VBA (Visual Basic for Applications)

virus

◼ REVIEW QUESTIONS

TRUE / FALSE

Circle T if the statement is true or F if the statement is false.

T   F   **1.**   The default format for a Word document is macro-enabled.

T   F   **2.**   Word already has numerous macros available.

T   F   **3.**   When you delete a macro shortcut, the macro is also deleted.

T   F   **4.**   All macro buttons look the same.

T   F   **5.**   To rename a macro, you must edit the VBA code.

MULTIPLE CHOICE

Select the best response for the following statements.

1. When recording a macro, _____.

   A.   you can use the mouse to reposition the insertion point

   B.   you can use keyboard shortcuts to navigate through the document

   C.   you can use the mouse to select text

   D.   none of the above

2. When a macro is stored in a document template, _____.

   A.   the macro is available to only the active document

   B.   the macro is stored in the normal (default) template

   C.   the macro is available to all users and to all documents at any time

   D.   the macro is available when the document template is attached to a document or made global

3. When you store a macro in a document, _____.

   A.   a document template must be attached

   B.   the macro is available to all users for all documents at any time

   C.   the macro must first be listed as a trusted source

   D.   the document must be macro-enabled

4. By default, Word stores macros _____.

   A.   in a document template

   B.   in the current document

   C.   in the Normal (dotm) template

   D.   none of the above

5. If you want to choose when to enable the macro, in the macro security settings, you should choose the option to _____.

   A.   disable all macros without notification

   B.   disable all macros with notification

   C.   disable all macros except digitally signed macros

   D.   enable all macros

WRITTEN QUESTIONS

Write a brief answer to the following questions.

1. What are the advantages of storing macros in a document template?

2. Why will Word not accept the macro names *Print 4*, *4Copies*, or *Print4**?

3. When looking at a filename extension, how can you determine if the document is macro-enabled?

4. When you edit a macro, why does the VBA window open?

5. What happens when you create a new macro using an existing macro name?

■ PROJECTS

If you have a SAM 2010 user profile, your instructor may have assigned an autogradable version of the indicated project. If so, log into the SAM 2010 Web site at *www.cengage.com/sam2010* to download the instruction and start files.

PROJECT 16–1

1. Open the **Resume.docx** file from the drive and folder where your Data Files are stored. Save the document as a macro-enabled document and name the document **Final Resume**, followed by your initials. Make sure the file is saved with the extension .docm.

2. Click the File tab, and then click Options. In the left pane, click Trust Center, and then click Trust Center Settings. For Macro Settings, make sure the option Disable all macros with notification is enabled. Click Trusted Locations and make sure your solutions folder is included in the Trusted Locations list. Close all dialog boxes.

3. Create a new macro:
   a. Name the macro **SaveAs_XPS**.
   b. Store the macro in the current document.
   c. Describe the macro as **Save the document in XPS format**.
   d. Create a keyboard shortcut using the key combination Alt+6. (Make sure the changes are saved to the current document.)

4. Record the actions to save the document in the XPS format, using the same filename and folder where you save your solution files. (When the XPS document opens, close it and then stop recording.)

5. Add a new button for the *SaveAs_XPS* macro to the Quick Access Toolbar. Modify the button icon with a graphic of your choice.

6. Center the content on the page vertically:
   a. Click the Page Layout tab.
   b. In the Page Setup group, click the Dialog Box Launcher.
   c. In the Page Setup dialog box, click the Layout tab.
   d. Under Page, in the Vertical alignment box, select Center.
   e. Click OK. If prompted about the margins set outside the printable area, click Ignore.

7. Save the changes to the document.

8. Run the *SaveAs_XPS* macro to create a new file in the XPS format. The new XPS file is saved with the same name as the previous XPS document. Every time you update the resume, you can run the macro to update the XPS version of the document.

9. Close the XPS document window and close the Final Resume document.

10. Open the folder where you save your solution files. You should see two solution files for this project: the *Final Resume.docm* file and the *Final Resume.xps* file. Close the folder.

SAM PROJECT 16–2

1. Open a new blank document and save it as a new macro-enabled template using the filename **Personal Template 3.dotm**.

2. If you are beginning a new Word session, click the File tab, then click Options. In the left pane, click Trust Center, and then click Trust Center Settings. For Macro Settings, make sure the option Disable all macros with notification is enabled. Make sure your solutions folder is included in the Trusted Locations list.

3. Make the Personal Template 3.dotm document template global. Close the Personal Template 3 document template.

4. Open a new blank document. To create random text, type **=rand(5,5)** and then press Enter.

5. Practice the required actions to format text in two columns with a line between the columns. Use the following tips as a guide:
   a. Open the Columns dialog box. (*Hint*: On the Page Layout tab, click the Columns button, then click More Columns.)
   b. Select the options for two columns with a line between the columns and click OK.

6. Close the document without saving the changes.

7. Open the **Personal Template 3** document template.

8. Create the new macro:
   a. Name the macro **Columns2**.
   b. Store the macro in your Personal Template 3 document template.
   c. Describe the macro as **Format text in columns with a line between the columns.**.
   d. Record the actions.
   e. Stop the recording.

9. Save the changes and then close the document template.

10. Open the **Profile.docx** file from the drive and folder where your Data Files are stored. Save the document as **Revised Profile 1**, followed by your initials. Make sure the file is saved with the extension .docx.

11. Attach your Personal Template 3.dotm document template to the document.

12. Create a keyboard shortcut for the Columns2 macro by applying the key combination Alt+5. Make sure you save the keyboard shortcut in your Personal Template 3.dotm document template.

13. Run the Columns2 macro.

14. Save the changes, and when prompted to save changes to the document template, click Yes. Close the document.

WARNING

If you are ending your Word session now, or any time before you complete the remaining Projects in this lesson, you must restore all the settings you changed. Go to Step-by-Step 16.12 and complete all seven steps to restore the changed settings.

PROJECT 16–3

1. If you are beginning a new Word session, click the File tab, then click Options. In the left pane, click Trust Center, and then click Trust Center Settings. For Macro Settings, make sure the option Disable all macros with notification is enabled. Make sure your solutions folder is included in the Trusted Locations list.

2. Open the **Personal Template 3** file from your solution files. Make the template global.

3. Open the Organizer dialog box. In the left pane, open the **Final Resume.docm** document from your solution files.

4. Rename the NewMacros project **SaveFormat**.

5. In the right pane of the Organizer dialog box, open your **Personal Template 3.dotm** file.

6. Copy the SaveFormat project from the Final Resume.docm file to your Personal Template 3.dotm document template.

7. Close the Organizer dialog box. When prompted to save the changes to the Final Resume.docx document, click Save. Save the changes to the Personal Template 3.dotm document template and leave the document open.

8. Edit the Columns2 macro:
   a. Open the Macros dialog box. Select the Columns2 macro and click Edit.
   b. In the first line of the code, change *Sub Columns2* to *Sub Columns3*.

   c. Change the Green heading from *Columns2 Macro* to *Columns3 Macro*.
   d. In the line reading *.SetCount NumColumns:=2*, change the number of columns to **3**.
   e. In the line reading *.Width = InchesToPoints (3)*, change the *3* to **1.5**.

9. Save the changes to the VBA code, and then close the VBA window and return to the Word application. Close the document template.

10. Open the **Revised Profile 1.docx** file from your solution files and save the document as **Revised Profile 2**, followed by your initials. Make sure the file is saved with the extension .docx.

11. Open the Macros dialog box and run the Columns3 macro.

12. Save the changes to the Revised Profile 2.docx file and close the file.

WARNING

If you are ending your Word session now, or any time before you complete the remaining Projects in this lesson, you must restore all the settings you changed. Go to Step-by-Step 16.12 and complete all seven steps to restore the changed settings.

PROJECT 16–4

1. Open the **Personal Template 3** file from your solution files.

2. Open a new blank document. Click the Insert tab, click the Screenshot button, and then click Screen Clipping.

3. Wait a moment for the active document to fade away. Drag the mouse pointer over the Quick Access Toolbar to identify the area to capture in the clipping. When you release the mouse button, the active document appears and the clipping is inserted in the document.

4. Save the document with the screenshot as **Quick Access Toolbar Screenshot**, followed by your initials. Make sure the file is saved with the extension .docx. Close the document.

5. Open the VBA application and attach your digital signature to the TemplateProject (Personal Template 3).

6. Save the changes in the VBA application window, and then return to the Word application.

7. Close the document template.

8. Go to Step-by-Step 16.12 and complete all seven steps to restore the settings you changed.

CRITICAL THINKING

ACTIVITY 16–1

Celeste was recording a macro when she was interrupted by a co-worker who needed some information. Celeste temporarily paused the recording to assist her co-worker. When Celeste returned to her document, she couldn't remember the last action before she stopped. What would you have done if you were Celeste?

ACTIVITY 16–2

Celeste always creates both keyboard shortcuts and buttons for all macros stored in the Normal.dotm template on all computers in the office. Five macros have been saved. Is it really necessary to create both types of shortcuts? Do you think this is a good idea? Explain why.

LESSON 17

Customizing Settings

■ OBJECTIVES

Upon completion of this lesson, you should be able to:

- Add and delete buttons on the Quick Access Toolbar.
- Customize the Ribbon.
- Modify the default document formats.
- Modify the document display settings.
- Change the edit settings.
- Change the save settings.
- Set AutoCorrect exceptions.
- Create a custom dictionary.

■ VOCABULARY

main tabs

tool tabs

The Word application has numerous commands and settings for displaying, editing, and saving documents. In the previous Word lessons, features have been introduced using the default settings. To improve your productivity as you work with Word, you can customize some of these settings to change how Word displays items and responds to your input.

Customizing the Quick Access Toolbar

The Quick Access Toolbar has been designed to provide quick access to the commands you use most often. You may find that you use commands that do not appear in the default Quick Access Toolbar. To save time accessing these commands, you can add buttons to the toolbar. In the previous lesson, you learned to add buttons to the Quick Access Toolbar to run macros. You can also add buttons for all other Word commands, including commands that don't appear on the Ribbon.

You can add an unlimited number of buttons to the Quick Access Toolbar, but putting too many buttons on it may defeat the purpose. So as you add new buttons, you may need to remove existing buttons. You can remove buttons individually, or you can remove multiple buttons you have added by resetting the toolbar to its default settings. When you reset the toolbar settings, any of the default buttons you removed will be restored on the toolbar.

When you customize the settings in Word, the changes are automatically saved to the application. However, it is easy to restore the default settings.

⚡ WARNING

As you work through the activities in this lesson, information will be provided to reset the Word application with the default settings. If you end the Word session before completing this lesson, be sure to restore the default settings before exiting Word.

Step-by-Step 17.1

1. Launch Word. Click the **File** tab, and then click **Options**. In the left pane of the Word Options dialog box, click **Quick Access Toolbar** to open the dialog box shown in **Figure 17–1**. Your settings may differ. A list of popular commands appears in the center pane, and a list of the current buttons on the Quick Access Toolbar appears in the right pane.

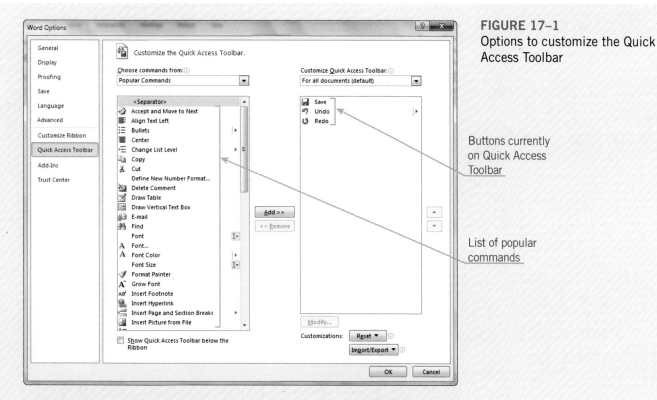

FIGURE 17–1
Options to customize the Quick Access Toolbar

Buttons currently on Quick Access Toolbar

List of popular commands

2. Scroll down in the list of popular commands and select **New**. Then click **Add** to add the New button to the toolbar. The New button, with an icon, now appears in the list of Quick Access Toolbar buttons in the right pane.

3. In the center pane, under Choose commands from, click the **list arrow** and then click **All Commands**. The list in the center pane changes. Scroll through the list. As you can see, the list is quite extensive.

4. Under Choose commands from, click the **list arrow** again to show the options for selecting commands, as shown in **Figure 17–2**. This list helps you quickly locate commands by first clicking the tab where the command appears on the Ribbon.

FIGURE 17–2
Options for choosing commands for the Quick Access Toolbar

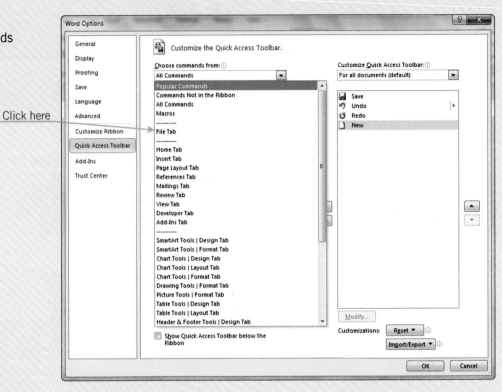

5. In the list of tabs in the center pane, click **File Tab**. The list now shows all the commands that can be accessed using the File tab on the Ribbon. In the center pane, scroll down and select **Quick Print**. Click **Add**. A new button with an icon is added to the list of buttons for the Quick Access Toolbar.

6. In the center pane, under Choose commands from, click the **list arrow** and then click **Commands Not in the Ribbon**. To access these commands, you must open dialog boxes or menus. Select **All Caps**, and then click **Add**. Scroll down farther in the list, select **Hanging Indent**, and then click **Add**. In the lower-right corner of the dialog box, click **OK**.

7. Four new buttons appear on the Quick Access Toolbar. Click the **New** button on the Quick Access Toolbar. A new document opens. Type the following sentence.
When the hanging indent format is applied to a paragraph, the first line of the paragraph is not indented, but all subsequent lines in the paragraph are indented from the left margin.

TIP

The Quick Print command sends the document to the printer without an opportunity to preview it.

TIP

If you don't recognize a button icon, you can position the mouse pointer over the button to view the ScreenTip.

8. Press **Enter** two times. Click the **All Caps** button on the Quick Access Toolbar to toggle on the font effect. Type your **first name**. Click the **All Caps** button again to toggle off the font effect, and then press the **spacebar** and type your **last name**.

9. Click anywhere in the first paragraph of text, and then click the **Hanging Indent** button. The hanging indent format is applied to the paragraph.

10. Right-click the **Save** button on the Quick Access Toolbar, and then click **Remove from Quick Access Toolbar**. The button no longer appears on the toolbar.

11. Click the **File** tab, and then click **Options**. In the left pane of the Word Options dialog box, click **Quick Access Toolbar**. In the right pane, in the list of current buttons, select **All Caps**. Then click **Remove**. The button is removed from the list.

12. In the lower-right corner of the dialog box, click **OK**. The All Caps button no longer appears on the Quick Access Toolbar, but the toolbar still contains three buttons that you added.

13. Click the **File** tab, and then click **Options**. In the left pane of the Word Options dialog box, click **Quick Access Toolbar**. In the lower-right corner of the dialog box, click **Reset**, and then click **Reset only Quick Access Toolbar**. When prompted to restore the Quick Access Toolbar to its default contents, click **Yes**, and then click **OK** to close the dialog box. All buttons you added are removed from the Quick Access Toolbar, and the default buttons are restored.

14. Close the document without saving the changes, and leave Word open for the next Step-by-Step.

Customizing the Ribbon

A new feature in Word 2010 enables you to customize the Ribbon. The Ribbon consists of two types of tabs: main tabs and tool tabs. The ***main tabs*** appear on the Ribbon when you launch the application. The ***tool tabs*** are contextual and appear on the Ribbon only when you select objects in a document.

    The default Ribbon is loaded with commonly used commands. You may not use all of those commands, and there may be other commands that you frequently use that do not appear on the Ribbon. You can reorganize the Ribbon so that your favorite commands appear together on a single tab.

▶ **VOCABULARY**
main tabs

tool tabs

Reorganizing Tabs, Groups, and Commands on the Ribbon

You can choose which tabs to display on the Ribbon, and you can rename all the default tabs. You can also rearrange the order of the tabs and/or the groups on the tabs. Reorganizing tabs and groups for the Ribbon is similar to rearranging document headings in Outline view. You can expand and collapse the names, and you can drag and drop the names to reorganize where the tabs and groups appear on the Ribbon. However, you cannot move default commands within a group or from one group to another. You also cannot change the icon assigned to a command button on a default tab or in a default group.

When you customize the Ribbon in Word, the changes are saved in the Word application; no changes will appear in the Ribbon for other applications such as Excel and PowerPoint. You can easily restore the default settings for an individual tab or for the entire Ribbon.

Step-by-Step 17.2

1. Click the **File** tab, and then click **Options**. In the left pane of the Word Options dialog box, click **Customize Ribbon**. The current configuration of the Ribbon appears in the right pane, as shown in **Figure 17–3**. Your settings may differ.

FIGURE 17–3
Options for customizing the Ribbon

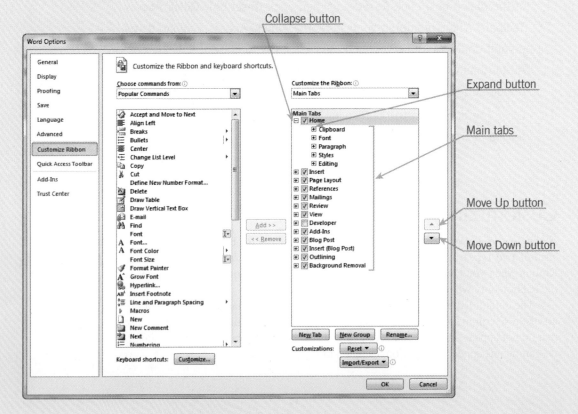

2. In the right pane, under Customize the Ribbon, click the **list arrow** and then click **Tool Tabs**. Scroll down to view all the default Tool Tabs that are available. Click the **list arrow** again, and then click **Main Tabs**.

3. In the right pane, under Main Tabs, click the **check box** next to Mailings to disable the tab. (When disabled, the check box is unchecked.)

4. In the right pane, under Main Tabs, select **Page Layout**. In the lower-right corner of the dialog box, click **Rename** to open the Rename dialog box. Type **Document Layout**, and then click **OK**. The tab name is now *Document Layout.*

5. In the right pane, drag and drop the **Review** tab name so it is repositioned just above the Insert tab name. To the left of the Review tab name, click the **Expand** button ⊞ to show all the groups on the Review tab.

6   In the list of groups on the Review tab, select **Proofing**. Then click the **Move Up** button on the right side of the pane five times to reposition the Proofing group just after the Clipboard group on the Home tab.

7. In the right pane, in the list of groups on the Review tab, select **Chinese Conversion**. Then click **Remove** (between the center and right panes). The group is removed from the tab.

8. In the right pane, in the list of groups on the Review tab, select **Language**. In the lower-right corner of the dialog box, click **Rename** to open the Rename dialog box. Type **Translate**, and then click **OK**. The group name is now *Translate.*

9. To the left of the Review tab name, click the **Collapse** button ⊟ to hide the list of groups on the tab.

10. In the lower-right corner of the screen, click **OK**. On the Ribbon, note that the Review tab is now positioned to the right of the Home tab, the Home tab now shows the Proofing group to the right of the Clipboard group, the Page Layout tab is now the Document Layout tab, and the Mailings tab is not shown.

11. Click the **File** tab, and then click **Options**. In the left pane, click **Customize Ribbon**. In the right pane, select **Review**.

12. In the lower-right corner of the dialog box, click **Reset** and then click **Reset only selected Ribbon tab**. In the right pane, next to the Review tab name, click the **Expand button** to show the list of groups. Note that the Proofing and Chinese Conversion groups are included in the list, and the name for the Language group was restored. No changes were made to the other tabs.

13. In the lower-right corner of the dialog box, click **Reset** and then click **Reset all customizations**. When prompted to delete all customizations, click **Yes**.

14. Click **OK** to accept the changes and close the Word Options dialog box. The entire Ribbon is restored to the default settings.

▶ **TIP**

To expand or collapse a tab or group, you can double-click the tab or group name.

▶ **EXTRA FOR EXPERTS**

The Proofing group also still appears under the Home tab, so you have essentially copied the Proofing group and it now appears on two different tabs in the Ribbon.

Adding and Removing Groups, Commands, and Tabs on the Ribbon

For quicker access to commands that you use frequently, you can customize the Ribbon by adding new commands. You cannot add new commands to default groups. To add new commands to a tab, you must first create a new custom group. You can create new groups on all tabs. When you add new commands to a custom group, you can assign custom icons to the buttons for the commands. If you want to add several new groups and commands, you can add new main tabs and tool tabs to the Ribbon.

You can remove all of the new tabs, groups, and commands that you create. You can also remove default commands and groups from all of Word's default tabs. However, you cannot remove the default tabs that appear on the Ribbon. If you don't want a default tab to appear on the Ribbon, you can hide the tab.

Step-by-Step 17.3

1. Click the **File** tab, and then click **Options**. In the left pane, click **Customize Ribbon**. If necessary, click the **Expand** button next to Home to show all the groups on the Home tab.

2. To create a new group on a default tab, first select the desired tab. In the right pane, select **Home**. In the lower-right corner of the dialog box, click **New Group**. The group name *New Group (Custom)* appears at the end of the list of groups on the Home tab.

3. To rename the new group, make sure the group name you want to change is selected. (*New Group (Custom)* is already selected.) Click **Rename**. In the Rename dialog box, type **My Stuff**, and then click **OK**. The new group name *My Stuff (Custom)* appears in the right pane. The word *(Custom)* will not appear on the Ribbon tab.

4. To add a command to the group, first select the group. (*My Stuff (Custom)* is already selected.) In the left pane, under Choose commands from, click the **list arrow** and then click **Commands Not in the Ribbon**. Scroll down in the list of commands and select **Close All**. Then click **Add**.

5. To change the button icon for the new Close All command, make sure the command is selected. (*Close All* is already selected.) Click **Rename** to open the Rename dialog box, as shown in **Figure 17–4**. At the end of the fourth row of icons, click the **hand** icon and then click **OK**. The new icon replaces the original icon in the right pane.

> **TIP**
>
> The Close All command will close all open documents at the same time. If one or more documents have unsaved changes, Word will prompt you before closing those documents.

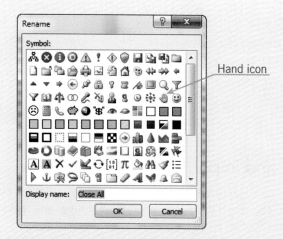

FIGURE 17–4
Rename dialog box with options
for icons

Hand icon

6. To create a new tab, select an existing tab. In the right pane, select **View**. In the lower-right corner of the dialog box, click **New Tab**. In the list of tabs in the right pane, *New Tab (Custom)* appears below the selected tab, and *New Group (Custom)* appears below the new tab entry. This new tab will appear to the right of the View tab on the Ribbon.

7. In the right pane, select **New Tab (Custom)**. Then, in the lower-right corner of the dialog box, click **New Group**. The new tab now has two groups. Select **New Tab (Custom)**. Click **Rename** and in the Rename dialog box, type your **first name** and **last name** and then click **OK**.

8. In the list of groups on the new tab, select the first **New Group (Custom)**. Then click **Rename**, type **Favorites**, and click **OK**.

9. The Favorites (Custom) group should still be selected. In the center pane, under Choose commands from, click the **list arrow**, and then click **Popular Commands**. Under Popular Commands, select **Copy** and click **Add**. Then add the **Paste (Paste)** command and the **Cut** command to the new Favorites group.

10. In the right pane, use the drag-and-drop method to reposition the commands in the Favorites group so they appear in this sequence: *Cut*, *Copy*, and *Paste*.

11. In the right pane, select **Cut** and then click **Remove**. The command is removed from the group.

12. Click **OK** to close Word Options. The new tab with two groups appears on the Ribbon.

13. Click the **File** tab, and then click **Options**. In the left pane of the Word Options dialog box, click **Customize Ribbon**. In the right pane, select the custom tab with your name and then click **Remove**. Click **OK** to close the Word Options dialog box. The tab and all the groups and commands on the tab are removed. However, the Custom group *My Stuff* still appears on the Home tab.

TIP

Hover the mouse over the command name to show a ScreenTip to distinguish the two Paste commands.

14. Leave Word open for the next Step-by-Step. If you are ending your Word session, restore the entire Ribbon to the Default settings. (In the Word Options dialog box, click Customize Ribbon, click Reset, and then click Reset all customizations. When prompted to delete all customizations, click Yes.)

Exporting and Importing Customizations

You can share your customized Ribbon and Quick Access Toolbar by exporting the settings to a file. Then other users can import those settings and replace their Ribbon and Quick Access Toolbar settings with the customized settings.

In the next Step-by-Step, you'll export custom Ribbon and Quick Access Toolbar settings to a new file. If you have restored the Ribbon to the default settings, you can still complete the steps.

Step-by-Step 17.4

1. Click the **File** tab, and then click **Options**. In the left pane of the Word Options dialog box, click **Customize Ribbon**.

2. In the lower-right corner of the dialog box, click **Import/Export** and then click **Export all customizations**. The File Save dialog box opens.

3. Navigate to the drive and folder where you save your solution files. In the File name box, change the filename to **Word Customizations**, followed by your initials. Note that Word assigns the document extension *.exportedUI*. Then click **Save**.

4. In the Word Options dialog box, click **Reset** and then click **Reset all customizations**. Click **Yes** to delete the customizations. Then click **OK** to accept the changes and close the Word Options dialog box.

5. Click the **File** tab, and then click **Options**. In the left pane, click **Customize Ribbon**.

6. Click **Import/Export**, and then click **Import customization file**. The File Open dialog box opens.

7. Navigate to the drive and folder where you save your solution files. Select the .exportedUI file you just saved and click **Open**. A prompt appears to confirm changing the settings. Click **Yes** and then click **OK** to close the Word Options dialog box. The Ribbon now shows the customized settings you saved.

8. Click the **File** tab, and then click **Options**. In the left pane, click **Customize Ribbon**. Click **Reset** and then click **Reset all customizations**. Click **Yes** and then click **OK** to accept the changes and close the Word Options dialog box. The custom group *My Stuff* no longer appears on the Home tab.

9. Leave Word open for the next Step-by-Step.

Modifying the Default Document Formats

As you already know, the font style and font size, paragraph line spacing, and document margins are always the same when you open a new blank document. The document formats are determined by the Normal.dotm template. Changing the default settings is easy, and you can save the new settings to the active template so that all new documents based on that template will be formatted with the new settings.

As you learned in Lesson 10, when you attach a template to a document, that template becomes the active template. In the next Step-by-Step, you create and attach a personal template to a document. Then as you change some default settings, the settings will be saved in the personal template and not in the Normal.dotm template. After saving settings to a template file, you can create new documents based on the template and you can share the template with colleagues.

WARNING

Throughout this lesson, if you are prompted to save changes to the Normal.dotm template, click No.

Step-by-Step 17.5

1. If necessary, open a new blank document. Click the **File** tab, and then click **Save As** to open the Save As dialog box.

2. Navigate to the drive and folder where you save your solution files. In the File name box, type **Personal Template 4**, followed by your initials. In the Save as type box, select **Word Template (*.dotx)**. Click **Save**.

3. On the Home tab, in the Font group, click the **Dialog Box Launcher** to open the Font dialog box. If necessary, click the **Font** tab to display the options shown in **Figure 17–5**.

FIGURE 17–5
Font tab in the Font dialog box

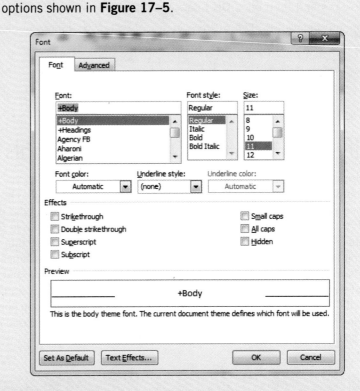

4. In the Font text box, type **g** to move down in the list to show all the fonts beginning with the letter *g*. Select **Georgia**. Under Size, select **12** point. Click **Set as Default**. A prompt appears asking you to confirm the changes, as shown in **Figure 17–6**.

FIGURE 17–6
Prompt to confirm default font change

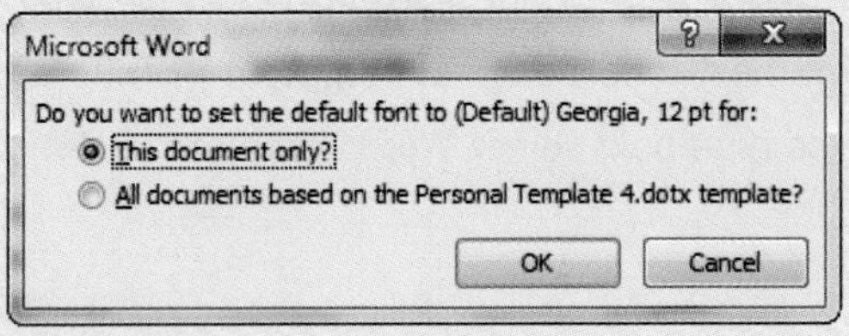

5. Select the **All documents in Personal Template 4.dotx template?** option, and then click **OK**.

6. In the Paragraph group, click the **Dialog Box Launcher** to open the Paragraph dialog box. Under Spacing, change the After setting to **0 pt**. Under Line spacing, change the setting to **Single**. Your settings should match those shown in **Figure 17–7**.

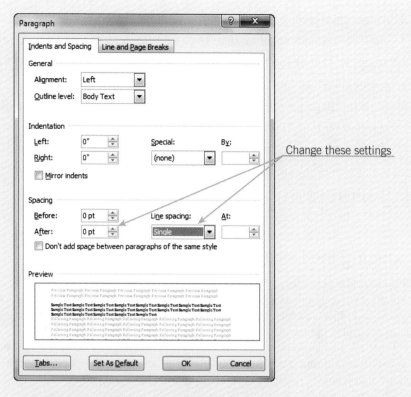

FIGURE 17-7
Paragraph dialog box

7. Click **Set As Default**. A prompt appears to confirm the changes. Select the **All documents in Personal Template 4.dotx template?** option, and then click **OK**.

8. Change the Page Setup settings:

   a. Click the **Page Layout** tab. In the Page Setup group, click the **Margins** button and then click **Custom Margins** to open the Page Setup dialog box.

   b. On the Margins tab, change the top margin to **1.5"**.

   c. In the Page Setup dialog box, click the **Paper** tab. Under Paper size, change the setting to **Legal**.

   d. In the Page Setup dialog box, click the **Layout** tab. Under Headers and footers, enable the **Different first page** option.

   e. Click **Set As Default**. A prompt appears to confirm the changes, which include all three Page Setup settings. Click **Yes**.

9. Save the changes to the document and then close the document.

10. To open a new document based on the document template, click the **File** tab and then click **New**. Under Available Templates, click the **New from existing** icon. The New from Existing Document dialog box opens.

11. If necessary, navigate to the drive and folder where you save your solution files. Select the file **Personal Template 4.dotx**, and then click **Create New**.

12. A new blank document opens. Type **=rand(3,3)** and press **Enter** to create three paragraphs of random text, with three sentences in each paragraph. Note that the font size is Georgia 12 point, and the paragraphs are single-spaced with no extra space between paragraphs.

13. Click the **Page Layout** tab, and then in the Page Setup group, click the **Margins** button. The top margin is set to *1.5"*. Click the document to close the menu. In the Page Setup group, click the **Size** button. The paper size is set at *Legal 8.5 x 14"*. Close the menu.

14. Close the document without saving the changes.

Changing the Document Display Settings

Everyone has a personal preference for how content displays on the screen, and Word offers several options to control the display. If you're not comfortable with the way text and objects appear on your screen, you can modify the settings using the document display options.

Table 17–1 lists several document display options and describes why you would want to enable or disable the options and how you can access the options in the Word Options dialog box.

TABLE 17–1   Document display options

OPTION	PURPOSE	LOCATION IN WORD OPTIONS DIALOG BOX
Show Mini Toolbar on selection	When enabled, a transparent image of the Mini toolbar appears when you select text. If you don't use the Mini toolbar and you find it gets in your way, you can disable this option.	General options, under User Interface options
Show white space between pages in Print Layout view	When you disable this option, in Print Layout view, the white space for the top and bottom margins does not appear. This saves space on your screen as you review the document.	Display options, under Page display options
Show highlighter marks	When disabled, highlighted content appears normal and the highlight color does not appear on the screen or in printed copies. This option is useful when you've marked content with highlights and you want to print the document without the highlights.	Display options, under Page display options
Show document tooltips on hover	When disabled, the ScreenTips that Word provides will not be displayed.	Display options, under Page display options

TABLE 17–1 Document display options (continued)

OPTION	PURPOSE	LOCATION IN WORD OPTIONS DIALOG BOX
Show text wrapped within the document window	When enabled, the flow of text changes to fit the window when the document window is resized. This option only affects the display when the document appears in Draft, Outline, and Web Layout views. In Page Layout view, even when the option is enabled, if the document window is not as wide as the line of text, some of the text does not show.	Advanced options, under Show document content
Show picture placeholders	If the document contains many graphics, you can scroll through the document more quickly by showing placeholders instead of the pictures.	Advanced options, under Show document content
Show text boundaries	When enabled, you won't need to use the rulers to estimate the text area. This option is useful when you are positioning objects on a page.	Advanced options, under Show document content
Use draft font in Draft and Outline views	Depending on the fonts used in the document, this option can make documents easier to read; it does not affect how the document prints.	Advanced options, under Show document content
Show this number of Recent Documents...	You can choose the number of recent documents that appear in the Recent Documents list in Backstage view. The number can be set between 0 and 50.	Advanced options, under Display
Show measurements in units of...	This option affects rulers and settings in dialog boxes. You can choose to show units in inches, centimeters, millimeters, points, and picas.	Advanced options, under Display

In the following Step-by-Step, you will enable and disable some of these options to see the effect on how content is displayed on your screen.

Step-by-Step 17.6

1. Open a new blank document. Type **=rand(14,5)** and press **Enter** to create 14 paragraphs of random text, with five sentences in each paragraph.

2. Position the insertion point at the top of the document. Insert a clip art image of a box. Resize the image so it is approximately 5 inches high by 5 inches wide.

3. Click the **View** tab. In the Zoom group, click the **One Page** button. Scroll to the bottom of the first page so you can view parts of both the first and second pages. Notice the white space at the bottom of the first page and at the top of the second page.

4. Click the **File** tab, and then click **Options**. In the left pane of the Word Options dialog box, click **Display** to display the options shown in **Figure 17–8**. If your settings differ, make a note of the differences, because at the end of the Step-by-Step, you will need to restore all the settings.

FIGURE 17–8
Options for display settings

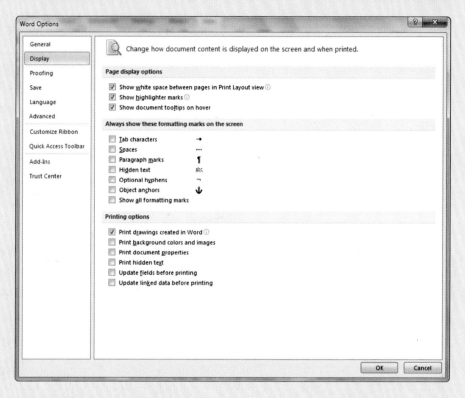

5. Under Page display options, disable the option **Show white space between pages in Print Layout view**. Click **OK** to close the Word Options dialog box.

6. If necessary, scroll down to show parts of both the first and second pages. Now the white space for the bottom and top margins no longer appears, and a divider line indicates the break between the two pages.

7. Point to the divider line. The mouse pointer changes to a double-headed arrow, as shown in **Figure 17–9**. Double-click the divider line and the white space appears.

FIGURE 17–9
Divider line between two pages

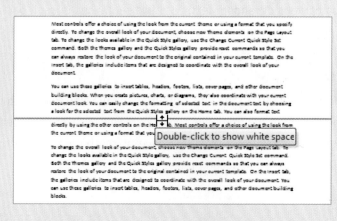

8. Position the mouse pointer in the break between the two pages. When the pointer changes to a double-headed arrow, double-click to hide the white space. Double-click the divider line again to show the white space and restore the default setting.

9. Click the **File** tab, and then click **Options**. In the left pane, click **Advanced**. Scroll down to the middle of the list to display the settings shown in **Figure 17–10**. If your settings differ, make a note of the differences, because at the end of the Step-by-Step, you will need to restore all the settings.

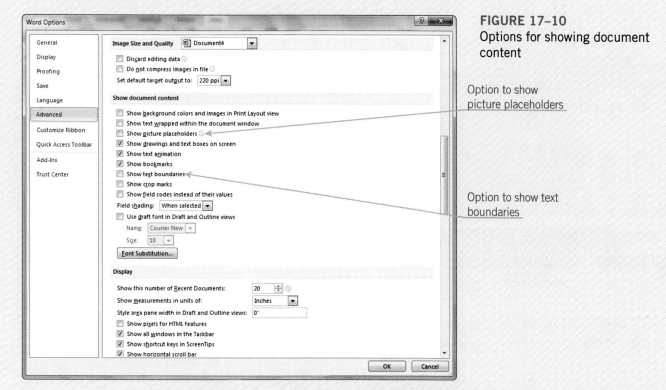

FIGURE 17–10
Options for showing document content

Option to show picture placeholders

Option to show text boundaries

10. Under Show document content, enable the options **Show text boundaries** and **Show picture placeholders**. Click **OK** to close the Word Options dialog box. Notice that the clip art image no longer appears, but a placeholder indicates where the image was inserted. Also, text boundaries now appear. These boundaries will not print.

11. Click the **File** tab, and then click **Options**. In the left pane, click **Advanced**. Scroll down to the middle of the list and, under Show document content, disable the options **Show text boundaries** and **Show picture placeholders**. Compare your settings for Advanced options to those in Figure 17–10 (and any differences you noted) to make sure the settings are the same as when you began working in this Step-by-Step. Make any necessary changes.

12. In the left pane, click **Display**. Compare your settings for Display options to those in Figure 17–8 (and any differences you noted) to make sure the settings are the same as when you began working in this Step-by-Step. Make any necessary changes, and then click **OK** to accept the changes and close the Word Options dialog box.

13. Leave the document open for the next Step-by-Step. (If you are ending your Word session now, you can close the document without saving the changes.)

Changing the Edit Settings

Word provides many default settings to help you edit document content. For example, you can drag and drop content, and you can quickly select text and replace it with different text. You may find that you need to change these settings to fit your needs for editing documents.

Table 17–2 lists several editing options; it describes why you would want to enable or disable the options and how you can access them. To access the editing options, click Advanced in the left pane of the Word Options dialog box.

TABLE 17–2   Editing options

OPTION	PURPOSE
Typing replaces selected text	When this option is disabled, the selected content is not removed and new content is inserted in front of the selected content.
When selecting, automatically select entire word	When enabled, whole words and the blank space after the word are selected when you double-click a word. Also, if you use the mouse to drag across text and you select part of one word and then continue to drag the mouse over part of the text in the next word, all the text in both words is automatically selected.
Allow text to be dragged and dropped	Some users prefer to use cut and paste instead of drag and drop. If you find you often accidentally drag and drop selected text, you can disable this option.
Use smart paragraph selection	If this option is enabled, when you triple-click to select a paragraph, the paragraph mark is included in the selection. The paragraph formatting is stored with the paragraph mark and, therefore, stays with the selected paragraph.
Use smart cursoring	When this option is enabled, the insertion point moves as you scroll through the document. Then, when you press the arrow keys to reposition the insertion point, the insertion point responds on the current page in view instead of its previous position.
Keep track of formatting	This option is useful when you need formatting to be consistent throughout a document. When formats are inconsistent, such as line spacing for paragraphs, Word will identify the paragraph with the inconsistent line spacing with a wavy blue underline.

TABLE 17–2   Editing options (continued)

OPTION	PURPOSE
Mark formatting inconsistencies	To use this option, you must also enable the Keep track of formatting option. When formatting is similar to, but not exactly the same as, other formatting in the document, the content will be underscored with a wavy blue underline.
Show AutoComplete suggestions	When enabled, this option provides ScreenTips that suggest text entries to complete the word or phrase.

In the following Step-by-Step, you will enable and disable various options to see how they affect some of the editing features in Word.

Step-by-Step 17.7

1. If necessary, open a new blank document, type **=rand(14,5)**, and press **Enter** to create 14 paragraphs with five sentences in each paragraph. If necessary, click the **View** tab, and in the Zoom group, click **One Page**.

2. Hold down **Ctrl** and press **Home** to reposition the insertion point at the top of the document.

TECHNOLOGY CAREERS

If you have fast and accurate typing skills and a good eye for detail, there are several data entry and information processing career opportunities for you. *Word processors and typists* work with word processing applications to create and edit a variety of documents such as correspondence, reports, forms, and contracts. In addition to typing skills, word processors and typists also need skills in proofreading documents, identifying and correcting spelling, grammar, and punctuation errors, and formatting documents. Data entry keyers enter numbers and information in a form, such as medical records and membership information. Accuracy is emphasized because inaccurate data leads to inaccurate records, and errors result in high business expenses. *Data entry keyers* are also often responsible for correcting errors and compiling and sorting data. Technology allows many data entry and information processing workers to work flexible hours, both part- and full-time, and the flexibility to work out of their homes.

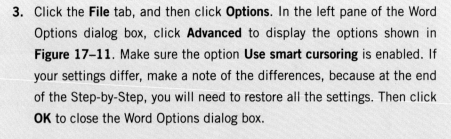

3. Click the **File** tab, and then click **Options**. In the left pane of the Word Options dialog box, click **Advanced** to display the options shown in **Figure 17–11**. Make sure the option **Use smart cursoring** is enabled. If your settings differ, make a note of the differences, because at the end of the Step-by-Step, you will need to restore all the settings. Then click **OK** to close the Word Options dialog box.

FIGURE 17–11
Options for editing

Option for smart
cursoring

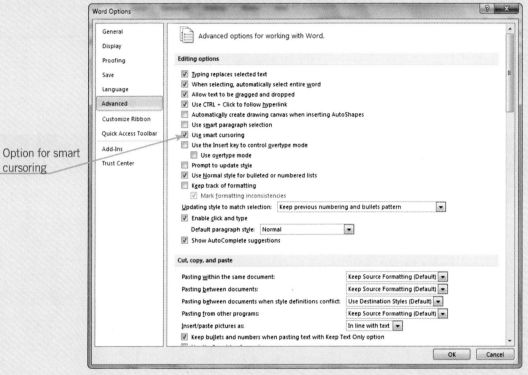

4. Use the mouse to scroll down in the document to view about half of the content on the second page. Press the **down arrow**. The insertion point is repositioned near the bottom of visible content on the second page. Scroll to the top of the document so you can view the first paragraph. Press the **up arrow**. The insertion point is repositioned at the top of the first page.

5. Click the **File** tab, and then click **Options**. In the left pane, click **Advanced**. Under Editing options, disable the option **Use smart cursoring**. Click **OK** to close the Word Options dialog box.

6. Use the mouse to scroll down in the document to view all the content on the second page. Press the **down arrow**. The view changes to show the first page of the document, and the insertion point is repositioned one line below its original position at the top of the first page. The insertion point did not move when you scrolled through the document using the mouse.

7. Click the **File** tab, and then click **Options**. In the left pane, click **Advanced**. Under Editing options, enable the option **Use smart cursoring**.

8. Under Editing options, enable the options **Keep track of formatting** and **Mark formatting inconsistencies**. Click **OK** to close the Word Options dialog box.

9. Position the insertion point at the end of the document. Then change the font point size from 11 to **12**.

10. Type your name. Because of the inconsistency in the font format, Word marks the new text with a wavy blue line.

11. Click the **File** tab, and then click **Options**. In the left pane, click **Advanced**. Under Editing options, disable the options **Mark formatting inconsistencies** and **Keep track of formatting**. Click **OK** to close the Word Options dialog box.

12. Close the document without saving the changes.

13. Click the **File** tab, and then click **Options**. In the left pane, click **Advanced**. Compare your settings for the Advanced options to those in Figure 17–11 (and any differences you noted) to make sure the settings are the same as when you began working in this Step-by-Step. Make any necessary changes, and then click **OK** to accept the changes and close the Word Options dialog box.

14. Leave Word open for the next Step-by-Step.

Changing the Save Settings

Word's default settings for saving documents include the file format and the drive and folder where files are saved. You can also specify a path to save draft files for offline editing.

Word automatically saves draft versions as you work with a document. The frequency of saving depends on your Word settings. For example, you can set the option to save a draft version every three minutes. When you close the document, the draft versions are deleted. You can also enable an option so that if you accidentally close a document without saving the changes, a draft version will automatically be saved, and then you would be able to access that draft version. Draft versions are useful if you are not tracking changes when you are creating or editing a document. If you've been working on the document for a long time, you can compare the current document with an earlier draft version of that same document to see the changes that you have made.

Table 17–3 lists several save options; it describes why you would want to enable or disable the options and how you can access them.

TABLE 17–3   Save options

OPTION	PURPOSE	LOCATION IN WORD OPTIONS DIALOG BOX
User name and Initials	The information provides the author name in the document properties.	General options, under Personalize your copy of Microsoft Office
Save AutoRecover information	This setting controls how frequently AutoRecover files are saved as you work with a document.	Save options, under Save documents
Default file location	The default file location is the My Documents folder. You can change the setting to save to a different drive and folder. You do not need to save all files in the default file location, but if you don't designate a different path, the file will be saved in the default file location.	Save options, under Save documents
Server drafts location	If you share documents using a document management server, you can designate a location to save server draft files.	Save options, under Offline editing options for document management server files
Embed fonts in the file	You can embed the fonts in the document file so other users can view and use the fonts, even if they don't have the fonts installed on their computers.	Save options, under Preserve fidelity when sharing this document

In the following Step-by-Step, you will explore how to access some of the save options in Word. You will not make any changes in the Word save settings in this Step-by-Step.

Step-by-Step 17.8

1. Open a new blank document.
2. Click the **File** tab, and then click **Options**. In the left pane of the Word Options dialog box, click **Save** to display the options shown in **Figure 17–12**. Your settings may differ.

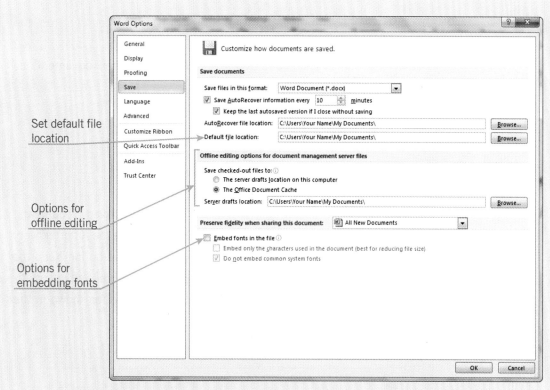

Set default file location

Options for offline editing

Options for embedding fonts

FIGURE 17–12
Options for saving documents

3. Under Save documents, you can change the default document format and the frequency of AutoRecover saving. You can also change the default settings for where the AutoRecover files and all other files are saved. Make a note of the drive and folder for the AutoRecover and Default file locations.

4. Note that under Offline editing options for document management server files, you can change the drive and folder for storing server drafts.

5. Note that under Preserve fidelity when sharing this document, you can choose to embed fonts in the file. By embedding fonts, you can be sure the document will show the fonts you used when you created the file, even if the user doesn't have those fonts installed on their computer.

6. Click **Cancel** to close the Word Options dialog box without making any changes.

7. Click the **File** tab to show the Backstage view. Depending on the AutoRecover settings, if you were working on a saved document, you may see one or more autosaved versions of the open document, as shown in **Figure 17–13**.

FIGURE 17–13
Autosaved versions in
Backstage view

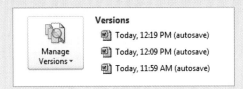

8. Click **Manage Versions**, and then click **Recover Unsaved Documents**. The Open dialog box opens and shows the folder where the AutoRecovery drafts are saved (as noted in Step 3 above). If the save option *Keep the last autosaved version if I close without saving* is enabled, an automatically saved version may appear in the Open dialog box, as shown in the example in **Figure 17–14**.

FIGURE 17–14
Open dialog box with example of an
AutoRecovery saved document

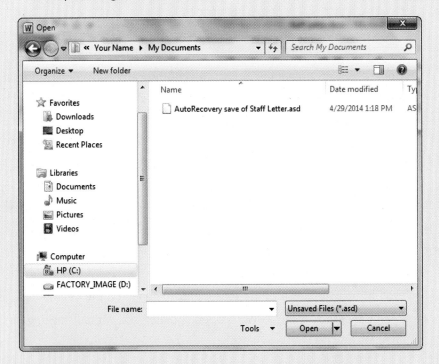

9. Click **Cancel** to close the dialog bog.

10. Click the **File** tab and leave Word open for the next Step-by-Step.

Customizing the AutoCorrect Feature

You already know that the AutoCorrect feature automatically corrects commonly misspelled words immediately after an error is typed. The default settings in Word provide a long list of AutoCorrect entries. You can customize the list by creating your own AutoCorrect entries. To illustrate, if you frequently type certain words incorrectly, you can add the misspelled words to the AutoCorrect list so Word will always correct your mistake.

You can also use AutoCorrect to quickly insert text you use over and over again. For example, you may frequently enter your full name in documents. You can create an AutoCorrect entry using your initials, and then every time you type your initials followed by a blank space, Word will automatically insert your full name.

Sometimes you frequently use terms and phrases that have unique spellings and/or capitalization, and you don't want Word to correct those spellings. For example, the spellings of personal, company, and product names cannot always be found in a dictionary. To store names that you do not want Word to correct automatically, you can create a list of exceptions for three different categories: (1) words or text after which you do not want Word to capitalize (such as an abbreviation that includes a period); (2) words or text in initial caps; and (3) other corrections that do not fall within the first two categories.

In the next Step-by-Step, you will add a new entry to the AutoCorrect list and you will create two AutoCorrect exceptions. However, because you may be sharing a computer, you will delete the new entry and the two exceptions at the end of the Step-by-Step.

Step-by-Step 17.9

1. If necessary, open a new blank document. Click the **File** tab, and then click **Options**. In the left pane of the Word Options dialog box, click **Proofing**.

2. Under AutoCorrect options, click **AutoCorrect Options**. The AutoCorrect dialog box opens, as shown in **Figure 17–15**. In the scrolling list at the bottom of the window, the text shown in the left column is automatically replaced with the text shown in the right column.

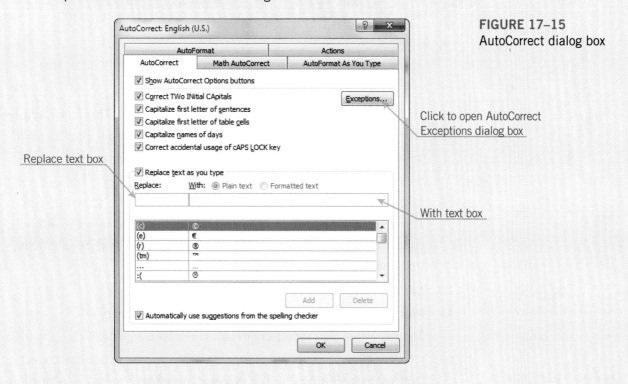

FIGURE 17–15
AutoCorrect dialog box

3. Scroll through the list of frequently misspelled words until you see *agian* in the left column. Note that Word will automatically correct this misspelling to *again*.

4. In the Replace text box, type **wrd**. In the With text box, type **word**. Click **Add**. Click **OK** to close the AutoCorrect dialog box, and then click **OK** to close the Word Options dialog box.

5. Type the following sentence exactly as shown with the misspelled words. Notice as you type that Word automatically corrects the misspelled words.

   Sometimes we misspell the same wrd agian and agian. As soon as you press the spacebar or end the sentence with a period, Word immediately corrects the misspellings.

6. Click the **File** tab, and then click **Options**. In the left pane, click **Proofing**, and then click **AutoCorrect Options**.

7. In the AutoCorrect dialog box, click **Exceptions**. The AutoCorrect Exceptions dialog box opens, as shown in **Figure 17–16**. Notice that Word already provides a list of exceptions for first-letter capitalization.

FIGURE 17–16
AutoCorrect Exceptions dialog box

8. In the text box under Don't capitalize after, type **Ltd.**. Then click **Add**. Normally, Word would capitalize the first letter in a word after a blank space following *Ltd.* due to the period, but this exception will prevent Word from capitalizing the next word that follows.

9. Click the **INitial CAps** tab. In the text box under Don't correct, type **EXcel** and then click **Add**. Normally, Word would lowercase the second capital letter in the word *EXcel*, but this exception will prevent Word from making that AutoCorrect change.

10. Click **OK** three times to close the dialog boxes.

11. Press the **spacebar** and then type the following sentence:
    The merger of EXcel and Durand Ltd. is almost complete.

12. Click the **File** tab, click **Options**, click **Proofing**, and then click **AutoCorrect Options**. In the Replace text box, type **wrd**. Word scrolls to that AutoCorrect entry in the list box. With the *wrd* entry selected, click **Delete**.

13. Click **Exceptions**. On the INitial CAps tab, select the entry **EXcel** and click **Delete**. Click the **First Letter** tab, and under Don't capitalize after, type the letter **l** (a lowercase L), select **ltd.**, and then click **Delete**. Click **OK** three times to close the dialog boxes and the Word Options.

14. Close the document without saving the changes.

Creating a Custom Dictionary

When you run a spelling checker, Word compares the text to a list of common words stored in a standard dictionary. When Word flags a possibly misspelled word, you can add the word to the dictionary, but it is not added to the standard dictionary. Instead, the word is added to a new custom dictionary named CUSTOM.DIC. If you frequently use proper names and acronyms that are not in Word's standard dictionary, you will find that adding those words to a custom dictionary is helpful so they aren't flagged as unknown or misspelled words during a spell check. When you add words to a dictionary, the words are added to the custom dictionary designated as the default dictionary.

Every Office 2010 application shares the file CUSTOM.DIC. If you share a computer, multiple individuals are contributing to the word list in the CUSTOM.DIC dictionary, and though it might be useful to have words added to the dictionary list, you don't have complete control of the list. To confirm that a word is in the list, you would need to review the list of words in the dictionary. An alternative solution is to create a separate custom dictionary. For example, you can create a custom dictionary for legal terms, one for medical terms, and another for engineering terms. Then you can add the new dictionary to Word's dictionary list and make it active. During a spell check, Word will check the standard dictionary, the default custom dictionary, and any other custom dictionaries that are active.

Step-by-Step 17.10

1. Open a new blank document. Click the **File** tab, and then click **Options**. In the left pane of the Word Options dialog box, click **Proofing**.

2. Under When correcting spelling in Microsoft Office programs, click **Custom Dictionaries**. The Custom Dictionaries dialog box opens, as shown in **Figure 17–17**. Your settings may differ. The CUSTOM.DIC default dictionary appears under Dictionary List.

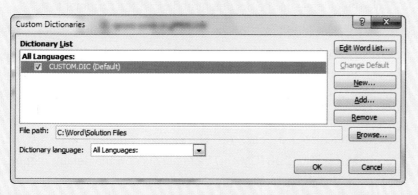

FIGURE 17–17
Custom Dictionaries dialog box

3. In the dialog box, click **New** to open the Create Custom Dictionary dialog box.

4. Navigate to the drive and folder where you save your solution files. In the File name box, type **UltraTech**, followed by your initials. Do not change the file type. Word will add the .dic extension to the filename. Click **Save**.

5. In the Custom Dictionaries dialog box, select the **UltraTech** dictionary. Click **Edit Word List**. A dialog box for the new UltraTech dictionary opens. Currently, the Dictionary list contains no words. In the Word(s) text box, type **UltraTech** and then click **Add**. The new word is added to the Dictionary list.

6. Add two more words to the list:
    a. Click the Word box, type **coextrusion**, and then click **Add**.
    b. Click the Word box, type **coextrusions**, and then click **Add**.
    c. Click **OK**.

7. Now the Dictionary List shows two dictionaries. Both dictionaries have check marks, so they are both active. Select the **UltraTech** dictionary. (Be sure not to uncheck it.) Click **Change Default**. The order of the dictionaries is changed, and the UltraTech dictionary is now the default dictionary.

8. Click **OK** twice to close the dialog boxes.

9. Open the **LLDPE Blends and Coextrusions** file from the drive and folder where your Data Files are stored. Save the document as **Revised LLDPE Blends and Coextrusions**, followed by your initials.

10. If your Proofing settings are set to check spelling as you type, a wavy red line will appear below unknown words. Right-click the first unknown word, **Lepri**. In the shortcut menu, click **Add to Dictionary**. The word is added to the UltraTech dictionary because that is the default dictionary.

11. Click the **Review** tab, and then click the Spelling & Grammar button. When the word *comonomer* is flagged as an unknown spelling, click **Add to Dictionary**. A prompt appears indicating that the spelling and grammar check is complete. If the proofing option to show readability statistics is enabled, the Readability Statistics dialog box opens. Click **OK** to complete the spell check.

12. Save the changes to the document and close the document.

13. Click the **File** tab, click **Options**, and then click **Proofing**. Click **Custom Dictionaries**. Select the dictionary **UltraTech**, and click **Edit Word List**. Note that the words *Lepri* and *comonomer* appear in the Dictionary list. Click **OK**.

14. In the Custom Dictionaries dialog box, in the Dictionary list under All Languages, disable the **UltraTech** dictionary. When prompted to remove the custom dictionary, click **Yes**. The dictionary remains in the list, but it is not active. The CUSTOM.DIC dictionary is now the default dictionary. Click **OK** two times to close the dialog boxes.

WARNING

If you are prompted to save changes to the Normal.dotm template upon exiting Word, click No.

SUMMARY

In this lesson, you learned:

■ You can customize the Quick Access Toolbar by adding and deleting command buttons.

■ You can customize the Ribbon by rearranging the order of the tabs and the groups and commands on the tabs.

■ You can add new groups and new commands to the default Ribbon tabs, and you can create new custom tabs on the Ribbon.

■ To share customized Ribbon and Quick Access Toolbar settings, you can export the settings to a file.

■ You can save default settings to a document template so the settings are available for other documents and on other computers without changing the default settings in the Normal.dotm template.

■ If you're not comfortable with the way text and objects appear on the screen, you can modify the display settings.

■ Word offers several options for editing documents, and you can customize the editing settings to fit your needs.

■ The default save settings include the document file format and location. For offline editing, you can also designate a location for saving documents on a document management server.

■ You can customize the list of AutoCorrect entries, and you can also create a list of exceptions so Word does not correct the spelling or capitalization for unique terms and phrases.

■ If you often type terms that are not in the main dictionary, you can save time using the spelling checker by creating a custom dictionary to store these terms.

 VOCABULARY REVIEW

Define the following terms:

main tabs   tool tabs

 REVIEW QUESTIONS

TRUE / FALSE

Circle T if the statement is true or F if the statement is false.

T   F   **1.** When restoring Ribbon settings, you can reset an individual tab without making changes to the other tabs.

T   F   **2.** You can choose which tabs to display on the Ribbon.

T   F   **3.** When you customize the settings in Word, the changes are automatically saved to the application.

T   F   **4.** When you customize the Ribbon in Word, the changes will also appear in the Ribbon for other applications such as Excel and PowerPoint.

T   F   **5.** Word automatically checks all custom dictionaries when the spelling checker is run.

MULTIPLE CHOICE

Select the best response for the following statements.

1. When adding buttons to the Quick Access Toolbar, the buttons _____.

   A. can be for commands that appear on the Ribbon

   B. can be for commands that do not appear on the Ribbon

   C. can be for popular commands

   D. all of the above

2. When reorganizing default commands on the Ribbon, you _____.

   A. can copy and paste the commands to other groups

   B. can move the commands within a group

   C. can move the commands from one group to another

   D. cannot move the commands within a default group or from one default group to another

3. To add a new command to the Ribbon, you must _____.

   A. add the command to a default group

   B. make sure the command does not appear somewhere else on the Ribbon

   C. create a custom group and then add the new command to the new group

   D. create a new tab, then create a new custom group, and then add the new command to the new group

4. The AutoCorrect feature automatically corrects _____.

   A. commonly misspelled words

   B. all misspelled words

   C. only words included in the default dictionary or an active custom dictionary

   D. repetitive errors in a document

5. _____ appear on the Ribbon only when you select objects in a document.

   A. Main tabs

   B. Default tabs

   C. Tool tabs

   D. Auxiliary tabs

WRITTEN QUESTIONS

Write a brief answer to the following questions.

1. The Ribbon already provides the most commonly used commands. Why would anyone want to customize the Ribbon?

2. How is reorganizing the tabs, groups, and commands on the Ribbon similar to rearranging document headings in Outline view?

3. How does the AutoCorrect feature save you time when entering frequently used text?

4. What is the purpose of the list of exceptions for AutoCorrect?

5. What is the maximum number of buttons you can add to the Quick Access Toolbar?

■ PROJECTS

If you have a SAM 2010 user profile, your instructor may have assigned an autogradable version of the indicated project. If so, log into the SAM 2010 Web site at *www.cengage.com/sam2010* to download the instruction and start files.

PROJECT 17–1

1. Open a new blank document. Make a note of the buttons that appear on the Quick Access Toolbar.

2. Add three new buttons to the Quick Access Toolbar. Choose commands that are not already on the Ribbon.

3. Remove the Undo button from the Quick Access Toolbar.

4. Open another new blank document. Click the Insert tab, click the Screenshot button, and then click Screen Clipping. Wait a moment for the active document to fade away. Drag the mouse pointer over the Quick Access Toolbar to identify the area to capture in the clipping. When you release the mouse button, the active document appears and the clipping is inserted in the document.

5. Save the document with the screenshot as Toolbar Screenshot, followed by your initials, and then close the document.

6. Restore the Quick Access Toolbar to its original settings by removing the three new buttons and adding the Undo button. (If the Quick Access Toolbar only showed three buttons at the beginning of the Project—Save, Undo, and Redo—you can use the Reset only Quick Access Toolbar option.)

SAM PROJECT 17–2

1. If necessary, open a new blank document.

2. Hide the References tab on the Ribbon.

3. Create a new tab on the Ribbon, and position it between the Review and the View tabs. Name the new tab Popular.

4. Rename the new custom group Editing.

5. Add a second new group to the Popular tab, and name the new group Formatting.

6. In the custom group Editing, add the Cut, Copy, Paste (Paste), and Find commands. In the custom group Formatting, add the commands Bold, Italic, and All Caps. If desired, assign custom icons to the buttons.

7. Move the View tab on the Ribbon so it appears to the right of the Home tab.

8. Close the Word Options dialog box.

9. Click the Popular tab.

10. Open another new blank document. Click the Insert tab, click the Screenshot button arrow, and then click Screen Clipping. Wait a moment for the active document to fade away. Drag the mouse pointer over the Ribbon to identify the area to capture in the clipping. Include all the Ribbon tabs in the capture. When you release the mouse button, the active document appears and the clipping is inserted in the document.

11. Save the document with the screenshot as **Custom Ribbon Screenshot**, followed by your initials. Then close the document.

12. Export the customized settings to a file. Name the file **Custom Ribbon Settings**, followed by your initials.

13. Reset all customizations to the Ribbon, and close the Word Options dialog box.

PROJECT 17–3

1. Create a custom dictionary titled **Members**, followed by your initials. Make sure you save the dictionary where you save your solution files.

2. Add the following names to the new dictionary:

   Cuffman

   Fulcom

   Harison

   Osbun

   Alano

   Irwig

   Ji

   Salvino

   Ogg

   Terrion

   Cimone

3. Make the Members dictionary the default dictionary. Close the Custom Dictionaries and Word Options dialog boxes.

4. Open the file **Member Directory** from the drive and folder where your Data Files are stored. Save the document as **Revised Member Directory**, followed by your initials.

5. Run the spelling checker and add the unknown member names to the dictionary.

6. Save the changes and close the document.

7. Open the Members custom dictionary to confirm that the new names were saved to the correct dictionary.

8. Uncheck the Members dictionary in the list of dictionaries so it is no longer active. Close any open dialog boxes.

9. Exit Word. If prompted to save changes to the Normal.dotm template when exiting Word, click No.

■ CRITICAL THINKING

ACTIVITY 17–1

Describe the difference between AutoCorrect and AutoComplete.

ACTIVITY 17–2

List three commands that you think should appear on the Quick Access Toolbar, and explain why you would add each command button to the toolbar.

UNIT REVIEW

Advanced Microsoft Word

◼ REVIEW QUESTIONS

MATCHING

Match the correct term in Column 2 to its description in Column 1.

Column 1

_____ 1. a ghost image that appears behind the content of a document

_____ 2. a set of predefined formats you can apply to characters, paragraphs, tables, and numbered and bulleted lists

_____ 3. a collection of variable information to be used in a merge

_____ 4. the last line of a multiline paragraph that is split from the other lines in the paragraph and wraps to the next page or column

_____ 5. a group of related fields, or a single field, treated as a unit in a data source

_____ 6. an object that accesses data stored in the source file

_____ 7. a format developed by Microsoft that preserves the visual appearance and layout of each page and enables fast viewing and printing

_____ 8. a group of sequential commands and actions combined as a single command to automatically complete a task

_____ 9. a file that affects the basic structure of a document and contains document settings (such as fonts, line spacing, margins, and page layout)

_____ 10. an excerpted line or phrase used to draw attention in a document

Column 2

A. record

B. data source

C. template

D. pull quote

E. watermark

F. widow

G. orphan

H. sidebar

I. XML Paper Specification (XPS)

J. macro

K. style

L. metadata

M. embedded object

N. Portable Document Format (PDF)

O. linked object

MULTIPLE CHOICE

Select the best response for the following statements.

1. You create a hyperlink to _____.

    A.   navigate to a Web page

    B.   navigate to another location in the same document

    C.   navigate to a location in another document

    D.   all of the above

2. To create a price list or a catalog, you use the _____ document type in the mail merge process.

    A.   Labels

    B.   Directory

    C.   Catalog

    D.   Letters

3. The numbered labels for table captions are automatically updated when _____.

    A.   tables are moved within the document

    B.   tables are deleted from the document

    C.   new tables are inserted in the document

    D.   all of the above

4. A summary of tracked changes appears _____.

    A.   in the markup area

    B.   in the Review Pane and in the markup area

    C.   only in the Review Pane

    D.   in the document properties that appear in Backstage view

5. When sorting content in a table, _____.

    A.   you can sort a single column without rearranging the data for the remaining columns

    B.   you can sort all the data based on a specified column

    C.   the sort can be based on three criteria in multiple columns

    D.   all of the above

6. A section break controls the formatting for the _____.

    A.   content that follows the break

    B.   content that precedes the break

    C.   content that follows and precedes the break

    D.   current page

7. A _____ is a section format.

    A.   page border

    B.   header and footer

    C.   page number

    D.   all of the above

8. If you want to change a macro, you can _____.

    A.   edit the VBA code

    B.   re-record the macro using the same macro name

    C.   re-record the macro using a new macro name

    D.   A or B

9. Themes define _____ in a document.

   A.   styles

   B.   document formats

   C.   colors, fonts, and effects

   D.   all of the above

10. When you copy and paste data from an Excel worksheet, _____.

   A.   you have access to all of Excel's data formatting and calculation options

   B.   the data is converted to a table

   C.   the data is linked to the Excel worksheet and will automatically be updated

   D.   you cannot edit the data in the Word document

WRITTEN QUESTIONS

Write a brief answer to the following questions.

1. Explain how using the Navigation Pane to reorganize document content is similar to using Outline view to reorganize document content.

2. How can you protect a document from being edited before distributing it within a workgroup?

3. What is the difference between a document template and a global template?

4. What is the difference between linking and embedding an object?

5. If a chart in a Word document is linked to an Excel worksheet, how do you update changes in the chart data?

6. If you plan to create a table of contents and an index, which should you complete first and why?

7. What are the benefits of creating a custom dictionary?

8. Why would you use the filtering process when completing a mail merge process?

9. Name three paragraph formats that control text flow and explain how they control the text flow.

10. Why is it recommended that you attach a digital signature to a macro project?

■ PROJECTS

PROJECT 1

1. Create a new macro-enabled document template and save the file as **Personal Template 5.dotm**, followed by your initials.

2. Open the **Ski Club** file from the drive and folder where your Data Files are stored. Save the document as **Ski Club Flyer**, followed by your initials.

3. Attach the Personal Template 5 template to the document.

4. Create two sidebars. Cut and paste the *Show Schedule* text and the *Contact Information* text to the sidebars.

5. Create custom styles for the title, subtitle, and headings. Name the styles **Flyer Title**, **Flyer Subtitle**, and **Flyer Heading**, and save the new styles to the Personal Template 5 template.

6. Under the heading *Practices*, after *Outdoor practices are scheduled as follows:*, convert the five lines of text to a table and then AutoFit the table contents.

7. Insert the picture file Pyramid.JPG from the drive and folder where your Data Files are stored. Resize and format the picture as necessary.

8. Create a macro to apply a custom bullet format. Choose a symbol for the bullet, and apply a color format for the symbol. Name the macro **Bullets**, and save the macro in the Personal Template 5 template.

9. Arrange the content on the page and further enhance the document so it can be used as a one-page flyer to recruit new members. For example, add a page border and/or a page color, justify the text alignment, and add a border to the picture.

10. Save the changes to the document and to the document template. Then save the document in the XPS format.

11. Close the XPS document, and then close the Word document and the document template.

PROJECT 2

1. Open the **Kick City** file from the drive and folder where your Data Files are stored. Save the document as **Final Kick City**, followed by your initials.

2. Apply a style to the headings at the top of each page. Modify the style(s) as needed and add paragraph borders if desired. (You can use a variety of formats for the headings; they do not have to be formatted the same.)

3. Apply a theme. Format a page background and modify settings as desired.

4. On the first page, format all the paragraphs between the title and the table in two columns.

5. Justify the alignment of all text in the document, and then automatically hyphenate the entire document.

6. AutoFit the contents in each table. Apply table styles to each of the tables and modify the table style(s) as desired. (You can use a variety of formats for the tables; they do not have to be formatted the same.)

7. Edit the first table by moving the rows for *Girls U10* and *Girls U8* to the bottom of the table. Then center the table horizontally at the bottom of the first page.

8. If necessary, change the page margins and adjust spacing above and below paragraphs so that the first table fits on the first page. If necessary, insert a column break. The second page should begin with the title *Kick City Soccer Day Camps*. If you change margin and paragraph formats, be sure to apply the changes to the entire document.

9. Edit the second table by deleting the first column.

10. Insert an appropriate clip art image to the right of the table on the second page. Resize the image as needed, and add a picture effect.

11. On the second page, in the first paragraph under the heading, insert a footnote after the word *instructors*. Choose a symbol for the reference mark. In the footnote pane, type **All instructors are certified by the United States Soccer Federation.**.

12. Make any other adjustments to enhance the appearance of the document.

13. Save the changes to the document. Then save the document in XPS format.

14. Close the XPS document, and then close the Word document.

PROJECT 3

1. Open the **Home Remedies** file from the drive and folder where your Data Files are stored. Save the document as **Final Home Remedies**, followed by your initials.

2. Mark the following words or groups of words that occur in the paragraphs below the headings. Do not apply the bold and italic formats for the page numbers format.

    a.   Under *Minor Ills*, mark **sore throat** and **relax**.

    b.   Under *Cure-Alls*, mark **bleeding gums**, **fever blister**, **eyestrain**, and **chicken pox**.

    c.   Under *Insect Bites*, mark **mosquito bite**.

3. AutoMark the remaining index entries using the file **Home Remedies Entries**, which is stored in the drive and folder where your Data Files are stored.

4. Insert a page break at the end of the document. Generate the index, using a style of your choice, and then add the heading **Index** above the index. Format the heading for a single column, apply the Heading 1 style, and center the heading.

5. Create a table of contents:

    a.   Insert a next page section break at the top of the document.

    b.   Generate the table of contents in the new section at the top of the document, using a style of your choice.

    c.   Add the heading **Table of Contents** above the table of contents. Apply the Heading 1 style and center the heading.

6. Add page numbers to the document:

    a.   In the table of contents section, format the page numbers in the lower-right corner of the document, using a footer style of your choice. Format the page numbers with lowercase roman numerals (i, ii, iii).

    b.   In the next section of the document, format a page number in the lower-right corner of the page, starting at number 1. Change the number to the 1, 2, 3 format, and show the page number on the first page.

    c.   Update the page numbers in the table of contents.

7. Save the changes and close the document.

PROJECT 4

1. Open the **Pet Travel 1** file from the drive and folder where your Data Files are stored. Save the document as **Final Pet Travel**, followed by your initials.

2. The source information for the document content is provided at the end of the document. Add the source to the master list and the current list in the Source Manager (using the MLA Sixth Edition style settings). Then delete the four lines that reference the source at the end of the document. (*Hint*: The author is a corporate author.)

3. At the end of the last paragraph, insert a citation to reference the source you just added.

4. Position the insertion point at the end of the document and then insert the contents of the *Pet Travel 2* file, which is stored in the drive and folder where your Data Files are stored.

5. The source information for the document content is provided at the end of the document. Add the source to the master list and the current list in the Source Manager (using the MLA Sixth Edition style settings). Then delete the five lines that reference the source at the added content at the end of the document.

6. At the end of the last paragraph in the document, insert a citation to reference the source you just added.

7. Insert a page break at the end of the document, and then create a works cited page on the last page of the document.

8. Add page numbers to the bottom of each page. Choose a page number format and footer style of your choice.

9. Save the changes and close the document.

■ SIMULATION

Charles Feenstra is the vice president of marketing for a distribution company. The sales figures for the first and second quarters are compiled, and Charles asks you to review a letter he drafted to the company's four regional managers.

JOB 1

1. Open the **Sales Letter** file from the drive and folder where your Data Files are stored. Save the document as **Revised Sales Letter**, followed by your initials.

2. Convert the sales data to a table.

3. Format and sort the table contents:

   a. Center and bold the column headings.

   b. Add another row to the end of the table, and in the cell directly below *Southern*, type **Total**. Apply bold formatting to the *Total* row heading.

   c. Calculate the row and column totals.

   d. AutoFit the columns for contents, and center the table horizontally.

   e. Right-align the numbers in the *Year to Date* column.

   f. Sort the table contents in ascending alphabetic order based on the region names. Do not include the column headings or the *Total* row in the sort.

   g. Remove the table borders so they do not print.

4. Create a new custom dictionary named **Marketing.dic**, followed by your initials, and save the new dictionary with your solution files. Add Feenstra to the custom dictionary.

5. Toggle on the Track Changes feature. (Make sure the user name and initials are yours.) Review the document and make any necessary changes to correct spelling, punctuation, and grammar. Read the document content thoroughly; Word does not flag all the errors.

6. Add at least one comment to the document. If you don't have any revisions that require a comment to explain or justify the edit, then make a comment about the letter. Remember, Mr. Feenstra is a colleague, so be positive!

7. Restrict access to the table data. Use the password **jck0429!**.

8. Remove your custom dictionary from the dictionary list.

9. Save the changes and leave the document open for the next Job.

JOB 2

Mr. Feenstra reviewed your edits and agreed to everything, but he doesn't have experience working with revision marks, so he asks you to finalize the document.

1. If necessary, open the **Revised Sales Letter** file from your solution files. Save the document as **Final Sales Letter**, followed by your initials.

2. Turn off editing restrictions, and accept all the changes in the document.

3. Delete all the comments from the document.

4. If necessary, toggle off the track changes feature.

5. The letter will be printed on company stationery. Insert seven blank lines at the top of the document.

6. Save the document, and then inspect it and remove personal information.

7. Mark the document as final.

8. Leave the document open for the next Job.

JOB 3

Mr. Feenstra asks you to prepare final copies for each of the regional managers. He provides a data source with the names and addresses for company managers.

1. Open the **Managers** file from the drive and folder where your Data Files are stored. Save the document as **Updated Managers 1**, followed by your initials. Close the document.

2. If necessary, open the **Final Sales Letter** file from your solution files. Enable the editing, and then save the document as **Sales Letter Main Document**, followed by your initials.

3. Position the insertion point at the top of the document and press the down arrow six times. Type **June 18,** and then press spacebar and type the current year.

4. Complete the mail merge process for letters:

   a. Use the Sales Letter Main Document file as the main document.

   b. Use the Updated Managers 1 file as the data source.

   c. Include all the records in the merge. Edit Edith Kleiber's record by changing her last name to **Hunter**.

   d. Sort the records in ascending alphabetic order by last name.

   e. Complete the main document by inserting individual fields for the name and address below the date, following the format below.
      <<Title>> <<FirstName>> <<LastName>>
      <<JobTitle>>
      <<Company>>
      <<Address1>>
      <<City>>, <<State>> <<PostalCode>>

   f. Use the GreetingLine field to insert a salution. This is a business letter, so punctuate the greeting line with a colon.

   g. Preview the results and make any necessary changes.

   h. Merge all the records to a new document.

5. Save the new document as **Merged Sales Letter 1**, followed by your initials, and close the merged document. Save changes to the main document and close it. When prompted to save the changes to the *Updated Managers 1* data source file, click Yes.

6. Open a new blank document. Save the document as **Envelopes Main Document**, followed by your initials.

7. Complete the mail merge process for envelopes:

   a. Use the settings for size 10 envelopes.

   b. Use the same recipient list you used in Step 4.

   c. Preprinted envelopes will be used, so you do not need to include a return address. Complete the main document by inserting individual fields for the name and address, following the format below.
       <<Title>> <<FirstName>> <<LastName>>
       <<JobTitle>>
       <<Company>>
       <<Address1>>
       <<City>>, <<State>> <<PostalCode>>

   d. Preview the envelopes and make any necessary changes.

   e. Merge all the records to a new document. Save the new file as **Merged Sales Letter Envelopes 1**, followed by your initials.

8. Close the merged envelopes document. Then save the changes and close the main document.

JOB 4

Mr. Feenstra recently hired three new district managers, and he asks you to create copies of the letter for each of them.

1. Open the **Updated Managers 1** file from your solution files. Save the document as **Updated Managers 2**, followed by your initials.

2. Add the following names and addresses to the table, and then save the changes and close the document.

   Ms. Heidi Baldridge
   District Manager
   Micro Innovations
   233 Maple Avenue
   Trenton, NJ 08618-3401
   Region: **Eastern**

   Mr. Mike Heitkamp
   District Manager
   Micro Innovations
   18 Lownes Lane
   Springfield, PA 19064-5545
   Region: **Eastern**

   Ms. Marjorie Lashley
   District Manager
   Micro Innovations
   16620 SE 27th Street
   Bellevue, WA 98008-8856
   Region: **Western**

3. Open the **Sales Letter Main Document** file from your solution files. When prompted to place data from your database and continue, click Yes.

4. Complete the mail merge process for letters:

   a. Use the Updated Managers 2 file as the data source.

   b. Sort the data source in ascending alphabetic order by last name.

   c. Filter the data source for the job title District Manager.

   d. Preview the results and make any necessary changes.

   e. Merge all the records to a new document and save the new document as **Merged Sales Letter 2**, followed by your initials.

5. Close the merged document. Then close the main document, saving the changes.

6. Open the **Envelopes Main Document** file from your solution files. If prompted to place data from your database and continue, click Yes.

7. Complete the mail merge process for envelopes:

    a.   Use the Updated Managers 2 file as the data source.

    b.   Filter the data source for district managers.

    c.   Preview the results and make any necessary changes.

    d.   Merge all the records to a new document. Save the new file as **Merged Sales Letter Envelopes 2**, followed by your initials.

8. Close the merged envelopes document. Then close the main document, saving changes. If prompted to save the changes to the data source, click Yes.

JOB 5

Mr. Feenstra is preparing for a meeting with the regional and district managers. He asks you to create a bar chart using the table data that was included in the sales letter.

1. Open a new blank document.

2. Insert a bar chart, and then enter the table data provided in the Sales Letter Main Document file. Only use the region names and the first and second quarter sales figures. Do not chart the *Year to Date* column or the *Total* row.

3. Above the chart, add the chart title **First and Second Quarter Sales**.

4. Reposition the legend at the lower-right corner of the chart.

5. Change the page layout to landscape orientation, and resize the chart to fill the page.

6. Change the chart type to a column chart. Apply a style that you think best presents the data, and adjust chart elements if necessary.

7. Save the document as **Quarterly Sales Chart**, followed by your initials. Close the document.

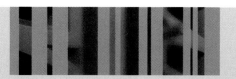

APPENDIX A

Computer Concepts

The Computer: An Overview

A computer is a machine that is used to store, retrieve, and manipulate data. A computer takes *input*, uses instructions to *process* and *store* that data, and then produces *output*. You enter the data into the computer through a variety of input devices, such as a keyboard or mouse. The processor processes the data to produce information. Information is output presented in many ways such as an image on a monitor, printed pages from a printer, or sound through speakers. Computer *software* is stored instructions or programming that runs the computer. *Memory* inside the computer stores the programs or instructions that run the computer as well as the data and information. Various *storage devices* are used to transfer or safely store the data and information on *storage media*.

A *computer system* is made up of components that include the computer, input, and output devices. Computer systems come in many shapes, sizes, and configurations. The computer you use at home or in school is often called a *personal computer*. *Desktop computers* often have a 'computer case' or a *system unit*, which contains

APPENDIX A

processing devices, memory, and some storage devices. **Figure A–1** shows a typical desktop computer. Input devices such as the mouse or pointing device, and keyboard are attached to the system unit by cables or wires. Output devices, such as the monitor (display device), speakers, and printer are also attached to the system unit by cables or wires. *Wireless technology* makes it possible to eliminate wires and use the airwaves to connect devices. *Laptop* or *notebook* computers have all the essential parts: the keyboard, pointing device, and display device all in one unit. See **Figure A–2** for a typical notebook computer.

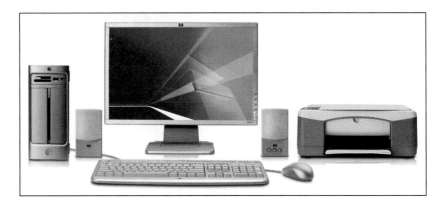

FIGURE A–1   A desktop computer system

FIGURE A–2   A laptop computer

When learning about computers, it is helpful to organize the topics into a discussion about the hardware and the software, and then how the computer processes the data.

Computer Hardware

The physical components, devices, or parts of the computer are called *hardware*. Computer hardware includes the essential components found on all computers such as the central processing unit (CPU), the monitor, the keyboard, and the mouse. Hardware can be divided into categories: Input devices, processors, storage devices, and output devices. ***Peripheral devices*** are additional components, such as printers, speakers, and scanners that enhance the computing experience. Peripherals are not essential to the computer, but provide additional functions for the computer.

Input Devices

There are many different types of input devices. You enter information into a computer by typing on a keyboard or by pointing, clicking, or dragging a mouse. A ***mouse*** is a handheld device used to move a pointer on the computer screen. Similar to a mouse, a ***trackball*** has a roller ball that turns to control a pointer on the screen. Tracking devices, such as a ***touchpad***, are an alternative to the trackball or mouse. Situated on the keyboard of a laptop computer, they allow you to simply move and tap your finger on a small electronic pad to control the pointer on the screen.

    Tablet PCs allow you to input data by writing directly on the computer screen. Handwriting recognition technology converts handwritten writing to text. Many computers have a microphone or other ***sound input device*** which accepts speech or sounds as input and converts the speech to text or data. For example, when you telephone a company or bank for customer service, you often have the option to say your requests or account number. That is ***speech recognition technology*** at work!

    Other input devices include scanners and bar code readers. You can use a ***scanner*** to convert text or graphics from a printed page into code that a computer can process. You have probably seen ***bar code readers*** being used in stores. These are used to read bar codes, such as the UPC (Universal Product Code), to track merchandise or other inventory in a store. See **Figure A–3**.

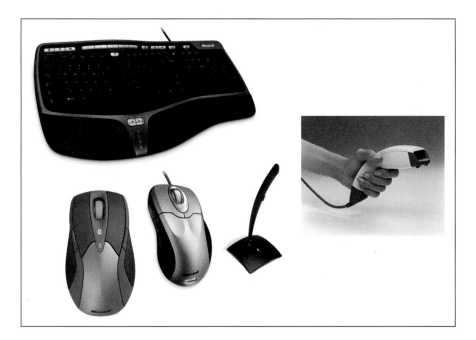

FIGURE A–3   Examples of input devices

APPENDIX A

Processing Devices

Processing devices are mounted inside the system unit of the computer. The *motherboard* is where the computer memory and other vital electronic parts are stored. See **Figure A–4**. The *central processing unit* (**CPU**) is a silicon chip that processes data and carries out instructions given to the computer. The CPU is stored on the motherboard of the computer. The *data bus* includes the wiring and pathways by which the CPU communicates with the peripherals and components of the computer.

FIGURE A–4   A motherboard

Storage Devices

Computers have to store and retrieve data for them to be of any use at all. Storage devices are both input and output devices. A *storage medium* holds data. Storage media include hard drives, tape, memory cards, solid state flash drives, CDs, and DVDs. A *storage device* is the hardware that stores and retrieves data from a storage medium. Storage devices include hard drives, card readers, tape drives, and CD and DVD drives.

Storage devices use magnetic, optical, or solid state technologies. Magnetic storage uses magnetic fields to store data and can be erased and used over and over again. Optical technology uses light to store data. Optical storage media use one of three technologies: read-only (ROM), recordable (R), or rewritable (RW). Solid state storage uses no moving parts and can be used over and over again. There are advantages and disadvantages to each technology.

Most computers have more than one type of storage device. The main storage device for a computer is the *hard drive* that is usually inside the system unit. Hard drives use magnetic storage. The hard drive reads and writes data to and from a round magnetic platter, or disk. **Figure A–5** shows a fixed storage unit. It is not removable from the computer.

FIGURE A–5   An internal hard drive

External and removable hard drives that can plug into the USB port on the system unit are also available. External drives offer flexibility; allowing you to transfer data between computers easily. See **Figure A–6**. At the time this book was written, typical hard drives for a computer system that you might buy for your personal home use range from 500 gigabytes (GB) to 2 terabytes.

FIGURE A–6   An external hard drive

APPENDIX A

The *floppy disk drive* is older technology that is no longer available on new computers. Some older computers still have a floppy disk drive which is mounted in the system unit with access to the outside. A floppy disk is the medium that stores the data. You put the floppy disk into the floppy disk drive so the computer can read and write the data. The floppy disk's main advantage was portability. You can store data on a floppy disk and transport it for use on another computer. A floppy disk can hold up to 1.4MB (megabytes) of information. A Zip disk is similar to a floppy disk. A *Zip disk* is also an older portable disk technology that was contained in a plastic sleeve. Each disk held 100MB or 250MB of information. A special disk drive called a *Zip drive* is required to read and write data to a Zip disk.

Optical storage devices include the *CD drive* or *DVD drive* or *Blu-ray drive*. CDs, DVDs, and *Blu-ray drive (BD)* use optical storage technology. See **Figure A–7**.

FIGURE A–7   A CD/DVD/Blu-ray drive

These drives are typically mounted inside the system unit, although external versions of these devices are also available. Most new computers are equipped with CD/DVD burners. That means they have read and write capabilities. You use a CD/DVD drive to read and write CDs and DVDs. A *CD* is a compact disc, which is a form of optical storage. Compact discs can store 700 MB of data. These discs have a great advantage over other forms of removable storage as they can hold vast quantities of information—the entire contents of a small library, for instance. They are also fairly durable. Another advantage of CDs is their ability to hold graphic information, including moving pictures, with the highest quality stereo sound. A *DVD* is also an optical disc that looks like a CD. It is a high-capacity storage device that can contain up to 4.7GB of data, which is a seven-fold increase over a CD. There are two variations of DVDs that offer even more storage—a 2-layer version with 9.4GB capacity and double-sided discs with 17GB capacity. A DVD holds 133 minutes of data on each side, which means that two two-hour full-length feature movies can be stored on one disc. Information is encoded on the disk by a laser and read by a CD/DVD drive in the computer. ***Blu-ray discs (BD)*** offer even more storage capacity. These highest-capacity discs are designed to record full-length high-definition feature films. As of this writing, a BD can store upwards of 35GB of data. Special Blu-ray hardware, including disc players available in gaming systems and Blu-ray burners, are needed to read Blu-ray discs.

A CD drive only reads CDs, a DVD drive can read CDs and DVDs, a Blu-ray drive reads BDs, CDs, and DVDs. CD/DVD/BD drives look quite similar, as do the discs. See **Figure A–8**.

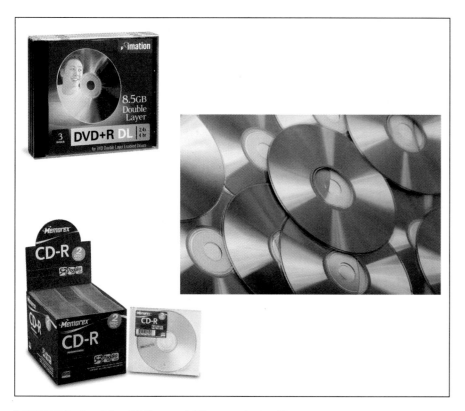

FIGURE A–8   CDs, DVDs, and Blu-rays look alike

APPENDIX A

Solid state storage is another popular storage technology. A ***USB flash drive*** is a very portable small store device that works both as a drive and medium. It plugs directly into a USB port on the computer system unit. You read and write data to the flash drive. See **Figure A–9**.

FIGURE A–9   A flash drive

Solid state card readers are devices that can read solid state cards. Solid state storage is often used in cameras. See **Figure A–10**.

FIGURE A–10   Solid state card and card reader

Magnetic tape is a medium most commonly used for backing up a computer system, which means making a copy of files from a hard drive. Although it is relatively rare for data on a hard drive to be completely lost in a crash (that is, for the data or pointers to the data to be partially or totally destroyed), it can and does happen. Therefore, most businesses and some individuals routinely back up files on tape. If you have a small hard drive, you can use DVDs or CD-ROMs or solid state storage such as a flash drive or memory card to back up your system. **Figure A–11** shows a tape storage system.

FIGURE A–11   Tape storage system

Output Devices

The *monitor* on which you view your computer work is an output device. It provides a visual representation of the information stored in or produced by your computer. The typical monitor for today's system is a flat-screen monitor similar to a television. Computer monitors typically use *LCD technology*. LCD stands for Liquid Crystal Display. See **Figure A–12**. LCD monitors provide a very sharp picture because of the large number of tiny dots, called *pixels*, which make up the display as well as its ability to present the full spectrum of colors. *Resolution* is the term that tells you how clear an image will be on the screen. Resolution is measured in pixels. A typical resolution is 1024 × 768. A high-quality monitor may have a resolution of 1920 × 1080, or 2560 × 1440 or higher. Monitors come in different sizes. The size of a monitor is determined by measuring the diagonal of the screen. Laptops have smaller monitors than desktop computers. A laptop monitor may be 13", 15", or 17". Desktop monitors can be as large as 19"–27" or even larger.

FIGURE A–12   An LCD monitor

Printers are a type of output device. They let you produce a paper printout of information contained in the computer. Today, most printers use either inkjet or laser technology to produce high-quality print. Like a copy machine, a *laser printer* uses heat to fuse a powdery substance called *toner* to the page. *Ink-jet printers* use a spray of ink to print. Laser printers give the sharpest image and often print more pages per minute (ppm) than ink-jet printers. Ink-jet printers provide nearly as sharp an image, but the wet printouts can smear when they first are printed. Most color printers, or photo printers for printing photographs, are ink-jet printers. Color laser printers are more costly. These printers allow you to print information in a full array of colors, just as you see it on your monitor. See **Figure A–13**.

FIGURE A–13   Printers

Laptop or Notebook Computer

A *laptop computer*, also called a *notebook computer*, is a small folding computer that can literally fit in a person's lap or in a backpack. Within the fold-up case of a laptop is the CPU, data bus, monitor (built into the lid), hard drive (sometimes removable), USB ports, CD/DVD drive, and trackball or digital tracking device. The advantage of the laptop is its portability—you can work anywhere because you can use power either from an outlet or from the computer's internal, rechargeable batteries. Almost all laptops have wireless Internet access built into the system. The drawbacks are the smaller keyboard, smaller monitor, smaller capacity, and higher price, though some laptops offer full-sized keyboards and higher quality monitors. As technology allows, storage capacity on smaller devices is making it possible to offer laptops with as much power and storage as a full-sized computer. See **Figure A–14**.

FIGURE A–14   Laptop computers

Personal Digital Assistants (PDA) and Smartphones

A *Personal Digital Assistant (PDA)* is a pocket-sized electronic organizer that helps you to manage addresses, appointments, expenses, tasks, and memos. If you own a cell phone, chances are it is a *Smartphone* and it can do more than just make and receive phone calls. Today, many handheld devices, such as cell phones and Personal Digital Assistants include features such as a full keypad for text messaging and writing notes, e-mail, a browser for Web access, a calendar and address book to manage contacts and appointments, a digital camera, radio, and digital music player. Most handheld devices also include software for games, financial management, personal organizer, GPS, and maps. See **Figure A–15**.

FIGURE A–15   Smartphones

The common input devices for PDAs and some Smartphones include touch-sensitive screens that accept input through a stylus pen or small keyboards that are either built in to the device or available as software on the screen. Data and information can be shared with a Windows-based or Macintosh computer through a process called synchronization. By placing your handheld in a cradle or through a USB port attached to your computer, you can transfer data from your PDA's calendar, address book, or memo program into your computer's information manager program and vice versa. The information is updated on both sides, making your handheld device a portable extension of your computer.

How Computers Work

All input, processing, storage, and output devices function together to make the manipulation, storage, and distribution of data and information possible. Data is information entered into and manipulated or processed within a computer. Processing includes computation, such as adding, subtracting, multiplying, and dividing; analysis planning, such as sorting data; and reporting, such as presenting data for others in a chart or graph. This next section explains how computers work.

Memory

Computers have two types of memory—RAM and ROM. **RAM**, or **random access memory**, is the silicon chips in the system unit that temporarily store information when the computer is turned on. RAM is what keeps the software programs up and running and provides visuals that appear on your screen. You work with data in RAM up until you save it to a storage media such as a hard disk, CD, DVD, or solid state storage such as flash drive.

Computers have sophisticated application programs that include a lot of graphics, video, and data. In order to run these programs, computers require a lot of memory. Therefore, computers have a minimum of 512MB of RAM. Typical computers include between 2GB and 4GB of RAM to be able to run most programs. Most computer systems are expandable and you can add on RAM after you buy the computer. The more RAM available for the programs, the faster and more efficiently the machine will be able to operate. RAM chips are shown in **Figure A–16**.

FIGURE A–16 RAM chips

ROM, or ***read-only memory***, is the memory that stays in the computer when it is turned off. It is ROM that stores the programs that run the computer as it starts or "boots up." ROM holds the instructions that tell the computer how to begin to load its operating system software programs.

Speed

The speed of a computer is measured by how fast the computer processes each instruction. There are several factors that affect the performance of a computer: the speed of the processor, or the ***clock speed***, the ***front side bus speed***—the speed of the bus that connects the processor to main memory—the speed in which data is written and retrieved from the hard drive or other storage media, and the speed of the graphics card if you are working on programs that use a lot of graphic images. These all factor into a computer's performance.

The speed of a computer is measured in ***megahertz (MHz)*** and ***gigahertz (GHz)***. Processor speed is part of the specifications when you buy a computer. For example, to run Windows 7 on a computer, you need a processor that has 1 gigahertz (GHz) or faster 32-bit (x86) or 64-bit (x64) processor. Processors are sold by name and each brand or series has its own specifications. Processor manufacturers include AMD, Intel, and Motorola.

APPENDIX A

Networks

Computers have expanded the world of communications. A *network* is defined as two or more computers connected to share data. *LANs (local area networks)* connect computers within a small area such as a home, office, school, or building. Networks can be wired or wireless. The *Internet* is the largest network in the world connecting millions of computers across the globe. Using the Internet, people can communicate across the world instantly.

Networks require various communication devices and software. *Modems* allow computers to communicate with each other by telephone lines. Modem is an acronym that stands for "MOdulator/DEModulator." Modems convert data in bytes to sound media in order to send data over the phone lines and then convert it back to bytes after receiving data. Modems operate at various rates or speeds. *Network cards* in the system unit allow computers to access networks. A *router* is an electronic device that joins two or more networks. For example, a home network can use a router and a modem to connect the home's LAN to the Internet. A *server* is the computer hardware and software that "serves" the computers on a network. Network technology is sometimes called "client-server." A personal computer that requests data from a server is referred to as a *client*. The computer that stores the data is the *server*. On the Internet, the computer that stores Web pages is the *Web server*. **Figure A–17** shows a network diagram.

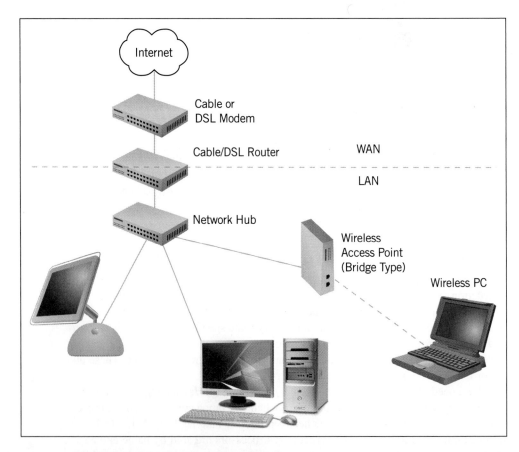

FIGURE A–17   Diagram of a network

Networks have certain advantages over stand-alone computers: they allow communication among the computers; they allow smaller capacity computers to access the larger capacity of the server computers on the network; they allow several computers to share peripherals, such as one printer; and they can make it possible for all computers on the network to have access to the Internet.

Connect to the Internet

To connect to the Internet you need to subscribe to an ***Internet Service Provider (ISP)***. There are several technologies available. Connection speeds are measured in bits per second. Upload speeds are slower than download speeds. ***Dial-up*** is the oldest, and the slowest Internet access technology that is offered by local telephone companies. To get access to the Internet, your computer has to dial out through a phone line. Many people have moved to ***always-on connection technologies***. The computer is always connected to the Internet if you turn the computer on, so you don't have to dial out. These always-on faster technologies, known as a ***Digital Subscriber Line (DSL)***, include cable connections, satellites, and fiber optic. They are offered by telephone and cable television companies, as well as satellite service providers. It can be noted that satellite Internet access is the most expensive and dialup is the cheapest. DSL is through phone lines. **Table A–1** shows a brief comparison of these technologies based on the time this book was written and average speed assessments.

TABLE A–1   Comparing average Internet access options

FEATURE	SATELLITE	DSL	CABLE	FIBER OPTIC
Max. High Speed	Download speeds ranging anywhere from 768 Kbps up to 5.0 Mbps	Download speed 10 Mbps/ upload speed 5 Mbps	Download speed 30 Mbps/ upload speed 10 Mbps	Download speed 50 Mbps/ upload speed 20 Mbps
Access is through	Satellite dish	Existing phone line	Existing TV cable	Fiber-optic phone lines
Availability	Available in all areas; note that satellite service is sensitive to weather conditions	Generally available in populated areas	Might not be available in rural areas	Might not be available in all areas as fiber-optic lines are still being installed in many areas

Software

A ***program*** is a set of instructions that the computer uses to operate. ***Software*** is the collection of programs and other data input that tells the computer how to run its devices, how to manipulate, store, and output information, and how to accept the input you give it. Software fits into two basic categories: systems software and applications software. A third category, network software, is really a type of application.

Systems Software

The ***operating system*** is the main software or ***system software*** that runs a computer and often defines the type of computer. There are two main types or platforms for personal computers. The Macintosh computer, or Mac, is produced by Apple Computer, Inc. and runs the Mac operating system. The PC is a Windows-based

APPENDIX A

computer produced by many different companies, but which runs the Microsoft Windows operating system.

Systems software refers to the operating system of the computer. The operating system is a group of programs that is automatically copied in from the time the computer is turned on until the computer is turned off. Operating systems serve two functions: they control data flow among computer parts, and they provide the platform on which application and network software work—in effect, they allow the "space" for software and translate its commands to the computer. The most popular operating systems in use today are the Macintosh operating system, MAC OS X and several different versions of Microsoft Windows, such as Windows XP, Windows Vista, or Windows 7. See **Figure A–18** and **Figure A–19**.

FIGURE A–18   Windows 7 operating system

FIGURE A–19   Mac OS

Since its introduction in the mid-1970s, Macintosh has used its own operating system, a graphical user interface (GUI) system that has evolved over the years. The OS is designed so users "click" with a mouse on pictures, called icons, or on text to give commands to the system. Data is available to you in the WYSIWYG (what-you-see-is-what-you-get) format; that is, you can see on-screen what a document will look like when it is printed. Graphics and other kinds of data, such as spreadsheets, can be placed into text documents. However, GUIs take a great deal of RAM to keep all of the graphics and programs operating.

The original OS for IBM and IBM-compatible computers (machines made by other companies that operate similarly) was DOS (disk operating system). It did not have a graphical interface. The GUI system, Windows™, was developed to make using the IBM/IBM-compatible computer more "friendly." Today's Windows applications are the logical evolution of GUI for IBM and IBM-compatible machines. Windows is a point-and-click system that automatically configures hardware to work together. You should note, however, that with all of its abilities comes the need for more RAM, or a system running Windows will operate slowly.

Applications Software

When you use a computer program to perform a data manipulation or processing task, you are using applications software. Word processors, databases, spreadsheets, graphics programs, desktop publishers, fax systems, and Internet browsers are all applications software.

Network Software

A traditional network is a group of computers that are hardwired (connected together with cables) to communicate and operate together. Today, some computer networks use RF (radio frequency) wireless technology to communicate with each other. This is called a *wireless network*, because you do not need to physically hook the network together with cables. In a typical network, one computer acts as the server, controlling the flow of data among the other computers, called nodes, or clients on the network. Network software manages this flow of information.

History of the Computer

Though various types of calculating machines were developed in the nineteenth century, the history of the modern computer begins about the middle of the last century. The strides made in developing today's personal computer have been truly astounding.

Early Development

The ENIAC, or Electronic Numerical Integrator and Computer, (see **Figure A–20**) was designed for military use in calculating ballistic trajectories and was the first electronic, digital computer to be developed in the United States. For its day, 1946, it was quite a marvel because it was able to accomplish a task in 20 seconds that normally would take a human three days to complete. However, it was an enormous machine that weighed more than 20 tons and contained thousands of vacuum tubes, which often failed. The tasks that it could accomplish were limited, as well.

FIGURE A–20   The ENIAC

From this awkward beginning, however, the seeds of an information revolution grew. The invention of the silicon chip in 1971, and the release of the first personal computer in 1974, launched the fast-paced information revolution in which we now all live and participate.

Significant dates in the history of computer development are listed in **Table A–2**.

TABLE A–2 Milestones in the development of computers

YEAR	DEVELOPMENT
1948	First electronically stored program
1951	First junction transistor
1953	Replacement of tubes with magnetic cores
1957	First high-level computer language
1961	First integrated circuit
1965	First minicomputer
1971	Invention of the microprocessor (the silicon chip) and floppy disk
1974	First personal computer (made possible by the microprocessor)

The Personal Computer

The PC, or personal computer, was mass marketed by Apple beginning in 1977, and by IBM in 1981. It is this desktop device with which people are so familiar and which, today, contains much more power and ability than did the original computer that took up an entire room. The PC is a small computer (desktop size or less) that uses a microprocessor to manipulate data. PCs may stand alone, be linked together in a network, or be attached to a large mainframe computer. See **Figure A–21**.

FIGURE A–21 An early IBM PC

Computer Utilities and System Maintenance

Computer operating systems let you run certain utilities and perform system mainte-nance to keep your computer running well. When you add hardware or software, you make changes in the way the system operates. With Plug and Play, most configura-tion changes are done automatically. The *drivers*, software that runs the peripherals, are installed automatically when your computer identifies the new hardware. When you install new software, many changes are made to the system automatically that determine how the software starts and runs.

In addition, you might want to customize the way the new software or hard-ware works with your system. You use *utility software* to make changes to the way hardware and software works. For example, you can change the speed at which your mouse clicks, how quickly or slowly keys repeat on the keyboard, and the resolution of the screen display. Utilities are included with your operating system. If you are running Windows XP, Windows Vista, or Windows 7, the Windows Control Panel provides access to the many Windows operating system utilities. **Figure A–22** shows the System and Security utilities in the Control Panel for Windows 7.

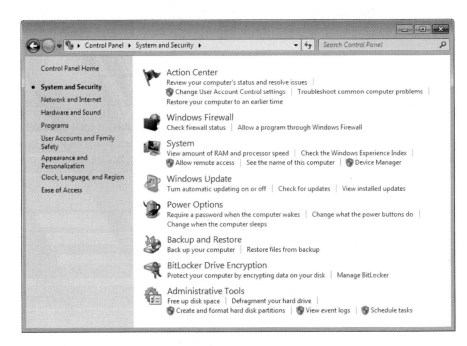

FIGURE A–22 Control Panel for Windows 7

Virus and Spyware Protection

Certain maintenance should be performed regularly on computers. *Viruses* are mali-cious software programs that can damage the programs on your computer causing the computer to either stop working or run slowly. These programs are created by people, called *hackers*, who send the programs out solely to do harm to computers. Viruses are loaded onto your computer without your knowledge and run against your wishes. *Spyware* is also a form of a program that can harm your computer. There are utilities and programs called *antispyware* and *antivirus* programs that protect your computer from spyware and viruses.

You should install and update your antivirus and spyware protection software regularly, and scan all new disks and any incoming information from online sources for viruses. Some systems do this automatically; others require you to install soft-ware to do it.

Disk Maintenance

From time to time, you should run a program that scans or checks the hard drive to see that there are not bad sectors (areas) and look for corrupted files. Optimizing or defragmenting the hard disk is another way to keep your computer running at its best. Scanning and checking programs often offers the option of "fixing" the bad areas or problems, although you should be aware that this could result in data loss.

Society and Computers

The electronic information era has had global effects and influenced global change in all areas of people's lives including education, government, society, and commerce. With the changes of this era have come many new questions and responsibilities. There are issues of ethics, security, and privacy.

Ethics

When you access information—whether online, in the workplace, or via purchased software—you have a responsibility to respect the rights of the person or people who created that information. Digital information, text, images, and sound are very easy to copy and share, however, that does not make it right to do so. You have to treat electronic information with respect. Often images, text, and sound are copyrighted. *Copyright* is the legal method for protecting the intellectual property of the author— the same way as you would a book, article, or painting. For instance, you must give credit when you copy information from the Web or another person's document.

If you come across another person's personal information, you must treat it with respect. Do not share personal information unless you have that person's permission. For example, if you happen to pass a computer where a person left personal banking information software open on the computer or a personal calendar available, you should not share that information. If e-mail comes to you erroneously, you should delete it before reading it.

When you use equipment that belongs to your school, a company for which you work, or others, here are some rules you should follow:

1. Do not damage computer hardware.

2. Do not add or remove equipment without permission.

3. Do not use an access code or equipment without permission.

4. Do not read others' e-mail.

5. Do not alter data belonging to someone else without permission.

6. Do not use the computer for play during work hours or use it for personal profit.

7. Do not access the Internet for nonbusiness related activities during work hours.

8. Do not install or uninstall software without permission.

9. Do not make unauthorized copies of data or software or copy company files or procedures for personal use.

10. Do not copy software programs to use at home or at another site in the company without permission.

APPENDIX A

Security and Privacy

The Internet provides access to business and life-enhancing resources, such as distance learning, remote medical diagnostics, and the ability to work from home more effectively. Businesses, colleges and universities, and governments throughout the world depend on the Internet every day to get work done. Disruptions in the Internet can create havoc and dramatically decrease productivity.

With more and more financial transactions taking place online, *identity theft* is a growing problem, proving a person's online identity relies heavily upon their usernames and passwords. If you do online banking, there are several levels of security that you must pass through, verifying that you are who you claim to be, before gaining access to your accounts. If you divulge your usernames and passwords, someone can easily access your accounts online with devastating effects to your credit rating and to your accounts.

Phishing is a criminal activity that is used by people to fraudulently obtain your personal information, such as usernames, passwords, credit card details, and your Social Security information. Your Social Security number should never be given out online. Phishers send e-mails that look legitimate, but in fact are not. Phishing e-mails will often include fake information saying that your account needs your immediate attention because of unusual or suspected fraudulent activity. You are asked to click a link in the e-mail to access a Web site where you are then instructed to enter personal information. See **Figure A–23** and **Figure A–24**. Phishing e-mail might also come with a promise of winning some money or gifts. When you get mail from people you don't know, the rules to remember are "you never get something for nothing," and "if it looks too good to be true, it's most likely not true."

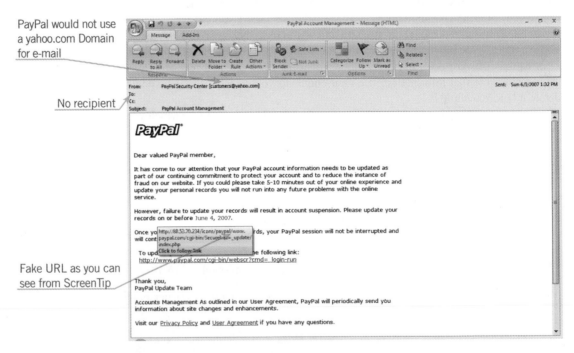

PayPal would not use a yahoo.com Domain for e-mail

No recipient

Fake URL as you can see from ScreenTip

FIGURE A–23   Fake PayPal e-mail for phishing

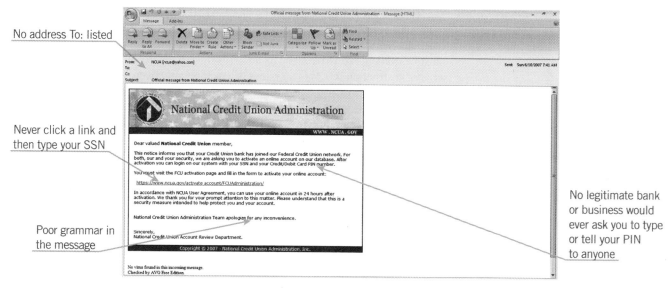

No address To: listed

Never click a link and then type your SSN

Poor grammar in the message

No legitimate bank or business would ever ask you to type or tell your PIN to anyone

FIGURE A–24   Fake Credit Union e-mail for phishing

Whatever the ruse, when you click the link provided in the phishing e-mail, your browser will open a Web site that looks real, perhaps like your bank's site, eBay, or PayPal. But, in fact, this is a fake site set up to get you to give up your personal information. Phishing sites are growing. You should never click a link provided in an e-mail to get to sites such as your bank, eBay, or PayPal. Your bank or any other legitimate Web site will never ask you to type personal information on a page linked from an e-mail message. Always type the Web page address directly in the browser. Banks and Web sites have been trying to stop phishing sites through technology. Other attempts to reduce the growing number of reported phishing incidents include legislation and simply educating users about the practice.

Just as you would not open someone else's mail, you must respect the privacy of e-mail sent to others. When interacting with others online, you must keep confidential information confidential. Do not endanger your privacy, safety, or financial security by giving out personal information to someone you do not know.

Career Opportunities

In one way or another, all careers involve the computer. Whether you are a grocery store clerk using a scanner to read the prices, a busy executive writing a report that includes charts, graphics, and detailed analysis on a laptop on an airplane, or a programmer writing new software—almost everyone uses computers in their jobs. Farmers use computers to optimize crops and order seeds and feed. Most scientific research is done using computers.

There are specific careers available if you want to work with computers in the computer industry. Schools offer degrees in computer programming, computer repair, computer engineering, and software design. The most popular jobs are systems analysts, computer operators, database managers, database specialists, and programmers. Analysts figure out ways to make computers work (or work better) for a particular business or type of business. Computer operators use the programs and devices to conduct business with computers. Programmers write the software for applications or new systems. There are degrees and jobs for people who want to create and maintain Web sites. Working for a company maintaining their Web site can be a very exciting career.

▣ EXTRA FOR EXPERTS

Ebay is an online auction Web site that provides people a way to buy and sell merchandise through the Internet. PayPal is a financial services Web site that provides a way to transfer funds between people who perform financial transactions on the Internet.

APPENDIX A

There are courses of study in using CAD (computer-aided design) and CAM (computer-aided manufacturing). There are positions available to instruct others in computer software use within companies and schools. Technical writers and editors must be available to write manuals about using computers and software. Computer-assisted instruction (CAI) is a system of teaching any given subject using the computer. Designing video games is another exciting and ever-growing field of computer work. And these are just a few of the possible career opportunities in an ever-changing work environment. See **Figure A–25**.

FIGURE A–25   Working in the computer field

What Does the Future Hold?

The possibilities for computer development and application are endless. Things that were dreams or science fiction only 10 or 20 years ago are now reality. New technologies are emerging constantly. Some new technologies are replacing old ways of doing things; others are merging with those older methods and devices. Some new technologies are creating new markets. The Internet (more specifically, the Web), cell phones, and DVD videos are just a few inventions of the past decades that did not have counterparts prior to their inventions. We are learning new ways to work and play because of the computer. It is definitely a device that has become part of our offices, our homes, and our lives.

Social networking has moved from the streets and onto the Web. People meet and greet through the Internet using sites such as MySpace, Facebook, and Twitter.

Emerging Technologies

Today the various technologies and systems are coming together to operate more efficiently. Convergence is the merging of these technologies. Telephone communication is being combined with computer e-mail and Web browsing so users can set a time to meet online and, with the addition of voice technology, actually speak to each other using one small portable device.

The Web, now an important part of commerce and education, began as a one-way vehicle where users visited to view Web pages and get information. It has evolved into sites where shopping and commerce takes place and is now evolving into a technology where users create the content. Web 2.0 and sites such as Facebook.com, flickr.com, LinkedIn.com, twitter.com, wikipedia.com, and youtube.com have content generated by the people that visit the Web sites. See **Figure A–26**.

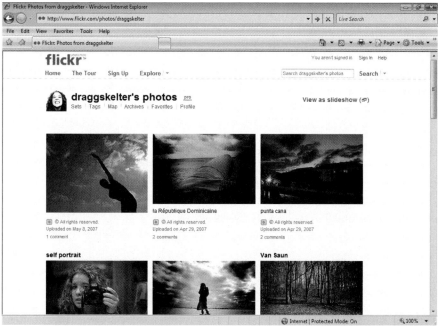

FIGURE A–26   User generated content

Computers have radically changed the way the medical profession delivers health care. Through the medical community, computers have enhanced medicine and healthcare throughout the world.

Trends

There are many trends that drive the computer industry. One trend is for larger and faster storage. From megabytes, to gigabytes, to terabytes, storage is becoming less an issue as the cost of storage is also dropping. RAM today is increasing exponentially. The trend is to sell larger blocks of RAM with every new personal computer. Newer processors also operate at speeds that are faster than the previous generation processors.

The actual size of computers is decreasing. Technology is allowing more powerful components to fit into smaller devices—laptops are lighter, monitors take up less space on the desktop, and flash drives can fit in your pocket and store gigabytes of data.

Home Offices

More and more frequently, people are working out of their homes—whether they are employees who are linked to their office in another location or individuals running their own businesses. *Telecommuting* meets the needs of many industries. Many companies allow workers to have a computer at home that is linked to their office and employees can use laptop computers to work both from home and on the road as they travel. A laptop computer, in combination with a wireless network, allows an employee to work from virtually anywhere and still keep in constant contact with her or his employer and customers.

Business communication is primarily by e-mail and telephone. It is very common for serious business transactions and communications to occur via e-mail rather than through the regular mail. Such an arrangement saves companies time and workspace and, thus, money.

Home Use

More and more households have personal computers. The statistics are constantly proving that a computer is an essential household appliance. Computers are used to access the Internet for shopping, education, and leisure. Computers are used to maintain financial records, manage household accounts, and record and manage personal information. More and more people are using electronic banking. Games and other computer applications offer another way to spend leisure dollars, and the convergence of television, the Internet, and the computer will find more households using their computers for media such as movies and music.

The future is computing. It's clear that this technology will continue to expand and provide us with new and exciting trends.

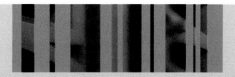

APPENDIX B

Keyboarding Touch System Improvement

Introduction

- *Your Goal—Improve your keyboarding skills using the touch system so you are able to type without looking at the keyboard.*

Why Improve Your Keyboarding Skills?

- To type faster and more accurately every time you use the computer
- To increase your enjoyment while using the computer

Instead of looking back and forth from the page to see the text you have to type and then turning back to the keyboard and pressing keys with one or two fingers, using the touch system you will type faster and more accurately.

 WARNING

Using two fingers to type while looking at the keyboard is called the "hunt and peck" system and is not efficient when typing large documents.

Getting Ready to Build Skills

In order to get ready you should:

1. **Prepare your desk and computer area.**
   a. Clear your desk of all clutter, except your book, a pencil or pen, the keyboard, the mouse, and the monitor.
   b. Position your keyboard and book so that you are comfortable and able to move your hands and fingers freely on the keyboard and read the book at the same time.
   c. Keep your feet flat on the floor, sit with your back straight, and rest your arms slightly bent with your finger tips on the keyboard.
   d. Start a word-processing program, such as Microsoft Word, or any other text editor. You can also use any simple program such as the Microsoft Works word processor or WordPad that is part of the Windows operating system. Ask your teacher for assistance.

2. Take a two-minute timed typing test according to your teacher's directions.

3. Calculate your words a minute (WAM) and errors a minute (EAM) using the instructions on the timed typing progress chart. This will be the base score you will compare to future timed typing.

4. Record today's Date, WAM, and EAM on the Base Score line of the writing progress chart.

5. Repeat the timed typing test many times to see improvements in your score.

6. Record each attempt on the Introduction line of the chart.

Getting Started

Keyboarding is an essential skill in today's workplace. No matter what your job, most likely you have to learn to be an effective typist. Follow the hints below to help you achieve this goal:

- Ignore errors.
- To complete the following exercises, you will type text that is bold and is not italicized and looks **like this**.
- If you have difficulty reaching for any key, for example the y key, practice by looking at the reach your fingertips make from the j key to the y key until the reach is visualized in your mind. The reach will become natural with very little practice.
- To start on a new line, press Enter.

Skill Builder 1

Your Goal—Use the touch system to type the letters j u y h n m and to learn to press the spacebar.

Keys

What to Do

1. Place your fingertips on the home row keys as shown in **Figure B–1**.

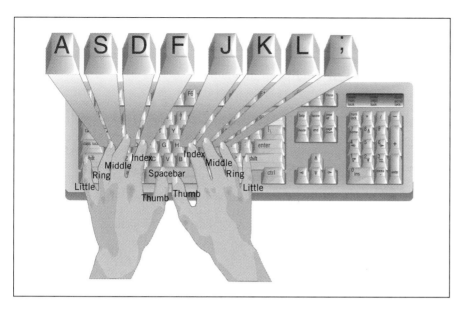

FIGURE B–1   Place your fingertips on the Home Row keys

2. Look at **Figure B–2**. In step 3, you will press the letter keys j u y h n m. To press these keys, you use your right index finger. You will press the spacebar after typing each letter three times. The spacebar is the long bar beneath the bottom row of letter keys. You will press the spacebar with your right thumb.

> **TIP**
>
> The home row keys are where you rest your fingertips when they are not typing. The index finger of your right hand rests on the J key. The index finger of your left hand rests on the F key. Feel the slight bump on these keys to help find the home row keys without looking at the keyboard.

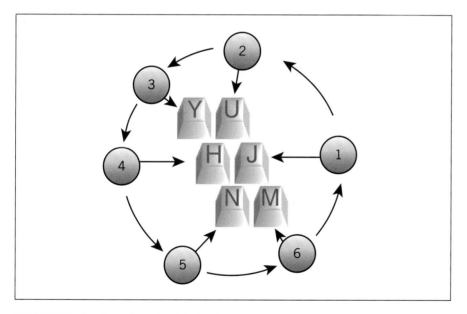

FIGURE B–2   Pressing the J U Y H N M keys

3. Look at your keyboard. Repeat the letters silently to yourself as you move your right index finger from the j key to press each key three times, and then press the spacebar. Start typing:

jjj uuu jjj yyy jjj hhh jjj nnn jjj mmm

jjj uuu jjj yyy jjj hhh jjj nnn jjj mmm jjj

4. Repeat the same drill as many times as it takes for you to reach your comfort level.

   jjj uuu jjj yyy jjj hhh jjj nnn jjj mmm

   jjj uuu jjj yyy jjj hhh jjj nnn jjj mmm jjj

5. Close your eyes and visualize each key under each finger as you repeat the drill in step 4.

6. Look at the following two lines and type:

   jjj jjj jjj juj juj juj jyj jyj jyj jhj jhj jhj jnj jnj jnj jmj jmj jmj

   jjj jjj jjj juj juj juj jyj jyj jyj jhj jhj jhj jnj jnj jnj jmj jmj jmj

7. Repeat step 6, this time concentrating on the rhythmic pattern of the keys.

8. Close your eyes and visualize the keys under your fingertips as you type the drill in step 4 from memory.

9. Look at the following two lines and type these groups of letters:

   j ju juj j jy jyj j jh jhj j jn jnj j jm jmj j ju juj j jy jyj j jh jhj j jn jnj j jm jmj

   jjj ju jhj jn jm ju jm jh jnj jm ju jmj jy ju jh j u ju juj jy jh jnj ju jm jmj jy

10. You may want to repeat Skill Builder 1, striving to improve typing letters that are most difficult for you.

Skill Builder 2

The left index finger is used to type the letters f r t g b v. Always return your left index finger to the f key on the home row after pressing the other keys.

Your Goal—Use the touch system to type f r t g b v .

Keys

What to Do

1. Place your fingertips on the home row keys as you did in Skill Builder 1, Figure B–1.

2. Look at **Figure B–3**. Notice how you will type the letters f r t g b v and then press the spacebar with your right thumb.

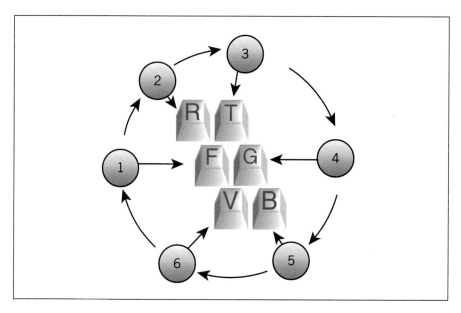

FIGURE B–3   Pressing the F R T G B V keys

3. Look at your keyboard. To press these keys, you use your left index finger. You will press the spacebar after typing each letter three times. The spacebar is the long bar beneath the bottom row of letter keys. You will press the spacebar with your right thumb.

   After pressing each letter in the circle, press the home key f three times as shown. Don't worry about errors. Ignore them.

   fff rrr fff ttt fff ggg fff bbb fff vvv

   fff rrr fff ttt fff ggg fff bbb fff vvv fff

4. Repeat the same drill two more times using a quicker, sharper stroke.

   fff rrr fff ttt fff ggg fff bbb fff vvv

   fff rrr fff ttt fff ggg fff bbb fff vvv fff

5. Close your eyes and visualize each key under each finger as you repeat the drill in step 4.

6. Look at the following two lines and key these groups of letters:

   fff fff fff frf frf frf ftf ftf ftf fgf fgf fgf fbf fbf fbf fvf fvf fvf

   fff fff fff frf frf frf ftf ftf ftf fgf fgf fgf fbf fbf fbf fvf fvf fvf

7. Repeat step 6, this time concentrating on a rhythmic pattern of the keys.

8. Close your eyes and visualize the keys under your fingertips as you type the drill in step 4 from memory.

9. Look at the following two lines and type these groups of letters:

   fr frf ft ftf fg fgf fb fbf fv fvf

   ft fgf fv frf ft fbf fv frf ft fgf

10. You are about ready to type your first words. Look at the following lines and type these groups of letters (remember to press the spacebar after each group):

jjj juj jug jug jug rrr rur rug rug rug

ttt tut tug tug tug rrr rur rub rub rub

ggg gug gum gum gum mmm mum

mug mug mug hhh huh hum hum hum

11. Complete the Keyboarding Technique Checklist.

Skill Builder 3

Your Goal—Use the touch system to type k i , d e c.

Keys ⟨K⟩ ⟨I⟩ ⟨,⟩ (comma)

What to Do

1. Place your fingertips on the home row keys. The home row key for the left middle finger is d. The home row key for the right middle finger is k. You use your left middle finger to type d, e, c. You use your right middle finger to type k, i, , as shown in **Figure B–4**.

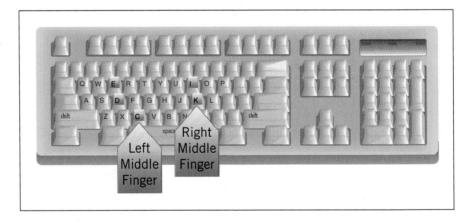

FIGURE B–4 Pressing the K I , D E C keys

2. Look at your keyboard and locate these keys: k i , (the letter k key, the letter i key, and the comma key).

3. Look at your keyboard. Repeat the letters silently to yourself as you press each key three times and put a space between each set of letters and the comma to type:

kkk iii kkk ,,, kkk iii kkk ,,, kkk iii kkk ,,, kkk iii kkk ,,, kkk iii kkk ,,, kkk

4. Look at the characters in step 3 and repeat the drill two more times using a quicker, sharper stroke.

5. Close your eyes and repeat the drill in step 3 as you visualize each key under each finger.

6. Repeat step 3, do not look at the keyboard, and concentrate on the rhythmic pattern of the keys.

Keys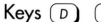

What to Do

1. Place your fingertips on the home row keys.

2. Look at your keyboard and locate these keys: d e c (the letter d key, the letter e key, and the letter c key).

3. Look at your keyboard. Repeat the letters silently to yourself as you press each key three times and put a space between each set of letters to type:

   ddd eee ddd ccc ddd eee ddd ccc ddd eee ddd ccc ddd eee ddd ccc ddd

4. Look at the letters in step 3 and repeat the drill two more times using a quicker, sharper stroke.

5. Close your eyes and repeat the drill in step 3 as you visualize each key under each finger.

6. Repeat step 3, do not look at the keyboard, and concentrate on the rhythmic pattern of the keys.

7. Look at the following lines of letters and type these groups of letters and words:

   fff fuf fun fun fun ddd ded den den den

   ccc cuc cub cub cub vvv vev vet

   fff fuf fun fun fun ddd ded den den den

   ccc cuc cub cub cub vvv vev vet

8. Complete the Keyboarding Technique Checklist.

Skill Builder 4

Your Goal—Use the touch system to type l o . s w x and to press the left Shift key.

Keys   (period)

APPENDIX B

What to Do

1. Place your fingertips on the home row keys. The home row key for the left ring finger is s. The home row key for the right ring finger is l. You use your left ring finger to type s w x. You use your right ring finger to type l o . as shown in **Figure B–5**.

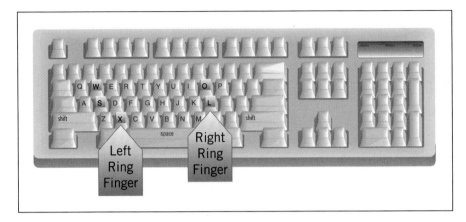

FIGURE B–5   Pressing the L O . S W X keys

2. Look at your keyboard and locate the following keys: l o . (the letter l key, the letter o key, and the period key).

3. Look at your keyboard. Repeat the letters silently to yourself as you press each key three times and put a space between each set of letters and the periods to type:

   lll ooo lll ... lll ooo lll ... lll ooo lll ... lll ooo lll ... lll ooo lll ... lll ooo lll ... lll

4. Look at the line in step 3 and repeat the drill two more times using a quicker, sharper stroke.

5. Close your eyes and repeat the drill in step 3 as you visualize each key under each finger.

6. Repeat step 3, do not look at the keyboard, and concentrate on the rhythmic pattern of the keys.

Keys ⟨ S ⟩ ⟨ W ⟩ ⟨ X ⟩

1. Place your fingertips on the home row keys.

2. Look at your keyboard and locate the following letter keys: s w x

3. Look at your keyboard. Repeat the letters silently to yourself as you press each key three times and put a space between each set of letters to type:

   sss www sss xxx sss www sss xxx sss www sss xxx sss www sss xxx sss

4. Look at the line in step 3 and repeat the same drill two more times using a quicker, sharper stroke.

5. Close your eyes and repeat the drill in step 3 as you visualize each key under each finger.

6. Repeat step 3, do not look at the keyboard, and concentrate on the rhythmic pattern of the keys.

Key Shift (SHIFT) (Left Shift Key)

You press and hold the Shift key as you press a letter key to type a capital letter. You press and hold the Shift key to type the character that appears above the numbers in the top row of the keyboard and on a few other keys that show two characters.

Press and hold down the left Shift key with the little finger on your left hand while you press each letter to type capital letters for keys that are typed with the fingertips on your right hand. See **Figure B–6**.

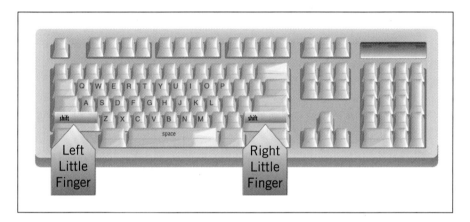

FIGURE B–6   Using the Shift keys

1. Type the following groups of letters and the sentence that follows.

   jjj JJJ jjj JJJ yyy YYY yyy YYY nnn NNN nnn NNN mmm MMM

   Just look in the book. You can see well.

2. Complete a column in the Keyboarding Technique Checklist.

Skill Builder 5

Your Goal—Use the touch system to type a q z ; p / and to press the right Shift key.

Keys (;) (Semi-Colon) (P) (/)

APPENDIX B

What to Do

1. Place your fingertips on the home row keys. The home row key for the left little finger is a. The home row key for the right little finger is ;. You use your left little finger to type a q z. You use your right little finger to type ; p / as shown in **Figure B–7**.

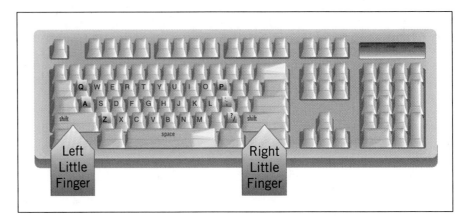

FIGURE B–7   Pressing the A Q Z ; P / and the right Shift key

2. Look at your keyboard and locate the following keys: ; p / (the semi-colon, the letter p, and the forward slash).

3. Repeat the letters silently to yourself as you press each key three times and put a space between each set of characters to type:

   ;;; ppp ;;; /// ;;; ppp ;;; /// ;;; ppp ;;; ///

   ;;; ppp ;;; /// ;;; ppp ;;; /// ;;; ppp ;;; /// ;;;

4. Look at the lines in step 3 and repeat the drill two more times using a quicker, sharper stroke.

5. Close your eyes and repeat the drill in step 3 as you visualize each key under each finger.

6. Repeat step 3, do not look at the keyboard, and concentrate on a rhythmic pattern of the keys.

Keys (A) (Q) (Z)

1. Place your fingertips on the home row keys.

2. Look at your keyboard and locate the following keys: a q z (the letter a, the letter q, and the letter z).

3. Look at your keyboard. Repeat the letters silently to yourself as you press each key three times and put a space between each set of letters and type:

   aaa qqq aaa zzz aaa qqq aaa zzz aaa qqq aaa zzz aaa qqq aaa zzz aaa

4. Look at the line in step 3 and repeat the same drill two more times using a quicker, sharper stroke.

5. Close your eyes and repeat the drill in step 3 as you visualize each key under each finger.

6. Repeat step 3, do not look at the keyboard, and concentrate on the rhythmic pattern of the keys.

Key Shift (SHIFT) (Right Shift Key)

Press and hold down the right Shift key with the little finger on your right hand while you press each letter to type capital letters for keys that are typed with the fingertips on your left hand.

1. Type the following lines. Press and hold down the right Shift key with the little finger of your right hand to make capitals of letters you type with the fingertips on your left hand.

   sss SSS rrr RRR

   Press each key quickly. Relax when you type.

2. Complete another column in the Keyboarding Technique Checklist.

Skill Builder 6

You will probably have to type slowly at first, but with practice you will learn to type faster and accurately.

Your Goal—Use the touch system to type all letters of the alphabet.

What to Do

1. Close your eyes. Do not look at the keyboard and type all letters of the alphabet in groups of three with a space between each set as shown:

   aaa bbb ccc ddd eee fff ggg hhh iii jjj

   kkk lll mmm nnn ooo ppp qqq rrr sss

   ttt uuu vvv www xxx yyy zzz

2. Repeat step 1, concentrating on a rhythmic pattern of the keys.

3. Repeat step 1, but faster than you did for step 2.

4. Type the following sets of letters, all letters of the alphabet in groups of two with a space between each set as shown:

   aa bb cc dd ee ff gg hh ii jj kk ll mm nn oo pp qq rr ss tt uu vv ww xx yy zz

5. Type the following letters, all letters of the alphabet with a space between each letter as shown:

   a b c d e f g h i j k l m n o p q r s t u v w x y z

6. Continue to look at this book. Do not look at the keyboard, and type all letters of the alphabet backwards in groups of three with a space between each set as shown:

zzz yyy xxx www vvv uuu ttt sss rrr

qqq ppp ooo nnn mmm lll kkk jjj iii

hhh ggg fff eee ddd ccc bbb aaa

7. Repeat step 6, but faster than the last time.

8. Type each letter of the alphabet once backwards:

z y x w v u t s r q p o n m l k j i h g f e d c b a

9. Think about the letters that took you the most amount of time to find the key on the keyboard. Go back to the Skill Builder for those letters, and repeat the drills until you are confident about their locations.

Timed Typing

Prepare to take the timed typing test, according to your teacher's directions.

1. **Prepare your desk and computer area.**
   a. Clear your desk of all clutter except your book, a pencil or pen, the keyboard, the mouse, the monitor, and the computer if it is located on the desk.
   b. Position your keyboard and book so that you are comfortable and able to move your hands and fingertips freely.
   c. Keep your feet flat on the floor, sitting with your back straight, resting your arms slightly bent with your fingertips on the keyboard.

2. Take a two-minute timed typing test according to your teacher's directions.

3. Calculate your words a minute (WAM) and errors a minute (EAM) scores using the instructions on the Timed Typing Progress Chart in this book.

4. Record the date, WAM, and EAM on the Skill Builder 6 line in the Timed Typing Progress Chart printed at the end of this appendix.

5. Repeat the timed typing test as many times as you can and record each attempt in the Timed Typing Progress Chart.

Skill Builder 7

Your Goal—Improve your typing techniques—which is the secret for improving your speed and accuracy.

What to Do

1. Rate yourself for each item on the Keyboarding Technique Checklist printed at the end of this appendix.

2. Do not time yourself as you concentrate on a single technique you marked with a "0." Type only the first paragraph of the timed typing.

3. Repeat step 2 as many times as possible for each of the items marked with an "0" that need improvement.

4. Take a two-minute timed typing test. Record your WAM and EAM on the Timed Typing Progress Chart as 1st Attempt on the Skill Builder 7 line. Compare this score with your base score.

5. Looking only at the book and using your best techniques, type the following technique sentence for one minute:

   .   2   .   4   .   6   .   8   .   10   .   12   .   14   .   16

   Now is the time for all good men and women to come to the aid of their country.

6. Record your WAM and EAM in the Timed Typing Progress Chart on the 7 Technique Sentence line.

7. Repeat steps 5 and 6 as many times as you can and record your scores in the Timed Typing Progress Chart.

Skill Builder 8

Your Goal—Increase your words a minute (WAM) score.

What to Do

You can now type letters in the speed line very well and with confidence. Practicing all of the other letters of the alphabet will further increase your skill and confidence in keyboarding.

1. Take a two-minute timed typing test.

2. Record your WAM and EAM scores as the 1st Attempt in the Timed Typing Progress Chart.

3. Type only the first paragraph only one time as fast as you can. Ignore errors.

4. Type only the first and second paragraphs only one time as fast as you can. Ignore errors.

5. Take a two-minute timed typing test again. Ignore errors.

6. Record only your WAM score as the 2nd Attempt in the Timed Typing Progress Chart. Compare only this WAM with your 1st Attempt WAM and your base score WAM.

Get Your Best WAM

1. To get your best WAM on easy text for 15 seconds, type the following speed line as fast as you can, as many times as you can. Ignore errors.

   .   2   .   4   .   6   .   8   .   10

   Now is the time, now is the time, now is the time,

2. Multiply the number of words typed by four to get your WAM (15 seconds × 4 = 1 minute). For example, if you type 12 words for 15 seconds, 12 × 4 = 48 WAM.

3. Record only your WAM in the 8 Speed Line box in the Timed Typing Progress Chart.

4. Repeat steps 1–3 as many times as you can to get your very best WAM. Ignore errors.

5. Record only your WAM for each attempt in the Timed Typing Progress Chart.

Skill Builder 9

Your Goal—Decrease errors a minute (EAM) score.

What to Do

TIP

How much you improve depends upon how much you want to improve.

1. Take a two-minute timed typing test.

2. Record your WAM and EAM as the 1st Attempt in the Timed Typing Progress Chart.

3. Type only the first paragraph only one time at a controlled rate of speed so you reduce errors. Ignore speed.

4. Type only the first and second paragraphs only one time at a controlled rate of speed so you reduce errors. Ignore speed.

5. Take a two-minute timed typing test again. Ignore speed.

6. Record only your EAM score as the 2nd Attempt in the Timed Typing Progress Chart. Compare only the EAM with your 1st Attempt EAM and your base score EAM.

Get Your Best EAM

1. To get your best EAM, type the following accuracy sentence (same as the technique sentence) for one minute. Ignore speed.

   Now is the time for all good men and women to come to the aid of their country.

2. Record only your EAM score on the Accuracy Sentence 9 line in the Timed Typing Progress Chart.

3. Repeat step 1 as many times as you can to get your best EAM. Ignore speed.

4. Record only your EAM score for each attempt in the Timed Typing Progress Chart.

Skill Builder 10

Your Goal—Use the touch system and your best techniques to type faster and more accurately than you have ever typed before.

What to Do

1. Take a one-minute timed typing test.

2. Record your WAM and EAM as the 1st Attempt on the Skill Builder 10 line in the Timed Typing Progress Chart.

3. Repeat the timed typing test for two minutes as many times as necessary to get your best ever WAM with no more than one EAM. Record your scores as 2nd, 3rd, and 4th Attempts.

> **TIP**
>
> You may want to get advice regarding which techniques you need to improve from a classmate or your instructor.

Assessing Your Improvement

1. Circle your best timed typing test for Skill Builders 6-10 in the Timed Typing Progress Chart.

2. Record your best score and your base score. Compare the two scores. Did you improve?

	WAM	EAM
Best Score	_____	_____
Base Score	_____	_____

3. Use the Keyboarding Technique Checklist to identify techniques you still need to improve. You may want to practice these techniques now to increase your WAM or decrease your EAM.

Timed Typing

Every five strokes in a timed typing test is a word, including punctuation marks and spaces. Use the scale above each line to tell you how many words you typed.

```
        .      2     .     4     .     6      .
If you learn how to key well now, it
    8    .    10    .    12    .    14    .       16
is a skill that will help you for the rest
        .    18    .    20    .    22    .     24
of your life. How you sit will help you key
  .     26    .    28    .    30    .       32    .     34
with more speed and less errors.  Sit with your
        .    36    .    38    .    40    .     42    .
feet flat on the floor and your back erect.
      44    .    46    .    48    .    50
To key fast by touch, try to keep your
   .    52    .    54    .    56    .    58     .
eyes on the copy and not on your hands or
    60    .    62    .    64    .    66    .    68
the screen.  Curve your fingers and make sharp,
    .      70      .
quick strokes.
  72    .    74    .    76    .     78      .
Work for speed first.  If you make more
    80    .    82    .    84    .    86    .     88
than two errors a minute, you are keying too
   .    90    .    92    .    94    .    96     .
fast. Slow down to get fewer errors. If you
     98    .    100    .    102    .    104     .
get fewer than two errors a minute, go for
  106     .
speed.
```

Timed Typing Progress Chart

Timed Writing Progress Chart

Last Name: _____   *First Name:* _____

Instructions

Calculate your scores as shown in the following sample. Repeat timed writings as many times as you can and record your scores for each attempt.

Base Score	Date	WAM	EAM	Time

To calculate WAM: Divide words keyed by number of minutes to get WAM. For example: 44 words keyed in 2 minutes = 22 WAM [44/2=22]

To calculate EAM: Divide errors made by minutes of typing to get EAM

For example: 7 errors made in 2 minutes of typing = 3.5 EAM [7/2=3.5]

Skill Builder	Date	1st Attempt (a) WAM	1st Attempt (b) EAM	2nd Attempt WAM	2nd Attempt EAM	3rd Attempt WAM	3rd Attempt EAM	4th Attempt WAM	4th Attempt EAM
Sample	9/2	22	3.5	23	2.0	25	1.0	29	2.0
Introduction									
6									
7									
8						-----			
9					-----				
10									
7 Technique Sentence									
8 Speed Line			-----		-----		-----		-----
9 Accuracy Sentence		-----		-----		-----		-----	

Keyboarding Technique Checklist

Last Name: _____   *First Name:* _____

Instructions

1. Write the Skill Builder number, the date, and the initials of the evaluator in the proper spaces.

2. Place a check mark (✓) after a technique that is performed satisfactorily.

3. Place a large zero (0) after a technique that needs improvement.

Technique											
Skill Builder Number:	Sample										
Date:	9/1										
Evaluator:	SL										
Attitude											
1. Enthusiastic about learning	✓										
2. Optimistic about improving	✓										
3. Alert but relaxed	✓										
4. Sticks to the task; not distracted	✓										
Getting Ready	✓										
1. Desk uncluttered											
2. Properly positions keyboard and book	✓										
3. Feet flat on the floor	✓										
4. Body erect, but relaxed	0										
Keyboarding											
1. Curves fingers	0										
2. Keeps eyes on the book	✓										
3. Taps the keys lightly; does not "pound" them	0										
4. Makes quick, "bouncy," strokes	0										
5. Smooth rhythm	0										
6. Minimum pauses between strokes	✓										

APPENDIX C

Differences between Windows 7, Windows Vista, and Windows XP

The Windows Experience

- Microsoft offers many new features in Windows 7 that are not available in Windows XP and Windows Vista.
- The overall Windows experience has been vastly improved from Windows XP to Windows 7. If you make the jump from XP to Windows 7, you will discover a great number of changes that are for the better. In addition, many of the new features introduced in Windows Vista were retained in this latest version of the popular operating system. Upgrading to Windows 7 is also an easier, more streamlined transition.

APPENDIX C

- With Windows 7, Microsoft has simplified everyday tasks and works more efficiently. This is all in response to issues users had with the Windows XP and Windows Vista experience. The major differences between Windows XP, Windows Vista, and Windows 7 are in the Start menu, dynamic navigation, desktop gadgets, improved security, search options, parental controls, and firewall, as well as improvements to the Windows Aero feature, see **Figure C–1**.

FIGURE C–1 Windows 7 Features

Windows Aero

- Windows Aero is a new graphic interface feature which gives a "transparent" quality to windows, dialog boxes, and other items in the Windows Vista and Windows 7 environment.

- Flip 3-D, or simply Flip, shows mini versions of windows and thumbnails in the Windows 7 environment when turned on.

Windows XP users had to download Windows Desktop Enhancements and PowerTools from the Microsoft Web site to change their Windows experience. Windows Vista and Windows 7 now have many different themes and options built into the operating system, making it easy to modify the Windows experience. One theme, introduced in Windows Vista is Aero.

Windows Aero is a feature which was first introduced in Windows Vista and is not available in the Windows XP operating system. Windows Aero, enabled by default in Windows 7, is a more aesthetically pleasing user interface to Windows Vista and Windows 7 systems. For example, Windows XP utilizes ScreenTips only when pointing to items on the Taskbar, Desktop, and Menus. The basic ScreenTips found in Windows XP have been enhanced to show live "sneak-previews" of windows with a simple point to the icon on the taskbar , as shown in **Figure C–2**.

Windows 7 made major improvements to the function of Aero. These new features include Aero Peek, Aero Shake, Aero Snap, Touch UI, and many other visual effects covered in this section. Compare the evolution of the Taskbar ScreenTip in Windows XP to Windows Vista and finally in Windows 7 in the figures below.

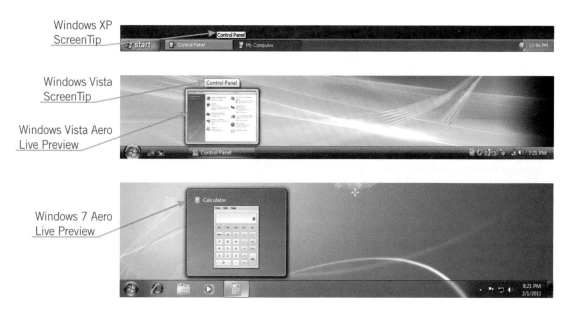

FIGURE C–2 Comparing Windows XP taskbar with Windows Vista and Windows 7

Understanding the Desktop

- Gadgets, introduced in Windows Vista, and Jump Lists, introduced in Windows 7, are two new desktop features.

- Windows 7 also includes multiple Aero themes to customize your desktop including the Desktop Background Slideshow.

APPENDIX C

At first glance, the Windows XP desktop only appears to differ slightly from that of Windows Vista, but the new features available with Windows 7 are substantial. The icons, shortcuts, folders, and files are generally the same; however, there are major aesthetic visual differences in this version. The most obvious addition from XP to Vista is the desktop gadget. Gadgets were not available in Windows XP. In **Figure C–4**, notice the appearance of three gadgets on the sidebar. Desktop gadgets are also available in Windows 7; however the sidebar function has been abandoned. Users simply add the gadget to the desktop.

The Taskbar in Windows XP includes the notification area, quick launch (when enabled), Start button, and icon(s) representing open programs. Beginning with Windows 7, you can now easily pin items to the Taskbar instead of using a quick launch feature. Jump lists, Aero themes and the Desktop Background Slideshow, explained in this chapter, are also new features to Windows 7.

FIGURE C–3 Windows XP Start menu and Desktop

The Start menu has been slightly enhanced from Windows XP to Windows 7. All Programs no longer appears on an additional menu, it has been merged with the Start menu. Windows Vista introduced a search function built into the Start menu, which allows users to search the computer easily for documents, applications, and help. Compare the evolution in desktops from Windows XP to Windows 7 in **Figures C–3, C–4,** and **C–5**.

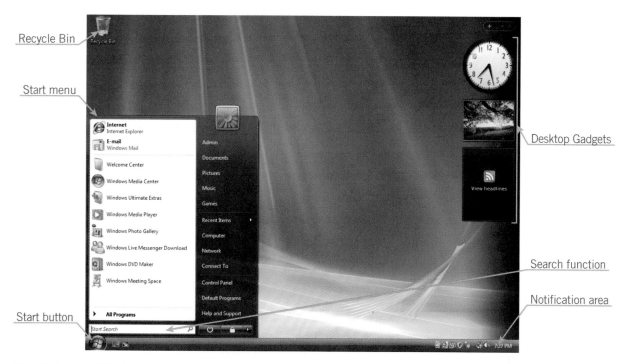

FIGURE C–4 Windows Vista Start menu and Desktop

FIGURE C–5 Windows 7 Start menu and Desktop

Navigating in Windows

- The Address bar in Windows 7 now functions differently, with more direct navigation functions.
- Windows 7 now includes a comprehensive Navigation pane in Windows Explorer.

Windows Explorer provides the tools to navigate and locate items on your computer. The Address bar has been upgraded from Windows XP to allow for easier movement between folders. In Windows XP, the only available methods were the Back button and drop-down arrow. See **Figure C–6**. A big difference is in the function of the path. You may now click the folder in your path to move back. You may also begin a search directly from the Address bar, which is a new Windows 7 feature. Windows XP users' only option to search was to utilize the Search Companion.

The Navigation pane, which provides links to common or recently used folders, is dramatically different in Windows 7, compared to Windows XP, which only featured Favorites. "My Documents", the default user folder in Windows XP, is now a collection of folders grouped in Libraries in Windows 7. These folders, as well as Favorites, are easily found on the new Navigation pane and are easily customizable.

To switch between open programs easily, Windows XP's only option aside from clicking the icon on the Taskbar, was to tab through available programs, in a basic method with no preview of the program state. Windows Flip, introduced in Windows Vista, allows you to move to an open file, window or program by pressing the Alt+Tab keys, while showing a preview of the program's current state in Aero. The Windows Vista version of Flip was enhanced for Windows 7 users, although the function remains the same. See **Figures C–8** and **C-9** on the following pages.

FIGURE C–6   Windows Explorer as seen in Windows XP

FIGURE C–7 Windows Explorer as seen in Windows Vista

FIGURE C–8 Flip in Windows Vista

Aero Flip 3-D tabs through open programs

Taskbar buttons for open programs

FIGURE C–9   Flip 3-D in Windows 7

Using Windows

- The new Aero Shake and Aero Snap allow you to easily move, resize, minimize and maximize open windows.
- The Control Panel now includes additional descriptive links, making it easy to find the item you are looking to modify.

Moving and resizing windows in Windows 7 provides the same essential functions as it did in previous Windows versions, with a few additions. In Windows XP and Vista, you had to manipulate each window individually, by clicking and dragging. You can still click and drag to resize and move windows; however this function has been upgraded and revamped in Windows 7. Aero Shake allows you to "shake" all open windows except that particular window to a minimized state. Aero Snap is a new way to easily resize open windows to expand vertically, or side-by-side.

The Control Panel, revamped in Windows Vista, has a new look in Windows 7, compared to that in Windows XP. The Search text box allows you to search for the Control Panel task you wish to perform. There are also descriptive linked items now replacing the "classic" icon format. **Figures C–10**, **C–11**, and **C–12**, which are shown on the following pages, illustrate the differences in the Control Panel from Windows XP to Windows 7.

Switch to Classic
View for basic icon
arrangement

Control Panel

Grouped categories

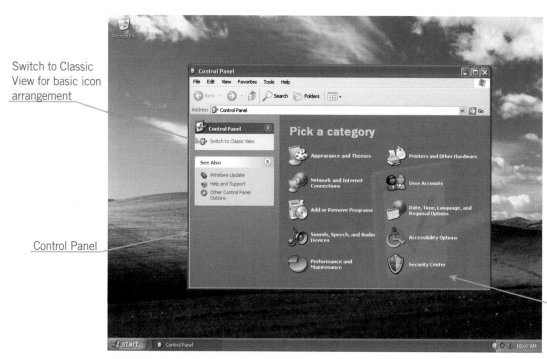

FIGURE C–10 Windows XP Control Panel

Switch to Classic
View for basic icon
arrangement

Control Panel

Search text box

Descriptive Grouped
categories with links

FIGURE C–11 Windows Vista Control Panel

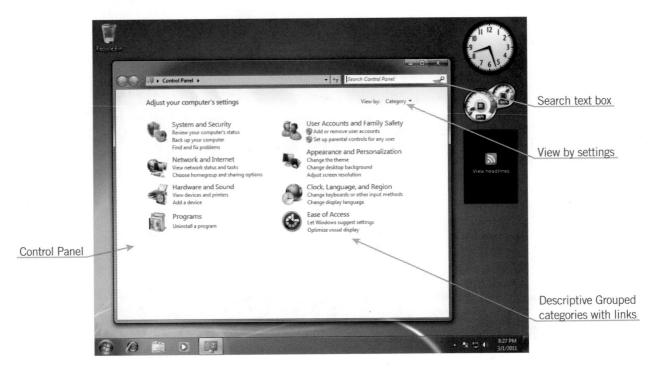

Search text box

View by settings

Control Panel

Descriptive Grouped categories with links

FIGURE C–12   Windows 7 Control Panel

Managing Your Computer

■ The Action Center is a new feature in Windows 7 which consolidates message traffic from Windows maintenance and security features.

■ Basic system utilities, such as Disk Cleanup and Disk Defragmenter, remain essentially the same from Windows XP to Windows 7.

Windows XP and Windows Vista's only method of receiving information on security and maintenance was the Security Center, available from the Control Panel. Windows 7 has improved this function, by creating a new Action Center, which communicates with the firewall, spyware protection, and antivirus software. Windows 7 users can now navigate to the Action Center by visiting the System and Security section of the Control Panel to view computer status and resolve issues. The Action Center is also pre-configured in Windows 7 to send important alerts to the Notification area of the taskbar.

One of the major upgrades in Windows 7 is in performance. Windows 7 was designed to run on less memory, shutting down services when not in use. In the Control Panel of Windows 7, there is a new Performance and Information Tools section. If you are a previous Windows XP user, you should familiarize yourself with this new feature. You will be able to assess your computer's performance, adjust settings, run disk cleanup, and launch advanced tools to manage your computer.

Windows Defender, introduced in Windows Vista is Microsoft's answer to spyware protection. This was not available for Windows XP users, pre Windows XP Service Pack 2. Windows XP Service Pack 2 users could download it from the Microsoft Web site and install it manually. Windows 7 also includes Windows Defender by default.

Windows Update, introduced in Windows XP has remained the same throughout the transitions through Windows Vista and Windows 7. Windows Update, which automatically downloads and installs important updates, was one of the only ways

Microsoft offered to maintain a secure PC with Windows XP. Now, in Windows 7, the Action Center, Performance Information and Tools, Windows Defender, and Windows Update work together to keep your computer secure. **Figures C–13**, **C–14**, and **C–15**, which are shown on the next few pages, compare Windows XP and Vista's Security Centers with Windows 7 Security Center and Action Center.

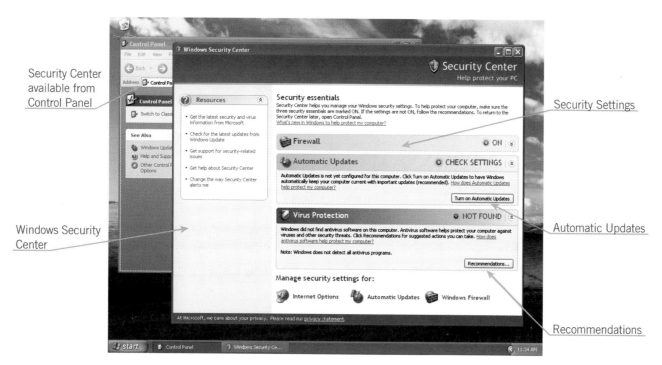

FIGURE C–13   Windows XP Security Center

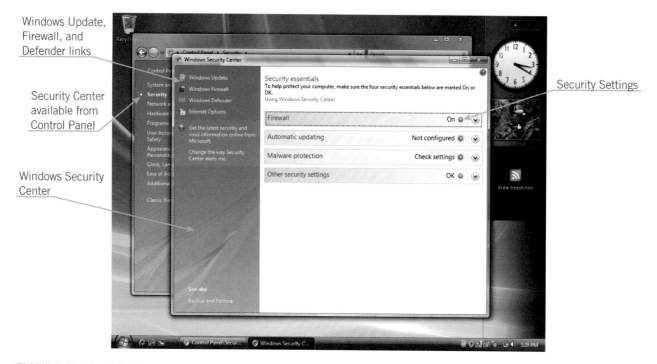

FIGURE C–14   Windows Vista Security Center

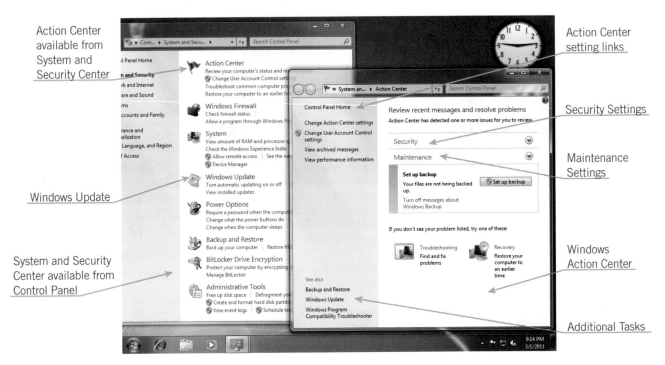

FIGURE C–15 Windows 7 Security Center and Action Center

APPENDIX D

Using SkyDrive and Office Web Apps

■ OBJECTIVES

Upon completion of this lesson, you should be able to:

- Explore cloud computing and Windows Live.
- Obtain a Windows Live ID and sign in to Windows Live.
- Upload files to SkyDrive.
- Use Office Web Apps View and Edit modes.
- Create folders on SkyDrive.
- Organize files on SkyDrive.
- Give permission for access to a folder on your SkyDrive.
- Co-author using the Excel Web App.

■ VOCABULARY

cloud computing

co-author

Office Web Apps

OneNote

SkyDrive

Windows Live

If the computer you are using has an active Internet connection, you can go to the Microsoft Windows Live Web site and use SkyDrive to store and share files. From SkyDrive, you can also use Office Web Apps to create and edit Word, PowerPoint, Excel, and OneNote files, even when you are using a computer that does not have Office 2010 installed. In this Appendix, you will learn how to obtain a Windows Live ID, how to share files with others on SkyDrive, and how to use the Word, Excel, and PowerPoint Web Apps, including co-authoring in the Excel Web App.

Understanding Cloud Computing and Windows Live

▶ **VOCABULARY**
cloud computing
Windows Live

Cloud computing refers to data, applications, and even resources that are stored on servers that you access over the Internet rather than on your own computer. With cloud computing, you access only what you need when you need it. Many individuals and companies are moving towards "the cloud" for at least some of their needs. For example, some companies provide space and computing power to developers for a fee. Individuals might subscribe to an online backup service so that data is automatically backed up on a computer at the physical location of the companies that provide that service.

Windows Live is a collection of services and Web applications that you can use to help you be more productive both personally and professionally. For example, you can use Windows Live to send and receive email, chat with friends via instant messaging, share photos, create a blog, and store and edit files. Windows Live is a free service that you sign up for. When you sign up, you receive a Windows Live ID, which you use to sign into your Windows Live account. **Table D–1** describes the services available on Windows Live.

TABLE D–1 Services available via Windows Live

SERVICE	DESCRIPTION
Email	Send and receive e-mail using a Hotmail account
Instant Messaging	Use Messenger to chat with friends, share photos, and play games
SkyDrive	Store files, work on files using Web Apps, and share files with people in your network
Photos	Upload and share photos with friends
People	Develop a network of friends and coworkers and use it to distribute information and stay in touch
Downloads	Access a variety of free programs available for download to a PC
Mobile Device	Access applications for a mobile device: text messaging, using Hotmail, networking, and sharing photos

SkyDrive is an online storage and file sharing service. With a Windows Live account, you receive access to your own SkyDrive, which is your personal storage area on the Internet. You upload files to your SkyDrive so you can share the files with other people, access the files from another computer, or use SkyDrive's additional storage. On your SkyDrive, you are given space to store up to 25 GB of data online. Each file can be a maximum size of 50 MB. You can also use your SkyDrive to share files with friends and coworkers. After you upload a file to your SkyDrive, you can choose to make the file visible to the public, to anyone you invite to share your files, or only to yourself. You can also use SkyDrive to access Office Web Apps. When you save files to SkyDrive on Windows Live, you are saving your files to an online location. SkyDrive is like having a personal hard drive "in the cloud."

Office Web Apps are versions of Microsoft Word, Excel, PowerPoint, and *OneNote*, an electronic notebook program included with Microsoft Office, that you can access online from your SkyDrive. Office Web Apps offer basic functionality, allowing you to create and edit files created in Word, PowerPoint, and Excel online in your Web browser. An Office Web App does not include all of the features and functions included with the full Office version of its associated application. However, you can use the Office Web Apps from any computer that is connected to the Internet, even if Microsoft Office 2010 is not installed on that computer.

Obtaining a Windows Live ID

To save files to SkyDrive or to use Office Web Apps, you need a Windows Live ID. You obtain a Windows Live ID by going to the Windows Live Web site and creating a new account.

Note: If you already have a Windows Live ID, you can skip Step-by-Step D.1.

> **VOCABULARY**
> **SkyDrive**
> **Office Web Apps**
> **OneNote**

Step-by-Step D.1

1. Start Internet Explorer. Click in the Address bar, type **www.windowslive.com**, and then press **Enter**. The page where you can sign into Windows Live opens.

2. Click the **Sign up** button. The Create your Windows Live ID page opens.

3. Follow the instructions on the screen to create an ID with a new, live.com email address or create an ID using an existing email address.

4. After completing the process, if you signed up with an existing email address, open your email program or go to your Web-based email home page, and open the email message automatically sent to you from the Windows Live site. Click the link to open the Sign In page again, sign in with your user name and password if necessary, and then click the **OK** button in the page that appears telling you that your email address is verified.

5. Exit Internet Explorer.

> **WARNING**
>
> If the URL doesn't bring you to the page where you can sign into Windows Live, use a search engine to search for *Windows Live*.

Uploading Files to SkyDrive

You can access your SkyDrive from the Windows Live page in your browser after you signed in with your Windows Live ID, or from Word, Excel, PowerPoint, or OneNote. Then you can upload a file to a private or public folder on your SkyDrive.

Uploading a File to SkyDrive from Backstage View

If you are working in a file in Word, Excel, or PowerPoint, you can save the file to your SkyDrive from Backstage view. To do this, you click the File tab, click Save & Send in the navigation bar, and then click Save to Web. After you do this, the right pane changes to display a Sign In button that you can use to sign in to your Windows Live account. See **Figure D–1**.

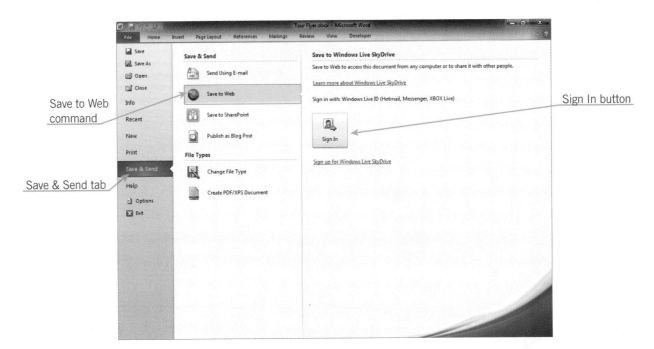

FIGURE D–1   Save & Send tab in Backstage view in Word after clicking Save to Web

Click the Sign In button to sign into Windows Live. After you enter your user name and password, the right pane in Backstage view changes to list the folders on your SkyDrive and a Save As button now appears in the right pane. See **Figure D–2**.

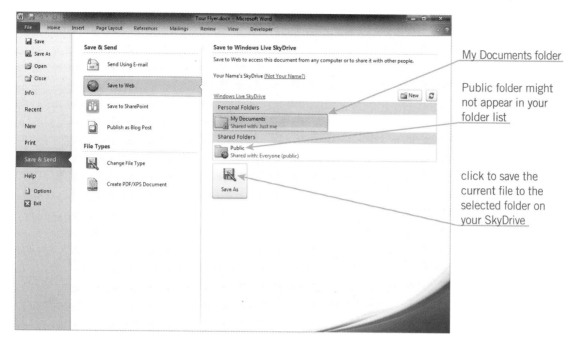

My Documents folder

Public folder might not appear in your folder list

click to save the current file to the selected folder on your SkyDrive

FIGURE D–2   Save & Send tab after connecting to Windows Live

To save the file, click the correct folder, and then click the Save As button.

Step-by-Step D.2

1. Start Word. Open the file named **Tour Flyer.docx** document from the drive and folder where your Data Files are stored.

2. Click the **File** tab, and then click **Save & Send** on the navigation bar. The Save & Send options appear in Backstage view as shown in Figure D–1.

3. Under Save & Send, click **Save to Web**.

4. Click the **Sign In** button. The Connecting to docs.live.net dialog box opens. See **Figure D–3**. If you are already signed into Windows Live, you will see the folders in your SkyDrive account listed instead of the Sign In button. Skip this step (Step 4) and Step 5.

FIGURE D–3
Connecting to docs.live.net dialog box

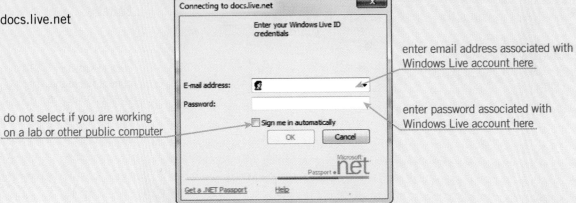

5. In the E-mail address box, type the email address associated with your Windows Live ID account. Press **Tab**, and then type the password associated with your Windows Live account in the Password box. Click the **OK** button. The dialog box closes, and another dialog box appears briefly while you connect to the Windows Live server. After you are connected, the folders on your SkyDrive appear in the right pane in Backstage view, as shown in Figure D–2.

6. In the right pane, click the **My Documents** folder, and then click the **Save As** button. Backstage view closes, and then after a few moments, the Save As dialog box opens. The path in the Address bar identifies the Public folder location on your SkyDrive.

7. Click the **Save** button. The dialog box closes and the Tour Flyer file is saved to the My Documents folder on your SkyDrive.

8. Exit Word.

Uploading a File to SkyDrive in a Browser

You can also add files to SkyDrive by starting from an Internet Explorer window. To do this, go to www.windowslive.com, and then log in to your Windows Live account. See **Figure D–4**.

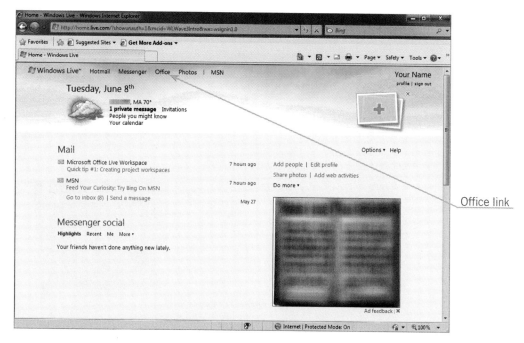

Office link

FIGURE D–4   Windows Live home page

To get to your SkyDrive, you click the Office link in the list of navigation links at the top of the window. To see all the folders on your SkyDrive, click View all in the Folders list on the left. See **Figure D–5**.

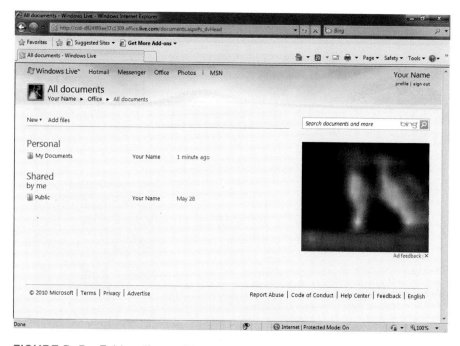

FIGURE D–5   Folders list on SkyDrive

Click the folder to which you want to add the file to open it. See **Figure D–6**.

click to add files
to this folder

contents of folder
are listed here

FIGURE D–6 My Documents folder page on SkyDrive

Click the Add files link to open the Add documents to *Folder Name* page; for example, if you click the Add files link in the My Documents folder, the Add documents to My Documents page appears. See **Figure D–7**.

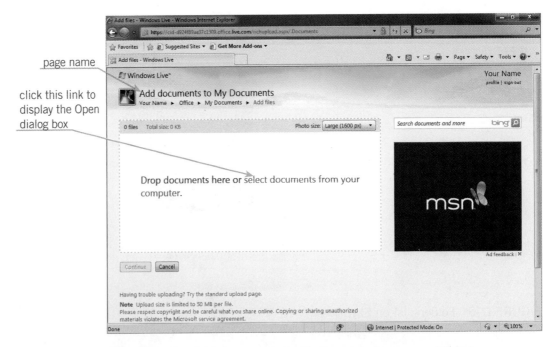

page name

click this link to
display the Open
dialog box

FIGURE D–7 Add documents to My Documents page on SkyDrive

Click the "select documents from your computer" link to display the Open dialog box. Locate the drive and folder where the file is stored, click it, and then click Open. The file uploads and is listed in the box. Click Continue to display the folder containing the files you uploaded to your SkyDrive.

Step-by-Step D.3

1. Start Internet Explorer. Click in the Address bar, type **www.windowslive. com**, and then press **Enter**.

2. If the Sign In page appears, type your Windows Live ID user name and password in the appropriate boxes, and then click **Sign in**. Your Windows Live home page appears similar to the one shown in Figure D–4.

3. In the list of command links at the top of the window, click **Office**. Your SkyDrive page appears.

4. In the list under Folders on the left, click **View all**. All the folders on your SkyDrive appear, similar to Figure D–5.

5. Click the **My Documents** folder. The My Documents page appears, similar to Figure D–6.

6. In the list of command links, click the **Add files** link. The Add documents to My Documents page appears, as shown in Figure D–7.

7. Click the **select documents from your computer** link, navigate to the drive and folder where your Data Files are stored, click **Tour Sales.pptx**, and then click the **Open** button. The file uploads and appears in the box on the Add documents to My Documents page.

8. At the bottom of the box, click the **select more documents from your computer** link. In the Open dialog box, click **Tour Data.xlsx**, and then click **Open**. The Excel file is listed in the box along with the PowerPoint file.

9. Below the box, click **Continue**. The My Documents folder page appears listing the files in that folder.

10. Keep the My Documents folder page displayed in Internet Explorer for the next Step-by-Step.

APPENDIX D

Using Office Web Apps

There are two ways to work with files using the Office Web Apps. You can view a file or you can edit it using its corresponding Office Web App. From your SkyDrive, you can also open the document directly in the full Office 2010 application if the application is installed on the computer you are using. You do not need to have Microsoft Office 2010 programs installed on the computer you use to access Office Web Apps.

Using a Web App in View Mode

To use a Web App in View mode, simply click its filename in the folder. This opens the file in View mode in the Web App. **Figure D–8** shows the Tour Flyer Word file open in the Word Web App in View mode.

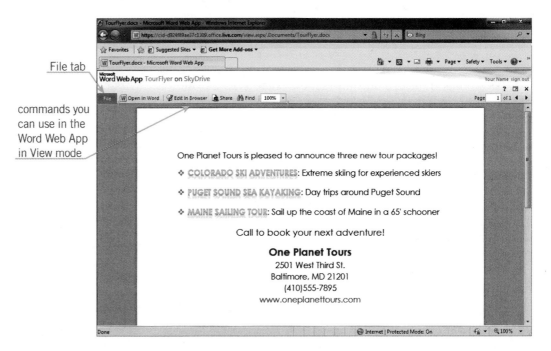

FIGURE D–8   Tour Flyer document open in View mode in Word Web App

Step-by-Step D.4

1. Click **Tour Flyer**. The Tour Flyer document opens in the Word Web App in View mode, as shown in Figure D–8.

2. Click anywhere in the document window, and then type any character. Nothing happens because you are allowed only to view the document in View mode.

3. Click the **File** tab. A list of commands opens. Note that you can print the document using the Print command on this menu.

4. Click **Close**. The document closes and the My Documents folder page appears again.

5. Leave the My Documents folder page open for the next Step-by-Step.

TIP

Position the mouse over a file icon to see the full filename and other details about the file.

Using a Web App in Edit Mode

You can also edit documents in the Office Web Apps. Although the interface for each Office Web App is similar to the interface of the full-featured program on your computer, a limited number of commands are available for editing documents using the Office Web App for each program. To edit a file in a Web App, point to the file in the folder page, and then click the Edit in browser link. You will see a Ribbon with a limited number of tabs and commands on the tabs. **Figure D–9** shows the file Tour Sales open in the PowerPoint Web App in Edit mode.

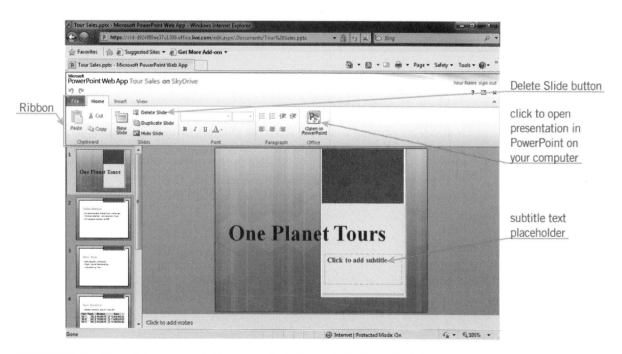

FIGURE D–9 Tour Sales presentation open in Edit mode in PowerPoint Web App

Step-by-Step D.5

TIP

To create a new file on SkyDrive using an Office Web App, open a folder, click the New link, and then select the appropriate Office Web App.

TIP

When you make changes to a file using a Web App, you do not need to save your changes before you close it because changes are saved automatically.

1. In the list of files in the My Documents folder, point to **Tour Sales**. A list of commands for working with the file appears.

2. In the list of commands, click the **Edit in browser** link. The Tour Sales presentation appears in the PowerPoint Web App in Edit mode, as shown in Figure D–9. In Edit mode, you see a version of the familiar Ribbon.

3. In the Slide pane, click in the subtitle text placeholder, and then type your name.

4. In the Slides tab, click **Slide 3** to display it in the Slide pane. The slide title is *New Tours*.

5. On the Home tab, in the Slides group, click the **Delete Slide** button. The *New Tours* slide is deleted from the presentation and the new Slide 3 (*Tour Revenue*) appears in the Slide pane. Now you will examine the other two tabs available to you in the PowerPoint Web App.

6. Click the **Insert** tab on the Ribbon. The only objects you can insert in a slide using the PowerPoint Web App in Edit mode are pictures and SmartArt. You can also create a hyperlink.

7. Click the View tab. Note that you cannot switch to Slide Master view in the PowerPoint Web App.

8. Leave the Tour Sales file open in the PowerPoint Web App for the next Step-by-Step.

Editing a File Stored on SkyDrive in the Program on Your Computer

If you are working with a file stored on your SkyDrive and you want to use a command that is available in the full-featured program on your computer but is not available in the Web App, you need to open the file in the full-featured program on your computer. You can do this from the corresponding Office Web App by clicking the Open in *Program Name* button on the Home tab on the Web App Ribbon.

Step-by-Step D.6

1. Click the **Home** tab. In the Office group, click the **Open in PowerPoint** button. The Open Document dialog box appears warning you that some files can harm your computer. This dialog box opens when you try to open a document stored on a Web site.

2. Click the **OK** button. PowerPoint starts on your computer and the revised version of the Tour Sales presentation opens on your computer. The presentation is in Protected view because it is not stored on the local computer you are using.

3. In the yellow Protected View bar, click the **Enable Editing** button. Now you can insert a footer on the slides.

4. Click the **Insert** tab, and then click the **Header & Footer** button in the Text group.

5. Click the **Footer** check box, type **2013 Sales Projections** in the Footer box, and then click the **Apply to All** button. When you use the full-featured version of a program, you do need to save the changes you made, even when it is stored in a folder on your SkyDrive.

6. On the Quick Access Toolbar, click the **Save** button ⊟. The modified file is saved to your SkyDrive.

7. In the PowerPoint window title bar, click the **Close** button [X]. The PowerPoint program closes and you see your browser window listing the contents of the My Documents folder.

8. Click the **Tour Sales** file. Slide 1 of the Tour Sales file appears in the PowerPoint Web app in View mode.

9. At the bottom of the window, click the **Next Slide** button ▶ twice. Slide 3 (*Tour Revenue*) appears in the window. Remember that you deleted the original Slide 3, *New Tours*. Also note that the footer you added is on the slide.

10. Click the **File** tab, and then click **Close**. The PowerPoint Web App closes and the My Documents page appears.

11. Leave the My Documents page open for the next Step-by-Step.

WARNING

You can also open a document stored on your SkyDrive in the program stored on your computer from View mode in the corresponding Office Web App.

WARNING

If the Connecting to dialog box opens asking for your Windows Live ID credentials, type the email address associated with your Windows Live ID in the E-mail address box, type your password in the Password box, and then click the OK button.

Creating Folders on Your SkyDrive

You can keep your SkyDrive organized by using file management techniques, similar to the way you organize files on your computer's hard drive. You can create a folder in your SkyDrive in the Internet Explorer window or from Backstage view in the program on your computer.

To create a folder on your SkyDrive in Internet Explorer, click the New link in the list of commands, and then click Folder to open the Create a new folder page on your SkyDrive. See **Figure D–10**.

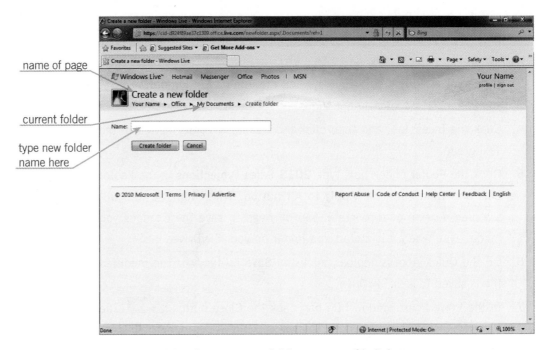

name of page

current folder

type new folder name here

FIGURE D–10   Create a new folder page on SkyDrive

To create a new folder on your SkyDrive from the Save & Send tab in Backstage view in an application, click the New button in the upper-right. This opens the same Create a new folder page shown in Figure D–10.

Type the name for the new folder in the Name box, and then click Next. The Add files to *Folder Name* page that you saw earlier appears. If you want to upload a file to the new folder, you can do so at this point. If you don't, you can click the link for the new folder or click the SkyDrive link to return to your SkyDrive home page.

Step-by-Step D.7

1. In the list of command links, click the **New** link, and then click **Folder**. The Create a new folder page appears with the insertion point in the Name box.

2. In the Name box, type **Sales**, and then click **Create folder**. The new empty folder is displayed in the browser window. You can see that you are looking at the contents of the new folder by looking at the navigation links. See **Figure D–11**.

navigation links

command links

FIGURE D–11
Sales folder on SkyDrive

Sales folder is the current folder

3. Leave the Sales folder page open for the next Step-by-Step.

Organizing Files on Your SkyDrive

As on your hard drive, you can move and delete files on your SkyDrive. To move or delete a file, first display the commands for working with the file by pointing to its name in the file list in the folder. To move a file, click the More link, and then click Move to open the "Where would you like to move *File Name*?" page. See **Figure D–12**.

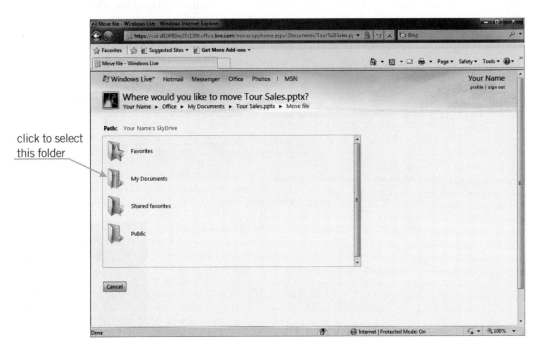

FIGURE D–12   Folder list that appears when moving a file

In the list of folders, click a folder. Then, at the top of the list, click the "Move this file into *Folder Name*" command. The folder into which you moved the file appears, along with a message telling you that the file was moved.

To delete a file, point to it to display the commands for working with the file, and then click the Delete button in the list of command links.

Step-by-Step D.8

1. In the list of navigation links, click the **My Documents** link. Point to **Tour Sales**. The commands for working with this file appear.

2. In the list of command links, click the **More** link, and then click **Move**. The "Where would you like to move Tour Sales.pptx?" page appears, and a list of folders on your SkyDrive appears.

3. In the list of folders, click the **My Documents** folder to display the list of folders located inside that folder. Click the **Sales** folder. The contents of the Sales folder appear in the list of folders. Because this folder does not contain any additional folders, you see only a command to create a New folder and the command to move the file.

4. In the list of folders, click **Move this file into Sales**. After a moment, the contents of the Sales folder appear, along with a message telling you that you have moved the Tour Sales file from the My Documents folder.

5. In the list of navigation links, click the **My Documents** link. The contents of the My Documents folder appear.

6. Point to **Tour Flyer**. In the list of command links, click the **Delete** button . A dialog box opens warning you that you are about to permanently delete the file.

7. Click **OK**. The dialog box closes, the file is deleted from the My Documents folder on your SkyDrive.

8. Leave the My Documents folder page open for the next Step-by-Step.

> **WARNING**
>
> Depending on the resolution of your computer, you might not need to click the More link to access the Move command.

Giving Permission for Access to a Folder on Your SkyDrive

If you upload a file to a private folder, you can grant permission to access the file to anyone else with a Windows Live ID. You can grant permission to folders located at the same level as the My Documents folder. You cannot grant permission to individual files or to folders located inside a locked folder. If you grant permission to someone to access a folder, that person will have access to all the files in that folder.

To grant permission to someone, click the folder to display its contents, click the Share link in the list of navigation links, and then click Edit permissions. The Edit permissions for *Folder Name* page appears. You can use the slider bar to make the contents of the new folder public by sharing it with everyone, your friends as listed on your Windows Live ID account and their friends, just your friends, or only some friends. You can also share it only with specific people that you list in the box in the Add Specific People section. When you type someone's name or email address associated with the person's Windows Live ID account in the box in the Add specific people section, and then press Enter, the person's name appears in a box below with a check box next to the name or email address. The box to the right of the person's name or email address indicates that the person can view files in the shared folder. You can then click the arrow to change this so that the person can view, edit, or delete files. See **Figure D–13**. Click Save at the bottom of the window to save the permissions you set.

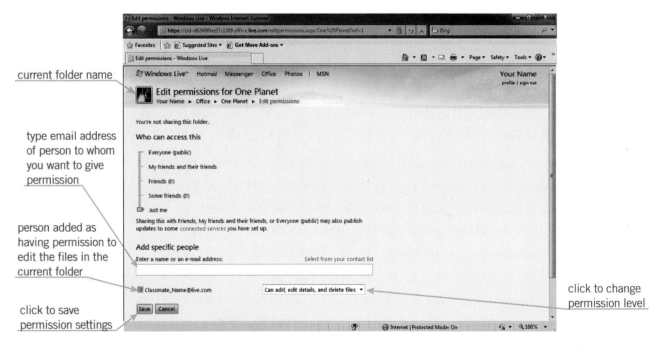

FIGURE D–13 Edit permissions for One Planet page on SkyDrive

To complete the next Step-by-Step, you need to work with a partner who also has a Windows Live ID account.

Step-by-Step D.9

1. In the list of navigation links, click the **Office** link, and then in the list of links on the left, click **View all**. The All documents page appears.

2. In the list of command links, click the **New** link, and the click **Folder**. The Create a folder page appears with a temporary folder name in the Name box. The temporary name is selected, so you can just type the new name.

3. In the Name box, type **One Planet**. Click **Next**. The One Planet folder page appears.

4. In the list of navigation links, click the **Office** link. In the list of folders on the left, click the **My Documents** link. The My Documents folder page appears.

5. In the file list, point to **Tour Data**, click the **More** link, and then click **Move**. The Where would you like to move Tour Data.xlsx? page appears.

6. In the list of folders, click **One Planet**. In the new list that appears, click the **Move this file into One Planet**. The One Planet page appears with the Tour Data file listed.

7. In the list of command links, click the **Share** link. Click **Edit permissions**. The Edit permissions for One Planet page appears.

8. Under Add specific people, click in the **Enter a name or an e-mail address** box, type the email address of your partner, and then press **Enter**. The email address you typed appears below the box. A check box next to the email address is selected, and a list box to the right identifies the level of access for this person. The default is Can add, edit details, and delete files, similar to Figure D–13. You want your partner to be able to edit the file, so you don't need to change this.

9. At the bottom of the window, click **Save**. The Send a notification for One Planet page appears. You can send a notification to each individual when you grant permission to access your files. This is a good idea so that each person will have the URL of your folder. Your partner's email address appears in the To box.

TIP

Because you are creating a folder at the same level as the My Documents folder, there is a Share with box below the Name box. You can set the permissions when you create the folder if you want.

TIP

To make the contents of the folder available to anyone, drag the slider up to the top so it is next to the Everyone (public).

10. Click in the Include your own message box, type **You can now access the contents of the One Planet folder on my SkyDrive.**, and then click **Send**. Your partner will receive an email message from you advising him or her that you have shared your One Planet folder. If your partner is completing the steps at the same time, you will receive an email message from your partner.

11. Check your email for a message from your partner advising you that your partner has shared his or her Sales folder with you. The subject of the email message will be "*Your Partner's Name* has shared documents with you."

12. If you have received the email, click the **View folder** button in the email message, and then sign in to Windows Live if you are requested to do so. You are now able to access your partner's One Planet folder on his or her SkyDrive. See **Figure D–14**.

FIGURE D–14
One Planet folder on someone else's SkyDrive

name of person who gave you permission to access the One Planet folder on his or her SkyDrive

your Windows Live name appears here

current folder

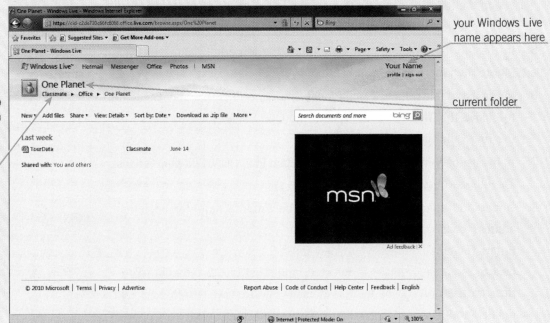

13. Leave Internet Explorer open for the next Step-by-Step.

Co-Authoring with the Excel Web App

When you work with the Excel Web App, you can use its *co-authoring* feature to simultaneously edit an Excel workbook at the same time as a colleague. When you co-author a workbook, a list of the people currently co-authoring the workbook appears at the bottom of the window. Co-authoring is not available in the Word or PowerPoint Web Apps. When you open a file in the Excel Web App, a notification appears at the right end of the status bar notifying you that two people are editing the document. See **Figure D–15**. You can click this to see the email addresses of the people currently editing the workbook.

▶ **VOCABULARY**
co-author

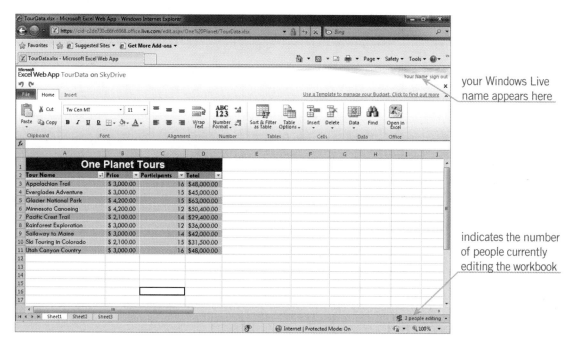

your Windows Live name appears here

indicates the number of people currently editing the workbook

FIGURE D–15   Tour Data file open in Edit mode in Excel Web App with two people editing

To complete this next Step-by-Step, you need to continue working with the partner who has permission to access the One Planet folder on your SkyDrive and who gave you permission to access his or her One Planet folder.

Step-by-Step D.10

1. Decide with your partner whether you will modify the Tour Data file stored on your SkyDrive or on his or her SkyDrive. After you decide the SkyDrive account with which you are going to work, both of you display the contents of that One Planet folder.

2. Point to **Tour Data**, and then in the list of command links, click the **Edit in browser** link.

3. In the status bar, click the **2 people editing** button. A list pops up identifying you and your partner as the two people editing the document.

   Decide with your partner which one of you will execute Step 4. The other person will then execute Step 5.

4. Either you or your partner click cell **A12**, type **Gulf Islands Sailing**, press **Tab**, type **3000**, press **Tab**, type **10**, and then press **Tab**. The formula in the other cells in column D is copied automatically to cell D12 because the data in the original Excel file was created and formatted as an Excel table. Both you and your partner see the data entered in row 12.

   If you entered the data in row 12, you partner should execute Step 5; if your partner entered the data in row 12, you should execute Step 5.

5. Either you or your partner—the person who did not execute Step 4—click cell **B12**, type **3700**, and then press **Tab**. The data entered is reformatted in the Accounting number format, and the total in cell D12 is recalculated. Again, both you and your partner see the change executed.

   Both you and your partner should execute the rest of the steps in this section.

6. Click the **File** tab, and then click **Close**. The changes you made to the Excel workbook are saved automatically on the current SkyDrive account. You are finished working with the Office Web Apps, so you can sign out of Windows Live.

7. In the upper-right of the SkyDrive window, click the **sign out** link. You are signed out of Windows Live.

8. In the title bar of your Web browser window, click the **Close** button ▮ **X** ▮ to exit your Web browser.

OneNote Web App

The other Office Web App is OneNote. As with Word, Excel, and PowerPoint files, you can share OneNote files on SkyDrive directly from OneNote. Note that you need to click the Share tab in the navigation bar in Backstage view, and then click Web and specify Windows Live as the Web location. After you upload a OneNote file to SkyDrive, you can work with it in its corresponding Web App.

GLOSSARY

A

alignment   The position of text between the margins.

aspect ratio   The relationship of an object's height to its width.

attribute   A formatting feature that affects how a font looks, such as a style, the color, or an effect.

AutoComplete   A feature in Word that guesses names of calendar items, such as the days of the week and months, as you type them, and then suggests the complete word.

AutoCorrect   A feature in Word that corrects errors as you type.

AutoFormat As You Type   A feature in Word that applies built-in formats as you type.

automatic grammar checking   A feature in Word that checks your document for grammatical errors as you type, and flags them with a green, wavy underline.

automatic spell checking   A feature in Word that checks your document for spelling errors as you type, and flags them with a red or blue wavy underline.

B

bibliography   A list of source materials that are used in the preparation of a work. (*See also* works cited page)

boilerplate text   Standard text that is reusable in documents, such as contracts and correspondence.

bookmark   An item or a location in a document that you identify and name for future reference so you can jump quickly to a specific location within the same document.

building block   Document parts that you can store in Word and reuse.

bullet   Any small character that appears before an item in a list.

C

callout   A special type of label in a drawing that consists of a text box with an attached line to point to something in the drawing.

caption   A label that identifies or describes an illustration, a table, or a picture.

case-sensitive   When entering a password, the upper- and lowercasing of the letters must be identical to the casing of the letters in the assigned password.

cell   The intersection of a column and a row in a table or worksheet.

center   To position text so that it is centered between the left and right margins.

chain   A series of links that let the story flow from one text box to the next, enabling you to continue a story elsewhere in the document.

chart   A graphical representation of data.

citation   A reference in a document that credits the source of information or other content, such as a picture or a chart, or references specific legal causes or statutes.

clip art   Graphics available for use in documents; the term clip art refers not only to drawn images, but also to photographs, movie clips, and sound files.

Clipboard   A temporary storage place in the computer's memory, available to all the programs, which can hold only one selection at a time; to place items on the Clipboard, you use the Cut or Copy command. An item on the Clipboard can be pasted into the file. *Also called* system Clipboard.

code   A set of instructions and data for a computer program.

color palette   A coordinated set of colors available for use in a document.

comment   An annotation that is added within a document by the author or reviewer.

content control   A special placeholder designed to contain a specific type of text, such as a date or the page number.

contextual spell checking   A feature in Word that checks your document for words that are spelled correctly, but that might be misused, and flags them with a blue, wavy underline.

copy   To place a copy of selected text on the Clipboard or the Office Clipboard.

crop   To remove part of a picture.

cross-reference   A reference from one part of a document to related material in another part of the document; an index reference; in an index, a cross-reference refers the reader to another index entry.

cut   To remove selected text and place it on the Clipboard or the Office Clipboard.

D

data source   The file used in a mail merge that contains the information that varies in each document.

destination file   The file to which you are transferring data when you move data between applications.

diagram   A visual representation of data to help readers better understand relationships among data.

digital signature   An attachment to a file or e-mail message that certifies that the information in the file is authentic and safe.

document template   Template type containing document settings, content, and styles that are available only to documents based on that template.

document workspace site   A central location for storing and sharing documents.

draft view   A way of viewing a document on screen that shows only the text of a document; you don't see headers and footers, margins, columns, or graphics.

drag   To select text by positioning the I-beam pointer to the left of the first character of the text you want to select, holding down the left button on the mouse, dragging the pointer to the end of the text you want to select, and then releasing the button.

drag-and-drop   To drag selected text from one place in a document to another.

drop cap   A letter or word at the beginning of a paragraph that is larger than the rest of the text and used to draw attention to the content.

E

embedded object   An object that becomes part of the destination file; an embedded object can be edited in the destination file.

encryption   A standard method for encoding data.

endnote   A note placed along with other notes at the end of a document to provide additional information to a document or cite the source of content.

F

field   One or more characters that create a piece of information, such as a first name, a last name, or a telephone number.

field name   A label identifying a field in a data source.

filter   A tool to screen records by identifying criteria that must be met before the records are included in a merge.

first-line indent   A description of the indent in a paragraph when only the first line of text in the paragraph is indented.

floating object   An object in a document that acts as if it were sitting in a separate layer on the page and can be repositioned anywhere on the page.

font   The design of text.

font effect   *See* text effect.

font size   The height of characters in points.

font style   A formatting feature you can apply to a font to change its appearance; common font styles are bold, italic, and underlining.

footer   Text that is printed at the bottom of each page.

footnote   A note that appears at the bottom of the same page where it is referenced to provide additional information to a document or cite the source of content.

format   To change the appearance or look of text.

Format Painter   A feature that copies format attributes such as colors, borders, and fill effects from an object, text, or cell to apply the same formatting to another object, text, or cell.

Full Screen Reading view   A way of viewing a document on screen that shows text on the screen in a form that is easy to read; the Ribbon is replaced by a small bar called a toolbar that contains only a few relevant commands.

G

global template   Template type containing document settings and styles that are available to all documents.

gradient fill   A gradual blending together of two or more fill colors.

graphic   A picture that helps illustrate the meaning of the text and make the page more attractive; graphics include predefined shapes, diagrams, and charts, as well as photographs and drawings.

gridlines   The lines in a table that form the rows and columns.

gutter margin   *See* inside margin.

H

hanging indent   A description of the indent in a paragraph when the first line of text is not indented but all of the following lines in the paragraph are.

header   Text that is printed at the top of each page.

hyphenation   A setting that allows a word at the end of a line to split between syllables.

I

import   To bring data into a document from another compatible application.

incremental search   A search that returns matches for the string of characters in the document as you type; as the search text is augmented, the matches in the document change.

indent   The space between text and the margin.

index   An alphabetic listing, usually at the end of a document, of pertinent words and phrases contained in a document, that references the page numbers where the related topics appear in the document.

inline object   An object in a document that can be repositioned as if it were a character in the line of text.

insertion point   A blinking vertical line that shows where text will appear when you begin typing.

inside margin   The right margin on a left page and the left margin on the right page when a document is set up with mirrored margins. *Also called* gutter margin.

J

justify   To format a paragraph so the text is distributed evenly across the page between the left and right margins and both the left and right edges of the paragraph are aligned at the margins.

K

keyword   A word or phrase used in a search.

L

landscape orientation   A page or worksheet rotated so it is wider than it is long.

leader   A solid, dotted, or dashed line that fills the blank space before a tab stop.

left-align   To position text so that it is aligned along the left margin.

linked object   An object that accesses data stored in the source file; a linked object must be edited in the source file.

M

macro   A group of sequential commands and actions combined as a single command to automatically complete a task.

mail merge   A process that combines a document with information that personalizes it.

main document   The file used in a mail merge that contains the information that does not vary from one document to the next.

main tabs   Tabs that appear on the Ribbon when the application is launched.

MAPI (Messaging Application Programming Interface)   A Windows programming interface that enables programs to send e-mails.

margin   Blank space around the top, bottom, and sides of a page.

markup Revision marks and annotations that Word places in a document.

merge field A placeholder in the main document in a mail merge that is replaced with data from the data source when you perform the merge.

metadata Data that describes other data.

mirrored margins Margins on left and right pages that are identical—"mirror" each other—when facing each other; usually used in books and magazines.

multilevel list A list with two or more levels of bullets or numbering. *Also called* outline numbered list.

N

negative indent A description of an indent in a paragraph in which the left indent marker is past the left margin. *Also called* outdent.

nonbreaking hyphen A nonprinting special formatting character used to indicate hyphenated words that should not be split if the hyphen falls at the end of a line.

nonbreaking space A nonprinting special formatting character used to indicate words that should not be split between lines.

Normal template Word's default global template.

O

object Anything that can be manipulated as a whole, such as clip art or another graphic you insert into a document; objects can be inserted, modified, resized, repositioned, and deleted.

Office Clipboard A special clipboard available only to Microsoft Office programs, on which you can collect up to 24 items.

optional hyphen A nonprinting special formatting character used to indicate where a word can be divided if all the characters in the word do not fit on the same line.

orphan The first line of a multi-line paragraph that is split from the other lines in the paragraph and appears at the bottom of a page or a column.

outdent *See* negative indent.

outline numbered list *See* multilevel list.

Outline view A way of viewing a document on screen that displays headings and text in outline form so you can see the structure of your document and reorganize easily; headers and footers, page boundaries, graphics, and backgrounds do not appear.

outside margin The left margin on the left page and the right margin on the right page when a document is set up with mirrored margins.

P

page break The place where one page ends and another begins.

pagination The system by which text and objects are manipulated to create the page layout.

passim A word used in annotations to indicate that terms, passages, or page references occur frequently in the work cited; in Word the default setting *Use passim* formats multiple page references on the same line in a table of authorities.

paste To copy an item stored on the Clipboard or the Office Clipboard to a location in a file.

point The unit of measurement for fonts.

Portable Document Format (PDF) A format developed by Adobe Systems designed to preserve the visual appearance and layout of each page and enable fast viewing and printing.

portrait orientation A page or worksheet rotated so it is longer than it is wide.

Print Layout view The most common way of viewing a document on screen; it shows how a document will look when it is printed, and you can work with headers and footers, margins, columns, and graphics, which are all displayed.

property Identifying information about a file that is saved along with the file, such as the author's name and the date the file was created.

pull quote A line or phrase excerpted from the main text and used to draw attention in a document.

Q

Quick Access Toolbar A small customizable toolbar at the top of the screen with buttons for common commands such as Save and Undo.

Quick Part A building block stored in the Quick Parts gallery and available when you click the Quick Parts button in the Text group on the Insert tab.

Quick Style A predefined format that you can apply by clicking a button in the Styles group on the Home tab.

R

read-only document A document users are able to open and read, but to which they are unable to make changes.

record A group of related fields, or a single field, treated as a unit in a data source, such as all the contact information for one individual.

reference marker A superscript number or custom character, such as an asterisk, inserted in the document to reference a footnote or endnote.

revision bar A vertical line that appears in the left margin of a Word document, indicating that there is a tracked change or comment related to the paragraph.

Ribbon An area at the top of an Office program window that contains commands for working with the open file; the commands are organized under tabs.

right-align To position text so that it is aligned along the right margin.

rotation handle A green circle that appears connected to a selection rectangle around an object and that you can drag to rotate the object.

S

sans serif fonts Fonts that do not include serifs.

section A part of a document where you can apply a layout, headers and footers, page numbers, margins, orientation, and other formatting features different from the rest of the document.

section break A formatting code that used to divide a document into sections.

select To highlight a block of text.

selection rectangle The box that appears around an object when it is selected.

separator line A line that separates the body text from the footnote area.

serif   A small line or curl at the end of a font character that embellishes the character.

serif fonts   Fonts that have serifs.

sidebar   Text set off from the main body of text in a text box that provides additional information for the reader.

sizing handle   A square, circle, or set of three dots that appears on a selection rectangle around an object and that you can drag to resize the object.

SmartArt   A predesigned chart or diagram that visually illustrates text and includes formatted graphics.

source file   The document file from which you are transferring data when you move data between applications.

sort   To arrange a list of words or numbers in ascending or descending order.

status bar   A bar at the bottom of the program window that provides information about the current file and process.

story   The text contained within a text box.

style   A set of predefined formats you can apply to characters, paragraphs, tables, and numbered and bulleted lists.

style sheet   A list of all styles that are used in a document or available in a template.

switch   A special instruction that modifies a field result.

System Clipboard   *See* Clipboard.

T

tab   *See* tab stop.

tab stop   An indicator in a paragraph that marks the place where the insertion point will stop when you press the Tab key. *Also called* tab.

table   An arrangement of text or numbers in rows and columns, similar to a spreadsheet.

table of authorities   A summary of the references used in a legal document to cite cases, statutes, rules and other sources.

table of contents   A sequential list of contents that provides an overview of the topics in a document.

table of figures   A sequential list of all the figures (such as tables, equations, pictures, charts, graphs, and other illustrations) included in a document.

template   A file that already contains the basic elements of a document, such as page and paragraph formatting, fonts, and text and from which you can create a new document.

text box   A shape specifically designed to hold text.

text effect   Formatting for text that is similar to font styles and can help enhance or clarify text. *Also called* font effect.

theme   A coordinated set of fonts, styles, and colors in a document that determines the default font, the colors applied to headings, and other features of the document.

Thesaurus   A built-in reference for finding synonyms for words in a document.

toggle   To switch between two options or to turn a feature on or off.

toolbar   A small bar that appears at the top or bottom of a window instead of the Ribbon; it displays buttons you can click to quickly choose a command.

tool tabs   Contextual tabs that appear on the Ribbon when objects are selected in a document.

Track Changes   A tool in Word that keeps a record of any changes you or a reviewer makes in a document by formatting inserted text in a color and underlined, and deleted and moved text in a balloon in the right margin.

V

VBA (Visual Basic for Applications)   A computer programming language and environment designed for use within Office and other Microsoft applications.

vertical alignment   The position of text on a page between the top and bottom margins.

view buttons   In an Office program window, buttons that you can click to change views quickly.

virus   A computer program designed to replicate itself; often causes damage to computer data, documents, and the computer operating system.

W

watermark   A ghost image that appears behind the content of a document. A watermark image can also be created by impressing text or a graphic image in the paper when the paper is manufactured.

Web Layout view   A way of viewing a document on screen that simulates the way a document will look when it is viewed as a Web page; text and graphics appear the way they would in a Web browser, and backgrounds are visible.

widow   The last line of a multi-line paragraph that is split from the other lines in the paragraph and wraps to the next page or column.

word processing   The use of a computer and software to enter and edit text and produce documents such as letters, memos, forms, and reports.

Word wrap   A feature in Word that automatically wraps words around to the next line when they will not fit on the current line.

WordArt   Stylized text that is treated as an object.

workgroup collaboration   The process of working together in teams, sharing comments, and exchanging ideas for a common purpose.

works cited page   A list of source materials that are used in the preparation of a work. (*See also* bibliography)

X

XML Paper Specification (XPS)   A format developed by Microsoft designed to preserve the visual appearance and layout of each page and to enable fast viewing and printing.

Z

zoom   The percentage the file is magnified or reduced on the screen; 100% zoom represents the normal size; percentages higher than 100% mean the document appears larger on screen; percentages lower than 100% mean the document appears smaller on screen.

INDEX

Note: Boldface entries include definitions.